D0001085

UNDERSTANDING
ADMINISTRATIVE LAW

LEXISNEXIS LAW SCHOOL ADVISORY BOARD

William Araiza
Professor of Law
Brooklyn Law School

Ruth Colker
Distinguished University Professor & Heck-Faust Memorial Chair in Constitutional Law
Ohio State University, Moritz College of Law

Olympia Duhart
Associate Professor of Law
Nova Southeastern University, Shepard Broad Law School

Samuel Estreicher
Dwight D. Opperman Professor of Law
Director, Center for Labor and Employment Law
NYU School of Law

David Gamage
Assistant Professor of Law
UC Berkeley School of Law

Joan Heminway
College of Law Distinguished Professor of Law
University of Tennessee College of Law

Edward Imwinkelried
Edward L. Barrett, Jr. Professor of Law
UC Davis School of Law

Paul Marcus
Haynes Professor of Law
William and Mary Law School

Melissa Weresh
Director of Legal Writing and Professor of Law
Drake University Law School

UNDERSTANDING
ADMINISTRATIVE LAW

SIXTH EDITION

William F. Fox
Visiting Professor of Law
Penn State University
Dickinson School of Law

 LexisNexis®

ISBN: 978-1-4224-9865-1

Library of Congress Cataloging-in-Publication Data
Fox, William F. Understanding administrative law / William F. Fox. -- 6th ed. p. cm. Includes index. ISBN 978-1-4224-9865-1 (softbound) 1. Administrative law--United States. 2. Administrative procedure--United States. I. Title. KF5402.F68 2012 342.73'06--dc23   2012016980

This publication is designed to provide authoritative information in regard to the subject matter covered. It is sold with the understanding that the publisher is not engaged in rendering legal, accounting, or other professional services. If legal advice or other expert assistance is required, the services of a competent professional should be sought.

LexisNexis and the Knowledge Burst logo are registered trademarks of Reed Elsevier Properties Inc., used under license. Matthew Bender and the Matthew Bender Flame Design are registered trademarks of Matthew Bender Properties Inc.

Copyright © 2012 Matthew Bender & Company, Inc., a member of LexisNexis. All Rights Reserved.
2012

No copyright is claimed by LexisNexis or Matthew Bender & Company, Inc., in the text of statutes, regulations, and excerpts from court opinions quoted within this work. Permission to copy material may be licensed for a fee from the Copyright Clearance Center, 222 Rosewood Drive, Danvers, Mass. 01923, telephone (978) 750-8400.

NOTE TO USERS

To ensure that you are using the latest materials available in this area, please be sure to periodically check the LexisNexis Law School web site for downloadable updates and supplements at www.lexisnexis.com/lawschool.

Editorial Offices
121 Chanlon Rd., New Providence, NJ 07974 (908) 464-6800
201 Mission St., San Francisco, CA 94105-1831 (415) 908-3200
www.lexisnexis.com

MATTHEW◊BENDER

PREFACE

Students react in various ways to the study of administrative law. Some elect the course because they anticipate employment in a federal or state administrative agency; some choose the course merely because it is a subject tested on the bar examination; others have some abstract interest in a course that deals with the manner in which agencies make policy and decide individual cases. Often it is not until a student graduates and begins the practice of law that the pervasiveness of various administrative decision-making models becomes apparent. These models are not limited to the federal government, but may be found at the state and regional level, in municipal governments and even in many private entities such as corporations and educational institutions. For that reason this text includes a certain amount of state-based material. Students who go into a state administrative practice will encounter concepts and terminology nearly identical with federal practice.

Law professors also approach the subject from different angles: some emphasize the administrative system of a single state; others focus exclusively on the federal system; still others explore only one or two specific administrative agencies, in the belief that the administrative *process* can be understood best in the context of a specific agency carrying out a specific assigned mission.

This book will help the reader grasp the fundamental concepts of administrative law regardless of the approach taken by an instructor and regardless of the reader's personal motivation for electing the course. By and large the book concentrates on the *process* of administrative decision-making in contrast to the substantive law of a particular agency. But as a student moves through the course and later enters practice, he or she will find that substance and procedure become more and more intertwined and, in many instances, become almost inextricable. An awareness that there is no bright line between substance and procedure, particularly in an administrative agency context, is especially helpful for a thorough understanding of the subject.

Students should also realize that the practicing bar has serious reservations as to the utility of the typical administrative law course. One prominent Washington, D.C. lawyer commented that if he ever got to the point in handling a case before an administrative agency that he needed to use or refer to anything he had been taught in his administrative law course in law school, he probably would have failed his client.[1] For this reason, this book contains a number of attempts to sensitize law students to the lawyering operations involved in administrative law — *i.e.*, to the manner in which a client's problem moves through a typical agency and the manner in which a lawyer copes with the various problems and issues encountered in representing clients before administrative agencies. The relative informality of the administrative process and the fact that agencies exercise both adjudicative and legislative powers means that an administrative lawyer must often be far more creative and adaptable in dealing with an agency dispute than in handling a piece of civil litigation. Moreover, many agencies are beginning to experiment with alternative dispute resolution techniques so a well-trained lawyer needs to know something about regulatory negotiation, arbitration and mediation.

---

[1] Comments of Peter Barton Hutt, as quoted in Peter L. Strauss, *Teaching Administrative Law: The Wonder of the Unknown*, 33 J. LEGAL EDUC. 1 (1983).

PREFACE

In addition, the book contains a significant amount of material on trends in administrative law such as deregulation and regulatory reform. Many governmental entities, including a number of federal agencies, have begun to move away from traditional models for exercising governmental power (the so-called "command and control" regulatory techniques) toward concepts of policymaking and decisional processes that take full advantage of the marketplace as regulator. Students anticipating thirty to forty more years of practice must realize that many areas of practice involving deregulation and regulatory reform are in fact fertile fields for a legal practice. In many cases these trends have enhanced, rather than diminished, the lawyer's role.

A good deal of the material in this book consists of suggestions on ways to identify administrative problems and ways to organize the reader's thinking after the problem is identified. The book does not, of course, ignore the statutory and case law basis of administrative law; but often, whether the reader is a student or practitioner, a guide on how to think through a problem is more helpful than a mere paraphrase of a statute or recitation of a case holding. Since one of the assumptions of the author is that most readers will be using this book as an adjunct to a course in administrative law and thus will have access to a casebook, lengthy verbatim quotations from cases are kept to an absolute minimum.

This book should also prove helpful to practitioners who either missed the course in law school or find themselves dealing with topics not covered in their course. In those instances, a practicing lawyer might profitably read at least a bit of the full text of any case discussed.

Hopefully, most readers will concur that there are no insoluble mysteries in administrative law, although as in all areas of law, there are many schools of thought, a large number of differing (and often conflicting) viewpoints and a great deal controversy. But there should not be very much mystery as you dig through the issues and concepts. As the author has often remarked: students are just as bright and capable as teachers, it's just that a teacher has usually covered the same ground before; and it's always easier to walk through a maze with someone who has already been there than to attempt the journey on your own.

This book may be used with any of the existing commercially-published casebooks on administrative law. While this Book's tables of contents and chapter headings may not correspond directly with some of the headings used in the casebooks, there is a generally accepted core of administrative law topics that virtually every casebook covers and for which there is a standard vocabulary. There are two ways for a reader to use this book without reading it from cover to cover. First, if an outline heading in this book corresponds to a similar heading in a casebook (for example, the topic of "delegation"), the reader may move immediately to that topic. If there seems to be no correspondence between this book's outline headings and those headings used in the casebook, the most efficient mechanism for finding relevant discussion is to match the case in the casebook against the table of cases in this book.

My thinking on administrative law has been shaped by all those who have walked the ground before me. I am especially grateful to the many students at my former academic home, The Catholic University of America, who took my course, who challenged me in class, and who sent me scurrying back to the library and to practice for answers to their questions. My current students at Penn State-Dickinson School of Law keep me busy and engaged with all of their questions, comments and insights. I have been enriched by an

PREFACE

association with the many lawyers I encounter in Washington practice. I owe a great debt to a number of other people who helped me grow as a lawyer and law professor: Professors Clinton Bamberger, Albert J. Broderick, and Harvey Zuckman, Judge Benigno C. Hernandez, Counselors William T. Simmons, and Theodore Voorhees, Sr. A number of research assistants, now all practicing law, were indispensable. They include: Andrew Palmieri, Scott Squillace, B. Erin Sullivan, and Roman Majtan. My most recent research assistant, Madison Cassels, was enormously helpful in preparing the manuscript for the sixth edition.

Table of Contents

Table of Contents

Table of Contents

Table of Contents

Table of Contents

Table of Contents

Table of Contents

Table of Contents

Table of Contents

Table of Contents

Chapter 1

INTRODUCTION

§ 1.01 STUDYING AND PRACTICING ADMINISTRATIVE LAW

[A] An Overview of Administrative Law

In the broadest sense, administrative law involves the study of how those parts of our system of government that are neither legislatures nor courts make decisions. These entities, referred to as administrative agencies, are normally located in the executive branch of government and are usually charged with the day-to-day details of governing. Agencies are created and assigned specific tasks by the legislature. The agencies carry out these tasks by making decisions of various sorts and supervising the procedures by which the decisions are carried out. For example, Congress has charged the United States Social Security Administration (SSA) with the administration of the federal government's social security program. Under that mandate, SSA does two things: (1) it makes general social security policy (within the terms of the SSA statute, of course) and (2) it processes individual applications for, and terminations of, social security benefits. Affected persons who disagree with the agency's decisions on either the substance of the social security program or the procedures under which that program is implemented-and whose grievances are not resolved within the agency-are permitted to take their dispute into federal court for resolution. Occasionally, aggrieved persons return to the legislative branch in an attempt to persuade Congress to alter the statute under which the social security program functions.

This brief outline is the basic model for the American administrative process; and whether you are studying federal administrative law, a state administrative system, or even a single administrative agency, the process of decision-making is likely to be similar even when the missions of the agencies differ. It is the unifying force of the administrative *process* — in dramatic contrast to the wide variety of substantive problems with which agencies deal-that has persuaded most administrative law professors to concentrate on agency procedure rather than agency substance. Accordingly, most contemporary administrative law courses analyze the manner in which matters move through an agency, rather than the wisdom of the matters themselves. In other words, the manner in which the Federal Department of Transportation decided to impose a passive-restraint system on automobile manufacturers is a fascinating case history of the administrative process, irrespective of anyone's personal position on the wisdom of air bags versus seat belts. Recognizing that the focus of most administrative law courses is on how decisions are made (rather than what those decisions are) should help you more readily understand the themes of the typical course in administrative law.[1]

[B]   The Study and Practice of Administrative Law

Administrative law can be approached in much the same fashion as many other law school courses. If you regard the field merely as a collection of discrete legal doctrines, it may make a great deal of sense simply to memorize various general principles, to apply those principles to a final examination or a bar examination, and then forget about the topic. This book can be used in that fashion. However, a more profitable approach, to truly understanding administrative law — and for practicing administrative law after your admission to the bar — is to keep two questions in mind: (1) What are the rules of the game, both substantive and procedural; and (2) how may I best represent my client before an administrative agency? Thinking through the twin issues of doctrine and the application of that doctrine through the lawyering process will make you a much better practitioner, even if it doesn't necessarily have an immediate payoff in your law school course or on the bar examination.[2]

The administrative law course itself will be less fuzzy if you keep in mind a few other fundamentals. First, under our constitutional system, agencies are creatures of the legislature. They do not spring up on their own, and they cannot be created by courts. Agencies function only insofar as a legislature has given them the authority to function. That authority may be exceptionally broad (e.g., telling an agency to regulate railroads by applying the standard of "public convenience and necessity") or incredibly narrow (e.g., when Congress sets the specific income levels and other criteria for those persons who qualify for certain government benefits; or when Congress passes a Coal Mine Safety and Health Act containing provisions that tell mine operators what size of mine roofing bolts to install).

Federal administrative agencies are typically endowed with broad, general powers. By contrast, state legislatures frequently enact far more detailed agency statutes because of a lingering reluctance to give state agencies unfettered power. For example, the Nebraska legislature once enacted a statute prescribing the thickness of the walls of metal milk cans presumably because the legislature did not trust the cognizant administrative agency to make a sound decision on the issue. This kind of statutory detail often signals a legislature's distrust of a

---

[1] One respected casebook, now unfortunately out of print, disagrees with this approach and postulates that administrative law can be properly understood only if one studies an individual agency in depth, both substantively and procedurally. GLEN O. ROBINSON, ERNEST GELLHORN & HAROLD H. BRUFF, THE ADMINISTRATIVE PROCESS (4th ed. 1993). Two other distinguished administrative law scholars believe that "[a]dministrative law scholarship has reached the end of the questions it may pose and answer." The authors contend that we have reached this end-game because basic administrative law instruction concentrates on the process of administrative agencies to the detriment of studying "the substantive scope and nature of regulatory government." Joseph P. Tomain & Sidney A. Shapiro, *Analyzing Government Regulation*, 49 ADMIN. L. REV. 377, 380 (1977).

[2] Administrative law questions on the bar examination tend to be very much like law school examination questions. Practitioners will find additional hints on practicing before federal agencies in William Fox, *Some Considerations in Representing Clients Before Federal Agencies*, Law Practice Notes (Barrister Mag., ABA) 21–26 (Summer, 1981).

particular agency, or possibly, with the administrative process in general. While common in state administrative systems, it is much less frequent in the federal government. Congress rarely gets involved in the minutiae of administering a particular federal regulatory program because it usually has substantial confidence in the federal agencies that it creates.

Irrespective of what form a new administrative agency takes or what mission it is given, the legislature *must* enact a statute creating the agency. This statute, sometimes called an agency's *organic act* but more frequently referred to as an agency's *enabling act*, is the fundamental source of an agency's power. This principle — that the legislature creates agencies and sets limits on their authority — should be regarded as cardinal rule number one of administrative law. Far too many people in law school and, on occasion, far too many experienced practitioners lose sight of this fundamental principal. A misunderstanding of this basic concept can lead to erroneous assumptions about an agency's ability to deal with a particular issue or problem.

Some enabling acts set out specific agency procedures; but more often than not, the legislature creates an agency with a particular substantive mission but with procedures that are established in a general procedural statute that controls all or most of the agencies in that jurisdiction. The governing procedural statute at the federal level is the Administrative Procedure Act (APA),[3] in place since 1946 and normally the doctrinal thread that holds most law school administrative law courses together. While state administrative procedure statutes differ considerably, a prototype statute, the Model State Administrative Procedure Act,[4] has been promulgated; and many states either have adopted the Model Act *in toto* or incorporated substantial portions of it into their existing administrative procedure statutes. Thus, you are likely to find a fair amount of procedural uniformity even among the states. Those students whose courses emphasize a single state's administrative system would do well to make constant reference to that state's administrative procedure act as they work through their course and this book. They will probably see many similarities between the state act and the Federal APA but with enough differences to make generalizations dangerous.[5]

Some law professors understandably disagree with an exclusively "federal" approach to understanding administrative law. Professor Arthur Bonfield of the University of Iowa College of Law believes that a proper study of the state administrative process would pay large dividends for both students and professors. He has urged, among other things, that administrative law is best appreciated through a comparative approach to the topic, that there is a great deal of creativity (what he calls "state solutions") in state administrative systems that are never

---

[3] 5 U.S.C. §§ 551–808. *See* Appendix A.

[4] *See* Appendix B.

[5] *See, e.g.*, William Fox & Leonard Carson, *A Comparison of the Florida and Federal Administrative Procedure Acts*, 11 FLA. B.J. 699 (1980). Florida has more recently engaged in a great deal of administrative reform. The Florida APA has occasionally been amended to reflect current administrative scholarship. *See, e.g.*, David M. Greenbaum & Lawrence E. Sellers, Jr., *1999 Amendments to the Florida Administrative Procedure Act: Phantom Menace or Much Ado About Nothing?*, 27 FLA. ST. U. L. REV. 499 (2000); Lawrence E. Sellers, Jr., *The 2003 Amendments to the Florida APA*, 77 FLA. B.J. 74 (2003).

implemented by the stodgier, less innovative federal agencies, and perhaps most importantly:

> State administrative processes operate under different circumstances than does the federal administrative process; consequently, some of the problems presented [in the states] differ either in degree or kind from those presented in the federal process. Many of the feasible or effective solutions to federal administrative law problems are not feasible or effective in the state context. Therefore, a study of problems and solutions in the federal administrative process cannot be an adequate vehicle to prepare students for dealing with all of the major problems presented in the state administrative process.[6]

But no matter how a legislature at either the federal or state level chooses to set up an agency, as a law student and as a practicing attorney, your first task is simple: *Read the agency's enabling act and that jurisdiction's administrative procedure act.* One way to create a lot of trouble for yourself, even at the beginning of the course, is to be casual about reading the applicable statutes. Reading and trying to understand the statutes should be regarded as cardinal rule 1-A for understanding administrative law.

Agencies make a great deal of policy within the boundaries of their enabling acts. Within the boundaries of their generic administrative procedure act, they also establish procedures for efficient and fair decision-making. Remember that enabling acts and administrative procedure acts often establish only *minimum* standards and requirements for individual agencies. These statutes are often so broadly phrased that agencies have enormous leeway to fill in the gaps — both procedural and substantive — of the legislation so long as they keep within the terms of the governing statutes. The areas in which many agencies are free to set their own policies and procedures are quite extensive. We refer to this freedom of action as *agency discretion.* Agency discretion is a yet another fundamental concept to keep constantly in mind.

Sadly, agency discretion is one of the least studied and most poorly understood aspects of administrative law. It is so little analyzed that it is frequently referred to as "the hidden component" of administrative law. Nevertheless, it is a phenomenon that both students and practitioners need to appreciate if they are to have a thorough understanding of an agency. You can begin to grasp agency discretion by first realizing that the vast majority of agency decisions are never reviewed by either the courts or the legislature. Other parts of the executive branch, such as the president, governor or attorney general, occasionally get involved with agency action, but for the most part agencies function on their own, often with only sporadic outside scrutiny and accountability.

---

[6] Arthur E. Bonfield, *State Law in the Teaching of Administrative Law: A Critical Analysis of the Status Quo*, 61 TEX. L. REV. 95, 103–04 (1982). Professor Peter Strauss has suggested that administrative law is one of the "hidden" comparative law courses in law school because it combines and requires comparisons between a large number of other law school courses. Peter L. Strauss, *Administrative Law: The Hidden Comparative Law Course*, 46 J. LEGAL EDUC. 478 (1996).

A third fundamental that should never be forgotten is that courts have a relatively limited role in supervising agency conduct. These days, the federal courts and many state courts are required to take what amounts to a "hands off" attitude toward the agencies. The days when a free-wheeling court could substitute its judgment for that of the agency are largely over, irrespective of whether the issue before the court is substantive or procedural. The United States Supreme Court has been hammering this message home to the lower federal courts for years.[7] Most if not all state courts have adopted a similar posture.

This is not to say that judicial review of agency action is unimportant. As we will see, it is the tail that wags the dog in many cases. But the mere fact that a dispute *may* be taken to court is no excuse for sloppy lawyering at the agency level. Too many lawyers make the fatal mistake of thinking that a reviewing court will correct any and all mistakes in the proceedings below, or indeed, that a court has plenary review powers over agency action. That is simply not the case. The ability of a court to change an agency decision is so limited these days that the second cardinal rule for agency practice is: *A lawyer must win a case at the agency or likely will not win it at all.*[8] A legislative solution for your client's problem may be theoretically possible, but you should remain realistic about actually achieving a favorable result as a result of legislative action. In studying and practicing administrative law you should try to avoid wishful thinking. If you have a problem within the jurisdiction of an administrative agency, that problem will likely begin with the agency and conclude with the agency with your client stuck with whatever result the agency dictates.

§ 1.02   THE NATURE OF ADMINISTRATIVE AGENCIES

[A]   Addressing Legal Disputes

There is hardly any function of modern government that does not involve, in some way, an administrative agency. The reason for this is really very simple: agencies are the only government entities equipped to deal with the day-to-day minutiae of governing. It is one thing for Congress to decide that transportation companies should be regulated, but the last thing that Congress wants to decide is how much Company X may charge to carry a package from New York to Chicago.

---

[7] See, e.g., *Vt. Yankee Nuclear Power Corp. v. Natural Res. Def. Council, Inc. (NRDC)*, 435 U.S. 519 (1978), discussed in Chapter 7, § 7.03.

[8] The author recognizes that this statement really goes out on a limb. Many readers, both lawyers and students, will throw back all sorts of instances when courts overturned agency action. That's true, but whether one addresses this issue by analyzing the doctrinal limitations placed on judicial review or merely looks at the statistics (*i.e.*, the number of all agency decisions overturned by courts), he or she will find that the vast bulk of agency decisions are either never taken to court or are simply affirmed when they get there. Thus, the message of cardinal rule number two should not be forgotten: cases are normally won or lost *at the agency.* Courts usually are not the answer nor is the legislature. However, lawyers should not ignore the possibility of a legislative solution. If agencies are creatures of statute, one of the most effective places to turn for relief-at least on a prospective basis-is the legislature. But here again, a wise practitioner will consider whether the legislature will pay any attention to the grievance. Most legislatures are far too busy with more generic issues such as budget and taxes. They are often reluctant to involve themselves in the detail of government.

Rigorous protection of the environment is now a matter of national consensus, but a court is unlikely to have the technical expertise necessary to decide precisely which specific air pollution control equipment is best suited for coal-fired power plants. Two themes that continually repeat in administrative law with regard to administrative agencies are: (1) the agency is charged with the detail of regulation and (2) the agency is expected to develop expertise in a particular area of regulation.

Understanding the nature of administrative agencies first requires an analysis of the way in which disputes are typically addressed by our legal system. Consider, for example, the case of a creative business executive who sees a need for privately-owned space vehicles that might serve various industrial and commercial purposes.[9] One option for the business executive under our system of government might be simply to start building and flying space vehicles without seeking anyone's permission to do so. It could be that only good things will result from this activity and nothing bad will ever happen. However, a wise entrepreneur always considers the potential liability of a business undertaking.

In a legal system such as ours we frequently leave disputes in the hands of the common la: if some harm does occur the common law can grapple with any disputes that arise through the application of general principles of tort or contract liability. For example, the nineteenth century British courts had no trouble dealing with a water storage tank that broke and flooded some nearby property, even though Parliament had never spoken on the issue, and even though no previous court had addressed the problem. When injury to an individual's property interest occurs, principles drawn from tort law permit a court to dispose of both the issue of liability and the issue of remedy, even if the case is one of first impression.[10] Common law dispute resolution may be triggered by any injured person who feels strongly enough about his or her injury to file a formal action in court and who has a strong enough case to convince the court that liability exists and that some type of monetary relief ought to be granted. Applying this *common law* solution to the space vehicle scenario means that the cumulative effect of a number of reported court decisions will eventually establish a body of legal rules for the construction and operation of private space vehicles without any other government action. Concededly, court decisions are not perfect. Judge-made rules may be overly-narrow or too sketchy to give comprehensive guidance on how an entrepreneur ought to proceed. Still, many problems in our society are handled precisely in this fashion, and it is not necessarily a bad way to handle disputes. The common law solution is flexible enough to react to changing circumstances and predictable enough to give people at least a little warning before they get into trouble.

Looking at the problem realistically, however, a business executive will likely want more predictability and stability than the common law system offers. Courts can take years or even generations to develop a comprehensive body of law on a particular issue. Most businesses can't wait this long and most businesses need some security and stability for the immediate future. It is highly doubtful, for

---

[9] This hypothetical was suggested by an analogous problem on rainmaking contained in WALTER GELLHORN, CLARK BYSE & PAUL VERKUIL, ADMINISTRATIVE LAW PROBLEMS (1974).

[10] *Rylands v. Fletcher*, 3 Eng. Rep. (H.L.) 330 (1823).

example, whether a bank would lend our executive any money for a brand new business activity involving as dangerous an activity as space flight without at least some protection from liability. One option would be to go to a legislature for assistance. Armed with enough political clout, our business executive might persuade the legislature simply to authorize the activity. In other words, the legislature could pass a statute simply stating: "Private corporations may build and operate space vehicles." This statute will clearly authorize the activity, but notice that it does absolutely nothing to resolve issues of liability. If the business executive is worried about liability and accountability, she might ask the legislature not only to expressly permit the activity but also to set a cap on possible liability stemming from any accidents involving the private rockets.[11] We can refer to this as a "pure" *legislative* solution — i.e., where the legislature resolves the problem on its own without referring the issue to any other branch of government. But, we all know that actions of any given legislature are frequently unpredictable. Rather than approving private space flight, the legislature could decide that the activity is so fraught with danger and with hidden social and economic costs that it could decide to simply *prohibit* private space vehicles. Legislators might become so frightened of this activity that they categorically prohibit the activity and impose criminal penalties on anyone who engages in the activity. Legislative prohibitions of this type don't occur all that often, but readers may recall that cocaine was once sold to the American public on an over-the-counter basis and once was a primary ingredient in a still-popular soft drink. In the mid 1920s, Congress and the state legislatures became sufficiently aware of the dangers of cocaine that they made use, possession and sale of the substance a prohibited criminal act. Indeed, for quite a number of years, Congress did just that with regard to private space flight. It simply prohibited private sector initiatives.

[B] Legislative Choices Involving Administrative Agencies

The legislature has other alternatives for dealing with private spaceships. It might decide that the problem should be put in the hands of an executive branch agency. In this instance, the legislature has a broad spectrum of choices. In making a choice, a legislature will typically analyze:

1. The task to be assigned to the agency (often referred to as the agency's "mission").

There are two factors that are usually considered in this analysis: **a.** what is the nature of the specific business or industry to be regulated (*e.g.*, firms manufacturing drugs, firearms or space vehicles); and **b.** in what manner should the regulation be carried out (by licensing, monitoring, or performing the actual work at issue);

2. How the agency itself should be structured (whether, for example, it is to be headed by a single administrator or by a multi-person commission and what its internal organization will be); and

---

[11] For example, the Price-Anderson Act, 42 U.S.C. § 2210(c), sets a cap of $560 million on any accident occurring in a civilian nuclear power plant.

3. The placement of the agency within the existing system of government (*e.g.*, whether it is to be a separate cabinet-level agency, a component of an existing agency or an independent regulatory commission).

The choices are plentiful. The legislature could decide to prohibit any private sector activity whatsoever and to establish a government agency to perform the entire task. Congress has taken this approach in a few intances. For example, Congress initially made private space flight unlawful and gave the task solely to a government agency (initially NASA, the National Aeronautics and Space Administration). This alternative exemplifies one of the tightest forms of government control because the private sector is flatly forbidden to engage in the activity in question.

By contrast, if the legislature decided that only limited control of the business activity was necessary, it could create an administrative mechanism at the other end of the "control" spectrum requiring only that those persons wishing to conduct private space flights identify themselves, register with some governmental entity and report periodically on their space flight activities. We usually refer to this model as a *registration-and-reporting* mechanism. The Lobbying Disclosure Act of 1995[12] is a good example of this kind of minimalist control mechanism.

The legislature might decide that it wants more governmental control over the activity in question than is permitted by a registration-and-reporting statute, but not the categorical prohibition found in the NASA model. As it investigates the phenomenon of private space flight, it might conclude that the only aspect of this activity that requires some control is the credentialing of rocket engineers. In other words, the legislature could decide that this was an activity suitable for the private sector, but was still complicated enough and dangerous enough that only a select group of professionals should be permitted to engage in the activity. Based upon this assumption, the legislature could establish a *professional licensing* process for rocket engineers. All other persons would be expressly forbidden from participating. Under this model, certified rocket engineers would have the exclusive right to engage in the activity and any licensed engineer who committed an error could be sued for professional malpractice. Law students in particular should instantly recognize this model and should be especially sensitive to regulation in the form of professional licensing.

---

[12] 2 U.S.C. §§ 1601–1612. The 1995 act, with important 1988 amendments, repealed the older Federal Lobbyist Registration Act. Readers should understand that one of the principal reasons for the relaxed controls on lobbyists springs from the First Amendment right to petition the government. Indeed, the 1995 act expressly provides: "Nothing in this Act shall be construed to prohibit or interfere with-(1) the right to petition the Government for the redress of grievances; (2) the right to express a personal opinion; or (3) the right of association, protected by the first amendment to the Constitution." Most other forms of private sector activity, particularly business activity, are not protected nearly as much by the Constitution. There are relatively few registration and reporting statutes on either the federal or state level that pertain to businesses. One of the few such examples is a registration and reporting activity under the Federal Pesticide Act, 7 U.S.C. § 136(2) for farmers who intend to administer pesticides on their own lands.

[C] "Command-and-Control Regulation"

Another alternative is the administrative model that is characteristic of a great deal of the current regulatory activity of both state and federal governments and whose analysis often constitutes the major portion of the traditional course in administrative law. Under this model an administrative agency is given powers to regulate a particular industry under a broad statutory mandate (*i.e.*, "in the public interest," or "consistent with public health and safety") by first authorizing individual private-sector firms to perform the activity in question and then by policing the day-to-day operations of that industry. We usually refer to this type of mechanism as *command-and-control regulation*. When the now-defunct Interstate Commerce Commission was created Congress gave the ICC the authority to license individual firms to carry freight and also the authority to approve the prices those companies charged for the transportation. There are a number of variations on this theme. Some agencies — for example, the Environmental Protection Agency (EPA) — are given regulatory powers that extend to setting standards for pollution control but without the authority to decide which companies should be permitted to perform a particular function. The EPA has no broad general licensing powers. It cannot, for example, decide whether a particular steel manufacturing plant may be built and operated but it does have the power to regulate that plant's air emissions once the plant is up and running. This is not to say that the EPA never issues permits. It can do so in certain instances, but its permitting process does not extend to deciding whether or not that particular firm may exist and do business. The National Labor Relations Board and the Federal Trade Commission perform similar tasks in policing unfair labor and trade practices.

[D] Licensing Agencies

Typical licensing agencies on the federal level are the Federal Communications Commission (broadcast licenses) and the Federal Energy Regulatory Commission (hydroelectric facility licenses, among other things). Licensing agencies frequently also regulate many of the day-to-day activities of individual companies, such as rates that licensed companies may charge their customers. On the state level, licensing agencies, such as state public utility commissions, are sometimes given regulatory powers involving health and safety issues as well as economic issues.

[E] The Structure of an Agency

The legislature never stops with a mere statement of agency powers. It must also decide on the agency's structure and that agency's position within the government. For example, in setting up a new administrative agency, Congress will decide whether to make the agency one of the cabinet-level departments or merely a component of one of the existing departments. One of the newest federal *cabinet* agencies is the Department of Veterans Affairs, an agency that had existed prior to 1988 as the sub-cabinet administrative agency known as the Veterans Administration. The newest cabinet-level agency, the Department of Homeland Security, is an amalgam of government entities that were either free-standing agencies or existed within other cabinet departments. With regard to agency organization, on the federal level, a *Secretary* presides over a cabinet agency. These entities typically have a large bureaucracy administering many different programs. On occasion Congress will create a free-standing agency — the EPA is perhaps the best-known example — that is within the executive branch but not part of any cabinet department. The President as the chief executive has nearly total control over executive branch agencies. He or she can normally appoint and fire the department's highest officials. The President has control over departmental policy and a great deal of control over the department's budget, once Congress approves that department's budget.

There are, however, some instances when Congress wants a new agency to have some independence from presidential control. In that case, it can create an *independent regulatory commission*, such as the Federal Maritime Commission or the Securities and Exchange Commission. On a few occasions, Congress will establish an agency as an independent regulatory commission, but place it within an existing cabinet department — e.g., the Federal Energy Regulatory Commission, an independent regulatory agency that exists within the cabinet-level Department of Energy. FERC has exclusive responsibility for certain areas of regulation, such as wholesale electric ratemaking. In other matters, the enabling act permits FERC to issue orders that constitute final agency action for the Department of Energy.[13] In other matters, different components of the Department of Energy function completely independently from FERC.[14] On the federal level, independent regulatory commissions are headed by a multiple-person commission and staffed by a bureaucracy that is usually much smaller than a cabinet agency.

An agency's status as independent regulatory commission restricts some of the President's prerogatives in controlling the agency. While the President may appoint commissioners, they typically serve for fixed terms and may not be removed other than on the specific grounds set out in the agency's enabling act. Many independent regulatory agencies, by statute, must have a mixture of Republicans and Democrats commissioners, so the President may not be free to appoint commissioners solely from within his own political party. These constraints on the appointment and removal process in theory make the commissions "independent" of the President, but in practice and over time simply by filling vacancies on the commission with like-minded people the President can have a substantial effect on that agency's policymaking.

Students will encounter many different examples at the federal level and in state and local government. There is no single type of structure or control that characterizes an administrative agency, be it on the federal, state or municipal level but understanding just where an agency fits is one of the first steps in fully appreciating that agency's role and function.

---

[13] *See* the Department of Energy Organization Act, 42 U.S.C. § 7101.

[14] There are occasional attempts towards executive branch reorganization often with the goal of eliminating or minimizing jurisdictional overlap. *See, e.g., Toward a Logical Governing Structure: Restoring Executive Reorganization Authority, Before the Comm. on Gov't Reform*, 108th Cong. (2003).

§ 1.03 JUSTIFICATIONS FOR REGULATION

[A] Economic Justification

Free markets are one of the basic premises of the American economy. Thus, a decision to create an administrative agency to regulate a particular business activity implies a failure on the part of the marketplace to deal adequately with some problem. One way to develop a better understanding of any particular administrative agency is to ask why the legislature created a particular agency. Typically, an agency's regulatory mission — its reason for being — will be explained in the early portions of its enabling act or in its legislative history. For example, when Congress initiated price regulation of the petroleum industry following the Arab oil embargo in 1973-1974, it explained as one of its goals (or justifications) the necessity of protecting U.S. consumers from unconscionable price gouging on the part of the oil companies. This justification was spelled out in the underlying statute, the Emergency Petroleum Allocation Act,[15] but was only one of several goals stated in the first section of that statute. On occasion, a legislature will not state its justifications expressly, but on close examination of an agency's enabling act and the Act's legislative history, justifications can almost always be discerned. This analysis is important to a practicing lawyer because an understanding of an agency's reason for being is often helpful in understanding how the agency functions.

In his now classic work on regulation, now Supreme Court Justice Stephen Breyer created a list of possible justifications for regulation.[16] These include, among others:

a. to control monopoly power;

b. to control excess profits;

c. to compensate for externalities;

d. to compensate for inadequate information;

e. to inhibit excessive competition; and

f. to compensate for unequal bargaining power.[17]

A statute need not be based solely on one of these justifications, but can be a blend of two or more. Many of Breyer's justifications are self-explanatory, but a few examples may make the others a little clearer. "Externalities," occasionally referred to as "spillovers," occur when the cost of producing something does not reflect the true cost to society for producing the good. One example is a manufacturing process that creates air pollution-for which society pays the clean up costs. A single firm, however high-minded, cannot take it upon itself to install

---

[15] 15 U.S.C. § 751 (the regulatory programs authorized by this statute were cancelled by Executive Order in 1981; the statute is no longer operative).

[16] STEPHEN BREYER, REGULATION AND ITS REFORM (1982). *See also*, Andrew P. Morriss, Bruce Yandle & Andrew Dorchak, *Choosing How to Regulate*, 29 HARV. ENVTL. L. REV. 179 (2005).

[17] BREYER, *supra* note 16, at 12–35.

costly pollution control equipment, if no other firm invests in the equipment, because to do so will drive up that firm's costs to the point where it cannot compete successfully with lower cost goods manufactured by firms that continue to pollute. Some entity, usually the government, must require all firms to make these investments in order to spread the costs of pollution control over the entire industry. The attempt under the Clean Air Act to establish certain national standards for air and water pollution applicable to all firms within particular industries is a recognition of the concept of spillover.

Compensating for inadequate information is a justification for a great deal of current consumer protection legislation. Laypersons do not have the wherewithal to analyze children's sleepwear for flammability. Purchasers of food cannot analyze the nutritional content or the health hazards of various food products. Buyers of major appliances cannot themselves calculate the energy efficiency of a particular model of refrigerator. The Food and Drug Administration's product approval requirements and the Consumer Product Safety Commission's and Department of Energy's labeling regulations reflect this justification. Similarly, compensating for unequal bargaining power is the justification for many of the "truth in lending" regulations issued by the federal banking regulation agencies.

[B]   Political Justifications

There are also political explanations for regulation that are conceptually distinct from economic justifications. One political justification for regulation is that certain matters within our society ought to be subject to the control of persons who are under some obligation of political accountability. It is doubtful, for example, that we would turn over the voting process to a private-sector company. In theory, the most politically accountable branch of government is the legislature, but even the executive branch and the judiciary reflect various concepts of political accountability. Agencies derive their political accountability from the actions of the legislature (in establishing and monitoring the agency) and the executive (through the appointment power). Political accountability helps insure that the agencies function in the public interest, rather than in the interest of narrow single-issue groups. While there is a lot of debate as to whether agencies, in truth, represent the public interest, this concept lies at the heart of the theory of the administrative process.[18] An elaborate inquiry along these lines is usually outside the scope of the typical law school course in administrative law, but only the bitterest cynics will assert that the concept of the public interest is meaningless. Moreover, there are occasions when terms such as *public interest* become important as a matter of statutory interpretation. For that reason alone, law students should not disregard the more theoretical aspects of the administrative process.[19]

---

[18] For a further discussion on understanding and improving administrative rulemaking, see Cary Coglianese, *Empirical and Experimental Methods of Law: Empirical Analysis and Administrative Law*, 2002 U. ILL. L. REV. 1111 (2002).

[19] The first edition of this book was both praised and criticized for taking a highly practical approach to understanding administrative law. While that approach clearly reflects the author's bias and predilections, the more enthusiastic students of administrative law should not disregard some of the fine writing that has been published on the more theoretical and conceptual issues of administrative law.

[C]   Evolution of Regulatory Philosophy

The American public seems to have developed a renewed faith in the market mechanism as a proper control device and simultaneously seems to have abandoned the idea that command-and-control economic regulation by government agencies is the best way to deal with many problems. This movement, often referred to as *deregulation*, began in the mid-1970s during the Ford and Carter administrations and reached full flower during the Reagan years. That same spirit continued into the Clinton administration as President Clinton declared that the era of big government is over. President George W. Bush expressed similar views. The push toward deregulation in the late 1970s and early 1980s has raised doubts about the wisdom and rationale of many of Justice Breyer's justifications for regulation. A number of prominent failures of the regulatory process (for example, in the area of regulation of the interstate transportation of natural gas-a program that for years actually created natural gas shortages) have weakened public interest in traditional regulatory mechanisms. In the late 1980s and early 1990s there was much discussion of taking regulatory powers away from the federal government and giving those powers to the states through the process known as *devolution*.[20]

At the same time, it is clear that the American public has not given up its consensus on such matters as clean air and water and employee and consumer safety. The tensions between a perceived need for some control and monitoring and the tight, often irrational and economically-inhibiting forms of traditional economic

---

Some book-length writings on the theory of our administrative system that a careful student might wish to read are: JAMES LANDIS, THE ADMINISTRATIVE PROCESS (1938); KENNETH CULP DAVIS, DISCRETIONARY JUSTICE: A PRELIMINARY INQUIRY (1969); ROBERT L. RABIN, PERSPECTIVES ON THE ADMINISTRATIVE PROCESS (1979); JERRY L. MASHAW, BUREAUCRATIC JUSTICE: MANAGING SOCIAL SECURITY DISABILITY CLAIMS (1983); JERRY L. MASHAW, DUE PROCESS IN THE ADMINISTRATIVE STATE (1985); JAMES WILSON, BUREAUCRACY: WHAT GOVERNMENT AGENCIES DO AND WHY THEY DO IT (1989); PETER L. STRAUSS, AN INTRODUCTION TO ADMINISTRATIVE JUSTICE IN THE UNITED STATES (1989); CASS R. SUNSTEIN, AFTER THE RIGHTS REVOLUTION: RECONCEIVING THE REGULATORY STATE (1990); Christopher F. Edley, Jr., ADMINISTRATIVE LAW: RETHINKING JUDICIAL CONTROL OF BUREAUCRACY (1990); GLEN O. ROBINSON, AMERICAN BUREAUCRACY: PUBLIC CHOICE AND PUBLIC LAW (1991); SUSAN ROSE-ACKERMAN, RETHINKING THE PROGRESSIVE AGENDA: THE REFORM OF THE AMERICAN REGULATORY STATE (1992); PETER H. SCHUCK, FOUNDATIONS OF ADMINISTRATIVE LAW (1994). Some frequently cited law review articles on broad themes of administrative law are: Robert B. Stewart, *The Reformation of American Administrative Law*, 88 HARV. L. REV. 1669 (1975); Robert L. Rabin, *Federal Regulation in Historical Perspective*, 38 STAN. L. REV. 1189 (1986); Gerald E. Frug, *Administrative Democracy*, 40 U. TORONTO L.J. 559 (1990); Mark Seidenfeld, *A Civic Republican Justification for the Bureaucratic State*, 105 HARV. L. REV. 1511 (1992); Richard H. Pildes & Cass R. Sunstein, *Reinventing the Regulatory State*, 62 U. CHI. L. REV. 1 (1995); Cynthia R. Farina, *The Consent of the Governed: Against Simple Rules for a Complex World*, 72 CHI.-KENT L. REV. 987 (1997); Steven P. Croley, *Theories of Regulation: Incorporating the Administrative Process*, 98 COLUM. L. REV. 1 (1998); Elena Kagan, *Presidential Administration*, 114 HARV. L. REV. 2245 (2001); Lisa Schultz Bressman, Symposium, *Getting Beyond Cynicism: New Theories of the Regulatory State Disciplining Delegation After* Whitman v. American Trucking Ass'ns, 87 CORNELL L. REV. 452 (2002); Orly Lobel, *The Renew Deal: The Fall of Regulation and the Rise of Governance in Contemporary Legal Thought*, 89 MINN. L. REV. 342 (2004); Evan J. Criddle, *Fiduciary Foundations of Administrative Law*, 54 UCLA L. REV. 117 (2006); Rachel E. Barkow, *The Ascent of the Administrative State and the Demise of Mercy*, 121 HARV. L. REV. 1332 (2008).

[20] There is considerable debate as to the meaning of devolution and whether or not it has already occurred. *See, e.g.,* Mary A. Gade, *The Devolution Revolution Has Already Occurred*, ST. ENVTL. MONITOR, Mar. 4, 1996.

regulation have provoked a search for different types of controls and new administrative mechanisms.[21]

There are some discernible trends toward new methods of regulation on both the state and federal levels. Interest in economic regulation — such as setting railroad freight rates or establishing the price natural gas pipelines charge to transport natural *gas* — has greatly diminished. One such agency, the Interstate Commerce Commission (ICC), an entity that regulated railroads and interstate trucking companies, among other businesses, has been abolished. Another agency, the Federal Energy Regulatory Commission (FERC), (regulation of natural gas pipelines, and wholesale electric rates) spends most of its time these days developing initiatives that promote market entry and competition and enhance market mechanisms, rather than focusing on price controls and limitations on entry as its basic regulatory philosophy. Congress has occasionally entered this fray. Prior to the demise of the ICC, deregulation had been prompted by two important Congressional enactments, the Motor Carrier Act of 1980[22] and the Staggers Rail Act of 1980.[23] In contrast, FERC has attempted many of its reforms by changing its rules without an earlier change in the agency's enabling acts.[24]

There are many bills introduced in every session of Congress to do away with most federal economic regulation. On occasion, one or another of these bills will succeed. In 1980, Congress abolished an entire major regulatory agency charged with economic regulation of the airline industry. Originally established in the heyday of the New Deal, the Civil Aeronautics Board (CAB) went completely out of business in January, 1985, following an elaborate phase-out timetable mandated by Congress. The CAB does not seem to be a grievous loss. Many of the consumer protection programs established by the CAB simply were transferred to the Department of Transportation. Safety regulation of airlines is still enforced by the Federal Aviation Administration. While we remain in the midst of a continuing debate as to the impact of deregulation on aviation safety, there seems to be virtually no interest in reviving the CAB. The abolition of the ICC did not engender any large-scale public outcry.[25] A small number of ICC functions were transferred to the Department of Transportation. Some commentators, disheartened by the performance of the Federal Emergency Management Agency (a component of the Department of Homeland Security) during Hurricane Katrina, have urged its abolition.

The debate continues.[26] In the first edition of this book, the author surmised: "The lessons learned from the CAB experience (that deregulation may enhance

---

[21] *See, e.g.*, Susan Rose-Ackerman, Foreword, *Regulatory Reform: Where Are We Going*, 31 WAKE FOREST L. REV. 581 (1996); LARRY N. GERSTON ET AL., THE DEREGULATED SOCIETY (1988); Thomas O. McGarity, *Regulatory Reform in the Reagan Era*, 45 MD. L. REV. 253 (1986).

[22] 49 U.S.C. §§ 10101–11917.

[23] Pub. L. No. 94-210, 90 Stat. 31 (codified in various sections of 49 U.S.C.).

[24] *See, e.g.*, William Fox, *Transforming an Industry by Agency Rule: Regulation of Natural Gas by the Federal Energy Regulatory Commission*, 23 LAND & WATER L. REV. 113 (1988).

[25] President Clinton signed the Interstate Commerce Commission Termination Act, 109 Stat. 803 (1995), codified in 49 U.S.C., on December 29, 1995.

[26] *See, e.g.*, Frank B. Cross, *The Judiciary and Public Choice*, 50 HASTINGS L.J. 355 (1999) (Public

rather than destroy an industry) suggest that it is entirely possible that other federal agencies that engage in economic regulation such as the ICC and the Federal Maritime Commission may be abolished in the near future."[27] The Federal Maritime Commission remains in existence — albeit a constant target of deregulators.[28] There seem, however, to be few cheerleaders for any renewal of economic controls. President Reagan's attempts to abolish the Departments of Education and Energy did not succeed. Subsequent Presidents, particularly George W. Bush, have diminished the power of various agencies by failing to fill important personnel vacancies or by appointing agency executives who take a "do-nothing" stance with regard to the agency's mission.

In the past several years, we have seen more than a little public and legislative interest in what has been called *reregulation*.[29] In a small number of instances, such as nuclear power, food and drug products, banking and savings and loan institutions, and hazardous waste sites, public interest in some type of continuing regulation has persisted. These days, many commentators have expressed interest not in abolishing, but merely in "fixing" government regulation, possibly by developing concepts of *regulatory flexibility*.[30] A number of people in and out of government have begun to explore *performance-based* regulations as an alternative to classic command and control regulation. Performance-based regulation sets certain goals or that need to be accomplished while permitting the regulated entity relatively free rein in achieving those goals.[31] Since September 11, 2001 and the destruction of the World Trade Center in New York City, virtually all the new initiatives in regulation have been sparked by international terrorism — a phenomenon that has created sharp new interest in regulation that relates directly

---

choice theory has assumed nearly preeminent importance in legal analysis and often has been employed to justify an expansive role for the judiciary and litigation in law interpretation.); IAN AYRES & JOHN BRAITHWAITE, RESPONSIVE REGULATION: TRANSCENDING THE DEREGULATION DEBATE (1992); PETER KAHN, *The Politics of Unregulation: Public Choice and Limits on Government*, 75 CORNELL L. REV. 280 (1990).

[27] WILLIAM FOX, UNDERSTANDING ADMINISTRATIVE LAW 9 (1st ed. 1986).

[28] For a discussion on recent developments in maritime legislation, see Constantine G. Papavizas & Lawrence I. Kiern, *2001-2002 U.S. Maritime Legislative Developments*, 34 J. MAR. L. & COM. 451 (2003).

[29] Killing the CAB was symbolically important because the agency was established in that flurry of New Deal legislation that helped create many of the federal agencies referred to as the "Big Seven"-the CAB, Federal Communications Commission, Federal Power Commission (now Federal Energy Regulatory Commission), Federal Trade Commission (established in 1914), Interstate Commerce Commission (established in 1887 and now abolished), National Labor Relations Board and Securities and Exchange Commission. This does not mean that U.S. airlines are totally unregulated. They remain subject to all other forms of government control (*i.e.*, safety requirements, labor and equal employment laws, antitrust statutes, and the like). Thus, the term *deregulation* frequently refers solely to termination of economic regulation: It does not mean the total absence of regulation.

[30] *See, e.g.*, Symposium on Regulatory Reform, *supra* note 21; Marshall J. Breger, *Regulatory Flexibility and the Administrative State*, 32 TULSA L.J. 325 (1996); Douglas C. Michael, *Cooperative Implementation of Federal Regulations*, 13 YALE J. ON REG. 535, 541 (1996) ("The government would rely on the regulated entities to develop specific and individual implementation plans, and would thus restrict its role to assisting in and providing incentives for self-implementation programs, and to maintaining a credible residual program of detection, surveillance and enforcement.").

[31] *See, e.g.*, Cary Coglianese, Jennifer Nash & Todd Olmstead, *Performance-Based Regulation: Prospects and Limitations in Health, Safety, and Environmental Protection*, 55 ADMIN. L. REV. 705 (2003).

to public safety and which prompted the formation of the Department of Homeland Security.[32]

Now almost three years into the administration of President Barack Obama, we have seen some attempts at regulation of the banking and securities industry through the formation of a new consumer finance protection agency. The Dodd-Frank Wall Street Reform and Consumer Protection Act[33] has been described as the most sweeping change in financial regulation since the New Deal. Among other things, the act created the Bureau of Consumer Financial Protection within the Federal Reserve System. As this edition goes to press, the new Bureau is just getting started. In addition to financial regulation, the off-shore oil platform explosion in the Gulf Coast on a rig owned by BP has triggered some renewed interest in fresh regulation of the off-shore oil industry. The 2010 earthquake in Fukushima, Japan and the resultant leak of radioactive gases from some nearby nuclear power plants has sparked additional interest and comment on regulation of nuclear power.

No matter what form these new developments take, they are healthy because they force everyone to re-examine some of the fundamental assumptions of the administrative system of government. Putting agencies' specific regulatory programs and conventional administrative procedures under the microscope will help us develop more creative and effective solutions for the problems of twenty-first century America.[34] But even so, as we near the end of the first decade of the twenty first century, the federal government and most state and local governments look a lot like they did during Franklin Roosevelt's time.

§ 1.04   THE ADMINISTRATIVE PROCESS

[A]   Generally

Much of the discussion in the first three sections of this chapter has focused on matters that involve the substance of administrative law. The substance of regulation is always the primary concern of clients and of the American public. Limits on the amount of social security benefits, changes in water quality standards for the lead smelting industry and prohibitions on the use of flammable fabrics in children's sleepwear are the things that most directly interest companies and individuals. However, lawyers who practice before agencies are always equally concerned with the way an agency decides these matters. You will be surprised as you begin to practice administrative law how often the manner in which an agency decision is made affects the substance of that decision.

The administrative *process* is governed mainly by the language of an agency's enabling act, the relevant administrative procedure act (APA)[35] and the procedural

---

[32] *See* Phillip A. Karber, *Re-Constructing Global Aviation in an Era of the Civil Aircraft as a Weapon of Destruction*, 25 HARV. J.L. & PUB. POL'Y 781 (2002).

[33] Pub. L. No. 111-203, 124 Stat. 1376 (2010).

[34] Many of these innovations are discussed in more detail in Chapter 15.

[35] Students concentrating on the administrative law of a particular state should take care to

rules adopted by the agency. Many agencies use specific procedures for individual matters, so it is dangerous to over-generalize on a particular agency's process of decision-making. In some instances, courts have required that agencies follow certain specified procedures.[36]

There are essentially three components to agency decision-making: *rulemaking*, *adjudication* and *informal action* (frequently referred to as informal *adjudication*). Agency procedures normally vary depending on the type of decision-making in which the agency is engaged.

[B] Rulemaking

When an agency exercises its legislative functions by making rules, the process normally used is a relatively simple system known as *notice and comment* or *informal* rulemaking.[37] This process requires the agency (1) to give the general public notification that a rule is being contemplated and the language or a general description of the proposed rule, and (2) to invite any interested person to submit comments on the proposed rule. The agency considers the comments and then promulgates a final rule. There are some limited instances on the federal level when rules may be promulgated only after an agency follows the adjudication procedures described in the next paragraph (so-called *formal* rulemaking), as well as instances when an agency's enabling act requires procedures somewhere between informal and formal rulemaking. This in-between procedure is usually referred to as *hybrid* rulemaking.

[C] Adjudication

When the agency exercises its judicial function by engaging in what is sometimes called formal adjudication, it uses a process that is very much like a civil bench trial in court. These proceedings-while subject to some variation depending on whether the agency is at the federal or state level and on the precise identity of the agency and the matter being adjudicated-typically permit an oral hearing with direct-and cross-examination, testimony under oath, the development of a complete and exclusive record on which the decision is to be based and the presence of a neutral presiding officer (sometimes referred to as an administrative judge or an administrative law judge). However, court and agency procedures are not identical. Unlike civil courts, most agencies do not use formal rules of evidence or permit the comprehensive discovery allowed under, for example, the Federal Rules of Civil Procedure. Elaborate pre-trial and post-trial procedures are rare, and juries are unheard of. Nonetheless, the similarities between agency adjudication and civil litigation are still far greater than the differences.

---

determine the scope of their state's act. Many state administrative procedure acts apply to specific agencies only if the legislature expressly provides, in the enabling act, that the state APA governs. Other states follow the model of the Federal APA and make the APA applicable to all agencies unless a specific agency is expressly exempted from the terms of the APA.

[36] The Supreme Court in *Goldberg v. Kelly*, 397 U.S. 254 (1970), required that state agencies wishing to terminate certain welfare benefits-aid to families with dependent children-adopt an elaborate hearing procedure for termination disputes. *See* the discussion of constitutional due process in Chapter 5.

[37] Rulemaking is discussed extensively in Chapter 7.

[D]   Informal Agency Action

Procedures used when an agency engages in informal action (sometimes referred to as informal *adjudication* because most of these decisions involve the deciding of individual cases rather than generic policymaking) vary considerably. Minimal procedures include merely giving reasons for a decision — as, for example, when a federal agency denies certain applications for benefits. Other actions can require the giving of notice and some opportunity to comment in writing or providing an oral hearing for aggrieved persons. Although procedures for rulemaking and formal adjudication are often tightly controlled by either an enabling act or the relevant APA, procedures governing informal agency action are often established by the procedural rules of the agency.

[E]   Alternative Dispute Resolution

Much like the current ferment in the substantive law of administrative agencies, traditional agency procedures are under serious re-examination. For some time, a number of agencies, such as the Environmental Protection Agency and the Federal Aviation Administration, have experimented with a new process known as *regulatory negotiation* to make rules. This procedure, in essence, brings representatives of all the major groups affected by a rulemaking around a table for face-to-face negotiation on the terms of the proposed rule, prior to its being published in the *Federal Register.*[38] In 1990, Congress codified regulatory negotiation by adding the Negotiated Rulemaking Act to the Administrative Procedure Act (APA).[39] In the next several years, agency practitioners will have even more procedural devices at their disposal. After a number of proposals to adapt alternative dispute resolution (ADR) techniques to agency decision-making surfaced during the 1980s,[40] Congress acknowledged that ADR could become an important part of agency process by enacting in 1990, and substantially amending in 1996, the Administrative Dispute Resolution Act.[41] In appropriate circumstances, such techniques as arbitration, mediation and mini-trial may now be used as part of the agency dispute resolution process.

---

[38] *See, e.g.*, Neil Eisner, *Regulatory Negotiation: A Real World Experience*, 31 FED. B. NEWS & J. 371 (1984), and the more elaborate description of regulatory negotiation in Chapter 7.

[39] 5 U.S.C. §§ 570–581. The Negotiated Rulemaking Act was permanently reauthorized in late 1996. Pub. L. No. 104-320.

[40] *See, e.g.*, Philip Harter, *Dispute Resolution and Administrative Law: The History, Needs, and Future of a Complex Relationship*, 29 VILL. L. REV. 1393 (1984) and the discussion of alternative dispute resolution techniques in Chapter 8.

[41] 5 U.S.C. §§ 571–583. The ADR Act was permanently reauthorized in late 1996. Pub. L. No. 104-320.

§ 1.05　JUDICIAL REVIEW OF AGENCY ACTION

[A]　Effect of Judicial Review

Lawyers should never lose sight of the important role that courts play in the development of administrative law. The creation of a new agency by the legislature almost always triggers an attack on the constitutionality of the agency, a dispute that can be resolved with finality only by the courts. The validity of each new regulatory program and many individual agency decisions can be challenged by persons affected by the action who are dissatisfied with the agency decision. Indeed, in most administrative systems there are very few agency decisions that are exempt from judicial review. It is almost unheard of for Congress to enact a new administrative statute without also providing for some type of judicial review. Reflecting the standard federal practice, state administrative systems also favor judicial review.

For law students and lawyers alike, it is possible to make both too much and too little of judicial review. Some of the traditional teaching in administrative law over-emphasized judicial review to the point that many students and practitioners were deceived into thinking that the only truly important component in an administrative law system is the judiciary. Even now, students may get the wrong idea that courts review everything and correct all errors because so many of the administrative law casebooks use large numbers of written appellate judicial decisions as the primary materials for the course. In actual agency practice, nothing could be further from the truth. The vast majority of agency decisions are never taken to court, and those that are taken to court usually come away with nothing more than an affirmance of the agency's action.[42] The United States Supreme Court has sent some extraordinarily strong signals to the lower federal courts (and in particular, to the United States Court of Appeals for the District of Columbia Circuit, the court that reviews a disproportionate number of federal agency appeals) to leave agency decisions alone, absent a clear showing that the agency acted erroneously.[43] State courts have not taken quite the hands-off attitude of the Supreme Court, but a quick review of a number of recent state court decisions suggests that a number of state supreme courts are tightening standards for reversing state agency action.

When analyzing judicial review of agency action, a lawyer typically confronts three types of issues: (1) *whether* judicial review is available at all for a particular

---

[42] There has been some criticism of judicial review of agency actions. *See, e.g.*, Alan Charles Raul & Julie Zampa Dwyer, *"Regulatory Daubert": A Proposal to Enhance Judicial Review of Agency Science by Incorporating* Daubert *Principles into Administrative Law*, 66 LAW & CONTEMP. PROBS. 7 (2003); Jerry L. Mashaw, *Small Things Like Reasons Are Put in a Jar: Reason and Legitimacy in the Administrative State*, 70 FORDHAM L. REV. 17 (2001).

[43] With regard to judicial review of the substance of agency action, *see Baltimore Gas & Elec. Co. v. Natural Res. Def. Council, Inc.*, 462 U.S. 87 (1983) (the courts have no business substituting their judgments for the scientific and technical decisions of the agencies); *Vt. Yankee Nuclear Power Corp. v. Natural Res. Def. Council, Inc. (NRDC)*, 435 U.S. 519 (1978) (reviewing an earlier stage of the *Baltimore Gas* case, the Court instructed lower federal courts that they were not to impose, by judicial fiat, more rulemaking procedures on agencies than those established under the Federal APA "absent extraordinary circumstances").

case, (2) the timing of judicial review (*i.e.*, *when* judicial review may take place), and (3) if judicial review is both permissible and timely, *what standard* of review a court should apply to the merits of the case. Since most enabling acts provide for some type of judicial review, and since both the Federal APA and most state APAs provide for judicial review even if the enabling act is silent, the question of whether or not a court may take a case is almost always answered in the affirmative. On the federal level, because federal courts are courts of limited jurisdiction, you must always identify and cite a specific grant of subject matter jurisdiction. Doing so is rarely difficult.

[B] Preclusion from Judicial Review

But finding a jurisdictional statute is not the end of this inquiry. There are instances when an agency decision may be precluded from judicial review because the legislature has specifically prohibited judicial review or because a matter is deemed totally within the agency's discretion. On occasion, a person seeking judicial review of a particular agency determination may not be able to prove that she is sufficiently affected by the agency's action to have the requisite standing to bring the action on her own behalf. The normal test applied in the federal courts is whether a person can show "personal injury in fact, economic or otherwise" stemming from the agency's action.[44]

[C] Other Barriers to Judicial Review

[1] Statutory and Common Law Barriers

Even if jurisdiction and standing exists and the decision is not precluded from review, a court may not be permitted to act at the time judicial review is sought. The doctrine of primary jurisdiction requires that most disputes within an agency's jurisdiction first go to the agency and not directly into court. If a party starts with the agency, the dispute will have to stay in the agency until the agency has taken final agency action. Two doctrines apply here. First, the litigant must exhaust the decisional possibilities within the agency. If there remains a decisional step within the agency not yet taken, a court will often stay its hand pending further agency action. Second, the doctrine of ripeness, a concept related to but not identical with exhaustion, prohibits judicial review if a dispute is not yet a legal (as opposed to a scientific or technical) issue.[45]

The litigant who survives these threshold barriers still has few prospects of getting the agency action reversed. Both statutes and case law significantly curb a court's authority to reverse agency action on the merits. In a limited number of cases, judicial review is virtually unfettered and a court may review agency action *de novo*. However, *de novo* review is normally permitted only when a statute expressly allows it. The vast majority of agency decisions are not reviewed *de novo*.

---

[44] These matters are extensively discussed in Chapter 10.

[45] These doctrines are discussed in Chapter 11.

For those cases, the Federal APA permits a court to overturn agency action on the following grounds:[46]

1. the action violates a statute (including statutes establishing the agency's jurisdiction and authority), the Constitution, or some procedure established by law;

2. the action is unsupported by substantial evidence;

3. the action is arbitrary, capricious, an abuse of discretion, or otherwise not in accordance with law.

This list may seem comprehensive, but there are comparatively few agency actions that give rise to statutory, procedural or constitutional violations. Accordingly, in practice, judicial review is largely limited to either *substantial evidence* review (undertaken if the agency has made the decision after conducting a formal rulemaking or adjudication) or *arbitrary/capricious* review. Both of these grounds are highly deferential to the determinations of the agency and generally require a court to uphold the agency's decision if the decision is one that a reasonable person could have made, irrespective of whether the court itself would have made the same decision.[47]

[2]   Odds of Judicial Reversal of Agency Decision

There are few meaningful statistics available on the proportion of agency decisions reversed by courts on either the substantial evidence or arbitrary/capricious ground. The author's personal experience, both as a practitioner and an academic, suggests that less than 10 percent of agency decisions are reversed on these grounds. The threshold barriers to judicial review sometimes make it difficult even to get into court; once there, a party is hard-pressed to get a reversal on the merits. If this statistical estimate is even close to being correct, judicial review should never be seen as a safety valve in planning a case strategy. The prospects of winning in court, having lost before the agency, are far too slim. As you read the remainder of this book, you should constantly remember cardinal rule number two of agency practice: You win your case at the agency or probably not at all.

There is yet a third cardinal rule for practicing before administrative agencies that needs to be set out here, even though it is probably obvious to any one who has read this far in this chapter. There is no substitute for having a thorough understanding of the manner in which the agency functions. Many practitioners obtain this knowledge over time; but even if this case marks your first experience with a particular agency, you are not excused from getting a good grip on that agency's behavior. As the following section explains, proper research is vital, and, these days with so much information available electronically, not all that difficult. So always keep in mind the third cardinal rule: "Know your agency."

---

[46] For convenience, these grounds paraphrase the principal grounds available under 5 U.S.C. § 706. These issues are discussed in much greater length in Chapter 12.

[47] The constantly cited Supreme Court decision in *Citizens to Preserve Overton Park, Inc. v. Volpe*, 401 U.S. 402 (1971), contains a good review of each of these grounds. *See also* Chapter 12.

§ 1.06   RESEARCHING ADMINISTRATIVE LAW

[A]   Student Awareness of Administrative Materials

Most teachers of administrative law are surprised by the lack of attention to administrative materials in most first-year legal writing and research courses. Many students come into their first administrative law course knowing virtually nothing about the primary materials of the course and absolutely nothing of the secondary materials. The following is a brief guide to federal materials available for those who are not already familiar with the sources.

[B]   Official Materials

[1]   *The United States Code*

The essence of administrative law is to be found primarily in government documents. First and foremost of these is the compilation of federal statutes, the *United States Code* (U.S.C.) and its various sources of legislative history such as committee reports. Floor debates transcribed in the Congressional Record are sometimes useful. These materials contain the language of the agency's enabling act and the pre-enactment comments on that act by members of Congress and other persons.

The primary federal procedural statute, the Administrative Procedure Act (APA), was first enacted in 1946, but had been the subject of intense discussion for almost ten years prior to enactment as lawyers, agency officials and members of Congress adjusted to many of the procedural lessons learned during the New Deal. One central feature of this debate, on which there was virtually a consensus, was the need for a uniform procedure applicable to most if not all federal agencies. At the same time, the APA does not control every aspect of every agency process. These days, an agency's enabling act will contain many specific procedures directly applicable to that agency. Some of the enabling act requirements may not be consistent with the APA. For example, practice before some highly proceduralized agencies, such as the National Labor Relations Board, almost never requires reference to the APA because the agency's statutes and internal procedural rules are so detailed and sophisticated. For most agencies, however, the APA has a strong bearing on the process by which the agency makes decisions.

The APA is contained in 5 U.S.C. §§ 551 *et seq.*, and its legislative history may be found in Administrative Procedure Act — Legislative History 1944–46, S. Doc. No. 248, 79th Cong., 2d Sess. (1946). A crucial executive branch committee report is also widely regarded as part of the APA's legislative history: Final Report of the Attorney General's Committee on Administrative Procedure, S. Doc. No. 8, 77th Cong., 1st Sess. (1941). Both the House and Senate reports on the APA will be found in the Attorney General's report, all of which are reprinted in a basic loose-leaf service, Pike & Fischer, Administrative Law (Desk Book).

[2] *The Federal Register*

Agencies announce proposed and final rules and various other information on their day-to-day functioning in the *Federal Register.*[48] This document was established by Congress during the New Deal because at the time there was no central repository of important agency pronouncements. Indeed, many agency rules could only be found in the desk drawers of agency employees. The *Federal Register* is published five days each week.

[3] *The Code of Federal Regulations*

The *Code of Federal Regulations* (CFR) is published annually and contains the agency's current rules in force.[49] Rules and certain other documents, such as agency interpretations and rulings published initially in the *Federal Register*, eventually find their way into CFR. For agencies whose rules change only infrequently, CFR is often the primary research tool used by practitioners; however, readers should be warned that there often are substantial delays between publication of a final rule in the *Federal Register* and codification of that rule in CFR. Because of this delay, most agency practitioners subscribe to various commercial publications that track rule and policy changes on a day-to-day basis, such as the Bureau of National Affairs' *Environment Reporter* or Commerce Clearinghouse's labor reporters.

[4] Agency Decisions

Most federal agencies publish some kind of official reporter that includes the reports of agency adjudications. These compilations look much like court reporters and carry titles such as "*I.C.C. Reports,*" "*FCC 2d*" and the like. Again, most practitioners subscribe to the official agency reporter but depend on proprietary loose-leaf services (*see* § [2] *above*) for up-to-the-minute information. In many circumstances, the value of using reported agency adjudications as controlling authority is questionable because most agencies do not consider themselves wholly bound by judicially-developed doctrines such as *stare decisis.* Nonetheless, careful lawyers pay close attention to these decisions to determine the current trend of agency thinking. Most agencies now publish these decisions on their individual websites.

[5] Other Agency Publications

Agencies always publish a great deal of information outside the *Federal Register* or CFR that can be enormously helpful. Documents such as internal agency newsletters, annual reports, and statistical summaries are useful in developing a comprehensive understanding of the entire agency. The Government Printing Office publishes a *Monthly Catalog of United States Government Publications* that lists many of these documents. The GPO also publishes THE UNITED STATES GOVERNMENT ORGANIZATION MANUAL, a single volume compilation of basic information on virtually all government agencies.

---

[48] *Federal Register* is available online *at* http://www.fdsys.gov.

[49] The *Code of Federal Regulations* is available *at* http://www.fdsys.gov.

These days there is a great deal of agency information available over the Internet. Virtually every federal agency has a Web site that may be mined for a great deal of basic information on that particular agency. A good basic source for links to the various agencies is provided by the Library of Congress: http://www.loc.gov/rr/news/fedgov.html. A private sector Internet source for similar information is a site maintained by Louisiana State University (http://www.lib.lsu.edu/gov/).

[6] Presidential Documents

The President figures importantly in the work of administrative agencies. Accordingly, executive orders and presidential proclamations, along with reorganization plans and executive agreements, must often be closely analyzed. These documents may occasionally be found in the Federal Register, but more likely are to be found in the *Weekly Compilation of Presidential Documents*, published by the Government Printing Office.

[7] Opinions of the Attorney General

The Attorney General of the United States is often asked to provide interpretations of treaties, statutes, presidential documents and other official material, as well as to advise on other matters of agency functioning. While the precise legal impact of an attorney general's opinion never has been conclusively determined, the Attorney General's pronouncements carry great weight both inside and outside the executive branch. Most opinions are published in a compilation called the Opinions of the Attorneys General of the United States.

[C] Unofficial Commercial Services

By definition, government documents are the official source of information on administrative agencies, but there is at least one privately-published service available for virtually every major federal regulatory agency. Most practitioners regard these services as indispensable because they are not subject to many of the publication delays associated with government publications. Published by such companies as Bureau of National Affairs and Commerce Clearing House, they are gold mines of information on the agencies, containing a wide range of documents and information from proposed and final rules, to adjudications, to agency gossip.

A vast amount of additional information on administrative law in general and on specific agencies may be found in the casebooks and treatises listed in the preface and in law journal articles. Serious students of administrative law never disregard these sources.

Chapter 2

EXTERNAL CONTROLS ON ADMINISTRATIVE AGENCIES — THE LEGISLATIVE BRANCH

§ 2.01 INTRODUCTION

Modern administrative agencies have numerous prerogatives and may exercise a great deal of discretion. But they do not create themselves, and they are subject to a substantial number of external controls. Each branch of government has an impact on agencies. Since all agencies are created by the legislature, they are obviously subject to the terms of the agency's enabling act; but that is only one of many ways a legislature can exert influence. Agencies are normally located within the executive branch of government, so they are constrained by various entities within that branch, such as the President and the Attorney General. Components of the cabinet-level agencies are, by definition, under the control of the cabinet officer for that agency. Even the nominally "independent" regulatory commissions are subject to a large number of executive controls, exercised mainly through the presidential appointment power and the President's control of the budgetary process. The judicial branch exerts control over agencies by way of judicial review of agency action on an after-the-fact, case-by-case basis; but the power of the courts is no less significant for coming at the end of the administrative process.

The form of these controls range from the obvious to the subtle. Virtually everyone with an elementary understanding of the United States' system of government realizes that a legislature may amend an enabling act, and that the chief executive may appoint cabinet officers and regulatory commissioners. Even so, the less-obvious controls can be just as compelling. These include the power of the legislature to conduct investigations, the power of the attorney general to order agencies to do — or refrain from doing — certain things and the power of the courts to write language in judicial opinions that, while not necessarily compelling agency action, may gently persuade an agency to mend its ways.

This Chapter considers the matter of legislative controls; Chapter 3 discusses executive controls on agency action. Judicial controls are discussed in several chapters, principally Chapter 5, and Chapters 9 through 12.

§ 2.02   CONSTITUTIONAL LIMITATIONS ON THE CREATION OF AGENCIES — THE DELEGATION ISSUE

[A]   Legislative Authority

On both the state and federal levels, the legislative branch is responsible for establishing agencies and endowing those agencies with a great deal of power and discretion. This authority does not, however, give the legislature carte blanche. The United States Constitution and most, if not all, state constitutions impose some limits upon when and under what circumstances a legislature may delegate powers to an agency. Most administrative law casebooks refer to this as the *non-delegation* doctrine. Non-delegation is a principle based on the premise that under our Constitution a legislature may delegate its powers to an agency only under carefully controlled conditions and that those conditions are to be expressly set out in the agency's enabling act.

[B]   Federal Agencies and the Non-Delegation Doctrine — The Early Cases

On the federal level, the Supreme Court has tussled with the non-delegation doctrine for years, even though the general rule — that a legislature may not delegate full legislative power to an agency — was established very early in our history. The source of the doctrine is the Constitution itself. Article I, § 1 provides that "[a]ll legislative powers herein granted shall be vested in a Congress of the United States . . . ." Section 8 of Article I provides that Congress has the power "[t]o make all laws which shall be necessary and proper for carrying into execution" the other powers in Article I. Reviewing these two provisions on their face suggests some of the tensions that have persisted for nearly two hundred years. § 1 could be read to give legislative powers *exclusively* to the Congress — i.e., that Congress may never pass on any of those powers to other components of the government. However, § 8 gives Congress the authority to carry out its powers by appropriate legislation. Section 8 arguably allows a busy Congress to authorize other governmental entities to act on its behalf, even if those delegated actions look very much like the exercise of legislative power.

The Supreme Court moved very gingerly on this issue in the first few decades following ratification of the Constitution, but it could not realistically deny the existence of the earliest executive branch agencies, such as the customs office and the treasury, because many of these offices pre-dated the Constitution and were clearly essential to the functioning of national government. Chief Justice Marshall, writing in *Wayman v. Southard*,[1] recognized that Congress could not by itself possibly exercise or even meaningfully supervise on a day-to day basis every detail of the functioning of a national government; thus, some delegation was a compelling necessity. Nonetheless, Chief Justice Marshall set certain boundaries on delegation-the traces of which still can be seen today. He insisted that Congress

---

[1] 23 U.S. (10 Wheat.) 1 (1825).

must establish the general outline of a regulatory program, but may leave to the agency the authority "to fill up the details."[2]

Subsequent cases paid lip service to the non-delegation principle, but generally upheld Congressional enactments that gave duties to administrative agencies. In *Marshall Field & Co. v. Clark*,[3] the Court upheld a delegation to the President for suspension of certain favorable tariffs on the goods of countries that did not reciprocate favorable treatment. The saving grace of the enabling act in that case was, in the Court's view, that the agency was limited to making purely factual determinations. Later cases permitted the delegation if the agency was limited to determining a "contingency"[4] or where Congress, by statute, set the "primary standard,"[5] or delegations in which Congress stated "an intelligible principle"[6] for agency decision-making.

The trend of these decisions is obvious. The Supreme Court had little or no interest in interfering in the day-to-day workings of the executive branch. Even before the turn of the twentieth century, the federal government dealt with so many complicated matters that a heavy-handed application of the non-delegation principle could have stopped the executive branch in its tracks. It is also clear that the Court realized that Congress should not have to burden itself with excessive detail. But at the same time, the Court was totally unwilling to do away with the non-delegation principle itself — probably because the doctrine is based on the express language of Article I, § 1. Not for the first or the last time in its history, the Court preserved a theoretical facade (the idea that Congressional power could not be delegated) while deciding individual delegation cases realistically.

[C] The New Deal Cases

[1] Background

What was not anticipated was that these early cases preserved just enough of the non-delegation doctrine to permit a Supreme Court that was hostile to the politics of Congress or the executive branch to invalidate on non-delegation grounds enabling acts that might otherwise have survived. That opportunity came in the early stages of President Franklin Roosevelt's New Deal when several Supreme Court Justices who reviled the President's new economic policies used the non-delegation doctrine to strike down a number of the agencies charged with implementing the New Deal.[7]

---

[2] *Id.* at 16.

[3] 143 U.S. 649 (1892).

[4] *The Brig Aurora*, 11 U.S. (7 Cranch) 382 (1813).

[5] *Buttfield v. Stranahan*, 192 U.S. 470 (1904) (standards of purity and fitness of tea imported into the United States). Students interested in the minutiae of government will be delighted to know that until recently the federal government employed a contingent of tea tasters to carry out the duties at issue in the *Buttfield* case.

[6] *J. W. Hampton, Jr., & Co. v. United States*, 276 U.S. 394 (1928) (tariff duties).

[7] This sentence may sound like a political statement. It is not meant to be. There is ample literature on the history of the New Deal documenting the Court's hostility. Students with additional interest in this

[2]   The Litigation Arising from the National Industrial Recovery Act of 1933

The most dramatic confrontation between the Justices and the President came in 1935 when two portions of what was probably the centerpiece of the New Deal, the National Industrial Recovery Act of 1933 (NIRA), reached the Court. In both cases, *Panama Refining Co. v. Ryan*[8] (the "Hot Oil" case), and *A.L.A. Schechter Poultry Corp. v. United States*[9] (the "sick chicken" case), the Supreme Court used the non-delegation doctrine to strike down two separate portions of the NIRA. Since these two cases are often used as the take-off point for administrative law courses, they warrant close analysis by students. They are also good vehicles for a discussion of legislative drafting and for an introduction to the administrative process itself.

The two opinions appear murky on first reading but are not that difficult to parse. *Panama Refining* ought to be viewed in context. It was an early attempt to establish a coherent federal energy policy in conjunction with existing state regulation of the oil industry. In states with large oil reserves, the state legislatures established state regulatory commissions (for example, the Texas Railroad Commission) with significant powers to control oil and natural gas production. Among other things, those commissions were authorized to enforce production levels for individual oil wells. These production limits, which are still imposed by many states, had two purposes: (1) they held down total production, and thus, increased the price per barrel of the oil actually produced and (2) they functioned as oil conservation measures because it is usually possible to get more oil out of a well that produces its oil slowly than it is to get oil from a well that is permitted to produce at a rapid rate. This is a scientific principle established early in the history of oil production by petroleum geologists, rather than merely a tenet of government regulation. Whatever one might think of regulatory agencies, it is indisputable that the state oil and gas commissions had a great deal of experience in what they were doing and that there was a rational basis for this type of regulation. Moreover, production levels had been set by the state agencies for years and were neither creations of the New Deal nor the federal government.

Section 9 of the NIRA, the only section of the statute under review in *Panama Refining*, did only one thing. It permitted the President, acting through the NIRA's jurisdictional agency, the National Recovery Administration (NRA), to write a regulation prohibiting oil producers from shipping in interstate commerce any oil produced from a well in excess of these state-established production levels. Obviously, Congress hoped that controlling excess oil production would have a beneficial effect on the national economy, but did not want to exercise the Supremacy Clause to interfere with the states' setting of the production levels — an activity that had always been carried out by the state oil and gas commissions. Instead, Congress chose to control the one part of the process that was within its

---

fascinating chapter in American history should consult, *e.g.*, Louis Jaffe, Judicial Control of Administrative Action 51–62 (1965) or Ernest Hawley, The New Deal and the Problem of Monopoly 12–34 (1966).

[8]   293 U.S. 388 (1935).

[9]   295 U.S. 495 (1935).

jurisdiction: the interstate commerce aspects of oil transportation and sale. Remember that a state's authority to regulate business under our Constitution normally stops at the state's boundaries. The federal government is the only entity that may regulate *interstate* commerce under the Commerce Clause.

Thus, there was nothing totally outlandish in what the states had been doing all along or in what Congress attempted to do under the Commerce Clause. Using the language of existing case law, the Supreme Court could have preserved the constitutionality of NIRA § 9 in a number of different ways. For example, the Court could have looked closely at what the President was asked to do — *i.e.*, determine the applicable state-mandated production level and issue an order prohibiting interstate shipment of any oil in excess of that level — as merely the "ascertainment of a fact." The "fact" that the NRA would be ascertaining would simply be the level of permissible production for a well or group of wells as established by the appropriate state oil and gas commission. As an alternative, the Court could have viewed the state production limitations and the use of those production quotas as principles that conserve natural resources and thereby constitute the necessary "intelligible principle" that created the requisite boundaries on executive action.

However, a majority of the Court refused to adopt any of this reasoning and held § 9 unconstitutional as a violation of the non-delegation principle. The Court majority viewed § 9 as a statute giving the President "unlimited authority" to act, with no boundaries set on his discretion. In the Court's words, § 9 set no conditions, established no criteria, nor required any specific findings before the President could act.[10]

In *Schechter*, the Court reviewed another section of the NIRA and came to the same conclusion as it did in *Panama Refining*. *Schechter* involved § 3 of the Act, in which Congress authorized private bodies, essentially trade associations, to develop standards (or "codes") of fair competition. When these codes were completed, they were handed to the President, and upon Presidential approval, became binding (that is, they had the force of law) on the industry as a whole.[11] As in *Panama Refining*, the Court concluded initially that § 3 lacked an appropriate standard for setting out boundaries for executive branch discretion and was thereby unconstitutional.

Moreover, the *Schechter* Court was also troubled by the statute's giving governmental decision-making powers to private entities, although it did not dwell

---

[10] Congress reacted quickly to the decision in *Panama Refining*. Shortly after the opinion was announced, Congress passed the Connolly Hot Oil Act setting out essentially the same prohibition on the interstate transportation of oil produced in excess of state quotas. The Connolly Hot Oil Act never was successfully challenged and remains on the books to this day at 15 U.S.C. § 715c. This statute required the President to make findings on the effect on interstate commerce of shipments of hot oil before prohibiting those shipments.

[11] Students should not conclude that Franklin Roosevelt personally reviewed these codes. To the extent that they were reviewed by the executive branch, they were reviewed by the National Recovery Administration even though the statute directs the President to perform the review. This is an example, frequently utilized by the executive branch of so-called *sub-delegation:* the handing down of powers within the executive branch from a senior official to an official or office further down the organizational chart.

on this defect in the opinion. One year later, in *Carter v. Carter Coal Co.*,[12] the Court re-emphasized the "no-delegation-to-private-parties" rule by invalidating a portion of the Bituminous Coal Conservation Act because that statute permitted binding wage and hour standards to be promulgated for the whole industry by private sector groups comprised of management and labor representatives.

The majority opinions in both *Panama Refining* and *Schechter* were probably politically motivated — *i.e.*, a majority of the justices were exceptionally hostile to President Roosevelt's economic programs and were looking for any halfway plausible basis for invalidating them. Because of this hostility, the opinions are characterized by what most commentators regard as a wooden application of the non-delegation principle in the face of years of flexible application of the doctrine in earlier Court opinions. For these reasons, most administrative law courses spend a lot of the time on the New Deal delegation cases by discussing the separate opinions by Justice Benjamin Cardozo, who dissented in *Panama Refining* and merely concurred in *Schechter*. Cardozo, unlike the *Panama Refining* majority, was willing to read § 9 in light of the statement of purpose for the NIRA contained in § 1 of the statute. Section 1 set out, among many other things, a need to conserve natural resources. Cardozo accepted this as a standard for curbing executive discretion and thereby concluded that the statute set appropriate boundaries for executive branch action. However, he was unwilling to use § 1 in similar fashion in *Schechter*, pointing out that Presidential authority to promulgate the codes of competition was not properly "canalized" and deemed § 3 "delegation run riot."

Superficially, Cardozo simply could not find a proper standard in *Schechter*. Yet, when a judge as distinguished as Cardozo believes that one part of a statute (§ 9) is constitutional and another part (§ 3) is unconstitutional, a more sophisticated analysis of his opinion ought to be made. Looking closely at Cardozo's two opinions, at least three distinguishing factors are present.

First, the Hot Oil provision (§ 9) was a *prohibition* on business conduct, while the Sick Chicken provision (§ 3) was essentially an *admonition* to industry to do good. Consistent with the traditional view of the manner in which American business ought to be regulated, Cardozo viewed the proper role of government as *prohibiting* bad practices, rather than a somewhat fuzzy encouragement of the best possible behavior.

Second, the Hot Oil statute was directed toward a *single industry* and reflected an understanding of conventional practices in that industry (*i.e.*, the setting of production levels by the state agencies), while the Sick Chicken statute affected virtually all American business.

Third, the Sick Chicken statute seemed to permit private parties to make decisions that should be reserved for the government, even though the President had to approve the standards before they went into effect. Cardozo apparently believed that the President's role would be largely a matter of rubber-stamping the private decisions.[13]

---

[12] 298 U.S. 238 (1936).

[13] Be wary of according undue importance to this analysis. The procedure for promulgating the codes

This is where matters came to rest, however. After the *Carter Coal* decision in 1936 and Roosevelt's unsuccessful attempt to pack the Supreme Court, there were noticeable changes in the Court's attitude toward New Deal legislation, possibly triggered by a number of changes in the Supreme Court's membership.[14] These changes, combined with more care in drafting legislation on the part of Congress (Congress these days is always careful to include some standard, however broad), prompted the Court to stop invalidating Congressional legislation, at least on Commerce Clause and delegation grounds. Since *Carter Coal*, the Supreme Court has not overturned any statute on the basis of the non-delegation principle.

[D] Delegation Since the New Deal

Between 1936 and the late 1970s, the non-delegation doctrine was certainly a dormant, if not a dead, issue. In 1947, the Court upheld an exceptionally vague statutory standard in *Fahey v. Mallonee*,[15] in part because the implementing regulations were detailed and explicit, and in part because the statute did not contain criminal penalties. In 1974, in *National Cable Television Ass'n v. United States*,[16] the Court hinted that a statute setting fees for certain cable television operations might have problems under the non-delegation principle, but remanded the case to the Federal Communications Commission on other grounds. In the same case, two dissenters characterized the non-delegation doctrine as "moribund."

However, in the early 1980s the non-delegation doctrine surfaced again. In two separate opinions, Justice William Rehnquist (who subsequently served as Chief Justice until his death in 2005) suggested that the Court resuscitate the non-delegation principle in an attempt to force Congress to be more careful when it drafts enabling legislation. He surprised the legal community in his separate opinion on this issue in *Industrial Department AFL-CIO v. American Petroleum Institute*,[17] when he suggested that Congress had invalidly delegated to the Department of Labor virtually unfettered authority to set certain employee safety and health standards. More to the point, Justice Rehnquist indicated his respect for *Panama Refining* and his sympathy for the non-delegation doctrine by calling attention to the doctrine's underlying purposes. In his view, a proper application of the doctrine: (1) forces the elected representatives of the people — Congress — to make the important choices of social and economic policy; (2) guarantees that any delegation to an agency will be accompanied by an intelligible principle guiding the

---

of fair competition is not too different from the current procedure for promulgating agency rules under the Administrative Procedure Act. *See* 5 U.S.C. § 553 and all the discussion of rulemaking procedure in Chapter 5. Agencies frequently accept suggestions from private parties as to the language of proposed rules and then make those suggestions part of the final rule.

There may also be a delegation problem when Congress gives executive branch powers to a member of the legislative branch. *See* the discussion of the Supreme Court's decision invalidating a portion of the Gramm-Rudman-Hollings budget balancing statute, *Bowsher v. Synar*, 478 U.S. 714 (1986), discussed in [E] below.

[14] *See* JAFFE, *supra* note 7, at 51–62.

[15] 332 U.S. 245 (1947).

[16] 415 U.S. 336 (1974).

[17] 448 U.S. 607 (1980).

agency's discretion; and (3) enhances judicial review by giving the courts a standard against which to weigh the exercise of the agency's discretion.[18]

Of course, it is possible to make both too much and too little of the Rehnquist opinions. On the one hand, he was writing in dissent when he was only an associate justice. As Chief Justice, he never saw fit (or perhaps never had the occasion) to repeat these views in later cases.

The Rehnquist position is not totally implausible. Congress sometimes fails to take sufficient care in writing legislation. A number of years ago, in an action signaling distrust of agency policymaking, Congress attempted to impose after-the-fact controls on agency conduct through the use of the legislative veto (by which Congress could disapprove agency rules after those rules were promulgated). The legislative veto was overturned by the Supreme Court in 1983.[19] Had Congress drafted more explicit standards in the enabling act, a legislative veto might not be necessary.

A majority of the Court, however, has consistently refused to apply the non-delegation doctrine rigidly because it realizes that Congress cannot legislate with precision in all areas of public policy. Indeed, it may be enough for Congress to identify a problem without prescribing its solution, so long as a competent agency is established to deal with it, and providing that *some* standard, however minimal and ambiguous, is put into the enabling act. This was essentially the message the Supreme Court sent to the American public when it upheld, in 1989, the United States Sentencing Commission and the somewhat flawed criminal sentencing requirements imposed on federal court under the Commission's hotly debated federal sentencing "guidelines."

In *Mistretta v. United States,*[20] the Court noted: "In light of our approval of [all the earlier] broad delegations, we harbor no doubt that Congress' delegation of authority to the Sentencing Commission is sufficiently specific and detailed to meet constitutional requirements . . . . We cannot dispute petitioner's contention that the Commission enjoys significant discretion in formulating guidelines . . . . but our cases do not at all suggest that delegations of this type may not carry with them the need to exercise judgment on matters of policy . . . . Only if we could say that there is an *absence of standards* for the guidance of the Administrator's action . . . would we be justified in overriding [Congress'] choice of means for affecting its declared purpose."[21] Of course, these days Mistretta itself is probably only of

---

[18] Justice Rehnquist reiterated his position on delegation the next term in his dissent in *Am. Textile Manufacturers Inst. v. Donovan,* 452 U.S. 490 (1981). He stated that the post-New Deal Supreme Court was too quick to consign the non-delegation principle to the junk heap along with substantive due process, for which even Rehnquist has no particular affection. The non-delegation principle, by contrast, has certain utility in containing Congress' penchant for ambiguity.

[19] *Immigration and Naturalization Serv. v. Chadha,* 462 U.S. 919 (1983). In the past, Congress has made an attempt to reintroduce the legislative veto. This legislation is discussed in § 2.04 *below.*

[20] 488 U.S. 361 (1989).

[21] *Id.* at 378 (emphasis supplied). In *Loving v. United States,* 517 U.S. 748 (1996), the Court took up a case involving a presidential executive order that established procedures for military courts martial in imposing the death penalty. The petitioners, among other things, argued that the non-delegation principle invalidated the procedures. Justice Kennedy, writing for eight of the justices, commented: "We

historical interest. In *United States v. Booker*,[22] the Supreme Court determined that the Sentencing Guidelines were advisory in nature because they interfered with a defendant's right to be convicted and sentenced only on facts proved beyond a reasonable doubt at trial. The *Booker* court did not revisit any of the delegation discussion set out in *Mistretta*.

In 2001, the Supreme Court in *Whitman v. American Trucking Ass'ns, Inc.*,[23] refused to deviate from the traditional non-delegation jurisprudence. Justice Scalia writing for a unanimous Court, stated that the proper standard of review in a delegation challenge is to determine whether Congress had legislated an "intelligible principle" to which the agency's decision-making must conform, or whether the statute was so broad and lacked any standard as to be unconstitutional. Reviewing portions of the Clean Air Act, the Court examined language in the Act that authorized the Environmental Protection Agency to set air quality standards that are "requisite to protect public health from the adverse effects of the pollutant in the ambient air." Justice Scalia invoked a 1991 decision, *Touby v. United States*,[24] in which a similar delegation to the Attorney General to designate certain drugs as controlled substances was upheld. Justice Scalia commented that the delegation in Whitman was "in fact well within the outer limits of our nondelegation precedents"[25] and noted that the Court had invalidated only two statutes on non-delegation grounds (*Panama Refining* and *Schechter*).

Everything discussed so far has involved the issue of standards. Remember, however, that there is another component of non-delegation: an inquiry as *to whom* the decision-making power is given. This other aspect of the non-delegation

---

find no fault . . . with the delegation in this case . . . . The President's duties as Commander-in-Chief . . . require him to take responsible and continuing action to superintend the military, including the courts-martial. The delegated duty, then, is interlinked with duties already assigned to the President by express terms of the Constitution, and the same limitations on delegation do not apply 'where the entity exercising the delegated authority itself possesses independent authority over the subject matter.' " *Id.* at 762. Delegation continues to attract the attention of a number of administrative law scholars. *See, e.g.*, Cass R. Sunstein, *Constitutionalism After the New Deal*, 101 Harv. L. Rev. 421 (1987); David Schoenbrod, Symposium, *The Phoenix Rises Again: The Nondelegation Doctrine from Constitutional and Policy Perspectives: Delegation and Democracy: A Reply to My Critics*, 20 Cardozo L. Rev. 731 (1999); Frona M. Powell, *The Supreme Court Rejects the New Nondelegation Doctrine: Implications for the Administrative State*, 71 Miss. L.J. 729 (2002). In another provocative article confirming that the non-delegation doctrine has very little modern utility, Professor Sunstein notes that the non-delegation doctrine had "one good year and 211 bad ones (and counting)." Cass R. Sunstein, *Nondelegation Canons*, 67 U. Chi. L. Rev. 315, 322 (2000).

[22] 543 U.S. 220 (2005). Justice Scalia also asserted that the agency itself cannot cure an otherwise defective delegation by promulgating rules that narrow its scope of authority. *Id.* at 227.

[23] 531 U.S. 457 (2001).

[24] 500 U.S. 160 (1991).

[25] 543 U.S. at 228. There is some evidence that lower federal courts have used the nondelegation doctrine as a tool to narrow certain statutes so as to preserve them against a nondelegation attack. In *International Union v. Occupational Safety & Health Adm'n*, 938 F.2d 1310 (D.C. Cir. 1991), Judge Stephen Williams determined that certain interpretations by OSHA were "so broad as to be unreasonable" but went on to conclude that at least one of the OSHA interpretations was "reasonable and consistent with the nondelegation doctrine." *Id.* at 1317. *See* Richard J. Pierce, Jr., *The Inherent Limits on Judicial Control of Agency Discretion: The D.C. Circuit and the Nondelegation Doctrine*, 52 Admin. L. Rev. 63 (2000).

doctrine figured in a very important decision, *Bowsher v. Synar*,[26] overturning a budget balancing statute known as the Gramm-Rudman-Hollings Act.[27] In *Synar*, the Supreme Court reviewed a statute giving the Comptroller General (CG), the chief officer of the General Accounting Office (now called the "Government Accountability Office" or GAO), certain powers of review over the executive branch budget. The court determined that the GAO is properly part of the legislative branch (the CG is appointed by the President but removable only by Congress) and therefore was not permitted under the Constitution to make executive branch decisions-decisions that affect the execution of the law — because the President lacked the authority to remove the CG. Although this type of delegation is somewhat different from the delegation to private parties issue decided in *Schechter* and in *Carter Coal*, *Synar* is a landmark decision for the proposition that delegation *to whom* is still an important matter. The *Synar* case, as well as the statements of Justice Scalia and the earlier comments of then-Justice Rehnquist, suggest that the non-delegation doctrine is still not completely dead, even on the federal level.

[E]   Delegation in State Administrative Systems

While broad generalizations about state administrative law are understandably suspect, most observers believe that the non-delegation doctrine has more force and effect at the state level than it currently enjoys at the federal level. For example, in his seminal book on state administrative law, Professor Frank Cooper lists a number of factors that, in his view, have prompted state courts to be tougher on their legislatures than the Supreme Court has been on Congress.[28] Professor Cooper believes that state courts have a stronger interest in limiting the activities of state agencies because state courts tend to trust state agencies less than Congress and the Supreme Court trust federal agencies.

However, when state delegation cases are read individually, it appears that state courts are mainly hostile only to totally standardless delegation — *i.e.*, statutes that give an agency the power to regulate without specifying how, when or where- or to delegations of governmental decision-making power to private persons. This is much the same pattern as established by the United States Supreme Court.[29] As a consequence, most of the state cases seem to involve what appear to be mere mistakes in legislative drafting (the failure to include a standard), rather than outright hostility on the part of state courts toward state agencies.

Moreover, even though there are numerically far more state decisions striking down state statutes on non-delegation grounds, remember that there are numerically more state statutes to be reviewed. If you only examine the decisions

---

[26] 478 U.S. 714 (1986).

[27] Gramm-Rudman is formally called the Balanced Budget and Emergency Deficit Control Act of 1985, Pub. L. No. 99-177, 99 Stat. 1037.

[28] FRANK COOPER, STATE ADMINISTRATIVE LAW 73–91 (1965).

[29] *See, e.g., Sarasota County v. Barg*, 302 So. 2d 737 (Fla. 1974); *State Compensation Fund v. De La Fuente*, 18 Ariz. App. 246, 501 P.2d 422 (1972). One state court has invalidated a delegation that established a public interest standard without any further elaboration. *Bell Tel. Co. v. Driscoll*, 343 Pa. 109, 21 A.2d 912 (1941) (but readers should take note of the date of this decision).

of a single state supreme court, you normally find no more cases invalidating state laws on non-delegation grounds than you do on the federal level. In other words, most state courts seem to invalidate statutes on non-delegation grounds about as often as the Supreme Court has done. Lawyers wondering what a court might do with a statute should keep in mind a principle of judicial review much more important than the non-delegation doctrine — *i.e.*, courts are always reluctant to hold statutes unconstitutional regardless of the ground on which the statute is attacked.

The vast majority of delegations of legislative power to administrative agencies, whether state or federal, have been upheld. Some states seem to be willing to let due process requirements in a statute (requirements that order an agency to deal fairly and correctly with persons who come before it) to substitute for *public interest* or *public convenience* standards. For example, the Maine Supreme Court upheld a 1974 statute, commenting:

> We are of the opinion that, in such cases in which the statutory enactment of detailed specific standards is impossible, the presence of adequate procedural safeguards to protect against an abuse of discretion by the administrators of the law, compensates substantially for the want of precise legislative guidelines and may be taken into consideration in resolving the constitutionality of the delegation of power.[30]

[F] Solving a Delegation Problem

[1] Identifying a Delegation Issue

Delegation issues are sometimes difficult to spot, but once spotted they are rarely difficult to analyze. To spot a delegation issue, first consider:

1. What is the *standard* set out in the statute, if any?

2. *To whom* is the decision-making power given? Each of these questions must be separated for proper discussion.

[2] Resolving the Standards Issue

Spotting and resolving the issue of a proper standard is a matter of searching the enabling act in question for words that appear to set out a standard. At least in theory, this inquiry is to be limited to the face of the statute. There are numerous cases that hold that no amount of subsequent agency action, no matter how reasonable, can cure an otherwise defective delegation.[31] If absolutely no standard,

---

[30] *Finks v. Me. St. Highway Comm'n*, 328 A.2d 791 (Me. 1974).

[31] For example, the regulations at issue in *Panama Refining* had been inadvertently repealed by the NIRA before the case reached the Supreme Court, so they were never at issue in the case. For a longer description of this aspect of the case, *see* Chapter 7, § 37 (the requirement of publication of agency rules). *See also Yakus v. United States*, 321 U.S. 414 (1944), one of the cases that signaled the end of the Supreme Court's hostility to the New Deal legislation. In upholding the constitutionality of the Emergency Price Control Act against various challenges, including a delegation argument, the Court stated: "[The Act's constitutionality] depends not . . . [upon the administrative officer's findings] but

however loose or ambiguous, can be found, there may be serious problems with the delegation, even on the federal level. But consider this from the standpoint of common sense. Most, if not all, legislative drafters are at least faintly aware of *Panama Refining* and *Schechter.* Consequently, they can be expected to put language in the statute that at least appears to be some kind of standard. One way to work through the standard issue is simply to review the language of the standards that have passed muster.

Agency	Standard in Enabling Act
Federal Maritime Commission	"public convenience & necessity"
FTC	"unfair methods of trade/competition"
Energy Dep't	"national security" (oil imports)
OSHA	"protect health to the extent feasible"[32]
EPA	protect human health & environment "to an adequate degree of safety"

If a new statute contains language such as the language in these examples, in all likelihood it contains a valid standard, and your inquiry so far as this first aspect of the non-delegation doctrine is concerned is at an end. Note that every one of the agencies listed in this chart, except for the Interstate Commerce Commission, are alive and kicking. If their statutes have survived an attack on non-delegation grounds, it is highly likely that similar language in a new enabling act will also survive. If the statute does not contain even this much enabling language, the non-delegation doctrine might be used to invalidate the statute, but only if a reviewing court sees fit to resuscitate *Panama Refining* and *Schechter.* A modern court will likely bend over backward to discern some kind of standard, however slight, anywhere in the statute, as did Justice Cardozo in *Panama Refining.*

[3]   Resolving the Delegation to Whom Issue

The second part of the delegation inquiry may be a bit more troublesome. To whom has the power been given? The enabling act must be examined to determine precisely who will make the decisions under the enabling act. There are three possibilities to review:

1.   A delegation to the "President" or to the "Secretary of Transportation;"

---

upon . . . whether the [statutory] definition sufficiently marks the field within which the administrator is to act. . . ." *But see Zemel v. Rusk*, 381 U.S. 1 (1965) (another case upholding an exceptionally broad delegation of authority to the Secretary of State to restrict travel to Cuba), in which the Court drew a distinction between administration of domestic matters and administration of foreign affairs and discussed the statutory standard "in light of prior administrative practice." *Zemel* may not be a good basis for generalizing, however. Throughout the course in administrative law, students should be leery of using cases that deal with immigration or other foreign affairs matters as a basis for developing general principles of administrative law. These cases may occupy a category all their own. Moreover, the Court referred to Congress' acceptance of past administrative practices to uphold the standard, rather than prospective administrative action.

[32] This was the standard at issue in *Indus. Dep't AFL-CIO v. Am. Petroleum Inst.*, 448 U.S. 607 (1980), that gave Justice Rehnquist so much trouble. A majority of the Court had no trouble with it, however.

2.   A subsequent delegation to another officer within the agency (the so-called *subdelegation* issue);

3.   A delegation to private entities or to an entity in a branch of government other than the executive branch.

There are no constitutional problems with possibilities 1 or 2. The first alternative is the normal course of action. The second possibility, subdelegation, is now mainly of historical interest. A number of early Supreme Court decisions[33] suggested that the officer to whom Congress delegated authority must be the person who actually decides. These days it is virtually unquestioned that the federal officer named in the statute may hand over day-to-day decision-making to lower echelon officials within that agency.[34]

The second two possibilities require a bit more analysis. With regard to giving over governmental decision-making powers to the private sector, the principle appeared, until just recently, to be straightforward and unambiguous. The general rule grew out of the *Schechter* and *Carter Coal* cases: it is impermissible under our constitutional system for Congress to give governmental decision-making powers to private entities.

But even a principle as seemingly strong as this may be giving way to the practical necessities of decision-making. In a 1982 case, *Schweiker v. McClure*,[35] the Supreme Court reviewed the use of private sector insurance carriers to provide hearings (and decisions) on disputed claims for Medicare payments under the Social Security System. The Court dealt with the case purely in terms of due process considerations and concluded that the company's hearing officers did not have any existing pecuniary bias or prior involvement with the cases that would require them to be disqualified from sitting in the capacity of administrative judges to decide the Medicare claims. There was no discussion whatsoever of the delegation-to-private-persons issue. On the one hand, this may simply re-affirm the fact that the Court has no affection for either *Schechter* or *Carter Coal.* Even though the cases have never been overruled expressly, they have long been given the silent treatment by the Court. On the other hand, the Court may have determined-again silently-that there was really no government policy being made by these private sector judges. All of the policy seems to have been made by the Department of Health and Human Services. The insurance carrier personnel were really just functioning in a kind of fact-gathering or investigative capacity. In other words, HHS was then the agency that determined, as a matter of policy, the classes of persons who are eligible for Medicare (these decisions are now made by the independent Social Security Administration); the insurance carriers simply decide whether a particular indi-

---

[33]   *See, e.g., Runkle v. United States*, 122 U.S. 543 (1887) (a statutory delegation to "the President" in cases of officers being dismissed from the military services after court martial requires the exercise of the President's personal judgment).

[34]   Congress has resolved this by enacting 5 U.S.C. § 302 which expressly permits sub-delegation. *See also United States v. Cottman Co.*, 190 F.2d 805 (4th Cir. 1951), *cert. denied*, 342 U.S. 903 (1952). When analyzing the statute, be careful to insure that the sub-delegate is a government official and that he or she is employed in the agency in question. It is possible that a sub-delegation by the Secretary of the Treasury to a Department of Commerce employee may be invalid.

[35]   456 U.S. 188 (1982).

vidual fits the profile established by the agency.

In another case, *Thomas v. Union Carbide Agricultural Products Co.*,[36] the Court approved the use of private sector arbitrators to render decisions in controversies under the Federal Insecticide, Fungicide, and Rodenticide Act (FIFRA). Once again, the Court did not squarely address the delegation to private parties issue in the parlance of *Schechter* and *Carter Coal*, but rather determined that not all government determinations confer an automatic right to a full-blown agency hearing followed by comprehensive review by an Article III court. Instead, as the Court put it:

> Congress, acting for a valid legislative purpose . . . may create a seemingly "private" right that is so closely integrated into a public regulatory scheme as to be a matter appropriate for agency resolution with limited involve-ment by the Article III judiciary. To hold otherwise would be to erect a rigid and formalistic restraint on the ability of Congress to adopt innovative measures such as negotiation and arbitration with respect to rights created by a regulatory scheme.[37]

The underlying reasoning here may be much like that of the *Schweiker* case: the private sector people are not really making policy; they're simply applying the policy to individual disputes. *Thomas* may also reflect the Court's growing awareness of and affection for alternative dispute resolution techniques as a mechanism for coping with court congestion. Generally, when the Supreme Court has had the opportunity to move disputes out of the courts and into ADR settings, it has done so. Alternative dispute resolution in the context of federal administrative agencies is more elaborately discussed in Chapter 8, § 8.02.[38]

What is less certain is whether these two cases suggest a full-blown retreat from the basic principle of no delegation to private persons. That is unlikely. Recall that in *Schechter* and *Carter Coal*, the private sector entities were actually setting policy that would bind the industry as a whole. In other words, the private sector was functioning in a rulemaking capacity. The Court wisely held that this was constitutionally impermissible. It is far more difficult to see that same policymaking role handed to the private sector in either *Schweiker* or *Thomas*. Of course, if the insurance carrier hearing officers or the private sector arbitrators begin making policy through their case decisions, we may have moved into a private sector policymaking setting without full consideration of the constitutional issues at hand.[39]

---

[36] 473 U.S. 568 (1985).

[37] *Id. Thomas* gave great impetus to the move toward the use of alternative dispute resolution procedures in federal agencies, culminating in 1991 with the enactment of a statute approving ADR techniques for general agency use. *See* the discussion on the ADR act *below* at § 8.02.

[38] *See, e.g., Mitsubishi Motors Corp. v. Soler Chrysler-Plymouth, Inc.*, 473 U.S. 614 (1985) (even federal antitrust disputes must be submitted to arbitration when a contract contains an arbitration clause).

[39] For a provocative article that takes the "delegation to whom" issue far beyond the scope of this chapter, see Gillian E. Metzger, *Privatization as Delegation*, 103 COLUM. L. REV. 1367 (2003).

[4]   Delegation Outside the Executive Branch — The Separation of Powers Muddle

The Supreme Court has frequently considered Congress's creation of decision-making entities that cross the boundaries between the legislative, executive and judicial branches. In one case, *Humphrey's Executor v. United States*,[40] involving the President's power to remove a member of an independent regulatory agency, the Federal Trade Commission, the Supreme Court concluded that an independent regulatory commission exercised powers in certain cases as an agency for either the legislature ("quasi-legislative" powers) or the courts ("quasi-judicial" powers), and thus, Congress could shield an FTC commissioner from unfettered removal by the President, even though the President appoints FTC commissioners. The effect of the *Humphrey's Executor* decision was to shore up the status of the independent regulatory commission, but at the expense of cluttering the constitutional doctrine of separation of powers.

The Court in recent years has only increased the difficulties in parsing the doctrine of separation of powers. Consider the following cases, set out, for lack of a better order, chronologically. In *Buckley v. Valeo*,[41] the Supreme Court invalidated a part of the Federal Election Campaign Act because Congress retained for itself the power to appoint several of the members of the jurisdictional agency, the Federal Election Commission. The Court held that only "officers of the United States" appointed by the President could exercise the powers of election oversight conferred by the Act. In *Immigration and Naturalization Service v. Chadha*,[42] (discussed below), the Court invalidated Congress' attempt to give itself veto power over rules promulgated by executive branch agencies. In *Chadha*, the Court reasoned that the separation of powers doctrine reserved a veto to the President and that Congress' only power was to enact legislation that is presented to the President for signature.

In *Bowsher v. Synar*,[43] decided three years after *Chadha*, the Court held that it is impermissible for Congress to give to a legislative branch officer, the Comptroller General (the head of what is now called the Government Accountability Office), decision-making powers with regard to the executive branch's budget that properly belong solely to the President. In *Bowsher*, the Court looked closely at the office of Comptroller General and concluded that the Comptroller General was essentially an officer of the legislative branch. Thus, Congress had attempted to give one of its own agents powers that were reserved solely for the executive branch. These cases were not unanimous. Justice White, for example, sharply criticized the Court for creating almost impenetrable boundaries around each branch of government and in the process interfering with Congress's attempts to deal creatively with important problems of governing. He found the majority's reasoning excessively formalistic.

---

[40] 295 U.S. 602 (1935).

[41] 424 U.S. 1 (1976).

[42] 462 U.S. 919 (1983).

[43] 478 U.S. 714 (1986).

If the Court had stopped with *Bowsher*, it might have preserved a thread of consistency in its separation of powers decisions, with *Humphrey's Executor* one of the few aberrations. But since 1986, the Court has decided even more separation of powers cases, creating doctrinal twists and turns that exist in few other areas of constitutional law. Consider, for example, the opinions issued in *Morrison v. Olson*[44] and *Mistretta v. United States*.[45] In *Morrison*, the Court reviewed the Office of Independent Counsel (OIC) created by a portion of the Ethics in Government Act.[46] Under the statute, members of Congress may recommend to the Attorney General the appointment of an independent counsel. If the AG concurs, the AG convenes the judges who make up the special division to make the ultimate appointment. Simply stated, the independent counsel is an attorney normally from the private sector who is appointed as a federal prosecutor (an office within the executive branch) by a "Special Division" — a court comprised of Article III judicial officers.

The former federal officials challenged the OIC's constitutionality along the same lines set out above-that it is unconstitutional for an entity (the special division) outside the executive branch to appoint an *officer* of the United States (*i.e.*, the independent counsel). In this instance, the Court upheld the OIC, insisting that "we have never held that the Constitution requires that the three Branches of Government operate with absolute independence." The Court went on to emphasize that in the case of OIC, Congress did not reserve any meaningful powers of appointment for itself, but simply permitted its members to recommend the appointment. On the other hand, the Court concluded that the appointment of a prosecutor by the judges in the special division was not inappropriate because the special division may do so only when the AG so recommends, and the AG's refusal to recommend appointment is not reviewable in court.

In *Mistretta*, the entire newly promulgated federal criminal sentencing scheme, the *Federal Sentencing Guidelines*, was at stake. In this instance, the so-called *Guidelines* (actually hard and fast rules permitting very little exercise of judicial discretion in criminal sentencing) were promulgated by the United States Sentencing Commission. The Commission is established by statute as an independent commission within the judicial branch. It has seven voting members appointed by the President and confirmed by the Senate. Under the statute, at least three members must be federal judges selected by the President from a list compiled by the Judicial Conference of the United States, and the remainder may be non-judges, including private sector lawyers.

The Court in *Mistretta* took an approach to the delegation/separation of powers issues similar to that advanced in this book. It first examined the delegation to assure itself that appropriate standards existed for framing the guidelines. Noting the statutory language, such as "to provide certainty and fairness" and to "avoid unwarranted sentencing disparities," the Court quickly concluded that the statutory standards were sufficient. The Court went on to examine the nature of the sentencing commission and determined that its appointment did not violate the

---

[44] 487 U.S. 654 (1988).

[45] 488 U.S. 361 (1989).

[46] The actual work of the OIC is discussed in Chapter 3, § 3.05.

separation of powers doctrine. On this issue, the Court commented:

> According to petitioner, Congress may not upset the balance among the Branches by co-opting federal judges into the quintessentially political work of establishing sentencing guidelines, by subjecting those judges to the political whims of the Chief Executive, and by forcing judges to share their power with non-judges. [However,] [a]lthough the unique composition and responsibilities of the Sentencing Commission give rise to serious concerns about a disruption of the appropriate branch of governmental power . . . we conclude, upon close inspection, that petitioner's fears for the fundamental structural protections of the Constitution prove, at least in this case, to be "more smoke than fire" and do not compel us to invalidate Congress' considered scheme for resolving the seemingly intractable dilemma of excessive disparity in criminal sentencing.[47]

Thus, the appointment of the sentencing commission did not violate separation of powers doctrine.[48]

The separation of powers doctrine remains in this somewhat confused posture. In 1991 the Supreme Court reviewed congressional action in establishing an airport authority for the two major airports in the Washington, D.C. metropolitan area, National Airport and Dulles Airport. In transferring control of the airports to local authority, Congress created a Metropolitan Washington Airports Authority, which in turn was directed to create a Board of Review. Among other things, the Board of Review was empowered to consider whether too much air traffic was being diverted from very busy National Airport (a few minutes' drive from Capitol Hill) to Dulles Airport, which lies nearly thirty miles outside Washington. The Board of Review was to consist of nine members of Congress who served on the various Congressional transportation committees. The Authority was empowered to select the Board's nine members from a list provided by Congress. The Board could then exercise veto power over many decisions made by the Authority.

In deciding the validity of the new Authority in *Metropolitan Wash. Airports Auth. v. Citizens for the Abatement of Aircraft Noise, Inc. (MWAA)*,[49] the Court looked at this scheme and said "no." After examining the historical underpinnings of separation of powers and some, but not all, of its own separation of powers case law, the Court concluded that here Congress had arrogated too much power to itself. But once again, the Court was not unanimous. In a strongly worded opinion by Justice White (joined by Chief Justice Rehnquist and Justice Marshall), the

---

[47] For a lengthier discussion of the guidelines and *Mistretta*, see Ronald F. Wright, *Sentencers, Bureaucrats, and the Administrative Law Perspective on the Federal Sentencing Commission*, 79 CAL. L. REV. 1 (1991).

[48] As noted above, more recently the Supreme Court held that the Sentencing Guidelines are merely advisory. *United States v. Booker*, 543 U.S. 220 (2005).

[49] 501 U.S. 252 (1991). Another separation of powers case is *Edmond v. United States*, 520 U.S. 651 (1997), a case in which the plaintiffs challenged the Secretary of Transportation's appointment of civilian members to the Coast Guard's Court of Criminal Appeals a court that deals exclusively with military justice matters involving uniformed members of the Coast Guard. The Supreme Court sustained the appointments. The opinion is notable mainly for a lengthy discussion of the "principal/inferior" officer distinction that has occasionally factored in separation of powers cases.

dissent began: "Today the Court strikes down yet another innovative and otherwise lawful governmental experiment in the name of separation of powers." Justice White went on to point out that MWAA was the first occasion when the Court overturned on separation of powers grounds an administrative body that was created essentially under state law.

It is difficult to know exactly what to make of all of this. It may be possible simply to take refuge in statistics. The bulk of Congressional enactments are upheld when challenged on separation of powers grounds. The administrative mechanisms discussed here are outside the mainstream of federal administrative law. Still, there is no question that it is difficult to harmonize these decisions. One valiant attempt has been made by the late Professor Thomas Sargentich who distinguished between two separation of powers themes: the separation theme, and the checks and balances theme.[50] The separation theme essentially requires nearly absolute barriers between the three branches. But this theme is not especially favored by contemporary administrative scholars. For example, agency rulemaking arguably crosses over into a pure legislative function and thus, might be invalid under a separation concept. By contrast, the checks and balances approach simply tries to curb excessive concentration of power in any one of the branches. By judicious application of the checks and balances concept, courts may be able to approve some of the innovations enacted by Congress without doing terrible violence to our fundamental notions of separation of powers.

The Sargentich analysis is intriguing and helpful, but even its insights do not fully suffice to explain the Supreme Court's twists and turns. From a problem-solving standpoint, about all one can do is examine any new administrative model in light of this incredible muddle of cases and make her best guess as to how the Supreme Court might decide the new dispute.

There is one final consideration in spotting delegation issues. Delegation, a dormant if not moribund issue, should not be confused with the *ultra vires* doctrine (discussed in Chapter 3 and elsewhere), a doctrine that asks whether an agency is functioning within its statutory powers. One easy way to distinguish these two issues is to keep in mind that the non-delegation principle involves a look at the face of the enabling act and does not normally inquire into subsequent actions taken by the administrator. *Ultra vires*, by contrast, presumes that the enabling act contains a proper standard, *i.e.*, that it is constitutional on its face, and then investigates subsequent agency action to see whether that action is authorized by the enabling act. For example, the Federal Aviation Administration (a component of the Department of Transportation) is authorized to regulate the safety of aircraft. There is no question that the Federal Aviation Act (the FAA's enabling act) contains adequate standards. Thus, it does not violate the delegation doctrine, and the FAA is a fully constitutional administrative agency. However, if the FAA attempted to regulate railroad safety, it would be functioning outside the scope of its enabling act and thus, would be engaged in *ultra vires* activity. It is rare to see successful attacks

---

[50] *See* three articles by Thomas O. Sargentich, *The Limits of the Parliamentary Critique of the Separations of Powers*, 34 Wm. & Mary L. Rev. 679 (1993), *The Contemporary Debate About Legislative-Executive Separation of Powers*, 72 Cornell L. Rev. 430 (1987), *The Delegation Debate and Competing Ideals of the Administrative Process*, 36 Am. U. L. Rev. 419 (1987).

on agencies brought under the non-delegation principle; but *ultra vires* challenges are much more common and occasionally succeed.

[G]   Delegation in the Future

It is too soon to bury the non-delegation doctrine, although it clearly has had at least one and one-half feet in the grave for the past forty or fifty years. The Supreme Court has shown no particular affection for the doctrine, even with Justice Rehnquist's attempts to revive it.[51] Moreover, Congress learned a few lessons from *Panama Refining* and *Schechter.* When Congress enacts enabling legislation these days, the legislation invariably contains some kind of intelligible standard and normally delegates power to government officials in the executive branch (some of the separation of powers decisions described above notwithstanding). That is normally enough, and it appears to be enough to satisfy even the pickiest Supreme Court for the foreseeable future. Lawyers who now argue that statutes are invalid because they violate the non-delegation doctrine are probably wasting a great deal of their client's time and money.

However, as a matter of administrative policy, students should consider whether there are not disadvantages in permitting Congress to legislate too loosely.[52] In recent years, Congress has found it nearly impossible to perform even those two tasks central to its responsibility-enactment of a proper budget and establishment of a rational system of federal taxation. A lack of precise standards emanating from Congress permits the exercise of virtually unfettered discretion by non-elected agency officials. This was part of the message of Justice Rehnquist's dissent in *Industrial Department AFL-CIO v. American Petroleum Institute*, a message that has been echoed by a number of distinguished observers of the federal system.[53] On the one hand, we may marvel at a system that runs reasonably well, even in the face of arguable abdication of Congress' responsibilities. On the other hand, we may wonder about the concentration of enormous power and influence in persons (agency officials) not directly answerable to the voting public.

---

[51] For a discussion of administrative law and its role in addressing the delegation issue, *see* Lisa Schultz Bressman, *New Theories of the Regulatory State Disciplining Delegation After* Whitman v. American Trucking Ass'ns, 87 CORNELL L. REV. 452 (2002). *See also* Tongue Watts, *Agency Rules with the Force of Law: The Original Convention,* 116 HARV. L. REV. 467 (2002); Sandra B. Zellmer, *The Nondelegation Doctrine: Fledgling Phoenix or Ill-Fated Albatross?,* 31 ENVTL. L. REP. 1115 (2001); Frona M. Powell, *The Supreme Court Rejects the New Nondelegation Doctrine: Implications for the Administrative State,* 71 MISS. L.J. 729 (2002); Eric A. Posner & Adrian Vermeule, *Interring the Nondelegation Doctrine,* 69 U. CHI. L. REV. 1721 (2002); Michael B. Rappaport, *The Selective Nondelegation Doctrine and the Line Item Veto: A New Approach to the Nondelegation Doctrine and Its Implications for* Clinton v. City of New York, 76 TUL. L. REV. 265 (2001). For a very fresh view on delegation and other separation of powers issues, *see* Patrick M. Garry, *The Unannounced Revolution: How the Court Has Indirectly Effected a Shift in the Separation of Powers,* 37 ALA. L. REV. 689 (2006).

[52] For a discussion on permitting Congress to legislate too loosely, *see Does Congress Delegate Too Much Power to Agencies and What Should Be Done About It? Before the Comm. on Gov't Reform,* 106th Cong. (2000), *at* http://gpo.gov/congress/house.

[53] *See, e.g.,* DAVID SCHOENBROD, DELEGATION AND ITS DISCONTENTS: POWER WITHOUT RESPONSIBILITY (1993); JOHN HART ELY, DEMOCRACY & DISTRUST, 133–34 (1980); THEODORE J. LOWI, THE END OF LIBERALISM 125–55 (1969).

§ 2.03   OTHER LEGISLATIVE CONTROLS

[A]   Congressional Devices for Policing Administrative Agencies

No one should shed any tears over the demise of the non-delegation doctrine. Congress has many far more meaningful devices for policing the activities of administrative agencies and for curbing what the members of Congress might deem excessive agency discretion. First, Congress has the ability to write elaborate enabling acts, prescribing minute standards of agency behavior. The non-delegation cases involved statutes that prescribed only the minimum statutory requirements. Congress may always write with far more detail.

Second, the enabling act can prescribe the credentials of the persons who are to occupy important positions in the agency. For example, the Department of Energy Organization Act requires that the President appoint persons with knowledge of the energy industry to the Federal Energy Regulatory Commission.[54]

Third, Congress and the state legislatures may specify the lifetime of an agency through provisions known as sunset legislation.[55] State legislatures have employed sunset legislation even more frequently than the federal government. The process is not complicated. The legislature may simply provide in the enabling act a date certain for closing the agency.[56] A milder form of sunset legislation requires an agency to submit an extensive report to the legislature on its activities as a condition of its survival. In this second option, the legislature reviews the sunset report and then determines whether the agency should continue in business.

[B]   The Power to Investigate and the Doctrine of Executive Privilege

Congress has the power to investigate agencies, either through its own hearing and subpoena power or through its auditing and investigative arm, the General Accounting Office. Congressional investigations tend to be evaluated in terms of whose ox is being gored. Recall the controversy over such prominent congressional investigations as the McCarthy subversives-in-government hearings of the early 1950s, the Kefauver-organized crime investigations of the 1960s, the Senate Watergate hearings in 1973 and the so-called "Whitewatergate" and foreign election contribution investigations during the two Clinton administrations. Each investigation has had its proponents and detractors whose views of the

---

[54]   42 U.S.C. § 7101.

[55]   Sunset legislation appears to wax and wane in popularity at both the federal and state levels. For some good discussion of this important legislative drafting and agency control concept, *see, e.g.*, Mark B. Blickle, *The National Sunset Movement*, 9 SETON HALL LEGIS. J. 209 (1986); Lewis A. Davis, *Review Procedures and Public Accountability in Sunset Legislation: An Analysis and Proposal for Reform*, 33 ADMIN. L. REV. 393 (1981).

[56]   For example, Congress expressly provided that the Department of Energy's oil price control program (in existence from 1973 to 1981) would terminate in September, 1981. The President was also given the power to terminate the program by executive order at an earlier date. President Reagan did so in January, 1981. *See* Emergency Petroleum Allocation Act of 1973, 15 U.S.C. §§ 751 *et seq.*

investigative process seem governed only by which side they support. This narrow view of the propriety of Congressional investigations is unfortunate because it would be absurd to deny the legislative branch the power to inform itself on issues of importance.

For our purposes, it is important to keep in mind that Congress has the power to investigate and to compel the attendance of witnesses and the production of documents through its own subpoena power.[57] The troublesome issue is whether the executive branch has a right to resist giving Congress information. When it comes to administrative agencies, the short answer might appear to be a flat "no" because agencies are purely creatures of Congress. However, the answer is not quite that simple because of the placement of agencies in the executive branch of the government, largely, although not exclusively, under the control of the President.

The President, as the chief executive officer of the executive branch, may arguably have the constitutional power to refuse to disclose privileged information to a co-equal branch of government. The underlying theory is that the executive branch could not function properly if its deliberations-the crucial "give-and-take" so necessary to the effective development of policy-had to be disclosed to the public. This issue, now referred to as the doctrine of *executive privilege*, reflects many of the tensions between Congress and the executive branch. But prior to the Watergate controversy, executive privilege had never been the subject of a head-on confrontation between the two branches because, in the past, either the President or Congress took steps to avoid confrontation.[58]

While many earlier presidents hinted at the existence of the doctrine, executive privilege was not formally recognized by the Supreme Court until the Watergate controversy forced the Court to determine whether President Nixon had the right to withhold certain White House tapes from the Senate Watergate Committee. In *United States v. Nixon*,[59] the Court conceded that the privilege exists, but appears to have limited it to military or diplomatic affairs or matters of national security. Thus, the privilege is not absolute. However, it cannot be invoked by a President to refuse to disclose information that may bear on criminal activity within the executive branch.

The *Nixon* decision established the privilege but did not spell out its precise boundaries. Since then there have been few confrontations on this issue, although

---

[57] For a good discussion of the congressional subpoena power, *see Senate Select Committee v. Nixon*, 498 F.2d 725 (D.C. Cir. 1974).

[58] During the Civil war, one congressional committee was investigating certain allegations that Mrs. Lincoln was a spy for the Confederacy. President Lincoln apparently walked unannounced into the committee hearing and gave the committee members his personal word that the allegations were untrue. Immediately after his statement, the committee terminated the investigation. For this and other stories on the historical antecedents of executive privilege, *see* RAOUL BERGER, EXECUTIVE PRIVILEGE (1974). Students of the American legal system should pay close attention to all those instances in which public officials have sought to avoid conflict on issues that could severely test the glue holding our system of government together. In many cases, our system has survived because of someone's reluctance to provoke confrontation. An excellent and full-blown discussion of executive privilege is MARK J. ROZELL, EXECUTIVE PRIVILEGE: THE DILEMMA OF SECRECY AND DEMOCRATIC ACCOUNTABILITY (1994).

[59] 418 U.S. 683 (1974).

in the first term of the Reagan administration, the doctrine was invoked by certain administration spokespersons in attempting to prevent certain officials in the Environmental Protection Agency from giving over documents to congressional committees investigating claims of mismanagement and improper conduct on the part of EPA officials. The confrontation was defused, however, when virtually all of the EPA officers resigned. Currently, all we know is that executive privilege may be invoked by the executive branch, but we know little about the precise dimensions of the privilege.

The doctrine of executive privilege was elaborated upon in two decisions that involved subpoenas issued to the White House by the Office of Independent Counsel[60] to persons on the White House staff and to Hillary Rodham Clinton, the wife of the former President. In the decision involving an investigation into the activities of the Secretary of Agriculture and subpoenas to the White House, the District of Columbia Circuit broke the concept of executive privilege into two different components: (1) the "deliberative process" privilege; and (2) protection of the confidentiality of presidential communications privilege.[61] The court acknowledged the legitimacy of both concepts, noted in passing that the most frequently invoked of the two was the deliberative process privilege and held that neither is absolute. However, the court did not conclusively resolve any of the issues presented, but instead remanded the case for a further analysis of the contents of the documents requested.

In a case decided by the United States Court of Appeals for the Eighth Circuit, the Office of Independent Counsel sought documents in the hands of Mrs. Clinton and in the possession of other White House staff members. The court determined that neither the fundamental attorney-client privilege, nor the "presidential confidentiality" branch of executive privilege warranted a refusal to disclose the documents. A petition for certiorari to the Supreme Court was denied shortly after the Eighth Circuit decided the case.[62]

[C] The Oversight Process

Congress polices day-to-day agency action through what is known as the *oversight* process. Oversight is simply the monitoring of agency activities by the standing committees of Congress, such as the House Committee on Foreign and Interstate Commerce and the Senate Energy Committee. Both members of Congress and, in particular, persons employed as committee staff members become well versed in the operations of the agencies under each committee's jurisdiction. This familiarity permits them to conduct investigations, hold hearings, and engage in informal contact with agency officials to insure that the agency is carrying out its mission. Although the effectiveness of the process varies, depending on the make-up and enthusiasm of the committee members, it is now an integral part of the on-going relationship between Congress and the agencies.

---

[60] The Office of Independent Counsel is discussed at length in Chapter 3, § 3.05.

[61] *In re Sealed Case*, 107 F.3d 46 (D.C. Cir. 1997).

[62] *In re Grand Jury Subpoena Duces Tecum*, 112 F.3d 910 (8th Cir.), *cert. denied*, 521 U.S. 1105 (1997).

Investigations and oversight hearings often result in amendments to the enabling act.[63]

[D] Agency Budgets and Specific Statutory Controls

There are many other instruments of congressional control. Agencies cannot function without money. The power to set an agency's budget may be as important as all the other controls combined. On numerous occasions, Congress has expanded or contracted an agency's budget, depending on how much in favor or out of favor that agency happens to be. Congress has on numerous occasions directed agencies to spend or not to spend money on particular activities.

Congress has also enacted many statutes with a specific purpose that have a substantial impact on agency action, such as the Ethics in Government Act,[64] the Freedom of Information Act (FOIA),[65] the Federal Privacy Act[66] and the Government in the Sunshine Act.[67] Each of these statutes imposes constraints on various agency activities. The list can be lengthened to include the National Environmental Policy Act (NEPA),[68] the Regulatory Flexibility Act,[69] and the

---

[63] Members of Congress are sometimes criticized for too much interference in the workings of the agencies, particularly as agency action affects their constituents. Some agencies such as the Federal Communications Commission have taken steps to reduce congressional influence over individual licensing cases. For a number of case histories, and some good discussion, see RANDALL L. CALVERT, MARK J. MORAN & BARRY R. WEINGAST, CONGRESSIONAL INFLUENCE OVER POLICY MAKING: THE CASE OF THE FTC, IN CONGRESS, STRUCTURE AND POLICY (1987); Mark Bagnoli & Michael McKee, Controlling the Game: Political Sponsors and Bureaus, 7 J.L. ECON. & ORG. 229 (1991) For one member of Congress' view that Congress should be even more aggressive in exerting authority over administrative agencies, see Nick Smith, Restoration of Congressional Authority and Responsibility over the Regulatory Process, 33 HARV. J. ON LEGIS. 323 (1996).

[64] 5 U.S.C. App. § 401–405. The Ethics Act is discussed in Chapter 3.

[65] 5 U.S.C. § 552. The FOIA permits persons outside the government to have access to government information. The act, among many other things, presumes that an agency ought to disclose information and permits an agency to refuse to disclose only under a number of tightly controlled circumstances. The FOIA is discussed extensively in Chapter 14.

[66] This statute requires agencies to take special care in collecting, storing and disseminating information in its possession pertaining to individuals. It is discussed at length in Chapter 14.

[67] 5 U.S.C. § 552b. The Sunshine Act requires an agency to conduct most of its business in the open. It is discussed at greater length in Chapter 14. The Federal Advisory Committee Act, 5 U.S.C. App. 2, is also an attempt to promote more public government decision making when agencies use bodies of private persons to help them formulate policy.

[68] 42 U.S.C. §§ 4321 et seq. NEPA requires an agency to evaluate the environmental consequences of its activities and to prepare an environmental impact statement when an activity "significantly affects the quality of the human environment."

[69] 5 U.S.C. § 601. This statute requires agencies to consider the economic impact of its rulemaking activities on small businesses. The Regulatory Flexibility Act was amended to give it more strength in forcing agencies to consider the impact of their rules on small business by the Small Business Regulatory Enforcement Fairness Act. Pub. L. No. 104-121, 110 Stat. 857 (to be codified at 5 U.S.C. § 611(a)). In an attempt to give certain small businesses and individuals who have relatively small net worths some leverage against the agencies in litigating the validity of agency rules, Congress has passed the Equal Access to Justice Act, 5 U.S.C. § 504(a) statute that permits, in certain carefully controlled circumstances, a private small business or individual to recover his or her attorneys fees if the private party substantially prevails in litigation that challenges agency rules.

Paperwork Reduction Act.[70]

In the past, Congress has been disturbed by the imposition of regulatory obligations on state and local governments and Indian tribes without any attention paid to the costs of carrying out these federal "mandates." The Unfunded Mandates Reform Act,[71] requires an agency to place, in its notice of proposed rulemaking, certain explanations of the costs, benefits and burdens of the anticipated rule, to solicit the views of various entities, including state and local governments, and to explore any less-burdensome alternatives to the proposed rule. Persons who follow the federal regulatory process have already begun to see these "statements of significant regulatory action" in the *Federal Register.*

The point of this recitation is simple: Congress has placed an enormous number of restrictions on agency action that have nothing to do with the non-delegation doctrine. Indeed, many people now worry that the agencies may be too tightly controlled by an entity, Congress, that has no real understanding of their day-to-day problems. Readers should not lose sight of all the strings Congress has attached to agency functioning. The fear of Justice Cardozo and his *Schechter* colleagues that agencies will "run riot" does not seem to be a realistic possibility these days.

§ 2.04   THE SPECIAL PROBLEM OF THE LEGISLATIVE VETO

[A]   Streamlining Agency Rulemaking

Since the turn of the century, Congress has created a large number of administrative agencies to perform an enormous number of tasks. As discussed in Section 1.04 *above*, agencies make basic policy through their rulemaking powers, following the elementary procedures known as *notice and comment* or *informal rulemaking*. Agency rules have proliferated in near logarithmic fashion-*i.e.*, the increase in the quantity of agency rules is far greater than the increase in agencies.[72]

Several years ago, in searching for ways to keep some kind of handle on agency rulemaking, apart from its normal prerogatives of amending either the agency's enabling act or the APA, Congress hit on the idea of the legislative veto. As it was originally conceived, the veto worked in the following manner:

---

[70] 44 U.S.C. §§ 3501 *et seq.* This statute was a reaction to the proliferation of agencies and the consequent proliferation of agency reporting and recordkeeping requirements. It is discussed in Chapter 4.

[71] 2 U.S.C. §§ 658, 1501–1571.

[72] Presidents Reagan and Bush Sr. took great pride in having reduced the size of the Federal Register (the government publication in which rules and other announcements are made) by over one-third compared with the size of the *Federal Register* in the last years of the Carter Administration. President Clinton echoed the notion that less government is better government. Even so, the *Federal Register* exceeds 50,000 pages each year.

Step 1. Congress writes an enabling act authorizing an agency to make rules, but requires the agency to hand its rules over to Congress for review prior to implementing the rules.

Step 2. Congress may strike the rules by a resolution of disapproval passed by either House of Congress (the unicameral or single-house veto) or by a resolution of disapproval passed by both houses (the bicameral veto); the veto resolution may be passed by simple majority vote.

Step 3. An agency makes a rule and hands it over to Congress.

Step 4. Congress or one house of Congress passes the requisite resolution of disapproval. The rules therefore may not be implemented.

Over the past fifty years, Congress inserted either unicameral or bicameral legislative vetoes in approximately 200 different statutes, although Congress has actually voted resolutions of disapproval in a relatively few number of cases.[73]

The congressional interest in the veto is apparent. It's what you might call a last-ditch device for controlling agency action prior to the agency action actually going into effect. Moreover, it can be, at least in theory, less arduous and time-consuming than amending the agency's enabling act-a maneuver that requires not only assent by both houses but also the signature of the President. The unicameral veto dispenses even with the need to secure the assent of the other House.

[B] *Immigration and Naturalization Service v. Chadha* and *Process Gas Consumers Group v. Consumers Energy Council of America*

In 1975, and again in 1982, Congress exercised its legislative veto powers in two cases that eventually made their way to the United States Supreme Court. The 1975 veto arose out of an application for permission to remain in the United States filed by Jagdish Rai Chadha, a man of Indian descent born in Kenya and originally admitted to the United States on a student visa. When his student visa expired, the Immigration and Naturalization Service (INS) took steps to deport Chadha. The Attorney General of the United States then used statutory authority conferred by the immigration statutes to suspend Chadha's deportation proceedings.[74]

However, the statute also required that the Attorney General's decision be transmitted to Congress and permitted either House to veto the Attorney General's suspension (recall, this is the so-called "unicameral" legislative veto). For reasons that remain unclear, Representative Joshua Eilberg, a member of Congress from Pennsylvania, introduced a House resolution disapproving six

---

[73] The seminal article on the legislative veto prior to *Chadha* (discussed below) is Harold Bruff & Ernest Gellhorn, *Congressional Control of Administrative Regulation: A Study of Legislative Vetoes*, 90 HARV. L. REV. 1369 (1977).

[74] Title 8 U.S.C. § 244(a)(1) provides that the Attorney General "may, in his discretion, suspend deportation and adjust the status" of an alien who applies for suspension and who qualifies under the other terms of the statute (*i.e.*, that he lived in the U.S. continuously for at least seven years, that he is of good moral character and that deportation would work a great hardship on him).

suspension cases including Chadha's.[75] The House approved the Eilberg veto resolution on a voice vote. Chadha then took his case into the federal courts, arguing, among other things, that the legislative veto itself was unconstitutional.

In 1980, in an entirely different regulatory setting, the House of Representatives vetoed regulations issued by the Federal Energy Regulatory Commission under the Natural Gas Policy Act of 1978,[76] placing additional cost burdens on certain natural gas consumers. These rules, under a now defunct program known as incremental pricing, were controversial among energy specialists and affected industries but were, much like the situation involved Mr. Chadha, largely unknown to the general public. An intermediate appellate court held that this unicameral legislative veto was unconstitutional;[77] and the Supreme Court agreed to review both Chadha's case and the natural gas case, ultimately choosing *Chadha* as the primary vehicle for invalidating the legislative veto in its entirety.

The majority opinion in *Immigration and Naturalization Service v. Chadha*,[78] written by Chief Justice Burger, is probably best described as a workmanlike tour through basic provisions in Article I of the Constitution. There are three clauses in Article I at issue here: (1) the Legislative Powers Clause (Art. I, § 1) that vests the legislative power of the government in both the House and the Senate; (2) the First Presentment Clause (Art. 1, § 7, cl. 2) that requires that a bill passed by both Houses be presented to the President for signature; and (3) the Second Presentment Clause (Art. 1, § 7, cl. 3) that requires the President either to sign or to veto legislation and permits Congress to override a veto only by a two-thirds vote of each House.

At the outset, the Court made a threshold determination-a legislative veto is the exercise of legislative power-that essentially disposed of the remainder of the case. The Court then held that a one-house legislative veto, such as exercised in *Chadha*: (1) violated the principle of bicameralism inherent in the legislative powers clause because the exercise of legislative power requires assent by both houses; and (2) the veto violated both Presentment Clauses because it was an attempt to exercise legislative power without the requisite participation of the President.

Bicameralism, in the Court's view, was of fundamental importance in the framing of the 1787 Constitution. Quoting from the *Federalist Papers* and early commentaries on the Constitution by Joseph Story, the Court determined that bicameralism was a prime necessity to the Framers as a check against "legislative

---

[75] Eilberg stated on the floor of the House that his subcommittee had reviewed approximately 340 cases and that these six cases, including *Chadha*, did not satisfy the hardship requirement in the statute. There is virtually no other explanation for his actions in the record.

[76] 15 U.S.C. §§ 3301–3432. Readers interested in the nuances of FERC's incremental pricing program, the subject of the FERC rules, may refer to WILLIAM F. FOX, FEDERAL REGULATION OF ENERGY 473–85 (1983).

[77] *Consumer Energy Council of Am. v. FERC*, 673 F.2d 425 (D.C. Cir. 1982), *aff'd sub nom. Process Gas Consumers Group v. Consumers Energy Council of Am.*, 463 U.S. 1216 (1983).

[78] 462 U.S. 919 (1983).

despotism."[79] But on the issue of the Presentment clauses, the Court took a slightly different tack. These clauses are essential, in the Court's view, to preserve the doctrine of separation of powers. First, they enhance the system of checks and balances that is central to our system of government; and second, they insure, in the Court's words, "that a 'national' perspective is grafted on the legislative process."

The majority opinion is not difficult to understand. The harder question is whether the majority's conclusions were as inescapable as the Chief Justice seemed to believe. Justice White suggested a different analysis by questioning whether the veto is actually the exercise of legislative power because the veto procedure is found in an enabling act previously passed by Congress and signed by the President. Moreover, if Congress is free to delegate certain aspects of legislative power to the executive branch, is it not free to retain certain prerogatives, such as the legislative veto, for itself? If so, in White's view, the veto should survive. Worse, there are serious practical effects flowing from *Chadha*. As Justice White noted:

> [The *Chadha* majority opinion] reflects a profoundly different conception of the Constitution than that held by the Courts which sanctioned the modern administrative state. [*Chadha*] strikes down in one fell swoop provisions in more laws enacted by Congress than the Court has cumulatively invalidated in its history . . . .[80]

The legislative veto in the natural gas case was invalidated without full opinion a few days after *Chadha* was handed down. Nonetheless, it provided Justice White — again writing in dissent — with an opportunity to present another argument for the validity of the veto. In his view, the second presentment clause is not applicable because the President has no authority to veto agency regulations, so his veto power was really not at issue.[81]

[C] Issues Unresolved After Chadha

From the perspective of past experience with *Chadha*, Justice White's worst fears have not materialized; but as with most landmark Court decisions, the opinion left open as many questions as it answered. First, *Chadha* did not directly address the validity of the bicameral veto, although the majority's reliance on the Presentment clauses for part of the decision suggests that bicameral vetoes are also invalid. Second, the Court's rigid and formalistic discussion of separation of powers provided a basis for invalidating the Gramm-Rudman-Hollings Balanced

---

[79] The Court noted only three express exceptions to the requirement of bicameralism in the Constitution: (1) the initiation of charges of impeachment by the House; (2) the trial on impeachment charges vested in the Senate; and (3) the power to approve or disapprove certain presidential appointments vested exclusively in the Senate. Unquestionably, the legislative veto fits within none of these exceptions.

[80] 462 U.S. at 1002.

[81] *Process Gas Consumers Group v. Consumers Energy Council of Am.*, 463 U.S. 1216, 1217–18 (1983).

Budget Act in early 1986.[82]

Perhaps most importantly, the Court was not especially helpful on the crucial question of severability. After the *Chadha* decision was handed down, two hundred statutes contained a legislative veto provision that was presumptively invalid. Does the *Chadha* decision mean that the entire statute is defective? The Court in *Chadha* held that the statute in question was severable-*i.e.*, the remainder of the statute survives even if the legislative veto provision is no good-in part because the statute contained a severability clause. But what of statutes that lack a severability clause? The lower courts are split on this question. In one instance, *Exxon Corp. v. Department of Energy*,[83] the Temporary Emergency Court of Appeals held that *Chadha* should not be given retroactive effect (the enabling act in question had expired prior to *Chadha* even though enforcement actions for violations during the life of the statute continued) and that, in any event, the statute was severable even without an express severability clause. Two other circuits split on the validity of the 1977 Equal Employment Opportunity Commission Reorganization Act, another statute without a severability clause.[84]

In the years since *Chadha*, a number of people, in and out of Congress, have tried to think up alternatives to the legislative veto that might permit some Congressional action disapproving agency rules without running afoul of Article I of the Constitution. One suggestion was to require agencies to postpone implementation of regulations while Congress examines them. Congress could vote a joint resolution of disapproval (with Presidential signature) if Congress did not want the rules to take effect. Other proposals have suggested express sunset legislation for certain specific regulatory initiatives. Recall that sunset legislation triggers the end of a program or an entire agency merely by the passage of time so long as Congress does nothing to reauthorize the program or agency.

Getting around *Chadha* is an exceptionally difficult task, given the breadth of the *Chadha* opinion. Many readers of *Chadha* suggested that Congress simply forget about the legislative veto and concentrate on alternate statutory mechanisms for controlling agency action, such as writing more precise standards into the enabling act or establishing additional rulemaking procedures. Certainly, the Supreme Court has not signaled any interest in departing from the central tenets of *Chadha*.

But perhaps illustrating that old dictum that hope springs eternal, Congress revisited the entire matter and enacted, in 1996, a lengthy statute entitled "The Contract with America Advancement Act of 1996."[85] Within Title II (the Small Business Regulatory Enforcement Fairness Act) is an addition to Title 5 of the U.S. Code that most commentators refer to as the Congressional Review of Agency Rulemaking Act "Congressional Review Act"). This statute[86] is an attempt to get

---

[82] *See* the discussion of G-R-H in § 2.03.

[83] 744 F.2d 98 (Temp. Emer. Ct. App.), *cert. denied*, 459 U.S. 1127 (1984).

[84] *EEOC v. CBS, Inc.*, 743 F.2d 969 (2d Cir. 1984); *Muller Optical Co. v. EEOC*, 743 F.2d 380 (6th Cir. 1984).

[85] Pub. L. No. 104-121, 110 Stat. 847 (1996).

[86] The statute is to be codified at 5 U.S.C. §§ 801–808. A good basic description of the operation of the

around the limitations imposed by *Chadha* and to permit Congress to review agency rules prior to their implementation.

The Congressional Review Act contains detailed provisions that are best understood by reading the actual statutory language, but in outline form, it works this way:

Step One: Presidential agencies and independent regulatory commissions must submit their substantive rules (and possibly interpretative and other types of rules), accompanied by a written report[87] to Congress and the Government Accountability Office (GAO) prior to the rules going into effect. If the rule is not a major rule, the rule may take effect as required by the agency (although Congress may still disapprove non-major rules by the process described below). However, for major rules additional requirements are established. "Major" rules are defined with some precision.[88]

Step Two: For major rules, the GAO is given 15 days from receipt of the original agency report to submit its own report to Congress. The GAO report is to include the GAO's assessment of whether the agency has complied with all of its statutory obligations in making the rule. While this part of the process is going on, all major rules have their effective dates suspended for at least 60 days.[89]

Step Three: During this review procedure, Congress may vote a joint resolution of disapproval under detailed procedures set out in the Act.[90]

Step Four: The joint resolution is presented to the President, who may veto the joint resolution of disapproval.

---

act may be found in Daniel Cohen & Peter L. Strauss, *Congressional Review of Agency Regulations*, 49 ADMIN. L. REV. 95 (1997). For some commentary whose title gives away its viewpoint, *see* Morton Rosenberg, *Whatever Happened to Congressional Review of Agency Rulemaking?: A Brief Overview, Assessment, and Proposal for Reform*, 51 ADMIN. L. REV. 1051 (1999).

[87] The entire package of information to be submitted is: (1) a copy of the rule; (2) a "concise general statement" relating to the rule, including a statement (*see below*) as to whether it is a "major" rule; (3) the proposed effective date of the rule. 5 U.S.C. § 801(a)(1)(A). In addition to this report, the agency is required to submit to the General Accounting Office and make available to the Congress (1) a complete copy of any cost benefit analysis; (2) agency actions relevant to the Regulatory Flexibility Act and the Unfunded Mandates Act and any other information required under any other statute or executive order. 5 U.S.C. § 801(a)(1)(B).

[88] A "major" rule is one that (1) has an annual effect on the U.S. economy of $100 million or more; (2) results in a major increase in costs or prices for consumers, individual industries, federal, state or local government agencies, or geographic regions, or (3) has significant adverse effects on competition, employment, investment, productivity, innovation, or on the ability of United States-based enterprises to compete with foreign-based enterprises in domestic and export markets. 5 U.S.C. § 804(2).

[89] 5 U.S.C. § 801(a)(2). There are some fascinating exceptions to the 60 day rule. For example, there need not be any delay in an agency rule "that establishes, modifies, opens, closes, or conducts a regulatory program for a commercial, recreational, or subsistence activity relating to hunting, fishing, or camping." 5 U.S.C. § 808(1). Another exception is when the agency "for good cause finds [and includes such finding in its report] that notice and public procedure thereon are impracticable, unnecessary, or contrary to the public interest." 5 U.S.C. § 808(1)(2). There are other exception for rules that are issued under statutory or judicially imposed deadlines. 5 U.S.C. § 803.

[90] The procedures involving the joint resolution of disapproval are too intricate to set out here. Section 802 of the Act contains all of that detail.

Step Five: Congress may overturn the veto of the joint resolution of disapproval by the normal veto override procedure.[91]

Some things are obvious. The act gets around *Chadha* by subjecting the resolution of disapproval to the conventional process by which laws are enacted under our Constitution. Unicameralism, of course, is completely eliminated. It remains to be seen how many, if any, rules are subject to these procedures and how often a President vetoes the "veto" and, of course, how often Congress might gather the necessary two-thirds votes to override the Presidential veto. Only time will tell.

---

[91] These last two steps are not clearly expressed in the statute itself. However, they are implicit under the normal procedures for Presidential consideration of Congressional joint resolutions. There are additional provisions in the Act that bar judicial review of any "determination, finding, action, or omission under [the Act]." 5 U.S.C. § 805. Nor may any inferences be drawn from Congressional inaction under the statute. 5 U.S.C. § 801(g).

Chapter 3

EXTERNAL CONTROLS ON ADMINISTRATIVE AGENCIES — THE EXECUTIVE BRANCH

§ 3.01 INTRODUCTION

The executive branch of government exerts numerous and powerful controls over both nominally "independent" administrative agencies and those squarely within the executive branch. These controls run the gamut, from the power of appointment and termination of agency officials, to supervision of an agency's rulemaking authority, to the rendering of opinions by the attorney general. Controls such as these along with the crucial question of ethical conduct by agency appointees are the topics discussed in this chapter.

§ 3.02 AN EXCURSUS ON AGENCY ORGANIZATION

[A] Introduction

Before getting into the various methods the President and others in the executive branch use to control the actions of administrative agencies, it is important to recall some fundamentals on agency structure and organization. This inquiry first requires a close look at the actions of Congress even though this chapter is mainly devoted to executive branch controls. The place to start is with the Administrative Procedure Act (APA).

The APA defines *agency* mainly in terms of what an agency is *not*. Section 551 of the APA states: "*Agency* means each authority of the Government . . . whether or not it is within or subject to review by another agency, but does not include — (A) the Congress, (B) the courts of the United States, (C) the governments of the territories or possessions of the United States, (D) the government of the District of Columbia." This exceptionally broad definition tells us virtually nothing about agency structure and organization. Instead, your analysis of what constitutes an agency should proceed from the basic premise that the agency model that Congress ultimately chooses reflects congressional thinking on at least three issues: (1) the task or mission that Congress assigns to the agency, (2) the type of accountability Congress wishes to impose on the agency and (3) the realities of the political process.[1]

---

[1] For a more detailed explanation of operation of Federal Agencies, *see* Marshall J. Breger & Gary J. Edles, *Established by Practice: The Theory and Operation of Independent Federal Agencies*, 52 ADMIN. L. REV. 1111 (2000).

[B] The Agency's Mission

An agency's task or mission is always limited to a set of specific functions. For example, the Federal Aviation Administration regulates the safety and efficiency of air travel by, among other things, licensing pilots, setting standards for the construction and maintenance of aircraft and supervising the operation of airports. The FAA has nothing to do with railroads or with ships. Those functions are dealt with, respectively, by the Federal Railroad Administration, and the Coast Guard and Federal Maritime Administration. A quick glance at the United States Government Organizational Manual or the Federal Register will give anyone not already familiar with agency activities a good idea of the breadth and depth of federal agency operations.[2]

[C] Agency Accountability

An agency's accountability is determined by its enabling act and its designation as either an executive branch agency or an independent regulatory commission. Independence, in this regard, is primarily determined either by Congress' expressly labeling an agency "independent", as it has done in a number of statutes or, in the absence of express labeling, by the limitations, if any, the statute places on the powers of the President to remove the principal officers of that agency. Thus, if the President's powers are limited to removing a commissioner for negligence or malfeasance in office (as contrasted with totally discretionary removal, as in the case of cabinet secretaries), the agency will probably be deemed an independent regulatory commission. The major independent regulatory commissions are all collegially governed — that is, they are headed by multi-member commissions rather than by single administrators — but there seems to be no special reason why Congress could not create an independent regulatory agency with a single administrator at the head.

There is little rhyme or reason as to Congress' designation of a particular agency as either a cabinet agency or an independent regulatory commission. The federal government is filled with aberrations. For example, the entity charged with regulation of many of the environmental aspects of the nuclear power industry, the Nuclear Regulatory Commission, is an independent regulatory commission. The entity charged with supervision of many other environmental statutes, the Environmental Protection Agency, is an executive agency, even though the administrator of the EPA does not have cabinet status. Congress' choices are dictated by the political realities and the legislative give-and-take that occurs when a particular agency is created.

Another important factor in the organization of the multi-member commissions is the make-up of the commission itself. In virtually all instances, the commissioners sit for staggered terms, often from five to seven years. The membership of the commission normally must include persons from each of the two

---

[2] There has been more debate about the Office of Management and Budget's Office of Information and Regulatory Affairs and its role in overseeing agency information dissemination. *See, e.g.,* James T. O'Reilly, *The 411 on 515: How OIRA's Expanded Information Roles in 2002 will Impact Rulemaking and Agency Publicity Actions,* 54 ADMIN. L. REV. 835 (2002).

major political parties, which insures that each political party will preserve some influence within the agencies, even when it does not hold the Presidency. The parties accomplish this by requiring in an agency's enabling act, that some of the seats on each commission be held by persons who are members of the party out of power. Most, if not all, of the independent regulatory commissioners are nominated by the President, but must also be confirmed by the Senate, thereby giving Congress additional control.

Today, the major independent commissions — i.e., those that have traditionally engaged in economic regulation of business — are particularly vulnerable to abolition attempts because much of what they do involves economic regulation of business — a particularly disfavored form of regulation at the present time. One of the so-called "Big Seven," the Civil Aeronautics Board, was abolished on January 1, 1985, although some of its consumer protection functions were transferred to the Department of Transportation rather than eliminated. Another, the Interstate Commerce Commission, the regulatory body that was the first of the traditional regulatory agencies, was abolished in 1995. Some observers believe that the Federal Maritime Commission may be the next agency to be eliminated.[3]

Most other federal administrative agencies are part of cabinet-level departments and subject to the control of the departmental Secretary who, of course, serves at the pleasure of the President. They are normally referred to as executive branch agencies. However, there are a few aberrations, such as the Federal Energy Regulatory Commission, which is expressly an independent regulatory commission but still a component — for certain purposes — of the cabinet-level Department of Energy. The Environmental Protection Agency, an agency whose administrator is totally subject to Presidential control, is what might be called a "free-standing" executive branch agency and is not located within any cabinet department. Congress occasionally changes its mind. In 1995, the Social Security Administration was removed from the cabinet-level Department of Health and Human Services and given the same free-standing status as that of the EPA.

[D] Political Considerations

Political considerations have an important impact on the organizational process. When Congress decides to establish an agency, it can create an entirely new entity, as, for example, when the Interstate Commerce Commission was set up; or it can create an agency by reorganizing existing components of the executive branch. The Federal Departments of Transportation and Education, and to a certain extent the Department of Energy, were formed by combining a number of existing entities into a single cabinet-level department. The newest cabinet department, the Department of Homeland Security, is mainly an amalgam of pre-existing agencies that were placed within the new organization.

---

[3] The "Big Seven" were originally: The Civil Aeronautics Board (now abolished), Federal Communications Commission, Federal Power Commission (now the Federal Energy Regulatory Commission located within the Department of Energy), the Federal Trade Commission, the Interstate Commerce Commission (now abolished), the National Labor Relations Board and the Securities and Exchange Commission.

Political decisions also affect the components that are left out of a new agency. For example, when Congress established the Department of Transportation, it decided to preserve the Civil Aeronautics Board and the Interstate Commerce Commission as independent regulatory agencies, even though these two agencies had a great deal to do with transportation.

There is often little consistency in what Congress does. When the Department of Energy (DOE) was formed, Congress granted President Carter's express request that the Environmental Protection Agency (retained as a free-standing executive branch agency) and the Nuclear Regulatory Commission (which remained an independent regulatory commission) be retained as agencies separate from the DOE. The President believed that these two agencies should remain separate entities so that their important regulatory duties would not be affected by the energy promotion mission of the DOE. But this is only a partial explanation for the EPA's and NRC's continued independence. In contrast to Congress' treatment of these agencies, consider its actions in renaming the old Federal Power Commission, an agency with heavy regulatory obligations, as the Federal Energy Regulatory Commission and merging it with the Department of Energy, albeit as a nominally independent regulatory commission. Sometimes, and often without explanation, Congress splits agency jurisdiction over matters that seem to cry out for unified treatment. For example, jurisdiction over national forests is vested in the Forest Service — a component of the Department of Agriculture — while jurisdiction over national parks is given to the Department of Interior.

Once the decisions on agency head and basic organization are made, Congress may legislate more specifically on organization. If it does, it may prescribe internal components of the organization and leave other aspects of organization to be fleshed out by the President or the agency itself. For example, Congress prescribed that the Department of Energy would contain a number of specific components, including the Energy Information Administration and the Economic Regulatory Administration. In other cabinet departments, Congress has specified the number and titles of the assistant secretaries, but leaves the organization and make-up of the remainder of the agency up to the secretary. Again, there is little rhyme or reason for the specifics of organization.

Excessive generalization about agency structure can get a lawyer or law student into analytical trouble. For example, the Environmental Protection Agency contains "offices" that report to "assistant administrators." Another agency may contain "divisions" that report to "bureaus" that report to "administrators" who report to "assistant secretaries" who report to a "deputy secretary" who reports to the "secretary."

There are similarities, of course. A typical cabinet-level agency organizational chart will look something like the Department of Transportation:[4]

---

[4] A fine source of such basic information on agencies is the *United States Government Organizational Manual* (published annually by the Government Printing Office), *available at* http://www.gpoaccess.gov/gmanual/index.html.

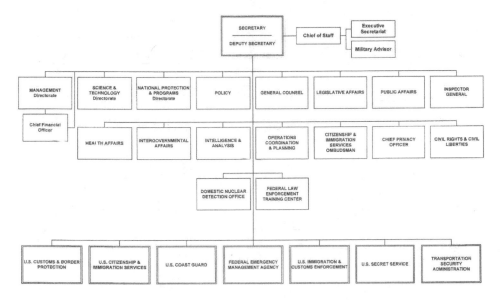

U.S. DEPARTMENT OF HOMELAND SECURITY

A typical independent regulatory commission will look something like the Federal Trade Commission:

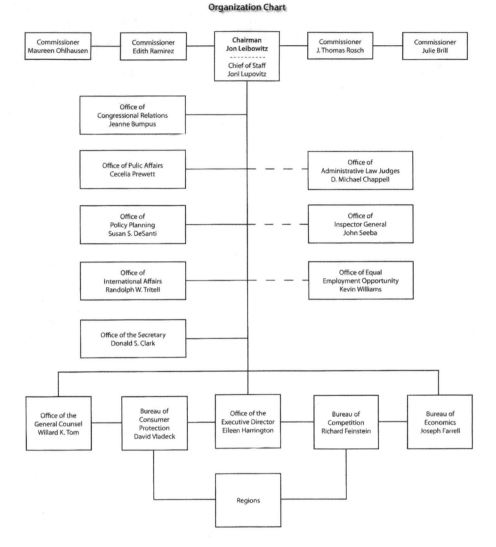

FEDERAL TRADE COMMISSION

Organization Chart

Students with special interest in these matters can work through the congressional floor debates and legislative histories of these agencies usually transcribed in the *Congressional Record* and *U.S. Code Congressional & Administrative News* to garner the precise reasons why congressional and executive branch decisions on agency structure and organization were made. For the purposes of this chapter, it is enough to understand that Congress has a broad spectrum of options and makes myriad choices for many different reasons. The nuances and some of the legal impact of many of these issues are discussed below.

§ 3.03   THE APPOINTMENT AND REMOVAL PROCESS

[A]   The Appointment Process

Article II of the United States Constitution sets out a number of Presidential powers: the President may, with the advice and consent of the Senate, appoint and commission "officers of the United States." The President may demand "the opinion in writing, of the principal officer in each of the executive departments, upon any subject relating to the duties of their respective offices." Some commentators view these statements as impossibly brief and ambiguous,[5] but when viewed closely and in conjunction with the admonition to the President to faithfully execute the laws of the nation, they establish several important constitutional principles. First, the President is the chief executive officer to whom all others in the executive branch report. Second, the Framers clearly envisioned that executive departments would be created by Congress. Third, the power to appoint executive branch officers is vested exclusively in the President. It is not really necessary for the Constitution to say more. There is nothing wrong with leaving to Congress and the executive the power to fill in the details.

The power to appoint and remove cabinet department officers is plenary-except, of course, when the Senate must consent to the appointment. Every executive branch political appointee (*i.e.*, those persons who are not given civil service protection) serves at the pleasure of the President. No one should be fooled by the protocol of the appointment or removal process and believe that simply because a President announces in the public press that he has "asked for" the resignation of a certain person that somehow he could not fire that person forthwith. He can and occasionally does.

The more complicated legal issues spring from the President's appointment of persons to the independent regulatory commissions. For example, the Federal Trade Commission Act provides that the FTC is to be headed by a five-person commission appointed by the President for seven-year terms with the advice and consent of the Senate.[6] No more than three of the five commission members may be members of the same political party. To insure that all the commission members do not come up for reappointment at the same time, the terms are staggered. To preserve staggered terms, the President may appoint a person to an unexpired term only for the duration of that term.[7] The commissioners, rather than the President, choose their own chair.

---

[5] One of the commentators who has problems with this language is John M. Burkoff, *Appointment and Removal Under the Federal Constitution: The Impact of* Buckley v. Valeo, 22 WAYNE L. REV. 1335 (1976).

[6] 15 U.S.C. §§ 41, 42.

[7] When an agency initially is formed, the enabling act typically provides for one term of three years, one of four years, one of five years and so on, to ensure that the commissioners sit in staggered terms from the outset. Staggering has two effects, one practical and one political: it enhances continuity at the highest agency levels over one or more presidential terms and it prevents the President from appointing a completely new commission in a single term (unless, of course, individual commissioners resign before the expiration of their terms).

A quick look at these requirements shows the length to which Congress has gone to preserve a strong degree of independence, while providing some accountability to the President. At the same time, the presidential appointment power is considerable, even when dealing with an agency like the FTC.[8] Commissioners sometimes die or resign before their terms are up, so staggered terms are often not a major inhibition on the President's influence. The limitation on the number of commissioners from the same political party sounds like a check on the President's power, but, in reality, a President can find members of either party who are fully sympathetic with the current administration's positions. The length of an FTC commissioner's term stretches nearly across two presidential terms, but it provides independence only so long as the commissioner wishes to keep the seat. New commissioners chosen by the President may make a commissioner appointed under a prior administration so uncomfortable that she resigns prematurely.

The requirement of Senate approval has occasionally stymied Presidents, but the typical appointment sails through the Senate with few dissenting votes. Only those few highly publicized instances of the Senate refusing to approve a presidential appointee suggest otherwise. The 1989 rejection of former Senator John Tower as President Bush's Secretary of Defense is an example. The fact is that the President has virtually unfettered discretion to choose whomever he wishes for appointive office. There are few other areas of government where a President can exercise so much control.

[B]   Termination of Officers

[1]   Statutory Limitations on Removal of Federal Personnel

For the first 100 years or so of our constitutional history, the presidential power to terminate executive branch officers was rarely at issue, mainly because of the broad language in *Shurtleff v. United States*,[9] confirming the President's power to remove executive branch officers such as postmasters. In the late nineteenth century, Congress became concerned that a new President's power to summarily remove large numbers of low-ranking government employees on political grounds was interfering with the effective running of the government. The spoils system was wreaking havoc with the continuity of government operations, and the lack of personnel standards had a detrimental effect on the quality of government services.

---

[8] For materials on executive branch agency actions concluded just before a new President takes office, *see* Nina A. Mendelson, *Agency Burrowing: Entrenching Policies and Personnel Before a New President Arrives*, 78 N.Y.U. L. Rev. 557 (2003); Robin Kundis Craig, *The Bush Administration's Use and Abuse of Rulemaking, Part I: The Rise of OIRA*, 28 Admin. & Reg. L. News 8 (Summer, 2003); William M. Jack, *Taking Care that Presidential Oversight of the Regulatory Process Is Faithfully Executed: A Review of Rule Withdrawals and Rule Suspensions Under the Bush Administration's Card Memorandum*, 54 Admin. L. Rev. 1479 (2002); Memorandum for the Heads and Acting Heads of Executive Departments and Agencies, 66 Fed. Reg. 7702 (Jan. 24, 2001).

[9] 189 U.S. 311 (1903). *Shurtleff* held that a customs officer who did not serve a specific term was removable at the discretion of the President. Among other things, the Court feared that any other result might guarantee persons like Shurtleff life-time employment in the Post Office.

Congress reacted by passing the Civil Service Act of 1883 (often referred to as the Pendleton Act),[10] which created the Civil Service Commission to develop a professional corps of government employees who could not be removed for purely political reasons. Persons with civil service protection may be fired only for cause.[11] Virtually all the state governments have similar systems.

In reaction to what many Presidents and quite a few members of Congress perceived as too much insulation and too little accountability on the part of high level civil servants, Congress enacted the Civil Service Reform Act of 1978,[12] which established the Senior Executive Service (SES). The 1978 legislation also contained provisions establishing special protection for federal employees who face adverse action for reporting agency misconduct, the so-called *whistleblowers*.[13] The SES is a group of senior level federal officers who serve without conventional civil service job protections, but who may reap many rewards, such as higher salaries and performance bonuses not now available to lower echelon employees. Removing the SES's job protections would likely promote far greater accountability among the senior officers. The greater financial rewards should stimulate increased attention and productivity on the part of senior level officials, who in turn would provoke greater efforts on the part of the people that they supervise.

At the present time, approximately 80 percent of all federal employees are insulated from summary removal due to the considerable number of statutory limitations on the President's removal power and the protections afforded them under the Pendleton Act. The entity that supervises federal personnel is now called the Office of Personnel Management.

[2] Constitutional Limitations on Removal

The parallel question of whether the Constitution also limits the President's power of removal was tested in two cases earlier in this century, *Myers v. United States*,[14] decided in 1926, and *Humphrey's Executor v. United States*,[15] decided in 1935. *Myers* involved a postmaster appointed by the President with the consent of the Senate. Under the terms of the postal service statutes, a class-one postmaster, such as Frank Myers, served for a four-year term and could be removed during that term only with the consent of the Senate. President Wilson fired Myers without seeking Senate approval. Myers (who died during the litigation) retaliated by bringing a lawsuit in the Court of Claims, seeking the salary that would have been paid him had he not been removed. Chief Justice Taft (recall that he had been President himself) wrote the Court's majority opinion, holding that the requirement in the statute that the Senate gives its consent for removal for this type of executive branch office was unconstitutional.

---

[10] 5 U.S.C. §§ 1101–1105.

[11] *See, e.g.*, DAVID H. ROSENBLOOM, FEDERAL SERVICE AND THE CONSTITUTION (1971).

[12] Pub. L. No. 95-454, 92 Stat. 1111 (codified at 5 U.S.C. §§ 101–105).

[13] *See* Robert G. Vaughn, *Statutory Protection of Whistleblowers in the Federal Executive Branch*, 1982 U. ILL. L. REV. 615 (1982).

[14] 272 U.S. 52 (1926).

[15] 295 U.S. 602 (1935).

The basis for the decision was straightforward. In a 6-3 decision with Justices Brandeis, Holmes and McReynolds dissenting, the majority cited those Article II provisions that vest the executive power in the President and admonish the President to "take care" that the laws are properly executed. The majority then concluded that the President's removal power is virtually unfettered under the constitution. The dissenters in *Myers* contended that this gave the President too much power over federal employees and thus, tilted the balance of power too much in the President's favor.

Myers may have been right on its facts but much of the language of that opinion proved to be too broad for a subsequent Court. In 1935, the same Court that demonstrated such hostility to President Roosevelt's economic programs in the *Panama Refining* and *Schechter* cases[16] showed equal hostility to his power to remove a member of an independent regulatory commission. William Humphrey had been appointed to a second seven-year term on the Federal Trade Commission by President Hoover in 1931. Because Humphrey clearly disagreed with Roosevelt's ideas for the FTC and because he refused to resign as requested by the President, Roosevelt fired him on October 7, 1933. Like Myers, Humphrey sued in the Court of Claims for his salary, insisting that his "removal" by Roosevelt was invalid; but before the suit reached the Supreme Court, Humphrey died, and his estate (thus the use of the word *executor* in the caption of the Supreme Court opinion) pursued the action.[17]

Humphrey's Executor has both a statutory and a constitutional dimension. The Federal Trade Commission Act provides that commissioners are to be appointed by the President with the consent of the Senate, that they shall serve for staggered seven-year terms and shall be removed by the President only for "inefficiency, neglect of duty or malfeasance in office."[18] Clearly, Roosevelt could not invoke any of these grounds. What then was the purpose of the statutory provisions? Justice Sutherland, writing for the majority, decided that Congress wanted to make it difficult for a President to remove an FTC commissioner because the Commission was to function as an expert in certain matters of commerce and trade, free from Presidential interference. In Sutherland's words:

> [The statutory language shows an intent] to create a body of experts who shall gain experience by length of service — a body that shall be independent of executive authority, except in its selection, and free to exercise its judgment without the leave or hindrance of any other official or any department of government.[19]

According to Sutherland, this was Congress' intent and easily discerned, but the harder question was the issue of the statute's constitutionality. The *Shurtleff* opinion contained some exceptionally broad language enhancing the President's

---

[16] *See* Chapter 2, § 2.02.

[17] The amount in controversy was approximately $60,000 — a healthy sum in the Great Depression. Humphrey had served about two years of a seven-year term. His yearly salary was $10,000. No wonder Mrs. Humphrey fought so fiercely.

[18] 15 U.S.C. § 41.

[19] 295 U.S. at 625.

removal powers that Sutherland had to circumvent because the Court was apparently not ready to overrule that case. Sutherland accomplished this by going back to the FTC's enabling act and determining that the FTC was to carry out its duties to police unfair methods of competition by exercising "quasi-legislative" and "quasi-judicial" powers. Thus, when the Commission exercises legislative powers, it functions as an arm (or agent) of Congress, and when it exercises judicial powers it functions as an agent of the courts. As such, the President had only limited control over the FTC, and any attempt to remove officers in contravention of the FTC statute (*i.e.*, any move to fire an officer on grounds other than inefficiency, neglect of duty or malfeasance) was a violation of the Constitution's doctrine of separation of powers because the President was interfering with an "agent" of the other two branches of government.

At first glance, this reasoning strikes most people as exceptionally contrived and convoluted. It is. *Humphrey's Executor* may rank as one of the most artificial decisions in Supreme Court history. First, there is a good chance that it was entirely politically motivated.[20] It is probably not pure coincidence that *Humphrey's Executor* was handed down the same day as *Schechter.* Second, while Congress wanted some independence from the executive for the FTC, it is unlikely that Congress really viewed the FTC as either its own agent or an agent of the courts. There is virtually nothing in the FTC Act's legislative history supporting this idea, although concededly Sutherland participated in the Act's debates as a Senator and, thus, might be expected to have some special insight on this issue. Third, in constructing a basis for the decision, Justice Sutherland did a terrible disservice to agencies themselves and to generations of lawyers and law students by labeling agency powers as merely "quasi." Most of the remainder of this book will demonstrate that there is nothing *quasi* (particularly if one thinks that the word *quasi* carries connotations of *artificial* or *weak*) about an agency's powers. As will be seen, persons within an agency's jurisdiction violate agency requirements at their peril. An agency's exercise of its power can be an awesome experience for a regulated party.[21] Finally, the case added another label to administrative law. Since the decision in *Humphrey's Executor*, many people have taken to calling the independent regulatory commissions the "headless Fourth Branch" of government.

---

[20] For example, Professors Jaffe and Nathanson point out that Justice Sutherland, as a Senator, had participated in the debates on the original FTC enabling legislation. LOUIS L. JAFFE & NATHANIEL L. NATHANSON, ADMINISTRATIVE LAW CASES & MATERIALS 157–59 (4th ed. 1976). Of course there were strong political feelings on both sides. Commenting on Roosevelt's attempt to pack the Supreme Court after the *Panama, Schechter* and *Humphrey's Executor* decisions, Justice Jackson (then Roosevelt's Attorney General) commented: "I really think the decision that made Roosevelt madder at the Court than any other decision was that damn little case of *Humphrey's Executor.* The President thought they went out of their way to spite him personally and they were giving him a different kind of deal than they were giving Taft." EUGENE C. GERHART, AMERICA'S ADVOCATE: ROBERT H. JACKSON 99 (1958). For additional comments on *Humphrey's Executor, see* David M. Driesen, *Toward a Duty-Based Theory of Executive Power*, 78 FORDHAM L. REV. 71 (2009).

[21] Justice Jackson, dissenting in *FTC v. Ruberoid Co.*, 343 U.S. 470 (1952), noted that: "The mere retreat to the qualifying 'quasi' is implicit with confession that all recognized classifications have broken down and 'quasi' is a smooth cover which we draw over our confusion as we might use a counterpane to conceal a disordered bed." *Id.* at 487–88.

Since the mid-1930s, *Humphrey's Executor*, has rarely been invoked by the Supreme Court, mainly because both agency appointees and Presidents appear to try to avoid confrontation. The holding of the case appears to have some vitality, however. In one case, decided twenty years later, Justice Frankfurter (who was one of Roosevelt's principal New Deal advisers and who presumably would have agreed with the attempted removal of Humphrey) wrote the majority opinion in *Weiner v. United States*,[22] a dispute involving the removal of a member of the War Claims Commission who had been appointed by President Truman and fired by President Eisenhower. In *Weiner*, Frankfurter held the removal invalid and noted that the Commission functioned essentially as a court, and thus the President's discretion to fire members of the commission was severely limited after *Humphrey's Executor*. In language that was nearly as sweeping (albeit in the other direction) as the 1926 *Myers* decision, Frankfurter stated:

> [I]f, as one must take for granted, the War Claims Act precluded the President from influencing the Commission in passing on a particular claim, *a fortiori* it must be inferred that Congress did not wish to have hang over the Commission the Damocles' sword of removal by the President for no reason other than that he preferred to have on that Commission men of his own choosing.

Weiner is one of the last cases to reach the Supreme Court in which the President's power of removal was at issue. There have, however, been some recent controversies that have involved the removal power. During the Watergate controversy, President Nixon attempted to remove Special Prosecutor Archibald Cox. The Attorney General had established the office of Special Prosecutor and had written an agency rule providing that the prosecutor could be removed only for "extraordinary improprieties."[23] When Nixon fired Cox, a public interest group challenged the firing in court. Without reaching the constitutional issues, a lower federal court held the firing improper because the agency rule had been violated.[24]

A number of years ago, *Humphrey's Executor* figured in the controversy over the constitutionality of the Gramm-Rudman-Hollings Act because the Comptroller General (the principal officer of the General Accounting Office, now the Government Accountability Office or GAO) arguably exercised executive powers, but was, in fact, a member of the legislative branch.[25] The three-judge district court that held this portion of the Act unconstitutional determined that the caselaw establishes three classes of federal officer:

> 1. purely executive officers, such as Myers, who are unquestionably part of the executive branch and who serve totally at the pleasure of the President;

---

[22] 357 U.S. 349 (1958).

[23] *See* 38 Fed. Reg. 14,688 (1973).

[24] *Nader v. Bork*, 366 F. Supp. 104 (D.D.C. 1973). *See also United States v. Nixon*, 418 U.S. 683 (1974) (discussed in Chapter 7, *infra* § 7.09).

[25] Under the original version of Gramm-Rudman-Hollings, the Comptroller General imposes mandatory cuts on the executive branch's budget. However, the Comptroller General may be removed from office only by action of Congress. The terms of the Comptroller General's appointment and removal led the Court to conclude that he was a member of the legislative branch.

2. members of an independent regulatory commission, such as Humphrey, who exercise only legislative and judicial functions; and

3. officers, such as the Comptroller General, who appear to fit neither category 1 nor category 2.

The anomalous status of the Comptroller General doomed that portion of Gramm-Rudman-Hollings, at both the district court and Supreme Court levels.

In *Bowsher v. Synar*,[26] the Supreme Court conducted a thorough analysis of the status of the Comptroller General as the head of the GAO and concluded that there was no doubt that the Comptroller General was an agent of Congress and had been such since the creation of the office in 1921. Having affirmed that finding, the Court then reviewed virtually all of the case law discussed above and concluded that "Congress cannot reserve for itself the power of removal of an officer charged with the execution of the laws except by impeachment." Coupling the holding in *Bowsher* with its earlier decision invalidating the legislative veto, *Immigration and Naturalization Service v. Chadha* (discussed in Chapter 2, § 2.04 *above*), the Court went on to state in the most unambiguous terms:

> To permit an officer controlled by Congress to execute the laws would be, in essence, to permit a congressional veto. Congress could simply remove, or threaten to remove, an officer for executing the laws in any fashion found unsatisfactory to Congress. This kind of congressional control over the execution of the laws . . . is unconstitutionally impermissible.

Bowsher was not the first instance of this kind of analysis. In a case decided ten years earlier, *Buckley v. Valeo*,[27] the Supreme Court struck down a proposed Federal Election Commission established to police federal campaign contributions because the members, largely appointed by the Congress, were deemed to exercise executive branch powers. Even more recent separation of powers cases such as *Morrison v. Olson*, involving the appointment process, are discussed in Chapter 2, § 2.02.

These cases have had some interesting and perhaps unanticipated results. A few scholars have questioned the legitimacy and reasoning of *Humphrey's Executor* and have asked whether the independent regulatory agencies are constitutional in that their members cannot be summarily dismissed by the President. However, the current Supreme Court has shown absolutely no sign that it would go this far.[28] In other words, the Fourth Branch may be too independent for good government. While these arguments often turn on whose ox is being gored, we do know that the controversies over the status of the Fourth Branch and the whole doctrine of separation of powers is far from over. The cases discussed here, and the additional cases discussed in Chapter 2, suggest that the Supreme Court still has not resolved, with any clarity, the separation of powers muddle.

---

[26] *Synar v. United States*, 626 F. Supp. 1374 (D.D.C. 1986), *aff'd sub nom. Bowsher v. Synar*, 478 U.S. 714 (1986).

[27] 424 U.S. 1 (1976).

[28] One of the best comments on separation of powers in this context is Peter L. Strauss, *The Place of Agencies in Government: Separation of Powers and the Fourth Branch*, 84 COLUM. L. REV. 573 (1984).

§ 3.04   OTHER PRESIDENTIAL POWERS

[A]   Presidential Powers Generally

In the early 1950s, during the Korean War, President Truman seized the nation's steel mills in order to avert a strike that in his opinion would have endangered the national security. Prior to the seizure, Truman had asked Congress for seizure authority and had been refused. Truman took over the mills anyway and ran them with military personnel. Most students of constitutional law know that the Supreme Court, in *Youngstown Sheet & Tube Co. v. Sawyer*,[29] held the seizure unconstitutional because Truman exceeded his Presidential powers. More instructive for administrative law is the perceptive concurrence by Justice Jackson that outlined three categories of Presidential power for further analysis:

> 1. When the President acts under an express or implied grant of power from Congress, the President has maximum authority — *i.e.*, all his own authority plus all that Congress delegates. The only time these acts could be called into question is when the Constitution categorically forbids the Federal Government to exercise these powers.

> 2. At the other end of the spectrum, when the President acts contrary to the express or implied wishes of Congress, presidential power "is at its lowest ebb" because the only powers that can be exercised are those solely possessed by the President. This is the *Youngstown* case and such actions "must be scrutinized with caution."

> 3. There is, however, a "zone of twilight" where Congress has not acted and where the President arguably has independent powers. In these cases, the realities of the situation may require some kind of governmental action. Unfortunately, actions that fit within this zone of twilight are "likely to depend on the imperatives of events and contemporary imponderables rather than on abstract theories of law."[30]

The "zone of twilight" is often fertile ground for enforceable executive orders and proclamations. For example, the President's power to establish certain labor management rules for federal employees has been upheld, as has an executive order prohibiting the award of government contracts to certain firms that violate what the President labeled "voluntary" wage and price controls.[31] There are numerous other controls that the President exercises. For example, the Office of Management and Budget, an entity within the Executive Office of the President, now exercises a great deal of control over executive branch rulemaking through a series of executive orders, even though its authority does not extend to the independent regulatory commissions.[32]

---

[29] 343 U.S. 579 (1952).

[30] *Id.* at 635–38.

[31] *See, e.g., Old Dominion Branch No. 496 v. Austin*, 418 U.S. 264 (1974); *AFL-CIO v. Kahn*, 618 F.2d 784 (D.C. Cir.), *cert. denied*, 443 U.S. 915 (1979).

[32] *See* Chapter 7, *infra* § 7.06.

The President has plenary control over foreign airline routes through his foreign affairs powers. Congress often gives the President power to reorganize certain agencies or groups of agencies. The Department of Justice has sole authority (except where otherwise authorized by Congress) to appear in court on behalf of the United States, giving Justice substantial control over litigation involving many other agencies, including some of the independent regulatory commissions.[33]

Another power that President Clinton attempted to exercise was the authority given to him by a recent Congressional statute to veto individual or "line items" in congressional legislation. The President, exercising this power, vetoed (or, in the parlance of the statute, "cancelled") two items in a 700-page Omnibus Budget Reconciliation Act. His action was quickly challenged in court and, on review by the Supreme Court, the Court held the line-item veto power to be unconstitutional. Although the opinion was lengthy, the ultimate conclusion was simply stated:

> [O]ur decision rests on the narrow ground that the procedures authorized by the Line Item Veto Act are not authorized by the Constitution. . . . If there is to be a new procedure in which the President will play a different role in determining the final text of what may "become a law," such change must come not by legislation but through the amendment procedures . . . of the Constitution.[34]

[B] The Role of the Executive Order

Frequently, the President issues directives to cabinet-level agencies through the device of the executive order. Executive orders are issued over the signature of the President and reviewed prior to issuance by the Office of Legal Counsel in the Department of Justice. The Justice Department believes that the President's authority to issue executive orders derives from Article II, § 3, requiring the President to "take Care that the Laws be faithfully executed." The Justice Department frequently quotes from the *Myers* case to the effect that the President has an obligation to "supervise and guide Executive officers in their construction of the statutes under which they act in order to secure that unitary and uniform execution of the laws which Article II of the Constitution evidently contemplated in vesting general executive powers in the President alone."[35]

While not having the force and effect of law, executive orders are compelling documents that agencies ignore at their peril. For example, during the early 1970s, President Nixon established a "voluntary" wage and price control program by executive order. In that order, the President required that agencies deny government contracts to any firm that did not comply with the wage and price controls. In *AFL-CIO v. Kahn*,[36] the D.C. Circuit upheld the executive order's

---

[33] Recently, there has been a trend to increased presidents' participation in administrative process, *see, e.g.*, Elena Kagan, *Presidential Administration*, 114 HARV. L. REV. 2245 (2001); John O. McGinnis, *Presidential Review as Constitutional Restoration*, 51 DUKE L.J. 901 (2001); Steven Croley, *White House Review of Agency Rulemaking: An Empirical Investigation*, 70 U. Chi. L. Rev. 821 (2003).

[34] *Clinton v. City of New York*, 524 U.S. 417 (1998).

[35] *Myers v. U.S.*, 272 U.S. 52, 135 (1926).

[36] 618 F.2d 784 (D.C. Cir.), *cert. denied*, 443 U.S. 915 (1979).

validity even though it was neither expressly authorized nor compelled by statute. The court reasoned that the federal procurement acts gave the President broad authority to manage government contracts through the device of the executive order. President Reagan attempted to exert broad authority over executive branch rulemaking through executive orders that established certain cost-benefit analysis requirements for executive branch agencies.[37]

The more difficult issue is whether an executive order may govern the activities of the independent regulatory commissions. In its analysis of the Reagan cost-benefit executive order, the Department of Justice concluded that it could argue that an executive order could control the actions of independent agencies, but "an attempt to exercise supervision of these agencies [through an executive order] would be lawful only if the Supreme Court is prepared to repudiate certain expansive dicta [in *Humphrey's Executor*] and [would trigger] a confrontation with Congress, which has historically been jealous of its prerogatives with regard to [the independent agencies]."[38] Most presidents have respected this arm's-length distance between the chief executive and the independent regulatory agencies.

[C]   The Special Role of the Attorney General

The Department of Justice under the leadership of the Attorney General of the United States plays a more substantial role in the administration of executive branch agencies than any other department.[39] As noted, the Department of Justice functions as the law firm for executive branch agencies in court. The Department also functions as the principal law enforcement agency for the federal government. The chief executive officer in the Department, the Attorney General (AG), was one of the original members of the President's cabinet in an office established by the 1789 Judiciary Act, although the Department of Justice itself was not established until 1870, over 100 years later.[40] The Attorney General must be someone

> learned in the law . . . whose duty it shall be to prosecute and conduct all suits in the Supreme Court in which the United States shall be concerned, and *to give his advice and opinion upon questions of law* when required by the President of the United States, or when requested by the

---

[37] *See, e.g.*, Peter M. Shane, *Presidential Regulatory Oversight and the Separation of Powers: The Constitutionality of Executive Order No. 12,291*, 23 ARIZ. L. REV. 1235 (1981).

[38] Memorandum of the Office of Legal Counsel, Department of Justice on Implementation of Executive Order 12,291 (1981).

[39] One of the best studies of the Office of Attorney General is DANIEL J. MEADOR, THE PRESIDENT, THE ATTORNEY GENERAL, AND THE DEPARTMENT OF JUSTICE (1980); a fascinating shorter article on the origins of the Department of Justice is Susan L. Bloch, *The Early Role of the Attorney General in Our Constitutional Scheme*, 1989 DUKE L.J. 561 (1989).

[40] Bloch *supra* note 39, at 566 & 619. While this is not the place to get into the intricacies of the U.S. law enforcement organizational structure, some detail is necessary to appreciate the full scope of the Department's authority. To a certain extent, the Office of United States Attorney in each federal judicial district functions as a kind of field office for the Department of Justice in both civil and criminal matters. However, each United States Attorney is separately appointed by the President and confirmed by the Senate and consequently enjoys a fair amount of independence from the Department of Justice itself. *See, e.g.*, PETER L. STRAUSS, AN INTRODUCTION TO ADMINISTRATIVE JUSTICE IN THE UNITED STATES 101 n.151 (1989).

heads of any departments, touching any matters that may concern their departments . . .[41]

It is this advice-giving prerogative-the power to issue Attorney General Opinions-that gives the AG substantial influence over the remainder of the executive branch. The issuance of an Attorney General's opinion is frequently used to settle inter-agency disputes or to resolve a broad administrative question that covers a number of agencies. Professor Peter Strauss suggests: "Once the agencies have received advice from the Attorney General, they may lack the means to generate valid litigation that would test its correctness; but if the issue later arises in a proper dispute, say between a citizen and an agency, the Attorney General's prior expression of view would have only persuasive authority for a court."[42] While the issue is not conclusively resolved, many agencies regard AG's opinions to be binding on them until rescinded or removed by judicial action.

[E]   The Unresolved Theory of the "Unitary Executive"

Over the past several years and stretching over a number of presidential administrations, a theory of presidential power called the unitary executive has been propounded[43] by some and debunked[44] by others. The concept is a fascinating one, advanced in particular by Justice Scalia, but not totally accepted by others. The theory has historical antecedents. Prior to the drafting and ratification of the current United States Constitution, the Articles of Confederation established a weak national executive that has been characterized as "executive by committee." There is some evidence stemming from the constitutional debates and other sources that the founders wished to vest all the powers of the executive branch in a single person — the President of the United States. The theory involves at least three separate acts on the part of the President: (1) the power to remove lower-ranking executive branch officials; (2) the power to dictate to subordinates the making of executive branch policy, and the power to veto or nullify exercise of discretionary actions on the part of lower-ranking persons within the executive branch.[45]

The theory derives from the language in Article II, Section 1 of the United States Constitution: "The executive Power shall be vested in the President of the United States of America." There is no question that the Framers adopted this language instead of counter proposals that would have created some kind of executive council. Article II, Section 2 gives the President the authority to "require the Opinion, in writing, of the principal Officer in each of the executive

---

[41]   Judiciary Act of 1789, ch. 20, 1 Stat. 73, 92–93.

[42]   Strauss, *supra* note 28, at 101 n.152.

[43]   *See, e.g.*, Christopher S. Yoo, Steven G. Calabresi & Anthony J. Colangelo, *The Unitary Executive in the Modern Era, 1945-2004*, 90 Iowa L. Rev. 601 (2005). This article is the final article in a series of historical studies by the same authors that begins with Steven G. Calabresi & Christopher S. Yoo, *The Unitary Executive During the First Half-Century*, 47 Case W. Res. 1451 (1997).

[44]   *See, e.g.*, Robert V. Percival, *Presidential Management of the Administrative State: The Not-So-Unitary Executive*, 51 Duke L.J. 963 (2001).

[45]   This entire section borrows from the Yoo, Calabresi & Colangelo article, *supra* note 43, and the Percival article, *id.*

Departments, upon any Subject relating to the Duties of their respective Offices." Article II, Section 3 requires that the *President* "shall take Care that the Laws be faithfully executed." Some have read the sum of these provisions as giving the President virtually unfettered authority within the executive branch. In his dissenting opinion in *Morrison v. Olson*,[46] the decision upholding the independent counsel statute (recall the counsel was appointed by a panel of Article III judges; see the more elaborate discussion in subsection 305(c) below), Justice Scalia cited Article II's vesting clause and noted that "this does not mean *some* of the executive power but *all* of the executive power . . . The President's constitutionally assigned duties include *complete* control over the investigation and prosecution of violations of the law."[47]

For the purposes of this book perhaps the most difficult of the questions posed is whether the president has the power to dictate policy decisions made by lower-ranking officials in the executive branch even though he clearly has the power to appoint and to fire such persons. At least one commentator urges that "the president may advise agency heads concerning his views on particular rules but the president has no authority to dictate regulatory decisions entrusted to them [the lower-ranking officers] by law."

As of mid-2012, there are a number of presidential decisions working their way through the federal judiciary. A number of them implicate the unitary executive theory. We may get an answer from the Supreme Court in the next few years.

§ 3.05   ETHICS IN GOVERNMENT SERVICE

[A]   Ethical Issues Arising Facing Administrative Lawyers

Ethical questions arise frequently in administrative practice both on the part of government attorneys and on the part of private practitioners. Lawyers have too often been insensitive to these concerns, probably resulting in the generally low opinion many members of the public have for lawyers in general and certain agency practitioners in particular. There may be serious limits to what statutes and rules can accomplish in this area, but there is no excuse for personal callousness on the part of individual lawyers.

There is probably no better place in this book to discuss some of the concerns that Congress, the executive branch and the general public have expressed regarding the conduct of federal employees, and more importantly, the conduct of lawyers who work for the Federal Government. To begin with, there are numerous controls on lawyers' conduct, such as the Code of Professional Responsibility or the newer Model Rules of Professional Conduct, that apply irrespective of whether a lawyer is a government employee. Thus, no lawyer, whether in the government or in the private sector, may commit fraud or engage in illegal conduct or violate any of the other canons or rules of professional ethics. In addition, there are statutory provisions and agency rules that prohibit federal employees dealing with matters

---

[46] 487 U.S. 654 (1988).

[47] *Id.* at 705 & 711 (emphasis in the original).

in which the employee has a financial interest. An executive order forbids employee conduct that might impair the integrity of the government.[48] There are special protections for whistleblowers in the Civil Service Reform Act.[49]

[B] The Ethics in Government Act

One of the most important problems in present-day administrative practice is the so-called revolving door phenomenon. This is the practice by which agency personnel leave government for high positions in the industries their agencies regulate, and industry executives move into those same agencies for a few years as political appointees. This movement creates a number of difficulties for the agency. For example, if the revolving door is completely uncontrolled and too cozy, it can result in a "captive" agency that reflects more the interests of the businesses being regulated than the concerns of the general public. By contrast, an agency cannot function capably if its personnel are so insulated that they are totally ignorant of regulated industry.

The revolving door phenomenon places ethical pressures on the officials exiting the government. There have been a number of highly publicized incidents at the federal level, such as the prosecution of former Reagan White House Aide, Michael Deaver, that suggest that many former government officials trade on the contacts and prestige they developed and enjoyed as government officers-again, to the detriment of the general public.[50]

In an attempt to curb the worst revolving door abuses, Congress in 1978 enacted the Ethics in Government Act,[51] a statute that bears close study by anyone contemplating entering or leaving government service. First, the Act requires current high-level government employees (generally those who are political appointees or serving in grades of GS-15 or higher) to file financial disclosure forms for both themselves and their close family members. Second, any employee who was personally and substantially involved in a particular matter is barred for life from appearing in any representative capacity on that matter for any party. (Rulemaking, however, is not regarded as a particular "matter" within the scope of the act). There are also prohibitions against a former employee representing persons on *any* matter before his or her agency for two years after leaving the government.[52]

---

[48] Exec. Order 11,222 (codified at 3 C.F.R. § 306).

[49] 5 U.S.C. § 1101. A good illustration of how some of the statutory whistleblower provisions work in practice is the discussion by Judge Patricia Wald in *Borrell v. United States Int'l Communications Agency*, 682 F.2d 981 (D.C. Cir. 1982).

[50] One conviction of a Reagan-era presidential aide, F. C. "Lynn" Nofziger was reversed with instructions to dismiss the indictment. *United States v. Nofziger*, 878 F.2d 442 (D.C. Cir. 1989).

[51] Pub. L. No. 95-521, 92 Stat. 1824 as amended (codified in scattered portions of U.S.C.). Two excellent articles discussing government ethics in general and the Ethics in Government Act specifically are: Kathleen Clark, *Do We Have Enough Ethics in Government Yet? An Answer from Fiduciary Theory*, 1996 U. ILL. L. REV. 57; ABA Committee on Government Standards, *Keeping Faith: Government Ethics & Government Ethics Regulation*, 45 ADMIN. L. REV. 287 (1993) (Professor Cynthia R. Farina served as the reporter for this comprehensive report).

[52] The Supreme Court held that the subsection of Ethics in Government Act prohibiting receipt of

The statute has not been uniformly praised. In fact, the statute may have the effect of reducing the number of persons interested in government service. It is not entirely clear whether the act, even after 25 years of operation, is truly effective or properly administered. Nonetheless, it is a start and is, at the very least, a statement by Congress that these matters are important.

[C]   The Office of Independent Counsel

In 1973, in a series of Presidential actions that have been referred to as the Saturday Night Massacre, President Nixon fired Archibald Cox, a special prosecutor who had been appointed by executive order to investigate and ultimately prosecute various people involved in the Watergate controversy. Nixon's actions prompted Congress to consider statutory authorization for special prosecutors, and after lengthy debate, Congress, in 1978, enacted an independent counsel provision in the original Ethics in Government Act. However, the Office of Independent Counsel was subject to a sunset provision that required Congressional reauthorization in 1987. The Bush Administration permitted the Act to lapse, but the statute was reenacted by Congress in 1994 as the Independent Counsel Reauthorization Act of 1994.

The Office of Independent Counsel (OIC) is a peculiar office that has triggered an important Supreme Court debate over separation of powers, *Morrison v. Olson*,[53] even though the ultimate effect of *Morrison* was to uphold the constitutionality of the independent counsel's office in all respects. The statute[54] is highly detailed. It expired as of June, 1999, and Congress has shown no interest in reviving it. However, it figured so importantly in the operation of the federal government for so many years that the following discussion is preserved, perhaps in a paraphrase of Santayana, that those who cannot remember the past will be condemned to repeat it.

In essence, the Independent Counsel statute worked in the following manner. When the Attorney General receives information of malfeasance or misfeasance on the part of high-ranking executive branch officials, he makes a preliminary inquiry to determine whether there are grounds to investigate the matter further. After the preliminary investigation is completed (but in no event later than ninety days from the day he initially received the derogatory information), he must file a report with the Independent Counsel Division of the United States Court of Appeals for the D.C. Circuit. The D.C. Circuit is constituted as a *special court* under the act, that either recommends or declines to recommend the appointment of an independent counsel. In the alternative, a majority of either political party's members on either the House or the Senate Judiciary Committee may request that the AG appoint the independent counsel.

Upon receiving the request for appointment of an independent counsel, the special court (composed of three Article III judges designated by the Chief Justice

---

honoraria by government employees was unconstitutional. *See U.S. v. Nat'l Treasury Employees Union*, 513 U.S. 454 (1995).

[53]   487 U.S. 654 (1988), discussed in Chapter 2, § 2.02.

[54]   The OIC statute is codified at 28 U.S.C. §§ 591–599.

of the United States) selects the person to serve as independent counsel and determines the scope of the counsel's duties. After his or her appointment, the independent counsel assumes full and independent responsibility for the investigation and prosecution of any individuals who come within the independent counsel's scope of authority. Accordingly, the operation of the OIC has two distinct phases. Phase I is the preliminary investigation by the AG, and Phase II is the investigation and prosecution that may result after the appointment of the independent counsel.

The wisdom of the OIC mechanism was never universally applauded. As noted above, there is no question that the office is constitutional; but that does not answer the more difficult question as to whether the establishment of the office is wise as a matter of public policy. Congress has not seen fit to reauthorize it. The record of the office is mixed at best. The investigations performed by various independent counsels have resulted in some convictions (notably of President Reagan's close adviser, Michael Deaver) and a number of acquittals (notably of another of President Reagan's close advisers, Lynn Nofziger). One independent counsel investigating the President Clinton's Department of Housing and Urban Development (HUD) was in existence for more than ten years and over $15 million with only one indictment to show for that work. The investigation by Independent Counsel Kenneth Starr led to President Clinton's impeachment by the House of Representatives after which he was acquitted by the Senate. The Starr investigation was so controversial that it may have permanently killed the OIC statute. The OIC statute may never be resuscitated, but it contributed so much debate and controversy to the federal administrative system that it bears mention if only for historical purposes.

[D] Presidential Signing Statements

Following on some initiatives launched by President Reagan, President George W. Bush frequently used a technique of executive decision making that partially substitutes for the President's lack of a line-item veto power.[55] When Congress enacted legislation that contained certain provisions that President Bush did *not* like, he accompanied his signature on the legislation with a "Presidential Signing Statement." The Presidential Signing Statement declared his intent not to implement or enforce some of the provisions of the law that he had just signed. For example, when Congress enacted some amendments to a Department of Defense appropriations act prohibiting the federal government from engaging in torture of detained persons (including those detained as enemy combatants at Guantanamo Bay, Cuba), President Bush objected because in his view this language interfered with his prerogatives as commander-in-chief. President Reagan used signing statements only sporadically, but one report states that President George W. Bush used signing statements questioning provisions in more than 100 separate pieces of legislation.

---

[55] One of the first analyses of the Reagan-era signing statements was Marc N. Garber & Kurt A. Wimmer, *Presidential Signing Statements as Interpretations of Legislative Intent: An Executive Aggrandizement of Power*, 24 Harv. J. on Legis. 363 (1987).

While the earliest signing statements were essentially innocuous pronouncements by Presidents as they signed legislation, as used by President Bush, signing statements assert that certain provisions of the legislation are unconstitutional and, thereby, will not be enforced or implemented by the executive branch. There is clearly no basis in the constitution for such statements, and the few lower federal courts that have addressed the issue have been unsure as to how to review the statements. As of late 2011, the Supreme Court has not addressed the validity or scope of the signing statements.[56] Any such review, if it comes, will be interesting because one of the strong proponents of such statements when he was in charge of the Department of Justice's Office of Legal Counsel is now-Justice Samuel Alito. Whether such statements are constitutionally permissible remain to be seen. President Obama, now nearly three years into his administration, has apparently not used the signing statement device.

---

[56] Nicholas J. Leddy, *Determining Due Deference: Examining When Courts Should Defer to Agency Use of Presidential Signing Statements*, 59 ADMIN. L. REV. 869 (2007).

Chapter 4

THE EXERCISE OF AGENCY POWER

§ 4.01 INTRODUCTION

The topics discussed in Chapters 2 and 3 involve the legitimacy and fundamental nature of administrative agencies. But questions of delegation and executive control are typically issues that have long since been settled in existing administrative agencies. Most of the real controversies in administrative law involve the agency in action. This chapter begins an analysis of agency action by examining certain limits on agency power, including issues that are often not clearly addressed in many administrative law casebooks but that are vital to a full understanding of individual agencies and of the administrative process as a whole.

Two basic concepts should be kept in mind as you work through this chapter and the remainder of the book. First, feel free to presume that there are no problems with the nondelegation issue — i.e., that the enabling act contains a valid standard and that the powers delegated are delegated only to government officials, not to private parties. This is the situation with virtually all agencies now in operation. Challenges to an agency's basic functions are usually resolved early in its existence. Subsequent controversies regarding such things as delegation usually arise only when the legislature gives the agency brand new authority or jurisdiction.

Second, this chapter is not an exclusive or exhaustive statement of the limitations on agency powers but merely a review of some of those limitations that do not easily fit into later chapters. Many limitations on agency functions are explored in the chapters on decision-making and judicial review and are not discussed here.

Humphrey's Executor v. United States[1] recognized that administrative agencies engage in a number of different activities, some of which look much like the drafting and promulgation of statutes (a legislative function) and some of which involve the resolution of individual claims and grievances brought by private persons who are affected by agency action (essentially a judicial function). Tragically, in writing the majority opinion in *Humphrey's Executor*, Justice Sutherland chose to refer to these powers as *quasi*-legislative and *quasi*-judicial, suggesting to many neophytes that there is something less legitimate about agency legislation or adjudication than might be the case if the same pronouncement came from Congress or a federal court. The term *quasi* also suggests that an agency pronouncement may be taken much more casually than one from a legislature or a court. Nothing could be further from the truth. To the extent that an agency is functioning under a proper

---

[1] 295 U.S. 602 (1935) (*Humphrey's Executor* is discussed fully in Chapter 3, *supra* § 3.03).

delegation and within the jurisdiction established by its enabling act, its rulings are not to be regarded lightly.

§ 4.02   AGENCY JURISDICTION-THE *ULTRA VIRES* DOCTRINE

The Federal Administrative Procedure Act expressly permits a court to determine whether an agency is functioning within its jurisdiction. Section 706(2)(C) authorizes judicial review of whether an agency action is "in excess of statutory jurisdiction, authority, or limitations, or short of statutory right." The authority of courts to review jurisdictional questions of this kind was established by the Supreme Court in *Crowell v. Benson*,[2] a case which is now disdained by most administrative law scholars for other reasons. If an agency is acting outside its jurisdictional limits, it is said to be functioning in an *ultra vires* manner.

The term *ultra vires* is borrowed from corporate law and must be sharply distinguished from the nondelegation doctrine. A delegation analysis looks at the face of the enabling act and asks whether the statute *itself* contains a proper standard curbing unfettered agency discretion. As we saw in Chapter 2 (§ 2.02) there is not much vitality left in the non-delegation doctrine on the federal level. By contrast, the issue of whether an agency is acting *ultra vires* assumes that there is a proper delegation in the statute and then analyzes specific action taken by the agency to see whether that action is within the limits set by the enabling act. Courts often overturn agency action because the action is outside the agency's boundaries.

But how does one know whether an agency is functioning within its jurisdiction? The first place to look is the agency's enabling act. To the extent that the Shipping Act expressly gives the Federal Maritime Commission the authority to regulate ocean shipping but not airlines, the Commission will be limited to regulating ocean shippers. Most of the time, the enabling acts are clear as to the substantive boundaries of an agency's jurisdiction. For example, in one of its most important *ultra vires* decisions, *Board of Governors, Federal Reserve System v. Dimension Financial Corp.*,[3] the Supreme Court determined that the Federal Reserve Board's authority to regulate "banks," as that term was defined in the underlying statute, did not give the Board the authority to regulate certain savings and loan institutions. As the Court put it: "If the statute is clear and unambiguous [with regard to an agency's authority] that is the end of the matter . . . ."

But sometimes, the issue is not so clear-cut. The old Federal Power Commission (FPC) (now the Federal Energy Regulatory Commission) was given statutory authority to regulate rates for the interstate shipment of natural gas in 1938. For a number of reasons, the FPC believed that its authority permitted it to regulate only interstate natural gas pipelines and firmly insisted that this jurisdiction did not

---

[2] 285 U.S. 22 (1932). This case should be approached with extreme care. It does establish the authority of courts to review an agency's jurisdiction, but much of the language in the case dealing with the concept of "constitutional" or "jurisdictional" fact (suggesting that a court can review these matters *de novo, i.e.*, with no reference whatsoever to what the agency said) is probably not acceptable today. Those aspects of *Crowell v. Benson* are discussed in Chapter 12.

[3] 474 U.S. 361 (1986).

extend to the regulation of prices charged by natural gas *wells* whose production was sold in interstate commerce. It took a Supreme Court decision in 1954 to prompt the FPC to exercise its wellhead jurisdiction.[4]

Occasionally, an aggressive new agency will deliberately test the limits of its jurisdiction in the first few years of existence. The Consumer Product Safety Commission decided that it had jurisdiction to regulate the use of aluminum electric wiring in new home construction as a safety hazard, asserting that aluminum wiring was a *consumer product*, consistent with the definition of "consumer product" in the Consumer Product Safety Act. The aluminum manufacturers and the construction industry strongly objected, but eventually a federal court of appeals determined that aluminum wiring did fit within the statutory definition of consumer product.[5] In another instance, the predecessor agency of the Department of Energy thought that it could regulate the rents charged for gasoline service station premises under a statute giving it jurisdiction to control petroleum prices. A federal court of appeals determined that nothing in the statutory language could possibly extend to something as peripheral to petroleum prices as the amount of rent paid by gas station operators.[6]

Ultra vires issues mainly involve statutory interpretation and require a close look at the express language of the statute, particularly those provisions that tell the agency what it may regulate. Statutory interpretation, in turn, often requires an examination of the enabling act's legislative history. Moreover, a court will pay some attention to what an agency has to say about its own jurisdiction although a reviewing court is not bound by the agency's decision.[7]

Ultra vires issues arise infrequently in day-to-day agency practice. The jurisdiction of older administrative agencies is normally well established, and new jurisdictional issues usually arise only when the agency's enabling act is amended. The more conservative new agencies are careful not to test the outer limits of their jurisdiction: first, because they normally want to avoid confrontation in the first few years of their existence, and second, because they usually have more than enough to do on matters squarely within their boundaries.

There are some recent exceptions, of course. For example, in 2000, the venerable United States Food and Drug Administration (FDA) got slapped down by the Supreme Court for going beyond its jurisdictional boundaries. In *Food and Drug Administration v. Brown & Williamson Tobacco Corp.*,[8] the FDA attempted to regulate tobacco products as they came within the FDA's statutory power to regulate "drugs" and certain "drug delivery devices." Looking at the precise language of Congressional legislation that prohibited the removal of tobacco

---

[4] *Phillips Petroleum Co. v. Wisconsin*, 347 U.S. 672 (1954).

[5] *Kaiser Alum. & Chem. Corp. v. Consumer Prod. Safety Comm'n*, 574 F.2d 178 (3d Cir.), *cert. denied*, 439 U.S. 881 (1978).

[6] *Shell Oil Co. v. FEA*, 527 F.2d 1243 (Temp. Emer. Ct. App. 1975).

[7] *See Chevron, U.S.A., Inc. v. Natural Res. Def. Council, Inc.*, 467 U.S. 837 (1984) (an agency's pronouncements will be given a great deal of weight, particularly when the underlying statute is ambiguous).

[8] 529 U.S. 120 (2000).

products from consumer markets, the Court determined that Congress had effectively prohibited any FDA regulation of tobacco products and any FDA ban on such products "would therefore plainly contradict congressional policy."[9]

§ 4.03 AGENCY EXERCISE OF LEGISLATIVE POWER

Recall that in *Humphrey's Executor*, Justice Sutherland characterized certain of the activities of the Federal Trade Commission as *quasi*-legislative. In truth, at that point in its history, the only legislative power the FTC exercised was the power to conduct certain investigations to determine whether to recommend to Congress changes in the enabling act. But in the early 1960s, after nearly fifty years of making agency policy by bringing individual adjudications asserting unfair or deceptive trade practices or unfair methods of competition against individual companies, the FTC decided that it would make policy by announcing broad, generally applicable rules relating to unfair and deceptive trade practices (to be known as *trade regulation rules*) rather than relying exclusively on case-by-case policy development. Unfortunately, the FTC's enabling act did not give the Commission exlress permission to make rules. The only language arguably giving the FTC rulemaking power was section 6(g) of the FTC Act that states: the Commission may "[f]rom time to time . . . classify corporations and . . . make rules and regulations for the purpose of carrying out the provisions of . . . this title."[10]

The language of section 6 created a number of interpretative difficulties. This section was placed in the act at a time when the two major independent regulatory commissions (the Interstate Commerce Commission and the FTC) did virtually nothing but adjudicate. It is unlikely, therefore, that many members of Congress who voted for the act regarded section 6 as allowing a commission to write legislative rules. Moreover, for fifty years, the FTC itself had interpreted this portion of the statute merely to give it power to promulgate rules governing agency procedures or housekeeping matters. Thus, the agency's own inaction arguably created an inference that legislative rules were not authorized by section 6.

Nonetheless, in 1962, the Commission began issuing trade regulation rules separately from its conventional adjudications. In 1971, after some less-than-complimentary reports on its activities and after significant changes in Commission personnel the Commission really began to flex its rulemaking muscles. One of its most controversial was a trade regulation rule that, in effect, ordered gasoline service stations to post octane ratings on gasoline pumps.[11] The rule deemed a station's failure to post octane ratings an unfair or deceptive trade practice that could lead to civil penalties.[12]

---

[9] *Id.* at 132.

[10] FTC Act § 6(g), codified at 15 U.S.C. § 46(g).

[11] There was a rational basis for this rule. The FTC's investigation showed that consumers were purchasing inappropriate grades of gasoline because they had no idea of the gasoline's octane rating. Some were buying more expensive premium gasoline when they really didn't need it, and others were buying low octane gasoline for high performance engines and thereby doing serious damage to their cars.

[12] Note that the FTC would still have to pursue an offending service station operator in an individual enforcement action to collect penalties for the violation. But no one in his right mind was going to

When the controversy reached the federal courts in *National Petroleum Refiners Ass'n v. FTC*,[13] the district court reviewed the section 6 language, its legislative history and previous FTC interpretations of the section and concluded that the Commission had rulemaking power only for "housekeeping chores and investigative responsibilities. But on appeal, the D.C. Circuit looked at these same materials (noting, for example, that nothing in the Act's history said the FTC could *not* make trade regulation rules) and waxed eloquent on the benefits of an agency's issuing rules, rather than doing all its policymaking by adjudication. In *National Petroleum Refiners*, the FTC's authority to promulgate legislative rules, even under the skeletal language of section 6, was upheld by the D.C. Circuit. Since *National Petroleum Refiners*, the issue is hardly worth questioning: an agency with a conventional enabling act may exercise rulemaking powers.

§ 4.04   AGENCY EXERCISE OF JUDICIAL POWER

[A]   The Basic Power to Adjudicate

In *Humphrey's Executor*, Justice Sutherland also talked about an agency exercising *quasi*-judicial powers. For many years, this was virtually all that the major regulatory agencies did. The proliferation of agency rules (measurable by comparing the length of the *Federal Register* between, say, 1960 and 2008) is a relatively new phenomenon. The basic power to decide individual cases was rarely questioned because virtually all enabling acts make specific reference to the agency's adjudication authority. The FTC Act, for example, provides that the Commission may police unfair or deceptive trade practices by drafting a complaint, holding a hearing, making findings of fact and issuing a cease-and-desist order.[14] Other agencies function under similar statutory language.[15]

Are there any general limitations on an agency's power to adjudicate? One would think there should be some because the Constitution does limit the judicial power of the United States exercised by the federal courts, and virtually all state constitutions contain similar limiting provisions. Justice Sutherland declined to impose general restrictions on federal agencies by holding that agencies that adjudicate are operating as *agents* of courts. This may be a wholly artificial way to dispose of the issue but it has seems to have worked for the the federal administrative agencies. At least one state appears to have taken a different approach. In the face of the precedent of *Humphrey's Executor*, the New Mexico

---

intentionally disregard the FTC's rule if it were held valid in a pre-enforcement proceeding (a pre-enforcement proceeding permits a court to review an agency's rule before it is applied to any individual in an enforcement action).

[13] 482 F.2d 672 (D.C. Cir. 1973), *cert. denied*, 415 U.S. 951 (1974), *rev'g* 340 F. Supp. 1343 (D.D.C. 1972).

[14] Section 5(b) of the FTC Act, codified at 15 U.S.C. § 45(b).

[15] For a further discussion on agency exercise of judicial power, *see* David B. Spence & Frank Cross, *A Public Choice Case for the Administrative State*, 89 Geo. L.J. 97 (2000); Jason Nichols, *"Sorry! What the Regulation Really Means Is . . .": Administrative Agencies' Ability to Alter an Existing Regulatory Landscape Trough Reinterpretation of Rules*, 80 Tex. L. Rev. 951 (2002); *Tennessee Valley Auth. v. Whitman*, 336 F.3d 1236 (11th Cir. 2003).

Supreme Court in *State v. Mechem*,[16] held squarely that workers compensation actions may be tried only in a court (as opposed to an administrative agency) because those actions are exclusively within the *court's* judicial power. *Mechem*, however, has been subject to a great deal of criticism (some administrative law casebooks turn the case into some kind of joke), and its approach apparently has not been adopted by any other court, federal or state, in the past forty-seven years. Even New Mexico has changed its mind. In 1986, the Supreme Court of New Mexico overruled *Mechem* and held that creation of Workmen's Compensation Administration and vesting in it the power to determine controversies was valid exercise of legislative power.[17]

By the mid-1970s, one would have thought that there was no question that federal administrative agencies could decide cases, even if that power was merely quasi-judicial. But new agencies are always subject to various attacks by persons who disagree with their creation. In 1977, the Supreme Court, in *Atlas Roofing Co. v. Occupational Safety and Health Review Comm'n*,[18] provided a few answers to some of the unresolved issues relating to an agency's power to adjudicate cases.

Atlas Roofing is a strange duck. It probably can't be understood without a little background. In the late 1960s, Congressional investigations revealed that state workers compensation programs — which are mainly private insurance programs governed by state statute — were not doing all they could to protect the health and safety of workers. Moreover, state-based statutory or common law tort systems were also somewhat ineffective. Following these investigations, Congress passed the Occupational Safety and Health Act of 1969, a statute requiring employers to maintain safe and healthy workplaces for workers in businesses affecting interstate commerce.[19]

The Occupational Safety legislation was signed by President Nixon in 1969. It had been bitterly opposed in Congress by a broad spectrum of American industry. Industry resistance continued as OSHA commenced its rulemaking activities and continued into the Commission as OSHA began its initial enforcement actions. It is almost axiomatic that American industry will immediately challenge the constitutionality of any new administrative agency before industry reaches an accommodation with the agency. On one level, *Atlas Roofing* may fairly be read as simply one instance of this widespread resistance movement.

To implement occupational safety and health programs, Congress created two entities: the Occupational Safety and Health Administration (OSHA) — a component of the Department of Labor — to make policy, conduct investigations and assess penalties; and the Occupational Safety and Health Review Commission

---

[16] 63 N.M. 250, 316 P.2d 1069 (1957), *overruled by Wylie Corp. v. Mowrer*, 726 P.2d 1381 (N.M. 1986). *Mechem* is another case that might be referred to as a Lawyer's Full-Employment Act because workers compensation cases in court can be handled only by lawyers (unless the complainant is filing *pro se*). Many state and some federal agencies permit non-lawyers to represent parties.

[17] 726 P.2d 1381 (N.M. 1986).

[18] 430 U.S. 442 (1977).

[19] For a comprehensive description and analysis of the OSH Act, *see* BENJAMIN MINTZ, OSHA: HISTORY, LAW & POLICY (1984).

as an independent regulatory commission with the authority to adjudicate contested OSHA penalty assessments. Pressed by corporate management entities, Congress bowed to the idea that separation of the investigative function and the adjudication function required the creation of two entirely separate administrative agencies.

The problem industry faced in mounting a constitutional attack on the OSH Act was that there were few such attacks that could be taken seriously enough to pass the laugh test. An attack based on nondelegation on wouldn't work. There were express albeit general standards in the statute. An attack based on the Commerce Clause was equally ineffective. The Commerce Clause had been virtually useless as a basis for attacking a federal regulatory program since the New Deal. Other constitutionally-based attacks such as due process were inapt. Indeed, the act was, in fact, brimming over with due process protections for affected companies. But that didn't stop industry from trying to shut down the agencies.

The facts of *Atlas Roofing* are not particularly complicated. The company had been cited for a violation of an OSHA rule that required construction companies to implement certain techniques for shoring up trenches dug in soft or unstable soil. One worker had died as a result of the company's failure to adequately shore its trenches. OSHA proposed a $7500 penalty which the company disputed. After a full trial-type hearing before the Occupational Safety and Health Review Commission, the Commission upheld a penalty of $5000 against one of the individuals involved and $500 against the company. The company then took the dispute to federal court on a number of grounds.

The most striking argument claimed that the OSH Act was unconstitutional because the creation of the Commission and the delegation of the program's adjudicative functions to the Commission (a mere administrative agency) violated the company's right to a *civil jury trial* under the Seventh Amendment to the United States Constitution.[20] The Seventh Amendment provides in part: "[I]n suits at common law, where the value in controversy shall exceed twenty dollars, the right of trial by jury shall be preserved." One would be hard pressed to find a more obscure or infrequently-utilized provision in the Bill of Rights (unless it be the Third Amendment's prohibition against the quartering of soldiers in civilian dwellings) on which to base a claim that an administrative agency was unconstitutional. In the end, the Supreme Court agreed that the company's arguments were not viable but probably gave the company's argument more consideration in the opinion than it really deserved.

In the first place, reasoned the Court, the OSH Act creates an entirely new scheme of statutory rights and obligations, providing for monetary penalty assessments and committing to the Commission the exclusive function to resolve assessment disputes. This new program, in effect, creates a batch of "public rights" as contrasted with "private rights." In the Court's view the Seventh Amendment simply does not apply to this new set of public rights. Moreover, the Court viewed

---

[20] The Seventh Amendment is one of the few provisions in the Bill of Rights not made applicable to the states through the Fourteenth Amendment. For additional insights, *see* Caleb E. Nelson, *Adjudication in the Political Branches*, 107 COLUM. L. REV. 559 (2007); Ellen E. Sward, *Legislative Courts, Article III, and the Seventh Amendment*, 77 N.C. L. REV. 1037 (1999).

the Seventh Amendment as a doctrine frozen in time. In other words, the Amendment was declaratory of the law existing in 1791 — i.e., the law in place at the time of its ratification and requires a jury trial only for those disputes that were afforded jury trials when the amendment was ratified. Thus, the Seventh Amendment does not extend to a new federal remedial program not in existence when the amendment was framed.

Atlas Roofing is intentionally a broad decision. Arguably, it gives Congress a green light to establish an administrative dispute resolution mechanism for virtually any social problem, and thereby, to dispense with a civil jury trial in federal court. Even if it is not so broad, it clearly eliminates any question that Congress has the power to delegate adjudicative functions to agencies and that agencies have the power to adjudicate those disputes. This does not, of course, eliminate judicial review of agency action. It merely permits the agency to adjudicate the dispute in the first instance. A disgruntled party may always seek review in federal court, although as will be seen in subsequent chapters, the grounds on which a reviewing court may overturn the agency's decision will likely be limited.

The *Atlas Roofing* decision saved OSHA and the Commission but some of its language on the public versus private right distinction has led to other problems. For example, in *Thomas v. Union Carbide Agricultural Products Co.*,[21] the Court reviewed an administrative program under the Federal Pesticide Act. The Act requires companies to submit certain proprietary information on pesticides to the Environmental Protection Agency. The Act further provides that the EPA must pay compensation to these companies when it uses that proprietary data. Disputes as to the amount of compensation are to be resolved through binding arbitration. The arbitration is conducted by private sector arbitrators. Challenging the arbitration process, the companies argued that they should be permitted to litigate their claims in an Article III court, rather than be required to submit to binding arbitration.

In *Thomas*, the companies relied heavily on the Court's earlier decision in *Northern Pipeline Constr. Co. v. Marathon Pipe Line Co.*,[22] a plurality decision with an elaborate discussion of separation of powers issues. In *Northern Pipeline*, a plurality decision, the Court determined that United States bankruptcy judges, while affiliated with federal district courts, are not themselves Article III judges. The *Northern Pipeline* plurality went on to hold that Congress could not constitutionally give the right to resolve all matters arising in a bankruptcy context to non-Article III judges.

At issue in *Northern Pipeline* was a contract claim based in state law. For this type of claim, labeled by Justice Brennan (the author of the plurality opinion) as a *private* right, the Constitution requires adjudication in an Article III court. Justice Brennan made a valiant attempt to state the instances in which Congress could give disputes to non-Article III courts. He suggested that the only disputes that could be referred to non-Article III courts are matters that (1) arise in territorial

---

[21] 473 U.S. 568 (1985).

[22] 458 U.S. 50 (1982).

courts, (2) arise in military courts martial, and (3) arise in the context of *public* rights that are adjudicated in legislative courts and administrative agencies. However, Justice Brennan's private/public distinctions were not adopted by a number of other justices who were only willing to concur in the result.

This was the posture of the case law when the Court addressed the validity of mandatory arbitration in *Thomas*. Making some slightly shaky distinctions relating to the earlier cases, the Court — unanimously this time — concluded that the arbitration did affect a *private* right, but in this case, a private right expressly created by Congress in enacting the Federal Pesticide Act. As such, it was a matter that did not require adjudication in an Article III court, but could properly and constitutionally be handled in arbitration.[23] In the Court's own words: "Congress, acting for a valid legislative purpose pursuant to its constitutional powers under Article I, may create a seemingly private right that is so closely integrated into a public regulatory scheme as to be a matter appropriate for agency resolution with limited involvement by the Article III judiciary."

In 1986, in *Commodity Futures Trading Commission v. Schor*,[24] Justice O'Connor seems to have repudiated much of the reasoning of *Northern Pipeline* by permitting the adjudication of state law counterclaims growing out of so-called reparations proceedings at the Commodity Futures Trading Commission (CFTC). Citing *Northern Pipeline*, Schor, the aggrieved party, argued that these state law claims (as *private* rights) were required to be litigated in an Article III court. This time the Court disagreed. Writing for a solid majority, Justice O'Connor concluded that the CFTC deals only with a "particularized area of the law, whereas bankruptcy judges may face broad-based state law claims. Justice O'Connor was relatively casual about the public/private right distinction, suggesting that the distinction "reflects simply a pragmatic understanding that when Congress selects a quasi-judicial [Heaven help us, the *Humphrey's Executor* language revived yet again!] method of resolving matters . . . the danger of encroaching on the judicial powers is less than when private rights [are adjudicated in a non-Article III court]. As might be expected, Justice Brennan, the author of *Northern Pipeline*, dissented in *Schor*.

All of this sounds great. You are probably ready to conclude that *Atlas Roofing* has been revalidated by *Thomas* and *Schor*. That may be the case, but any reader of these cases must now take into consideration a 1987 Supreme Court decision, *Tull v. United States*.[25] In *Tull*, the Court reviewed the imposition of civil penalties by the Environmental Protection Agency under the Clean Water Act. In this instance, EPA investigates the matter and administratively assesses the penalty but must then go to federal court for enforcement of the penalty if the violator does not voluntarily pay. Mr. Tull refused to pay and demanded a jury trial in federal court under the Seventh Amendment. After denying the jury demand, the district court conducted a fifteen-day bench trial to determine that Tull had violated the Act and that the penalty assessment was proper. The Supreme Court split the

---

[23] The Court's decision in *Thomas* provided additional impetus to Congress' enactment of the Administrative Dispute Resolution Act in 1990, discussed in Chapter 8.

[24] 478 U.S. 833 (1986).

[25] 481 U.S. 412 (1987).

controversy into two parts, determining that (1) Tull had a Seventh Amendment right to trial by jury on the issue of *liability* (*i.e.*, whether he, in fact, violated the Clean Air Act), but (2) Tull did not get a jury trial under the Seventh Amendment for the *penalty assessment* phase of the trial. In other words, a jury must determine the violation, but the amount of the penalty could be set by a judge sitting alone. The Court cited *Atlas Roofing* only in a minor footnote. Moreover, it did not invoke or elaborate on the private right/public right distinction.

Tull is so lacking in analysis and in citation to preexisting case law that it is difficult to parse. One possible distinction between *Tull* and *Atlas Roofing* is that the EPA has no internal adjudicatory structure for penalty disputes equivalent to the Occupational Safety and Health Review Commission. Second, the private right/ public right distinction may not be relevant here because it was conceded that Mr. Tull was permitted to adjudicate the dispute in an Article III court in the first instance.

The much narrower question in *Tull* was merely whether or not the violator was entitled to a jury trial. The bifurcation of the opinion, as between the violation or liability phase, and the penalty assessment phase was explained by the Court in the following manner. A Clean Air Act violation, leading to the imposition of a civil monetary penalty is "a type of remedy at common law that could only be enforced in courts of law." In the Court's view, such a penalty dispute is not, as the government argued, essentially an equitable proceeding which would not have triggered a jury trial when the Seventh Amendment was ratified. With regard to the actual assessment of the dollar amount of the penalty, the Court stated: "The assessment of a civil penalty is not one of the most fundamental elements [of a jury trial]. [Therefore] Congress' assignment of the determination of the amount of civil penalties to trial judges . . . does not infringe on the constitutional right to a jury trial."

As of 2007, the Supreme Court has not further addressed these issues in the context of administrative agency action.[26] The lower federal courts try their best. For example, in *Austin v. Shalala*,[27] the Fifth Circuit reviewed a dispute in which a social security recipient argued that she should have a jury trial for an action in which the government sought recovery of overpayments. The overpayment action was a hearing before an administrative law judge within the Social Security Administration. The *Austin* court conceded that she would have had a right to a jury trial had the action been commenced in court, but went on to conclude that here "Congress has created a public right for the government to recover the overpayment of social security benefits, and the SSA has special competence in this field . . . [W]e conclude that Congress may properly assign the relevant determinations to an administrative agency, and a jury trial is not required."

---

[26] In *Granfinanciera v. Nordberg*, 492 U.S. 33 (1989), a case involving two private parties involved in a bankruptcy proceeding, the Court determined that "public" rights may be implicated even when the government is not a party to the action. In this instance, the Seventh Amendment does not require a jury trial.

[27] 994 F.2d 1170 (5th Cir. 1993).

It is difficult, at this juncture, to harmonize these cases or even to predict a trend in this area of the law. In all likelihood, we have not seen the last of the jury trial/bench trial problem or of the public rights/private rights distinction.

Students interested in state administrative law may see some equally interesting cases. Many states have considered establishing administrative agencies to deal with workers compensation, certain gambling and drug offenses, traffic violations and other low-echelon violations of state law. Does *Atlas Roofing* approve the use of an administrative agency to handle these disputes? The short answer is that no one knows for sure. *Atlas Roofing* is based solely on one part of the Constitution — the Seventh Amendment — that has never applied to the states. State constitutions may have different, more compelling provisions that forbid giving such controversies to administrative agencies. Also, gambling offenses and traffic violations have traditionally been regarded as part of the criminal process, rather than a matter of adjudication of private sector civil disputes. If a matter is criminal in nature, those provisions in either the federal or state constitutions that guarantee certain procedures in criminal court apply.

[B]   Penalty Assessments and Other Remedies

Atlas Roofing tells us that agencies may adjudicate various controversies within their jurisdiction. But what power does an agency have to grant remedies or to penalize wrongdoers? Early case law suggested that administrative agencies had no right to assess flexible, civil penalties because that gave excessive discretion to the agencies. In contrast, modern enabling acts, such as the OSH Act, give the agency the power to assess penalties of, for example, "not more than $10,000 per violation . . . or "up to $25,000 per day." These provisions are now clearly permissible, at least on the federal level. In *National Independent Coal Operators Ass'n v. Kleppe*,[28] the Supreme Court approved the assessment of flexible monetary civil penalties under the Federal Coal Mine Safety and Health Act,[29] a statute much like the Occupational Safety and Health Act, and presumably settled the flexible penalty issue once and for all.

However, the penalties should be proportionate to the actual violation. The Supreme Court made the proposition somewhat clear in *United States v. Bajakajian*.[30] In *Bajakajian*, an international traveler attempted to board a flight carrying more than $350,000. He was detained and cited for failure to report to Customs officials that he was carrying more than $10,000 in currency. The traveler pleaded guilty to this offense. However, as an additional citation, the government attempted to declare the entire amount of $357,144 forfeited because the traveler

---

[28] 423 U.S. 388 (1976).

[29] 30 U.S.C. § 813(a).

[30] 524 U.S. 321 (1998). *Bajakajian* has an interesting pedigree. In *United States v. Halper*, 490 U.S. 435 (1989), the Court, in a somewhat muddled opinion, held that civil monetary penalties coupled with a criminal conviction for the same conduct violated the Double Jeopardy Clause. The Court reasoned that the civil penalty was totally disproportionate to the loss suffered by the government and thus, constituted an additional punishment for the same conduct. *Halper* proved so problematic for the federal courts that the Supreme Court, in *Hudson v. United States*, 522 U.S. 93 (1997) overruled *Halper*, holding that a civil remedy, even if coupled with a criminal penalty, does not violate Double Jeopardy.

willfully violated the statute and the funds were directly "involved in" the offense. On review, the Court concluded that the forfeiture constituted punishment and as such it fell within the "Excessive Fines" clause of the United States Constitution. Because the amount of the forfeiture was deemed to be excessive, it was overturned by the Court.

There are other remedies that may be given to an agency by its enabling act. The FTC, for example, has the power to issue *cease and desist* orders to persons found to have committed unfair or deceptive trade practices. These orders are in the nature of injunctions and have been uniformly upheld by the courts. Many agencies find the device of the consent order (by which a party refuses to admit liability but agrees to discontinue the practice) helpful. Some agencies that engage in economic regulation of a particular industry may order restitution of overcharges. There is little doubt that an agency may do any of these things so long as Congress approves.

The more difficult question is not whether an agency may assess a penalty or issue a cease and desist order, but rather whether a party is subject to instant discipline if she refuses to pay the penalty or defies an order. In other words, do agencies have the inherent authority to *enforce* their sanctions? In some cases, as for example, when a party is requesting permission from the agency to do something, such as asking the Federal Communications Commission for a broadcast license, the agency may sanction the party by merely denying the license. But in most other instances, the agency may not enforce civil sanctions. If compliance by the private party is not voluntary, virtually all agencies must ask an appropriate court to enforce the penalty or sanction against the party. This takes a separate court proceeding even though that proceeding may nevertheless be short and sweet. Judges are rarely happy with people who defy the legitimate commands of administrative agencies.

[C]   Agencies and Criminal Sanctions

May an agency put someone in jail? The short answer is no; no agency has *independent* authority to impose criminal penalties of any sort. However, this blurs an issue that many lawyers and law students never quite grasp. Even if the agency itself may not put your client in jail, your client still may go to jail for a willful violation of an agency requirement if the agency's enabling act expressly provides for criminal penalties and if a court determines that the violation was intentional.[31] Forgetting this basic proposition can have drastic consequences for lawyer and client alike.

The criminal violation process works as follows. Consider that a typical agency enabling act permits an agency to develop a regulatory program through its rule making authority. For example, the Environmental Protection Agency is permitted under the Clean Air Act[32] to develop rules restricting the amount of sulfur oxide

---

[31] Some people have become concerned that agencies are imposing punishments traditionally reserved for the criminal justice system, *see* Jason M. Day, *The Intertwining of Administrative Actions and the Criminal Justice System*, 4 Tex. Tech. J. Tex. Admin. L. 99 (Spring, 2003).

[32] 42 U.S.C. §§ 7401–7626.

emissions from coal-burning power plants. The Clean Air Act permits the assessment of civil monetary penalties and authorizes both criminal fines and jail sentences for violators who intentionally violate the statute (or, by derivation, the agency's rule implementing the statute). Assume that EPA writes a rule setting the maximum discharge of sulfur oxide at 1 part per cubic foot of total air emissions from a particular type of power plant. Assume further that XYZ, Inc., a corporation subject to the Clean Air Act and to this rule, knows about the rule and intentionally permits emissions from its plant totaling 126 parts per cubic foot.

The EPA may do one of two things: it may use its own enforcement authority to assess civil penalties against XYZ, or it may refer the case to the Department of Justice for criminal prosecution. To the extent that the agency has already compiled data on XYZ's pollution control practices, that information will probably be introduced at trial. Granting that XYZ has all the procedural rights given to criminal defendants (such as right to counsel, proof beyond a reasonable doubt, etc.), it must still defend against EPA's charges. If the government can prove both the violation itself and the requisite state of mind for criminal conviction (intentional violation), XYZ and its officers are subject to both fines and jail sentences.

This sounds like a simple and unquestionable scenario. It was not always so. Before the turn of the twentieth century, in *ICC v. Brimson*,[33] the Supreme Court stated in dicta: "[An administrative agency] could not, under our system of government, and consistently with due process of law, be invested with authority to compel obedience to its orders by a judgment of fine or imprisonment." Some early readers of *Brimson* took this comment to mean that no criminal sanctions whatsoever could flow from a violation of an agency requirement even if the criminal action was brought in a proper court.

Not quite fifteen years after *Brimson*, the Court decided *United States v. Grimaud*[34] mainly to remove this uncertainty. Mr. Grimaud had intentionally violated a Department of Agriculture order forbidding grazing of cattle on national forest land without a permit. Charged with a criminal violation in federal court, he argued that the Department did not have the constitutional power to define the terms of any crime — *i.e.*, that an agency rule could not be used as the substantive basis for a criminal conviction. The Court disagreed and upheld the conviction based upon very simple reasoning: It is Congress that authorizes the criminal penalty by making any violation of a proper agency rule unlawful. Thus, the authority for the criminal sanction springs from the legislature and not from the agency itself even if the agency writes the rule upon which the conviction is based.

Everyone should be aware that there are some aberrations in this line of case law that grow out of the activities of federal immigration and naturalization programs. Most of these programs are now administered by two components of the Department of Homeland Security, the United States Citizenship and Immigration Services and the Immigration and Customs Enforcement. The agency formerly handling these activities was called the Immigration and Naturalization Service

---

[33]　154 U.S. 447 (1894).

[34]　220 U.S. 506 (1911).

(INS). A great deal of the agency's authority springs from the plenary power to conduct foreign affairs vested in the executive branch by the Constitution. The agency exercises vast powers over persons who are in the United States illegally. As a result, certain actions taken by the agency involving the process of deportation or exclusion of aliens come very close to criminal sanctions. In certain cases, the agency may detain people, may issue warrants and may physically remove people from the United States without providing those persons with the full panoply of procedural rights that would be given to persons charged with crimes who are legally in the U.S.

Much of the broad authority given to the agency has been upheld in cases, such as *Abel v. United States.*[35] The narrow holding of *Abel* permits the introduction in an immigration hearing of evidence seized under an agency warrant that would have been defective if it had been issued as a criminal warrant. In a criminal case, evidence seized as a result of a defective warrant must be suppressed. But *Abel* and related cases contain additional language that appears to approve broad powers over illegal aliens that go well beyond the powers given to other federal agencies.

Lawyers should always be cautious in using immigration cases as a basis for creating general principles of administrative law. Our immigration agencies are unique among federal administrative agencies because their work is so heavily intertwined with the plenary power to conduct foreign affairs, and little decisional authority springing from their activities is useful in cases involving garden-variety federal administrative agencies.

It is also clear that an administrative action and a criminal proceeding may go forward at the same time in most instances and the government agency involved and the prosecutor of the criminal action may share information on the same case as the two go forward. In *SEC v. Dresser Indus., Inc.,*[36] the District of Columbia Circuit made quite clear that there has always been significant overlap between the regulatory and criminal laws of the United States. While a court may have discretion to stay a parallel civil or administrative proceeding pending the outcome of a criminal case, it is not required to do so.

[D]   Agency Regulation of Attorney Conduct

Regardless of specialty, the behavior of all U.S. lawyers, including administrative law practitioners, is governed by a code of ethics. In the United States, there exist two principal ethical codes, both promulgated as models by the American Bar Association (ABA) and formally adopted, sometimes with significant revisions, by various state bars and supreme courts.

The Model Code of Professional Responsibility has been in existence in various forms for a number of years and-with state-by-state variations-applies in some states. In the 1970s, the ABA spent a great deal of time and effort attempting to develop a new set of ethical constraints better attuned to the practice of law in the United States in the latter half of the twentieth century. That set of principles, the

---

[35]   362 U.S. 217 (1960).

[36]   628 F.2d 1368 (D.C. Cir.), *cert. denied,* 449 U.S. 993 (1980).

Model Rules of Professional Conduct, has been adopted throughout the United States with the notable exception of California. Because lawyers who practice before agencies must be admitted in at least one state, one or the other of these two sets of ethical principles will have a significant effect on their behavior as lawyers.

At least one jurisdiction, the District of Columbia, has modified the Model Rules of Professional Conduct for members of the D.C. Bar. The D.C. rules, based on the Model Rules, include special and somewhat innovative provisions directed specifically toward lawyers whose practices involve the federal government or who take and then leave government service (the so-called "revolving door"). Because so many lawyers in D.C. have administrative agency practices, the D.C. rules may provide a model for regulating the conduct of lawyers in other states with a heavy administrative practice.

There may be additional constraints on lawyer behavior. Most agencies have the power to regulate the conduct of attorneys who appear before the agency. Congress made this clear a number of years ago when it enacted a portion of Title 5 of the *United States Code* that is often not reproduced in administrative law casebooks. Title 5 U.S.C. § 500(d)(2) provides that the APA "does not authorize or limit the discipline, including disbarment, of individuals who appear in a representative capacity before an agency."[37]

A few agencies have used this provision and other portions of their own enabling acts to promulgate ethical rules for attorneys, strictly for their respective agencies. The Securities and Exchange Commission, for example, has had under consideration for a number of years an ethical code for lawyers who practice before the SEC.[38] The now-defunct Interstate Commerce Commission had a code of professional behavior that had been used on occasion as the basis for agency-imposed discipline. In one instance, the ICC ordered a six-month suspension for a lawyer who represented two clients with conflicting interests before the Commission without the permission or knowledge of those clients. The lawyer challenged the authority of the ICC to administer any discipline whatsoever and pursued that challenge into the D.C. Circuit. In a decision dripping with incredulity and sarcasm, the Circuit very nearly held his appeal frivolous, noting that the existence of § 500 makes it abundantly clear that an agency may discipline attorneys who appear before it and who engage in improper conduct.[39]

Moreover, the power of agencies to sanction lawyers for misbehavior, even in the absence of a formal code of ethics, has been implicitly recognized by the Supreme

---

[37] Another part of § 500 provides that an agency cannot require more than mere admission to a state bar as a qualification for practicing before the agency.

[38] *See* LEGAL TIMES, Dec. 7, 1981, at 20. The subcommittee on federal agency discipline of the ABA's Standing Committee on Professional Discipline promulgated a draft code of ethical behavior for all attorneys practicing before federal agencies. *See* LEGAL TIMES, Apr. 6, 1981, at 22. The draft code, however, has not yet been implemented. For some general discussion of many of these issues, *see* Harold Levinson, *Professional Responsibility Issues in Administrative Adjudication*, 2 BYU J. PUB. L. 219 (1988).

[39] *Polydoroff v. ICC*, 773 F.2d 372 (D.C. Cir. 1985).

Court. In *Steadman v. SEC*,[40] the Court reviewed a suspension levied against a broker in the securities industry by the Securities and Exchange Commission. The suspended broker had argued that no personal sanction could be imposed unless the Commission could show fraud on his part that met the evidentiary standard of clear and convincing proof. The Court essentially accepted, with little discussion, the notion that the SEC had the inherent power to invoke the sanction against the broker. The Court went on to the narrow issue that grows out of the case, limiting the standard of proof in agency actions (absent a different statutory standard) to mere preponderance of the evidence (the broker had argued that he could be sanctioned only on the basis of clear and convincing evidence of a violation).

Accordingly, agencies have tremendous internal powers. These powers extend not just to members of the regulated industry but also to lawyers who practice before the agency. New agency lawyers should take special care to determine whether the agency has a special code of ethics and to ascertain the terms of that code prior to engaging in practice before the agency. Even if no special code exists, lawyers should never forget the applicability of the Code of Professional Responsibility or the Rules of Professional Conduct to administrative practice.

§ 4.05 AGENCY ACQUISITION OF INFORMATION — AN OVERVIEW

[A] Congress' and the Courts' Recognition of Agency Need for Information

One of the ways an agency first begins flexing its muscles (or "exercising its powers" in the parlance of law professors) is by demanding information from persons within its jurisdiction. This is not surprising because it is axiomatic that agencies cannot function without information. But it is equally axiomatic that many persons regulated by administrative agencies dislike providing information, particularly information that touches on sensitive personal or business matters. Congress and the courts have acknowledged these tensions, but have generally resolved the issues in favor of the agencies — in clear recognition that agencies simply cannot perform their missions without a great deal of information.

There are basically four devices available to most agencies for obtaining information as discussed below.

[B] Recordkeeping Requirements

These are agency rules that require people to maintain and preserve certain records. Perhaps the best known example of a recordkeeping requirement is the multitude of records that must be kept (on automobiles, personal computers and the like) by persons who seek to deduct expenses on their tax returns. Note that these requirements merely oblige a person to develop and maintain the records but not necessarily to turn them over to the government. Records such as these get

---

[40] 450 U.S. 91 (1981).

into the hands of the government under normal circumstances only when a dispute arises between the private person and the agency.

[C]   Reporting Requirements

These rules require persons to file periodic reports with the agency. Again, one of the best examples of a reporting requirement is the IRS Form 1040 by which taxpayers inform the IRS of their yearly income and expenditures. Another example pertains to persons holding federal licenses — such as television broadcast licenses or hydroelectric power licenses — who must file periodic reports on their activities. These reports are typically much more detailed than the information requested on the IRS Form 1040. There are usually penalties connected with failure to file the required reports that may be imposed separately from any other penalty.

[D]   Subpoenas

Most administrative agencies have the power to issue their own subpoenas through language in the enabling act and through § 555(d) of the Administrative Procedure Act. Many state agencies have parallel subpoena power. A subpoena may simply require the presence of an individual before some kind of agency hearing to give testimony (the classic subpoena *ad testificandum*) or may be issued in the form of a subpoena *duces tecum*, which requires that individual to appear as well as to present to the agency certain specified records. When an agency is engaged in a formal adjudication, it frequently invokes its own discovery rules to take depositions or to submit interrogatories as a device for acquiring information.[41]

[E]   Physical Inspections

Many agencies can do their job only if they can actually view the operations of a business. For example, the government decided long ago that many aspects of coal mine health and safety could be policed only by on-premises inspections of operating coal mines. In some instances, the Environmental Protection Agency can determine whether certain industries are releasing impermissible amounts of air or water pollution only by looking at the factory. For these reasons, many agencies conduct periodic, and usually unannounced, inspections of persons and businesses within their jurisdiction.

[F]   Other Forms of Information Gathering

There are many other ways that an agency acquires information. Any time an agency conducts a major rulemaking, it is given reams of data by interested persons who submit comments on the proposed rules. Quite often, that information is useful for broad agency purposes not just for the rule under consideration. When agencies open participation in adjudications to persons other than the original parties, they may acquire considerable material in the nature of *amicus curiae*

---

[41] Discovery in agency proceedings is discussed in Chapter 8, § 8.04 *below.*

(friend of the court) briefs. Moreover, agency personnel closely follow the activities of regulated industries through Congressional hearings and investigations, much of which becomes part of the agency's store of knowledge. In reality, an agency's problem is frequently too much information and too little analysis rather than the other way around.

In 1978, Congress created a wholly new entity within most major federal agencies, the Inspector General (IG).[42] Under the Act, each major federal agency now contains an IG appointed by the President with the advice and consent of the Senate. Among other things, the IG is empowered to conduct audits within the agency, investigate instances of fraud and abuse in the agency's programs and to report on and make various recommendations relating to those audits or investigations to the agency head. Agency inspectors general are also required to report periodically to Congress.

Since the inception of the Office of Inspector General, and particularly since a 1988 amendment to the IG Act strengthened the IG's powers considerably, the agency Inspector General has become a power to be reckoned with in all of the major agencies. The IG's investigating powers have created a whole new structure of information gathering and employee discipline within each of these agencies. While, in theory, the IG is an officer who deals with the internal governance of each agency, because so many IG reports eventually become public knowledge, the activities of the IG have also become an important source of information about the agency for both Congress and the general public.

§ 4.06 RECORDKEEPING AND REPORTING REQUIREMENTS

[A] Information Requests Generally

The primary source of authority for establishing recordkeeping and reporting requirements is the rules of the agency in question. Congress occasionally writes such requirements into an agency's enabling act. However, even when it does so, it sets out the requirements in fairly sketchy terms. The particulars of any information-gathering requirement are generally respected by persons regulated by the agency. One of the reasons these requirements are not often questioned is that, as will be seen, there are not many plausible grounds on which a person can resist keeping records or making reports if the agency requires her to do so.

Around the beginning of the twentieth century, the Supreme Court wrote a number of opinions, often under the pen of Justice Oliver Wendell Holmes, containing language that raised some significant doubts about the scope of an agency's power to retrieve information. In *Harriman v. ICC*,[43] Justice Holmes suggested that an agency could compel the release of information only when the

---

[42] The IG Act is set out at 5 U.S.C. Appendix. For a compilation of existing literature on the work of the inspectors general, *see* William S. Fields & Thomas E. Robinson, *Legal and Functional Influences on the Objectivity of the Inspector General Audit Process*, 2 GEO. MASON IND. L. REV. 97 (1993).

[43] 211 U.S. 407 (1908).

agency is able to allege a "specific breach of the law." However, specific legislation giving the Interstate Commerce Commission broader investigatory powers later eroded the *Harriman* holding.[44] Agency information-gathering continued to trouble Justice Holmes as late as the 1920s when he wrote what has become one of the classic (but little followed) decisions in this area, *FTC v. American Tobacco Co.*[45] In *American Tobacco*, the FTC asked for "all" letters and telegrams received by the company from its jobbers over a one-year period. The request stemmed from an FTC investigation into the company's business practices, although there was no ongoing enforcement action.

The case is famous mainly for Justice Holmes' comment that an agency's general power to investigate and to request documents does not permit "fishing expeditions into private papers on the possibility that [the papers] may disclose evidence of crime." The fishing expedition dictum of *American Tobacco* seems to be invoked every time private persons seek to resist an agency request for information. Today, invoking *American Tobacco* as a winning basis on which to resist an agency's request is usually not worth the time and effort of citing the case. More recent cases have confirmed the authority of an agency to request virtually any information from businesses within its jurisdiction.

In *United States v. Morton Salt Co.*,[46] for example, the FTC ordered a number of salt producers to file reports describing their compliance with an earlier cease and desist order. The producers refused to file the reports and took the FTC to court, and the dispute eventually reached the Supreme Court of the United States. Examining the Constitution, the Administrative Procedure Act and the FTC's regulations, Justice Jackson, writing for the Court, found absolutely no impediment to the Commission's request. As he put it: "It is sufficient if the inquiry is within the authority of the agency, the demand is not too indefinite and the information sought is reasonably relevant." Justice Jackson went on to make a very helpful suggestion that all counsel with similar problems should heed. If a company objects to an agency's request for information, it should first try to negotiate some limits on the request with the agency. A frontal attack on the request in court is not likely to prevail.[47]

[B] The Limitations of the Fifth Amendment Right Against Self-Incrimination

There are a few additional limitations on agency information gathering. The Fifth Amendment right against self-incrimination has been used on several occasions to block a reporting requirement, although the facts of the cases are so unique that they provide very little comfort for the average person subject to a conventional agency information request. Moreover, these cases must be read in

---

[44] *Smith v. ICC*, 245 U.S. 33 (1917).

[45] 264 U.S. 298 (1924).

[46] 338 U.S. 632 (1950).

[47] The *Morton Salt* holding was confirmed in litigation involving a vast information gathering project by the FTC. *In re FTC Line of Bus. Report Litig.*, 595 F.2d 685 (D.C. Cir.), *cert. denied*, 439 U.S. 958 (1978).

concert with a Supreme Court opinion of much broader applicability, *Shapiro v. United States.*[48]

Shapiro involved a prosecution for violation of some World War Two price controls. The defendant, Shapiro, was a seller of fruits and vegetables in New York who refused to give the agency certain business records on the grounds that being forced to give up the records violated his right against self-incrimination. The Court made short shrift of Mr. Shapiro's Fifth Amendment arguments. Specifically, the Court noted that (1) the records were simply conventional business records (that is, the records were the sort of records that business people would keep whether or not they were subject to price controls), (2) the activity in question, selling fruits and vegetables, was a legitimate business enterprise, and (3) the agency was functioning within the scope of its authority. The basic reasoning of the Court is quite simple: the government's request to see conventional records maintained for normal business purposes could not be equated with forcing someone to confess to the commission of a crime.

The difficulty with the application of the *Shapiro* holding stems from additional language added to the majority opinion by Chief Justice Vinson. In an apparent attempt to further bolster the broad holding of *Shapiro*, the Chief Justice claimed that whenever ordinary business records became subject to a mandatory government recordkeeping requirement they became "public records", over which persons such as Mr. Shapiro no longer had any control. This dictum horrified Justice Frankfurter, who saw it as far too overreaching. It was, in Justice Frankfurter's view, a proposition that arguably permits the government, under the *Shapiro* rationale, to require every citizen to keep a daily record of his or her activities and to turn over that record to any government official who asks for it. Recall *Shapiro*'s historical setting": the case arose during World War Two when the Allies were heavily engaged against Nazi Germany, a totalitarian state where constant inspections of one's "papers" by government officials was a standard and horrifying practice.

Justice Frankfurter's fears have not been realized — at least not as of the writing of this edition. Indeed, since *Shapiro* was written, persons in the United States have probably developed a heightened sense of personal privacy implemented as public policy by such statutes as the Federal Privacy Act (*see* Chapter 14, § 14.04). Still, there are many records which Americans are required to keep for certain purposes, and we quite often lose legal control over those records. For example, the Internal Revenue Service requires the maintaining of numerous records on business entertainment expenses, travel expenditures and the like by those persons who wish to qualify for certain tax deductions. Recordkeeping requirements imposed on certain professional groups as a matter of ethics and good business practices result in the compilation of highly detailed and voluminous records. The typical lawyer's time sheets closely resemble that daily diary that Justice Frankfurter had in mind.

There are some distinctions between these records and those at issue in the *Shapiro* case. The penalty, if one can call it that, for failing to keep car mileage and

---

[48] 335 U.S. 1 (1948).

business entertainment records is simply that the taxpayer may not legitimately claim those deductions on her tax return, whereas the records in Mr. Shapiro's case were being used as the basis for a criminal prosecution against him.

The Fifth Amendment right against self-incrimination is not easily invoked in any setting. For example, a private person's records may lose the protection of the Fifth Amendment if the records fall into the hands of third parties, such as banks. In *California Bankers Ass'n v. Shultz*,[49] the Supreme Court upheld a portion of the Bank Secrecy Act of 1970,[50] a statute that requires banks to preserve various depositors' records and to disclose those records to government employees, even though depositors have no say in whether the records are released.[51] Most importantly, the Court in recent years seems to have limited the right against self-incrimination to situations in which the incriminating testimony comes directly from the person's mouth or the person's actions. In *Andresen v. Maryland*,[52] a case involving records in the hands of a taxpayer's accountant, the Court reiterated much of the language of *California Bankers* for the proposition that records given to another person frequently lose their Fifth Amendment protection. However, in *Andresen*, the Court went on to emphasize that self-incrimination involves forcing a human being to do something or say something that may be an admission of criminal activity. A mere request by the government for otherwise legitimate records does not normally rise to this level.

There are, of course, a few cases holding to the contrary, but they must be invoked with the greatest of caution. Those decisions in which the Supreme Court has upheld a private person's invoking the right against self-incrimination in a recordkeeping or reporting setting were decided twenty years after *Shapiro* and should be read more as aberrations than as a general rule. In *Marchetti v. United States*,[53] the government tried to force Marchetti to fill out a form declaring his gambling earnings. Mr. Marchetti lived in a state where gambling was illegal. The Court observed that the mere filling out of the form would constitute the admission of a crime by Marchetti himself. Consequently, the Court permitted Marchetti to invoke his right against self-incrimination and to refuse to answer on that basis. Shortly after *Marchetti* was decided, the Court issued its decision in *Leary v.*

---

[49] 416 U.S. 21 (1974).

[50] 12 U.S.C. § 1829(b).

[51] Professor K.C. Davis enumerates five situations in which the Fifth Amendment cannot be used: (1) corporate records (corporations are not "persons" for purposes of the right against self-incrimination, although they are "persons" for purposes of Fifth and Fourteenth Amendment Due Process); (2) a *California Bankers* situation in which records are held by third persons (although records in the hands of an attorney normally are protected through the attorney-client privilege); (3) records that are not deemed "private papers"; (4) records that are required to be kept by statute or agency regulation; and (5) records pertaining to a person who has been given use immunity and who thereby can no longer invoke the right against self-incrimination. K.C. Davis, Administrative Law 567 (1977). Nor does the Fourth Amendment prohibition against unlawful searches and seizures work well here. In *United States v. Miller*, 425 U.S. 435 (1976), *superseded by statute (see also SEC v. Jerry T. O'Brien Inc.*, 467 U.S. 735 (1984)), an indicted taxpayer objected to a bank's voluntarily turning over his banking records to the IRS. The Court held that the Fourth Amendment does not protect records which the taxpayers willingly let the bank have, even if he had no idea that the bank might turn them over to the government.

[52] 427 U.S. 463 (1976).

[53] 390 U.S. 39 (1968).

United States.[54] In this instance, Dr. Timothy Leary was asked to fill out a tax form declaring the amount of marijuana he was importing into the United States from Mexico. Importation of marijuana was then and is now unlawful. Leary refused to execute the form on Fifth Amendment grounds, and litigation ensued. When the case reached the Supreme Court, the Court invoked its *Marchetti* rationale to permit Leary to refuse to make the declaration.[55]

The *Marchetti* and *Leary* cases cannot be pushed too far. In them, the government asked: (1) "Mr. Marchetti, have you gambled?" and (2) "Dr. Leary, are you importing marijuana?" It was essentially the *form* of these questions that gave rise to the Fifth Amendment defense.

Consider the result if the government had asked Mr. Marchetti: "How much money did you make last year?" What if the Customs Officer in El Paso had asked Dr. Leary: "What are you bringing across the border?" Could either Marchetti or Leary have refused to answer? Probably not, because merely responding to questions such as these does not, in and of itself, constitute admitting a crime. These hypothetical questions are more like the *Shapiro* question: "Mr. Shapiro, how much did you charge for carrots and apples last month?" Note that a question framed in this way does not give the private person a Fifth Amendment defense.

For the most part, the government has learned the lessons of *Marchetti* and *Shapiro* and has cleaned up its act. Lawyers can expect to run into very few reporting requirements such as those at issue in *Marchetti* and *Leary.* The vast majority of government inquiries are phrased like the inquiry in the *Shapiro* case.

There is an important corollary to all of this case law. When a person gives information to the government, that information had better be accurate. There are two federal criminal statutes, the False Statement Act[56] and the False Claims Act[57] that provide penalties for giving false information to the government. The False Claims Act, for example, punishes the willful uttering of "any false, fictitious, or fraudulent statements or representations," as well as the use of "any false writing or document" when the person making the statement knows that the document contains "any false, fictitious, or fraudulent statement or entry." It makes no difference to which agency the statement is made. The statute covers "any matter within the jurisdiction of any department or agency of the United States." Even when the utterance is a simple "no" to an inquiry of wrongdoing, the statute may come into play.[58]

This raises some important issues of client counseling. Lawyers new to administrative practice are sometimes reluctant to tell clients that they have to comply with certain agency requests. Clients do not like to be told that they must

---

[54]   395 U.S. 6 (1969).

[55]   *Marchetti* and *Leary* had some companion cases. *Grosso v. United States*, 390 U.S. 62 (1968) (federal excise tax form for gambling winnings); *Haynes v. United States*, 390 U.S. 85 (1968) (Treasury form for registering a sawed-off shotgun).

[56]   18 U.S.C. § 1001.

[57]   18 U.S.C. § 287. *See, e.g.*, Jordan L. Coyle & Tarnetta V. Jones, *False Statements and False Claims*, 43 Am. Crim. L. Rev. 461 (2006).

[58]   *See, e.g., Brogan v. United States*, 522 U.S. 398 (1998).

disclose confidential personal information or highly sensitive trade secrets to government employees. But a lawyer who does not appreciate that there are precious few grounds on which to resist a request for records is doing a great disservice to his client. Remember the message of *Morton Salt.* You may better help your client by negotiating with the government than by making a frontal constitutional attack on the request for information.

[C]   Limitations Imposed by the Paperwork Reduction Act

Congress has become much more sensitive to the burdens of government reporting and recordkeeping requirements in recent years. In 1980, Congress passed the Paperwork Reduction Act[59] in an attempt to limit the proliferation of agency requests for information or agency demands that records be kept. Briefly stated, the Act forbids an agency from conducting or sponsoring the collection of information from private persons without first obtaining clearance for that request from the Office of Management and Budget (OMB). OMB may not approve any request for more than three years at a time, and no person may be sanctioned or penalized in any way for refusing to comply with an information request that has not been approved by OMB.[60]

The theory behind the Act is that OMB will closely scrutinize all agency information gathering and will approve agency requests sparingly. There is a serious question whether the Act has accomplished that purpose. When the Act initially took effect, OMB essentially grandfathered all existing government forms and recordkeeping requirements.

In 1995, the Act was substantially amended.[61] To begin with, the 1995 Act establishes the jurisdictional agency, the Office of Information and Regulatory Affairs (OIRA), as an entity separate from the OMB. OIRA is expected to supervise other federal agencies in the dissemination, including electronic dissemination, of information to the general public. It oversees the compilation and publication of statistics, supervises agency archives and agencies' protection of private and confidential information. It continues the recordkeeping and report approval function under the original Paperwork Reduction Act.[62] There has been very little empirical study of the Act's effectiveness since its enactment. Although the 1995 amendments may be viewed as a congressional vote of confidence in the concept of paperwork reduction, the 1995 act is far broader than a mere paperwork approval process. Many people continue to be somewhat cynical as to the Act's true value.

---

[59] 44 U.S.C. §§ 3501–3520; for a hearing to amend the Paperwork Reduction Act, *see Paperwork and Regulatory Improvements Act of 2003*: Hearing on H.R. 2432 Before the Comm. on Gov't. Reform, 108th Cong. (2003).

[60] For a good discussion of the Act, *see* William Funk, *The Paperwork Reduction Act: Paperwork Reduction Meets Administrative Law,* 24 Harv. J. on Legis. 1 (1987).

[61] Pub. L. No. 104-13, 109 Stat. 163 (codified at 44 U.S.C. §§ 3501–3520).

[62] For a thorough description of the 1995 Act, *see* Jeffrey S. Lubbers, *Paperwork Redux: The (Stronger) Paperwork Reduction Act of 1995,* 49 Admin. L. Rev. 111 (1997).

§ 4.07   AGENCY SUBPOENAS

[A]   Some General Considerations

No one should read this section without first reviewing section 20 because much of the general case law on government information gathering has been developed in the context of subpoena enforcement cases. Some additional basic information is necessary to understand the nature of agency subpoenas. Subpoenas are authorized in an agency's enabling act and through § 555(d) of the Administrative Procedure Act (APA) which provides:

> Agency subpoenas *authorized by law* shall be issued to a *party* on request and, when required by rules of procedure, on a statement or showing of *general relevance and reasonable scope* of the evidence sought. On contest, the court shall sustain the subpoena or similar process or demand to the extent that it is found to be in accordance with law. In a proceeding for enforcement, the court shall issue an order requiring the appearance of the witness or the production of the evidence or data within a reasonable time under penalty of punishment for *contempt* in case of contumacious failure to comply. (emphasis added.)

This language, read carefully, tells us a great deal about agency subpoena practice. Working through the following questions is a good way to solve any subpoena problem:

1. Does an agency have subpoena power?

2. Who may invoke the agency's subpoena power?

3. What showing is necessary to obtain a subpoena?

4. To whom may a subpoena be addressed?

5. What may a subpoena compel?

6. Are there any ways to defend against a subpoena, and most importantly, what is the price paid for resisting a subpoena without a proper basis?

The APA, the relevant case law and common sense answer these questions.

[B]   Who May Issue Subpoenas?

An agency has the authority to issue subpoenas only if its enabling act or some other statutory provisions outside the APA give it the power to do so. Note the statutory language: "[A]n agency authorized by law." Virtually all major federal regulatory agencies have subpoena power, although many state and local government agencies, particularly the low-echelon agencies, do not. An agency's enabling act and other relevant statutes must be closely examined before concluding that it has subpoena authority.

[C]   Who May Utilize an Agency's Subpoena Power and What Showing Is Necessary to Obtain a Subpoena?

Under the APA, either the agency itself or a "party" (as defined in § 551 of the APA)[63] may utilize the agency's subpoena power. In practice, this means that lawyers involved in agency proceedings often carry pads of agency subpoenas and tear them off and fill them in as the need to subpoena someone arises. The showing necessary to obtain a subpoena is normally presumed if the requester is a party to an action. There are times, however, when grounds for issuing a subpoena are questioned. Possible grounds for resistance are detailed in subsection [E] *below.* Most agencies use similar forms for their subpoenas. The illustration below is a subpoena form used by the Department of Labor.

---

[63] Section 551 defines party as "a person or agency named or admitted as a party [or seeking intervention as a party] in an agency proceeding or . . . admitted by an agency as a party, for limited purposes." For an entirely different, yet equally compelling step-by-step analysis of the agency subpoena process, *see* PETER L. STRAUSS, TODD RAKOFF, ROY A. SCHOTLAND & CYNTHIA R. FARINA, GELLHORN & BYSE'S ADMINISTRATIVE LAW: CASES AND COMMENTS 892–908 (9th ed. 1995).

United States Department of Labor
OFFICE OF ADMINISTRATIVE LAW JUDGES

In Re:

_____

(Plaintiff/Complainant/Claimant)

v.

OALJ Case No:

_____

(Defendant/Respondent/Employer/Carrier)

SUBPOENA TO APPEAR AND TESTIFY AT A HEARING

To:

YOU ARE DIRECTED to appear at the time, date, and place set forth below to testify at a formal hearing in the above captioned proceeding. When you arrive, you must remain at the location of the proceeding until the judge or a court officer allows you to leave. If you are an organization that is not a party in this case, you must designate one or more officers, directors, or managing agents, or designate other persons who consent to testify on your behalf about the following matters, or those set forth in an attachment:

Date: _____

Place of Testimony: _____

Time: _____

YOU MUST ALSO BRING WITH YOU the following documents, electronically stored information, or objects (blank if not applicable):

The provisions of Code of Federal Regulations (CFR) 29 CFR §§18.24(c) 18.15 and 18.34(e) and Federal Rules of Civil Procedure (FRCP) Rule 45(c), relating to your protection as a person subject to a subpoena, and 29 CFR §§18.24(d) and 18.29(b) and FRCP Rule 45(d) and (e), relating to your duty to respond to this subpoena and the potential consequences of not doing so, are summarized at the end of this form.

This subpoena is issued upon the application of (indicate attorney/representative for named party):

(Person requesting subpoena)   (Address and Telephone Number)

Name _____

Address _____

City _____ State ____ Zip Code _____

Phone Number _____

IN WITNESS WHEREOF the undersigned United States Administrative Law Judge has hereunto set his/her hand and caused the seal of the United States Department of Labor to be affixed.

_____   _____

Signature of U.S. Administrative Law Judge   Date   To be valid, a raised USDOL Seal must appear here

PROOF OF SERVICE

Person served (print name)   Date of Service

Server (print name)   Place of Service

Title of Server   Manner of Service

Unless the subpoena was issued on behalf of the United States, or one of its officers or agents, I have also tendered to the witness fees for one day's attendance, and the mileage allowed by law, in the amount of _____ .

DECLARATION OF SERVER

I declare under penalty of perjury under the laws of the United States of America that the foregoing information contained in the Proof of Service is true and correct.

Address

Signature of Server   Date   City   State   Zip Code

NOTICE: This subpoena is only valid in proceedings before the Office of Administrative Law Judges or Office of Workers' Compensation Programs. To be valid, this subpoena must bear a raised United States Department of Labor (USDOL) seal, and the signature of a Department of Labor (DOL) administrative law judge.

Rules of Practice and Procedure for Administrative Hearings
Before the Office of Administrative Law Judges
[Code of Federal Regulations, Title 29, Part 18]

29 C.F.R. §18.24 Subpoenas
(c) *Motion to quash or limit subpoena.* Provides that within ten (10) days of receipt of a subpoena but not later than the date of the hearing, the person subject to a subpoena may file a motion to quash or limit the scope of the subpoena with the presiding judge. The motion must state the reasons why the subpoena should be withdrawn or limited in scope.

(d) *Failure to comply.* Provides that any person who fails to comply with an order to testify or a subpoena may be referred to a U.S. District Court for enforcement of the subpoena by the party adversely affected by such failure to comply, when authorized by statute or law.

29 C.F.R. §18.34 Representation
(e) *Rights of witnesses.* Any person compelled to testify in a proceeding in response to a subpoena may be accompanied, represented, and advised by counsel or other representative, and may purchase a transcript of his or her testimony.

29 C.F.R. §18.15 Protective orders
Provides that the person subject to the subpoena may file a motion to request the presiding judge to protect him or her from annoyance, embarrassment, oppression, undue burden or expense, or to protect trade secrets or other confidential research, development or commercial information.

29 C.F.R.§18.29 Authority of administrative law judge
(b) *Enforcement.* Provides that if any person disobeys or resists a lawful order or process, or neglects to produce, after having been ordered to do so, any pertinent book, paper or document, or refuses to appear after having been subpoenaed, or upon appearing refuses to be examined according to law, the presiding judge may certify facts to the U.S. District Court and request that Court impose appropriate remedies, where authorized by statute or law.

HIPPA NOTICE: In regard to the Privacy of Individually Identifiable Health Information under the Health Insurance Portability and Accountability Act of 1996, if this subpoena does not bear a raised USDOL seal and the signature of a DOL administrative law judge, it is not valid under 45 C.F.R. §§164.512(e), 164.512(f) or 164.512(l).
Federal Rules of Civil Procedure [Applied by 29 C.F.R. §18.1(a)]
Rule 45 Subpoena
(c) Protecting a Person Subject to a Subpoena.
(c)(1) Provides that the party or attorney responsible for issuing and serving a subpoena must take reasonable steps to avoid imposing undue burden or expense on a person subject to the subpoena and the issuing court must enforce this duty and impose an appropriate sanction on a party or attorney who fails to comply.
(c)(2) Provides that, unless ordered to appear for a deposition or hearing, a person ordered to produce documents, electronically stored information, or tangible things, or to permit inspection of premises, need be present at the place of production or inspection. The person subject to the subpoena may also object to producing the documents, electronically stored information, or tangible things, or to permit inspection of premises, by giving written notice to the party or attorney responsible for issuing and serving the subpoena. The written objection must be made before the date of requested performance or 14 days from receiving the subpoena, whichever is earlier.
(c)(3) Provides that the person subject to the subpoena may file a motion to quash (stop) or limit the scope of a subpoena because there is not enough time to comply with the subpoena, the person would incur substantial expense requiring travel more than 100 miles to comply, privileged or protected matter would be disclosed, or other undue burden would result.
(d) Duties in Responding to a Subpoena.
(d)(1) Requires that the person responding to the subpoena produce documents as they are kept in the ordinary course of business or must organize and label them to correspond to the categories in the subpoena. If the subpoena does not specify a form for producing electronically stored information, the person responding must produce it in the form in which it is usually maintained or in another reasonably usable form.
(d)(2) Require that a person withholding subpoenaed information because it is privileged information or subject to protection as trial-preparation material must expressly make such claim and describe the nature of the withheld documents, communications, or tangible things in a manner that, without revealing the privileged or protected information, will enable the parties to assess the claim of privilege or protection.
(e) Contempt. Provided that a U.S. District Court may hold a person in contempt if the person fails to obey the subpoena without adequate excuse, such as those reasons in Rule 45(c)(3).

Because an agency subpoena is so easy to obtain and often looks deceptively simple, it is sometimes taken casually. Treating an agency subpoena casually is one of the most dangerous things a lawyer can do. Always remember: *In most circumstances, an agency subpoena has just as much power and authority as a subpoena issued by a court.*

[D] What May a Subpoena Compel and to Whom May it Be Addressed?

As noted earlier, a subpoena may be used to compel the attendance of a particular person at a hearing (sometimes referred to by its classic Latin name, *subpoena ad testificandum*) or issued in the form of a *subpoena duces tecum*, requiring that person to appear at the hearing and to produce certain specified records. Most of the questions concerning a subpoena's scope and direction have been addressed by the Supreme Court and answered in the broadest possible fashion.

Two cases decided by the Supreme Court during World War Two make this abundantly clear. In *Endicott Johnson Corp. v. Perkins*,[64] decided in 1943, the Court dealt with a subpoena issued by the Department of Labor under the authority conferred on the Department by the Walsh-Healy Act.[65] The Walsh-Healy Act gives the Department of Labor the authority to police minimum wage and labor standards among private companies that obtain government contracts. The company resisted the subpoena by invoking the *American Tobacco* "fishing expedition" language, the Fifth Amendment and, most importantly, by claiming that the agency had no jurisdiction over the company. Nonetheless, the Court permitted the subpoena to be enforced and summarily rejected the fishing expedition and Fifth Amendment claims. The Court spent most of its time on the narrower question of whether the agency exceeded its jurisdiction in issuing the subpoena. Jurisdictional arguments, the Court held, simply did not apply to subpoena enforcement cases. The time to argue about jurisdiction is when and if the agency decides to bring an enforcement action, not when it is merely requesting information.

Oklahoma Press Publishing Co. v. Walling,[66] decided three years later, said almost exactly the same thing. In *Oklahoma Press*, the newspaper argued that, as a newspaper, it was not subject to the Fair Labor Standards Act and more importantly, the subpoena had been issued before the Department of Labor had any grounds for believing the newspaper had violated the statute. The Supreme Court paid no attention to either argument, pointing out that the jurisdictional argument had been addressed in *Endicott Johnson* and that an agency subpoena does not have to be supported by the kind of probable cause necessary to obtain a search warrant. Subpoenas may be used to develop facts, even when the agency is not yet certain it has a case.

These two decisions were enough to give the agencies the broadest possible powers of inquiry. But possibly to reemphasize that point, the Court, in 1957, granted certiorari in *Civil Aeronautics Board v. Hermann*,[67] reversing the Ninth Circuit's quashing of an agency subpoena on the grounds that less drastic information gathering techniques should be used before an agency resorts to a

---

[64] 317 U.S. 501 (1943).

[65] 41 U.S.C. §§ 35–45.

[66] 327 U.S. 186 (1946).

[67] 353 U.S. 322 (1957) (*per curiam*).

subpoena. The Supreme Court, *per curiam*, thought differently. The subpoenas had been reviewed by the hearing examiner, the CAB itself, and a federal district judge. Each of these entities had determined that (1) the subpoenas described the documents requested, (2) with sufficient particularity, (3) were reasonable in scope and (4) were not found to be oppressive (*i.e.*, overly burdensome). As a consequence, the Court ordered the subpoenas enforced.

Part of what happened in *Hermann* springs from comments in dicta by Justice Holmes in the old *American Tobacco* case to the effect that a subpoena cannot be so broad and oppressive that it disrupts a company's ability to carry on its business. Obviously, a company could not long survive if an agency is able to seize all of its original and current accounts receivable records. There is additional language in *American Tobacco* and other cases, stating that a subpoena must be particularized and cannot simply request "all" of a company's records.

The first dictum has probably not survived the photocopying machine. Original records no longer have to be seized, and the "burden" of making copies has not persuaded many courts to find compliance with a large record request to be oppressive. The second dictum may still be valid in theory; a subpoena's request for documents must be particularized. But an examination of the actual subpoena in the *Hermann* case suggests that the sum total of the requests came very close to a request for all of the company's records.[68] The *Hermann* decision has led many observers of the agency subpoena process to conclude that all of a company's records can be requested if one simply creates an itemized list of records-even if that list eventually totals 100 percent of the contents of a company's files.

[E]   May a Subpoena be Resisted and, if Resisted, What Are the Dangers of Impermissible Resistance?

A private party resists an agency subpoena at his or her peril. The mechanics of the enforcement process, at least on the federal level, are relatively simple. Once an agency determines that voluntary compliance with the subpoena is not forthcoming, it refers the matter to the Justice Department. Justice lawyers file a *show cause* action in an appropriate federal district court against the person subject to the subpoena. A private party who cannot show proper cause for noncompliance with the subpoena and who continues to resist is likely to be hit with a contempt of court citation.

Lawyers who participate in frivolous resistance face real dangers. For several years, the Department of Energy administered its now-defunct petroleum price controls through an auditing system that relied in part on agency subpoenas. The oil companies repeatedly refused to comply; and strenuously resisted the subpoenas in federal court enforcement actions. After disposing of countless subpoena resistance cases in favor of the Department of Energy, the Temporary Emergency Court of Appeals finally lost its temper and began threatening lawyers,

---

[68] The text of the subpoena can be found in the circuit decision, *Hermann v. Civil Aeronautics Bd.*, 237 F.2d 359 (9th Cir. 1956), *rev'd*, 353 U.S. 322 (1957), and included, among many other things: all general ledgers, all audit reports, all bank statements and canceled checks, all correspondence between Hermann and a long list of other companies, all individual personnel and payroll records, etc.

who brought cases involving resistance to the agency's subpoena, with sanctions for filing frivolous actions, including the sanctions of bar discipline and payment of the government's attorneys fees.[69]

One prominent administrative law casebook lists five arguments that might be interposed against a subpoena: (1) the subpoena is not issued pursuant to an authorized objective; (2) the evidence sought is not germane to a lawful subject of inquiry; (3) the demands made are unduly burdensome or unreasonable; (4) the subpoena violates a personal right not to speak or act, such as the right against self-incrimination; and (5) the subpoena is not issued in proper form.[70] These are arguments that a lawyer might conceivably advance in court; but remember that most of the cases cited for each of these propositions were decisions that supported the validity of the subpoena.

If, after all of these warnings and admonitions, a lawyer decides to resist a subpoena, what can be done? There have been instances in which subpoenas have been quashed where an agency attempted to function entirely without jurisdiction. In *FTC v. Miller*,[71] for example, the court quashed a subpoena when the Federal Trade Commission (an agency with civil antitrust jurisdiction shared concurrently with the Department of Justice) attempted to obtain information from a common carrier subject to Interstate Commerce Commission jurisdiction. Common carrier status under an ICC license carries with it antitrust immunity.

Smart lawyers think through the subpoena process as a component of overall case strategy. Give some thought to whether you want to break your sword on a generally futile resistance action when you could be marshaling a more plausible attack against the agency on other grounds, such as whether the violation actually occurred. Remember that no matter what the case law says, negotiation is always possible. Don't forget the penalties, both monetary and professional, for bringing frivolous actions.

§ 4.08 PHYSICAL INSPECTIONS

[A] Background and Preliminary Analysis

Agencies, particularly agencies concerned with public health and safety, must, as a matter of course, conduct hundreds of thousands of inspections of premises. There are certain aspects of health and safety compliance that can be enforced only by taking a close look at a factory or a private residence. Most of these inspections do not result in controversy. Since the early 1970s, however, a few private persons have successfully used the Fourth Amendment prohibition against unreasonable searches and seizures as a defense against agency inspections.

Recall that the Fourth Amendment provides:

---

[69] *See, e.g., United States v. Merit Petroleum Co., Inc.*, 731 F.2d 901 (Temp. Emer. Ct. App. 1984).

[70] STRAUSS ET AL., *supra* note 63.

[71] 549 F.2d 452 (7th Cir. 1977).

The right of the people to be secure in their persons, houses, papers, and effects, against [i] *unreasonable* searches and seizures, shall not be violated, and no [ii] *Warrants shall issue*, but [iii] upon *probable cause*, [iv] supported by *Oath or Affirmation* and [v] *particularly describing* the place to be searched, and the persons or things to be seized.[72]

The italicized portions of the quoted language identify the crucial elements of the Fourth Amendment and provide a good issue-spotting outline for resolving[HAC1] an administrative search question. First, is the inspection an "unreasonable search"? If the answer is "no," the inquiry is at an end. If the answer is "yes," a person who is about to be searched has the right to refuse the search. If the search is refused, you must analyze the amendment's warrant requirements: first, a warrant must be obtained (generally, from a federal magistrate-judge for federal agency inspections); second, the warrant must be supported by a sworn affidavit from someone in the agency (typically, the person who wishes to conduct the inspection); and third, that affidavit must explain with some precision the necessity for the search.

Before 1970, no administrative lawyer had to worry about these issues because the Supreme Court had consistently held administrative inspections per se reasonable and therefore not subject to the warrant requirements of the Fourth Amendment.[73] In 1967, however, the Court changed its mind and decided, in two companion cases, *Camara v. Municipal Court*[74] (an inspection of a private residence for housing code violations) and *See v. City of Seattle*[75] (an inspection of a business for fire code violations), that administrative inspections were searches within the meaning of the Fourth Amendment, that they were not always reasonable, and that in certain circumstances a warrant would be required.

Camara and *See* launched a flurry of Supreme Court litigation that is not yet ended. Although there are some loose ends still to be tied up by the Court, the "law" of administrative searches is now relatively clear. To begin the analysis, one now starts from the position that the general rule requires a warrant. In other words, whenever an administrative agency-either federal, state or local-wishes to conduct a physical inspection of private premises, that inspection is assumed to be an unreasonable search, and a warrant must be obtained unless the agency may avail itself of some recognized exception to the warrant requirement.

There has been a flurry of cases involving searches of individuals in an employment or educational setting that do not easily fit the categories enumerated below. These cases are occasionally referred to as "special needs" searches. In the companion cases of *Skinner v. Railway Labor Executives' Ass'n*[76] and *National Treasury Employees Union v. Von Rabb*,[77] the Supreme Court upheld mandatory

---

[72] Emphasis and bracketed materials supplied.

[73] The prototype case is *Frank v. Maryland*, 359 U.S. 360 (1959). It was *Frank* that was expressly overruled by the subsequent *See* and *Camara* decisions.

[74] 387 U.S. 523 (1967).

[75] 387 U.S. 541 (1967).

[76] 489 U.S. 602 (1989).

[77] 489 U.S. 656 (1989).

warrantless searches, in *Skinner*, of (1) railroad crew members immediately after an accident, and (2) permissive breath and urine tests of those employees involved in violations or suspected of impairment; and, in *Von Rabb* urine testing of Customs Service employees who were being considered for transfer or promotion to positions involving drug interdiction or possession of firearms. A case involving a warrantless inspection of the desk of a state hospital executive director was remanded for an inquiry as to whether the search was reasonable given that "actual office practices" may reduce that employee's reasonable expectation of privacy.[78] Non-voluntary urinalysis of public school athletes was upheld in *Vernonia School District 47J v. Acton.*[79] The holding of *Vernonia* was echoed, over a very powerful dissent, by *Board of Education of Pottawatomie County v. Earls,*[80] upholding an exceptionally broad drug testing program for all public school students who wished to participate in athletic programs or extra-curricular activities.

[B]   Analyzing the Exceptions to the Warrant Requirement

[1]   Categories of Exceptions

Any instance in which a warrant is not required should be treated as an exception to the general warrant rule. As in so many other instances, the Court has worked out the exceptions on a case-by-case basis. The exceptions, however, are now so numerous that they have come close to swallowing the rule. The exceptions can be placed in six broad categories.

[2]   Consent

As ominous as *See* and *Camara* might have seemed to agency enforcement staffs in 1967, those decisions have not impeded most subsequent inspection efforts. The vast majority of agency inspections are not objected to. In other words, when the agency inspector presents herself at someone's door, she is granted entry. Remember that anyone may voluntarily give up a constitutional right, and if that consent/waiver is knowing and intelligent, that's the end of the matter.

Of course, there are gradations of awareness of Fourth Amendment rights in terms of agency inspections. By now, business people are aware of *See* and *Camara* and the other cases discussed below. They occasionally refuse to admit an inspector on constitutional grounds. Most non-business people are unaware of their right to refuse admittance, and the Court has *never* contemplated any kind of *Miranda* warning for administrative inspections.[81]

Moreover, a good lawyer should think of the advantages and disadvantages of counseling his or her clients to refuse entry to an agency inspector. A refusal, as will be seen below, may simply mean that the inspector makes a quick stop in a

---

[78] *O'Connor v. Ortega*, 480 U.S. 709 (1987).

[79] 515 U.S. 646 (1995).

[80] 536 U.S. 822 (2002).

[81] *See, e.g., United States v. Thriftimart, Inc.*, 429 F.2d 1006 (9th Cir.), *cert. denied*, 400 U.S. 926 (1970) (no need for agency inspectors to inform a company official of his right to refuse entry).

magistrate's office and returns with a warrant. It may also make the inspector a little more grouchy when she does gain admittance.[82] Many inspectors are voluntarily admitted by people who understand their rights fully.

[3] Emergency

The Court has determined several times that inspections for poisonous food or entry to fight fires are not activities requiring a warrant. When an emergency requires instant access, consent is not necessary.[83]

[4] Border searches

Customs officers who conduct routine inspections of vehicles crossing the U.S. borders do not need a warrant.[84]

[5] Welfare inspections

It might be wise to place an asterisk beside this exception. *Wyman v. James,*[85] decided in 1971, contained language that is very difficult to reconcile with earlier Supreme Court case law. Here, the Supreme Court held that an inspection of a private residence to determine whether certain AFDC (Aid for Families with Dependent Children) funds were being spent properly was not a search, and even if it were a search, it was not unreasonable. The Court based its reasoning in part on the premise that American taxpayers have a right to determine whether something that is in the nature of a public gratuity, such as AFDC, is being abused.[86]

Public interest lawyers viewed *Wyman* with great alarm when it was first decided, but it has not since been a topic of great controversy. The fears were mainly that *Wyman* authorized the so-called midnight raid, a late-night unconsented-to inspection to determine the physical presence of an able-bodied wage earner on the premises, a fact that would thereby render the AFDC recipient ineligible for benefits. These fears were unfounded. Justice Blackmun, writing for the Court in *Wyman,* was very careful to limit the holding to the *Wyman* facts-a daytime request for entry by a qualified social worker.[87]

---

[82] In defense of agencies, most of them claim not to retaliate because of having to go back and get a warrant.

[83] *See, e.g., Michigan v. Tyler,* 436 U.S. 499 (1978) (No warrant necessary to inspect premises immediately after fire to determine the cause of the fire. However, warrant might be necessary if inspectors wait too long after the emergency to inspect.).

[84] *United States v. Martinez-Fuerte,* 428 U.S. 543 (1976).

[85] 400 U.S. 309 (1971).

[86] This reasoning appears to be something of an aberration — just one year earlier, in *Goldberg v. Kelly,* 397 U.S. 254 (1970), the Court held that AFDC was a federal "entitlement", the termination of which warranted exceptional due process protection. *See* Chapter 5, § 5.03 *below* for an extended discussion of *Goldberg.*

[87] *See* Note, *Administrative Investigations of Welfare Recipients,* 22 CASE W. RES. L. REV. 581 (1971).

[6] Plain view inspections

This exception grew out of parallel criminal search warrant cases. If the thing inspected is something that anyone can see — *i.e.*, "plain view" — the person's expectation of privacy is greatly diminished. In a criminal setting, the example often used is the illegal automatic rifle laying on the back seat of a car that has just been stopped for speeding. In an administrative context, the fact patterns are somewhat different, but the result is generally the same. In *Air Pollution Variance Board v. Western Alfalfa Corp.*,[88] an inspector had entered private property to make an inspection of smoke emitted from smokestacks visible for miles.[89] In other words, the object being inspected could be seen by virtually anyone in the vicinity and was not a matter that incorporated a reasonable expectation of privacy. As a result, the Court held that no warrant was necessary. Several years later, the Supreme Court decided, in *Dow Chemical Co. v. United States*,[90] that an Environmental Protection Agency inspection of a factory made by flying over the premises and taking various measurements from the air was not a "search" for Fourth Amendment purposes. The Court reasoned that the open areas of an industrial complex are comparable to an "open field" in which an individual may not legitimately demand privacy. The company objected to the warrantless fly-over, in part because the inspections could also reveal proprietary chemical manufacturing methods. That possibility did not seem to carry much weight with the court. The factory was located in an area where planes were permitted to fly (it was not within a closed airspace); EPA, therefore, was permitted to make an over flight for inspection purposes.

[7] Pervasively regulated industries

Since the Supreme Court decided *See* and *Camara*, it has spent a substantial amount of time construing this exception (recently the Court seems to favor the word "closely" rather than the word "pervasively"). In *Colonnade Catering Corp. v. United States*[91] and *United States v. Biswell*,[92] two cases decided shortly after *See* and *Camara*, the Court refused to require warrants for inspections of licensed liquor dealers (*Colonnade*) or registered gun dealers (*Biswell*) on the grounds that each business was a pervasively regulated industry and was not the sort of commercial enterprise that had any legitimate expectation of privacy. The doctrine is essentially an outgrowth of the waiver/consent doctrine. By voluntarily engaging in a heavily regulated business, you give up your privacy expectations. These holdings were certainly justified in context of the early cases, but have led to an enormous amount of trouble for lower courts which now must decide what constitutes a pervasively (or closely) regulated business activity.

---

[88] 416 U.S. 861 (1974).

[89] The inspection was to measure the opacity of the "smoke-one" method for determining what pollutants were being given off by the chimneys.

[90] 476 U.S. 227 (1986).

[91] 397 U.S. 72 (1970).

[92] 406 U.S. 311 (1972).

In what has become one of the classic administrative search cases, *Marshall v. Barlow's, Inc.*,[93] the Court reviewed a company's refusal to admit an Occupational Safety and Health Administration (OSHA) inspector without a warrant, notwithstanding a statute that permitted an inspector "to inspect and investigate during regular working hours and at other reasonable times, and within reasonable limits and in a reasonable manner, any [place of employment]." The only requirement for entry was that the inspector present "appropriate credentials."[94]

One can see from the statutory language that Congress was attempting to avoid any Fourth Amendment problems by surrounding the conditions of inspection in reasonableness. The OSH Act is tied to the Commerce Clause and presumptively applies to all businesses engaged in or affecting interstate commerce, virtually the whole of American business enterprise. In *Barlow's*, the government tried to argue that the warrantless inspection statute could be preserved by the pervasively regulated industry exception. The Court raised an eyebrow at this-Barlow's, Inc. was an electrical and plumbing contractor. Moreover, the Court reiterated that *Biswell* and *Colonnade Catering* were to be narrowly-drawn exceptions. Extending the exception to virtually the whole of American business would effectively do away with the *See/Camara* rule that warrants are normally required when consent is not forthcoming.

What, then, is a pervasively regulated business? In *Barlow's* the Court hinted at three possible factors: (1) that the business in question has been historically regulated by some level of government; (2) that the regulation is substantial, *i.e.*, something more than merely obtaining a municipal license to do business;[95] and (3) that the statute in question be limited to single industries.

Three years after *Barlow's* the Court took up the exception in a case, *Donovan v. Dewey*,[96] involving warrantless inspections of coal mines under the Federal Coal Mine Safety and Health Act.[97] The language of the statute was not much different from the OSH Act's language, so *Donovan* could pass muster, if at all, only on the basis of the pervasively regulated exception. This time, the Court determined that the coal mine business was pervasively regulated by analyzing the purpose of the Safety and Health Act-to improve health and safety conditions, in both surface and underground mines, in an industry with "a notorious history of serious accidents and unhealthful working conditions." Thus, a mine owner must surely realize that the business is going to be subject to close government scrutiny.

Donovan is a good case to read for a summary of the decisions from *See* and *Camara* and is used as such by many administrative law casebooks. However, it is not terribly helpful in getting a sense of how to define "pervasively regulated" or

---

[93] 436 U.S. 307 (1978).

[94] This is from 29 U.S.C. § 657(a), the Occupational Safety and Health Act, a statute intended to insure American workers a safe and healthful workplace (or at least to prohibit unsafe and unhealthy workplaces). The OSH Act is also discussed in § 4.03 of this chapter.

[95] Note that these are possible factors gleaned from a close reading of *Biswell*, *Colonnade*, and *Barlow's*. This is not necessarily a *test* for the exception.

[96] 452 U.S. 594 (1981).

[97] 30 U.S.C. § 813(a).

"*closely regulated*" because the Court arrived at that conclusion without a great deal of analysis. As a result of the decision in *Donovan*, the only thing we knew positively is that three industries (liquor, firearms and coal mines) are pervasively regulated. Faced with this situation, a lawyer must simply ask whether some other industry is more like an electrical and plumbing contractor (Barlow's, Inc.) or more like the firearms, liquor or coal mines industries.

It was at this point that the Supreme Court really muddied the waters by holding that a junkyard was a closely regulated industry. In *New York v. Burger*,[98] the owner of a Brooklyn junkyard denied access to his premises to state inspectors who sought evidence of impermissible vehicle dismantling (a so-called "chop shop" operation). According to the Supreme Court, Mr. Burger was first asked to produce his business license and his "police book" (a required record of his inventory of junked cars and vehicle parts). Mr. Burger informed the inspectors that he had neither. The inspectors then told Burger that they were going to conduct an inspection of the serial numbers of various cars and parts of cars in his yard. According to the Court, Burger did not object to this inquiry.

As you might expect, the inspection revealed that many of the cars and parts were stolen, and Burger was arrested and tried for possession of stolen property, a criminal violation. At his trial in state court, Burger objected to the inspection on Fourth Amendment grounds. On appeal, the New York Court of Appeals held that his Fourth Amendment rights had been violated. The Supreme Court granted certiorari.

The Supreme Court spent no time on Mr. Burger's apparent consent to the search, but rather devoted virtually the whole of its opinion to the issue of what constitutes a closely regulated industry (the Court used the terms "closely regulated" and "pervasively regulated" interchangeably). Justice Blackmun's opinion for the Court began the analysis by noting that the expectation of privacy in business premises was something less than the expectation of privacy in a residence. The owner of a closely regulated business has even less of a privacy expectation.

What, then, constitutes a closely regulated business? It is at this point that the opinion's analysis breaks down, at least when compared with the analysis of what is not a closely regulated industry, as discussed in *Marshall v. Barlow's, Inc.* The Court noted three things: (1) an operator of a junkyard must have a license: (2) an operator must maintain a police book and (3) an operator must display his registration number prominently at his place of business. These three things, in the Court's view, coupled with "the history of regulation of related industries," make a junkyard a closely regulated business.

The problem with the Court's analysis in *Burger* is that these components of regulation are required of virtually every business. Compare a junkyard operator with a plumbing and electrical contractor (the business at issue in *Barlow's*). Plumbing contractors in most jurisdictions must be licensed. Typically, those licenses are more difficult to obtain than the rather *de minimis* permit required to operate a junkyard. While a plumbing contractor does not have to keep a police book, local governments impose stringent quality control standards on plumbing

---

[98]   482 U.S. 691 (1987).

and electrical contractors-regulating such things as the type of electrical wiring that may be installed, the methods of plumbing and the like. A plumbing contractor is normally required to display a registration number, as is a junkyard operator. If junkyard operators have been historically subject to regulation, as Mr. Justice Blackmun seems to think, have not plumbers been exposed to regulation over an equally long period of time?

Under close scrutiny, this part of *Burger* makes absolutely no sense. Even worse, the remainder of the opinion is devoted mainly to a justification for warrantless searches. The Court, for example, noted that: (1) the state has a substantial interest in keeping tabs on chop shops, (2) regulation of vehicle dismantlers serves the state's interest in eradicating automobile theft and (3) a warrant requirement would interfere with the state's enforcement of anti-chop shop laws. But even if a reader concedes all of this, and simply substitutes the label "plumber" wherever Justice Blackmun uses the term "vehicle dismantler," you arrive at precisely the same result.

What seems to have been truly troubling for the Court — and a point that cries out for better discussion — is the Court's fear that if inspectors were refused access and had to obtain a warrant, the chop shop could probably hide much of its contraband before the inspectors returned with the warrant. This may be a meaningful distinction between a junkyard and a plumbing contractor. It may be easier to get rid of stolen car parts than it is to hide an unsafe condition in a plumbing shop, but there is little in the *Burger* record that supports this proposition.

The *Burger* opinion deserves much criticism. The Court should have more carefully distinguished *Barlow's* from *Burger.* It did not. The Court may have little affection left for *Barlow's.* But if that is the case, the Court should simply have overruled *Barlow's.* For the practicing lawyer, finding meaningful differences between junkyards and plumbers for the purpose of assessing a company's Fourth Amendment posture is nearly impossible. This is one instance when the Court could have done a better job.

On this issue, the New York Court of Appeals took some corrective action. After the U.S. Supreme Court's decision in the *Burger* case, the New York court decided *People v. Scott.*[99] In *Scott,* by a 4 to 3 vote, the New York Court of Appeals applied the search and seizure provision in the New York state constitution and determined that warrantless searches of junkyards violated the owner's *state* constitutional rights. The majority opinion in *Scott* was virtually the same as the dissent in *New York v. Burger.* The U.S. Supreme Court should have no institutional problems with this decision, given that it reflects some honored and fundamental doctrines of federalism.[100]

---

[99] 79 N.Y.2d 474, 583 N.Y.S.2d 920, 593 N.E.2d 1328 (1992).

[100] Some state courts reacted to *Burger* negatively, *see, e.g., People v. Scott,* 79 N.Y.2d 474 (1992); *People v. Keta,* 538 N.Y.S.2d 417 (Sup. Ct. 1989); *State v. Welch,* 160 Vt. 70 (1992); *Pinney v. Phillips,* 230 Cal. App. 3d 1570 (1991); *Ascolese v. Southeastern Pennsylvania Transp. Auth.,* 902 F. Supp. 533 (E.D. Pa. 1995); *State v. Russo,* 259 Conn. 436 (2002); *People v. Kenway,* 219 Cal. App. 3d 441 (1990); *Commonwealth v. Slaton,* 530 Pa. 207 (1992).

[C]   Analyzing the Warrant Requirement

What does a lawyer do when his client is in a business to which the warrant requirement applies? Sometimes this is a matter of "think fast" law. Clients will call with an inspector actually on the premises asking to be let in without a warrant. In the discussion of consent, we noted that most businesses simply consent — in part because there are risks for not consenting — but also because it is not difficult for an agency inspector to obtain a warrant. In other words, an inspector who is refused entry may simply drive to a magistrate-judge's chambers, swear out an appropriate affidavit, get her warrant, and return. If an inspector comes back armed with the warrant, there is no way to fight entry short of risking a contempt of court citation.

The previous paragraph illustrates the mechanics of obtaining a warrant. The *law* of administrative warrants is a little less clear. Once again, *See/Camara* set the stage by noting that the requirements for obtaining an administrative inspection warrant are much less stringent than the probable cause requirement necessary for a criminal warrant.[101] These two cases and *Barlow's* address probable cause only in terms of reasonableness, leading some courts and commentators, probably erroneously, to discuss administrative warrants in terms of a requirement of "reasonable" cause.[102] Other writers seem to prefer the concept of "administrative probable cause." Neither of these terms is particularly striking or helpful in our analysis, but whatever term is used, it is clear that an administrative affidavit is examined by a court in a much more relaxed fashion than a criminal warrant affidavit.

There are two issues not yet completely resolved. What must the affidavit contain and may a warrant be obtained by an agency on an ex parte basis (*i.e.*, without the knowledge of the company to be inspected)? The affidavit requirements are discussed at length in *Barlow's*. The test appears to be whether the affidavit is supported either by (1) specific evidence of an existing violation (generally shown by complaints against the specific business) or (2) a general administrative plan derived from neutral sources.

Does this mean that an agency may randomly inspect businesses? The answer is probably "no," even though the Supreme Court has yet to address all the nuances of this issue. For example, in a revealing lower court opinion, the court required an explanation of the need for inspecting a particular business and suggested that more than mere randomness is necessary.[103] However, the same court of appeals has approved warrants that are issued by choosing businesses for full inspections under what the court characterized as a "neutral" administrative scheme for

---

[101] The cases explicating "probable cause" in a criminal setting are endless. One good prototype is *Illinois v. Gates*, 462 U.S. 213 (1983).

[102] This is an error because the Constitution uses the term "probable cause" and does not distinguish between administrative inspections and criminal searches. *See* Justice Stevens' dissenting opinion in *Barlow's* for this proposition.

[103] *Brock v. Gretna Mach. & Ironworks, Inc.*, 769 F.2d 1110 (5th Cir. 1985) (information suggesting that a particular business has a worse than normal safety record might suffice).

selecting such businesses.[104]

May an agency get an ex parte warrant? One federal administrative agency, OSHA, has long claimed that it may do so; but that authority has not been squarely confirmed by the courts. Because most agencies first attempt entry and seek a warrant only if entry is refused, the company will be on notice that the agency is seeking to inspect. Accordingly, the company will also be aware that a warrant is being sought. In this posture, the company may demand to participate in the actual court proceeding in which the warrant is sought.[105] While the final word on ex parte warrants has not yet been written, most warrants are obtained outside the presence of the company's lawyers. In this fashion, administrative warrants do not differ from criminal warrants. Criminal warrants are normally obtained ex parte on the quite plausible rationale that a person who knows he or she is about to be searched under a warrant will destroy the evidence or flee. Courts have used similar reasoning for approving the ex parte agency warrants.

Think carefully about counseling clients in an inspection setting. Many inspections are performed under one of the numerous exceptions to the warrant requirement, so many businesses may not refuse entry under any circumstances. Even if a warrant is necessary, it is not difficult to obtain: probable cause for administrative searches is far easier to show than probable cause for a criminal warrant. A client might obtain some leverage later on in the proceeding by consenting to the inspection, thereby demonstrating her good faith in cooperating with the agency, rather than by objecting and alienating agency personnel.

§ 4.09   AN AGENCY'S USE OF INFORMATION AS A SANCTION

If we accept the idea that agencies are to look out for the public interest, it makes sense that an agency occasionally will have to warn the general public when dangerous conditions exist, no matter what impact that warning may have on a particular company or industry. Capsules that look like normal painkillers but contain cyanide have to be taken off the market instantly, and purchasers must be warned immediately. There is no time for elaborate investigations and extensive fact-finding proceedings prior to the announcement.

Occasionally, agencies release information to the press as a kind of sanction against a particular business or industry. The Consumer Product Safety Commission, not too many years ago, made a number of public comments on the safety of skateboards long before they had completed an investigation of their safety. In other circumstances, an agency's announcement may have nothing to do with health or safety. It could concern business practices that the agency does not approve of and would like to see halted. Some business enterprises are so delicate that a simple announcement that the company is under agency investigation for, say, unfair trade practices or impermissible securities transactions, can harm a company.

---

[104] *In re Establishment Inspection of Trinity Indus.*, 898 F.2d 1049 (5th Cir. 1990).

[105] A good discussion of these issues may be found in William J. Stuntz, *Implicit Bargains, Government Power, and the Fourth Amendment*, 44 STAN. L. REV. 553 (1992).

Agency press releases are a two-edged sword. If there is a true danger, virtually no one would question the agency's right to tell the public. But what if the agency is wrong? Adverse publicity can kill a business without any opportunity for that business to contradict the release. Is it possible for a company to go into court to enjoin an adverse press release? The general rule is no. Most courts reason that an agency has a duty to warn the public in many instances, even when it does not yet have all the facts necessary to pursue a conventional enforcement action.[106]

There are a few cases that have permitted injunctions when the company can prove that it has been improperly singled out, or when the agency is conducting some kind of vendetta against it or when the agency has deliberately misrepresented the facts.[107] These cases, however, are few and far between, and their reasoning has never been reviewed by the Supreme Court.[108] This is one instance when court-ordered relief is not likely to be forthcoming. Is there anything else that can be done? One possibility, if an attorney has advance warning of the adverse press release, is to try to negotiate a number of things with the agency such as:

a.   a delay of the release until corrective action can be taken; or

b.   cancellation of the release if corrective action can immediately take care of the problem; or

c.   an agreement to have the agency release accompanied by some kind of response on the company's part.

There may be some help from the agencies themselves. A few agencies have recognized the truly awesome power of their press releases and have voluntarily limited their own actions by rule. The Consumer Product Safety Commission, for example, typically gives an affected company notice and an opportunity to comment prior to issuing a press release except when an emergency exists.[109] Most agencies are not so kind, however. This is one area in which private clients are simply at the mercy of the agency. Fortunately, there have been relatively few instances of abuse of the press release device.

---

[106]   *See, e.g., Ajay Nutrition Foods, Inc. v. FDA*, 378 F. Supp. 210 (D.N.J. 1974), *aff'd*, 513 F.2d 625 (3d Cir. 1975).

[107]   *See, e.g., Silver King Mines, Inc. v. Cohen*, 261 F. Supp. 666 (D. Utah 1966); *B.C. Morton Int'l Corp. v. FDIC*, 305 F.2d 692 (1st Cir. 1962).

[108]   One administrative law scholar who has touched on these issues is Lars Noah, *Administrative Arm-Twisting in the Shadow of Congressional Delegations of Authority*, 1997 Wis. L. Rev. 873.

[109]   16 C.F.R. § 115.15(c).

Chapter 5

AGENCY DECISION-MAKING: THE CONSTITUTIONAL LIMITATIONS

§ 5.01 AN INTRODUCTION TO CONSTITUTIONAL DUE PROCESS

[A] Issues Pertaining to Due Process

The typical course in administrative law is a course that concentrates on agency procedure. For this reason and other less frequently articulated reasons, most administrative law professors spend a great deal of time on the issues of constitutional due process.[1] However these issues interest the academics, it is entirely possible for an administrative law *practitioner* to spend thirty or forty years in practice without ever encountering a constitutional due process issue. Keep in mind that the Constitution sets procedural *minimums* for all administrative agencies at every level of government. By contrast, the procedural rules governing day-to-day administrative practice grow out of the applicable administrative procedure act and additional procedures implemented by the individual agencies. Most of the time, the combination of a jurisdiction's administrative procedure act requirements and an agency's internal procedures far exceed the constitutional threshold. For this reason, constitutional due process claims in practice are relatively rare.

Nonetheless, an administrative law student must confront issues of constitutional due process. A close look at some of the cases and concepts will pay dividends in many areas far removed from agency practice. One benefit is the insights into the Supreme Court's decisional process provided by the procedural due process cases. Another benefit is the exposure these cases bring to the fascinating historical evolution of deliberately ambiguous constitutional language. Due process in the last decade of the twentieth century is a very different concept from due process in the late 1800s.

Before getting into specific cases and issues, it is a good idea to think through some fundamentals of constitutional law. First, when the Supreme Court declares a matter to be of constitutional dimension, that pronouncement may not be altered

---

[1] The doctrine is judge-made, rather than statutory or regulatory, and thus, can be dealt with on a comfortable four cases-a-day basis, much like almost every other course in law school. You can spend a lifetime analyzing just the Supreme Court decisions in this area. Those students anticipating an administrative practice after law school would be well advised to spend more time on statutory and regulatory analysis — a far more productive inquiry for practicing lawyers.

except (1) by constitutional amendment or (2) by the Supreme Court's overruling of the earlier decision. Second, when the Court speaks on a matter of constitutional dimension, that pronouncement applies to all levels of government throughout the United States. These are the messages of *Marbury v. Madison*[2] and other early Supreme Court decisions. It is always surprising how many law students and lawyers forget these basic propositions when working through more sophisticated administrative law problems.

Another fundamental often disregarded is the language of the Constitution. When working with a due process problem on the federal or state level, you apply the due process clause of either the Fifth (federal level) or the Fourteenth Amendment (state level). Those clauses state:

Fifth Amendment: "No person . . . [shall] be deprived of life, liberty, or property, without due process of law . . ."

Fourteenth Amendment: "[N]or shall any State deprive any person of life, liberty, or property, without due process of law . . ."

Finally, don't forget that the deprivation of due process must be at the hands of the government, not at the hands of private persons. This is the requirement of *state action*.[3] In most administrative law problems state action is a given because the action under review is normally that of a government agency. Furthermore, the action of the agency must trigger the deprivation of either *life, liberty* or *property*. Because the Fifth and Fourteenth Amendments' use of the term "life" is generally restricted to the matter of capital punishment,[4] virtually all administrative due process questions involve liberty and property interests. It is much easier to understand the nuances of due process when these fundamentals are kept in mind.

How do you spot due process issues? There are a number of ways to work through a problem, but it may be helpful to think through the issues with the following progression of questions:

1.   *Whether* due process, of any kind, is required?

2.   *When* the process is due?

3.   *What kind* of process is due?

While a bit simplistic, these questions touch on virtually every due process issue that is likely to arise, either in an administrative law course or out in practice. Like most simple concepts, they warrant further explanation.

---

[2]   5 U.S. (1 Cranch) 137 (1803).

[3]   Anyone who is unclear as to this factor should review the discussion of the state action requirement in, *e.g.*, *Jackson v. Metro. Edison Co.*, 419 U.S. 345 (1974) (actions in terminating utility services by a private utility that was merely licensed to do business by a state agency was not state action under the Fourteenth Amendment).

[4]   One intriguing case, however, involved certain plaintiffs arguing that certain custodial practices followed by a nursing home deprived the nursing home patients of "life." *Town Court Nursing Ctr. v. Beal*, 586 F.2d 280 (3d Cir. 1978), *rev'd*, 447 U.S. 773 (1980).

[B] *Whether*

This is the threshold analysis. It must be answered in the affirmative before moving on to questions 2 and 3. It relates directly to the constitutional language recited above. The answer to the *whether* is "yes" (*i.e.*, some process is due) if an agency is seeking to deprive someone of his or her liberty or property interests. At the same time, identifying a liberty or property interest is not necessarily easy.[5]

[C] *When*

This is a question of *timing*, *i.e.*, the point in the agency's decision-making process at which the process is implemented. There are certain instances when the Supreme Court has directed that due process be provided before an agency makes a decision and certain instances when the Court permits some or all of the process to be given after the agency makes a decision. This question is to be analyzed simultaneously with the next question.

[D] *What Kind*

This question gets into the specific elements of an agency's procedure. For example, an agency may choose merely to give persons notice of some proposed agency action and an opportunity to comment on that proposal in writing. Another agency dealing with a different matter may permit an oral hearing, but without the right to direct and cross-examination of witnesses. In at least one case, the Supreme Court has determined that the due process clause requires direct and cross-examination of witnesses. Supreme Court case law, discussed below, suggests that the minimum due process required (if any process whatsoever is due) is at least notice *plus* some opportunity to comment (either in writing or orally). As a result, notice and opportunity to comment is a starting point for analysis of the *what kind* question.

Recall again that you do not move into questions 2 and 3 until you answer question 1 in the affirmative. That threshold analysis requires an understanding of some of the more prominent Supreme Court decisions.

§ 5.02 THE EARLY DECISIONS

Before moving on to some of the more sophisticated due process problems, most administrative law courses begin with an analysis of two Supreme Court opinions written in the early part of the century. Although these cases have a certain historical interest, they may not necessarily be the law today, even though they have never been expressly overruled. Both decisions are useful to show how far we have

---

[5] Because due process is triggered by either a property or liberty interest, it is rarely productive to try to distinguish between the two. The true distinction is between something that is either a property or a liberty interest and something which is *neither* a property nor a liberty interest. Nonetheless, there are times when you need to address the distinction to determine whether you have one or the other. Some of the cases discussed below will help you sort out the difference between a property and liberty interest. That discussion may be helpful in determining whether either of the interests is at stake.

come in our thinking on agency process, and for that reason alone they are quite instructive.

For roughly the first one hundred years of U.S. constitutional history, the Supreme Court did not seem particularly interested in questions of agency procedure. It was only in 1908 that the Court squarely addressed agency procedures in light of the due process protections to be afforded private persons. In *Londoner v. City of Denver*,[6] the Court confronted state agency action in the context of local government assessments for making street improvements. A municipal agency, the Board of Public Works in Denver, Colorado, was permitted to order street paving when a majority of the abutting land owners requested that a particular street be paved. The paving was paid for by an assessment based on the proportionate benefit enjoyed by the individual landowners after paving — i.e., each assessment reflected the length of the landowner's frontage on the paved street as compared with the other owners. However, the assessment was required from all abutting landowners, not just those who requested the paving. All the landowners were given notice of the specific dollar amounts of their individual assessment, but were permitted to object to these assessments only in writing. There was no provision whatsoever for an oral proceeding.

The aggrieved landowners who objected to those assessments took the dispute to court, arguing that the Fourteenth Amendment's due process clause gave them the right to an oral hearing. In a decision that may have been surprising at the time, the Supreme Court agreed. The Court acknowledged the notice and opportunity to comment in writing, but declared, without much analysis, that in these circumstances something more was required for the aggrieved landowners. The additional procedure involved at least "the right to support his allegations by [oral] argument, however brief; and, if need be, by proof, however informal."[7]

In terms of our three-step due process analysis, note that *Londoner* is not a *whether* case.[8] Rather it is a *what kind* case because the Court acknowledges that the landowners were already given some kind of hearing. That process was simply not sufficient. The *Londoner* Court determined that some degree of what we now refer to as "orality" must be provided and some mechanism permitting the landowners to get evidence into the record must be furnished. The Court did not, however, prescribe the procedural mechanisms necessary to satisfy these two requirements, nor did the Court demand elaborate mechanisms; it demanded only a little process "however brief and however informal."

Londoner was followed, seven years later, by a striking decision written by Oliver Wendell Holmes, *Bi-Metallic Inv. Co. v. Colorado*.[9] Like *Londoner*, the case began in Denver, Colorado. This time it involved a generic or across-the-board increase of

---

[6]   210 U.S. 373 (1908).

[7]   *Id.* at 386.

[8]   To be fair, some readers of *Londoner* believe that the process offered by the City of Denver is not an acceptable process in any situation in which an agency is dealing with individuals. Accordingly, some people read *Londoner* as a *whether* case, even though the Court went on to discuss what it might accept as the elements of minimal Due process-essentially an analysis of the *what kind* issue.

[9]   239 U.S. 441 (1915).

approximately 40% in the valuation of all taxable real estate in the city of Denver.[10] In other words, individual property values were irrelevant to this determination. The government simply increased the valuation of *all* taxable property by 40%. The decision was made by a Denver Board of Equalization that did not hear from individual landowners prior to making its decision. One of the landowners, invoking the *Londoner* decision, argued that he had a due process right to be heard, in some fashion, before the decision was made.[11]

The Court held that no process was due. Justice Holmes acknowledged the existence of *Londoner*, but distinguished that case on the basis of (1) the huge numbers of people to which the Board would have had to listen, (2) the fact that the landowners were also voters in Denver and could remove their elected representatives if they didn't like the Board's actions, (3) that the decision was a generic, or across-the-board matter, having nothing to do with individualized determinations of the specific valuation of particular plots of land, and (4) that, in any event, the real estate owners had the opportunity to contest individual assessments when they received their tax bills.

Unlike *Londoner*, *Bi-Metallic* is a true *whether* case, and a case that answered the *whether* question in the negative: no process was due. In an analysis of constitutional due process, if the answer is that no process is due, any further inquiry into the timing of the agency decision or the elements of due process is superfluous.

In addition, the *Bi-Metallic* opinion is often cited for the proposition that when an agency functions in a *legislative* capacity — when it makes an across-the-board rule — it is not required to provide individualized due process. As will be seen in Chapter 6, some states have taken the *Bi-Metallic* holding to mean that they have no obligation to provide any process whatsoever to persons affected by their rules — *i.e.*, even notice is not necessary, much less any kind of hearing or opportunity to comment. Whether a *total* lack of process, even in a rulemaking context, squares with due process in the twenty-first century remains to be seen.

---

[10] One of the reasons many students have difficulty understanding *Bi-Metallic* is that they do not understand the basic mechanism of state property taxation. Described briefly, the process works like this: (1) taxable property is identified and given a valuation-*e.g.*, the house and lot at 123 Cedar Street shall be valued at $15,000 (that valuation traditionally was something considerably less than fair market value, although most governments currently are moving to what is known as a fair market value level of valuation); (2) the government decides how much tax to assess against each dollar of taxable property (for instance, 2 cents per dollar of valuation (in this hypothetical, the tax would be $15,000 × $.02=$300)); and (3) the landowner is sent a bill for that tax ($300). The taxpayer is allowed to contest that final tax bill mainly with arguments, such as "my house is not worth that much" or "your arithmetic is wrong." Under *Londoner*, the government would be required to provide some type of hearing for the individual tax bills.

[11] 239 U.S. at 445.

§ 5.03   THE IMPACT OF *GOLDBERG v. KELLY*

While the Court occasionally tinkered with agency due process over the next fifty years, the so-called "due process explosion" did not begin until the Court's 1970 decision in *Goldberg v. Kelly*.[12] *Goldberg* remains one of the fundamental cases in this area and warrants close scrutiny by anyone seeking to understand procedural due process. The facts were complicated initially and became even more convoluted as the case worked its way through the lower federal courts because the agency being sued by the welfare recipients changed its mind as to how termination proceedings should be conducted as the case was being litigated. Although the agency initially argued that no process was due, midway through the litigation, it identified additional procedures that it would be willing to provide the recipients.

The dispute arose out of certain state-based welfare programs and out of the program known as Aid to Families with Dependent Children (AFDC), a program established by federal statute but largely administered through state welfare agencies and subsequently abolished by the Clinton administration. In its simplest terms, AFDC provided money for families with children when the family's income falls below a certain level. People receive AFDC money by qualifying under certain statutory criteria, including (1) level of income, (2) number of dependent children, and (3) the absence of an able-bodied supporting parent. Once a person can show that he or she qualifies, the agency must provide monetary support, assuming funds are available. The agency normally has no discretion to deny the benefits if a person is qualified under the statutory criteria. In 1996, Congress abolished the AFDC program and essentially engaged in an act of what is now referred to as "devolution." States are now permitted to create and administer welfare programs of their own choosing that do not necessarily have to be consistent with the now-defunct AFDC program. However, because *Goldberg* is a constitutional decision, it follows that any state welfare program that is modeled after AFDC would have to abide by the principles articulated by the Supreme Court in *Goldberg*.

Grounds for termination of AFDC benefits also varied. In most cases, recipients were terminated because they no longer meet the statutory criteria. Occasionally, welfare agencies terminated benefits for other reasons, such as improper use of the funds. For example, one of the plaintiffs in *Goldberg* was threatened with termination because she refused to sue her absent spouse for child and spousal support. Another *Goldberg* plaintiff was terminated because he refused to participate in a drug counseling and rehabilitation program.

A number of recipients who were either terminated or threatened with termination filed suit against the State of New York (the administering agency) in federal district court in New York, arguing, among other things, that termination without a pre-termination hearing was unconstitutional. In the beginning, New York provided no process whatsoever. The agencies had simply issued notices of termination. After the *Goldberg* lawsuit was filed, the state changed its mind and adopted new rules that gave recipients (1) notice of termination, (2) reasons for the termination, and (3) if requested by the recipient, either a review of the case by an office supervisor or an opportunity for the terminated recipient to comment on the

---

[12] 397 U.S. 254 (1970).

termination in writing. In some cases, the recipient would be able to have the case reviewed and to comment. After termination, the state promised recipients a fairly elaborate oral hearing with direct and cross-examination, among other procedures.

In *Goldberg v. Kelly*, the Supreme Court held both alternatives unconstitutional. The Court, in a majority opinion authored by Justice Brennan, required elaborate hearing procedures as a matter of constitutional law. As a result, *Goldberg* is simultaneously a *whether, when,* and *what kind* case. Although *Goldberg* is not favored by the current Supreme Court, it remains highly important because it sets the outer limits for constitutional due process.

The Court's reasoning warrants close examination. First, the Court determined that AFDC money is a statutory "entitlement" constituting a *property* interest under the Fifth and Fourteenth Amendments. The Court reached this conclusion by noting that AFDC benefits, in the modern American economic system, are far more than mere gratuities or *privileges*, which the state can provide or terminate solely in its discretion. Indeed, the Court hinted in a footnote that these statutory entitlements comprise a new form of property that deserve just as much constitutional protection as the more traditional forms of property ownership — *e.g.*, a car or a piece of real estate.[13] While the Court did not address the property interests inherent in applying for AFDC benefits, it held squarely that *termination* of these benefits was a protected constitutional interest. Thus, the Court's answer to the *whether* question was a most emphatic "yes."

The Court could have stopped there if it wished, simply by holding that a total absence of process or even the procedures offered to recipients by the State of New York after the litigation began were not enough. This would have permitted the state officials to experiment with new procedures and possibly to return to the Court in subsequent litigation if the recipients were not satisfied with the new procedures. Such a disposition would have been entirely consistent with the way the Court generally handles cases.

The Court, however, did not stop with a simple declaration of unconstitutionality. It addressed and resolved both of the other questions. On the question of timing (*when*), the Court determined that the due process must be afforded *prior* to termination, reasoning that AFDC benefits were so important as to mean the difference between survival and starvation-between life and death-for the recipients. In the Court's parlance, AFDC satisfies a "brutal need,"[14] and without those benefits recipients might die. Some welfare experts believe that such is not really

---

[13] This proposition originated from two law review articles written just a few years before *Goldberg* was decided: Charles A. Reich, *Individual Rights and Social Welfare: The Emerging Legal Issues*, 74 YALE L.J. 1245 (1965), and Charles A. Reich, *The New Property*, 73 YALE L.J. 733 (1964). In his majority opinion, Justice Brennan was also careful to move away from an outmoded distinction, discussed below, that things that a court can label a "privilege" are not protected by the Constitution, while something that a court is willing to label a "right" is deserving of a great deal of protection. Expunge those terms from your administrative law vocabulary. In 1988, Justice Brennan wrote a law review article that articulated some of his thinking in constructing the *Goldberg* opinion. William J. Brennan, Jr., *Reason, Passion, and "The Progress of the Law,"* 10 CARDOZO L. REV. 3 (1988).

[14] The expression "brutal need" is now regarded as a bit of Brennan-esque hyperbole that was not really necessary to the decision. The Supreme Court has never again held that a government benefit rose to the level of satisfying a "brutal need."

the case-that there exist a number of welfare programs that provide certain benefits, even if a person has lost his or her AFDC benefits.

The Court went on to hold that, because the need for AFDC benefits is so important and the risks involved in the government's making a wrong decision are so dire, due process must be provided not only before benefits are terminated, but that process must also be extraordinarily detailed. As a matter of constitutional law, Justice Brennan required as ingredients of a pre-termination hearing (the *what kind issue*) the following elements:

- Notice

- An oral hearing before an "impartial" decision-maker with direct and cross-examination

- retained counsel (although not appointed counsel)

- compilation of a record

- the use of that record as the exclusive basis for a decision

- a decision accompanied by a statement of reasons (although not by the sort of formal findings and conclusions that a trial judge must make).

Most students who read *Goldberg* today don't fully appreciate the nature of the case as a landmark.[15] No case, before or since, has required more due process as a matter of constitutional law. And recall your constitutional law fundamentals: this type of Court decision has the effect of carving these requirements in granite, either until the Constitution is amended or until the Court overrules *Goldberg*. Neither has occurred.

Thus, the Court's reasoning deserves even more explication. The Court regards notice and some kind of hearing as fundamental; but New York had already offered that much in the revised hearing procedures that it drafted and proposed after the litigation began. Justice Brennan wanted an oral hearing mainly because he concluded that the typical AFDC recipient is not a person who is likely to be able to handle a purely written proceeding. However, for an oral hearing to be meaningful, it must have other ingredients, such as confrontation and cross-examination. Beyond this, an agency compelled to provide a hearing should be forced to base its decision solely on the record of that hearing; otherwise, an agency could use external materials and information as the basis for its final decision and thereby, undercut the entire hearing process. Some degree of neutrality in the hearing officer is necessary, although the Court did not require complete independence. The hearing officer may be an agency employee so long as she was not involved in the case initially. Reasons for the decision must be given, especially if a decision is to be taken to a higher authority for review. A lawyer, trained in the adversary process, must be permitted to represent the claimant at the hearing, although the claimant has no constitutional right to appointed counsel.

---

[15] And no one reading *Goldberg* in the days after the Gramm-Rudman-Hollings Act (providing for automatic cuts in agencies' budgets to balance the federal budget) days should disregard the dissent of Justice Black. As Justice Black saw it, in a society of finite resources, every dollar spent on elaborate trial-type hearings is a dollar less that can be given to fully-qualified AFDC recipients.

At first glance, this sounds great; but there are some flaws in the Court's reasoning. To begin with, these hearings are expensive and time-consuming, perhaps severely detracting from the agency's primary mission-to deliver AFDC benefits to qualified recipients. Second, think about the dispute resolution aspects of this case. The Court has mandated essentially a trial-type proceeding (notwithstanding the fact that Justice Brennan keeps referring to a *Goldberg*-type hearing as an "informal" process) without requiring a lawyer.[16] But how can lay people-particularly lay people who, in the Court's own judgment, cannot deal adequately with a purely paper proceeding-expect to effectively and efficiently build a record, or deal with a hearing officer, or cross-examine adverse witnesses, or read a final decision with enough sophistication to decide whether to pursue an appeal? Without the participation of dispute resolution professionals, such as lawyers, doesn't the hearing become nearly meaningless? Most of these questions have no immediate answer. It is unlikely that the current Supreme Court has any interest in seeking the answers. Nonetheless, the questions should be pondered as we examine the third landmark case in the area.

The Supreme Court quickly lost whatever affection it may have had for *Goldberg*, but apparently those Justices who now probably despise *Goldberg* have not yet garnered the votes to overrule the decision. Because the case could not be completely nullified, the Court would have to work around it by careful distinguishing.

One outcome of *Goldberg* is what administrative law scholars now refer to as the *due process revolution*.[17] During the next half-dozen years following *Goldberg*, the Court decided a surprisingly large number of cases involving a wide range of government decision-making in which it determined that some process was due, including:

---

[16] This is another point with which some students have difficulty. Remember that this is a Fifth/Fourteenth Amendment Due process case. It is the Sixth Amendment that guarantees counsel in a criminal trial. In *Gagnon v. Scarpelli*, 411 U.S. 778 (1973), a decision that imposed virtually the same Due process elements on probation revocation proceedings that had been mandated in *Morrissey* for parole revocation, the Court addressed the issue of counsel: "[P]resumptively, it may be said that counsel should be provided in cases where, after being informed of his right to counsel, the probationer or parolee makes such a request . . . ." By contrast, in *Walters v. National Ass'n of Radiation Survivors*, 473 U.S. 305 (1985), the Court upheld a Civil War vintage statute prohibiting attorneys from recovering fees in excess of $10 per case for representing veterans before the Veterans Administration. In *Walters*, the Court relied heavily on statistics that suggested that cases handled by lawyers do not show a greater degree of success than cases handled by nonlawyers, lawyers, or by the veteran/claimants themselves. The Court structured its discussion in terms of the "risk of erroneous deprivation" factor set out in *Mathews v. Eldridge* (discussed *below*) and concluded that the statistics show that a lawyer's presence or absence in a veterans claim case did not significantly affect the risk of error.

[17] The phrase was coined by a distinguished and not-unsympathetic appeals court judge, Henry Friendly (of the Second Circuit), in one of the classic articles on administrative due process, Henry J. Friendly, *Some Kind of Hearing*, 123 U. Pa. L. Rev. 1267 (1973). As Judge Friendly put it, after *Goldberg* the tendency is to ask: "If there, why not here?" For a more recent commentary on the impact that the recent federal abolition of so-called "welfare" has had on cases such as Goldberg, *see* Cynthia R. Farina, *On Misusing "Revolution" and "Reform": Procedural Due Process and the New Welfare Act*, 50 Admin. L. Rev. 591 (1998).

- driver license revocation (*Bell v. Burson*)[18]

- parole revocation (*Morrissey v. Brewer*)[19]

- termination of a state university teacher's contract in a "*de facto*" tenure setting (*Perry v. Sindermann*)[20]

- certain prisoner's rights (*Wolff v. McDonnell*)[21]

- misconduct suspension of a public school student for ten days or less (*Goss v. Lopez*)[22]

This is an illustrative, rather than an exhaustive, list. Simultaneously, the lower federal courts, following the lead of the Supreme Court, were rapidly expanding the number of private interests accorded due process protection.[23]

By 1976, the membership of the Supreme Court had changed significantly. President Nixon, who ran on a platform of express distaste for the Warren Court, had the opportunity to appoint three new members of the Court, including the Chief Justice, Warren Burger. Some remaining justices, of course, had never been happy with *Goldberg*. The Court began searching for some way to stop the flood of due process cases before the "explosion" got completely out of hand. The first signals that the Court was in the process of rethinking administrative due process came in *Arnett v. Kennedy*,[24] a case involving a federal civil servant who argued that, as a non-probationary employee, he had not received sufficient due process in his termination proceeding.[25] The Court examined the process and found that he had received notice of termination and an opportunity to comment in writing before termination; and, if he continued to disagree with the decision, he could have a full trial-type hearing after termination. If he prevailed in the post-termination hearing, his rank would be restored and he would receive back pay to the date of termination.

---

[18] 402 U.S. 535 (1971).

[19] 408 U.S. 471 (1972).

[20] 408 U.S. 593 (1972). But in a companion case, *Board of Regents v. Roth*, 408 U.S. 564 (1972), a teacher with a one-year contract without a *de facto* tenure scheme was held not to have a protected due process interest in continued employment. Consider also, *Bishop v. Wood*, 426 U.S. 341 (1976), which held that "mere" employment by a governmental body is not a protected interest.

[21] 418 U.S. 539 (1974). There is something of a backlash brewing on this point, given the trend toward "privatization" of prison facilities. *See, e.g.*, Warren L. Ratliff, *The Due Process Failure of America's Prison Privatization Statutes*, 21 SETON HALL LEGIS. J. 371 (1997). The entire issue of Due process in the context of correctional facilities may be undergoing a re-examination by the Supreme Court. In *Sandin v. Conner*, 515 U.S. 472 (1995), the Court held that a prisoner who was serving an indeterminate sentence of 30 years to life did not have a constitutionally-protected liberty interest in his challenge to a prison decision to place him in segregated confinement.

[22] 419 U.S. 565 (1975).

[23] *Caulder v. Durham Housing Auth.*, 433 F.2d 998 (4th Cir. 1970), *cert. denied*, 401 U.S. 1003 (1971) (eviction from public housing).

[24] 416 U.S. 134 (1974).

[25] In the federal civil service, new hires must stay on the job for one year in probationary status, during which they may be fired without a great deal of trouble for virtually any reason. However, after a civil servant survives his first year, the process of termination is quite elaborate.

In an interesting 3-3-3 decision, six members of the Court determined that the employee did have a protected interest in his status as a federal employee (*i.e.*, the answer to the *whether* question was "yes"), but because his interest did not rise to the *Goldberg* level of "brutal need," the pre-termination due process he received was sufficient, and, in any event, he received elaborate post-termination due process that would restore his status and pay if he prevailed at the post-termination hearing. In a separate opinion, Justice Thurgood Marshall suggested that any time a government agency adversely affects the interests of a private person, at least *some* process is due. The *Arnett* dissenters, by contrast, urged (as had Justice Black as far back as *Goldberg*) that government efficiency, while not an exclusive consideration, at least ought to be a factor in framing a due process decision.

§ 5.04   THE CURRENT TEST FOR DUE PROCESS — *MATHEWS v. ELDRIDGE*

No one doing any work in the area of administrative due process can afford to disregard *Mathews v. Eldridge*.[26] The setting of the case was not too different from *Goldberg*. The Federal Social Security Administration (now a component of the Department of Health and Human Services) is charged with the administration of the social security system, including a program that pays social security disability (SSD) benefits to persons who qualify and who are no longer able to work. Persons employed in the United States pay into the social security system through payroll deductions (called "FICA"). Persons who have paid into the system for the requisite number of calendar quarters (forty quarters at the time the *Mathews* case arose) are eligible to claim disability benefits if, during their working careers, they become disabled to the point where they are not capable of gainful employment. This is not a workers' compensation system-the injury or illness does not have to be suffered on the job to trigger social security disability benefits; rather, it is a form of salary insurance that an eligible person receives in monthly payments from the social security system until she again becomes capable of gainful employment.

In *Mathews*, social security disability benefits were terminated after notice and the opportunity to comment in writing.[27] After termination, the recipient was given a trial-type hearing, and, as in *Arnett*, retroactive benefits would be paid if the recipient prevailed. The claimant argued that this form of process was constitutionally insufficient. The Supreme Court disagreed.

Mathews' bottom line is not a problem. The Court held, 6-2, that while a termination proceeding does trigger some kind of due process (more accurately, the government did not dispute the *whether* aspects of the case), Mr. Eldridge was not entitled to any more due process than he had already received. The Court reached this conclusion mainly by distinguishing *Goldberg* and *Mathews*, although reading between the lines, it is clear that a number of justices might have preferred to overrule *Goldberg* altogether.

---

[26] 424 U.S. 319 (1976). The reader should also consider all of the more recent cases cited and discussed in Richard J. Pierce, Jr., *The Due Process Counterrevolution of the 1990s?*, 96 Colum. L. Rev. 1973 (1996).

[27] 424 U.S. 319.

Some commentators find it difficult to accept a number of the distinctions. The Court was unwilling to equate the *brutal need* of AFDC benefits with social security disability (SSD) benefits. As the Court reiterated in *Mathews*, AFDC recipients are "on the very margin of subsistence." This is not the case for persons who have their SSD benefits terminated. That type of benefit does not equate with a brutal need; thus, a trial-type proceeding prior to termination is not constitutionally necessary. Beyond this, in the Court's view, an AFDC proceeding was more likely to turn on specific factual disputes where an oral hearing might be beneficial, while SSD benefits were more a matter of evaluating medical evidence that had already been committed to paper.[28] There is little need for an oral hearing in disputes based primarily on a paper record.

These comments on evidence are the one part of *Mathews* that puzzles many people who deal regularly with SSD termination proceedings. In practice, there is much paper generated, and a lot of decisions turn on those pieces of paper. But many cases involve medical evidence and expert witnesses presented by each side. Frequently, the issue becomes one of which expert to believe-a question particularly suitable for a face-to-face oral confrontation and often difficult to resolve solely on the basis of paper presentations. Moreover, there appears to be nothing in the *Mathews* record that supports the court's conclusion-that a paper hearing process was sufficient-as an across-the-board proposition. The Court apparently reached this conclusion without much factual or statistical support. This conclusion, however, served another important function: it helped the Court decide *Mathews* the way it wanted without having to overrule *Goldberg*.

To be completely fair to the Court, the significant part of *Mathews* is not the ultimate disposition of the case itself. Concededly, there are differences between SSD and AFDC, and there was a great deal of due process already afforded in the challenged procedures. Moreover, having conceded the *whether* question, the Court does have a certain amount of leeway in addressing the *when* and *what kind* issues. What is important, and what everyone reading *Mathews* and dealing with a procedural due process question in the future must address, is the three-part test first articulated in *Mathews* by which all federal courts now evaluate challenges to agency procedures. Due process questions are now to be weighed in terms of three factors:

1. the private interest affected by agency action;

2. the risk of error inherent in the agency's existing procedures; and

3. the government's interest in maintaining the existing procedures weighed in terms of both fiscal and administrative burdens that might be encountered if new procedures were mandated.

Remember: this test is a Supreme Court pronouncement and must be addressed any time you deal with an administrative due process question. For example, if you are writing a brief in federal court on an administrative due process issue, it is likely that you will organize the brief on the basis of these three factors. *Mathews* is now

---

[28] *Id.*

almost 30 years old now, and the Court does not seem to have retreated or even altered its basic formula.

Factor one has three components: (1) *identify* the "thing" (interest) in question with which the government is tampering. (Is it AFDC benefits, a driver's license or something else?); (2) *discuss* whether this interest is something that is either a property or a liberty interest (a discussion of the methodology for making this determination follows); (3) if the thing is a property or liberty interest, then *consider* how important is the thing to a person's well-being or survival. Recall that you are guaranteed a *Goldberg*-type result (pre-termination due process) only if the thing has something to do with survival — *i.e.*, satisfies a "brutal need."

Factor two requires an evaluation of the agency's procedures to determine whether those procedures lead to accurate results.[29] The touchstone is not total accuracy, however. Instead, this inquiry is really a blending of an analysis of (1) the interest involved and the importance of that interest to the private person and (2) whether the procedures assure to some reasonable degree that the government's decision is correct. Again, keep in mind the Court's language. The articulated test is "the risk of erroneous deprivation."

Factor three requires an analysis of what the Court refers to as either the *public* interest or the *government* interest. The Court seems to view the two terms as being synonymous, although it is possible to disagree with the Court on this point. A government agency may worry only about its budget and not give a hoot for establishing a fair procedure for those whose lives the agency affects. By contrast, the public may have just as strong an interest in insuring that agencies implement a fair and accurate decisional process as it does in guarding against unreasonable expenditures of government money. In factor three, the Court seems to treat the public interest only in terms of an interest in the public fisc.

What the justices are really getting at in factor three was never clearly articulated in the *Mathews* opinion. Recall Justice Black's point in *Goldberg*: How much do we want to burden the agency, both financially and administratively, simply to insure an additional increment of fairness or accuracy? The Court was quick to point out in *Mathews* that "[f]inancial cost alone is not a controlling weight in determining whether due process requires a particular procedural safeguard . . . But the Government's interest, and hence that of the public in conserving scarce fiscal and administrative resources is a factor that must be weighed."

Mathews was a watershed case. Since then, the Court has not cut back on any of the due process protections decided during the explosion years, but it has sent clear signals that it does not intend to go too much further. For example, there is no case that extends beyond the protections provided by *Goldberg*. The case that is probably closest to *Goldberg* in terms of mandating strict procedure is *Morrissey v. Brewer* (parole revocation).[30] When someone loses a parole hearing, he or she goes

---

[29] There is a classic law review article that takes up administrative procedures along the same lines as *Mathews*, but uses a slightly different vocabulary. Roger C. Cramton, *A Comment on Trial-Type Hearings in Nuclear Plant Siting*, 58 Va. L. Rev. 585 (1972). Professor Cramton prefers the terms: "accuracy" "efficiency" and "acceptability."

[30] The procedures required for parole revocation in *Morrissey v. Brewer*, 408 U.S. 471 (1972), are

back to jail. It would seem that the *Morrissey* Court viewed the loss of liberty to be nearly as important as the brutal need test enunciated in *Goldberg.*

More recently, the Court has taken a number of cases in which it finessed the *whether* question (*i.e.*, refused to deem the interest either a property or liberty interest) by going to the opposite end of the spectrum, seeing what kind of process the recipient was given and deeming that sufficient. For example, in *Board of Curators of the University of Missouri v. Horowitz,*[31] the Court reviewed the expulsion from a state medical school of a fourth-year medical student. Throughout the *Horowitz* opinion, the Court seemed to view the failure of Ms. Horowitz to satisfy academic criteria as the reason for the expulsion. It was obvious that the Court felt totally uncomfortable second-guessing the academic determinations of a medical faculty and simply affirmed Ms. Horowitz' expulsion. In reaching this result, the Court refused to reach the question of whether attendance at a state-supported medical school was a property or liberty interest by holding that the due process afforded Ms. Horowitz was all the Court would have given her, even if she had a property or liberty interest in medical school attendance.

This is not to say that the Court was wrong in its decision. Ms. Horowitz' clinical performance was reviewed at various times by: (1) the faculty, (2) a Council of Evaluation (three times), (3) an appeals board consisting of seven practicing physicians, (4) a faculty coordinating committee, (5) the Dean and (6) the University Provost. That is considerable due process by any standard. If one views due process, in part, as the making of a *careful* decision, it is difficult to find fault with the University of Missouri's procedures. In a more recent case, involving state-supported higher education (recall the state action requirement; in most respects the actions of private schools are not deemed *state action*), the Court again refused to reach the question of whether attendance in college is a property/liberty interest by following the same decisional method as in *Horowitz.*[32]

By contrast, the Court seems to view government employment somewhat differently. In *Cleveland Board of Education v. Loudermill,*[33] the Court reviewed the claim of a state civil servant that he was fired in violation of his right to procedural due process. In this case, the Court determined that Mr. Loudermill had a protected property interest in his employment and required that he be given at least minimal pre-termination due process. He had been given none by the state. In *Barry v. Barchi,*[34] the Court determined that a jockey suspended for fifteen days for alleged use of stimulants was not due any pre-decisional process, but did have a right to a prompt post-suspension hearing. In *Barry*, the Court seemed to view the issue of a jockey's suspension for possible drug use as an emergency matter. In other words, if the supervisors could not get a drug-using jockey off the track instantly, the safety of many other persons would be compromised.

---

virtually identical to the *Goldberg* procedures, but the Court has never gone beyond *Goldberg.*

[31] 435 U.S. 78 (1978).

[32] *Regents of the Univ. of Mich. v. Ewing*, 474 U.S. 214 (1985).

[33] 470 U.S. 532 (1985).

[34] 443 U.S. 55 (1979).

In dramatic contrast to the majority of recent due process cases, the Supreme Court recently held that the transfer of a state prisoner to a "supermax" prison in Ohio affected that prisoner's liberty interest and requires a due process hearing. In *Wilkinson v. Austin*,[35] the Court was clearly struck by the conditions of confinement in the prison: prohibition of virtually all human communication; lights on 24 hours each day; prisoners stay in their cells 23 hours every day with their "recreation" period limited to walking within an interior room; permanent placement in the supermax with only an annual review, etc. Nonetheless, the Court was satisfied with the procedures provided by Ohio prior to the transfer to supermax: hearing before a three-person committee; 48 hours notice prior to the hearing; inmate permitted to attend the hearing and provide information and argument on his or her behalf (but not call witnesses); a statement of findings and reasons by the committee if it orders transfer; further review by the prison warden; and a final decision by the state Bureau of Prisons before transfer is carried out. In reaching these conclusions, the Court used the three *Mathews* factors to conclude that the procedures satisfied the due process clause.

The war on terrorism has sparked a number of important judicial decisions. The Supreme Court's decision in *Hamdi v. Rumsfeld*,[36] is instructive on the issue of due process. Mr. Hamdi was born in the United States and eventually arrested by U.S. authorities in Afghanistan where, the government alleged, he took up arms on behalf of the Taliban. In a lengthy opinion, the Court first determined that the United States government does have the power to detain enemy combatants under Congressional authority enacted in 2002 which permitted the president to use all necessary and appropriate force" against persons who were associated with the September 11, 2001 terrorist attacks.

However, Mr. Hamdi asserted that he nonetheless had a right under the due process clause to challenge his enemy combatant status. The Court performed a standard *Matthews* three-part analysis to conclude that Hamdi did have a right to bring such a challenge. With regard to the threshold issue (private interest affected), the Court concluded that this is one of the "most elemental of liberty interests — the interest in being free from physical detention by one's own government." Not even war (the government's interest — step three) trumps this particular interest.

With regard to the risk of an erroneous determination (step two in *Matthews*), the Court reviewed the processes suggested by the government and determined that its procedures did not satisfy due process requirements. The Court ultimately required that a person in Hamdi's position, at the very least, be given "notice of the factual basis for his classification, and a fair opportunity to rebut the government's factual assertions before a neutral decisionmaker." However, the Court was willing to accept certain constraints on the hearing process. For example, it conceded that the admission of hearsay evidence might be necessary. It was willing to permit some kind of presumption in favor of the government's assertions. Nonetheless, it went on to reiterate its fundamental holding: even terrorism does not warrant deprivation of

---

[35] 545 U.S. 209 (2005).

[36] 542 U.S. 507 (2004).

at least the requirements of notice, some kind of hearing, and an independent decision maker.[37]

This is not to say that administrative due process issues have been conclusively settled by the Court. The Court decides a new procedural due process case about once every other term, mainly because state and local governments sometimes ignore or attempt to sidestep settled rules. The Court has never questioned the soundness of the *Mathews* analysis; the three-part *Mathews* test is always applicable. For lawyers, the important challenge is how to relate new fact patterns to the existing case law.

§ 5.05 RESOLVING ADMINISTRATIVE DUE PROCESS ISSUES

[A] Approaches

The *whether, when* and *what kind* questions help spot due process issues but don't really help resolve them.[38] There are a number of ways to work through due process issues. The following discussion contains some suggestions for doing so. One thing that is certain is that it is hard to talk about these concepts in the abstract.

You may find the following discussion almost impenetrable if you have not read the previous sections because it refers to the important due process cases by name. This section is not the place to begin. Anyone who arrives at this point without understanding the analysis of the landmark cases discussed in the preceding sections should go back to the beginning of the chapter. Application of the *whether, when* and *what kind* questions help sort out some of the basic issues, but you need to take your analysis several steps further to complete a full-blown resolution of any new due process question.

[B] Resolving a *Whether Issue*

Recall that the place to begin is with the language of the Fifth and Fourteenth Amendments and that the term *life* almost never figures into an administrative due process question because it is generally reserved for capital punishment cases. Thus, the question becomes: Does your client have a property or liberty interest protected by the Constitution? Most students strive mightily to distinguish between a property and a liberty interest. In the context of administrative due process, that's rarely a productive inquiry. The Supreme Court never has made up

---

[37] As might be expected, Hamdi generated an enormous amount of writing on the case. *See, e.g.*, Cass R. Sunstein, *Administrative Law Goes to War*, 118 HARV. L. REV. 2663 (2005); Edwin Chermerinsky, *Enemy Combatants and Separation of Powers*, 1 J. NAT'L SECURITY L. & POL'Y 73 (2005). Hamdi was eventually released under an agreement that he relinquish his U.S. citizenship.

[38] This is an elementary point that is too often lost on law students, even in the upper classes. Issue spotting is the process of identifying and categorizing legal questions by area of the law. Issue resolution, by contrast, is the analysis of a particular body of law to attempt to reach conclusions as to the validity of an agency's action. In other words, issue resolution is a matter of predicting how a court faced with this issue might decide it.

its mind on the distinction. In *Horowitz,* for example, not only did the Court refuse to address whether Ms. Horowitz had any protected interest whatsoever, but it also refused to speculate on whether such an interest might be a liberty or property interest. One way to understand the distinction is to examine the Court's decisions on a case-by-case basis. For example, AFDC benefits, federal non-probationary employment and a driver's license have all been deemed property interests. Being out on parole or obtaining good time credits while in prison have been recognized as liberty interests.[39] For most purposes, it is probably enough to identify interests as property/liberty interests, because people have due process rights if either interest is affected. It is only when *neither* a property nor a liberty interest is at stake that the agency does not have to confer due process.

Where do you find property/liberty interests? Justice Rehnquist's dissenting opinion in *Loudermill* is a good starting point, although his discussion was preceded by similar discussions in a number of earlier cases. As he explains it: " 'Property interests, of course, are not created by the Constitution. Rather, they are created and their dimensions are defined by existing rules or understandings that stem from an independent source such as state law . . . .'"[40] However, while state law is a good starting point for identifying protected interests, you cannot stop your inquiry there. Recall that *Goldberg* (AFDC), *Mathews* (social security benefits) and *Arnett* (federal employment) are interests that are created by federal statute (*i.e.,* actions of Congress). So, in certain circumstances, a property interest may be conferred by the federal government.[41] In other words, while state law is an important source of interests (perhaps the most important source), it is not the only place where protected interests may be found.[42]

In 2005, the Court revisited the issue of property interests in the context of enforcement of domestic violence restraining orders. In *Town of Castle Rock v. Gonzales,*[43] the petitioner, a woman estranged from her husband, got a restraining order from a state court ordering the husband, among other things, to stay at least

---

[39] Using *Morrissey* and *Goldberg* as guideposts, most administrative due process cases will likely involve property interests because most administrative agencies regulate either entitlement programs (*e.g.,* social security) or the licensure and conduct of business activities. The cases arising out of public school activities are muddled; it is presently unclear whether attendance at school (or suspension from school) is a property or liberty interest. Students who wish to take this discussion further may wish to consult: Richard B. Stewart & Cass R. Sunstein, *Public Programs and Private Rights,* 95 Harv. L. Rev. 1193 (1982); Henry P. Monaghan, *Of "Liberty" and "Property,"* 62 Cornell L. Rev. 405 (1977).

[40] 470 U.S. at 561, quoting *Bd. of Regents v. Roth,* 408 U.S. 564, 577 (1972).

[41] One of the earliest due process cases involved suspension of a company's right to enter into federal contracts. *Gonzalez v. Freeman,* 334 F.2d 570 (D.C. Cir. 1964).

[42] In 1996, Congress repealed a large number of federal welfare statutes including AFDC and by way of a process known as "devolution" returned a large role in welfare administration to the states while still preserving a large amount of federal funds for the various state programs. In the Personal Responsibility and Work Opportunity Reconciliation Act, Pub. L. No. 104-193, 110 Stat. 2105 (1996), codified in scattered sections of 42 U.S.C. This statute contains an express provision that purports to repudiate the concept of welfare benefits as a constitutionally-protected entitlement: the statute "shall not be interpreted to entitle any individual or family to assistance under any state program funded under this part." *See, e.g.,* Christine N. Cimini, *Welfare Entitlements in the Era of Devolution,* 9 Geo. J. on Poverty L. & Pol'y 89 (2002).

[43] 545 U.S. 748 (2005).

100 yards from the family home. The husband disobeyed the order, kidnapped the couple's three children, and ultimately murdered the children. The wife sued the town of Castle Rock, asserting that the town's police department customarily disregarded such orders and often failed to enforce them, thereby depriving her of due process.[44] In an opinion authored by Justice Scalia, the Court determined that the wife had no protected property interest in the enforcement of the protective order. Justice Scalia reviewed earlier case law such as *Roth* and *Paul* to note that a property interest is an entitlement that is not an abstract need or desire and such entitlements are "defined by existing rules or understandings that stem from an independent source such as state law."[45] The benefit here was not a protected interest because "a benefit is not a protected entitlement if government officials may grant or deny it in their discretion."[46] Looking closely at the Colorado statutes and applicable case law (and refusing to defer to the 10th Circuit's view of these issues[47]) the Court determined that nothing in the Colorado law made enforcement of protective orders *mandatory.* Accordingly, as a matter of state government discretion, there was no protected interest at stake.

In the case of liberty interests, the Court has suggested that "there are other interests, of course, protected not by virtue of their recognition by the law of a particular State but because they are guaranteed in one of the provisions of the Bill of Rights which has been 'incorporated' into the Fourteenth Amendment."[48] In recent years, the Court has grappled with the concept of liberty interest in the context of prisoners' rights. For example, in *Board of Pardons v. Allen,*[49] the Court reviewed a Montana statute that provided that the state parole board "shall release

---

[44] The wife asked for money damages under 42 U.S.C. § 1983 (the federal statute that permits a monetary recovery against state officers who violate constitutional rights under color of law).

[45] 545 U.S. at 756.

[46] *Id.*

[47] While not terribly relevant to administrative law, this concept of deference to a Circuit's construction of state law grows out of an important civil procedure concept first articulated in *Erie Railroad v. Tompkins,* 304 U.S. 64 (1938) (application of state substantive law to federal court cases arising in diversity). Following the *Erie Railroad* decision, the Supreme Court decided to let the federal circuit courts make the final determination of what state law said. Here, however, Justice Scalia determined that this was not a case requiring deference to state law but rather a matter of federal constitutional law (i.e., what constituted a protected interest under the United States Constitution).

[48] *Paul v. Davis,* 424 U.S. 693, 710 n.5 (1976). *Paul* is a case involving the distribution of flyers identifying certain people by name and mug shot as active shoplifters. Davis, one of the people whose picture and name were distributed to area businesses, argued that he had a Due process right to a hearing before the mug shots were sent out. The Supreme Court disagreed because the Court was unwilling to conclude that any liberty interest had been infringed. In *Board of Regents v. Roth,* 408 U.S. 564 (1972), the Court refused to find a property or liberty interest in a one-year teaching contract with no *de facto* tenure systems, but commented:

> [A liberty interest] denotes not merely freedom from bodily restraint but also the right of the individual to contract, to engage in any of the common occupations of life, to acquire useful knowledge, to marry, establish a home and bring up children, to worship God according to the dictates of one's own conscience, and generally to enjoy those privileges long recognized . . . as essential to the orderly pursuit of happiness by free men." [citations omitted].

Ingraham v. Wright, 430 U.S. 651 (1977) held that corporal punishment (paddling) in public schools implicated a liberty interest.

[49] 482 U.S. 369 (1987).

on parole . . . any person confined . . . when in its opinion there is reasonable probability that the prisoner can be released without detriment to the prisoner or community." The Court determined that the use of the mandatory verb *shall* created a liberty interest on the part of a prisoner seeking parole, even though the board enjoyed discretion in making the finding that upon release the prisoner would or would not be a danger to society. As the Court reasoned, the statute makes release mandatory after the requisite finding is made and thereby, creates a liberty interest. By contrast, just two years after *Allen*, the Court held that a prisoner's interest in being permitted to receive visitors in prison is not a liberty interest, even though the prison authorities tended to respect the rights of prisoners to have visitors.[50] The Court determined that the discretion of the prison officials was not narrowed by any statutory language (as it was in *Allen*) and that no constitutionally protected interest was created. More recently, a prisoner's transfer to a "supermax" prison triggers a liberty interest.[51] And in the now-seminal case of *Hamdi v. Rumsfeld*,[52] the Court commented: "Hamdi's private interest . . . affected by the official action is the most elemental of liberty interests — the interest in being free from physical detention by one's own government. In our society, liberty is the norm and detention without trial is the carefully limited exception."[53]

There are other ways to grapple with these threshold issues. Sometimes a case-by-case analysis shows the difficulty of drawing hard, fast lines in this area. Consider the following lists:

Due Process Required	No Due Process Required
a) termination of non-probationary federal employment[54]	termination of federal employee's security clearance[55]
b) termination of a state school teacher in a system with de facto tenure[56]	termination of a teacher on a one — year contract[57]

---

[50] *Ky. Dep't of Corrections v. Thompson*, 490 U.S. 454 (1989).

[51] *Wilkinson v. Austin*, 545 U.S. 209 (2005). However, the Court noted in passing that the claim of a liberty interest was somewhat weak given that the prisoner was already confined and thus had suffered a loss of liberty from the initial incarceration.

[52] 542 U.S. 507 (2004).

[53] *Id.* at 518 (internal quotations omitted). For additional comments on this aspect of the *Hamdi* opinion, see Jesselyn A. Radack, *You Say Defendant, I Say Combatant: Opportunistic Treatment of Terrorism Suspects Held in the United States and the Need for Due Process*, 29 N.Y.U. Rev. L. & Soc. Change 525 (2005).

[54] *Arnett v. Kennedy*, 416 U.S. 134 (1974).

[55] *Cafeteria Workers v. McElroy*, 367 U.S. 886 (1961). While never overruled, there is serious doubt whether *Cafeteria Workers* would be decided the same way today.

[56] *Perry v. Sindermann*, 408 U.S. 593 (1972).

[57] *Board of Regents v. Roth*, 408 U.S. 564 (1972).

Due Process Required	No Due Process Required
c) automatic revocation of a driver's license because driver has no insurance[58]	automatic revocation of a driver's license after 3 suspensions in 10 years[59]
d) individualized tax assessment[60]	across — the — board increase in assessed value[61]
e) posting of a drunkard list[62]	posting of a shoplifters list[63]
f) public employment in a civil service system[64]	"mere" public employment[65]

This is an incredible jumble; it is extremely difficult to make heads or tails out of these cases without subjecting each to close scrutiny, because the distinctions between the cases on either side of the list are truly minute.

A slightly different analytical method to determine due process requirements starts from the general proposition that any time a government agency deals with private parties, it must provide some kind of due process. Recall that in his separate opinion in *Arnett v. Kennedy*, Justice Marshall suggested that whenever a government agency takes action that adversely affects a private citizen, that citizen is due some process. You can then view the cases that grant no process whatsoever as generic exceptions to this general rule.[66] The exceptions should be immediately recognizable to anyone who has tussled with everything previously discussed in this chapter.

The exceptions are:

a. *Waiver.* Recall that anyone can voluntarily relinquish a constitutional right.[67]

b. *Emergency.* This is a slightly more difficult concept to include as an exception. There are emergency cases involving adulterated food,[68] jockeys suspected of drug

---

[58] *Bell v. Burson*, 402 U.S. 535 (1971).

[59] *Dixon v. Love*, 431 U.S. 105 (1977).

[60] *Londoner v. City of Denver*, 210 U.S. 373 (1908).

[61] *Bi-Metallic Inv. Co. v. Colorado*, 239 U.S. 441 (1915).

[62] *Wisconsin v. Constantineau*, 400 U.S. 433 (1971).

[63] *Paul v. Davis*, 424 U.S. 693 (1976).

[64] *Cleveland Board of Education v. Loudermill*, 470 U.S. 532 (1985).

[65] *Bishop v. Wood*, 426 U.S. 341 (1976).

[66] A portion of this analysis was suggested by the late Professor Bernard Schwartz who used a version of this method in his casebook.

[67] *See, e.g., Nat'l Indep. Coal Operators' Ass'n v. Kleppe*, 423 U.S. 388 (1976). This is actually a case of waiver of a statutory right to a formal hearing when the mine operator failed to request a hearing. The Supreme Court acknowledged that the statute gives the mine operator the right to a hearing, but only when the operator requests a hearing (the operators had argued that the Mine Safety and Health Review Administration was required to provide a hearing even in the absence of a request). The waiver concept discussed in *Kleppe* is equally applicable in the context of federal constitutional rights.

[68] The case cited in virtually all of the casebooks is *N. Amn. Cold Storage Co. v. Chicago*, 211 U.S. 306 (1908), a case involving contaminated chickens. The Court said simply that the company's right to Due

use,[69] and unsafe coal mines.[70] However, a close analysis of each of the emergency cases suggests that what the Court is approving is merely post-decisional due process, rather than carving out an exception to the *whether* question. In each instance, the private party got at least some due process after the government action. Perhaps the emergency exception exists only insofar as the interest in question evaporates during the emergency. But examples of this kind of situation are few; so treat this exception carefully.

c. *Legislative-type actions.* *Bi-Metallic* has never been overruled, so we must cope with Justice Holmes' notion that when an agency is exercising its legislative powers, no process is due. An aggrieved party's recourse is in a subsequent, individualized enforcement action or through the voting booth. Some states have taken *Bi-Metallic* to mean that there are virtually no procedural restrictions on agency rulemaking, including such things as notice and publication requirements. The federal government provides at least notice and opportunity to comment in writing for agency rulemaking under the Administrative Procedure Act. Remember also Justice Holmes' suggestion in *Bi-Metallic* that the sheer numbers of people involved might justify an absence of individualized due process.

In *Atkins v. Parker*,[71] food stamp recipients objected to certain notice that they had received from a food stamp agency after Congress changed the percentage of a household's income that would be disregarded in computing food stamp eligibility from 20 to 18 percent. The recipients argued that they should have had advanced notice of the legislative change and precise notice of the change in the dollar amount of their individual benefits. The Supreme Court disagreed, commenting that "[t]he procedural component of the due process clause does not impose a constitutional limitation on the power of Congress to make substantive changes in the law of entitlement to public benefits."

It is equally clear that agencies may shorten trial-type proceedings by dealing generically with certain aspects of the proceeding. For example, in *United States v. Storer Broadcasting Co.*,[72] the Federal Communications Commission, by rule, limited the number of television stations any one person could own. Storer argued that such a generic limitation deprived it of its right to due process in an individual licensing proceeding. The Supreme Court disagreed, holding the FCC had power to deal with many issues by rulemaking and did not have to grant a hearing when an otherwise valid rule completely forecloses the application. Similarly, in *Heckler v. Campbell*,[73] the agency had promulgated generic medical-vocational guidelines to be used in social security disability hearings. The Supreme Court upheld the guidelines, even though they foreclosed a particular applicant from introducing certain evidence at hearing. In *Heckler*, the Court stated: "It is true that the statutory scheme contemplates that disability hearings will be individualized

---

process could not stand in the way of an emergency confiscation of the chickens to protect the public health.

[69] *Barry v. Barchi*, 443 U.S. 55 (1979).

[70] *Hodel v. Va. Surface Mining Ass'n*, 452 U.S. 264 (1981).

[71] 472 U.S. 115 (1985).

[72] 351 U.S. 192 (1956).

[73] 461 U.S. 458 (1983).

determinations based on evidence adduced at a hearing. But this does not bar the Secretary from relying on rulemaking to resolve certain classes of issues . . . ."

d. *No facts to be found.* The Supreme Court never has required an agency to engage in totally superfluous action. When a hearing would be meaningless, the due process clauses do not require one. This is the message of *Dixon v. Love* and a few other cases.[74] The late Professor Kenneth Culp Davis liked to distinguish between what he calls *legislative facts* (generic historical conditions, market conditions, the overall state of an industry, etc.) and *adjudicative facts* (the who, what, where and when facts applicable to a particular individual), making the point that when an agency is dealing with legislative facts no individualized due process is required.[75]

e. *When a "privilege" is at stake.* Some people still like to talk about the difference between a right and a privilege, arguing that rights trigger due process, while privileges are matters of grace for which the government need provide nothing. The Supreme Court has made abundantly clear that the right/privilege doctrine is no longer a useful concept in its deliberations. *Goldberg* signaled the Court's distaste for this distinction; *Roth* and subsequent cases have referred to it as a useless, "wooden" doctrine.

The right/privilege distinction should not factor into anyone's discussion of the due process guaranteed by the Federal Constitution. However, a number of state courts have not embraced this view and continue to include the concept in the list of exceptions to the due process requirement.[76] A lawyer whose client needs some due process has no recourse except to try and persuade a reviewing court not to apply the privilege label to his client's interest.

f. *Immigration cases.* Some of the discussion of Fourth Amendment rights in Chapter 4 advised wariness of the use of principles derived from immigration cases as the basis for general administrative law rules. That message is equally applicable here. There are a number of suggestions in immigration cases that the government's conduct of foreign affairs is exempt from any due process requirement.

Similarly, a number of cases distinguish between the immigration process of exclusion (keeping someone out of the U.S.) and deportation (expelling someone from the U.S.). Deportation may require some constitutional due process; exclusion may require nothing.[77] Reading between the lines of some of the immigration cases also leads to the suspicion that the sheer number of people desiring entry into the U.S. may militate against individualized due process.

g. *Private action.* Recall that due process is not triggered unless the action in question is taken by the government. The Supreme Court has made clear that

---

[74] *See supra* note 47. *See also, e.g., Weinberger v. Hynson, Westcott & Dunning, Inc.*, 412 U.S. 609 (1973).

[75] Kenneth Culp Davis, Cases, Text and Problems on Administrative Law, 275–84 (6th ed. 1977).

[76] *Id.*

[77] *Compare Knauff v. Shaughnessy*, 338 U.S. 537 (1950) (no due process for exclusion), *with Kwong Hai Chew v. Colding*, 344 U.S. 590 (1953) (some due process necessary in a deportation case).

termination of utility services by a private utility carries no obligation to provide the terminated party with due process, while termination of services by a municipally-owned utility requires some pre-termination due process.[78] Persons who find this distinction outrageous, particularly when considering a person's need for heat during the winter, should take comfort from the fact that Congress requires some type of pre-termination hearing, even for private utilities, as a matter of statute-the Public Utility Regulatory Policies Act of 1978.[79] There is an important message here for administrative law practitioners. Don't forget the legislative solution. What the Court won't give you might be obtainable from Congress.

h. *Applications for government benefits.* Note that virtually all of the cases discussed in this chapter involve the government's taking away of something already in the hands of a private citizen. Is there any requirement that the government give you due process if it is merely saying "no" to your application for an entitlement? No one can be certain. The Supreme Court has never taken up an application case, and the lower federal courts have looked at the issue with mixed results.[80]

There are a number of ways to grapple with this issue. It is arguable that when the government sets up an entitlement program with fixed criteria, a person's right to that entitlement vests, so to speak (*i.e.,* becomes a right) when the person's situation fits the criteria. For example, assume that AFDC benefits require that (1) the parent must not earn more than $6000 per year, (2) the family must consist of at least two minor children and (3) the other parent must be absent from the residence. If these are the only criteria, an applicant is eligible when his personal facts fit the criteria, not when he applies for the benefit. Thus, a denial of the benefit without some opportunity to respond might be unconstitutional. However, if an agency has discretion to deny the benefit, even if an applicant meets all the threshold criteria, as in cases involving such things as broadcast licenses, nothing "vests" until the license is actually in the hands of the private person and thus, no process is due until the license is taken away.

Another approach uses some Supreme Court language. In his separate opinion in *Arnett*,[81] Justice Marshall suggested that whenever a government agency deals adversely with a private person some process, however minimal, is due that person.

---

[78] *Compare Jackson v. Metro. Edison Co.*, 419 U.S. 345 (1974) (private utility — no due process), *with Memphis Light, Gas & Water Div. v. Craft*, 436 U.S. 1 (1978) (public utility — due process required). A federal circuit court recently determined that the American Bar Association's law school accreditation function triggered a "common law" obligation to employ fair procedures in making accreditation decisions. In this instance, the ABA was given accreditation powers by the United States Department of Education. *Thomas M. Cooley Law School v. American Bar Ass'n*, 459 F.3d 705 (6th Cir. 2006).

[79] 16 U.S.C. § 2625(g).

[80] *Compare Alexander v. Silverman*, 356 F. Supp. 1179 (E.D. Wis. 1973) (some process due when an application for AFDC benefits is rejected), *with Griffeth v. Detrich*, 448 F. Supp. 1137 (S.D. Cal. 1978) (no constitutional process due to welfare applicant). In 1996, Congress enacted the Personal Responsibility and Work Opportunity Reconciliation Act. The Act leaves unanswered questions regarding the applicability of procedural due process doctrine. *See, e.g.,* Christine N. Cimini, *Welfare Entitlements in the Era of Devolution*, 9 Geo. J. on Poverty L. & Pol'y 89 (2002).

[81] *See supra* note 42.

The final alternative is simply the negative result: no process is due in an application setting.[82]

In the context of applications for federal benefits and due process the United States Court of Appeals for the Federal Circuit has recently issued two striking decisions involving the application for veterans' benefits under the jurisdiction of the Department of Veterans Affairs. In *Cushman v. Shinseki*,[83] and *Gambill v. Shinseki*,[84] the court of appeals held that due process is required in the specific context of veterans' disability claims. Among other things, the court commented on the special, nearly paternalistic attributes of the various veterans' statutes and the various promises that are made to military veterans when they are injured in the line of duty. The *Cushman* court reviewed nearly all of the cases cited in this section, noted that the Ninth Circuit had earlier determined that due process was required,[85] and concluded: "Veteran's disability benefits are nondiscretionary, statutorily mandated benefits. A veteran is entitled to disability benefits upon a showing that he meets the eligibility requirements set forth in the governing statutes and regulations. . . . Such entitlement to benefits is a property interest protected by the Due Process Clause of the Fifth Amendment . . . ."[86]

These different approaches may all be useful in answering the primary question of whether a private person is due any process. But this is only the first question. Recall that once you resolve the *whether* question in the affirmative you must deal with the questions of *when* and *what kind.*

[C] Resolving a *When Issue*

Unlike the matter of whether a private person has a liberty/property interest at stake, the *when* and *what kind* issues are usually discussed simultaneously. They tend to blend with each other; and no one should expect to find a bright line between the two concepts. Nonetheless, they are separate inquiries, and both must be analyzed to complete the due process inquiry.

Timing of due process can best be visualized by keeping in mind the following chart:

---

[82] On the federal level, the Administrative Procedure Act requires that anyone denied a federal application or petition in whole or in part, is at least due a "brief statement of the grounds for denial." 5 U.S.C. § 555(e). But remember: this is a statutory procedure; it is not a constitutional requirement. Thus, denial of an application by a state agency may not, per se, violate Due process.

[83] 576 F.3d 1290 (Fed. Cir. 2009).

[84] 576 F.3d 1307 (Fed. Cir. 2009).

[85] *Nat'l Assn of Radiation Survivors v. Derwinski*, 994 F.2d 583 (9th Cir. 1992).

[86] *Cushman*, 576 F.3d at 1298.

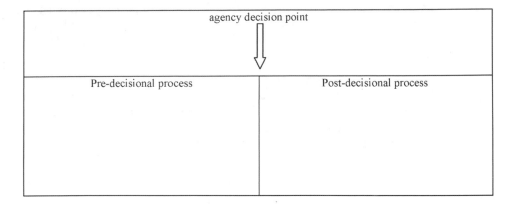

Set your fact pattern up on the chart by placing any procedures afforded by the agency prior to its making the decision on the left side of the chart and any procedures afforded after the decision is made on the right side. This allows you to compare your facts with the case law that analyzes when the process is due.

It does not, however, completely resolve the issue. The Court has never been completely clear on the timing question; but a case-by-case analysis can go a long way toward solving a new problem. To begin with, the Court now seems to be very suspicious of a total lack of due process prior to the agency decision. Note that the few cases in which the Court has permitted all the due process to be placed after the decision are the emergency cases such as *North American Cold Storage* (contaminated chickens) and *Barry v. Barchi* (jockey using drugs).

In every recent case other than *Barry*[87] there has been some due process prior to the decision. For example, in both *Arnett* and *Mathews*, pre-decisional due process consisted mainly of notice and the opportunity to comment in writing with a full-blown, trial-type proceeding following the decision. By contrast, in *Goss v. Lopez*[88] (ten-day public school suspension) and *Goldberg*, the Court insisted on pre-decisional due process without focusing on what might happen after making the decision.

The common thread in these cases is an assessment of the impact of termination on the individual. In both *Arnett* and *Mathews*, the benefits were essentially monetary and would be fully restored if the recipient prevailed in the post-decisional hearing.[89] By contrast, the Court decided that AFDC recipients might starve (remember the "brutal need" concept) if denied their benefits. *Goss* conveys a sense that lost school days are not easily made up, thereby triggering a requirement of pre-decisional due process. In *Constantineau*[90] (posting of drunk-

---

[87] 443 U.S. 55.

[88] 419 U.S. 565 (1975).

[89] A fascinating, yet unresolved, question is whether *Arnett* and *Mathews* would have been decided the same way if the only pre-decisional process the recipient received was notice of the action with reasons. *Loudermill* suggests that such action would be unconstitutional.

[90] 400 U.S. 433 (1971).

ard list), the person's reputation is injured immediately upon posting of the list. In *Morrissey*,[91] a post-decisional protest to a decision to revoke parole would have to be conducted from a jail cell. No amount of post-decisional due process can cure that sort of injury.

However, if the harm of revocation can effectively be remedied by a post-decisional hearing, the Court seems not to worry too much about what precedes the decision. But even in these cases, the Court will probably not tolerate a *total* absence of due process. If merely deciding the case adversely to the individual will have a substantial impact, the Court concentrates on what the agency provides before the decision.

Another question should be addressed at this point in the timing analysis. Occasionally, two individuals seek a government license that, for technical reasons, is mutually exclusive, such as television broadcast licenses or hydroelectric projects. If an agency hears initially from only one claimant and decides in that person's favor, the second claimant is effectively excluded from the process. The Supreme Court addressed this issue in *Ashbacker Radio Corp. v. FCC*,[92] a case in which the FCC heard from one applicant, granted the license to that applicant and then granted a hearing to the second applicant only to tell the second applicant that he could not have the license because it had already been awarded. The Court determined that an agency must hear from both applicants simultaneously in any situation involving a mutually-exclusive license in order to give both applicants a "meaningful hearing." *Ashbacker* is not a constitutional decision-the decision was based on the Court's construction of the language of the Federal Communications Act - but it is clear that the Court considers the proposition an important one. For most purposes, however, mutual exclusivity is fairly rare; thus *Ashbacker* has a relatively limited application. It is also not clear whether the present Supreme Court would have any interest in converting the *Ashbacker* concept into a matter of constitutional dimension by declaring the license a property interest, worthy of due process protection.

Most agencies deal with the problem of multiple applications for an exclusive license by announcing that they will receive applications and by establishing a cut-off date for those applications. Applicants who file after the cut-off date will not be heard; but timely applications will be heard simultaneously and will be disposed of on a comparative merit basis.[93]

[D] Resolving a *What Kind* Issue

Determining the kind of hearing given to an individual requires an analysis of all three *Mathews* factors, but concentrates mainly on the second and third factors (risk of error and government efficiency). To begin this inquiry, you should establish some generic boundaries and then proceed to a case-by-case analysis. Recall that Judge Friendly suggests that the rock-bottom minimum due process is

---

[91] 408 U.S. 471 (1972).

[92] 326 U.S. 327 (1945).

[93] *See* the Federal Communications Commission comparative hearing procedures at 47 C.F.R. §§ 1.221 *et seq.*

notice plus some opportunity to comment.[94] Whenever the *whether* question is resolved in the affirmative, at least this much must be provided.

In *Goss v. Lopez*,[95] the Court merely required notice plus an opportunity for the student to comment orally prior to suspension. The Court mentioned several times that this procedure was intended to provide at least some due process for the student while minimally interfering with the work of the school administrators. *Goss* comprises one of the shortest lists of procedures ever mandated by the Court.

The largest number of procedural elements ever required by the Court as a matter of constitutional due process is in *Goldberg* and more or less echoed in *Morrissey*. These procedures are set out in § 5.03, *above*, and include among other things, a neutral decision-maker, confrontation and an exclusive record. The generic term for such procedures is *trial-type* or *evidentiary* hearing. Language in more recent cases, such as *Mathews* and *Loudermill*, suggests that the Court at the present time has no interest in ever going beyond *Goldberg*. Indeed, the Court appears now mainly to be concerned with cutting back on *Goldberg* without actually overruling the case. Consider the following chart.

Interests and Procedures		
Minimum	Intermediate[96]	Maximum
(Notice & opportunity to comment)	(Notice, opportunity to comment, and something additional)	(Trial-type hearing)
1. school suspension 2. drunkard list[97]	1. civil service termination 2. academic suspension 3. prison discipline 4. social security disability 5. termination of utility services 6. revocation of de facto tenure 7. driver's license revocation	1. AFDC benefits 2. parole revocation 3. probation revocation

Once the boundaries of due process have been established, problem solving is simply a matter of fitting the new fact pattern in between *Goldberg* and *Goss*, with the understanding that for most agency actions the Court will likely not go as far as *Goldberg* in writing new procedures but probably will require something more

---

[94] *See, e.g.*, Henry J. Friendly, *Some Kind of Hearing*, 123 U. Pa. L. Rev. 1267 (1973).

[95] These procedures require something more than minimal notice and comment but less than those required by *Goldberg*. Each case has to be closely examined for the precise procedures required in each instance.

[96] These procedures require something more than minimal notice and comment but less than those required by *Goldberg*. Each case has to be closely examined for the precise procedures required in each instance.

[97] To be completely accurate, the Court in *Constantineau* held only that the total absence of process violated the Fourteenth Amendment. It did suggest that notice and some opportunity to comment would be required.

than the minimalist procedures of *Goss*. Moreover, the timing question blends into this inquiry. One of the reasons the Court tolerated the minimal pre-decisional procedures in *Arnett* and *Mathews* is because a trial-type hearing was granted after termination in a setting where full benefits could be restored retroactively.

No one can say with certainty where any new case will fit on the chart, although the obvious trend of the Court is away from elaborate constitutionally-mandated procedures. Fewer, rather than more, procedures seem to be the current rule.

Most of the preceding discussion has focused on the minimum due process procedures required by the Constitution. A legislature may grant far more procedures than the Court has ever required. For example, the trial-type procedures written into the Federal Administrative Procedure Act contain several more elements (testimony under oath, verbatim transcript and a truly independent administrative law judge) than the Court wrote into *Goldberg*.[98] Even in the absence of a statute, an agency, as a matter of its own discretion, can give persons more due process than the Constitution requires. Many federal agencies go even beyond the APA's procedural requirements to provide for pre-hearing discovery, rules of evidence, a highly structured intra-agency appellate process and the like. *Goldberg* and its progeny are important mainly because the cases set a national minimum for all administrative agencies wherever located.

§ 5.06   SUBSTANTIVE DUE PROCESS IN ADMINISTRATIVE LAW

[A]   Substantive Due process Generally

Constitutional law courses teach us that government action must be not only procedurally correct, but also must be based on intrinsically fair requirements. We usually refer to this concept of intrinsic fairness as *substantive due process*. There are some striking new developments in this field, discussed in subsection [B] *below*; but traditionally, substantive due process has not had much of an impact on administrative law mainly because there are other, more powerful doctrines that supplant it. As an example, the delegation doctrine requires an intelligible standard for agency behavior. The *ultra vires* doctrine requires an agency to stay within the boundaries of its enabling act. The APA requires an agency to give reasons for its actions. Those reasons, to a certain extent, are subject to examination by reviewing courts. There are numerous other principles discussed elsewhere in this book that constrain substantive agency action.

While court-developed concepts, such as *stare decisis*, *res judicata* and estoppel, have little utility in agency practice, agencies are held to some degree of definiteness and consistency in their policymaking, whether the policy is made by rule or through successive adjudications. For example, the Supreme Court reversed the Interstate Commerce Commission's approval of railroads' charging grain shippers an additional fee for inspection of the shipments when the prior

---

[98] *Compare Goldberg with* §§ 556–557 of the APA. *Compare Bi-Metallic with* the rulemaking procedures set out in § 553 of the APA.

policy had required that these charges be absorbed in the basic freight rate. The Court stated:

> There is, then, at least a presumption that . . . the settled rule [will be] adhered to. From this presumption flows the agency's duty to explain its departure from prior norms . . . . Whatever the ground for the departure from prior norms, however, it must be clearly set forth so that the review court may understand the basis of the agency's action and so may judge the consistency of that action with the agency's mandate.[99]

However, because this reasoning is based on statutory standards of review set out in the APA, it is difficult to elevate them to constitutional doctrine. Even so, definiteness and consistency also have roots in the concept of fundamental fairness, a central ingredient of due process.

Some courts in reviewing agency policymaking have suggested that the *void for vagueness* doctrine may have some applicability to agency rulemaking. In other words, an agency's rules may be constitutionally defective if they are not written with sufficient precision and accuracy. The dissenters in *Boyce Motor Lines, Inc. v. United States*[100] insisted that the regulation under review was excessively vague and that it was in the public interest and the interest of justice "to pronounce this vague regulation invalid." At least one lower federal court has held a state university regulation authorizing sanctions for misconduct void as a violation of the Fourteenth Amendment's due process Clause.[101]

A practitioner cannot rely heavily on these doctrines, however. Probably the better part of wisdom is to master the principles applicable to agency rulemaking discussed in the next chapter in order to be able to effectively participate in the policymaking process.

[B] The Impact of the "Takings" Doctrine

In recent years, the Supreme Court has breathed some life into a constitutional doctrine that flows directly from the Fifth and Fourteenth Amendments' due process clauses. Recall that the Constitution prohibits both the federal and state governments from *taking* private property without due process and just compensation. For years, most administrative law scholars and practitioners paid little attention to this doctrine in the context of government regulation. The standard assumption was that the mere imposition of government regulations had absolutely nothing to do with an unconstitutional taking of private property.

This assumption is gradually shifting, however, because of a number of Supreme Court decisions. In one of the more prominent cases, *Lucas v. South Carolina Coastal Council*,[102] the Court reviewed an interesting fact pattern that emerged from David Lucas' ownership of two residential lots on the beach in South Carolina.

---

[99] *Atchison, Topeka & Santa Fe Ry. Co. v. Wichita Bd. of Trade*, 412 U.S. 800 (1973).

[100] 342 U.S. 337 (1952).

[101] *Soglin v. Kauffman*, 295 F. Supp. 978 (E.D. Wis. 1968), *aff'd*, 418 F.2d 163 (7th Cir. 1969).

[102] 505 U.S. 1003 (1992).

Lucas intended to construct single family homes on this property, but before he could do so, the South Carolina legislature enacted a statute that prohibited the erection of any "habitable" structures on that portion of beach. Lucas challenged this regulation in court, arguing that the total prohibition rendered his property worthless for any economic purposes. The state argued that the statute was an environmental protection measure designed to prevent further erosion and deterioration of the beach itself and thus, fully permissible as an act of government. The trial court determined that the statute had the effect of making Lucas' property "valueless."

On review by the Supreme Court, the Court addressed squarely the issue of whether the statute constituted an unconstitutional taking in violation of the due process clause. In a lengthy opinion for the six member majority, Justice Scalia reviewed a great deal of the Court's existing takings case law and concluded that on remand the state courts must consider whether the action constitutes an impermissible taking on grounds different from those originally articulated by the lower courts.

In *Lucas*, Justice Scalia observed that the original view was that this portion of the constitution was violated only if there was an actual expropriation of the land in question, as opposed to mere government interference with the use of the property.[103] However, in 1922, the Court opened the window just slightly in *Pennsylvania Coal Co. v. Mahon*,[104] a case in which Justice Holmes recognized that there must be certain limits placed on a state's interference with the use of private property if the takings clause was to have any reasonable impact on governmental activity. But, as Justice Scalia stated in *Lucas*, the *Mahon* case was not really helpful in figuring out when the government has gone "too far" in its regulation. Indeed, until just recently the Court refused to formulate any kind of test for these actions, preferring that such issues be dealt with on a case-by-case basis. As might be expected, the Court granted review in very few takings cases, creating a climate in which virtually everyone-lower courts, practitioners and academics-believed that the entire doctrine was moribund, if not completely dead.

In 1987, that opinion began to shift when the Court decided a trilogy of takings cases in a single term.[105] The tensions are obvious: a landowner normally wishes to receive some economic benefit from his or her land ownership. At the same time, the government cannot be prevented from regulating some of the more damaging aspects of private land use (in the Court's words, the regulation of "harmful or noxious uses").

---

[103] *See, e.g., Legal Tender Cases*, 12 Wall. 457 (1871).

[104] 260 U.S. 393 (1922).

[105] *First Evangelical Lutheran Church of Glendale v. County of Los Angeles*, 482 U.S. 304 (1987) (even temporary deprivations of the use of land may constitute a compensable taking); *Keystone Bituminous Coal Ass'n v. DeBenedictis*, 480 U.S. 470 (1987) (where all beneficial or productive use of the land is denied, a taking may have occurred); *Nollan v. California Coastal Comm'n*, 483 U.S. 825 (1987) (essentially the same holding as *Keystone*). Note, of course, that these are only three of many Supreme Court takings decisions. The striking feature is that the Court felt compelled to take and decide three such cases in a single term. For further analysis of these cases, *see* Cass R. Sunstein, *Takings: Descent and Resurrection*, 1987 SUP. CT. REV. 1.

In *Lucas*, the Court was unwilling to characterize the South Carolina statute as a taking under the current posture of the case. Instead, the Court has essentially reformulated the necessary inquiry and remanded the case for further proceedings, thereby creating what Justice Scalia calls a "total taking inquiry" that requires reviewing courts to conduct a deep and searching examination of both the nature of the government regulation and the legal basis for that regulation. In the Court's words, government regulations that comprise a total deprivation of economically beneficial use of private property "must inhere in the title [to the land] itself, in the restrictions that background principles of the State's law of property and nuisance already place on land ownership."[106] Put in the context of the *Lucas* case: "[T]o win its case South Carolina must do more than proffer the legislature's declaration that the uses Lucas desires are inconsistent with the public interest, or the conclusory assertion that they violate a common-law . . . . South Carolina must identify background principles of nuisance and property law that prohibit the uses he now intends in the circumstances in which the property is presently found. Only on this showing can the State fairly claim that, in proscribing all such beneficial uses, the [statute] is taking nothing."[107]

The Court continues to develop a modern doctrine of takings. In 2005, in *Kelo v. City of New London*,[108] looked at takings in the context of eminent domain in circumstances in which a city took property from a property owner and then gave that same property to another private person. The reason advanced by the city was that it was pursuing a redevelopment plan for that particular area of the city and that the second property owner was better positioned to assist in this effort. The Supreme Court upheld the taking, pointing out that the constitution does not prohibit such action but inviting, in the opinion of Justice Stevens, state and local legislative action that could place limitations on this type of taking. *Kelo* generated a fury of negative commentary in the popular press and led to an attempt by some petitioners in Justice Souter's hometown to seize his home by eminent domain and give it to a private company who would build a luxury hotel on the property called the "Lost Liberty Hotel."[109] However, most legal scholars commenting on the case believe that it is fully consistent with takings precedent.

A takings case, *Lingle v. Chevron USA*,[110] decided just a month before *Kelo* involved a very different issue. In *Lingle*, the Hawaii legislature enacted a statute that limited the rent oil companies were permitted to charge gasoline service station operators who leased company-owned stations.[111] Chevron, one of the largest oil companies in Hawaii, challenged the enactment as an unconstitutional taking. Writing for a unanimous Court, Justice O'Connor discerned two separate categories for *per se* takings. The first category comprises instances in which the

---

[106] 505 U.S. at 1029.

[107] *Id.* at 1029–30.

[108] 545 U.S. 469 (2005).

[109] Beverly Wang, *For Souter, Seizure Ruling May Hit Home*, WASH. POST, July 25, 2005, at A4.

[110] 544 U.S. 528 (2005).

[111] Among other things, the Hawaii statute limited rents that Chevron could charge to 15 percent of a dealer's gross profits from gasoline sales plus 15 percent of the dealer's gross profits from sales of other than gasoline. *Id.* at 533.

government causes a property owner "to suffer a permanent physical invasion of her property – however minor."[112] When the government engages in such a taking it must provide just compensation. The second category is typified by *Lucas* and other cases and comprises instances when the government issues rules "that completely deprive an owner of '*all* economically beneficial use' of her property."[113] Apart from per se takings, the Court has established standards that require factor analysis. The most important of these factors is "the economic impact of the regulation on the claimant and, particularly, the extent to which the regulation has interfered with distinct investment-backed expectations."[114]

In ruling against Chevron, the Court rejected language that it had previously used to evaluate these claims (whether the taking "substantially advances" legitimate state interests) — Chevron had argued that the rent statute did not do so — and identified essentially four instances when a plaintiff could assert an unconstitutional taking: (1) an actual "physical" taking; (2) "a Lucas-type 'total regulatory taking', (3) a interference-with-expectations taking, or (4) "land-use exaction" taking.[115]

It appears that the Court is engaged in a major restatement, if not a refashioning, of its takings jurisprudence. It does appear to be writing a whole new chapter on substantive due process.[116]

---

[112] *Id.* at 538. The Court cites *Loretto v. Teleprompter Manhattan CATV Corp.*, 458 U.S. 419 (1982), as an example of this category.

[113] *Id.* (emphasis in the original).

[114] *Id.* at 538–39. Justice O'Connor cited *Penn Central Transp. Co. v. New York City*, 438 U.S. 104 (1978), for this proposition.

[115] *Id.* at 548.

[116] For a discussion on the recent developments in substantive due process jurisprudence and takings cases, *see, e.g.*, Gregory M. Stein, *Takings in the 21st Century: Reasonable Investment-Backed Expectations After* Palazzolo *and* Tahoe-Sierra, 69 TENN. L. REV. 891 (2002); Steven J. Eagle, *Substantive Due Process and Regulatory Takings: A Reappraisal*, 51 ALA. L. REV. 977 (2000); *Tahoe-Sierra Preserv. v. Tahoe Reg. Planning*, 535 U.S. 302 (2002); *Palazzolo v. Rhode Island*, 533 U.S. 606 (2001); *Boise Cascade Corp. v. U.S.*, 296 F.3d 1339 (Fed. Cir. 2002).

Chapter 6

AGENCY DECISION-MAKING: CHOOSING RULE OR ORDER

§ 6.01 INTRODUCTION

This chapter begins an analysis of material that is central to most law school courses in administrative law and crucial to an administrative law practitioner. Agencies conduct their business by making decisions. Lawyers need to know a great deal about how agencies make those decisions. Sometimes the decisions have broad policy implications for all persons who are regulated by the agency. Sometimes the decisions affect only a single individual.

On the federal level, most agencies have a national jurisdiction and, by definition, have large numbers of persons and companies under their control. Consider, for example, the millions of people affected by the Social Security Administration and the Internal Revenue Service, or the thousands of firms regulated by the Securities and Exchange Commission. Because agencies are generally required to treat similarly situated persons in a consistent manner, even agency pronouncements that seem to affect only one person may in reality reflect broader agency policy. As a consequence, most lawyers who practice before any of the federal agencies pay close attention to virtually anything the agency says, irrespective of either the label that the pronouncement carries or the person to whom that pronouncement is addressed. In other words, in practice you typically heed every nuance and pay attention to every raised eyebrow on the part of the agency. Even decisions nominally limited to a single fact pattern and a single individual may be very helpful in predicting future agency behavior. An appreciation of the subtleties of an agency's behavior is what separates the skilled agency practitioner from the merely mediocre.

This same rule — that you do not disregard anything an agency says — holds true for state administrative agencies, even though one of the primary difficulties in some state administrative practices is obtaining information from the agency. Some states, for example, have no general requirement that agency rules or decisions be published. By contrast, federal agencies generate so much material that the information is nearly impossible to collate and index, much less to master in its entirety.

Most federal and state agencies use two procedural vehicles for announcing agency policy: (1) a rule making or (2) an adjudication. This chapter begins our general policy-making analysis by examining the limitations on an agency's decision whether to choose a rule or an order (the outcome of an adjudication) to announce major policy decisions. The place to begin is with a familiar case. *Humphrey's*

Executor v. United States[1] established the fundamental authority of agencies to exercise both judicial and legislative powers — *i.e.*, by deciding individual cases (adjudication) or by making rules (rulemaking). *National Petroleum Refiners Asso. v. FTC*[2] established the authority of an agency (the Federal Trade Commission) to make agency policy by promulgating substantive rules, even though the FTC's enabling act was unclear as to its rulemaking authority, and even though the agency had never made rules in the first fifty years or so of its existence.

These days most agencies use an amalgam of rules and adjudication for policy-making. Their choices as to rule or order are normally let alone by the courts. But there is a lingering question, even now not fully resolved by the Supreme Court of the United States, as to whether an agency *must* choose rulemaking over adjudication, or vice versa. For all practical purposes, the agency is free to choose either vehicle, but the Court has hinted from time to time that the preferable course of action for announcing new policy is through the rulemaking process. The case law in this area is not terribly complicated, but it is sometimes difficult to understand without grasping some of the elementary distinctions between a rule (the outcome of a rulemaking) and an order (the outcome of an agency adjudication).

§ 6.02   SOME BASIC DISTINCTIONS BETWEEN A RULE AND AN ORDER

On the federal level, *rule* and *order* are defined by the Administrative Procedure Act. Under § 551(4), a rule is "the whole or part of an agency statement of *general* or *particular* applicability and *future effect* designed to implement, interpret, or *prescribe law or policy* or describing the organization, procedure, or practice requirements of an agency . . . ." (emphasis added). This chapter will concentrate on the use of rules or orders to make policy, rather than the use of these devices to prescribe agency procedures.

Basic rulemaking procedure on the federal level is a relatively simple notice and comment process. An agency announces a proposed rule, receives and considers comments from interested persons on that rule, and promulgates a final rule, normally effective no sooner than thirty days after the final rule is announced.[3] While this process has been strongly criticized for being too relaxed, it has the advantages of permitting any interested person (virtually anyone who cares to write into the agency) to comment on a proposed rule, requires the agency at least to consider the comments and then provides a lag-time of thirty days before the final rule goes into effect.

The final rule, in most instances, must be published in the *Federal Register*, so everyone in the United States, at least in theory, receives notice of the rule at the time of its publication. An agency rule is the direct analog of a congressional statute and is read and interpreted in much the same fashion as statutes. To state the advantages more colloquially, a person regulated by an agency has at least thirty

---

[1]   295 U.S. 602 (1935) (discussed at length in Chapter 3, § 3.03).

[2]   482 F.2d 672 (D.C. Cir. 1973) (discussed at length in Chapter 4, § 4.03).

[3]   3 APA § 553. For more on rulemaking procedure, *see* Chapter 7, § 7.02, *below.*

days to clean up his act before finding himself in violation of some new agency policy if that policy is announced in a rulemaking.

The definition of *order* is essentially a residual definition — *i.e.*, an order is an agency decision that is not a rule. Section 551(6) of the APA defines order as: "the whole or part of a final disposition, whether affirmative, negative, injunctive, or declaratory in form, of an agency in a matter *other than* rulemaking but including licensing" (emphasis added). Given such a broad definition, it is difficult to itemize all of the possible routes for obtaining an agency order.

Viewed in terms of procedure, an order is the outcome of an *adjudication*. The adjudication can be either a *trial-type proceeding* (sometimes referred to as an evidentiary hearing)[4] or what many law professors choose to call *informal adjudication*.[5] The Achilles' heel of adjudication is twofold: first, it frequently involves only a small number of participants; and second, orders are not normally required to be published in the *Federal Register* in the same fashion as proposed rules. While many agencies regularly announce their orders, and while many proprietary information services publish almost everything an agency issues, agency orders carry few formal publication requirements. Because agency orders are typically written in the same form as judicial opinions, spotting a new agency policy when the announcement of that new policy is buried in an order forces a lawyer to resort to common law techniques for analyzing cases. You have to worry about which language is *holding*, which is *dicta*, whether new case X overrules old case Z and the like. Worst of all, the grain of the new policy can get drowned in the chaff of a factual recitation. Highly experienced agency lawyers (those attorneys mentioned above who grasp all the nuances of an agency) will spot these changes easily. Neophyte lawyers have a much harder time identifying new policy in the context of adjudication. Lay persons are almost never aware of the impact of an agency order unless it happens to affect them personally.

Comparing rules and orders, it is not difficult to understand why rulemaking is usually viewed as a superior device for announcing agency policy. The legislative history of the Federal APA demonstrates that the entire APA was molded around the distinctions between rules and orders. The drafters of the APA expected that rules would be the vehicle "primarily concerned with policy considerations."[6] An

---

[4] Discussed extensively in Chapter 8.

[5] Informal adjudication is discussed in Chapter 9. It is not a term of art in administrative practice. Think of informal adjudication as an agency decision that results from a process that is *neither* a rulemaking nor a trial-type proceeding. For a discussion on how an emergence of informal, non-adversarial procedures in adjudications as well as the rise of rulemaking have contributed to the growth of administrative state, *see* Richard E. Levy & Sidney A. Shapiro, *Special Issue on the History of the Trial: Administrative Procedure and the Decline of the Trial*, 51 KAN. L. REV. 473 (2003).

[6] ATTORNEY GENERAL'S MANUAL ON THE ADMINISTRATIVE PROCEDURE ACT 9 (1947). This distinction, of course, is not the only basis for drafting an administrative procedure act. The Florida APA (seen by many as a very progressive and innovative statute) chooses to base most of its central distinctions on whether an agency action substantially affects individuals irrespective of the label, *rule* or *order*, that is placed on the procedure at issue. If the action has a substantial effect on private persons, the agency may be forced to conduct more formal proceedings to reach its decision. Fla. Stat. § 120.54. *See also* William F. Fox, Jr. & Leonard Carlson, *A Comparison of the Federal and Florida Systems of Administrative Procedure*, 1980 FLA. B.J. 699. A new Model State Administrative Procedure Act was promulgated in 2010 (See the

APA adjudication, by contrast, was viewed primarily as a device for applying agency policy to individual cases.

Many agencies, however, do not heed this admonition. Both before and after the enactment of the APA, the National Labor Relations Board and the Federal Trade Commission, among others, assiduously avoided rulemaking and continued to announce all of their policy in adjudications.[7] The issue of whether an agency might be compelled to make a rule rather than proceed by order did not come to a head until the late 1940s when the Supreme Court reviewed one of the most intricate cases in administrative law.

§ 6.03   THE SUPREME COURT'S VIEW: *CHENERY* AND *WYMAN-GORDON*

The landmark case, *SEC v. Chenery Corp.*,[8] grew out of the Securities and Exchange Commission's exercise of its authority under an obscure New Deal statute, the Public Utility Holding Company Act.[9] This statute gives the SEC the power to police mergers and acquisitions among large holding companies that had gobbled up many of the nation's private utilities after the First World War.

There are many ways to read *Chenery*. For one thing, it is a good example of the lengths to which people will go to pursue an argument when there is a great deal of money at stake. It tells us a lot about protracted administrative litigation and those things that can happen to a case when the case itself outlives agency commissioners and Supreme Court justices. The full *Chenery* road map looks like this:

---

full-text in Appendix B). In the 1981 version of the MSAA, section 2-104(4), the Act recommends that an agency "as soon as feasible and to the extent practicable, adopt rules to supersede principles of law or policy lawfully declared by the agency as the basis for its decisions in particular cases." The commentary in the 1981 version of the MSAPA is much more forceful than anything seen in the decisions of the United States Supreme Court:

"Only by the enactment of a statutory provision [such as] recommended here, therefore, can agencies be forced to codify in rules principles of law or policy they may lawfully declare in decisions in particular cases . . . Without such a provision they will be free, in many situations, to make their most controversial policies on a case-by-case basis in adjudications, and thereby avoid on a permanent basis rulemaking procedures and legislative and gubernatorial review."

Commissioners' Comment to the MSAPA.

[7] Two superior articles on this topic are: Colin S. Diver, *Policymaking Paradigms in Administrative Law*, 95 HARV. L. REV. 393 (1981), and the classic in the field, David Shapiro, *The Choice of Rulemaking or Adjudication in the Development of Administrative Policy*, 78 HARV. L. REV. 921 (1965).

[8] 332 U.S. 194 (1947). This case is *Chenery II*. The case discussed below, known as *Chenery I*, can be found at 318 U.S. 80 (1943). The case referred to as *Chenery III* (the final denial of certiorari by the Supreme Court) is found at 340 U.S. 831 (1950).

[9] 15 U.S.C. §§ 79h *et seq.*

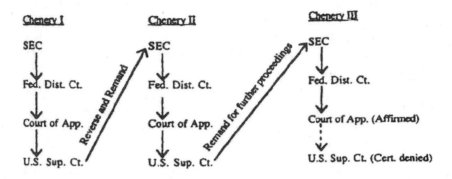

This chapter deals mainly with what the Supreme Court had to say about rule versus order in *Chenery II*, but an analysis of that decision requires a quick explanation of *Chenery I*.

In *Chenery I*, an existing utility holding company, called the Federal Water Service Corporation, wanted to reorganize into the Federal Water and Gas Corporation. The officers of the existing company filed an elaborate reorganization plan with the SEC. The SEC was required to police and approve such mergers under the Public Utility Holding Company Act. After a lengthy analysis of the proposed reorganization plan, the SEC objected to a portion of the plan by which the officers of the original corporation would be permitted to buy preferred stock in the original corporation (Federal Water Service) that, under the reorganization plan, would have been converted into the common stock of the reorganized holding company (Federal Water & Gas).

Most first-time readers of *Chenery* become intimidated at this point because they are not securities regulation experts. There's really no need to feel embarrassed; most administrative lawyers are just as much at sea because securities law is such a highly specialized practice. Stated a little more colloquially, the corporate officers expected to make a financial killing when the company was reorganized. It was a sweetheart deal for the officers, most likely at the expense of the regular shareholders of the existing company. Worse yet, there was obviously a great deal of money at stake here; the road map alone should tell you that.[10] The SEC determined that these officers were fiduciaries of the old company's shareholders and should not be permitted to profit personally from the reorganization to the possible detriment of the shareholders. In other words, their primary loyalty should be to the shareholders and not to their own pocketbooks. After the SEC objected, the reorganization plan was amended to prohibit the officers from converting their

---

[10] It is always helpful to try to look behind the printed appellate opinions in any casebook to try to determine exactly why people are angry with each other and why they are contending so strenuously before the agency and later in court. This behind-the-scenes analysis is really the only way anyone can understand how the lawyers in the case began thinking through the dispute. Litigation is incredibly costly these days and was similarly expensive in the 1940s. *Chenery* was not a *pro bono* or *in forma pauperis* case, so it is clear that large amounts of money were involved. Knowing this may help explain a great deal about this case that is not found in any of the *Chenery* opinions.

preferred shares. The SEC then approved the reorganization plan. That order of approval was based on a number of court decisions that discussed the *common law* of corporate fiduciary responsibilities, without paying any attention to the statutes and legislative history underlying the SEC's authority. The disgruntled officers then took the SEC to court.

In *Chenery I*, the Supreme Court held that the use of court decisions as the basis for the SEC's order was wrong because, in the Court's opinion, the SEC had misinterpreted the thrust of those decisions. The cases relied on by the SEC forbade officers to trade in stock of their own company only in instances in which there was fraud or mismanagement on the part of the officers. There was no such fraud or mismanagement here. On top of that, the Court noted that the SEC had never issued any *rule* forbidding this type of trading activity. Because the court decisions were inapposite, and because the agency had not previously announced a rule on point, the Court remanded the case to the SEC for further proceedings.

On remand, the SEC arrived at the same conclusion as it had the first time. It disapproved the reorganization so long as the corporate officers were permitted to convert their preferred shares to common stock in the new company. But this time the SEC, as the Court put it in *Chenery II*, "recast" its decision in terms of the language, purpose and legislative history of the Securities Act. It did not rely on common law fiduciary principles. The losing parties attacked this new determination, arguing that the SEC had only two choices on remand:

1. The Commission could issue a rule forbidding this type of officer trading. The rule would, of course, be purely prospective and thereby could not govern the reorganization of Federal Water Service; or

2. It could approve the reorganization as proposed.

In *Chenery II*, the Supreme Court upheld the Commission's action in an extraordinarily long and cumbersome opinion — that, by the way, led to Justice Jackson's famous pronouncement in dissent: "I give up. Now I realize fully what Mark Twain meant when he said, 'The more you explain it, the more I don't understand it.' " It takes some work to sift through the opinion to find the nugget affecting the rule versus order issue. The Court concluded that an agency could choose either rule or order as the vehicle for announcing new policy "in its informed discretion." The Court concluded that the new SEC rationale for its decision was satisfactory and that a new order was sufficient. In other words, the Commission did not have to promulgate a rule on corporate officer trading before it enforced its new policy in an adjudication, in this instance the *Chenery* adjudication.

The Court paid lip service to the APA's strong suggestion that agencies ought to use rules to announce new policy. But it recognized that there might be times when the agency would have to confront problems that it simply had not foreseen and thus, had not covered by rule. There may be other instances when the problems addressed by the agency are too specialized to permit a good rule to be drafted. As the Court noted: "In those situations, the agency must retain power to deal with the problem on a case-to-case basis if the administrative process is to be effective." Justice Jackson, in dissent, was far more cynical. He maintained that the only way to explain the difference in result between *Chenery I* and *Chenery II* was the intervening change in Supreme Court personnel.[11]

Even then, the losing parties in *Chenery II* were not satisfied and went back to the Commission on many of the same theories. After further SEC action, *Chenery III* made it to the Third Circuit, which upheld the Commission's action on the precedent of *Chenery II*, and four years after deciding *Chenery II*, the Supreme Court denied certiorari in *Chenery III*.

There are legitimate explanations for the *Chenery* decision without resorting to the cynicism of Justice Jackson. The Supreme Court was not that many years removed from the trauma of the *Panama* and *Schechter* decisions and the controversy of President Roosevelt's court-packing bill (discussed in Chapter 2, § 2.02). The SEC was one of the principal New Deal agencies, and the Public Utility Holding Company Act (the statute governing the Chenery dispute was viewed at the time as an important tool for breaking up some unusually large and very powerful energy conglomerates, over which the states were exercising no meaningful control. Remember that the *Chenery* controversy started in the early 1940s when the power of the SEC was just being established, even though the case took well over ten years to resolve completely.

Finally, the APA itself was new. It went into effect only one year prior to the *Chenery II* decision and had not yet been fully explicated by the courts. Older agencies, such as the FTC, had rarely promulgated rules and still functioned effectively. While the *legislative history* of the APA strongly suggests using rules to make policy, it's hard to find that strong a command in the language of the statute itself.

Matters remained unchanged for over twenty years. The SEC promulgated more and more rules, as did most of the other agencies. There were a few notable holdouts, however. The National Labor Relations Board, even to this day, prefers not to make policy through substantive rules. By 1969, the NLRB had practically twisted itself into a pretzel by its steadfast refusal to make rules.

In 1969, the Board was taken to the Supreme Court in *NLRB v. Wyman-Gordon Co.*[12] The tensions inherent in the *Wyman-Gordon* controversy become apparent when you consider some basic concepts of judicial decision making. Recall that when a court decides a case, it may frame its decision (more accurately, the disposition of the case) in one of three ways. It may:

1. Make the decision applicable to the parties to the case and to future persons similarly situated through the doctrine of *stare decisis*;

2. Make the decision prospective only (*i.e.*, applicable to persons in the future, but not applicable to the parties who brought the lawsuit); or

3. Make the decision fully retroactive.

Alternative Number One is classic common law judicial method. But some people are troubled by this method when a court decides to change one of its decisional

---

[11] Three *Chenery I* justices, namely Stone, Roberts and Byrnes, had departed and were replaced by Vinson, Burton and Rutledge.

[12] 394 U.S. 759 (1969).

principles. Consider, for example, the principle of law controlling the effectiveness of an acceptance in contract law. Assume that two people, Smith and Jones, have entered into a contract in a jurisdiction that has traditionally followed the principle that an acceptance is effective only upon receipt by the offeror. Smith and Jones get into a dispute as to whether a contract has been formed, and the case eventually gets to the state supreme court. Assume that the court has decided to adopt the so-called mailbox principle — i.e., that acceptance is effective upon posting, rather than upon receipt — and to announce that new principle in *Smith v. Jones*. If the court uses the common law method for announcing the new principle, one of the parties to the law suit is going to be penalized by her good faith reliance on the old rule. In all likelihood, the loser in the case will have had no advance warning that the reviewing court was going to change its mind on the doctrine of acceptance of offers. Such a result may not seem entirely fair to onlookers.[13]

Consider alternative Number Two. What if the court announces the new principle as purely prospective-i.e., not governing *Smith v. Jones* but controlling on all cases in the future?[14] There are two possible problems here. If the new principle is effective as soon as the *Smith v. Jones* opinion is published, some people who are just entering into contracts and who don't know about the decision might be hurt. More importantly, consider common law legal method. A statement in an opinion that is not necessary to the disposition of the case before the court is considered *dicta*, not holding, and under the doctrine of *stare decisis*, is not binding on any future court, including the court that announced the new principle. Even a slight change in court personnel before that court gets the chance to convert dicta to holding might kill the new principle.

---

[13] Professor Russell Weaver takes issue with the notion that such process is always unfair to some people. He comments:

> [The] process of rule creation and retroactive application is not always unfair. Unfairness depends on the extent to which the interpretation is novel and unanticipated, as well as on the severity of its impact. Retroactive application might be particularly necessary or appropriate when an initial interpretation proves to be totally unworkable or permits wholesale evasion of regulatory requirements. In such a situation, it may be desirable to replace that interpretation with a new one. It may also be appropriate to purge the initial interpretation immediately, especially if it produces particularly anomalous or undesirable results.

Russell L. Weaver, *Retroactive Regulatory Interpretations: An Analysis of Judicial Responses*, 61 NOTRE DAME L. REV. 167 (1986). For an interesting student article analyzing rule versus order in the context of a recent D.C. Circuit decision, *see* Kieran Ringgenberg, Comment, United States v. Chrysler: *The Conflict Between Fair Warning and Adjudicative Retroactivity in D.C. Circuit Administrative Law*, 74 N.Y.U. L. REV. 914 (1999). One author argues that the fairness concern is the only one justifying a judicial review of the agency's rulemaking/adjudication; William D. Araiza, *Agency Adjudication, the Importance of Facts, and the Limitations of Labels*, 57 WASH & LEE L. REV. 351 (2000). *See also* Jason Nichols, *"Sorry! What the Regulation Really Means Is . . .": Administrative Agencies' Ability to Alter an Existing Regulatory Landscape Through Reinterpretation of Rules*, 8 TEX. L. REV. 951 (2002). For additional, extensive commentary on *Chenery, see* Russell L. Weaver & Linda D. Jellum, *Chenery II and the Development of Federal Administrative Law*, 58 ADMIN. L. REV. 815 (2006).

[14] There is some fresh authority suggesting that Article III of the United States Constitution may not permit a purely prospective court by an Article III federal court decision. These issues were addressed in two recent cases, *Reynoldsville Casket Co. v. Hyde*, 514 U.S. 749 (1995), and *Harper v. Va. Dep't of Taxation*, 509 U.S. 86 (1993). In the *Harper* opinion, the Supreme Court stated: "When this Court applies a rule of federal law to the parties before it, that rule is the controlling interpretation of federal law and must be given full retroactive effect in all cases still open on direct review and as to all events, regardless of whether such events predate or postdate our announcement of the rule." 509 U.S. at 96.

With regard to alternative Number Three, even when a court renders a decision, very few judicial decisions are ever made fully retroactive. The Supreme Court sometimes makes a decision fully retroactive based upon the notion that the Court does not "make" constitutional rights but merely "discovers" rights in the Constitution itself. For example, the classic right to counsel case, *Gideon v. Wainwright*,[15] is one of the few Court decisions made retroactive. Fully retroactive *agency* action is even more unusual. A few agencies have tried it, usually without success.[16]

These were the choices confronting the NLRB in *Excelsior Underwear, Inc.*[17] decided just prior to the decision in *Wyman-Gordon*. In *Excelsior*, the Board decided that it would be a good idea for employers to provide to union organizers a list of the names and addresses of employees who are eligible to vote in what is frequently referred to as a unit election. These elections, with votes cast by eligible employees, determine whether the employees want a union and which union they prefer to represent them. Because the NLRB at that time did not make substantive rules, it announced in the *Excelsior* adjudication, a brand new principle. In the future, a failure to furnish a list of employees would be deemed an unfair labor practice leading to sanctions against the employer. However, because the Board sympathized with the Excelsior Company — a company that had obviously relied on the absence of any such principle when it engaged in the collective bargaining at issue — the Board made the disclosure of the list of employees mandatory only for *future* bargaining unit elections and not to the party to the adjudication. Even though the employee-disclosure requirement has become known to labor lawyers as the *Excelsior* list, the new requirement was never imposed on the Excelsior Company itself.

When the Wyman-Gordon Corporation became involved in a union election, the company refused to give over the list. Brought before the Board in an enforcement action and charged with an unfair labor practice, the company argued that the *Excelsior* list requirement was not enforceable agency policy. The requirement was not binding as an *order* because it had not been made applicable to the Excelsior Company in the *Excelsior* adjudication, and thus had no *stare decisis* effect. Moreover, the requirement of an employee list had never been properly promulgated as a *rule* so it had no future effect as an agency rule. In a plurality opinion, the Supreme Court reiterated the *Chenery* principle — that the choice of rule or order for policy making was within the agency's informed discretion — and upheld the Board's action.

---

[15] 372 U.S. 335 (1963).

[16] In 1988, the Supreme Court reviewed a rule promulgated by the Department of Health and Human Services purporting to have retroactive effect, and concluded that the rule could not be applied retroactively. *Bowen v. Georgetown Univ. Hosp.*, 488 U.S. 204 (1988) (discussed at greater length in Chapter 7, § 7.09). *Bowen* contained a strong general pronouncement: "Retroactivity is not favored in the law." *Id.* at 208. *See, e.g.*, the discussion of retroactivity in an agency setting in *Retail, Wholesale and Dep't Store Union v. NLRB*, 466 F.2d 380 (D.C. Cir. 1972), and *Mobil Oil Corp. v. Dep't of Energy*, 647 F.2d 142 (Temp. Emer. Ct. App. 1981). In a separate opinion in *Bowen*, Justice Scalia has suggested that the obverse is equally true. Reviewing the line of cases discussed in this chapter, particularly the *Wyman-Gordon* case, Justice Scalia believes that *Wyman-Gordon* stands for the proposition that agency adjudication may never be purely prospective because the only purely prospective vehicle recognized by the APA is rulemaking. *Bowen*, 488 U.S. at 220.

[17] 156 N.L.R.B. 1236 (1966).

The opinion itself is not that simple. *Wyman-Gordon* requires some pondering and some head counting to be properly understood. For example, Justices Douglas and Harlan simply dissented. Justice Harlan firmly believed that the NLRB — and the Court's support for the Board's position — had "trivialized" the presumption in the APA favoring rules as the appropriate vehicle for announcing policy shifts. While concluding that the Board had not abused its broad *Chenery* discretion, four other justices, namely Burger, Fortas, Stewart and White, were exceptionally critical of what the Board had done. Justice Fortas, who announced the Court's decision, wrote with unusual force: "The rule-making provisions of [the APA] which the Board would avoid were designed to assure fairness and mature consideration of rules of general application. There is no warrant in law for the Board to replace the statutory scheme with a rule-making procedure of its own invention." Clearly, these four justices would have overturned the Board's action but for the fact that the Board had issued a specific order to Wyman-Gordon to furnish the list of employees. That order had to be obeyed by the company, even if the policy announced in the *Excelsior* case had no effect.[18] By contrast, three other justices (Black, Brennan and Marshall), concurred in the result of the decision, but would not join Fortas' harsh criticism of the Board.

§ 6.04   THE CURRENT VIEW: *BELL AEROSPACE*

The *Wyman-Gordon* decision has been widely criticized;[19] and many observers thought it would be just a matter of time before the Supreme Court found an instance of an agency's using adjudication, rather than rule, to be so abusive that it would finally reverse an agency's choice. This prediction hasn't quite borne out. Five years after *Wyman-Gordon*, the Court granted certiorari in the case of *NLRB v. Bell Aerospace Co.*[20] and again approved NLRB policy making practices.

In *Bell Aerospace*, the Board seemed to be announcing a new policy by granting permission to form a collective bargaining unit to a group of the company's buyers (purchasing agents), even though these buyers, classified as *managerial employees* under the labor statutes, had traditionally not been given collective bargaining rights. The buyers had the authority to make purchases, to pledge the company's credit, to select actual sellers and to negotiate prices. The company argued that permitting employees who had this much decision making authority to join a union would create a conflict of interest between their duties as managers and their identity as union members. The Board disagreed, certified the union, and the case went to court.

The Second Circuit expressed some misgivings as to the Board's findings of fact, but decided to overturn the Board's action because of the Board's sudden change of position. Apparently, there had been a whole series of Board decisions in which the Board had been very reluctant to give any managerial employees union protection.

---

[18] This is why many labor lawyers believe the so-called *Excelsior* list ought, rightly, to be called the *Wyman-Gordon* list.

[19] *See, e.g.*, Merton C. Bernstein, *The NLRB's Adjudication-Rule Making Dilemma Under the Administrative Procedure Act*, 79 YALE L.J. 571 (1970).

[20] 416 U.S. 267 (1974).

In view of the drastic shift in the NLRB's position, the circuit held that the Board could announce this change only by writing and promulgating a rule under the APA.

The Supreme Court reversed the Second Circuit and approved the Board's decision to announce policy by order rather than by rule, holding expressly that the Board had not abused its discretion under *Chenery*. Some people who thought that, at long last, the Board was going to get its comeuppance were disappointed. However, the Court did make a superficial concession to its critics by writing a final paragraph in the *Bell Aerospace* opinion that set out, essentially for the first time, some criteria that appear to set the boundaries for weighing the exercise of agency discretion in the rule versus order setting.

First, the Court determined that the *diversity* and *complexity* of a problem may justify proceeding on a case-by-case basis. As the Court noted, the label *buyer* is not exactly a term of art in American industry. Duties of purchasing agents vary widely, depending on the industry and the specific company in question. It may be nearly impossible for an agency to develop a comprehensive definition ("any generalized standard") that could work across-the-board.

Second, there was very little evidence that the company had placed any great *reliance* on the earlier series of Board decisions (that refused to permit buyers to form a union). Certainly, the company could show no particular detriment, even if it had relied on the absence of some kind of Board definition of *buyer*.

Third, the change in policy did not involve any *new liability* that would be suffered because of a good faith reliance on the previous policy. The only injury here, if it could be called that, is that Bell Aerospace would have to contend with another group of unionized employees.

Fourth, this was not a case in which the company faced any *fines* or *damages* because of its reliance on the old policy. Again, all this case seeks to do is to confirm the legitimacy of the buyers' union. Bell Aerospace Company is not risking a monetary penalty for committing an unfair labor practice.

Although these criteria sound fine, this is a situation where you should watch what the Court does, not what it says. The Supreme Court has *never* squarely reversed an agency action for agency abuse of discretion in choosing order rather than rule. *Morton v. Ruiz*,[21] a decision announced during the same term as *Bell Aerospace*, has been read by some commentators as a Supreme Court decision that reversed agency action because the Bureau of Indian Affairs (BIA) developed a new policy on general assistance benefits to reservation Indians in the context of adjudication, rather than rulemaking. However, a close reading of *Ruiz* suggests that the Supreme Court was mainly troubled by the BIA's failure to publicize its new policy, rather than by the manner in which it had been announced.[22]

Following the Supreme Court's *Bell Aerospace* decision, the lower federal courts have essentially adhered to the *Chenery* notion that an agency's choice of rule or

---

[21] 415 U.S. 199 (1974).

[22] *See* Kenneth Culp Davis, *Administrative Law Surprises in the* Ruiz *Case*, 75 Colum. L. Rev. 823 (1975).

order is not to be disturbed. In one 1981 decision, *Ford Motor Co. v. FTC*,[23] the Ninth Circuit reviewed an attempt by the FTC, to stop practices of a car dealership that the FTC regarded as unfair trade practices. To enforce this theory, the FTC began adjudications against Ford and parallel actions against Chrysler and General Motors. After a strenuous battle, all the participants, except one dealership, Francis Ford, had settled with the FTC. On review, the Ninth Circuit concluded that the FTC was actually trying to promulgate a policy of general applicability for the entire retail automobile industry. The court determined that it was inappropriate to single out Francis Ford for a penalty when there had been no previous announcement of the policy. As the court boldly stated: "The FTC has exceeded its authority by proceeding to create new law by adjudication rather than by rule making."[24] One year later, in *Montgomery Ward v. FTC*,[25] the Ninth Circuit upheld a new retail store policy announced in an adjudication conducted by the FTC because the new policy was seen to have only a prospective effect on the private company. However, the Court simultaneously vacated the FTC's *cease and desist* order because, it reasoned, Montgomery Ward had had no advanced warning of the policy change.[26]

There were some, including the author of this book, who regarded that last paragraph in *Bell Aerospace* as a signal from the Supreme Court that it was seeking just the right case to finally throw out an agency's choice of procedure. But *Bell Aerospace* is now nearly thirty years old, and the current Supreme Court has shown absolutely no interest in this issue, inaction that suggests that the agency discretion first articulated in *Chenery* is virtually unfettered.

There are some signs that the NLRB is gradually changing its mind as to the efficacy of rules. In 1989, the Board promulgated its first substantive rule since 1935. The rule concerned the scope of an appropriate bargaining unit in acute care hospitals. As might be expected, the Board was quickly attacked in court as lacking the statutory authority to promulgate substantive rules. The Supreme Court affirmed the Board's general rulemaking authority in *American Hospital Ass'n v. NLRB*.[27]

Looking at the other side of the coin (those instances in which an agency might well have proceeded by adjudication rather than rule), the Court has upheld agency action when an agency has used rulemaking to sweep up some generic issues, even when the effect of those rules was to deny a party the right to a hearing for a

---

[23] 673 F.2d 1008 (9th Cir. 1981), *cert. denied*, 459 U.S. 999 (1982).

[24] *Id.* at 1010.

[25] 691 F.2d 1322 (9th Cir. 1982).

[26] There is yet another 9th Circuit decision that perhaps bears mention, *Patel v. INS*, 638 F.2d 1199 (9th Cir. 1980), a case that may more appropriately stand for the proposition that an agency must follow its own rules. The Ninth Circuit cases are elaborately discussed in William D. Araiza, *Limits on Agency Discretion to Choose Between Rulemaking and Adjudication: Reconsidering* Patel v. INS *and* Ford Motor Co. v. FTC, 58 ADMIN. L. REV. 899 (2006).

[27] 499 U.S. 606 (1991); *see* Mark H. Grunewald, *The NLRB's First Rulemaking: An Exercise in Pragmatism*, 41 DUKE L.J. 274 (1991). Even so, the poor NLRB continues to be strenuously criticized for the manner in which it makes policy. One scholar who accuses the NLRB of doing its "policymaking in the guise of factfinding" is Joan Flynn, *The Costs and Benefits of "Hiding the Ball": NLRB Policymaking and the Failure of Judicial Review*, 75 B.U. L. REV. 387 (1995).

television broadcast license. In *United States v. Storer Broadcasting Co.*,[28] the Federal Communications Commission promulgated multiple ownership rules that prevented persons owning more than a certain number of broadcast licenses from applying for additional licenses. Storer was at its limit under the rules but asked for a hearing on a new application notwithstanding the rule on the ground that the FCC could not deny it a hearing simply because the multiple ownership rules ostensibly prohibited it from acquiring any new licenses. The Supreme Court disagreed. It concluded that the FCC had the power to make multiple ownership rules, that the rules themselves were reasonable and that Storer could be automatically denied a hearing by the FCC because a hearing would simply be, in the Court's words, a "waste of time."[29]

§ 6.05 SOLVING A RULE VERSUS ORDER PROBLEM

Rule versus order problems come up more on law school and bar examinations than in practice. Practicing lawyers know that the NLRB is going to continue to make the vast bulk of its policy by adjudication unless Congress changes the Board's mind. Most of the other major federal agencies make their policy by rule. Thus, unlike the NLRB, they are probably not going to encounter trouble with the courts. When the rule/order issue arises in practice, most private-sector practitioners representing private clients know better than to waste their client's money on a rule versus order battle, because they will almost never win.

Thus, looking at the issue from the perspective of the agency lawyer is a good place to start. Assume that you are an FTC lawyer who is charged with developing some consumer protection principles for American supermarkets. We know that the FTC has the authority both to adjudicate and to make substantive rules. Thus, the agency may clearly proceed by rule or by order.

The FTC has the power to sanction supermarkets for engaging in what the enabling act calls unfair or deceptive trade practices. If the Commission chooses adjudication, it will bring an agency enforcement proceeding against a supermarket by charging that store with an unfair trade practice (*i.e.*, engaging in the retail practices that the FTC wants to stop). If the enforcement staff prevails at the agency level and in court, it will walk away with one reported judicial-style decision, presumably containing a description of what the store did that the Commission doesn't like. In the context of this action, it might be possible to persuade the Commission and the courts to penalize the store in some fashion during the adjudication as having engaged in an unfair/deceptive trade practice.

After a few such cases, there will be a body of FTC case law in place that makes the Commission's point very clearly. Because American businesses pay close attention to regulatory agencies, you can be assured that by the time the third or

---

[28] 351 U.S. 192 (1956).

[29] It may be that a reviewing court could adjust its standard of review of agency action based on its assessment of whether the agency should have proceeded by either rule or order. Professor Magill has suggested such an approach. *See* M. Elizabeth Magill, *Agency Choice of Policymaking Forum*, 71 U. Chi. L. Rev. 1383 (2004). *See also* Charles H. Koch, *Policy Making by the Administrative Judiciary*, 56 Ala. L. Rev. 693 (2005).

fourth enforcement action is completed, virtually all supermarkets in the United States will have gotten the message. People in business become very quickly aware of agency sanctions against other companies.

Notice, however, that the agency's actions have essentially trapped a few companies who were doing things that they did not realize were unfair trade practices until the Commission and the courts spoke. By contrast, trying to be gentle with the few stores who get caught in the agency's net can put the agency in the same dilemma as that in which the NLRB found itself in the *Excelsior* proceeding. If they forgive the targeted stores, they might not be able to enforce the new policy against other stores.

Would it make sense to try to write a rule? The bottom line on this issue is clearly established: Whether an agency adjudicates or makes rules, its choice of procedure is almost certain to be upheld by the courts. The Supreme Court has never squarely reversed an agency for an improper choice of rule or order.

Moreover, *Bell Aerospace* seems to emphasize the practicalities of the situation. First, are supermarkets throughout the United States too different from each other for an agency to write a meaningful rule? Obviously, it depends on what sort of practice the agency is trying to stop; but everyone who has shopped for groceries will acknowledge that supermarkets across the country are more alike than they are different. Supermarkets all have common traffic patterns, use shopping carts, have checkout stands and the like. A general rule might be an effective way to control the abusive practice.

Second, what will happen to the offending supermarkets? If the agency intends to declare the offending marketing practices unfair or deceptive trade practices and to seek fines or other sanctions for their violation, *Bell Aerospace* and the earlier cases strongly suggest a rulemaking if for no other reason than that it gives supermarkets at least thirty days to mend their ways before they are placed in jeopardy of a penalty.

In the long run, the agency's choice may not matter, because it can take a great deal of comfort from the fact that no matter what choice is made, it is virtually never going to be turned around on judicial review. Still, agency lawyers should recall the admonition of the *Wyman-Gordon* court: APA rulemaking is designed to assure fairness and mature consideration of rules of general application. To the extent that the agency accepts this admonition, it may have almost a public duty to proceed by rule. Future agency lawyers should remember the suggestion to prosecutors in the Model Code of Professional Responsibility: "The responsibility of a public prosecutor differs from that of the usual advocate; his duty is *to seek justice*, not merely to convict."[30]

---

[30] MODEL CODE OF PROF'L RESPONSIBILITY EC 7-13 (1980). The Model Rules of Professional Conduct state it a little differently: "A prosecutor has the responsibility of a minister of justice and not simply that of an advocate." MODEL RULES OF PROF'L CONDUCT R. 3.8 cmt. (1983).

Chapter 7

RULEMAKING

§ 7.01 INTRODUCTION

One of the preeminent administrative law scholars in the United States has called agency rulemaking "one of the greatest inventions of modern government."[1] Not everyone feels that way. A former professor of administrative law, now a Supreme Court justice, takes a less enthusiastic view, commenting that the bloom is now off the rose of rulemaking[2] Many private citizens and most practicing lawyers tend to view agency rulemaking more in terms of whose ox is being gored by the agency. Environmental groups gloat when the EPA writes tight air pollution control standards. The regulated industries cringe. Domestic oil producers are happy when the executive branch places import restrictions on foreign petroleum. Motorists who may be faced with higher gasoline prices are far less enthusiastic.

One of the best examples of the gored ox phenomenon comes out of the Federal Trade Commission. In the 1970s, when the consumer protection movement was at its peak and as the FTC became more and more aggressive in pursuing unfair and deceptive consumer marketing practices, many American businesses believed that existing rulemaking procedures made it too easy for the FTC to make rules. Companies lobbied hard in Congress and achieved enactment of a complicated and procedurally cumbersome statute known as the Magnuson-Moss Act, an act that made it much more difficult and time consuming for the FTC to make rules. But by late 1981, after President Reagan had changed a great deal of the FTC's regulatory philosophy by crucial appointments to the Commission, businesses decided that Magnuson-Moss made it too *hard* for the FTC to get rid of existing rules (the procedure for promulgating new rules and repealing old rules is the same) and asked Congress to repeal Magnuson-Moss, the statute that just a few years previously they had described in glowing terms.

---

[1] KENNETH CULP DAVIS, CASES, TEXT AND PROBLEMS ON ADMINISTRATIVE LAW 241 (6th ed. 1977). Readers who would like a very sophisticated analysis of current agency rulemaking should consult the following three articles, that have become near-classics in the field: Colin S. Diver, *Policymaking Paradigms in Administrative Law*, 95 HARV. L. REV. 393 (1981); James V. DeLong, *Informal Rulemaking and the Integration of Law and Policy*, 65 VA. L. REV. 257 (1979); William F. Pedersen, *Formal Records and Informal Rulemaking*, 85 YALE L.J. 38 (1975). For some further suggestions, *see* E. Donald Elliott, *Re-inventing Rulemaking*, 41 DUKE L.J. 1490 (1992); for a highly thorough and essentially empirical analysis, *see* CORNELIUS M. KERWIN, RULEMAKING (1994); for a good commentary on rulemaking, *see* Richard J. Pierce, Jr., *Rulemaking and the Administrative Procedure Act*, 32 TULSA L.J. 185 (1996). One of the most striking developments ever seen in federal administrative law is the use of the Internet for rulemaking by federal agencies. *See, e.g.*, a Department of Agriculture rulemaking to be found at www.ams.usda.gov/nop/.

[2] Antonin Scalia, *Making Law Without Making Rules*, REG. MAG. 25 (July/Aug. 1981).

This little war story says a lot about agency rulemaking. By and large, it is the substance of agency rules that make people happy or sad. Few people get terribly exercised about the procedure of making rules. But as we will see, it is very difficult to challenge the substance of an agency rule because the Supreme Court has admonished federal courts to defer to an agency's technical judgments. Lawyers know that there are two ways to invalidate an agency rule-by attacking either its substantive provisions or the procedure by which it was promulgated. If a rule is defective on either ground, it will not be put into effect.

For many years, challenges to agency rulemaking were as likely to be brought on procedural grounds as on substantive grounds. The difficulty with procedural challenges, as we will see, is that the Supreme Court has also made it very difficult to attack an agency for its rulemaking procedure. There is a message in all of this. Remember one of the cardinal rules of agency practice: if you don't like what an agency is proposing to do, the place to win your fight is at the agency. You will likely not get any great satisfaction out of a reviewing court.

This chapter first examines the procedure for making agency rules then it analyzes the legal effects of rules. The chapter concludes with a few basic techniques for writing agency rules. Because any statement of agency rulemaking is not complete without some discussion of how the courts react to rules, statements on judicial review of agency rulemaking are interspersed throughout the chapter. Readers seeking a thorough understanding of judicial review principles should also read Chapters 10 through 12.

§ 7.02 BASIC RULEMAKING PROCEDURE UNDER THE APA

[A] Triggering of Rulemaking Process

How does an agency begin? There are many ways the rulemaking process is triggered.[3] The agency may be commanded by its enabling act to write rules in a certain area. Most of the recent health and safety legislation passed by Congress requires agencies to promulgate rules, even though the agency has a great deal of discretion in determining what the final rules look like. In certain situations in which Congress thinks an emergency exists, Congress may write interim agency rules in the statute that will remain in place until the agency gets around to promulgating its own regulatory program.[4]

---

[3] One issue not discussed in this chapter is the refusal of an agency to make a rule and whether that refusal is reviewable in court. In *Heckler v. Chaney*, 470 U.S. 821 (1985), the Supreme Court held that an agency's refusal to launch an enforcement action was not reviewable, because such decisions are committed to agency discretion. *See* discussion of *Heckler* in Chapter 10, § 10.05. While *Heckler* did not involve a refusal to make a rule, many commentators have acknowledged its impact on the rulemaking process. *See* Ronald M. Levin, *Understanding Unreviewability in Administrative Law*, 74 MINN. L. REV. 689, 762–73 (1990). For a D.C. Circuit decision holding such refusal to be reviewable (more precisely determining that summary judgment was improper in this setting), see *American Horse Prot. Ass'n v. Lyng*, 812 F.2d 1 (D.C. Cir. 1987).

[4] Congress did this with the Mine Safety and Health Act of 1969, 30 U.S.C. §§ 801–960, and the Surface Mining Control and Reclamation Act of 1977, 30 U.S.C. §§ 1201–1328.

Quite often, an agency will determine that rules are needed when its own investigative processes show the need for additional regulatory activity in some area. Occasionally, even private citizens can get into the act. Section 553(e) of the APA gives any "interested person the right to petition for the issuance, amendment, or repeal of a rule."

As Chapter 6 has shown, the Federal Administrative Procedure Act emphasizes rulemaking as the basic process by which agencies should announce new policy, but that is not the only function of agency rules. The drafters of the APA contemplated many other roles for agency rules by writing a fairly broad definition. The APA defines a rule, in part, as "the whole or a part of an agency statement of general or particular applicability and future effect designed to implement, interpret, or prescribe law or policy or describing the organization, procedure, or practice requirements of an agency . . . ."[5]

The APA's normal rulemaking procedures are found in § 553.[6] Many people refer to normal APA procedure simply as *553 rulemaking*. Other labels frequently used for this type of procedure are *notice and comment* or *informal* rulemaking. To understand this crucially important vehicle, it is important to begin with a quick walk-through of § 553's important provisions.

[B]   The Scope of § 553

There are two limitations to keep in mind. First, note the scope of the APA itself, set out in § 551(1) of the APA in the definition of agency. For the purposes of this book, we assume that we are dealing with a governmental body that fits within the definition of agency. The second important exemption from § 553 procedures is set out in § 553(a). Agencies with activities having to do with military or foreign affairs, or instances in which an agency deals with management or personnel or public property, loans, grants, benefits or contracts are exempt from § 553 procedures.

This is a good place to begin reading the APA with as much sophistication as possible. A quick reading of § 553(a) could give the impression that the exemptions are themselves completely free of all controls. This is not at all true. There is a substantial body of statutes, case law and regulations that pertains to government contracts and grants. In many instances, those matters are subject to even tighter procedures than the APA. The exemptions in § 553(a) simply mean that the APA's rulemaking provisions are not applicable to those activities.[7]

---

[5] APA § 551(4). *See* JEFFREY S. LUBBERS, A GUIDE TO FEDERAL AGENCY RULEMAKING (American Bar Ass'n 4th ed. 2006). *See also* C.M. KERWIN, RULEMAKING: HOW GOVERNMENT AGENCIES WRITE LAW AND MAKE POLICY (2d ed. 1999). Another factor in agency rulemaking that must not be discounted is the role that agency lawyers play. It is highly important and rarely studied by legal scholars. For one excellent study, *see* Thomas O. McGarity, *Government Lawyering: The Role of Government Attorneys in Regulatory Agency Rulemaking*, 61 LAW & CONTEMP. PROBS. 19 (1998).

[6] For some good insights into the current climate of federal agency rulemaking, *see* Lisa Schultz Bressman, *Procedures as Politics in Administrative Law*, 107 COLUM. L. REV. 1749 (2007).

[7] Professor Arthur Bonfield of the University of Iowa College of Law has written two articles on these generic exceptions that are generally regarded as authoritative. Arthur E. Bonfield, *Military and Foreign Affairs Function Rulemaking Under the APA*, 71 MICH. L. REV. 221 (1972); Arthur E. Bonfield,

Moreover, no one should lose sight of what the agencies themselves may choose to do, irrespective of the commands of the APA. The Department of Defense may choose to use notice and comment rulemaking for its procedures, even if the APA does not demand that it do so. This does not necessarily mean that an agency is exempt from other portions of the APA. For example, an agency may still have to publish its rules in the Federal Register even though those regulations do not have to be promulgated under the § 553 procedures.[8]

[C] The Notice Requirement

The first principle of due process and the first requirement of § 553 is that the agency give notice to affected persons of its intent to publish a rule. Under normal circumstances this notice is placed in the *Federal Register.* If, however, an agency can give personal notice to all affected people (*e.g.*, in a situation where only ten companies are affected by a rule), individual notice is sufficient. The *Federal Register* notice has a number of mandatory ingredients:

1. A statement of the time, place, and nature of any public rulemaking proceedings;

2. A statement of the legal authority under which the agency proposes the rule;

3. The language of the proposed rule or merely a description of the topics and issues involved in the proposal; and

4. An invitation to any interested persons to submit comments on the rule, usually accompanied by a cut-off date for submitting the comments.

Requirements 1 and 2 are essentially boilerplate. The crucial parts of the notice for persons affected by the rule are the specific language of the proposed rule and the deadline for submitting comments.

It is rare for an agency to describe only the subject matter of a proposed rule. Normally, the agency includes the text of the rule that it proposes to issue. This permits far more pointed and specific comments to be submitted by interested persons. When an agency realizes that a problem exists within its jurisdiction, but does not yet have sufficient information to write a full-blown proposed rule, it generally refrains from publishing a proposed rule and instead publishes either: (1) a Notice of Inquiry, which includes a broad description of the area and issues for which it may write some kind of rule, or (2) an Advanced Notice of Proposed Rulemaking. While neither of these two terms are specifically authorized by the APA, they have evolved from agency custom and practice over the last several years.

Public Participation in Federal Rulemaking Relating to Public Property, Loans, Grants, Benefits, or Contracts, 118 U. Pa. L. Rev. 540 (1970).

[8] This is as good a place as any to confront a problem of terminology that sometimes troubles people new to administrative law concepts. The APA uses and defines only the term, *rule.* That definition is set out in § 551(4). Most practitioners and agency personnel use the term, *regulation*, interchangeably with *rule*, particularly after agency rules have been promulgated. The Government Printing Office, charged with the publication of the *Federal Register* and the *Code of Federal Regulations*, normally uses the term, *regulation*, only for those agency statements that are codified in the C.F.R. Generally, the term, *rule*, encompasses many more agency pronouncements than the term, *regulation*.

Examples of each appear frequently in the *Federal Register.*

The following illustration is an extract from an agency notice of proposed rulemaking, which was published in the *Federal Register.*

25952   Federal Register / Vol. 77, No. 85 / Wednesday, May 2, 2012 / Proposed Rules

rulemaking process and include them in the final rule.

List of Subjects in 30 CFR Part 943

Intergovernmental relations, Surface mining, Underground mining.

Dated: February 24, 2012.

Ervin J. Barchenger,

Regional Director, Mid-Continent Region.

[FR Doc. 2012–10572 Filed 5–1–12; 8:45 am]

BILLING CODE 4310–05–P

DEPARTMENT OF DEFENSE

Department of the Army, Corps of Engineers

33 CFR Part 334

Oregon Army National Guard, Camp Rilea, Clatsop County, OR; Danger Zone

AGENCY: U.S. Army Corps of Engineers, DoD.

ACTION: Notice of proposed rulemaking and request for comments.

SUMMARY: The U.S. Army Corps of Engineers is proposing to establish a new danger zone in the waters adjacent to Camp Rilea located in Clatsop County, Oregon. The regulation would prohibit any activity by the public within the danger zone during use of weapons training ranges. The new danger zone is necessary to ensure public safety and satisfy the Oregon National Guard operations requirements for small arms training.

DATES: Written comments must be submitted by June 1, 2012.

ADDRESSES: You may submit comments, identified by docket number COE–2011–0036, by any of the following methods:

Federal eRulemaking Portal: http:// www.regulations.gov. Follow the instructions for submitting comments.

Email: david.b.olson@usace.army.mil. Include the docket number, COE–2011–0036, in the subject line of the message.

Mail: U.S. Army Corps of Engineers, Attn: CECW–CO (David B. Olson), 441 G Street NW., Washington, DC 20314–1000.

Hand Delivery/Courier: Due to security requirements, we cannot receive comments by hand delivery or courier.

Instructions: Direct your comments to docket number COE–2011–0036. All comments received will be included in the public docket without change and may be made available on-line at *http://www.regulations.gov,* including any personal information provided,

unless the commenter indicates that the comment includes information claimed to be Confidential Business Information (CBI) or other information whose disclosure is restricted by statute. Do not submit information that you consider to be CBI, or otherwise protected, through regulations.gov or email. The regulations.gov web site is an anonymous access system, which means we will not know your identity or contact information unless you provide it in the body of your comment. If you send an email directly to the Corps without going through regulations.gov, your email address will be automatically captured and included as part of the comment that is placed in the public docket and made available on the Internet. If you submit an electronic comment, we recommend that you include your name and other contact information in the body of your comment and with any disk or CD–ROM you submit. If we cannot read your comment because of technical difficulties and cannot contact you for clarification, we may not be able to consider your comment. Electronic comments should avoid the use of any special characters, any form of encryption, and be free of any defects or viruses.

Docket: For access to the docket to read background documents or comments received, go to *www.regulations.gov.* All documents in the docket are listed. Although listed in the index, some information is not publicly available, such as CBI or other information whose disclosure is restricted by statute. Certain other material, such as copyrighted material, is not placed on the Internet and will be publicly available only in hard copy form.

FOR FURTHER INFORMATION CONTACT: Mr. David Olson, Headquarters, Operations and Regulatory Community of Practice, Washington, DC at 202–761–4922 or Mr. Steve Gagnon, U.S. Army Corps of Engineers, Portland District, Regulatory Branch, at 503–808–4379.

SUPPLEMENTARY INFORMATION: In response to a request from the Oregon Army National Guard, and pursuant to its authorities in Section 7 of the Rivers and Harbors Act of 1917 (40 Stat. 266; 33 U.S.C. 1) and Chapter XIX of the Army Appropriations Act of 1919 (40 Stat. 892; 33 U.S.C. 3), the Corps is proposing to amend the regulations at 33 CFR part 334 to establish a new danger zone. The proposed danger zone will prohibit access to waters adjacent to Camp Rilea during use of weapons training ranges, thereby ensuring that no

threat is posed to passing water traffic due to ricochet rounds.

Procedural Requirements

a. *Review Under Executive Order 12866.* The proposed rule is issued with respect to a military function of the Defense Department and the provisions of Executive Order 12866 do not apply.

b. *Review Under the Regulatory Flexibility Act.* This proposed rule has been reviewed under the Regulatory Flexibility Act (Pub. L. 96–354) which requires the preparation of a regulatory flexibility analysis for any regulation that will have a significant economic impact on a substantial number of small entities (i.e., small businesses and small governments). Unless information is obtained to the contrary during the public notice comment period, the Corps expects that this danger zone would have practically no economic impact on the public, and minimal anticipated navigational hazard or interference with existing waterway traffic. This proposed rule, if adopted, will have no significant economic impact on small entities.

c. *Review under the National Environmental Policy Act.* Due to the administrative nature of this action and because the proposed site for the danger zone is located in the Pacific Ocean and vessels may navigate around the prohibited area, the Corps expects that this regulation, if adopted, will not have a significant impact to the quality of the human environment and, therefore, preparation of an environmental impact statement will not be required. An environmental assessment will be prepared after the public notice period is closed and all comments have been received and considered.

d. *Unfunded Mandates Act.* This proposed rule does not impose an enforceable duty among the private sector and, therefore, it is not a Federal private section mandate and it is not subject to the requirements of either section 202 or Section 205 of the Unfunded Mandates Act. We have also found under Section 203 of the Act, that small governments will not be significantly and uniquely affected by this rulemaking.

List of Subjects in 33 CFR Part 334

Danger zones, Marine safety, Navigation (water), Restricted areas, Waterways.

For the reasons stated in the preamble, the Corps proposes to amend 33 CFR part 334 as follows:

A close reading of § 553(b) indicates that there are some exceptions to the notice requirement:

(1) When the agency is promulgating *interpretative* rules, *general statements of policy* or rules of *agency organization, procedure, or practice.* (There is more discussion on these distinctions in § 7.06, *below*); or

(2) When the agency makes what is known as a *good cause* finding that notice is *impracticable, unnecessary,* or *contrary to the public interest.* (More often than not, the courts simply defer to the agency's judgment on this point. But the finding must be published in order to be effective. Most agencies resort to this device very infrequently.)

[D]   Consideration of Comments

One of the hallmarks of rulemaking under the APA is solicitation of comments from all interested persons. This means very simply that an agency must accept comments from anyone who makes the effort to write a letter. Most agency comments are submitted in writing, although certain agencies, either because of a statutory requirement in the enabling act or through their own discretion, will conduct oral hearings to permit the submission of comments. The Magnuson-Moss Act (discussed in § 7.04) requires an oral hearing for most FTC rules.

The more difficult question is what the agency must do with these comments. The APA does not define the term *consider,* and the few courts that have reviewed disputes in this area have simply imposed a good faith requirement on the agency to at least log in all comments and to review carefully comments from major entities affected by the rule. This is not a totally hollow requirement. There are some cases in which agency rulemaking has been overturned because the agency failed to address significant comments in the preamble to the final rule. At the same time, most courts recognize that comments are written with a particular point of view and are, more often than not, pieces of advocacy rather than models of objectivity. One court has stated bluntly that neither agencies nor courts "need . . . accept at face value the self-serving comments of interested members of the [affected] industry."[10]

The view from outside the agency is a little different. Cynics who represent clients before federal agencies will probably tell you that *consider* for many agencies merely means placing a date-time stamp on the comments as they come in and tossing the comments into an appropriate filing cabinet.[11] It is abundantly clear that an agency is not bound absolutely by the comments, nor is an agency totally restricted to the comments in formulating a final rule. It can invoke its own expertise in writing a rule, even if the comments all suggest a contrary result. However, if an agency takes this approach, it must clearly explain itself. A reviewing court will be exceptionally suspicious of an agency rule that disregards all the commentary.

---

[10] *Nat'l Tire Dealers & Retreaders Ass'n v. Brinegar,* 491 F.2d 31, 39–40 (D.C. Cir. 1974).

[11] A hint for readers who anticipate practicing before agencies: make your comments as eye-catching as possible so they don't get lost in the shuffle. This hint may be more difficult to accomplish in an era that promotes electronic rulemaking. For some good insights into public participation, *see* Cary Coglianese, *Citizen Participation in Rulemaking: Past, Present, and Future,* 55 DUKE L.J. 943 (2006).

[E] Promulgation of a Final Rule

This step completes the basic rulemaking process. The step contains two important ingredients. First, the agency must prepare, after consideration of the comments and other matter in the rulemaking record, "a concise general statement of [the] basis and purpose" of the final rule. The statement of basis and purpose is usually incorporated in the preamble to the final rule and published along with the final rule in the *Federal Register.* But even though it is published only as a preamble, or occasionally just made part of the rulemaking record and not actually published, the statement of basis and purpose can be a crucial part of the rulemaking process if the rule is taken to court by disgruntled individuals.

The basis and purpose statement was seen by the drafters of the APA as an important part of the final rule, but they did not specify its ingredients. Congress suggested in the APA's legislative history that the agency was to "not only relate to the data so presented [*i.e.*, the comments and other matters in the record] but with reasonable fullness explain the actual basis and objectives of the rule."[12] Courts have taken this requirement seriously because the statement is sometimes one of the few pieces of information by which a court can analyze a rule if the validity of a rule is challenged before the agency enforces the rule on a case-by-case basis. For example, in *Automotive Parts & Accessories Ass'n v. Boyd,*[13] the District of Columbia Circuit looked at the words *concise* and *general* in the rule's statement of basis and purpose and concluded:

> These adjectives must be accommodated to the realities of judicial scrutiny, which do not contemplate that the court itself will, by a laborious examination of the record, formulate in the first instance the significant issues faced by the agency and articulate the rationale of their resolution. [In other words, the court won't do the agency's job just to try and preserve the rule.] We do not expect the agency to discuss every item of fact or opinion included in the submissions made to it in informal rule making. We do expect that, if the judicial review which Congress has thought it important to provide is to be meaningful, the [statement of basis and purpose] will enable us to see what major issues of policy were ventilated by the informal proceedings and why the agency reacted to them as it did.

The court was also careful to note that the reason for the statement is simple: it is to demonstrate to the public, and more importantly to reviewing courts that the agency has done its job "in a manner calculated to negate the dangers of arbitrariness and irrationality in the formulation of rules for general application in the future."[14]

---

[12] S. Doc. No. 79-248, at 259 (1946). The Attorney General's Manual on the APA noted that the statement was not to be in the nature of formal findings and conclusions (such as a federal district judge prepares in issuing a decision in a civil bench trial) but is mainly intended to "advise the public" of the basis and purpose of the rule. MANUAL at 32.

[13] 407 F.2d 330 (D.C. Cir. 1968).

[14] In *Independent U.S. Tanker Owners Committee v. Dole,* 809 F.2d 847 (D.C. Cir.), *cert. denied,* 484 U.S. 819 (1987), the D.C. Circuit reversed an agency for an inadequate statement of reasons for the rule, but did not depart in any substantial way from the Circuit's earlier language in *Boyd.*

Second, under normal circumstances, the rule goes into effect no earlier than thirty days after the rule's publication. Recall that this was one of the reasons why the Supreme Court has so strongly favored rulemaking for the announcement of new agency policy.[15] It gives someone subject to the new rule at least a month to get things in order before being in violation of the rule. However, Congress realized that on occasion an agency will have to move faster than that. Note carefully the exceptions in § 553(d) to the thirty-day delay period:

1. A rule that *provides an exemption* or *relieves a restriction.* These are instances in which the agency is easing up on a regulated party rather than imposing some new regulatory burden. Obviously, parties will welcome implementation as quickly as possible.

2. *Interpretative rules* and *statements of policy. See* § 7.06 for a discussion of these rules.

3. Upon a *finding of good cause* included in the publication of the final rule.

The following illustration is a portion of a final rule announced in the *Federal Register.*

---

[15] *See* cases discussed in Chapter 6.

25577

Rules and Regulations

Federal Register

Vol. 77, No. 84

Tuesday, May 1, 2012

This section of the FEDERAL REGISTER contains regulatory documents having general applicability and legal effect, most of which are keyed to and codified in the Code of Federal Regulations, which is published under 50 titles pursuant to 44 U.S.C. 1510.

The Code of Federal Regulations is sold by the Superintendent of Documents. Prices of new books are listed in the first FEDERAL REGISTER issue of each week.

FARM CREDIT ADMINISTRATION

12 CFR Part 618

RIN 3052–AC66

General Provisions; Operating and Strategic Business Planning

AGENCY: Farm Credit Administration.

ACTION: Final rule.

SUMMARY: The Farm Credit Administration (FCA, we, or our) amends its regulation requiring the board of directors of each Farm Credit System (FCS or System) institution to adopt an operational and strategic business plan (business plan or plan) to include, among other things, outreach toward diversity and inclusion. Each business plan must contain a human capital plan that describes the institution's workforce and management and assesses their strengths and weaknesses; describes succession programs; and includes strategies and actions to strive for diversity and inclusion within the institution's workforce and management. In addition, the business plan of each direct lender institution must include a marketing plan that discusses how the institution will further the objective that the FCS be responsive to the credit needs of all eligible and creditworthy agricultural producers and other eligible persons, with specific outreach toward diversity and inclusion. Further, the regulation requires including skills and diversity as part of the required assessment of the needs of the board of directors and establishes annual reporting requirements to the board.

DATES: *Effective Date:* This regulation will be effective 30 days after publication in the **Federal Register** during which either or both Houses of Congress are in session. We will publish a notice of the effective date in the **Federal Register**.

Compliance Date: System institutions must comply with this regulation no later than January 30, 2013.

FOR FURTHER INFORMATION CONTACT: Jacqueline R. Melvin, Policy Analyst, Office of Regulatory Policy, Farm Credit Administration, McLean, VA 22102–5090, (703) 883–4498, TTY (703) 883–4434, or

Jennifer A. Cohn, Senior Counsel, Office of General Counsel, Farm Credit Administration, McLean, VA 22102–5090, (703) 883–4020, TTY (703) 883–4020.

SUPPLEMENTARY INFORMATION:

I. Objectives

The objectives of this amendment are to ensure that:

• Each System institution promotes diversity and inclusion as critical to its success in the long term and incorporates diversity and inclusion as a vital component of its corporate culture;

• Skills and diversity are explicitly included in the assessment of the needs of the board of directors;

• Each System institution assesses the strengths and weaknesses of its current workforce and management; addresses succession planning; and develops strategies and actions to strive for diversity and inclusion within its workforce and management;

• Each System institution considers how it will further the objective of being responsive to the credit needs of all eligible and creditworthy agricultural producers and other eligible persons with specific outreach toward diversity and inclusion; and

• Each System institution's board of directors receives reports on the institution's progress in accomplishing the strategies and actions in its human capital and marketing plans, which will help the board establish accountability and plan new strategies and actions.

II. Background and Overview of Comments

On May 25, 2011, the FCA published a proposed rule to amend § 618.8440, which requires the board of directors of each System institution to adopt a business plan.[1] The proposed rule required, among other things, human capital and marketing plans that include

[1] *See* 76 FR 30280.

outreach toward diversity and inclusion.

We received approximately 75 comment letters from 48 System institutions. We also received two letters from the Farm Credit Council (Council), the trade association for the System.[2] Of the System letters, approximately eight opposed our proposed rule entirely and requested complete withdrawal of the proposal. Most of the remainder of the System commenters supported the premise of the proposed rule to consider human capital and marketing outreach, including diversity and inclusion, in the business plan, but they requested extensive revisions to the final rule or to the explanatory preamble to reduce what they viewed as undue burden. As discussed below, we are making a number of changes in the final rule in response to many of these comments. Many System commenters appeared to misunderstand some of the intended requirements of the proposed rule, because they opposed requirements that the rule would not have imposed. Throughout this preamble, we clarify the requirements of the final rule.

We received approximately 325 comments from non-System commenters, including sustainable agriculture advocacy and assistance groups, academics in the field of sustainable agriculture, small farmers, consumers, and others. The vast majority of these commenters supported the proposed rule. Many of these commenters requested that FCA include a number of specific requirements in the marketing plan provision that would, among other things, require institutions to train potential customers in business planning and financing; develop infrastructure such as cooperatives and farmers' markets; partner with governmental and non-governmental entities and investors for funding local and regional food systems (LRFS); set numerical investment goals for lending to LRFS; and make their marketing goals and progress assessments public.

We also received approximately 40 electronically submitted comment letters that contained the names and

[2] One Council letter was submitted on behalf of its membership, after soliciting input from all System institutions. The other Council letter was submitted on behalf of its President and CEO, with the endorsement and support of the Council Board of Directors.

[F]   Electronic Rulemaking

During the 1990s and continuing into the first decade of the twenty-first century, the Federal Government finally began appreciating the benefits (and to a lesser extent) the problems of the World Wide Web and the Internet. A few agencies began to appreciate that use of an exclusively hard copy process for rulemaking was enormously time-consuming, wasteful of natural resources and fairly inefficient.[16] These days every agency has a website. Large numbers of individuals

---

[16] For a description of some of the early initiatives in electronic rulemaking, *see* Barbara H. Brandon

and probably almost every business of any appreciable size have access to both e-mail and the Internet. There is no longer any reason not to take advantage of these devices for federal government administration. Rulemaking is a particularly appropriate candidate for electronic treatment.[17]

Electronic rulemaking for the federal government as a whole was mandated initially by a pronouncement of the Office of Management and Budget (OMB) in 2002 during the administration of President George W. Bush as part of what the OMB described as its "E-Government Strategy."[18] Most of the OMB's pronouncements were enacted by Congress that same year as the E-Government Act of 2002.[19] Early in 2003, the OMB created and announced a comprehensive website — "Regulations.gov" — to serve as a central electronic location for all federal agency rulemaking. As part of the creation of Regulations.gov., individual executive branch agencies were required to shut down their own websites. While the OMB pronouncements were technically limited to presidential agencies, many of the independent regulatory commissions chose to participate voluntarily. In sum, Regulations.gov. is a central, comprehensive site for all agencies' proposed rules, policy documents and other pieces of data relevant to the agencies' rulemaking activities. There is a separate password protected site, the Federal Docket Management System, within which the agencies store their rulemaking records in separately-numbered dockets. Within Regulations.gov. exists a subdirectory styled "Exchange" which, in turn, permits registered users to create a customized homepage called "MyRegulations."

Electronic rulemaking has played to generally strong reviews. One estimate suggests that it has saved federal agencies roughly $129 in the first five years of operation.[20] Other commentators, including a lengthy study commissioned by the American Bar Association, have been generally supportive and complimentary.[21] There is absolutely no question that e-rulemaking is here to stay and will, in the

---

& Robert D. Carlitz, *Online Rulemaking and Other Tools for Strengthening Our Civil Infrastructure*, 54 ADMIN. L. REV. 1421 (2002).

[17] *See, e.g.*, Cary Coglianese, *E-Rulemaking: Information Technology and the Regulatory Process*, 56 ADMIN. L. REV. 353 (2004).

[18] OFFICE OF MGMT. & BUDGET, EXEC. OFFICE OF THE PRESIDENT, E-GOVERNMENT STRATEGY (2002).

[19] Pub. L. No. 107-347, 116 Stat. 2899 (codified in scattered titles of U.S.C.).

[20] *See* the website itself: www.Regulations.gov. for this assertion and even more current information.

[21] CYNTHIA R. FARINA ET AL., ACHIEVING THE POTENTIAL: THE FUTURE OF FEDERAL E-RULEMAKING (ABA, 2008); Beth Simone Noveck, *The Future of Citizen Participation in the Electronic State*, 1 J.L. & POL'Y FOR INFO. SOC'Y 11 (2005); Beth Simone Noveck, *The Electronic Revolution in Rulemaking*, 53 EMORY L.J. 433 (2004). For a good recent article that raises a number of concerns with regard to user-friendly issues and transparency, *see* Gregory D. Jones, *Electronic Rulemaking in the New Age of Openness: Proposing a Voluntary Two-Tier Registration System for Regulations.Gov.*, 62 ADMIN. L. REV. 1261 (2010). For some agency reactions to this process, *see* Jeffrey S. Lubbers, *A Survey of Federal Agency Rulemakers' Attitudes About E-Rulemaking*, 62 ADMIN. L. REV. 451 (2010). Professor Lubbers reviewed a substantial number of agency questionnaires to conclude: "[A]gency rulemakers are generally receptive to e-rulemaking, although a common theme of their early evaluations was that the new system is a 'boon for the public but a bane for the agency'. . . . [Agencies] reported a general increase in rulemaking efficiency and a smaller majority reported a general increase in rulemaking quality." *Id.* at 474. For additional commentary, *see* Stuart Minor Benjamin, *The Role of the Internet in Agency Decision Making: Evaluating E-Rulemaking: Public Participation and Political Institutions*, 55 DUKE L.J. 893 (2006).

near future, replace hardcopy submissions and recordkeeping.

This is informal rulemaking procedure.[22] Many people believe it is too loose and informal-that the informality makes it too easy for agencies to promulgate careless and unthinking rules. A number of persons affected by agency rules have argued that agencies should have to provide more in the way of process. The Supreme Court disagrees and has written two major decisions on this point, one of which, *Vermont Yankee*, discussed in the following section, is enshrined as one of the most important Supreme Court opinions affecting the agency decisional process ever announced by the Court.

§ 7.03   THE IMPACT OF *FLORIDA EAST COAST RAILWAY* AND *VERMONT YANKEE* ON BASIC RULEMAKING PROCEDURE

[A]   *Formal* and *Hybrid* Rulemaking

There are three sources of authority for prescribing the process of agency rulemaking: Congress (through the agency's enabling act or the APA), the agency itself (through its discretion to set up its own internal procedural requirements), and the reviewing courts. Congress' power is virtually unfettered. Remember cardinal rule number one of administrative law: agencies are creatures of Congress and may function only insofar as Congress gives them authority to function. However, the agencies, once established, are generally given a great deal of discretion, particularly in establishing decisional procedures. Agencies frequently give affected persons more process than either the enabling act or the APA requires.

The tricky issue these days is whether courts may, of their own accord, impose additional rulemaking procedures on the agency apart from whatever is required by the enabling act, the APA or the agency's own rules. Make no mistake about this point: the general rule is NO! It took the Supreme Court two major decisions to make this clear to lower federal courts.

[B]   Formal Rulemaking and *Florida East Coast Railway*

In the first case, *United States v. Florida East Coast Railway*,[23] the now-abolished Interstate Commerce Commission (ICC) attempted to deal with a chronic, nationwide shortage of freight cars that was then having a serious detrimental affect on the nation's economy. A preliminary investigation by the ICC revealed that one of the reasons for the shortage was that many railroads kept and used freight cars belonging to other railroads without adequate compensation. It was simply cheaper to pay rent on the borrowed cars than to buy new cars. This practice discouraged railroads from investing in new freight cars because a large

---

[22] For an excellent recent analysis of "hands-on" rulemaking, *see* Wendy Wagner, Katherine Barnes & Lisa Peters, *Rulemaking in the Shade: An Empirical Study of EPA's Air Toxic Emission Standards*, 63 ADMIN. L. REV. 99 (2011).

[23] 410 U.S. 224 (1973).

part of their investment might be enjoyed by railroads that did not themselves invest, but who held onto cars belonging elsewhere.

To make a very long story short, the ICC promulgated rules requiring railroads that kept freight cars belonging to other companies to pay an incentive charge for the use of the cars. The Commission believed that this incentive charge would persuade railroads to return freight cars to their proper owners as quickly as possible. The affected companies challenged the rules in court on both substantive and procedural grounds, but the Supreme Court took up only the procedural issue.

The arguments were not complicated. The relevant portion of the Interstate Commerce Act stated that the ICC could promulgate rules "after hearing."[24] A number of railroads, including Florida East Coast, argued that this statutory language required the ICC to adopt rules only after a full-blown trial-type proceeding conducted under the terms of §§ 556–557 of the APA, a procedure often referred to as *formal rulemaking*. This was about the only way the rules could be deemed procedurally invalid because all of the parties to the case agreed that the Commission had used at least as much, and probably more, procedure than that required by § 553 (informal rulemaking).[25]

The Supreme Court resolved the procedural issue in favor of the ICC-the Commission was not required to hold oral hearings before promulgating the rule. The Court began by analyzing the language of both the Interstate Commerce Act (IC Act) and the APA. Its analysis warrants close attention.

The entire matter turns on the definition of the term *hearing* — a word used in both the APA and the IC Act. Section 553(c) of the APA requires an oral hearing (more precisely a §§ 556–557 proceeding)[26] only when a separate statute (usually the agency's enabling act) requires rules to be made "on the record after opportunity for an agency hearing." To the extent that the lower federal courts thought that the use of *hearing* in the IC Act triggered the formal hearing requirements of the APA, they were wrong, because the IC Act does not contain the additional language, "on the record after opportunity for agency hearing."

It is arguable that the IC Act itself somehow requires an oral hearing, irrespective of the APA. Remember that you generally analyze this type of problem by looking first at the enabling act, and if the enabling act is silent or ambiguous on procedures, you look at the APA. After a lengthy analysis of rulemaking principles, due process in a rulemaking setting, the original IC Act, and the IC Act as amended in 1966, the Court concluded that Congress used the term *hearing* in the IC Act in the same way as it uses the term in the APA. In other words, the IC Act does not require any *more* process than the railroads would enjoy under the APA.

---

[24] IC Act § 1(14)(a), recodified at 49 U.S.C. § 10101(14)(a) (repealed 1995).

[25] The ICC conducted a preliminary investigation in which written and oral statements were collected from the railroads. It then published notice of the rulemaking, directed railroads to collect sample information and held what the Court described as an "informal conference" in which the ICC discussed the proposals with the railroads. After all of this, and after getting a little push from Congress, the Commission announced the final rule.

[26] Recall that §§ 556–557 include direct and cross-examination, an administrative law judge as a presiding officer, testimony under oath, a verbatim transcript, etc.

This is a common method of statutory interpretation. When Congress uses the same term in two different, but related statutes, and does not expressly distinguish between the use of the word in each of the statutes, it is logical that Congress intended to use the same term the same way in both acts. In any event, we now know that the mere use of the term, *hearing*, in an enabling act requires nothing more in the way of rulemaking procedure than the procedures set out in § 553. It also makes exceptionally clear that formal rulemaking is never to be imposed on an agency unless Congress requires it with a precise formula of words.

[C]   "Hybrid" Rulemaking and *Vermont Yankee*

Florida East Coast dealt with the two polar positions in agency rulemaking-the distinction between informal (§ 553) procedures and formal (§§ 556–557) procedures. Is there anything in between? Of course there is. Many agencies and many legislatures, including Congress, have begun to experiment with procedures often referred to as *hybrid* rulemaking. This term is used to describe rulemaking procedures that are neither as skeletal as § 553, nor as elaborate and time-consuming as §§ 556–557. In administrative law, the term, *hybrid*, is not a term of art and is not mentioned anywhere in the APA. The term refers only to agency rulemaking procedures, whatever their specific elements, that stand somewhere between informal and formal rulemaking procedures.

The more difficult question is whether a reviewing court has the power to order an agency to adopt hybrid rulemaking procedures when the agency chooses not to do so and when Congress has said nothing in the enabling act. In 1978, the Supreme Court decided *Vermont Yankee Nuclear Power Corp. v. Natural Resources Defense Council, Inc.*,[27] a case that holds very plainly and simply:

> In the absence of "constitutional constraints or extremely compelling circumstances" a court MAY NOT impose rulemaking procedures on an agency beyond those set out in § 553 of the APA.

In other words, the procedures set out in § 553 are maximum rulemaking procedures unless Congress demands that the agency do more or unless the agency itself chooses, in its discretion, to provide more.

But this is working through *Vermont Yankee* backward. The initial dispute in the case stemmed from actions taken by the Nuclear Regulatory Commission in issuing a construction permit to Vermont Yankee Nuclear Power Corporation to begin building a nuclear power plant.[28] During the elaborate evidentiary proceedings that

---

[27]   435 U.S. 519 (1978).

[28]   You will get more out of *Vermont Yankee* if you understand the NRC licensing process that was in effect when *Vermont Yankee* was decided. Constructing nuclear power plants is expensive and controversial. Banks and other lending institutions are reluctant to lend money to a project without an assurance that the plant will be completed and the loans paid off through sales of electricity. To help applicants obtain funding-and to provide close monitoring of the project from start to finish-the NRC divided its licensing process into two parts: (1) An applicant applied for permission to construct the plant by filing an elaborate set of documents, including an environmental impact statement, blueprints, engineering specifications and many other things; (2) after lengthy review, the NRC could grant permission (the construction permit) to start construction. However, the plant could not begin operations

led to the issuance of the construction permit, a number of issues arose involving the disposal of the power plant's high-level radioactive waste and various other environmental concerns.

Recall that an agency has discretion to make new policy in either a rulemaking or an adjudication, so the NRC could have disposed of some of these issues in the Vermont Yankee license adjudication. It chose, however, to initiate a rulemaking for some of the environmental problems, and it is this rulemaking that led to the dispute finally resolved by the Supreme Court.

The NRC proposed to deal with certain power plant environmental effects through promulgation of what has since become known as the S-3 Table (a set of engineering and operating standards by which, in the Commission's judgment, the negative environmental consequences of nuclear waste disposal would be held to acceptable minimums). The NRC promulgated the S-3 Table after the following proceedings:

1. Notice of proposed rulemaking;

2. An oral hearing permitting interested persons to present their views to the Commission;

3. Opportunity afforded the participants to review not only all documents but also the written transcript; and

4. Filing of supplemental written comments.

Some of the parties, including the Natural Resources Defense Council, a feisty environmental organization, decided that even this was not sufficient process and asked the Commission to provide an opportunity for discovery and cross-examination before making the final rule. Because the NRC steadfastly refused to agree to any additional process, the D.C. Circuit vacated the S-3 table for procedural deficiencies. The Supreme Court granted certiorari and proceeded, unanimously, to write one of the strongest opinions of the past several decades, reversing the circuit and holding squarely that § 553 procedures are, under normal circumstances, all that an agency need follow.

Vermont Yankee can be understood on a number of different grounds. First, it may be seen as simply a reiteration of the doctrine stated in *Florida East Coast* that it is up to Congress or the agencies to require more than notice and comment procedures. Second, to the extent that an agency gives more process, it is within the agency's discretion to do so, not the court's. Third, readers should be aware of a hidden dimension. For a number of years, the Supreme Court has become far less patient with what was perceived by some justices as excessively free-wheeling decision-making on the part of the D.C. Circuit. To a certain extent, *Vermont Yankee* was a message to the D.C. Circuit to sit down and shut up.[29]

---

until the second phase of the process, the grant of the operating license, is complete.

[29] One year later, the circuit took up the same issue-the validity of the S-3 Table. This time the only possible argument was on substantive grounds-whether the NRC rule was arbitrary and capricious. The circuit held the table invalid as arbitrary agency action. The Supreme Court again reversed in an opinion filled with language that could have left no possible doubt that the Court wanted the circuit to leave the NRC alone. *See Baltimore Gas & Elec. Co. v. Natural Res. Def. Council, Inc.*, 462 U.S. 87 (1983).

Is there any daylight in *Vermont Yankee* that might permit a reviewing court to require more than § 553 procedures? For most practical purposes the answer is "no," although the Court was as careful, as usual, not to say "never."[30] The exception of constitutional constraints was probably inserted to accommodate *Goldberg v. Kelly*,[31] a case in which the Court mandated certain administrative hearing procedures as a matter of constitutional due process, although *Goldberg* was definitely *not* a case involving agency rulemaking.

The difficult test to apply is the *extremely compelling circumstances* exception. NRC deals with issues of nuclear safety, matters of exceptional public concern, particularly after the incidents at Three Mile Island and Chernobyl. Yet, it was precisely the setting of nuclear safety that the Court held not to be an extremely compelling circumstance. Visualizing any other instance of agency action more compelling than nuclear safety is difficult. This could be a meaningless exception inserted by the Court, simply because it did not want to close off some unforeseen future possibilities. In the Court's opinion, Justice Rehnquist hinted that "a totally unjustified departure from well settled agency procedures of long standing might require judicial correction." But he, and the Court, refused to elaborate on this concept, because it was not fairly raised on the *Vermont Yankee* facts.

At the same time, no one should read *Vermont Yankee* as apocalyptic or particularly ideological. Recall, first of all, that the decision was unanimous. Whatever else this case is about, it did not seem to trigger the profound liberal/conservative split that existed on the Supreme Court throughout the 1970s and 1980s. Second, recall that most courts have been reluctant to overturn agency rules for procedural deficiencies, both before and after *Vermont Yankee*. The case is probably most important as a signal to the lower federal courts to back away from using artificial and inappropriate grounds for overturning agency action. Most courts appear to have heeded the message.

§ 7.04 PROPER HYBRID AND FORMAL RULEMAKING

The message of *Vermont Yankee* is so clear and unambiguous that some students may make the mistake of thinking that no agency ever uses hybrid or formal rulemaking procedures. That is not the case at all. Many agencies do so because Congress has mandated hybrid procedures. Other agencies do so on their own initiative. Remember that the NRC used some oral process in developing the S-3 Table at issue in *Vermont Yankee* even though § 553 requires only written comments.

Perhaps the most frequently cited legitimate example of hybrid rulemaking is the Magnuson-Moss Act, also known as the Federal Trade Commission Improvements Act of 1975,[32] a statute that imposes detailed procedures on the Federal

---

[30] Students should be aware that Professor K.C. Davis disagreed with this analysis. He insists that courts have tacked procedures onto agency rulemaking both before and after *Vermont Yankee* and will likely continue to do so. KENNETH CULP DAVIS, ADMINISTRATIVE LAW TREATISE § 6:37 (1982 supp.).

[31] 397 U.S. 254 (1970); *see supra* § 5.03.

[32] 15 U.S.C. § 57a.

Trade Commission's promulgation of trade regulation rules. Briefly stated, Magnuson-Moss requires the following:

1. Notice of Proposed Rulemaking

2. Solicitation and submission of written comments

3. An informal hearing with the following ingredients:

   a) oral or written submissions or both;

   b) rebuttal evidence and cross-examination if issues of material fact are in dispute.

4. Promulgation of a final rule based on the rulemaking record accompanied by a statement of basis and purpose.

Note that these procedures are more detailed than § 553, but far less cumbersome than §§ 556–557; and, most importantly, they are prescribed by Congress. An example of congressionally-mandated formal rulemaking is the Fair Packaging and Labeling Act.[33] There is no problem with hybrid or formal rulemaking when it springs from legislative action or is a choice made by an agency.

§ 7.05 NEGOTIATED RULEMAKING AND OTHER STATUTORY CONTROLS ON AGENCY RULEMAKING

[A] Negotiated Rulemaking

There have been some important attempts to further rationalize the agency rulemaking process. A number of experiments, referred to as *regulatory negotiation*, were pioneered mainly by the Department of Transportation and the Environmental Protection Agency in the 1980s, and have attempted to provide a more structured, more closely-confined process for the development of rules in an attempt (1) to satisfy more of the groups directly affected by the rules and (2) to stave off some of the instant litigation that is triggered by disgruntled pressure groups as soon as the rules are issued in final form.[34]

Not all agencies have had a happy experience with notice and comment rulemaking. The submission of comments in written form sometimes makes it difficult to develop a dialogue on all the relevant issues. The invitation to all *interested persons* sounds nice in theory, but in reality there are usually only a small number of groups-at the federal level often represented by trade associations or other special interest groups-that have a true stake in the outcome of any rule. More importantly, the comments tend to come in only after the agency has expended considerable effort in writing a proposed rule and tend to focus on the defects and deficiencies in the proposed rule-to poke holes in the rule by way of

---

[33] 15 U.S.C. § 1455.

[34] *See, e.g.*, Neil Eisner, *Regulatory Negotiation: A Real World Experience*, 31 FED. B. NEWS & J. 371 (1984).

destructive, rather than constructive criticism. Finally, any well-financed group that feels abused by the final rule will, in all likelihood, try to tie up implementation of the rule in court.

A number of agency personnel and some sharper thinking private sector commentators[35] developed some innovative pilot programs that attempted to bring these special interest groups around a table to discuss and negotiate a possible rule, even in advance of the agency's publishing a notice of proposed rulemaking.[36] The movement toward regulatory negotiation (sometimes colloquially referred to as "reg neg") took off when the Administrative Conference of the United States began commissioning empirical and theoretical studies of the process.[37]

As one might expect, the process was not without its impediments. First of all, § 553 of the APA is silent on negotiated rulemaking. Second, peripheral statutes such as the Government in the Sunshine Act[38] and the Federal Advisory Committee Act[39] contained language that seemed to get in the way of negotiating rules. While none of these impediments halted a bona fide negotiated rulemaking in those agencies that were committed to the process, it made a number of other agencies a little hesitant about trying out this new concept. As a result, in late 1990, Congress decided that the entire matter needed legislative clarification and, for the first time in years, wrote extensive amendments to the APA that are known as the Negotiated Rulemaking Act of 1990.[40]

The Negotiated Rulemaking Act, reauthorized by Congress in 1996 and now a fully legitimate component of the APA, is not particularly complicated and may be best understood as an adjunct to normal notice and comment rulemaking for those instances in which an agency determines that reg neg would be a good thing. No

---

[35] *See, e.g.*, an article by Philip Harter, who might properly be called the private sector "father" of regulatory negotiation: Philip J. Harter, *Negotiating Regulations: A Cure for Malaise*, 71 Geo. L.J. 1 (1982).

[36] One of the pioneers of the technique was the Environmental Protection Agency. *See, e.g.*, Daniel J. Fiorino & Chris Kirtz, *Breaking Down Walls: Negotiated Rulemaking at EPA*, 4 Temp. Envtl. L. & Tech. J. 29 (1985).

[37] One of the primary sources of background material on regulatory negotiation is a thick volume compiled by the Conference: Acus, Negotiated Rulemaking Sourcebook (2d ed. 1995). The Administrative Conference was out of business for a number of years, but has now been reauthorized and currently funded by Congress. *See* 36 Administrative and Regulatory News 221 (2011).

[38] 5 U.S.C. § 552b. *See* the discussion of the Sunshine Act *infra* Chapter 14, § 14.04.

[39] 5 U.S.C. App. The FACA requires an agency to establish and publicize the appointment of a federal advisory committee if it intends to meet with more than one private sector individual on more than a single occasion to discuss agency policy making and to receive advice and recommendations on that policy from the private sector. The Act's purposes are salutary: it is designed to give notice to all interested persons that the agency is consulting with private sector persons to avoid the appearance of secret meetings with favored groups. However, much like the Government in the Sunshine Act, FACA is probably applied more in the breach than in the observance. For two excellent FACA articles that grew out of one of the last projects commissioned by the now-defunct Administrative Conference of the United States, *see* Steven P. Croley & William F. Funk, *The Federal Advisory Committee Act and Good Government*, 14 Yale J. on Reg. 451 (1997); Steven P. Croley, *Practical Guidance on the Applicability of the Federal Advisory Committee Act*, 10 Admin. L.J. Am. U. 111 (1996).

[40] Pub. L. No. 101-648, 104 Stat. 4969, amended by the Administrative Dispute Resolution Act of 1996, Pub. L. No. 104-320, now codified at 5 U.S.C. §§ 561–570.

agency is required under the act to utilize regulatory negotiation. No agency is required to publish either a proposed or a final rule merely because it is the product of regulatory negotiation. And an agency's decision, either to use or to forego regulatory negotiation, is exempt from judicial review as being a decision that is totally within the agency's discretion.[41]

Regulatory negotiation is commenced by the agency's making an initial determination that a particular rulemaking setting is a good prospect for reg neg. Section 596 of the Act suggests that the agency consider, among other things, whether: (1) there is a need for a rule; (2) there are a limited number of identifiable interests that will be significantly affected by the rule; (3) there is a reasonable likelihood that a committee can be convened with a balanced representation of persons who are proper representatives and show evidence of being able to negotiate in good faith; (4) the negotiating process will not delay promulgation or implementation of a final rule.

Note that these criteria hint at some of the advantages and disadvantages of *reg neg* that were discerned in the pilot projects. A rulemaking that will affect vast numbers of diversely situated persons is probably not a good prospect for *reg neg*. There must be a relatively small number of participants for the negotiated rulemaking to proceed smoothly. One of the successful projects at the Department of Transportation involved the Federal Aviation Administration's making of a rule involving maximum hours of flying time for pilots and other flight crew. A rule was necessary; there were a small number of groups actually affected by the proposals, all of whom were strongly and capably represented by trade associations; and, in the judgment of the FAA, a negotiation would likely speed up implementation, rather than delay it.[42] The Act permits the agency to obtain the services of a *convener* to assist in making these threshold determinations.[43]

Once a decision is made to proceed with *reg neg*, the agency must publish a notice in the *Federal Register* announcing the project, describing the subject of the negotiated rulemaking, setting out a list of the persons that it believes are proper participants and inviting other persons to apply for seats around the negotiating table.[44] To a certain extent, this may be one of the Achilles' heels of the negotiated rulemaking process. To be effective, the negotiation must involve a relatively small and relatively manageable group of participants. But there are few federal agency rulemakings that do not affect large numbers of individuals. Obviously, not all affected individuals can participate. One device for dealing with the problem of too many people is to look to trade associations and special interest groups as representatives of the individuals actually affected by the rulemaking. There is no reason to have all licensed airline pilots around the table if they can be adequately represented by the Airline Pilots Association. The Act limits membership on the committee to twenty-five members unless the agency determines that a larger

---

[41] 5 U.S.C. § 570. This section states: "Any agency action relating to establishing, assisting, or terminating a negotiated rulemaking committee under this subchapter shall not be subject to judicial review."

[42] This is one of the projects described in Eisner, *supra*, note 34.

[43] 5 U.S.C. § 563(b).

[44] 5 U.S.C. § 564.

group must be formed to represent adequately all significant interests. At least one member must be a representative of the agency.[45]

After publication of the notice and a final agency decision to commence the regulatory negotiation process, the committee is formed and begins deliberation under the guidance of what the Act, § 566(d), calls a *facilitator*. The facilitator may be a private sector person or a government employee, but whoever is nominated must be approved by the committee. The facilitator chairs the negotiating sessions and keeps the records of the proceeding. If the committee reaches a consensus on the text of a rule, it transmits this consensus to the agency in the form of a proposed rule. The text of the proposed rule may then be handled through the conventional notice and comment process, but with the *Federal Register* notice including information on the preceding negotiation. If the negotiation fails-as many of them do-the agency is at least armed with guidance from the committee on future pitfalls in its rulemaking.[46]

More than twenty five years after its initial enactment, negotiated rulemaking remains somewhat obscure and underutilized. Even now, agencies seem to shrink away from the process. Too many of the agencies are too comfortable with conventional notice-and-comment rulemaking (warts and all). At the same time, the 1996 permanent reauthorization of the statute at least signals congressional approval of the process; but even if only a few agencies use it successfully, it will stand as a significant departure, and properly handled an improvement, over the traditional notice-and-comment process.[47]

---

[45] 5 U.S.C. § 565.

[46] One of the real contributions of the *ACUS Sourcebook* is a number of communications from facilitators reporting on both successful and unsuccessful negotiations.

[47] See a distinguished report on negotiated rulemaking prepared under the auspices of the Administrative Conference: Cornelius Kerwin & Laura Langbein, *An Evaluation of Negotiated Rulemaking at the Environmental Protection Agency, Phase I*. This report was issued in September, 1995, and some of its conclusory language is striking: "This first phase of research has produced many results that advocates of negotiated rulemaking will find encouraging . . . [However,] [w]hat we cannot answer is whether in all or any dimensions of rulemaking studied here reg neg is superior to or even different from conventional techniques." Report at 48. In 1995, ACUS issued a revised reg neg sourcebook. Many of the significant contributions of the ACUS Sourcebook are embodied in a number of communications from facilitators reporting on both successful and unsuccessful negotiations. *See also* Cary Coglianese, *Assessing Consensus: The Promise and Performance of Negotiated Rulemaking*, 46 DUKE L.J. 1255 (1997). This article is notable for its citations to a number of statutes that *mandate* negotiated rulemaking. Philip Harter frequently admonishes the agencies for dragging their feet on negotiated rulemaking. Philip J. Harter, *Fear of Commitment: An Affliction of Adolescents*, 46 DUKE L.J. 1389 (1997). One sharply negative assessment of negotiated rulemaking is to be found in William Funk, *Bargaining Toward the New Millennium: Regulatory Negotiation and the Subversion of the Public Interest*, 46 DUKE L.J. 1351 (1997). An article much more complimentary of the process that recognizes negotiated rulemaking as part of the movement toward collaboration and away from the adversary model is Jody Freeman, *Collaborative Governance in the Administrative State*, 45 UCLA. L. REV. 1 (1997). *See also* Andrew P. Morris, Bruce Yandle & Andrew Dorchak, *Choosing How to Regulate*, 29 HARV. ENVTL. L. REV. 179, 192 (2005) ("Regulation by negotiation failed to live up to its proponents' enthusiastic predictions but . . . provides agencies with significant advantages [such as it] is cheaper to implement than [conventional rulemaking]"); Daniel P. Selmi, *The Promise and Limits of Negotiated Rulemaking: Evaluating the Negotiation of a Regional Air Quality Rule*, 35 ENVTL. L. 415 (2005).

[B]   Other Statutory Controls

There are a number of restrictions imposed on agency rulemaking by Congress apart from the APA. In certain circumstances, the Government in the Sunshine Act[48] may require some of the agency's deliberations to be conducted in open meetings. If the agency's action is a major federal action significantly affecting the quality of the human environment, the agency may have to complete an environmental impact statement under the National Environmental Policy Act.[49] If the new rule imposes additional record keeping or reporting requirements on affected persons, the agency may have to comply with the clearance procedures for new federal forms imposed by the Paperwork Reduction Act.[50] There were amendments made in 1995 to the Paperwork Reduction Act that some commentators believe substantially strengthens the role of the Office of Information and Regulatory Affairs (the supervising entity for the Act). The 1995 Act also deals more effectively with the now very important phenomenon of electronic forms and electronic information.[51]

Even if none of the above apply, agencies are now required to comply with the Regulatory Flexibility Act,[52] as now amended by the Small Business Regulatory Enforcement Fairness Act of 1996.[53] With the 1996 amendments, the Regulatory Flexibility Act has become one of the most important general requirements imposed on agency rulemaking apart from the APA itself. *Regflex*, as Washington lawyers like to call the statute, is intended to force agencies to make periodic comprehensive reviews of their regulatory activities by publishing a semi-annual agenda of proposed and continuing rulemaking. These agendas, published in the *Federal Register*, are a good source of information on many different agency proceedings and generally include a brief statement of what the rule encompasses, a chronology of rulemaking activities and proposed rulemaking completion dates. For anyone with clients who are anticipating rules to be issued, it can be a helpful publication. Agencies always have trouble setting these agendas.[54]

In addition, *Regflex* requires agencies to consider the impact their rules have on small businesses and to discuss that impact in the preamble to the rules prior to promulgation. While this requirement apparently is not an independent ground on

---

[48]   15 U.S.C. § 552b (described in detail in Chapter 14).

[49]   42 U.S.C. §§ 4321–4347.

[50]   44 U.S.C. §§ 3501–3520.

[51]   Paperwork Reduction Act of 1995, Pub. L. No. 104-13, 109 Stat. 163 (codified at 44 U.S.C. §§ 3501–3520. A good commentary on the 1995 changes is Jeffrey S. Lubbers, *Paperwork Redux: The (Stronger) Paperwork Reduction Act of 1995*, 49 ADMIN. L. REV. 111 (1997).

[52]   5 U.S.C. §§ 601–612.

[53]   Pub. L. No. 104-121, 1996 U.S.C.C.A.N. (110 Stat.) 857 (to be codified in scattered sections of 5 U.S.C., 15 U.S.C., and 28 U.S.C.). An excellent commentary on the 1996 Act is Thomas O. Sargentich, *Recent Developments: Regulatory Reform and the 104th Congress: The Small Business Regulatory Enforcement Fairness Act*, 49 ADMIN. L. REV. 123 (1997).

[54]   For a discussion of agendas and many other issues, *see* Sidney A. Shapiro, *Agency Priority Setting and the Review of Existing Agency Rules*, 48 ADMIN. L. REV. 370 (1996).

which to attack the validity of a rule, it does give certain agency rulemaking a new dimension.[55]

The Small Business Regulatory Enforcement Fairness Act of 1996 goes much further in terms of putting real teeth in the regflex concept. Briefly stated, the SBREFA provides the following: 1. Judicial review for: (a) the contents of the agency's regflex analysis; (b) the agency's certification that the rule does not have an impact on small entities; (c) any agency delay in completing its regflex analysis; (d) the agency's periodical review of its regulations. The statute, § 611, permits judicial review of these issues to be sought by aggrieved parties up to a year *after* the final agency action. 2. New requirements for the drafting of rules including so-called plain English language and the preparation of handbooks to guide compliance on the part of small businesses. 3. The establishment in the Small Business Administration of a "Small Business and Agriculture Regulatory Enforcement Ombudsman." This office is supposed to work with every other federal agency to see that each agency is properly attentive to the concerns of small business. 4. Amendment of the Equal Access to Justice Act to permit small entities to recover attorneys' fees against an agency when agency action is attributable to excessive and unreasonable demands in the agency's performance of its enforcement obligations. Not all commentators are sanguine about the SBREFA. Professor Sargentich, for example, believes that the Act "adds numerous new procedural requirements, a greater analytical burden on agencies, heightened prospects of searching judicial review, and broadened possibilities to stall and perhaps derail regulatory efforts . . . At bottom, the Act imposes burdensome layers of legal constraint on [agencies] already struggling mightily to meet minimal performance standards."[56] Not everyone views the new Act quite so drastically, although it is clear that the mere enactment of the 1996 legislation illustrates the continuing clout of small businesses in the United States. For lawyers representing small entities before federal agencies, it expands their leverage considerably.

§ 7.06   SUPERVISION OF EXECUTIVE BRANCH RULEMAKING BY THE OFFICE OF MANAGEMENT AND BUDGET

In the relatively short time he was in office, President Ford decided that agencies were not paying enough attention to the economic impact of their rulemaking activities, and he signed and implemented an executive order requiring executive branch agencies to prepare an inflation impact statement to accompany their rules. During President Carter's administration, a number of presidential advisers

---

[55] *Compare Small Refiner Lead Phase-Down Task Force v. Environmental Protection Agency*, 705 F.2d 506 (D.C. Cir. 1983) (rule might be struck down if there is a defect in Regflex analysis), *with Thompson v. Clark*, 741 F.2d 401 (D.C. Cir. 1984) (a failure in the Regflex analysis may not be an independent ground for declaring a rule invalid, but may help support an argument that a rule is otherwise arbitrary and capricious).

[56] Sargentich, *supra* note 53, at 137. For a lengthy article arguing against the policy wisdom of treating small business differently, *see* Richard J. Pierce, Jr., *Small Is Not Beautiful: The Case Against Special Regulatory Treatment of Small Firms*, 50 Admin. L. Rev. 537 (1998).

concluded that there was not enough coordination among federal agencies. Fights over territory, personality conflicts, self-aggrandizement and all of the other hidden (or non-legal) aspects of agency functioning began to hinder efficient agency action. President Carter attempted to rein in the executive branch agencies (*i.e.*, those agencies directly under the President's control, excluding the independent regulatory commissions) by signing an executive order that gave a great deal of supervisory control of agency rulemaking to the Office of Management and Budget (OMB).

OMB is well-known today mainly because of the activities of one or two of the personalities who have served as director and because of its central role in the Gramm-Rudman-Hollings controversy (discussed in Chapter 2). Most people have very little understanding of exactly how the agency works. Some explanation is required here before launching into a description of the OMB's impact on rulemaking.

Established just after World War One, OMB was originally called the Bureau of the Budget and was mainly involved in helping to set and administer executive branch expenditures. The OMB is formally designated on government organizational charts as a part of the Executive Office of the President and is led by a Director who is appointed by the President with the advice and consent of the Senate. In recent years, OMB has become a central institution in the executive branch, with power and influence ranging far beyond the numbers-crunching that was initially seen as its primary role.

In 1993, President Clinton issued an executive order governing OMB's role in agency rulemaking, Executive Order 12866,[57] that provides the framework for the current system of OMB review. EO 12866 borrowed heavily from the predecessor Reagan-Bush EOs and established the basic framework for OMB's assessment of agency rules. It required every executive branch agency to:

    a.   issue only those regulations that are necessary by law, to interpret the law, or "made necessary by compelling public need" such as market failures;

    b.   make regulations only after a thorough assessment of the costs and benefits of the regulations, both those costs and benefits that can be quantified and those that are difficult to quantify;

    c.   choose among regulatory alternatives that maximize the net benefits to society;

    d.   consider alternatives to direct [so-called "command and control"] regulation, including such possibilities as user fees or marketable permits;

    e.   tailor its regulations to impose the least burden on society, consistent with

---

[57] 58 Fed. Reg. 51,735 (1993) For an incisive commentary on the use of executive orders in the context of agency rulemaking, *see* Peter L. Strauss, *Presidential Rulemaking*, 72 CHI.-KENT L. REV. 965 (1997), and Peter L. Strauss, *From Expertise to Politics: The Transformation of American Rulemaking*, 31 WAKE FOREST L. REV. 745 (1996). The main executive order on the same topic in force during the Reagan-Bush administration was Exec. Order No. 12,291, 46 Fed. Reg. 13,193 (Feb. 19, 1981). For a concise review of requirements that an agency must consider when adopting a rule, *see* Mark Seidenfeld, *A Table of Requirements for Federal Administrative Rulemaking*, 27 FLA. ST. U. L. REV. 533 (2000).

the regulatory objectives of the regulation;

f. state the regulations in terms that are "simple and easy to understand, with the goal of minimizing the potential for uncertainty and litigation arising from such uncertainty."

The Executive Order went on to require agencies to develop a regulatory planning mechanism and a unified regulatory agenda. Each agency was directed to appoint a "regulatory policy officer" to work on regulations within the agency and serve as the crucial liaison with OMB's Office of Information and Regulatory Affairs (OIRA). Virtually all proposed agency regulations were to be submitted for full-blown, independent review to OIRA. The Obama Administration has preserved Executive Order 12886 and has issued a supplementary Executive Order 13563 that contains additional pronouncements on agency cost benefit analysis.[58]

Note that these standards are not mentioned in the APA. Few of them are expressly set out in enabling acts. Nonetheless, because it is an executive order, the executive branch agencies are governed by its terms.[59]

These Executive Orders have had a major impact on federal rulemaking. For the first time, agencies have been directed to do some kind of cost benefit evaluation of their rules.[60] Not all of these requirements have played to strong reviews.[61]

The most drastic change in federal rulemaking is the new OMB clearance requirement. Critics of the EO suggest that OMB has accumulated so much power through the clearance process that it has become in essence a "super agency" with powers clearly not contemplated by Congress when it first established OMB.[62] The practical effect of the clearance requirement has been to shift a great deal of the

---

[58] Exec. Order No. 13,563, 76 Fed. Reg. 3821 (Jan. 21, 2011). For a lengthy and exceptionally detailed analysis of this series of executive orders and the work of OMB Office of Information and Regulatory Affairs, see Symposium, *OIRA Thirtieth Anniversary Conference*, 63 ADMIN. L. REV. 1 (Special Edition 2011).

[59] Certain parts of the Clinton Executive Order purport to govern the activities of the independent regulatory commissions. It remains uncertain whether those agencies may be validly affected by a presidential executive order; but there is, of course, no doubt as to the compelling effect of such an order on the cabinet and so-called presidential agencies. *See also* Arthur Fraas & Randall Lutter, *On the Economic Analysis of Regulations at Independent Regulatory Commissions*, 63 ADMIN. L. REV. 213 (Special Edition, 2011).

[60] Vice President Gore has amplified many of these concepts in his various pronouncements on "reinventing government." The Clinton/Gore ideas on reinventing government are discussed below.

[61] In a lengthy analysis of the predecessor Reagan-Bush Executive Order, from which the Clinton order borrows heavily, Professors Sunstein and Pildes comment that the executive orders may have (1) caused an unlawful transfer of authority from the agencies to OMB; (2) made the regulatory analysis process far too secretive; (3) triggered huge delays in needed rulemaking; (4) overemphasized the device of cost-benefit analysis (discussed below). Cass R. Sunstein & Richard H. Pildes, *Reinventing the Regulatory State*, 62 U. CHI. L. REV. 1, 4–6 (1995). But recall the "gored ox" concept. A lot of people have praised these requirements as needed innovations in policing agencies that no longer reflect the public interest. In April, 1997, President Clinton issued Executive Order 13,045, requiring agencies that deal with environmental health and safety regulation to pay special heed to any risks that disproportionately affect children. This "child impact" analysis is in addition to the analysis required by Executive Order 12,866. As the Sixth Edition of this book goes to press, Professor Sunstein is the head of OIRA.

[62] *See infra* § 7.08, on ex parte contacts in agency rulemaking.

lobbying activities concerning agency rules from the agencies themselves to various people in OMB. Given that OMB personnel are not experts in the work of most agencies, some critics suspect that the OMB clearance process may have diluted the expertise of agency rulemaking. Moreover, it is still unclear whether a violation of the commands of the EO-or, conversely, an agency's refusal to follow the EO-is grounds for judicial review of administrative action. Whatever your personal evaluation, keep in mind that OMB is now a strong voice in rulemaking and will likely continue as such for the foreseeable future.[63]

After President Bush, Sr. took office in 1989, a Competitiveness Council was set up under the chairmanship of Vice President Quayle. This Council was composed of persons from the private sector, mainly representatives of large U.S. businesses, who have made a number of attempts-in the guise of protecting American competitiveness abroad -to halt or modify a number of major agency rulemakings, including some new rules issued by the Environmental Protection Agency under the amendments to the Clean Air Act. Given that President Bush served only one term, the actual impact of the council remains unclear.[64]

The idea of reinventing government sprang from President Clinton's premise that the federal government was too big and cost too much. Under the direction of Vice President Gore, the Clinton administration initiated a program called the National Performance Review. This review is a lengthy set of recommendations for cutting back on government regulation that has a statutory basis in the Government Performance and Results Act of 1993. This statute requires each agency head to develop and submit to OMB a strategic five-year plan that contains: (1) a comprehensive mission statement for the agency, (2) a statement of general goals and objectives, (3) a description of how those goals and objectives are to be achieved. In addition, each agency must submit to the OMB an annual performance plan accompanied by a report on results of performance. Virtually all of these initiatives have been continued in President Obama's administration. While the White House continues to trumpet these ventures, no one is quite sure whether government has truly been reinvented.[65]

---

[63] Much has been written on this topic. A number of the better articles are: Harold H. Bruff, *Presidential Management of Agency Rulemaking*, 57 GEO. WASH. L. REV. 533 (1989); Peter Raven-Hansen, *Making Agencies Follow Orders: Judicial Review of Agency Violations of Executive Order 12,191*, 1983 DUKE L.J. 285; Harold H. Bruff, *Presidential Power and Administrative Rulemaking*, 88 YALE L.J. 451 (1979).

[64] Many of these issues have been discussed in Bruff, *Presidential Management of Agency Rulemaking, supra* note 63.

[65] Many of these materials may be found on the White House's web pages: www.whitehouse.gov. A much more elaborate discussion of the early days of the Clinton/Gore reinventing government venture may be found in Colloquium, *The Fifth Annual Robert C. Byrd Conference on the Administrative Process: The First Year of Clinton/Gore: Reinventing Government or Refining Reagan/Bush Initiatives?*, 8 ADMIN L.J. AM. U. 23 (1994).

§ 7.07   COST-BENEFIT ANALYSIS

[A]   Cost-Benefit Methodology

The term, *cost-benefit analysis*, encompasses many different concepts and has engendered a lot of controversy. The whole idea is relatively new to agency decision making, even though a great deal of unconscious or unarticulated cost-benefit analysis has been done over the past 100 years or so since the advent of administrative agencies.

There are a number of ways to approach this topic. Perhaps the best way to start is to identify the different processes of analysis that sometimes fit under the general umbrella of cost-benefit analysis. Note that each of these processes is an attempt to accomplish an understandable goal-to get as much information and insight on a proposed government action as possible. The decision to take action comes later and is, or ought to be, a wholly separate process.

One expert on government policy making, Professor Lester Lave, professor of economics at Carnegie-Mellon's Graduate School of Industrial Administration, has identified five categories of regulatory analysis, many of which are often referred to as cost-benefit analysis and thus, frequently confused by students, lawyers and even government decision-makers: (1) no risk, (2) risk-risk, (3) risk-benefit, (4) regulatory budget and (5) formal cost-benefit analysis.[66] Each of these terms requires some explanation.

No risk analysis is a decision-making standard that requires agencies simply to eliminate all risk to the public. For example, there was, until repealed in 1996, a provision in the Federal Food, Drug and Cosmetic Act known as the Delaney Amendment or Delaney Clause[67] that prohibited the sale of any food containing even the slightest amount of a carcinogenic (cancer-causing) substance. There were no exceptions in this statute. Congress had written a categorical prohibition in order to maintain a regulatory standard that eliminates risk. In 1996, the provision was effectively repealed and a much more useful and less categorical risk assessment provision was put into the statute.

There may, however, be times when the consumption of minute quantities of one dangerous substance (nitrite, for example) may be necessary to protect persons from another hazard (botulism). Professor Lave refers to this as *risk-risk* analysis. Note that neither *no-risk*, nor *risk-risk* analysis has anything to do with the *cost* of regulation.

There are other times when an agency should know what a regulation is going to cost without worrying too much about its benefits in order to determine whether the proposal is the most efficient and effective method of dealing with the problem.

---

[66] Lester B. Lave, *Testimony Before the Subcommittee on Oversight and Investigations and Subcommittee on Consumer Protection and Finance, House Committee on Interstate and Foreign Commerce*, 96th Cong. 1st Sess. (July 1979). This discussion and much more may be found in Professor Lave's book, LESTER B. LAVE, THE STRATEGY OF SOCIAL REGULATION (1981).

[67] 21 U.S.C. § 321 (repealed 1996).

Some writers call this a *cost-assessment.* Professor Lave refers to it as *regulatory budget.*

The most intense, most highly quantified and most controversial analysis is formal *cost-benefit analysis.* It is easy to describe. A decision maker analyzes all costs associated with an action, as well as the benefits. Once the costs and benefits are established, she assigns a dollar-value to each. If the dollar value of the costs exceeds the dollar value of the benefits, the action should not be taken; if the benefits exceed the costs, the action is permissible.

As simple as this sounds, it horrifies some people because many government agencies deal with human health and safety and classic cost-benefit analysis, by definition, requires placing a dollar value on human life. But consider that many decision makers do that silently whether we like it or not. For example, an agency decision *not* to promulgate a regulation may be a matter of unarticulated cost-benefit analysis. Proponents of overt, on-the-record cost-benefit analysis argue that we should get this stuff out on the table and talk about it, rather than burying it.[68]

To see how cost-benefit analysis is actually done, consider the problem of acid rain. Acid rain is caused by the emission of airborne sulfur oxides by coal-fired factories and power plants. The airborne sulfur makes rainwater considerably more acidic and thereby, has a detrimental effect on plant life, including forests and agricultural operations. For example, many Canadians believe that acid rain emanating from coal-fired plants in the Ohio River Valley is killing a large part of the forests in Eastern Canada.

Assume that our research tells us that we can stop virtually all emissions of sulfur for a total cost of $500 billion. Assume further that our benefits estimates tell us that stopping all sulfur emissions will result in benefits quantified at $650 billion. Cost-benefit analysis then simply subtracts the $500 billion in costs from the $650 billion in benefits, for a positive gain in benefits of $150 billion. An agency administrator might use these calculations as a basis for going ahead with a rulemaking designed to halt all sulfur oxide emissions.

However, we can get even more sophisticated. Assume the following calculations:

$250 billion costs (to eliminate 65% of acid rain)

$390 billion benefits (of 65% removal)

[but notice the costs and benefits on the final 35%]

$250 billion costs (to eliminate last 35%)

$210 billion benefits

---

[68] The author of this book was discussing cost-benefit analysis with a young lawyer working on an occupational safety and health case. The lawyer commented that he really didn't believe in cost-benefit analysis but would not require an agency to promulgate a regulatory program that might cost industry $100, million but would save only ten lives. I responded: "You have just done a cost-benefit analysis. Whatever else you think about the regulation, you are telling me that, by your standards, one human life is worth something less than ten million dollars."

This is not an unrealistic scenario. It is often far more costly to achieve a total elimination of pollutant discharge than to merely reduce pollutants by some percentage. Doing this type of calculation suggests that an administrator might logically take steps to do away with 65% of acid rain. However, the administrator likely would not seek a rule that eliminated the final 35% because the costs of removing that last 35% do not result in a proportionate amount of benefits. These are basic cost benefit analysis calculations. Note that to a certain-and somewhat simplistic-extent, it is simply a matter of arithmetic. But while all this arithmetic sounds nice, it also points up the central problem with cost-benefit analysis. The dollar figures on the costs and benefits of acid rain were simply made up for this book. They may bear no relation whatsoever to the true figures. Even when figures have a more solid base than this, no one is ever quite sure what the numbers are. Costs are sometimes easy to estimate because in health and safety regulation, cost estimates often involve no more than figuring how much a new device, such as a better sulfur scrubber, will cost and then multiplying by the total number of chimneys that must install that scrubber.

The difficulty in estimating benefits makes true cost-benefit analysis very difficult, although the Environmental Protection Agency is one federal agency pioneering accurate benefits-estimation methodology. To its credit, EO 12,291 requires agencies to take this analysis only up to the point at which benefits and costs can be quantified and then asks the agencies merely to identify those costs and benefits that cannot properly be quantified. To this extent, the EO is clearly not demanding what this book calls formal cost-benefit analysis of the executive branch agencies.

[B] The Supreme Court and Cost-Benefit Analysis

The Supreme Court has dealt with the substantive aspects of cost-benefit analysis mainly in the context of occupational health and safety. Since 1980, it has decided two important cases that may have a significant impact on agencies' use of the technique. In *Industrial Department AFL-CIO v. American Petroleum Institute*,[69] the Court addressed the rulemaking power by the Occupational Safety and Health Administration to set an industrial worker exposure standard to a known carcinogenic, benzene, at a very low level. The OSH Act gave OSHA the power to set a standard "which most adequately assures, *to the extent feasible*, on the basis of the best available evidence, that no employee will suffer material impairment of health or functional capacity [even with regular exposure to the substance]."[70]

In a close decision, with four dissenting votes and no majority opinion, the Court overturned the standard on the basis of the language of the OSH Act. One opinion joined by four of the justices struck down the standard simply on the basis of inadequate findings in the record supporting the exceptionally tight benzene standard. However, in the view of three justices, the OSHA standard was not shown to be reasonably necessary or appropriate within the statute's language;

---

[69] 448 U.S. 607 (1980).

[70] 29 U.S.C. § 655(b)(5).

and, more importantly, the act did not give OSHA the discretion to create absolutely risk-free workplaces, regardless of costs. Moreover, the rulemaking record was devoid of any evidence that the agency had considered whether the expected benefits of the new standard bore any reasonable relationship to the costs imposed on employers.

The dissenters vigorously opposed these conclusions, noting that the proper test for evaluating this action was the substantial evidence test and, according to the dissenting justices, the benzene standard was supported by substantial evidence and was fully within the statutory power of OSHA to promulgate. The closeness of the decision and the lack of an authoritative majority opinion makes *Industrial Department* a poor gauge of the Court's sentiments on some of the central issues of cost-benefit analysis.

Two years later, probably because of *Industrial Department's* deficiencies, the Court took up another OSHA case, *American Textile Manufacturers Institute v. Donovan.*[71] *Donovan* also involved a health standard — in this case, a standard concerning the exposure to cotton dust by workers in textile manufacturing plants. The illness resulting from inhalation of cotton dust, byssinosis, or "brown lung," is similar to emphysema and just as debilitating.

Donovan, like *Industrial Department*, turned mainly on interpretation of the relevant statutory language — "to the extent feasible." But here the issue was stated in slightly different fashion. The unions argued that *feasible* meant only that something was technologically possible, *i.e.*, if it is technologically possible to build a machine that would reduce cotton dust exposure to the extent mandated by OSHA, the standard is feasible. The textile companies countered with the argument that "feasible" meant that OSHA was required to conduct a cost-benefit analysis of the standard and to promulgate an easier standard if the costs of complying with the tight standard were unreasonable, even if compliance is technologically possible.

The Court looked at the language of the OSH Act and at other statutes in which Congress had expressly mandated cost-benefit analysis.[72] Comparing language in other statutes that clearly required cost-benefit analysis with the lack of similar language in the OSH Act, the Court determined that there was no express cost-benefit requirement in the statute itself.

Largely because of this lack of express cost-benefit language, the Court then concluded that Congress had carried out all the cost-benefit analysis necessary when it drafted the statute. In the Court's view, when Congress used the term *feasible*, it meant simply "capable of being done." In other words, "Congress was fully aware that the Act would impose real and substantial costs of compliance on

---

[71] 452 U.S. 490 (1981).

[72] These statutes included the Flood Control Act of 1936, 33 U.S.C. § 701a ("if the benefits [of flood control] . . . are in excess of estimated costs . . .") and the Outer Continental Shelf Lands Act Amendments of 1978, 43 U.S.C. § 1347(b) (when benefits of certain equipment "are clearly insufficient to justify the incremental costs . . . .").

industry, and believed that such costs were part of the cost of doing business
. . . ."[73]

Donovan did not conclusively resolve all questions relating to cost benefit
analysis. For many years after Donovan, there was a lot of discussion among
administrative lawyers as to whether *Donovan prohibits* OSHA from doing a cost-
benefit analysis or merely tells OSHA that it does not have to do a cost-benefit
analysis *if it does not wish to do so*. Another view of *Donovan* suggests that the
Court prefers to let Congress live with the language it put into the enabling act.[74]
And Congress has, on occasion, inserted express cost-benefit requirements in
specific legislation without requiring such analysis as an across the board
regulatory requirement. For example, in the 1996 Accountable Pipeline Safety and
Partnership Act and the 1996 Safe Drinking Water Amendments,[75] Congress
inserted cost-benefit concepts. In the Safe Drinking Water Amendments, the
statutory language requires the Environmental Protection Agency to analyze
whether the benefits of certain water quality standards are justified in light of the
costs of implementing those standards. However, the agency is not prohibited from
choosing a standard whose benefits outweigh the costs. By contrast, in the Pipeline
Safety statute, the agency is permitted to adopt a safety rule "only upon a
reasoned determination that the benefits of the intended standard justify its costs."
Of great interest is the fact that it was the Department of Transportation (the
jurisdictional agency) that asked for this provision in the Pipeline Safety Act.

However, there is now some question as to the continuing validity of the
Donovan holding. In 2009, the Supreme Court decided *Entergy Corp. v.
Riverkeeper, Inc.*,[76] and provided significant new guidance on cost benefit analysis
in federal rulemaking. Entergy involved a review of a decision by the United States
Court of Appeals for the Second Circuit that invoked *Donovan* to conclude that the
Environmental Protection Agency could not use cost-benefit analysis in developing
base performance standards under the Clean Water Act.[77] The Entergy
Corporation operated a number of electric powerplants that employ cooling water
intake structures. These structures can have a detrimental impact on water quality.
Under the Clean Water Act, the EPA is required to establish performance
standards that reflect "the best technology available for minimizing adverse
environmental impact." In setting these standards, EPA considered two different
systems. One system referred to as a "closed-cycle" system was exceptionally
effective. An alternative approach, according to the EPA could approach but not
necessarily equal the closed-cycle systems. However, the EPA further determined
that the closed-cycle systems would cost roughly nine times the cost of an

---

[73] 452 U.S. at 514.

[74] *See, e.g.*, the famous snail darter case, *TVA v. Hill*, 437 U.S. 153 (1978), in which the Court decided
that Congress had written an inflexible command into the Endangered Species Act-the need to preserve
an endangered species, even as insignificant as the snail darter (a small freshwater fish), could block a
major hydroelectric project. The Court upheld that portion of the Act, even though application of the
statutory language led, arguably, to an absurd result.

[75] Pub. L. No. 104-304 and Pub. L. No. 104-182, respectively.

[76] 556 U.S. 208 (2009).

[77] 33 U.S.C. § 1326(b).

alternative technology. Examining the express language of the Clean Water Act, the Second Circuit (in a decision authored by then-judge, now Supreme Court Justice Sonia Sotomayor), could not discern any statutory authority for cost benefit analysis and, accordingly, remanded the case to the EPA to clarify whether or not it had, in fact, relied on cost benefit analysis in setting the standards.

By a vote of 5-4, with the majority opinion authored by Justice Scalia, the Supreme Court invoked the *Chevron* doctrine (discussed extensively in Section 12.05) and *Donovan* to conclude that even if a statute does not require an agency to perform cost benefit analysis this "does not mean that an agency is not permitted to do so."[78] Looking at several different sections of the Clean Water Act, the Court commented that "it was well within the bounds of reasonable interpretation for the EPA to conclude that cost-benefit analysis is not categorically forbidden."[79] The Court further observed that in weighing costs against benefits, the EPA "has been proceeding in essentially this fashion for over 30 years."[80] Thus, while Donovan was not expressly overruled, it would seem that the current Supreme Court strongly favors the notion what unless a statute expressly prohibits cost benefit analysis, an agency, proceeding in a reasonable fashion, may perform it in developing its regulatory structure.

[C] Cost Benefit Analysis Under Presidential Executive Orders

Additional impetus toward a much greater use of cost benefit analysis in presidential agencies comes from President Obama's Executive Order 13563 on Regulatory Review.[81] The Executive Order contains a number of requirements for supervision of presidential agency rulemaking by the OMB's Office of Information and Regulatory Affairs. Among those is the instruction that each agency shall adopt rules "only upon a reasoned determination that its benefits justify its costs (recognizing that some benefits and costs are difficult to quantify."[82]

In an era of shrinking government and country-wide financial difficulties, we have certainly not seen the last of cost-benefit analysis. In an age of finite resources, cost-benefit analysis is probably performed at both the federal and state level every day whether articulated or not. After *Entergy* and the Obama Executive Order, it will probably become a highly important technique for evaluating federal government regulations. It is likely that most states will follow the federal government's lead.[83]

---

[78] 556 U.S. at 223 (italics omitted).

[79] *Id.*

[80] *Id.* at 224, citing, among other cases, *Alaska Dep't of Environmental Conservation v. EPA*, 540 U.S. 461 (2004).

[81] 76 Fed. Reg. 3821 (Jan. 21, 2011).

[82] *Id. See also* Helen G. Boutrous, *Regulatory Review in the Obama Administration: Cost-Benefit Analysis for Everyone*, 62 ADMIN. L. REV. 243 (2010).

[83] A lengthy and seminal article on the sum and substance of cost-benefit analysis is Thomas O. McGarity, *A Cost-Benefit State*, 50 ADMIN. L. REV. 7 (1998).

§ 7.08 EX PARTE CONTACTS AND BIAS IN AGENCY RULEMAKING

[A] Ex Parte Contacts

By now, it should be apparent that federal agencies promulgate a multitude of rules that affect a substantial number of people. A difference of only a few words or a slightly altered technical standard or computational formula can mean millions of dollars in costs or savings for American industry. There is intense lobbying on agency rules both inside and outside the administrative agencies. This lobbying takes place on different levels and in different settings. A great deal of the lobbying effort in Congress is directed toward amending or repealing agency enabling acts. At the agency level, hundreds of informal contacts occur on a day-to-day basis because of the close relationship between many agencies and the companies regulated by those agencies. The so-called revolving door by which high-level industry officials take government positions and government administrators move out into industry is another mechanism of communication (and possible conflict of interest).

Long before agencies promulgate rules, they typically send signals to affected persons before making any kind of formal announcement in the *Federal Register.* Agency officials invite contact by making speeches before trade associations. Trade publications with inside-the-agency sources often publish agency plans long before an agency might wish to have the activity made public. To a certain extent, these activities are healthy, necessary and inevitable. But on the other hand, they can be harmful to the public interest if an agency listens only to one pressure group or accedes to the interests of only a segment of the industry it regulates.

Ralph Nader, as have many observers before him, has long advocated the thesis of the captive agency-*i.e.*, an agency that begins to identify with the companies that it is supposed to be regulating, at the expense of protecting the public. Merely becoming an expert in the industry that it regulates is a good thing. But a captive agency may listen too closely to or be too cozy with those it should be regulating thereby, forgetting that it represents the public interest, rather than the interests of the regulated industry.

When an agency acts as an adjudicatory body, the APA rules on unilateral or ex parte contacts with agency decision-makers are rather clear. Ex parte contacts in an adjudication are generally forbidden.[84] By contrast, one of the major goals in agency rulemaking is to encourage the agency to seek and listen to as wide a spectrum of opinion and expertise as possible when it is contemplating a rule. The main drawback with ex parte contacts is that they can go unrebutted and thus may carry more weight than they really should. Worst of all, they are often made in secret, thus, contributing to the sleaze element in administrative practice.

When important issues representing millions of dollars are at stake, ex parte contacts in agency rulemaking can become not only ugly, but also downright unfair if not properly handled. The APA is silent on this type of ex parte contact, but the

---

[84] *See infra* Chapter 8, § 8.07, for a discussion of ex parte contacts in agency adjudications.

federal courts, and particularly the D.C. Circuit, have occasionally taken up these issues and written a few opinions from which we can glean the dimensions of the problem, even if we can't articulate many hard, fast rules on ex parte contacts in agency rulemaking.

In the mid-1970s, the Federal Communications Commission began paying more attention to cable television and subscription television activities. After a long investigation, the Commission decided to promulgate some rules setting out certain programming limitations for these broadcasters. The new rules, as almost always happens, were immediately challenged in court.[85] The FCC went through the conventional rulemaking process and compiled a massive record. Comments and other information put into that record are always accessible to the public, and it is on the basis of that record that the Commission fashions the final rule.

However, in the case of the cable programming rules, a number of persons, mainly representatives of different segments of the industry, talked to individual commissioners and various FCC staff members in secret one-on-one sessions where they made additional comments on the rules. When the FCC finally promulgated the rules, it justified the rules only on the basis of the public record. The Commission neglected to mention even that the ex parte contacts had taken place. It said absolutely nothing about the substance of those contacts.

In *Home Box Office, Inc. v. FCC*,[86] the D.C. Circuit found these secret, off-the-record activities intolerable, vacated the rules and remanded the rulemaking proceeding to the Commission because it found the rules themselves fatally tainted by the ex parte contacts. As Judge Wright, speaking for the court, put it:

> [W]here, as here, an agency justifies its actions by reference only to information in the public file while failing to disclose the substance of other relevant information that has been represented to it, [the court] must treat the agency's justifications as a fictional account of the actual decision making process and must perforce find its actions arbitrary.

Analyze the case closely. Is the factor of secrecy the important thing? In other words, would it have sufficed for the FCC to disclose these contacts, and perhaps, even to disclose the substance of the conversations? According to the *Home Box Office* court, the answer is "no." It is very important, in the court's view, that statements and representations be weighed in the give-and-take of an open rulemaking proceeding, a proceeding in which all interested persons may participate. Merely docketing the contacts would probably not be enough.

Home Box Office caused a stir in all agencies, not just the FCC, because the general understanding among agency personnel prior to that decision was that ex parte contacts in rulemaking proceedings were generally permitted. Worse, some of the court's comments in the case seemed almost to force an agency into *formal* rulemaking procedures just to avoid any hassle with off-the-record comments.

---

[85] Challenges to FCC rulemaking are taken directly and exclusively to the United States Court of Appeals for the District of Columbia Circuit.

[86] 567 F.2d 9 (D.C. Cir.), *cert. denied*, 434 U.S. 829 (1977).

Just three months later, however, another panel on the D.C. Circuit tried to put a few things right. In *Action for Children's Television v. FCC*[87] (*ACT*) a three-judge panel that included Judge MacKinnon, the dissenter in *Home Box Office*, struck a more moderate tone. *ACT* involved FCC rules for television programs directed mainly toward children. In this instance, the Commission refused to promulgate a rule because it was convinced that voluntary standards and compliance efforts worked out by the networks would suffice. These voluntary efforts were proposed by network representatives in undisclosed meetings with individual commissioners. The general public had no knowledge of the meetings or of the substance of the proposals, and it had no opportunity to comment on the networks' proposals prior to the FCC's cancellation of the rulemaking.

The cancellation of the rulemaking was taken to court, where *Home Box Office* was cited as a basis for vacating the Commission's actions. It is apparent from some of the dicta in the *ACT* opinion that this D.C. Circuit panel was not happy with some of the broader comments in *Home Box Office*. The *ACT* panel refused to find the ex parte contacts impermissible and knocked down a few straw men on the way to its decision:

> If we go as far as *Home Box Office* . . . why not go further to require the decision maker to summarize and make available for public comment every status inquiry from a Congressman or any germane material-say a newspaper editorial-that he or she reads on their evening-hour rumina-tions? In the end, why not administer a lie-detector test to ascertain whether the required summary is an accurate and complete one?[88]

The *ACT* decision appears to be based on practicality (how can these things be policed meaningfully by a reviewing court?). The decision seems also to be based on the idea that no individual profited from the ex parte contacts. In other words, this was an instance when the Commission decided to do nothing. In the court's opinion, it was not a case of someone having secret conversations that enabled him to get a positive agency benefit, such as a broadcast license.

The policing argument makes sense. Moreover, if agency rulemaking is to remain informal, ex parte contacts are probably here to stay. But this does promote a certain cynicism in agency practitioners. The cynical message of *ACT* for most lawyers is to make sure to have your own ex parte contacts on behalf of your own client.

Other parts of the *ACT* analysis also fall flat. The court seems to think that no one profited by the refusal of the FCC to promulgate the rules. But didn't the networks prevail in the sense that they did not have to face tight Commission-imposed rules? Is it not a victory to have an agency scrap its own controls and tell you simply to regulate yourself? Freedom *from* regulation is almost always viewed as a benefit in our political system.

There are no easy conclusions to draw from these cases. The FCC itself has tried to address the problem by promulgating very detailed rules on ex parte contacts

---

[87] 564 F.2d 458 (D.C. Cir. 1977).

[88] *Id.* at 477.

that include rules on contacts during a rulemaking proceeding. A few other agencies have followed suit. But most courts are even more sanguine about the problem than the D.C. Circuit.[89]

Home Box Office and *ACT* involved contacts with the agency by representatives of the regulated industry. These are not the only contacts that take place in an agency proceeding. The other entities in the executive branch frequently want input into the agency's decisional process. Is it impermissible, say, for someone in the White House to contact the Environmental Protection Agency and express White House views on an EPA matter?

The D.C. Circuit recently permitted this sort of contact as within the bounds of proper governmental policy making. In *Sierra Club v. Costle*,[90] possibly one of the longest circuit decisions ever written, the court addressed the issue of ex parte contacts by White House personnel with EPA officials in a rulemaking proceeding of crucial importance to the coal industry. The court concluded that not only was it not wrong to have these contacts, but, to the contrary, it may be the wisest form of government: "Our form of government simply could not function effectively or rationally if key executive policy makers were isolated from each other and from the Chief Executive."[91] While there was a strong suggestion from the court, based on the statutory language controlling EPA rulemaking, that all such meetings and contacts be docketed in the rulemaking record, the contacts themselves were not seen by the Court as a proper basis on which to overturn the agency action.

Ex parte contacts often cause problems for young lawyers. On the one hand, you have an ethical obligation to represent your client zealously within the bounds of the law. On the other hand, you don't dare poison a client's case by engaging in impermissible ex parte contacts. There is no easy answer to these questions. You might begin with two separate presumptions: in adjudications and formal rulemaking you should presume that unilateral contacts are always forbidden; in informal rulemaking, absent special constraints in the agency rules, the statute, or relevant case law, you may presume that there is no absolute barrier to ex parte contacts, although you always want to be as sensitive as possible to negative fall-out. One rule of thumb followed by most of the careful lawyers in the District of Columbia is that you should not do anything that would embarrass you or your client if your actions became a front-page story in the *Washington Post* the next day.

[B] Agency Bias

One of the concerns of agency decision-making is that the decision-makers be fair to all parties concerned. Does that mean that a decider must be completely neutral or totally free from preconceived notions about the controversy? In one case, a member of the Federal Trade Commission, Michael Pertschuk, made speeches condemning network advertising practices in children's programs prior to his appointment to an FTC rulemaking involving children's advertising. The D.C.

---

[89] *See, e.g., Center for Science in the Public Interest v. Department of Treasury*, 573 F. Supp. 1168 (D.D.C. 1983). (An agency does not have to log congressional contacts in informal rulemaking.).

[90] 657 F.2d 298 (D.C. Cir. 1981).

[91] 657 F.2d at 406.

Circuit, in *Association of National Advertisers v. FTC*,[92] held that statements such as these were not sufficient to disqualify an agency decision maker, even though a different standard might apply to, for instance, a federal judge.

The court's reasoning was straightforward. First, there is a long-standing presumption of administrative regularity. It takes a great deal to prove actual bias on the part of an administrator. Second, "[t]he legitimate functions of a policymaker, unlike an adjudicator, demand interchange and discussion about important issues . . . . The mere discussion of policy or advocacy on a legal question, however, is not sufficient to disqualify an administrator." In other words, it is in the nature of persons charged with making policy to have ideas and value judgments and to want to advocate those conclusions. Thus, there is to be no disqualification of an administrator without "the most compelling proof that he is unable to carry out his duties in a constitutionally permissible manner."

Given this language, it is difficult to say that *National Advertisers* establishes a test for disqualification. At present, the standard may differ, depending on the nature of the rulemaking procedures used. In informal rulemaking it appears to be virtually impossible to disqualify a decision-maker for bias; but when an agency employs either tight hybrid procedures or uses formal rulemaking procedures, more neutrality may be required.[93]

§ 7.09 THE LEGAL EFFECT OF AGENCY RULES

[A] Distinguishing Between Substantive Rules and Other Types of Agency Pronouncements

Section 7.07, *above*, sets out some striking procedural distinctions between substantive (sometimes referred to as *legislative*) rules and other types of agency pronouncements. Substantive rules require notice and the opportunity for comment. Other agency statements do not. Substantive rules require a thirty-day delay between publication and effective date. Other agency statements do not. Later in this section, we will see some equally compelling differences in the legal effect of substantive rules compared with other types of agency pronouncements.

These important differences in legal effect tell us that it is very important to be able to distinguish between substantive rules and other agency statements. Unfortunately, this is one of the most difficult issues in administrative law and one on which neither Congress nor the courts have provided much useful guidance. For example, § 551 of the APA merely defines *rule* without drawing any distinctions between types of rules. The Attorney General's Manual on the APA makes some distinctions mainly by way of illustration. The Manual defines a substantive rule as:

> [R]ules, other than organizational or procedural rules . . . issued by an agency pursuant to statutory authority and which implement the statute,

---

[92] 627 F.2d 1151 (D.C. Cir. 1979), *cert. denied*, 447 U.S. 921 (1980).

[93] *See, e.g.*, Peter L. Strauss, *Disqualification of Decisional Officials in Rulemaking*, 80 COLUM. L. REV. 990 (1980).

as, for example, the proxy rules issued by the [SEC] pursuant to § 14 of the Securities Exchange Act of 1934. Such rules have the force and effect of law.

The Manual then defines interpretative rules as "rules or statements . . . to advise the public of the agency's construction of the statutes and rules which it administers." Statements of policy are defined as "statements . . . to advise the public prospectively of the manner in which the agency proposes to exercise a discretionary power."[94]

For most issues encountered by an administrative practitioner, the major task is to distinguish between substantive rules and all other types of pronouncements, because the APA makes only that distinction.[95] So, people who sit around trying to spot some bright lines separating statements of policy from interpretative rules are probably wasting a lot of their time.

In terms of the substantive/other-than-substantive distinction, the Supreme Court has offered some assistance but nothing in the way of a final, categorical pronouncement. In *Chrysler v. Brown*,[96] a case better known for its impact on the Freedom of Information Act,[97] the Court noted that most distinctions drawn by reviewing courts have been by negative inference rather than by positive definition, *i.e.*, a rule is substantive if it is not an interpretative rule or a statement of policy. If the Court wanted to be even more accurate in its summation of the existing case law, it might have pointed out that most suggested definitions are circular: substantive rules have the force and effect of law, so a rule is substantive if it has the force and effect of law.

Viewed a little differently, a substantive rule, according to the Court, is one that affects "individual rights and obligations."[98] This sounds like a nice formulation, but anyone involved in agency practice quickly realizes that virtually all pronounce-ments of a major regulatory agency affect individual rights and obligations. Consider, for example, letter rulings issued by the Internal Revenue Service. These rulings have never been considered to have the force and effect of law, yet they affect at least the individual who requests the ruling. Some lower federal courts have tried to finesse this definition by suggesting that an agency rule is substantive when it has a *substantial impact* on many members of a regulated industry, not just some individual companies.[99] But again, when a federal agency speaks on almost any topic, its comments generally have a substantial impact.

There are also some hints in *Chrysler* that the way an agency labels a rule should have some influence on a reviewing court because courts grant a fair amount of

---

[94] Attorney General's Manual on the Administrative Procedure Act 30 n.3 (1947).

[95] To eliminate the adverse consequences of the different procedures applicable to interpretative versus substantive rules, and in recognition of the fact that interpretative rules can have just as much impact as substantive rules, President Carter urged all agencies to put even interpretative rules and statements of policy through the regular § 553 notice and comment process. President Carter's Executive Order was rescinded by President Reagan.

[96] 441 U.S. 281 (1979).

[97] *See infra* Chapter 14, § 14.02.

[98] *Morton v. Ruiz*, 415 U.S. 199 (1974).

[99] *See, e.g., Standard Oil Co. v. Dep't of Energy*, 596 F.2d 1029 (Temp. Emer. Ct. App. 1978).

deference to agency pronouncements. But it seems strange to place so much weight solely on what the agency says the rule is. Other courts have let the agency's process dictate the definition by suggesting that substantive rules are those for which the agency has provided notice and opportunity for comment. There are no easy distinctions.[100]

[B] The Legal Effect of Substantive Rules

Even though it is very difficult to distinguish between substantive and nonsubstantive rules, the Supreme Court has left nothing to question on the effect of substantive rules. As the *Attorney General's Manual* points out, substantive rules have the force and effect of law. In practical terms, this means that your client can encounter as much trouble by violating an agency's substantive rule as he can by violating a federal statute. The Court made this absolutely clear in one of its Watergate decisions, *United States v. Nixon*,[101] the case in which President Nixon attempted to fire the first special prosecutor, Archibald Cox.

When Professor Cox was first hired as special prosecutor, he was sufficiently suspicious of the Nixon Administration to insist that his immediate supervisor, the Attorney General (AG), guarantee that he would not be fired simply because he was digging into activities that were very sensitive for the White House. To assure Cox's job security, the Justice Department promulgated a rule that specified, among other things, that the special prosecutor would not be fired for anything other than "extraordinary improprieties" and only after the President consulted with various members of Congress.

In ordinary circumstances, a lawyer in an executive branch agency would serve purely at the pleasure of the AG and the President. Moreover, in this instance there was no statute compelling the President to give Cox the assurances that he requested. Nonetheless, the AG published an agency rule in the *Federal Register* providing the guarantees sought by Cox.

Shortly after Cox was fired, in the now-famous Saturday Night Massacre, the propriety of his termination was taken into the federal courts and eventually reached the Supreme Court, where the Court held squarely that an agency's substantive rules have the force and effect of law. But you might ask, at this point, "So what? That's what the original APA said." It would seem a shame for the Court to have wasted everyone's time and effort in *Nixon* just to reiterate a proposition that had existed virtually without question, at least since 1946.

---

[100] Probably the most accurate judicial commentary on this problem came from Judge Patricia Wald of the D.C. Circuit who, in attempting to distinguish between different types of rules, wrote that this is "an extraordinarily case-specific endeavor." Worse, "analogizing to prior cases is often of limited utility in light of the exceptional degree to which decisions in this doctrinal area turn on their precise facts." *Am. Hosp. Ass'n v. Bowen*, 834 F.2d 1037, 1045 (D.C. Cir. 1987). Some of the best academic writing on the issues discussed here and in the following sections has been by Professor Robert Anthony. *See, e.g.*, Robert A. Anthony, *"Well, You Want the Permit, Don't You?" Agency Efforts to Make Nonlegislative Documents Bind the Public*, 44 Admin. L. Rev. 31 (1992); Robert A. Anthony, *Which Agency Interpretations Should Bind Citizens and the Courts?*, 7 Yale J. on Reg. 1 (1990).

[101] 418 U.S. 683 (1974).

Does *Nixon* contribute anything else to our understanding of agency rules? To a certain extent, it sets a few boundaries that were not clearly understood up to that time. First, it confirms that agency rules govern not only people regulated by an agency, but also the agency itself. The Court pointed out that neither the President, nor the AG, was obligated to give Cox these special protections, but did so out of an exercise of their discretion. But even if there was no initial obligation to treat Cox in this fashion, once they agreed to do so, they put curbs on their own discretion that could be enforced against them.

Second, *Nixon* makes clear that even if a rule springs from an exercise of agency discretion, it may not be amended or rescinded except by the same process required for its promulgation. In other words, the rule curbed the President's discretion until the rule was repealed in a procedurally correct manner. He was not free, for example, simply to pretend that the rule did not exist. The rule controlled the President's actions so long as it remained on the books.

[C]   Amending or Rescinding Substantive Rules

The *Nixon* case was an instance in which an agency put a rule on the books and then tried to disregard the rule when, in the President's view, the rule became politically unpalatable. Notice that the Court in *Nixon* was perfectly agreeable to the agency's changing the rule through proper procedures. The message of *Nixon* is simply that an agency just cannot ignore the rule when it so chooses.

Recently, there has been a strong push for deregulation of significant parts of American business activity. Begun in the Carter Administration and continued with great intensity under President Reagan, whose intensity has been echoed by President Clinton, deregulation has become one of the talismans of modern American administrative law. Most successful deregulation on the federal level has been implemented by congressional amendment of agency enabling acts and has affected mainly federal economic regulation, such as the now-defunct Interstate Commerce Commission's regulation of truck and rail rates and the Federal Energy Regulatory Commission's regulation of the wellhead price of natural gas. However, some agencies have made certain attempts to deregulate without changes in the underlying enabling acts. These experiments have met with mixed results on judicial review. One case, *Motor Vehicle Mfrs. Ass'n v. State Farm Mutual Automobile Ins. Co. (State Farm)*,[102] is a good example of what happens when an agency tries to loosen regulatory controls in the context of motor safety regulation.

In 1966, Congress passed the Motor Vehicle Safety Act,[103] giving the Department of Transportation the power to set vehicle safety standards. After some intensive fact-finding, DOT promulgated a 1967 requirement that all new automobiles be equipped with seat belts. But just a few years' experience with seat belts told DOT that belts were not enough. Most people didn't like them and most didn't use them. DOT began looking at a number of safety devices, known generically as "passive restraint systems," that were less dependent on drivers and passengers having to buckle up.

---

[102]   463 U.S. 29 (1983).

[103]   15 U.S.C. §§ 1381 *et seq.*

A passive restraint standard, known as Standard 208, was promulgated in 1969 on a carefully phased-in timetable beginning in 1969. By 1975, all new automobiles were to contain passive protection devices for all front seat passengers. Standard 208 led to a great deal of controversy, was postponed at least once, and by 1976, DOT had decided to begin an entirely new rulemaking process. However, in 1977, a new Secretary of Transportation, appointed by Jimmy Carter, scrapped the rulemaking and simply issued a modified passive restraint standard to be phased in between 1982 and 1984. The Modified 208 Standard left the basic choice of restraint system-either air bags or passive seat belts-up to manufacturers. Modified Standard 208 was firmly in place as of January, 1981 as a substantive agency rule.

Having considered the rulemaking history, now consider the political environment. The original standard had been promulgated by Secretary Coleman, a Ford appointee, and the modified standard had been promulgated by Secretary Adams, a member of the Carter administration. When President Reagan took office in 1981, his Secretary of Transportation, Drew Lewis, extended the standard's compliance deadline and published a notice in the *Federal Register* proposing to rescind the standard in its entirety. After holding hearings and considering written comments, DOT then rescinded the entire standard.

Recall that every substantive rule, or rescission of a substantive rule, must contain a statement of basis and purpose. In explaining its decision to rescind, DOT set out a kind of cost-benefit analysis. The department noted that virtually all manufacturers were electing passive seat restraints rather than air bags. These restraints could be detached and thus, would require some deliberate act on the part of the car's occupants to be effective. This would so greatly reduce the protection of the passive restraints that the costs of installation, estimated to be around $1 billion for the entire industry, did not justify the standard. Worse, according to DOT, a poorly-considered passive restraint standard might have a detrimental effect on public acceptance, in later years, of a proper restraint system.

Two insurance companies challenged the rescission in court, arguing that DOT's decision to rescind the standard was arbitrary and capricious because DOT did not adequately explain the rescission. The car manufacturers argued that the decision to rescind was really a decision simply to take no action and needed very little explanation. The Supreme Court agreed with the insurance companies, overturned the rescission and remanded the action to the agency for further consideration.

The Court's reasoning is not hard to follow. The underlying statute, the Motor Vehicle Safety Act, did not distinguish between promulgation and revocation of standards. In other words, the decisional process for making a rule or doing away with a rule was to be the same. The attempt to rescind was not a matter of an agency's deciding to take no action. The agency acted when the modified standard was promulgated, and the current DOT was attempting to revoke that action. More importantly, the agency's explanation of why the rescission was necessary was deficient and incomplete. While DOT is permitted to use cost-benefit analysis here and while any agency is free to change its mind on policy when the conditions underlying a particular agency policy change, the explanation for the change must be both plain on the face of the record and rational. Here, at bottom, DOT failed to provide the sort of "reasoned analysis" that the Court insists on for this type of rescission.

There are many ways to look at *State Farm*. Justice Rehnquist, concurring in part and dissenting in part, took perhaps the healthiest view of the case: DOT's actions were political and may be explained merely by the change in Presidential administrations. President Carter wanted the rule, President Reagan did not. Some commentators have looked upon *State Farm* with a great deal of distaste, viewing it as a modern parallel to the New Deal cases, *Panama Refining* and *Schechter*[104] — *i.e.*, a case in which a recalcitrant Supreme Court tries to stand in the way of the public will as expressed in the election of Ronald Reagan.[105] Others view the decision as a significant impediment to deregulation efforts taken by an agency when Congress has not changed the enabling act.

It is difficult to say that *State Farm* creates any new administrative law principles. The idea of a court closely scrutinizing an agency's explanation of its actions is not at all new. Nor is this the first time that the Court has been reluctant to accept, purely at face value, an agency's unsupported explanations for rescinding a rule. Note that the ultimate disposition of the case was unanimous. Even those justices who disagreed with some of the reasoning of the Court's opinion joined Justice Rehnquist in concluding that the Reagan DOT had provided no explanation whatsoever for its rescission of a standard that had been explicitly approved by its predecessor.

In a much different case, where the government was engaged in strong regulation of a particular professional group, the Supreme Court determined that an enabling act authorized the rules, even in the face of strong constitutional objections to the contrary. In *Rust v. Sullivan*,[106] the Department of Health and Human Services had promulgated rules under an enabling act that prohibited the use of federal funds in family-planning services "where abortion is a method of family planning." The agency rules prohibited any referral programs, counseling techniques or other patient-directed services that even mentioned abortion as an alternative to pregnancy. In *Rust*, the Court paid lip service to the constitutional objections of the health care providers (objecting on First Amendment, free-speech grounds), but chose to conclude that the statute approved the rules. The Court went on to comment that-in view of the constitutional objections — "every reasonable construction must be resorted to, in order to save a statute (and its accompanying substantive rules) from unconstitutionality."[107]

[D]   The Legal Effect of Other Than Substantive Rules

In concluding that substantive agency rules have the force and effect of law, the Court in *Nixon* essentially accepted the characterization of the special prosecutor rule as a substantive rule. The force and effect of interpretative rules or statements

---

[104]   *See supra* Chapter 2, § 2.02.

[105]   For a far more moderate view, *see* Cass R. Sunstein, *Deregulation and the Hard-Look Doctrine*, 1983 Sup. Ct. Rev. 177.

[106]   500 U.S. 173 (1991).

[107]   *Id.* at 190.

of policy is much more troublesome. They do not have the force and effect of law, although there is absolutely no question that they count for something. In the landmark case, *Skidmore v. Swift*,[108] the Supreme Court analyzed the impact of certain interpretative bulletins promulgated by the Department of Labor's Wage and Hour Division. The bulletins were clearly not substantive rules, although they did help people understand some of the more complicated aspects of the Department's minimum wage and overtime regulations.

In *Skidmore* the Court pondered the effect of the bulletins at some length and finally concluded that the bulletins, while not controlling (as might have been the case with a substantive rule), were certainly due some weight because an agency is not expected to waste a lot of time and effort on nothing. Staking out a middle ground between the polar positions of "nothing" and "force and effect of law," the Court determined that the bulletins, while not controlling on the issue, should be granted deference by reviewing courts in weighing the validity of agency action because interpretative rules and statements of policy "do constitute a body of experience and informed judgment to which courts and litigants may properly resort for guidance."[109]

[E]   The Retroactive Effect of Agency Rules

There is another matter that should be considered. Recall that the definition of *rule* in § 551 of the APA is a statement of general or particular applicability "and future effect." Thus, by definition, a rule controls prospective behavior of the regulated industry. This idea of prospective effect is also an important ingredient in the Supreme Court's admonition that agencies should make the bulk of their policy by rule, as opposed to adjudication.[110] It is extremely rare for an agency to attempt to give retroactive effect to its substantive rules, although some agencies faced with desperate circumstances have tried.[111]

By contrast, an interpretative rule, by definition, merely fleshes out what the agency said in the substantive rule and is thus, automatically retroactive.[112] Lest anyone think that this is much ado about nothing, consider the following hypothetical drawn from a number of disputes between individual oil companies and the Department of Energy, back when DOE had authority to establish maximum selling prices for various petroleum products, including gasoline.

---

[108] 323 U.S. 134 (1944).

[109] *Id.* at 140. See the lengthy discussion of *Skidmore, Christensen,* and *Mead* in Chapter 12, § 12.05.

[110] *See* discussion of rule versus order *supra* Chapter 6.

[111] The Department of Energy, faced with a court decision that severely undercut a major portion of one of its important regulatory programs, attempted to make a rule retroactive by applying criteria taken from a District of Columbia Circuit decision: (1) whether retroactive application represents a departure from well-established agency practices; (2) whether regulated parties relied on an earlier rule or the absence of a rule; (3) whether retroactivity imposes unreasonable burdens on the regulated industry; and (4) whether there is a compelling need for retroactive application. *See* 45 Fed. Reg. 58,871 (1980) *citing Retail, Wholesale and Dept. Store Union v. NLRB,* 466 F.2d 380 (D.C. Cir. 1972). This approach has still not been conclusively validated by reviewing courts. It has probably been severely undercut by the Supreme Court's decision in *Bowen v. Georgetown University Hosp.*

[112] *See, e.g., Standard Oil Co. v. Dep't of Energy,* 596 F.2d 1029 (Temp. Emer. Ct. App. 1978).

DOE's enabling act, the Emergency Petroleum Allocation Act of 1973,[113] permitted DOE to set the maximum retail pace of gasoline at, say, $1.00 per gallon. To be sure, the actual regulations were much more complicated; but for our purposes, merely assume a DOE rule announcing the maximum price is $1.00 plus "reasonable costs incurred by the service station owner." The rule, on its face, seems pretty clearly to be a substantive rule by any definition. It directly implements the statutory command to set a maximum price; it directly affects individual rights.

But how about a rule that tells service stations how to compute *reasonable costs*? DOE would probably argue that this was merely an interpretation of the earlier $1.00 per gallon rule. Now, assume further, that this *interpretative rule* was not announced until two years after the $1.00 per gallon rule and assume that a service station operator calculated his prices differently during the intervening two years. If the interpretative rule is given effect back to the date of the promulgation of the original $1.00 per gallon rule, the owner can be deemed to be in violation of the basic rule for the entire two-year period. This happened frequently while DOE was enforcing its price control rules.

The problem is this: without a bright line test for distinguishing between substantive and interpretative rules, an agency can slip substantive consequences into an interpretation and still enjoy the benefit of a fully retroactive effect. It is not unusual for agencies to write interpretations or rulings or statements of policy that, in effect, say to the regulated industry, "this is what we really meant when we promulgated the substantive rule, but were too inept to tell you at that time." Of course, conditions change, and no regulatory drafter can possibly be expected to anticipate all of the circumstances under which a rule will be applied. Nonetheless, careful drafting of substantive rules when initially promulgated can avoid many of the detrimental effects of fully retroactive interpretations. Agencies have an obligation to the industries they regulate to try to get it right the first time.

Some of these problems have been addressed in a major decision by the Supreme Court on the retroactive effect of agency rules. In *Bowen v. Georgetown University Hospital*,[114] the Department of Health and Human Services (HHS) promulgated rules that set limits on the reimbursable costs under the Medicaid program. While the details of the rules are too complex to be set out here, it is enough to understand that HHS had promulgated a cost schedule in 1981, excluding wages paid by government hospitals. In 1983, this rule was successfully challenged in court on the ground that HHS had not followed proper notice and comment procedures in promulgating the 1981 cost schedule. In 1984, HHS promulgated a final rule that essentially reinstated the 1981 schedule and attempted to recoup payments made between 1983 and 1984. In the Supreme Court's own words: "In effect, [HHS] had promulgated a rule retroactively, and the net result was as if the original rule had never been set aside."

While HHS attempted a number of justifications for this retroactivity, the department ran into a totally unsympathetic Supreme Court. The Court took a

---

[113] 15 U.S.C. §§ 751 *et seq.*

[114] 488 U.S. 204 (1988).

journeyman approach to this issue. It first looked at the enabling act and could find nothing in either the express language of the statute or its legislative history giving the department permission to write retroactive rules. Purporting to restrict its opinion to "the particular statutory scheme in question," the Court held squarely: "Our interpretation of the Medicare Act compels the conclusion that [HHS] has no authority to promulgate retroactive cost-limit rules."

Bowen v. Georgetown University Hospital may eventually be restricted to its facts; but it is of current importance to administrative law generally, in part because of a strong concurrence by Justice Scalia. Justice Scalia believes that the APA provides independent confirmation of the majority's holding in *Bowen*. As Justice Scalia reads the APA, the definition of *rule* is an agency statement of general or particular applicability *and future effect*. Taking a commonsense approach to the problem, he first noted that the concept of future effect must include *both* the idea of "taking effect in the future" and not having retroactive consequences. HHS had argued that, even if a rule goes into effect sometime after it is promulgated, it can, in certain appropriate circumstances, control behavior that has already occurred. As Justice Scalia sees it: "[T]here is really no alternative except the obvious meaning, that a rule is a statement that has legal consequences only for the future." However, he went on to emphasize that the concept of no retroactivity applies only to rulemaking-that an agency may, in proper circumstances, create a retroactive effect through adjudication. More importantly, for any agency that absolutely must have retroactive rulemaking authority, it may simply apply to Congress for the requisite authority.

The reader should understand that not all administrative law scholars are happy with Justice Scalia's conclusions. One commentator has labeled some of his reasoning "a wooden gloss" on the APA's definition of rule.[115]

There have been a few refinements on *Bowen* in the past few years. In *Landgraf v. USI Film Products*,[116] the Supreme Court tussled with the difficult task of determining just when a rule is being applied retroactively. As Justice Stevens, writing for the Court, noted:

> The conclusion that a particular rule operates 'retroactively' comes at the end of a process of judgment concerning the nature and extent of the change in the law and the degree of connection between the operation of the new rule and a relevant past event. Any test of retroactivity will leave room for disagreement in hard cases, and is unlikely to classify the enormous variety of legal changes with perfect philosophical clarity.[117]

---

[115] William V. Luneburg, *Retroactivity and Administrative Rulemaking*, 1991 DUKE L.J. 106.

[116] 511 U.S. 244 (1994).

[117] *Id.* at 270. For two other cases that address retroactivity issues but do not resolve any of the major questions, *compare Regions Hosp. v. Shalala*, 522 U.S. 448 (1998) (applying HHS' "reaudit" rule, the agency was permitted to retroactively adjust certain hospital expenses involved in Medicare reimbursement for medical education costs), *with Eastern Enterprises v. Apfel*, 524 U.S. 498 (1998) (Court held, in a series of mixed and muddled opinions, that certain application of the Coal Industry Retiree Health Benefit Act of 1992 was impermissibly retroactive.).

However, he went on to note that the normal assumption is that agency rules have only prospective effect and that rules may not be applied retroactively unless Congress permits such retroactivity in the underlying statute.

While this is a fascinating issue, students may take a great deal of comfort in the realization that the vast bulk of agency rules have only future consequences. It may be sometime before a vehicle emerges for further discussion of the retroactivity of rules.

§ 7.10   ESTOPPEL AGAINST THE GOVERNMENT

[A]   WARNING!

This is one section of this book that should be written entirely in capital letters. There is probably no other area of administrative law that can trap young lawyers more quickly than estoppel — *i.e.*, the legal principle that when a private person makes a decision or takes a position, he or she may be prevented from a change of mind at some later point in time. It is a topic that may not come up in an administrative law course or on the bar examination, but may become vitally important to a neophyte practitioner who is counseling clients in agency matters.

To make sure no one misunderstands the fundamental rule: absent extraordinary circumstances, the government may not be estopped. Rely on advice given by agency personnel at your own peril.

[B]   The Estoppel Case Law

This is one time when the Supreme Court has not vacillated. Begin with *Federal Crop Insurance Corp. v. Merrill*.[118] Merrill was a wheat farmer in Idaho who applied for crop insurance under the Federal Crop Insurance Act. The Act was administered by a government corporation, the Federal Crop Insurance Corp. (FCIC), that used local agents to carry out most of the program's terms. In this case, Merrill and other farmers worked through the Bonneville County Agricultural Conservation Committee, the local agent for the FCIC.

The FCIC had on its books certain rules that prohibited the insuring of any reseeded crops. The FCIC, however, accepted Merrill's application for insurance, leading Merrill to believe that his crops were fully insured. The FCIC said nothing to Merrill about the exception for reseeded crops, although the exception was plainly stated in the *Federal Register* announcement of the FCIC's rules. Merrill's crops were destroyed by drought, and the Corporation refused to pay, citing the exception in its regulations. Merrill didn't go quietly. He brought a lawsuit against the FCIC on the theory that a private insurance company, having accepted the application, would be estopped from denying coverage for something not personally disclosed to the insured party.

When the case reached the Supreme Court, the Court disagreed. While a private party would clearly be estopped in these circumstances, the Court refused

---

[118] 332 U.S. 380 (1947).

to invoke the doctrine of estoppel against a government agency because public policy requires that a different principle be applied to the government. First, the Court reasoned, whether Merrill had actual knowledge or not, he was on notice along with everyone else in the country as to the terms of the FCIC's rules when those rules were published in the *Federal Register.* As the Court put it, publication of rules in the *Federal Register* constitutes notice to all persons wherever situated as of the time of publication.

Second, permitting estoppel to be used against the federal government could prove to be a very serious impediment to efficient government operations. The government is such a vast operation and has so many employees (roughly three million civilian employees in the last decade of the twentieth century) that it cannot possibly know of all the representations made in its name. The only legitimate source of information for agency rules is the text of the rules themselves. Good faith reliance on either erroneous advice or a misreading of the rules (what some students like to call an "honest mistake") is simply irrelevant.[119]

The *Merrill* principle is still good law. The Supreme Court demonstrated that fact in a decision, *Schweiker v. Hansen,*[120] a case that provides a bit of a twist on *Merrill.* In *Schweiker,* an applicant applied for mother's insurance benefits but was told by a low echelon civil servant that she was not eligible. The applicant left the office without filing an application. Many months later, when she found that she in fact did qualify, she asked for benefits retroactive to her first oral conversation. Unfortunately, the relevant statute prohibited the payment of benefits unless an applicant had filed a written application. The Court was no more sympathetic to this applicant than it was to Merrill. In a relatively short *per curiam* opinion, the Court could find nothing in *Schweiker* that distinguished it from *Merrill.*

Occasionally, language contrary to the no estoppel rule creeps into the Supreme Court's language. For example, in *Heckler v. Community Health Services,*[121] the Court declined to adopt what it termed "a flat rule that estoppel may not in any circumstances run against the government." Justice O'Connor quoted this language a year later in a separate concurrence in *United States v. Locke,*[122] a mineral leasing case where long-term leaseholders relied on the representations of a Department of Interior employee; the Court, however, disposed of the case on other grounds. In *Locke,* Justice O'Connor seemed to be willing to entertain an estoppel argument (unfortunately it had not been raised below, but might, according to O'Connor, be brought up on remand) involving what she described as the extinguishing of "a vested property interest that has been legally held and actively maintained for more than twenty years."

---

[119] There is a sliver of authority to the contrary, to be found in two decisions in the 9th Circuit. *See, e.g., McFarlin v. Federal Crop Insurance Corp.,* 438 F.2d 1237 (9th Cir. 1971); *Brandt v. Hickel,* 427 F.2d 53 (9th Cir. 1970). These cases represent a drop in the bucket compared with the overwhelming number of decisions that have confirmed the legitimacy of *Merrill.*

[120] 450 U.S. 785 (1981).

[121] 467 U.S. 51 (1984).

[122] 471 U.S. 84 (1985).

Probably to put an end to any speculation that might have been prompted by these two pronouncements, the Court, in 1990, wrote yet another estoppel opinion, essentially confirming everything that had been said in *Merrill* and simply reemphasizing the proposition that there is to be no estoppel against the government. In *Office of Personnel Management v. Richmond*,[123] the Court reviewed a case in which a retired civilian employee of the Department of the Navy had qualified for disability payments from the government. Congress had passed a statute in 1982 that provided expressly for termination of disability payments to any retired person who earns-in another job-pay equivalent to at least 80 percent of his government salary before retirement. The law before 1982 was more complicated. It provided that the disability pay cutoff was not triggered unless the retired person met the 80 percent test in two consecutive years.

In 1986, four years after the statutory change, Mr. Richmond wanted to work overtime at his current job. He inquired at the agency, was given by an agency employee an erroneous opinion based on the law prior to 1982, worked the overtime, had his disability benefits cut off and took his claim to federal court. In a strong opinion by Justice Kennedy, the Supreme Court once again affirmed the *Merrill* principle. This time the Court went further by speculating on the possible impact of a legal principle that permitted the government to be estopped:

> To open the door to estoppel claims would only invite endless litigation over both real and imagined claims of misinformation by disgruntled citizens . . . . [Moreover,] [a] rule of estoppel might create not more reliable advice, but less advice. The natural consequence of a rule that made the Government liable for the statements of its agents would be a decision to cut back and impose strict controls upon Government provision of information in order to limit liability. Not only would valuable information programs be lost to the public, but the greatest impact of this loss would fall on those of limited means, who can least afford the alternative of private advice.

After *Richmond*, there should be little doubt in anyone's mind as to the Supreme Court's current view of estoppel. *Merrill* lives!

[C] Dealing With Estoppel as a Practitioner

The *Merrill* holding must give civil servants a great deal of comfort. They can say just about anything they like, however inaccurate, and never be held accountable. Fortunately, most civil servants are far more conscientious and reliable. Nonetheless, the difficulty is dealing with the *Merrill* doctrine as a private sector practitioner.

To begin with, consider the other side of the coin. Most agency practitioners have a problem just the opposite of *Merrill*. Most of the time, it's difficult, if not impossible, to get the agency to say anything to you. Agency personnel don't return telephone calls. They either fail to answer letters or take months to get an answer out. When you do receive a response, it is often an unintelligible or totally unhelpful

---

[123] 496 U.S. 414 (1990).

form letter. Even when an agency has some procedure for issuing more formal pronouncements, such as rulings or interpretations, the delay in obtaining one of these is generally so long that your client cannot afford to wait.

How do you deal with agency silence? More often than not, you simply have to make do with whatever is at hand. You try to find as much published agency data as possible. You make a stab at interpreting agency rules. You evaluate the political and philosophical climate that exists in the agency. You can, occasionally, find former agency employees who are willing to hazard a guess on your problem. Eventually, you cover yourself with an opinion letter to the client that has a sufficient number of disclaimers in it to absolve yourself of most malpractice consequences. This is not a very satisfying way to practice law.

What happens if your client insists on obtaining something from the agency? The first thing you should try to do is to reduce the matter on which you seek agency advice to the narrowest possible question. In other words, if your problem involves topics A, B, C & D, try to use publicly available and undisputed information such as statutory language, legislative history, existing agency regulations and other published agency statements to take care of, say, topics A, C, & D. § 1.05 *above* provides some guidance on this type of research. If there is still an informational gap with regard to topic B, you then should contact the agency to see what agency personnel have to say.

Using as much publicly available material as you can find should give you a very good idea of the parameters of the problem and should leave only a small portion of your problem to ad hoc agency advice. Part of Mr. Merrill's difficulty was that he relied *solely* on informal agency advice. Had Mr. Merrill read the FCIC rules, he might have been able to answer the question about reseeded crops himself. At the least, reading the rules would have created enough of a doubt to warrant pursuing the issue through formal agency channels until he got some reliable clarification.

Once you have done the maximum possible narrowing of the issues on your own and have decided to seek agency advice, the best way to deal with that advice is to think through a spectrum of possibilities, keeping the *Merrill* doctrine firmly in mind. For example:

a. Oral advice from an agency employee should not be relied upon, especially if that oral advice appears to cut against your own interpretation of agency rules. Oral advice that confirms what you have previously worked out may be a little comfort, but remember the message of *Merrill/Schweiker*: if you are later proven wrong, you cannot use the advice as an excuse.

b. Written advice in the form of a letter may be better. Think through this issue from the standpoint of the agency. The agency has the discretion *not* to use the *Merrill* defense. There are some situations in which an agency may choose to honor a written pronouncement as a matter of fairness to the private party, even if the pronouncement is inconsistent with agency policy. Obviously, the higher the rank of the writer, the greater the potential reliability. But continue to keep in mind the *Merrill* principle. There is virtually no distinction in the estoppel case law between oral and written advice or the rank of the officer giving the bad advice.

c. Many agencies have established procedures by which they will give advice that the agency agrees in advance to honor. For example, the Internal Revenue Service will issue letter rulings to persons on request. The Service considers itself bound by the terms of the letter ruling only for the person making the request. Nonetheless, a smart administrative lawyer knows that agencies tend not to indulge in abrupt shifts in position and that they try to treat similarly situated persons in a similar fashion. If your client has a tax situation precisely the same as the beneficiary of a letter ruling, you might decide to place at least some reliance on the ruling, absent any other signals that the agency is in the process of changing its position.

The difficulty with personalized decisions such as letter rulings is that they are incredibly time-consuming. Your application for a ruling may take a long time to prepare, and it may take an enormously long time for an agency to respond. Many problems in agency practice cannot wait the typical six months to a year for the agency to take action on an individual petition for clarification.

d. The agency declaratory order is another possibility. Under § 554(e) of the APA, an agency has the discretion to issue a declaratory order to terminate a controversy or remove uncertainty in cases that would otherwise be subject to a trial-type hearing. A declaratory order under the APA is the functional equivalent of the declaratory judgment in federal court civil practice. The declaratory order device is not always available, however. Agencies have to promulgate a rule establishing the procedure, and the proceedings can be as expensive, time-consuming and adversarial as any other evidentiary hearing. Nonetheless, when issued, a declaratory order binds the agency just as much as any other order it issues.[124]

§ 7.11 RULEMAKING IN THE STATES

There is a great deal of diversity in state rulemaking. Some states have relatively primitive administrative procedure acts; others, such as Florida, have APA's that are, in many respects, more sophisticated and well-thought-out than the Federal APA. Part of the reason for the diversity is that there is probably no constitutional due process applicable to state rulemaking.

In *Bi-Metallic Investment Co. v. Colorado*,[125] the Supreme Court suggested that a citizen's remedy for bad rulemaking is to kick out the decision makers in the next election. Because *Bi-Metallic* does not require it, some states still do not publish agency rules in a generally available publication. The text of the rules can be obtained by contacting the appropriate agency. Some states do not require notice and comment for agency rules on the assumption that disgruntled individuals can

---

[124] For a good general article on agency declaratory orders, see Burnele V. Powell, *Administratively Declaring Order: Some Practical Applications of the Administrative Procedure Act's Declaratory Order Process*, 64 N.C. L. Rev. 277 (1986).

[125] 239 U.S. 441 (1915). *Bi-Metallic* is extensively discussed in Chapter 5, § 5.02. For an excellent and comprehensive book on state rulemaking, *see* ARTHUR BONFIELD, STATE ADMINISTRATIVE RULEMAKING (1986). While not the only voice crying in the wilderness, Professor Bonfield deserves a great deal of credit for making the study and analysis of state administrative law a legitimate topic in American law schools.

always have the rules reviewed in a specific agency enforcement proceeding or in a court action.

The only proper way to deal with state administrative rulemaking is to check the provisions of the state's APA. Most states have administrative procedure acts that are similar to the federal APA, so most things discussed in this chapter will have relevance to both a state and a federal administrative practice.

There have been attempts at the state level to achieve some degree of uniformity. The National Conference of Commissioners on Uniform Laws promulgated a model state APA that provides for notice and comment rulemaking slightly different from the Federal APA.[126] Notice of the proposed rule must be published or served at least thirty days before the agency action. For certain rules, it must provide an opportunity for an oral hearing "if requested by 25 persons, by a governmental subdivision or agency, or by an association having not less than 25 members."[127] Prior to adoption of a rule, an agency must perform a regulatory analysis of the rule. On final promulgation, the agency must issue an explanatory statement along with the rule itself.

There are other innovative models on the state level. The state of Florida has a 25 year-old administrative procedure act that works around that sharp and sometimes artificial distinction in the federal APA between rulemaking and adjudication.[128] Florida rulemaking can be accomplished by notice and the opportunity for written comment, but a person whose interests are "substantially affected" may ask for a formal evidentiary hearing whenever a "disputed issue of material fact" exists.[129] In addition, the Florida APA permits the convening of an evidentiary hearing even for a proposed rule if a party whose interests are substantially affected can assert either (1) that the rule is in excess of agency authority (*ultra vires*); or (2) that the delegation of agency authority is somehow improper.[130]

No one should leave a course in administrative law thinking that the Federal APA is the only way an administrative system can be structured. The 1946 Federal APA was a great improvement in its time, but it has rarely been amended by Congress, in part because it works relatively well and in part because Congress has been far too busy with other more pressing matters. When Congress wants to deviate from the APA procedures, it normally writes the different procedures in an individual agency's enabling act.

---

[126] *See* §§ 3-101 *et seq.* of the Model Act in Appendix B.

[127] § 3-104 of the Model Act in Appendix B.

[128] Fla. Stat. ch. 120, as amended.

[129] This concept is related to the grounds for summary judgment in federal civil practice. *See* FED. R. CIV. P. 56. It also has roots in Professor K.C. Davis' famous, but difficult to implement, distinction between "legislative" and "adjudicative" facts.

[130] *See* William Fox & Leonard Carson, *A Comparison of the Federal and Florida Systems of Administrative Procedure*, 1980 FLA. B.J. 699. For an update on proposed and actual amendments to the Florida APA, *see* David M. Greenbaum & Lawrence E. Sellers, Jr., *1999 Amendments to the Florida Administrative Procedure Act: Phantom Menace or Much Ado About Nothing?*, 27 FLA. St. U. L. REV. 499 (2000). Lawrence E. Sellers, Jr., *The 2003 Amendments to the Florida APA*, 77 FLA. B.J. 74 (2003).

A great deal of recent innovation in administrative law has taken place at the state level. The model state administrative procedure act is frequently discussed by the Commissioners on Uniform State Laws, who are always receptive to suggestions for change, even if state legislatures do not always heed those suggestions. States such as Florida have gone beyond both the Federal APA and the model act to devise an administrative procedure act that is regarded as one of the most forward-looking statutes in the United States.

There is a lot of clear thinking on administrative procedure among the various state legislatures. Many of the modern state systems of administrative law were inspired by the Federal APA. It may now be time for Congress to look to the states for some lessons on how to deal with administrative agencies.

§ 7.12   DRAFTING A RULE

Most administrative law casebooks spend a great deal of time on the "law" of the administrative process without devoting much time to some of the things that lawyers work with every day. One such gap is the lack of attention paid to the techniques of drafting agency rules.

There are a number of reasons for this lapse. It is very difficult to communicate information on drafting techniques apart from actually drafting a rule. It is difficult to talk about drafting without having a specific drafting assignment to focus on. It is difficult to draft a rule without knowing a great deal about the administrative agency that is going to promulgate that rule. For all of these reasons, drafting is one of those things that most people learn by doing.

Nonetheless, regulatory drafting instruction could be improved. Before he left office, President Carter became very concerned that agency regulations were so poorly written that they could not be understood by those people who were subject to their commands, or even by reviewing courts. Saddest of all, they often could not be fully grasped even by the agencies who wrote them. To cope with these problems, the President issued an executive order directing executive branch agencies to write their regulations in plain English. This Executive Order was rescinded by President Reagan, although most agencies continue to try to write regulations that can be understood.

On the federal level, regulatory drafting has achieved some uniformity simply from the way the *Federal Register* is organized. For example, publication of agency rules begins with the part of the *Code of Federal Regulations* affected, followed by a title for the rule (*e.g.*, "resales of restricted and other securities"), the name of the agency (Securities and Exchange Commission) and the type of action taken ("final rule"). This introductory information is then followed by a summary of the action, names and telephone numbers of persons within the agency to contact for further information and the preamble to the rule.

The preamble, frequently used as the statement of basis and purpose in a final substantive rule, is often filled with information on the background of the rule, the agency's reasons for promulgating the rule and an explanation of comments received both in favor and opposed to the rule. The preamble is followed by the text of the rules themselves, followed by the name of the agency officer in charge of the promulgation and the date of promulgation.

But that's just the boilerplate. How about drafting the text of the rules themselves? The Government Printing Office, publisher of the *Federal Register* has published a guide called the *Legal Drafting Style Manual*[131] that is some help when faced with a regulatory drafting project. The *Manual* is too long to reproduce here, but some of its suggestions, paraphrased below, are well taken.

When first beginning the drafting process, prepare an outline of the matters to be covered by the rule and break the topics down into as many subdivisions as make sense. The less a subsection of a rule has to cover, the easier it is to draft and the easier it is to understand. Each subsection should be ordered in logical sequence. It is very important to think through the entire rule from start to finish in order to address the threshold matters first. For example, if you are drafting a rule setting up a monetary benefits program, don't write about setting the amount of individual benefits before you tell the reader the criteria for qualifying for the benefits.

As the *Manual* states: "Write short paragraphs, short sentences and use short words." Remember that the incredible prolixity of many legal documents began in the Middle Ages when many people could not write but needed certain written documents such as contracts or wills or court pleadings. A small industry of scriveners grew up and made their living by charging by the word. Hopefully, we have come a long way since then. The GPO *Manual* suggests as a rule of thumb keeping sentences to no more than twenty-five words and paragraphs to no more than seventy-five words with as few three-syllable words as possible.

If a rule contains a number of conditions, it is far better to state the conditions in outline form than to compress them into a single narrative sentence. For example, applicants for [the benefit] shall be:

(a) Over twenty-one years of age;

(b) with two or more children living with the applicant;

(c) and not gainfully employed.

Use the active voice and the present tense as often as possible. Make sure not to use different words to mean the same thing. Regulatory drafting is not the place to indulge yourself in a lot of synonyms, even if synonyms make your writing more interesting. If you say "motor vehicle" in one paragraph, use "motor vehicle" and not "automobile" every other time. By contrast, if your rule is to be limited to automobiles, don't say "motor vehicle" — a term that might include boats, airplanes and snowmobiles.

Many fledgling writers don't understand the proper use of ambiguity. Ambiguity is a defect when you mean thirty days and write "month" because some months are longer or shorter than thirty days. By contrast, ambiguity may be required when a drafter cannot foresee completely the application of the regulation. When the *Uniform Commercial Code* uses the term "good faith," when Congress establishes a standard of "public convenience and necessity" in an enabling act or when a court talks about a duty of "reasonable" care, each of these entities is using what is

---

[131] GPO, LEGAL DRAFTING STYLE MANUAL (undated).

frequently called *purposeful* or *deliberate* ambiguity.[132]

Deliberate ambiguity is not necessarily a crime in regulatory drafting even though agency rules are, by definition, supposed to be more detailed and more specific than statutes. You may intentionally incorporate an ambiguous phrase such as *good faith* in a rule, but you should have a very good reason for doing so, because without a reason, you do a great disservice to those regulated parties who are trying to modify their conduct to accommodate the rule.

Choose words carefully. Know the difference in legal drafting between the verbs *shall* and *may*. Avoid using *will* or *must* when you really mean *shall*. To please at least the author of this book, stay away from the adjective "said" as in "The motor vehicle shall be registered for two years and *said* motor vehicle shall . . . ." As the GPO Manual points out, the use of *said* in this context went out about the year 1500.

At present, it is generally ill-advised and objectionable to use gender specific words such as *he* or *his* when a rule is intended to cover both males and females. Most governments, federal, state and local, are also removing connotations of gender from job titles. The drafter should say "he or she" or simply remove these pronouns altogether and refer, for instance, to a police officer rather than a policeman. On occasion, it is possible to use the plural to avoid the gender specific pronouns.

This section could go on with writing suggestions to no great purpose. Just remember that writing agency rules requires as much care and thought as judges put into judicial opinions or as the legislatures put into drafting their statutes. State and federal agency regulations affect hundreds of thousands of people. The vast bulk of these regulations are never construed by courts or reviewed by legislatures. The only thing that makes them work is careful drafting.

§ 7.13 SOLVING RULEMAKING PROBLEMS

As everyone should recognize by now, agencies have vast discretion in formulating policy. More often than not, in "real life," an agency rule is going to stand as written. In law school courses and on bar examinations, agency rules are sometimes a little more difficult to predict. The following are just a few hints in the nature of a checklist for working through rulemaking problems.

(A) *Identify* the device that the agency is using for announcing its policy. Recall a theme discussed in Chapter 6: an agency may announce new policy either by rule or by order, and its choice is not likely to be disturbed by a reviewing court. If the device being used is rulemaking, consider the following:

(B) *Separate* the issues into (1) the *procedure* for promulgating the rule and (2) the contents of the rule-*i.e.*, its *substance*.

1. Procedural Considerations:

(a) *Evaluate* the procedures being used by the agency. Remember the message of *Vermont Yankee.* Unless Congress (in the enabling act) or the agency (through its

---

[132] *See, e.g.,* F. REED DICKERSON, LEGAL DRAFTING (1981).

own discretion) sets up special rulemaking procedures, the notice and comment procedures set out in § 553 of the APA are the *maximum* procedures to be followed, absent: (1) extraordinary circumstances or (2) constitutional considerations. For all practical purposes, you will not encounter problems that fall into either of these two exceptions. When all a statute mentions is a "hearing," an agency need only abide by § 553 procedures. Formal rulemaking requires some language, such as "on the record after opportunity for hearing."

(b) *Read* the enabling act. If an agency is commanded to promulgate rules following specific procedures set out in a statute, it must do so. If an agency has adopted specific rulemaking procedures and doesn't follow them, it will be deemed to have violated its own internal procedural rules (*Nixon*), and the rule itself will probably be held invalid. If an agency uses § 553 procedures, it must abide by the procedural commands of that section. Recall that in this sense, § 553 constitutes *both* the maximum procedures that an agency must use (*Vermont Yankee*) and the minimum procedures necessary to promulgate a valid rule. So, make sure that all the elements of § 553 are present. Skipping § 553 procedures means that the rule may be procedurally defective and thus, is likely to be held invalid. Remember that proper rulemaking procedures must be followed both for promulgating a rule and amending or rescinding a rule (*State Farm*).

(c) *Distinguish* between substantive rules and other than substantive rules, both for your procedural evaluation and later when you evaluate the substance of the agency's rule. There are very few procedural demands placed on non-substantive rules. But recall that it's often difficult to make the distinction, so some agencies err on the side of caution and put even rules that might be deemed interpretative through the notice and comment process. This eliminates all doubt and is probably the fairest way to treat the regulated industry. It is not, however, required by the APA.

(d) *Review* the record for ex parte contacts. They can, in the most egregious instances, poison a rulemaking, but truly fatal ex parte contacts are a rare occurrence.

2. *Consideration of the Substance of the Rules:*

(a) *Compare* what the rule says with the agency's authority under the enabling act. If the language of the rule exceeds the limits of the enabling act, an agency is acting in excess of statutory authority-*e.g.*, if the Interstate Commerce Commission (authority over trains and trucks) tries to write a rule regulating airlines.

(b) *Review* the agency's statement of basis and purpose. It is a crucial part of the rulemaking. If the agency has not provided a reasoned and rational explanation either for making a rule or for rescinding an existing rule (*State Farm*), a court will overturn the agency's action as arbitrary and capricious. Recall that courts take a "hard look" at the rulemaking record.

(c) *Do not forget* the message of *Merrill*: an agency may not be estopped for erroneous advice.

In the final analysis, agency rulemaking, while procedurally simple, can be fraught with difficulties for lawyers whether inside or outside the agency. You can cope more effectively with the issues you will encounter as a law student and as a practitioner if you first explore some of the rudiments of agency rulemaking discussed in this chapter and if you organize your issue resolution along the lines suggested by the preceding outline. One thing you can count on as a matter of certainty, whether it be as a lawyer or as a citizen of the United States in the twenty-first century, you are going to encounter-and have to deal with-large numbers of agency rules for the rest of your life.

Chapter 8

TRIAL-TYPE PROCEEDINGS

§ 8.01 INTRODUCTION

The first words out of my mouth in my first administrative hearing were: "Your honor, I respectfully move for a continuance." The presiding officer responded: "Mr. Fox, please. I'm not a judge, so don't call me 'your honor.' We don't have 'motions' in this agency, and I don't know what a 'continuance' is. If you want some more time to prepare, just ask for it." Pondering this exchange a few days later, I realized I had just been introduced to the administrative process. The hearing officer refused to give me any more time, by the way. I had to litigate the case that day, after only twenty-four hours notice and no discovery. That was another lesson in administrative action.

Many lawyers make fundamental mistakes in agency lawyering by regarding agency trial-type proceedings (also referred to as *evidentiary hearings* and occasionally as *formal adjudications*) as indistinguishable from the civil trial process. There are many similarities, but there are also a number of crucial differences. That is not to say that good trial skills are of no use in agency hearings. They are of tremendous importance, and, all other things being equal, the better trial lawyer will probably prevail in an agency hearing. Even so, a lawyer who does not fully grasp the differences between a trial and an agency hearing may compromise his client's case.

This chapter covers a number of matters relevant to evidentiary hearings in federal agencies. Most state evidentiary hearings are handled similarly, although there appears to be a greater degree of informality in many state procedural systems.[1] This chapter walks you through the important statutory provisions in the Federal Administrative Procedure Act. It then takes an administrative hearing apart piece by piece to make sure that you have a good understanding of the nuances of agency proceedings. Once that is accomplished, it provides an example of agency lawyering in a specific factual setting to illustrate the process of thinking through tactics and strategy in a hearing. Finally, it examines-again piece by piece-the process of making a decision based on an evidentiary hearing and provides some insights into how to draft an initial decision. Some of this material is standard fare for administrative law courses; other parts, especially the material on strategy and tactics and the suggestions on drafting an initial opinion, are new. All of it,

---

[1] The provisions for evidentiary hearings in the *Model State Administrative Procedure Act* are set out in §§ 9–14 of the Act. *See* Appendix B. For those of you contemplating practice in a specific state, make absolutely sure you check your own state APA. Not all states have adopted the Model Act. Keep in mind the admonitions in the text about looking closely at enabling acts and agency rules.

however, is essential for a successful agency practice.

§ 8.02 AN APA ROADMAP

[A] Agency Impact on Trial-Type Proceedings

This is tedious stuff, but it's vitally important. It will be very difficult to understand any of the sections that follow without understanding precisely what the Federal Administrative Procedure Act permits and forbids. In reading through this material, keep in mind that agency enabling acts and agency regulations have an important impact on trial-type proceedings. For example, to the extent that an agency provides formal rules of evidence or specific discovery tools, it will do so by rule. The APA has little to say about these two things except to mention that neither rules of evidence, nor elaborate discovery, is mandatory under the APA.

Agency enabling acts sometimes add to the provisions of the APA, particularly in the area of intra-agency review of initial decisions. A trial-type proceeding is an adversarial process intended to be similar to, but not identical with, a civil bench trial in federal court. Be alert for both the similarities and the differences. One thing you will not have to spend much time with in this area is constitutional due process. You will find, as you work through the APA provisions, that Congress has provided far more due process by statute than the Supreme Court has ever required as a matter of constitutional law.[2]

[B] The Scope of APA Adjudications

Begin the analysis by refreshing your recollection of the definition of *agency* in § 551(1) and "order" in § 551(6).[3] Next read thoroughly §§ 554, 555, 556, 557 and 558. These portions of the APA are the provisions that govern trial-type proceedings. The place to begin is § 554 (adjudications). With certain exceptions, agencies subject to the APA are to conduct adjudications when the agency's decision making proceedings are "required by statute to be determined on the record after opportunity for an agency hearing," with certain exceptions.

Not all components of the federal government are covered by the APA. There is no easy way to get a sense of which agency proceedings are covered other than to read individual enabling acts. As a general matter, an evidentiary hearing is granted for major federal licenses, such as for hydroelectric or nuclear power plants or water discharge permits, and for agency actions that terminate important

---

[2] Many law professors ask students to compare the procedures mandated for certain welfare benefit terminations set out in *Goldberg v. Kelly*, 397 U.S. 254 (1970), with the procedures set out in APA §§ 556–557. The APA list is longer, including such things as testimony under oath, a much more independent decider (an administrative law judge) and a verbatim transcript. For the *Goldberg* list, *see supra* Chapter 5, § 5.03.

[3] *Order* is a kind of catch-all category that includes virtually any kind of agency decision — expressly including a licensing decision-and that is not rulemaking. To this extent, the concept of order is a residual definition. If an agency makes a decision, and if that decision does not result in a rule, the agency has made an order.

federal benefits, such as civil service employment or social security disability payments.

The Supreme Court has not been of very much help in making this threshold determination. *Wong Yang Sung v. McGrath*,[4] an immigration case decided shortly after enactment of the APA, is a good statement of the trials and tribulations of getting a uniform agency procedure act through Congress. The Court seemed to suggest that §§ 556–557 hearings, including the requirement that the prosecutorial function be separated from the judicial function, are to be the rule rather than the exception in any instance in which individual rights (such as exclusion and deportation) are affected. But Congress overruled *Wong Yang Sung* legislatively just a few months after the decision by amending the statute to restrict the right to a hearing in certain immigration matters.[5]

The enabling act must be explicit on the right to an evidentiary hearing. In *United States v. Florida East Coast Railway*,[6] the Court held that the mere use of the word "hearing" in an enabling act was not enough to trigger formal rulemaking. The United States Court of Appeals for the First Circuit has recently changed its mind. In 1978, the Circuit decided *Seacoast Anti-Pollution League v. Costle*,[7] a case involving the Clean Water Act's requirement that nuclear power plants obtain water pollution discharge permits.[8] The Act is administered by the Environmental Protection Agency, but it is not clear on the face of the statute whether the EPA must hold evidentiary hearings on the permits. The Act requires "an opportunity for public hearing." This is language that doesn't even come close to the phrase "on the record after opportunity for an agency hearing," that was so important to the Supreme Court in *Florida East Coast Railway*.[9] In *Seacoast*, the Circuit decided that this language required a §§ 556–557 hearing because it also determined that a discharge permit was a license and that licensing is a form of agency adjudication[10] that involves an individualized determination on some matter such as a water discharge permit (the "license" at issue) for a specific facility. Accordingly, the *Seacoast* court decided there is a presumption in favor of an evidentiary hearing, unless the statute says something expressly to the contrary.

In 2003 the First Circuit looked at a proceeding involving the application for a water permit filed by an electric power station and came to a contrary position — thereby overruling *Seacoast*. In *Dominion Energy Brayton Point v. Johnson*,[11] the Circuit looked at the same language ("an opportunity for public hearing") and

---

[4] 339 U.S. 33, *modified in* ,339 U.S. 908 (1950).

[5] For some recent commentary suggesting that Wong Yang Sung should be revived, *see* William Funk, *The Rise and Purported Demise of Wong Yang Sung*, 58 ADMIN. L. REV. 881 (2006).

[6] 410 U.S. 224 (1973). *Florida East Coast* is discussed extensively in Chapter 7, § 7.03.

[7] 572 F.2d 872 (1st Cir.), *cert. denied*, 439 U.S. 824 (1978).

[8] 33 U.S.C. §§ 1251 *et seq.*

[9] Congress may also forbid the use of evidentiary hearings for specific agency actions. *See Marcello v. Bonds*, 349 U.S. 302 (1955).

[10] Note the definitions of both *order* and *adjudication* in § 551. An order includes a license and is the outcome of all adjudications.

[11] 443 F.3d 12 (1st Cir. 2006).

concluded that the Supreme Court's decision in *Chevron USA v. NRDC*[12] requiring deference to an agency's construction of its underlying statutes trumped the presumption in favor of an evidentiary hearing created by the *Seacoast* court.[13] The Dominion opinion is a straightforward application of the Chevron two-step. First, the court determined that the "public hearing" language was not plain and unambiguous on its face (*Chevron* step one). It clearly, as noted above, falls far short of the *Florida East Coast Railway* language. Second, when the statutory language is ambiguous, a reviewing court must defer to the interpretation given by the agency so long as that interpretation is reasonable (*Chevron* step two).[14]

The D.C. Circuit, in *United States Lines v. Federal Maritime Commission*,[15] took the opposite tack. There, the controversy was over the Federal Maritime Commission's (FMC) approval of an anti-competitive agreement. The statute requiring FMC approval did not expressly use the language "on the record after opportunity for hearing." Thus, the court determined that an evidentiary hearing was not required. The US Lines reasoning is echoed in the 7th Circuit's decision in *City of West Chicago v. NRDC*.[16]

Predicting future decisions may be a bit easier in the first decade of the twenty-first century. At the moment, *Chevron* is an enormously powerful case. But there is some countervailing pressure. The American Bar Association's Section of Administrative Law has urged agencies to use a trial-type hearing as the default mechanism when a statute calls for a hearing in the context of individual claims.[17] However, you can take some comfort from the fact that in most disputes involving established agencies and established proceedings, the issue never arises.[18]

This is not where the analysis of § 554's scope ends, however. Section 554 excepts certain proceedings, including the familiar military and foreign affairs exception,[19] an exception for certain federal personnel matters, one for certification of worker representatives,[20] two exceptions involving courts (where a person gets a trial *de novo* in court or where the administrative agency is functioning only as an

---

[12] 467 U.S. 837 (1984).

[13] The First Circuit was not a voice in the wilderness on this point. At least one other circuit came to essentially the same conclusion although with different reasoning. *Marathon Oil Co. v. EPA*, 564 F.2d 1253 (9th Cir. 1977).

[14] The EPA did a parallel Chevron analysis when it issued the final rule that dispensed with evidentiary hearings.

[15] 584 F.2d 519 (D.C. Cir. 1978).

[16] 701 F.2d 632 (7th Cir. 1983).

[17] *See* Michael Asimow, *The Spreading Umbrella: Extending the APA's Adjudication Provisions to All Evidentiary Hearings Required by Statute*, 56 ADMIN. L. REV. 1003 (2004); Cooley R. Howarth, Jr., *Restoring the Applicability of the APA's Adjudicatory Procedures*, 56 ADMIN. L. REV. 1043 (2004).

[18] There are instances, discussed in Chapter 10, that are considered adjudication, but require far less than a trial-type hearing.

[19] Section 553 rulemaking also contains a military/foreign affairs exception.

[20] Don't be misled by this exception. The federal labor statutes contain elaborate due process requirements. One successful labor lawyer of the author's acquaintance, with considerable work before the National Labor Relations Board, has practiced for many years in a heavily proceduralized agency setting without ever referring to or even having read the APA itself.

agent for the court) and one, slightly strange exception for proceedings in which the agency decision is based on inspections, tests or elections.[21] The exceptions are construed narrowly, so the requirement that an agency proceed in a dispute by adjudication will normally apply to many, if not most, of the individual disputes processed by the various agencies.

[C]   Pre-Hearing Matters

Section 554(b) requires that affected persons be given specific notice of the hearing, including time, place, nature of the hearing, legal authority for convening the hearing and in most circumstances, particularized information on the issues presented. The section also promotes settlement by requiring an agency to receive pre-hearing submissions, which may lead to a disposition of the controversy by consent.

Section 554(d) provides for strict separation of functions. This is one of the more important aspects of this portion of the APA. There must be a distinct separation between agency employees who may be involved in gathering information and serving as the agency equivalent of prosecutor or investigator and the agency employee designated as the presiding officer. As will be seen in subsequent sections of this chapter, when an administrative law judge is used as the presiding officer, he or she must be guaranteed even more independence and separation than that required by § 554. To enhance this separation, § 554 prohibits ex parte contacts between the parties and the presiding officer. Additional ex parte contact provisions are contained in § 558(d)(1).

Section 555(b) expressly provides a right to have counsel present; and to the extent that additional information is necessary, § 555(d) permits parties to a hearing to invoke the agency's subpoena power. The APA permits, and most agency rules provide for, a pre-hearing conference, although you should not necessarily expect a pre-trial conference in every proceeding in every agency.

[D]   The Hearing

Section 556 sets out the requirements for a hearing. Typically, an administrative law judge presides over an oral hearing by admitting documentary evidence and testimony under oath, permitting direct and cross-examination, ruling on evidentiary objections and the like. It is this part of the hearing process that most closely resembles a civil bench trial in federal court. Section 556(d) imposes the

---

[21] The *Attorney General's Manual* provides a number of obscure examples, such as locomotive inspections and the grading of grain by the Department of Agriculture. The sense of this provision is that the inspection or test is everything. The idea of this exception is that while it's not impossible to summon the inspector or tester into a hearing and require that person to swear under oath that she graded the grain in such a fashion or inspected the locomotive on such and such a date, the hearing wouldn't really provide anything meaningful that was not already provided in the report itself. As the *Manual* puts it: "The surest way to ascertain what is the grade of grain is for a skilled inspector to test it . . ." ATTORNEY GENERAL'S MANUAL ON THE ADMINISTRATIVE PROCEDURE ACT 45 (1947). Reasonable people might differ over this conclusion, however. Even experts occasionally make mistakes. There seems to be little reason to exclude these matters from the hearing process when other administrative hearings involve frequent clashes between experts as to the accuracy of a test or evaluation.

burden of proof on "the proponent of a rule or order." The hearing record is to be the sole basis for the ultimate decision.

[E] The Agency Decision

The outcome of an agency adjudication is referred to as an *order.* The process by which a hearing record is converted into an order is set out in § 557. Under normal circumstances, the Administrative Law Judge (ALJ) writes an initial decision that is reviewed by higher-ups in the agency if parties object to the initial decision. The agency decision is accompanied by formal findings of fact and conclusions of law (normally prepared by the ALJ but occasionally subject to modification within the agency) and is subject to judicial review.

This is an outline of a basic APA evidentiary hearing. The next several sections look closely at the important ingredients of the hearing and decisional process.

[F] Alternative Dispute Resolution in Federal Agencies

In late 1990, Congress enacted some important amendments to Title 5 of the United States Code that greatly broaden the procedural options for federal agency disputes. The statute is cited as the "Administrative Dispute Resolution Act"[22] and, for the first time, makes virtually all of the procedural vehicles available in private sector dispute resolution also available to agencies. The Act survived some tangential attacks and was permanently reauthorized in 1996. In essence, Congress was merely codifying what had become a growing number of agency experiments in ADR over the past several years.[23]

To a certain extent, the ADR Act is a strange development because you will recall that the administrative agencies themselves were supposed to be alternative dispute resolution entities. They were set up in the states and in the federal government because the courts were not up to dealing properly and expeditiously with the growing problems of regulating a large and complex society.

The ADR Act first confirms that the agency hearing process set up under the APA is now very cumbersome and time-consuming. Congress determined that many disputes could be resolved by some mechanism other than the elaborate evidentiary hearing process described in detail in the remainder of this chapter. Under the Act, agencies are now permitted-in appropriate circumstances-to employ ADR devices to resolve disputes.

---

[22] Pub. L. No. 101-552, 104 Stat. 2736, codified at 5 U.S.C. §§ 581 *et seq.*

[23] For a discussion of these experiments, *see* Philip J. Harter, *Dispute Resolution and Administrative Law: The History, Needs, and Future of a Complex Relationship*, 29 Vill. L. Rev. 1393 (1983). The Act also reflects a strong recommendation from the now abolished Administrative Conference of the United States (ACUS) that agencies adopt ADR techniques. ACUS produced a good — and lengthy — compendium of ADR materials in ACUS, Sourcebook: Federal Agency Use of Alternative Means of Dispute Resolution (1990). *See also* Robin J. Evans, Note, *The Administrative Dispute Resolution Act of 1996: Improving Federal Agency Use of Alternative Dispute Resolution Processes*, 50 Admin. L. Rev. 217 (1998).

Nothing about this Act is compulsory. The agency uses these alternative mechanisms at its election and only after careful consideration. Moreover, the parties to the dispute must agree to their use. The Act's general authority states: "an agency may use a dispute resolution proceeding for the resolution of an issue in controversy that relates to an administrative program, if the parties agree to such proceeding." This voluntary component is a major concession to the possibility that some ADR techniques, specifically arbitration, could run afoul of the delegation doctrine's prohibition on the use of private persons to make government decisions.

In this regard, the Act is probably overly cautious because in at least two separate instances the Supreme Court has approved the use of alternatives that employ private sector persons. In *Schweiker v. McClure*,[24] the Court approved the use of hearing examiners employed by private insurance carriers to dispose of claims filed under the Social Security Administration's Medicare program. The use of these private judges was attacked on due process rather than delegation grounds, and the Court upheld their use without addressing the delegation issues. In *Thomas v. Union Carbide Agricultural Products Co.*,[25] the Court approved the use of binding, private sector arbitration in disputes arising out of the payment of compensation for the use of company data in the registration of pesticides by the Environmental Protection Agency. In this instance, the Court held that not all disputes involving a government agency had to be tried in an Article III court.

The ADR Act now permits agencies to employ settlement negotiations, conciliation, facilitation, mediation, fact-finding, mini-trials and arbitration "or any combination thereof" in resolving disputes. Most of these proceedings will be presided over by what the Act calls a *neutral*. Neutrals may be either agency employees or private persons who are acceptable to the parties as unbiased and who are bound by certain statutory requirements of confidentiality with regard to the proceeding.[26]

It is obvious that Congress did not want many lawsuits arising out of the mere decision to use ADR, so an agency's decision to use ADR is committed to its discretion. Of course, the final agency action may be reviewable, but the decision to use ADR techniques is generally exempt from judicial review. Arbitral awards will be reviewed by a court under the terms of the federal arbitration act, rather than under the APA.[27]

The 1996 reauthorization and amendments made a number of contributions to the stability of the process. Congress eliminated the persistent reauthorization requirement, so it is now permissible to view the ADR Act as a permanent and integral component of the federal administrative process. This change alone may prompt a few more agencies to engage in alternative procedures. Agency heads are no longer permitted unilaterally to review arbitral awards. This change has the effect of making arbitral awards issued under the ADR Act the functional

---

[24] 456 U.S. 188 (1982).

[25] 473 U.S. 568 (1985).

[26] 5 U.S.C. § 583.

[27] 5 U.S.C. § 591. The Federal Arbitration Act, 9 U.S.C. §§ 10 *et seq.*, has been amended appropriately.

equivalent of arbitral awards issued in the private sector. In other words, arbitral awards will be essentially final and binding (subject, of course, to limited judicial review) when issued. Finally, the 1996 changes enhance the confidentiality of the proceeding, in particular by exempting materials in the hands of a neutral from disclosure under the Freedom of Information Act and other statutes.

The Act may not be a perfect statute. There is no perfect form of dispute resolution, whether it be ADR or an evidentiary hearing. Probably the Act's biggest contribution is that it gives federal agencies all the dispute resolution techniques that have been available in the private sector for years. As agencies become more comfortable with all their alternatives, we may see more rapid and efficient agency decision-making emerging from the process.

§ 8.03　INITIATION OF AN AGENCY ACTION

There are a number of ways to commence an agency adjudication. Frequently, an adjudication is begun by the filing of an application for some type of federal license, such as a television broadcast license (Federal Communications Commission) or a permit to construct a nuclear power plant (Nuclear Regulatory Commission). Many adjudications are commenced by the agency's charging some member of the regulated industry with a violation of an agency regulation. These proceedings are typically referred to as "enforcement actions" and frequently require the initiation of an evidentiary hearing at some point during the process. The Federal Trade Commission commences an enforcement action by filing and serving a company with an administrative complaint charging the company with an unfair or deceptive trade practice. The Department of Energy begins enforcement with the service of either a "notice of probable violation" or a "proposed remedial order." Other agencies use different labels.

The process is generally the same in all agencies. Based on information either produced by its own investigation or received from a grievance filed by someone outside the agency, the agency makes a preliminary internal determination as to whether an agency regulation has been violated. This determination is not too different, conceptually, from a probable cause determination in court, and many agencies permit the accused party to say something at this stage. These comments, however, are usually limited to some kind of written response, and even the written response is not mandated by the APA.

Once the in-house decision to issue a complaint is made, the offending party is notified by service of the complaint. Neither courts, nor the APA, impose a heavy requirement of detail on the initial complaint. It does not have to be as detailed as a criminal indictment, although most agencies voluntarily include a fair amount of detail as a matter of course. Because an agency proceeding is regarded as a civil matter, most courts insist only that the charging paper provide reasonable notice of the violation and the other details necessary to permit the accused party to participate in the remainder of the proceedings.[28] Very much like a complaint drawn under the Federal Rules of Civil Procedure, an agency complaint is almost always

---

[28] *See, e.g., Savina Home Industries v. Secretary of Labor*, 594 F.2d 1358 (10th Cir. 1979).

subject to amendment. Once notification takes place, parties are normally expected to respond in written form to the agency's claim, just as a defendant in court is expected to file an answer before anything else takes place.

In licensing proceedings, initial notification of potentially affected persons is accomplished in slightly different fashion. Typically, a federal agency will publish a notice of a license application in the *Federal Register* and invite other interested parties to submit parallel applications within a certain period of time or to file requests to participate in the proceeding, even if they don't want the license. In many cases, publication is required, either by rule or by statute, in newspapers in the vicinity of the applicant so that notice is given to as many persons as possible. Frequently, the applicant must pay for publication of the local notices. The published notice typically names the applicant, describes the license sought and provides a few details on the remaining procedures, including the scheduling of pre-hearing conferences and the location of where the evidentiary hearing will be held, as well as how the final decision will be made.

§ 8.04 PRE-HEARING ACTIVITIES

[A] Analysis of Pre-Hearing Process

Specific pre-hearing activities are normally governed by agency regulations. The APA requires an agency to provide participants in a hearing with an opportunity for "the submission and consideration of facts, arguments, offers of settlement or proposals of adjustment," but only when "time, the nature of the proceeding, and the public interest permit . . . ."[29] Even these matters are viewed more as settlement-provoking devices rather, than hearing-preparation devices.

Most agencies, however, provide more procedures. To a large extent, they do so because lawyers, both inside and outside the agencies, have been heavily involved with structuring agency process, and lawyers tend to impose procedures with which they already feel comfortable. More often than not, these procedures closely resemble civil trial procedures. There are three major facets of the pre-hearing process that require analysis: (1) participation, (2) discovery, and (3) the pre-hearing conference.

[B] Participation and Right to Counsel

[1] Participation

Many major federal agency proceedings include a lot of participants. Licensing proceedings attract parties because persons other than the original applicant decide that they too would like the license. The opportunity to construct and operate a television station is worth a great deal of money. Hydroelectric licensing applications typically have fewer applicants than television licenses, but hydro projects

---

[29] § 554(c)(1). Another reason for this language was to provide for agency consent orders, such as the Federal Trade Commission's cease and desist orders. This type of agency action permits the agency to force an entity to stop a particular practice without admitting to any violation.

tend to stir up environmental groups and state and municipal governments who want input into the licensing decision. Agency enforcement proceedings occasionally name more than one violator per notice and occasionally attract trade associations as participants.

Most agencies, as a matter of policy, are very lenient in permitting additional participants in the hearing process. Typically, a person who can show some connection between his or her situation and the matter under consideration will be allowed to participate at the hearing. But remember, if you wish to participate, you normally have to ask to do so. Agencies rarely provide for the automatic participation in a hearing of persons who have not been specifically named in the initial notification. There are a few instances when enabling acts or agency rules require the inclusion of state and local governments in certain licensing proceedings.

Every now and then the courts get into the act. The principal case in this area, *Office of Communication, United Church of Christ v. FCC*,[30] was authored by Chief Justice Burger when he was a judge on the D.C. Circuit. A television station in Jackson, Mississippi was before the FCC in a proceeding for renewal of its license (an undertaking that usually requires an evidentiary hearing). A number of people in Jackson had lodged complaints against the station for its lack of sensitivity to certain civil rights interests, for broadcasting programs urging a return to segregation and for other on-the-air remarks that suggested a racially discriminatory attitude on the part of station personnel.

The complainants asked the FCC for permission to participate in the license renewal proceeding, but were refused by the FCC. The Commission then proceeded to renew the station's license. At first glance, the FCC's action seems inexplicable, but it was really the outcome of settled agency policy on participation. Prior to *Church of Christ*, the Commission permitted intervention only by someone who would suffer electronic interference from the operation of the station in question or who could allege some kind of pocketbook injury from the grant or renewal of the license. Obviously, the complainants here could do no such thing.

The complaining parties then went to the D.C. Circuit, where Judge Burger wrote a sweeping opinion, in which he compared the more stringent requirements of standing to get into federal court and the standards for participating in agency action. While federal court standing is restricted by the terms of Article III of the Constitution and strictly controlled by the Supreme Court, agencies are not subject to the constitutional restrictions. Moreover, the purpose of the agencies is far different from federal courts. Agencies are supposed to look out for, and function on behalf of, the public interest. What better way to ascertain the public's interest than to permit very broad participation in agency adjudications? In any event, the exceptionally tight tests set up by the FCC were far too narrow. Listening to the public in an adjudication means more than just letting these people file written comments. If their participation is to be meaningful, they should be given party status and permitted the same scope of activity and freedom of action that the original parties are permitted.

---

[30] 359 F.2d 994 (D.C. Cir. 1966).

Church of Christ is a striking decision and one with which few would find fault. Nonetheless it should not be pushed too far. It is clear that there must be some connection between the agency action and the persons who seek to intervene. In *Church of Christ*, Judge Burger was impressed by the fact that the intervenors were people who lived in the Jackson area and watched the television station in question. Also, the organizations who wanted to come into the case claimed to represent a large portion of the potential audience of the station. Agency intervention may not require personal pocketbook injury, but it does require *some* linkage between the agency action and the status of the person seeking to participate. Potential participants should try to identify as many connections as possible between themselves and the agency proceeding.

There can be some difficulty implementing this idea of broad participation. Because federal agencies have nationwide jurisdiction over certain matters, it is entirely possible that hundreds and thousands of companies and individuals have interests identical with, or similar to, those of the parties to an agency action. Should they all be permitted to come in?[31] Wouldn't this destroy a meaningful hearing process? At least one court, writing after the *Church of Christ* case, in *National Welfare Rights Organization v. Finch*,[32] suggested that in most cases these questions are something of a chamber of horrors argument, not likely to be realized. Moreover, the agency can take steps to keep a hearing as efficient as possible. For example, an ALJ is empowered to exclude repetitious testimony. A pre-hearing conference can be used to align the various parties and to force them to agree to joint presentations. These devices, in the *Finch* court's view, are preferable to exclusion.

In 1986, the Administrative Conference of the United States issued a recommendation relating to intervention. The Conference noted that intervention "has been greatly broadened by statutes, administrative actions, and judicial decisions. To help an agency make an intervention determination, ACUS recommended that the following factors be considered: (1) the nature of the contested issues, (2) the intervener's precise interest in the adjudication, (3) the adequacy of representation of existing parties, (4) the ability of the prospective intervenor to present new or additional information, and (5) the effect of intervention on the agency's implementation of its statutory mandate.[33]

How about participation by poor persons? Is there any requirement that agencies pay the costs of participation for those who cannot afford it? Absent some statutory authority for payment of the costs of participation, courts have generally

---

[31] This could be the case in a rulemaking where any *interested person* may comment. *See* APA § 553.

[32] 429 F.2d 725 (D.C. Cir. 1970).

[33] ACUS, Public Participation in Administration Hearings (No. 71-6), reproduced in 1 C.F.R. § 305.71-6 (1986). A recent article on participation is Jim Rossi, *Participation Run Amok: The Costs of Mass Participation for Deliberative Agency Decisionmaking*, 92 Nw. U. L. Rev. 173 (1997). An even more recent study of adjudications in the context of social security decisionmaking is Jon C. Dubin, *Overcoming Gridlock:* Campbell *After a Quarter-Century and Bureaucratically Rational Gap-Filling in Mass Justice Adjudication in the Social Security Administration's Disability Programs*, 62 Admin. L. Rev. 937 (2010).

not required it. In *Greene County Planning Board v. Federal Power Commission*,[34] public interest intervenors asked the FPC to pay their attorneys' fees in a long, costly and controversial hydroelectric licensing proceeding. The court examined the relevant statutes and a decision by the General Accounting Office (the GAO has authority to determine the legitimacy of disbursement of federal funds in advance of any expenditure) that the FPC could pay the attorneys' fees and decided that there was no inherent or intrinsic authority for a federal agency to do so, absent express congressional authority.[35]

Congress reauthorized and amended the Equal Access to Justice Act (EAJA),[36] a controversial statute originally enacted in 1980 that permits courts to award attorneys' fees to certain classes of individuals and small businesses (determined to be such mainly on the basis of net worth and number of employees) who substantially prevail over federal agencies in litigation. The Act covers adversarial administrative proceedings as well as court cases, except for licensing and ratemaking matters. This is a difficult statute to invoke successfully, however. The government may escape liability for attorneys' fees by demonstrating that its position was *substantially justified.*[37] Private sector litigants have been successful in recovering fees under the EAJA, given the requirement of showing that they have substantially prevailed and that the agency's opposition was not substantially justified. Congress stepped into the fray in 1996 by inserting an EAJA amendment into the Small Business Regulatory Enforcement Fairness Act. The Small Business Act amended § 504(a) of the EAJA, inserting as new language:

> If, in an adversary adjudication . . . the demand by the agency is substantially in excess of the decision of the adjudicative officer and is unreasonable when compared with such decision, the adjudicative officer shall award to the party the fees and other expenses related to defending against the excessive demand, unless the party has committed a willful violation of law or otherwise acted in bad faith, or special circumstances make an award unjust.

This language may provoke a lot more EAJA litigation.

In certain licensing proceedings there is another consideration that significantly affects participation. Technical limitations in the industry may be such that only one license can be granted. Two radio stations using the same frequency cannot

---

[34] 559 F.2d 1227 (2d Cir. 1977), *(en banc) cert. denied,* 434 U.S. 1086 (1978).

[35] The court took a great deal of comfort from a Supreme Court opinion, *Alyeska Pipeline Service Co. v. Wilderness Society*, 421 U.S. 240 (1975), in which the Court invoked the "American Rule" (courts have no inherent power to award attorneys' fees as part of a costs award to a prevailing party) as grounds to deny an attorneys' fee request by the Wilderness Society, an organization that had prevailed in a lawsuit involving the Trans-Alaska Pipeline.

[36] 5 U.S.C. § 504, note; 28 U.S.C. § 2412, note.

[37] *See* John J. Sullivan, Note, *The Equal Access to Justice Act in the Federal Courts*, 84 COLUM. L. REV. 1089 (1984); For a discussion of the 1996 amendments to the EAJA, *see* Judith E. Kramer, *Equal Access to Justice Act Amendments of 1996: A New Avenue for Recovering Fees from the Government*, 51 ADMIN. L. REV. 363 (1999). The Administrative Conference has promulgated uniform rules for agency implementation of the EAJA. 46 Fed. Reg. 32,900 (1981), now codified in Title 5, C.F.R. It remains to be seen what will become of these regulations given the demise of the ACUS.

broadcast in the same geographical area without canceling each other out. Only one license can be granted for hydroelectric projects. The Supreme Court took up the issue of mutual exclusivity just after World War Two, in *Ashbacker Radio Corp. v. FCC*,[38] after the FCC granted a broadcast license to the first person to apply and then told a second applicant that a hearing would be meaningless because the license had already been given to someone else. Deciding the case on statutory, rather than constitutional grounds, the Court held that where license applications were mutually exclusive, a regulatory body must provide a *meaningful* hearing for both applicants.

Ashbacker prompted the FCC and a number of other agencies to adopt what is known as the comparative hearing process. The availability of a license is announced by the Commission, and a cut-off date is set for the receipt of applications. Any applicant who files before the cut-off date is given equal treatment with all other applicants. The agency compares each applicant's credentials and awards the license to whomever it determines is the most qualified.

Ashbacker is an important decision, and is probably not limited strictly to situations involving technical exclusivity, although the Supreme Court has never made this point clear. In addition, the Court has never made clear whether the *Ashbacker* principle is a matter of constitutional dimension. *Ashbacker* itself involved only the Court's interpretation of the Federal Communications Act. It would seem to be at least arguable that the comparative hearing process is a matter of constitutional due process. Some lower federal courts have hinted that any time two or more applicants for the same government permit apply at roughly the same time, the agency must accord all of them some kind of meaningful review.[39]

[2] Right to Counsel

The APA leaves no doubt on the right of participants to have counsel. Section 555(b) indicates: "A person compelled to appear . . . is entitled to be accompanied, represented and advised by counsel, or, if permitted by the agency, by other qualified representative. A party is entitled to appear in person or by or with counsel or other qualified representative in an agency proceeding." Note, however, that this means only that a person may retain counsel, not that counsel will be provided. The Supreme Court has never required appointed counsel in administrative proceedings because they are regarded as civil proceedings.[40] As discussed above, however, there are some instances in which attorneys' fees may be recovered from the agency.

In a 1985 opinion, *Walters v. National Association of Radiation Survivors*,[41] the Supreme Court reviewed a case in which veterans challenged a statutory limitation of $10 for attorneys' fees that could be paid for representing veterans before the Veterans Administration (now the Department of Veterans Affairs). This limitation had been inserted after the Civil War to prevent unscrupulous lawyers from

---

[38] 326 U.S. 327 (1945).

[39] *See, e.g., Railway Express Agency v. United States*, 205 F. Supp. 831 (S.D.N.Y. 1962).

[40] *See* discussion of the constitutional requirements in agency proceedings *supra* Chapter 5.

[41] 473 U.S. 305 (1985).

gouging helpless veterans as they pursued their veterans' benefits. The dollar amount had never been changed by Congress.

Veterans who had been exposed to nuclear bomb explosions in the 1950s challenged the $10 limit on fees on the basis of the Fifth Amendment's Due Process Clause and the First Amendment, claiming that it deprived them of their constitutional right to retain counsel of their choice in VA matters. After invoking standard Court boilerplate on the sensitivity of the Court's reviewing acts of Congress, Justice Rehnquist, writing for a 6-3 Court, held that the $10 limit did not infringe the Constitution. In this instance, the Court simply applied the three-part *Mathews* test (*see supra* Chapter 5, § 5.04), and concluded that there was no showing by the veterans that retained counsel were so important to the VA proceedings that it justified setting aside the statute. Recall also *Wolff v. McDonnell*,[42] where the Court held that certain agency proceedings may be so delicate (in this instance hearings involving internal prison discipline) that the agency may justify even the *exclusion* of lawyers. However, you are not likely to run into these settings in a garden-variety federal agency practice. The vast number of agency proceedings are attended by lawyers.

The Agency Practice Act,[43] forbids agencies to set any requirements for admission to practice for attorneys other than admission to the bar of at least one state. A few agencies permit non-lawyer representatives to practice, such as C.P.A.'s who become qualified to practice before the Internal Revenue Service as *enrolled agents*, and persons who pass an examination administered by the now-abolished Interstate Commerce Commission and became qualified as what the ICC called a "Class B Practitioner."[44] Although there are no uniform professional conduct rules for federal agency practitioners, many agencies have their own standards of ethics for practitioners.[45]

[C]   Discovery

The APA says very little about discovery in agency proceedings, although it does not prohibit it. The original understanding in the APA was that agency proceedings were not to be as complicated or cumbersome as trials. One of the things that makes trials costly and time-consuming is the elaborate pre-trial discovery in the *Federal Rules of Civil Procedure*.[46] The single discovery tool given major attention in the Act itself is the subpoena-a device available to the agency both before and during a hearing and available to parties in agency adjudications.[47] In § 556(c), a presiding judge is given authority to "take depositions or have depositions taken when the ends of justice would be served."

---

[42] 418 U.S. 539 (1974).

[43] 5 U.S.C. § 500 (1999).

[44] The IRS rules are codified at 31 C.F.R. pt. 10, the ICC's rules at 49 C.F.R. pt. 1103.

[45] *See* Michael P. Cox, *Regulation of Attorneys Practicing Before Federal Agencies*, 34 Case W. Res. L. Rev. 173 (1984).

[46] One of the primary reasons for setting up administrative agencies was that courts were not dealing efficiently and effectively with certain problems.

[47] *See supra* Chapter 4, § 4.07.

The *Attorney General's Manual* insists that private parties be given the same access to discovery enjoyed by the agency staff.[48] The *Manual's* statement was written in the section on subpoenas, but presumably would extend to any type of discovery made available by the agency. Beyond that, the APA is silent. This means that any available discovery flows from agency ruler-and, in certain rare instances, from the agency enabling act.

Agencies differ widely in the types of discovery permitted, although a search of every discovery rule written by every federal agency would probably reveal, somewhere, every discovery device available under the *Federal Rules of Civil Procedure.*[49] Always keep in mind that agency process is dominated by lawyers who tend to revert to the familiar. However, not every agency permits the use of all of these devices. The major licensing agencies tend to prefer to have as much of a case as possible committed to paper before moving to the oral discovery procedures, such as depositions. Many agencies recognize a number of discovery devices, but leave the actual shaping of discovery to the litigants and to the discretion of the administrative law judge. Many FCC judges, for example, force parties to choose either depositions or interrogatories, but not both, as their discovery tool.

There has been some push for uniformity. Nearly twenty years ago, the Administrative Conference of the United States recommended that agencies adopt certain minimum standards for discovery in agency adjudications, including, but not necessarily limited to, (1) depositions, (2) exchanges of prior witnesses' statements, (3) interrogatories, including interrogatories directed to the agency, (4) requests for admission, including requests directed to the agency, and (5) production of documents. As part of this recommendation, a pre-hearing conference would be held, during which the ALJ would be expected to help shape the discovery process and to issue protective orders to keep confidential any exchanged information that is particularly sensitive.[50]

The agencies that conduct large numbers of evidentiary hearings, such as the Federal Trade Commission, the Federal Communications Commission and the Federal Energy Regulatory Commission, responded to the Administrative Conference's proposal by providing many discovery tools to private parties.

---

[48] ATTORNEY GENERAL'S MANUAL ON THE ADMINISTRATIVE PROCEDURE ACT 67 (1947).

[49] Some examples: the FCC recognizes both oral depositions and depositions on written questions, interrogatories, production of documents and subpoenas. Protective orders are authorized. 47 C.F.R. §§ 1.311–1.340 (1982). The Federal Energy Regulatory Commission (formerly the Federal Power Commission) expressly recognizes only depositions and subpoenas. 18 C.F.R. §§ 1.24, 1.25. The Securities and Exchange Commission has rules for subpoenas, depositions and interrogatories. 17 C.F.R. §§ 201.14, 201.15.

[50] Administrative Conference Recommendation 70-4, codified at 1 C.F.R. § 305.70-4 (1985). For many years, the Conference is the official think-tank for federal agencies and has produced recommendations for various agency activities that are consistently thoughtful and sometimes even elegant. The Conference's recommendations and the law journal articles that spring from these reports represent some of the best thinking and writing on American administrative law. Unfortunately, many agencies fail to heed the Conference's admonitions. Congress abolished ACUS in 1995. It was revived and currently funded in 2010. For the consultant's report on discovery, *see* Edward A. Tomlinson, *Discovery in Agency Adjudication*, 1971 DUKE L.J. 89.

Hearings in those agencies have come, more and more, to resemble federal civil trials, particularly as elaborate discovery mechanisms have contributed to long delays in reaching a final agency decision in the same way that elaborate federal court discovery has contributed to court delay. At the same time, elaborate discovery has probably contributed to fairer and more accurate agency decisions. However, no lawyer should expect this kind of sophistication in every administrative agency.

Because not every agency has elaborate discovery rules, a lawyer needs to think through some of the alternatives. Fortunately, most federal agencies produce reams of written material about themselves. A wealth of information about the agency can be found in such things as statements of policy, preambles to rules published in the *Federal Register*, reports of the agency inspector general and the like. There are also two statutes, extensively discussed in Chapter 14 that may be used, in certain circumstances, as a discovery tool. The Freedom of Information Act[51] gives "any person" the right to request information in a federal agency's possession. The presumption under the FOIA is in favor of disclosure, although some information need not be disclosed by the agency if it is covered by one of nine exemptions in the Act. Agency investigative reports, for example, are normally very difficult to obtain through the FOIA because many of them are covered by the (b)(7) exemption in the Act.

For persons representing individuals before federal agencies, the Federal Privacy Act[52] establishes a statutory right of access to certain information about individuals held by the government. A person must request his or her own information-the right of access does not normally extend to files of third persons, but only to files relating to the requester-and there are some exceptions. In some instances involving agency action taken against an individual, a Privacy Act request can be highly productive.

One of the stumbling blocks to using the FOIA or the Privacy Act requests as a discovery tool in agency adjudications is that they proceed on an entirely different agency track with an entirely different agency time-span. Some agencies take a long time to come up with the information requested. While those delays may be litigated in a separate FOIA action in federal court, courts normally allow an agency a reasonable time to produce the documents. If this reasonable time does not coincide with the deadlines set in the adjudication, the FOIA request may prove useless.

[D] The Pre-Hearing Conference

Much like discovery, agencies vary greatly in their procedures for pre-hearing conferences. For those agencies that conduct pre-hearing conferences regularly, they tend to function much like pre-trial conferences under the *Federal Rules of Civil Procedure*. They can be used to discuss settlement, shape discovery, narrow the issues, receive stipulations, pass on pre-hearing motions of various sorts and establish the format for the hearing. This is another part of the hearing process

---

[51] 5 U.S.C. § 552.

[52] 5 U.S.C. § 552b.

that is very much subject to the discretion of the ALJ.

After giving notice of the pre-hearing conference, one retired ALJ suggests the following sequence for the conference: (1) opening statement by the ALJ, (2) the noting of appearances, (3) the raising and discussion of any preliminary matters by the judge or counsel, (4) ruling on requests to intervene, (5) shaping of discovery and exchange of various information, and (6) a discussion of the time, place and scope of the evidentiary hearing.[53]

§ 8.05   THE HEARING

[A]   Preparation for the Hearing

For most disputes, this is the most crucial phase of a formal adjudication. Remember the second cardinal rule of agency lawyering: by and large, this is where you win or lose your case. The worst possible attitude at this stage is to think you can be as sloppy and inattentive as you like because either higher-ups in the agency or a reviewing court will always bail you out. Agency review boards and courts occasionally reverse ALJs, but not as often as most people think. Even if you get a raw deal from an ALJ, the only way you can hope for a reversal on appeal is by building the best record possible at the hearing. Just as law professors cannot give credit on exams for blank space, appellate authorities cannot do much with an inadequate record.[54] Moreover, the lack of elaborate discovery tools or the absence of formal rules of evidence is no excuse. You must make do with what the agency gives you. Agencies have no obligation to behave exactly like courts.

This is litigation. Most lawyers prepare for an agency hearing in the same way they prepare for a civil trial, with briefing books, preparation of witnesses and rehearsing of opening and closing statements. § 8.08, *below*, will discuss some suggestions for lawyering in low-level agencies that give you very little in the nature of discovery or rules of evidence. This section and the following two sections will discuss some aspects of the "law" of the hearing process.

[B]   The Hearing Format

The APA does not impose a specific format on an agency hearing, leaving most of the hearing to the discretion of the ALJ, who may "regulate the course of the hearing."[55] A typical order of hearing is: (1) opening statements, (2) presentation of evidence and witnesses by the proponent (more on who is the proponent later), (3) presentation of evidence and witnesses by the defending party, (4) rebuttal

---

[53] 1 MERRITT H. RUHLEN, MANUAL FOR ADMINISTRATIVE LAW JUDGES (Rev. ed. 1982) (available from the Government Printing Office). More experienced practitioners may find some of Merritt Ruhlen's comments simplistic, but younger lawyers involved in agency practice in those agencies that conduct large numbers of formal adjudications would do well to keep the *Manual* on their bookshelves.

[54] *See, e.g.,* William Fox, *Some Considerations in Representing Clients Before Federal Agencies,* BARRISTER MAG. 21 (Summer, 1980). The original subtitle for this article was "Five Common Errors in Agency Practice." Error Number One is "Failure to Build a Proper Agency Record."

[55] APA § 556(c)(5).

evidence and witnesses as allowed by the ALJ, and (5) closing arguments.

[C]   Cross-Examination

There are some hidden pitfalls in the APA. Section 556(d) gives each party the right "to present his case or defense by oral or documentary evidence, to submit rebuttal evidence, and to conduct such cross-examination as may be required for a full and true disclosure of the facts." While most ALJs grant cross-examination as a matter of course, you have no absolute right to cross-examination under the APA itself. The *Attorney General's Manual* makes clear that no one has the right of unlimited cross-examination. Cross-examination is allowed in the discretion of the ALJ, and anyone seeking cross-examination has the burden of showing the need for it if it is not allowed automatically.[56]

Some agencies, such as the FCC, require that the bulk of each party's direct case be placed in evidence on paper (in the form of affidavits, engineering studies and demographic surveys) and then permit the other parties to cross-examine. As a guide for ALJs, Judge Ruhlen suggests that cross-examination be limited to clarifying exhibits, ascertaining the source of primary material and inquiring into the basis for the conclusions of the experts.[57]

[D]   Formal Rules of Evidence

The APA was never intended, on its own, to incorporate court-based rules of evidence. Other than a specific provision on official notice that will be discussed in the next subsection, the Act speaks only of "the exclusion of irrelevant, immaterial, or unduly repetitious evidence" and a decision supported by "reliable, probative, and substantial evidence."[58] Before moving on to some of the more difficult concepts, give this language some consideration.

The APA language establishes some boundaries on evidence. Evidence must be *relevant*, *reliable* and *probative*. Be cautious, however. For example, you should disregard, for the time being, the term *substantial evidence*. This is more accurately a concept of appellate review of agency action, not a concept properly involved in the hearing process. Also, the word *material* is now generally regarded as superfluous, even though there is a great deal of scholarship in the law of evidence devoted to distinguishing between *relevant* and *material*.[59] The APA's legislative history makes clear that the APA's use of these terms of evidence are concepts based on efficiency and common sense, rather than the basis for imposing technical rules of evidence. The House Report points out that "[t]hese are . . . principles usually applied tacitly and resting mainly upon common sense which

---

[56] Attorney General's Manual on the Administrative Procedure Act 78 (1947); *see also Am. Pub. Gas Ass'n v. Federal Power Comm'n*, 498 F.2d 718 (D.C. Cir. 1974).

[57] ALJ's Manual, *supra* note 53, at 37.

[58] APA § 556(d).

[59] *The Federal Rules of Evidence*, a recent compilation of evidence doctrine, does not use the word *material*.

people engaged in the conduct of responsible affairs instinctively understand."[60] At bottom, Congress seemed to view formal rules of evidence as principles applicable mainly to civil *jury* trials, in which the jurors need to be insulated from certain matters. Those considerations are not present in an agency hearing before a presumably expert ALJ. This conclusion was echoed by Judge Posner, writing for the Seventh Circuit, in *Peabody Coal Co. v. Director, Office of Workers' Compensation Programs.*[61] As Judge Posner put it:

> The rules of evidence are primarily designed to protect jurors, viewed as naive or inexperienced factfinders, from being muddled or inflamed by misleading, prejudicial, unreliable, confusing, or repetitious evidence. The reason these rules are not applicable to agencies is that being staffed by specialists the agencies are assumed to be less in need of evidentiary blinders than lay jurors or even professional, though usually unspecialized judges. Evidence that might merely confuse a lay fact-finder may be essential to the exercise of expert judgment by a specialized professional adjudicator.[62]

Even so, some agencies, such as the Federal Trade Commission and the National Labor Relations Board — agencies that regularly engage in large numbers of evidentiary hearings — have decided to use formal rules of evidence when practicable. Indeed, in a 1987 study, Professor Richard Pierce found 280 instances when an agency has tried to state rules of evidence. In thirty-seven of those instances, the agency refers expressly to the *Federal Rules of Evidence.*[63] But neither the APA, nor the Supreme Court, requires an agency to do so. Indeed, in one of the principal Supreme Court decisions on point, the Court took the opposite view.

Richardson v. Perales[64] involved a claim for social security disability benefits filed by Pedro Perales. The statute requires that a claimant demonstrate that he is disabled and unable to engage in gainful employment. Mr. Perales asserted that he had suffered a back injury on the job that prevented him from working. He filed a claim after seeing his own physician. The agency processed the claim and eventually denied it, triggering an evidentiary hearing request by Mr. Perales. Prior to the hearing, the following information came to the agency:

1. The report of an initial examination by Dr. Lampert, a consulting neurologist, who could find no objective evidence of a medical injury.

2. An examination by Dr. Morales, Perales' personal physician, whose report diagnosed Perales' injury as "back sprain-lumbro sacral spine, moderately severe, ruptured disk not ruled out."

---

[60] H.R. REP. No. 1980, 79th Cong., 2d Sess., at 270 (1946).

[61] 165 F.3d 1126 (7th Cir. 1999).

[62] *Id.* at 1128–29.

[63] Richard J. Pierce, *Use of the Federal Rules of Evidence in Federal Agency Adjudications*, 39 ADMIN. L. REV. 1 (1987); Elliott B. Glicksman, *The Modern Hearsay Rule Should Find Administrative Law Application*, 78 NEB. L. REV. 135 (1999).

[64] 402 U.S. 389 (1971).

3. An examination, commissioned by the agency, by Dr. Langston, who reported that Perales was not really injured.

4. An examination, again commissioned by the agency, by Dr. Bailey, a psychiatrist with a sub-specialty in neurology, who concluded that Mr. Perales had a "paranoid personality, manifested by hostility . . . ."

5. A second report based on electromyography studies by Dr. Langston and by a Dr. Mattson, both of whom concluded that Perales' problem was not job related or disabling.

After the agency denied the claim several times, Mr. Perales asked for, and received, an evidentiary hearing. The agency introduced various hospital records and the written reports filed by Langston, Bailey, Mattson and Lampert. However, the only one of these physicians to appear at the hearing and give oral testimony was Perales' own doctor, Morales. Instead, the agency gave the written reports to yet another physician, a Dr. Leavitt, who reviewed all the records and who testified orally as what the agency termed a medical adviser. Dr. Leavitt examined all the evidence and then offered an expert opinion on Perales' medical condition. Dr. Leavitt testified that in his opinion, Perales was suffering a "mild low-back syndrome of musculo-ligamentous origin." This is doctor-speak for a devastating legal conclusion — in Leavitt's opinion Perales was not hurt badly enough to get social security disability. But because Leavitt himself had not examined Perales, but merely reviewed the statements of the other physicians, his testimony was also hearsay testimony.

Following presentations by counsel, the social security hearing examiner (referred to as the ALJ for the remainder of our discussion) agreed with Leavitt's conclusion and denied the claim. Having objected to Leavitt's testimony, Perales' lawyer eventually took the case through a series of appeals all the way to the Supreme Court. The Court took the case to review only a single question: whether an agency decision based solely on hearsay evidence should be upheld on judicial review.

This point requires an excursus in both administrative hearings and appellate review before we can proceed with our *Perales* analysis. First, note carefully that the court is dealing with two separate concepts. The standard of proof in agency evidentiary hearings is the preponderance test (discussed in depth in subsection [H], *below*). This test requires the ALJ to determine whether an assertion made at hearing is more likely true than not. On the *Perales* record it is obvious that the ALJ believed that Leavitt's conclusion and the rest of the evidence more likely than not showed that Perales had not suffered a disabling injury.

However, that is not the test for judicial review of this type of agency decision. All the federal courts are authorized to examine is whether the agency decision is supported by *substantial evidence.*[65] This test is actually more relaxed than even the preponderance test. A court examines the entire record of the proceeding and determines if there is at least more than "a scintilla" of evidence supporting the agency's decision and if a reasonable person examining the same evidence could

---

[65] Substantial evidence is discussed in depth in Chapter 12.

have reached the same conclusion as the agency. If so, the agency's action must be upheld.

In *Perales*, the Court looked first at the Social Security Act, a statute that provides expressly for the receipt, by an ALJ, of evidence that might be "inadmissible under rules of evidence applicable to court procedure." But this provision deals only with the introduction of evidence and not with the use to which evidence is put in reaching a final agency decision. As the *Perales* Court characterized the decision, it rested solely on uncorroborated hearsay — something that an earlier Court decision, *Consolidated Edison Co. v. NLRB*,[66] suggested would not be sufficient, by itself, to support an agency decision.

The *Consolidated Edison* concept is generally referred to as the legal residuum rule. Stated simply, an agency need not adopt formal rules of evidence and may receive evidence that would not be admissible in court, but the final decision has to be supported by at least a little evidence, a *residue* of evidence, that would be accepted by a court.

The Court refused to apply this aspect of *Consolidated Edison* to the *Perales* case, although it did not expressly overrule the earlier case. Instead, it walked through the various reports described above, alluded to the fact that each of the reporting physicians did examine Perales, even if they were not available for cross-examination at hearing, cited the figures on the enormous workload of the Social Security Administration, and refused to condemn the device of the "medical adviser." At several points, the Court mentioned the reliability and probative worth of written medical reports and noted that Perales' lawyer could have subpoenaed the examining physicians and did not do so. While the Court did not completely dispose of the case (it remanded the case to the district court for a determination of whether, given the Court's opinion in *Perales*, the agency decision was supported by substantial evidence), it left little doubt as to its own sentiments on the issue.

There are many different ways to view the *Perales* opinion. On the one hand, the Court may simply have overruled *Consolidated Edison sub silentio*. The legal residuum test may now be dead on the federal level. But if the Court did so, it acted disingenuously, did it not? If the Court no longer applies the legal residuum test in any federal agency case, we deserve to know that.

On the other hand, the Court took several pages to comment favorably on the kind of evidence introduced in *Perales*. It noted, for example, that medical records are frequently regarded as an exception to the hearsay rule. As mentioned earlier, it took great pains to refer to this material and the use of Dr. Leavitt as reliable and probative. The Court may be hinting that this evidence might very well have been admissible in court. We can test this proposition by a quick reference to the Federal Rules of Evidence. The Federal Rules contain two hearsay rules, Rule 803 (availability of declarant immaterial) and Rule 804 (declarant unavailable). Rule 803(3) permits the admission of hearsay that has to do with a mental, emotional or physical condition; the next subsection, 803(4), permits hearsay involving statements for the purpose of medical diagnosis or treatment. Both Rules 803 and 804 have a residual category, 803(24) and 804(b)(5) that admit hearsay not specifically

---

[66] 305 U.S. 197 (1938).

mentioned but which has "equivalent circumstantial guarantees of trustworthiness." This may be the reason for the Court's iteration and reiteration of the reliable and probative language in *Perales.*

An alternative explanation calls into question the skills of Perales' lawyer at the agency hearing. Remember the Court's suggestion that the lawyer could have subpoenaed the doctors but did not. Thus, the lawyer may be the one primarily to blame. If his failure to subpoena the witnesses was an oversight or if he had some specific reason for not having the doctors there, the Court may have believed that this whole case was a matter of waiver-*i.e.*, Perales chose not to have the witnesses there for cross-examination and thus lost his right to object.

Yet another possible explanation, not articulated by the Court, but one that is familiar to litigators is to view Dr. Leavitt not as a fact witness giving hearsay testimony but as an expert witness who is permitted to render an opinion. That opinion may be in the context of a hypothetical presented to the expert by counsel. The hypothethical may comprise many of the facts underlying the case being adjudicated. If Dr. Leavitt was qualified as an expert, in most respects, the hearsay rule would not have been applied in any event to his testimony.

In any event, hearsay can come into agency hearings. It may be a substantial part of the proof. Most courts will not reject agency decisions merely because data which could be excluded in court comes onto a hearing record. You must be able to deal with this as an administrative lawyer without being devastated by the absence of formal rules of evidence.

[E]   Official Notice

One other type of evidence specifically mentioned in the APA is official notice. § 556(e) provides: "When an agency decision rests on official notice of a material fact not appearing in the evidence in the record, a party is entitled, on timely request, to an opportunity to show the contrary." However, this provision covers only those instances in which an ALJ proposes to take official notice of something not in the hearing record. It is clear that an ALJ may also officially notice something during the hearing in order to cut the hearing short. Although the APA does not expressly cover this situation, fundamental fairness dictates that the same opportunity to rebut be available.[67] Official notice should not be viewed lightly. When it is taken, it becomes just as much a basis for the final decision as anything else in the record.

The questions then become: (1) what sorts of things may be subject to official notice and (2) how does official notice relate to judicial notice? The Attorney General's Manual discusses official notice as a concept that is designed to circumvent the time-consuming efforts involved in proving "what is obvious and notorious." It is equally clear from the Manual and the other legislative history of the APA that official notice is intended to be broader than the related concept of

---

[67] *The Attorney General's Manual* addresses this: "Agencies may take official notice of facts at any stage in a proceeding-even in the final decision-but the matters thus noticed should be specified" and an opportunity to rebut offered. MANUAL, at 80.

judicial notice. However, the extent to which official notice departs from judicial notice is sometimes difficult to fathom.

Here, it might be easier to work backward because, presumably, anything that is a proper subject of judicial notice may also be officially noticed in an agency proceeding. By way of explicating judicial notice, the Federal Rules of Evidence borrow an administrative law concept — the distinction between *legislative* and *adjudicative* facts developed by Professor K.C. Davis — and provide for judicial notice of adjudicative facts.[68] Rule 201, Federal Rules of Evidence, limits the taking of judicial notice to a fact that is "not subject to reasonable dispute in that it is either (1) generally known within the territorial jurisdiction of the trial court or (2) capable of accurate and ready determination by resort to sources whose accuracy cannot reasonably be questioned." An example of (1), in the federal district of Hawaii, might be the fact that the attack on Pearl Harbor took place on December 7, 1941. An example of (2) might be the fact that the Alamo is in San Antonio, Texas (or, say, a trial in Anchorage, Alaska). A fact that could well be judicially noticed anywhere in the United States is the fact that the holiday of Christmas is celebrated in the United States on December 25.

For agency hearings, however, this is just a starting point. Remember that agencies are supposed to be experts in what they do and that they accumulate a vast store of information in files, libraries, and other reservoirs of information. An ALJ hearing a case involving medical evidence might like to know the statistics on congestive heart failure among white males between the ages of 40 and 55. A judge for the National Labor Relations Board might need some information on the number of representation elections supervised by the Board in 1984. Why force the parties to submit evidence on these matters when opening an agency file drawer may provide all the answers?

The Supreme Court has never completely resolved the problems with official notice. In 1937, in *Ohio Bell Telephone Co. v. Public Utilities Commission of Ohio*,[69] the Court refused to accept the taking of official notice involving land values and price trends by the Ohio Public Utilities Commission in a telephone rate case, because, in the words of Justice Cardozo, the agency decision was based on "facts not spread upon the record." But the rub here appears to be more the fact that the Commission refused to reveal the sources of this information rather than

---

[68] The legislative/adjudicative distinction can be a real can of worms, not too different from trying to distinguish between *procedural* and *substantive*. In fairness to Professor Davis, everyone should go to the source: Kenneth Culp Davis, *An Approach to Problems of Evidence in the Administrative Process*, 55 HARV. L. REV. 364 (1942). Briefly stated by your author (who has never been entirely sure of the distinction), adjudicative facts are those facts specifically related to the dispute at hand — the who, what, where, when of the controversy. In a social security proceeding these would be covered by questions, such as: what is the claimant's age, how many years has he paid into the social security system and what is his specific injury? Legislative facts, by contrast, are those generally accepted facts that address some of the generic or broad brush aspects of the regulatory program. For example, a legislative fact might include the determination that one of the purposes of the social security disability process is to compensate persons who are not able to work and thereby keep them off the welfare roles. Another legislative fact might be that the majority of employed persons in the United States pay into the Social Security System.

[69] 301 U.S. 292 (1937).

that the Commission proposed to officially notice facts. Eight years later, in *Market Street Railway v. Railroad Commission,*[70] the Court approved an agency's taking of official notice involving the potential effects on traffic of a rate reduction in street car and bus fares. In *Market Street*, Justice Jackson appears to have been persuaded by the expertise of the agency: "We cannot say that it is a denial of due process for a commission so experienced . . . to draw inferences as to the probable effect on traffic of a given rate decrease on such a record as we have here." A federal appeals court has permitted a federal agency to officially notice medical texts and certain figures derived from government studies on employment.[71]

Some of the federal Courts of Appeals have raised an eyebrow or two over the taking of official notice. In *United States Lines v. Federal Maritime Commission,*[72] the D.C. Circuit reversed a decision by the FMC in part because of the court's discomfort with FMC's taking judicial notice of material in its files (note, however, the more important part of this case dealt with impermissible ex parte contacts). In this case, the court faulted the agency for two errors: (1) failing to give the parties an adequate opportunity to respond to the official notice and (2) the fact that the material officially noticed was never specified with any precision by the agency. The FMC essentially said, "we have information in our files that persuades us." However, the Commission did not say what that information was or precisely how it assisted the FMC in its decision. Reviewed carefully, however, this case does not suggest that official notice taking is impermissible, only that the agency must be particularly careful in the manner in which it deals with official notice.[73] For example, in *Heckler v. Campbell,*[74] the Supreme Court permitted the Social Security Administration of the Department of Health and Human Services to rely on a set of medical-vocational guidelines (a kind of official notice) to decide a case, rather than proving at the hearing that the social security claimant could perform specific available jobs.[75] Of course, readers should understand that the Social Security Administration has such an overwhelmingly large caseload that techniques of proof that the Court may approve for that agency might not necessarily suffice in an agency with a smaller caseload consisting of larger, more factually complicated cases.

The message of these cases seems clear. Official notice is permitted on many things that might not necessarily be proper topics of judicial notice, although a conservative ALJ will, of course, be very cautious in moving too far beyond the judicial limits for noticing facts. The more compelling matter from the standpoint of fairness is the opportunity to rebut. For the party who is adversely affected by the taking of some official notice, all that may be necessary is to give that person

---

[70] 324 U.S. 548 (1945).

[71] *McDaniel v. Celebrezze*, 331 F.2d 426 (4th Cir. 1964).

[72] 584 F.2d 519 (D.C. Cir. 1978).

[73] *See also Air Products & Chemicals, Inc. v. FERC*, 650 F.2d 687 (5th Cir. 1981) (citing *United States Lines* with approval).

[74] 461 U.S. 458 (1983).

[75] It is also possible to view *Heckler*, not as an official notice case, but rather, as a case in which the agency takes care of generic issues that arise in adjudications by writing rules covering all similarly situated persons. This is the famous *Storer* doctrine discussed in subsection [F] *below*.

the opportunity to respond. Presumably, the party could mount a two-pronged attack: (1) that it is impermissible to official notice this particular fact or (2) that the fact itself is not accurate. Most ALJs are careful with such matters.

[F] Limiting Evidence at Hearing by Prior Rulemaking

An agency may also dispense with fact-finding during an evidentiary hearing by promulgating generic rules that eliminate the need for proof on certain aspects of a case. The Supreme Court has consistently approved this tactic. Perhaps the best example is the landmark case, *United States v. Storer Broadcasting Co.*,[76] a case in which the FCC promulgated multiple ownership rules that prohibited companies that already owned a certain number of television stations from acquiring any additional licenses. Storer Broadcasting Company applied for an additional license even though the new license, if granted, would have exceeded the FCC's ownership limits. Storer argued that the FCC still owed it a hearing on the application. The Supreme Court dispensed with this contention very quickly. If the agency's rules are reasonable and properly promulgated and if the rules make a hearing totally superfluous, no hearing is required. Obviously, if this principle applies to deny a hearing completely, as it did in *Storer*, it can also be invoked to dispense with evidence on particular issues in a hearing.

[G] Burden of Proof

The APA addresses burden of proof by stating: "Except as otherwise provided by statute, the proponent of a rule or order has the burden of proof."[77] The House Report on the APA equates *proponent* with the entity initiating the hearing.[78] This means that an agency commencing an enforcement proceeding has the burden of proof, but it also means that a person seeking a federal license has the burden of showing her suitability for the license.

The APA does not, on its terms, specifically distinguish between *burden of going forward* and *burden of persuasion*, even though this distinction is an important one.[79] On this topic, the APA's legislative history is not much help. The Senate Report on the APA makes clear that drafters of the APA recognized the matter of allocation of proof by pointing out that while the proponent has both the burden of coming forward and the burden of persuasion on the basic point of the hearing, other parties may bear the burden on other matters sought to be proved.

The few courts that have addressed this issue have handled it in conventional evidence terms by allocating proof to the entity which is in the best position to ascertain facts.[80] This is one aspect of administrative lawyering that requires you to go to basic sources on evidence. There are usually no special rules applicable to

---

[76] 351 U.S. 192 (1956).

[77] APA § 556(d).

[78] 1 H.R. Rep. No 79-1980, at 270 (1946).

[79] *See, e.g.*, McCormick on Evidence, §§ 36–41 (3d ed. 1984).

[80] *See, e.g.*, *NLRB v. Mastro Plastics Corp.*, 354 F.2d 170 (2d Cir. 1965), *cert. denied*, 384 U.S. 972 (1966).

agency proceedings to be found in the APA.[81] There may be some unique requirements in the procedural rules of certain agencies, however.

[H]   Standard of Proof

As thorough as the APA is on certain aspects of agency practice, it says absolutely nothing about the standard of proof applicable in trial-type proceedings. Recall that in judicial systems there are three standards of proof: (1) *beyond a reasonable doubt* (used almost exclusively in a criminal setting and with litigation), (2) *clear and convincing*, and (3) *preponderance*. No one knows for certain what these terms mean. They are designed mainly for jury trials, and you can find specific definitions in model jury instructions and in the various treatises on evidence. The standards appear to have far less effect and relevance in bench trials. For that same reason, they have had little practical impact on administrative proceedings. This may be why it took so long for the Supreme Court to write a clarifying decision.

That decision, *Steadman v. SEC*,[82] involved a registered broker who was sanctioned by the SEC for violating various provisions of the securities laws. One of the sanctions imposed on the broker included a permanent prohibition on affiliating with registered investment advisers or investment companies and a one-year prohibition on affiliating with any securities broker or dealer. The broker challenged his sanctions in part because the SEC had applied the preponderance of evidence test to his disciplinary proceeding. He argued that when an agency takes action affecting the professional status of a person functioning in a setting regulated by the agency, the agency should be held to the higher standard of proof, clear and convincing evidence.

The Supreme Court dealt quickly with this proposition. The Court noted that the APA does not include a standard of proof requirement. The Court pointed out that the APA's language on burden of proof and evidence tends to lean toward the minimum amount of evidence necessary to show to a reviewing body that the agency decision is supported by substantial evidence (remember: substantial evidence is a judicial review concept, *not* a concept applied to proof at hearing). *Steadman* is not a difficult decision to understand. The Court was straightforward in its holding-absent a statutory requirement or perhaps, an agency rule of practice[83] — the only standard of proof to be applied in agency proceedings is preponderance of the evidence.

---

[81] Statutes can sometimes help with problems of proof. In the late 1960s, Congress realized that the difficulties of proving that coal miners were suffering coal miner pneumoconiosis (so-called black lung), a compensable disease, as opposed to emphysema, a non-compensable ailment, were so great that a presumption in favor of the miners was necessary. In evidentiary hearings on black lung compensation, the miners who have worked in coal mines for at least ten years now enjoy a rebuttable presumption that the disease arose out of the miner's employment. 30 U.S.C. § 921(c) (1969). The Supreme Court upheld this program and the related presumptions in *Usery v. Turner Elkhorn Mining Co.*, 428 U.S. 1 (1976).

[82] 450 U.S. 91 (1981).

[83] One basis for the Court's decision in *Steadman* was the fact that the SEC had always used the preponderance standard in disciplinary proceedings.

[I] Hearings on a Purely Written Record

The overwhelming number of evidentiary hearings conducted by federal agencies have a substantial oral component. But not all hearings need necessarily be oral, even if they fit within the other strictures of §§ 556–557. In initial licensing proceedings, which are subject to §§ 556–557 procedures because of the specific language in § 558: "[A]n agency may, when a party will not be prejudiced thereby, adopt procedures for the submission of all or part of the evidence in written form."[84]

What the drafters of the APA had in mind were procedures used by the ICC and the Department of Agriculture prior to the enactment of the APA, sometimes referred to as *shortened procedure* or *modified procedure*. It is not a complicated process and is particularly well-suited for agency decisions in those matters that do not often involve controversies over adjudicative facts. The cases are dealt with on the basis of exchanged verified statements, with the opportunity for each party to rebut the statements of the other party. This pile of paper is then submitted to the ALJ for decision. Many lawyers react suspiciously to litigation conducted entirely on paper, but it can work in many instances.

Perhaps the best current example of a paper hearing process is the process by which the now & dash; defunct Interstate Commerce Commission dealt with applications from individual trucking companies for permission to haul freight from point to point under what are known as certificates of public convenience and necessity (PCN). In 1980, Congress enacted the Motor Carrier Act of 1980,[85] a statute that effectively deregulated a large portion of the motor freight industry. The Act deregulated, in part, by making it virtually impossible for existing carriers to challenge a new carrier application for a PCN certificate. Under the 1980 Act, a new applicant merely had to show that it is "fit" to perform the service it proposes. Under the pre-existing statute, a new carrier would have to convince the ICC of two things: that it was fit to perform the service and that the existing carriers were not satisfying the public's need for transportation services.

Because the standard for a PCN was so relaxed, the Commission accepted applications, dealt with any objections on the basis of the paper record and, in virtually all cases, issued the certificate. The changes in the statute obviated any need for an oral hearing because there are virtually no contested facts at issue.[86] It would seem that there are many other agency decisions that could be reduced to this type of procedure. However, very few other agencies have seen fit to implement or even experiment with the paper hearing process.

Even if the entire case cannot be reduced to paper submissions, many issues can be disposed of without an oral hearing in the same way that courts dispose of a great many pretrial issues through the devices of stipulation and summary judgment. A number of agencies incorporate summary judgment rules in their

---

[84] APA § 556(d).

[85] 49 U.S.C. §§ 10101–11917 (repealed).

[86] *See Am. Trucking Ass'n v. United States*, 642 F.2d 916 (5th Cir. 1981), for a description and approval of the new procedure.

procedural systems, although it is difficult to tell whether these devices are used as frequently as they are in civil trials.[87]

§ 8.06 THE ADMINISTRATIVE LAW JUDGE

[A] Establishing and Appointing ALJs

Prior to the enactment of the APA in 1946, evidentiary hearings were conducted by presiding officers called *hearing examiners*. There were few protections for these people. They tended to be subject to pressures and disciplinary actions within their agencies that had an impact on the way they decided cases. On many occasions, the person used as the hearing examiner was the same person who had conducted the initial investigation and written the initial complaint. As a result, many hearing examiners found themselves functioning in both a judicial and a prosecutorial capacity in the same case. Viewed from the perspective of the 1990s, this sounds terribly callous and insensitive on the part of the agencies. Much of the criticism is deserved, but much of it can be explained in terms of limited agency budgets and an overall sense that agencies did not have to function with the sophistication of courts. There is another partial explanation for the reduced status of hearing examiners. Prior to the APA, hearing officers often did no more than preside over the compilation of a hearing record that was then handed up to supervisors in the agency for decision. It was not until agencies began to proliferate and to conduct more and more evidentiary hearings that issues questioning the duties and independence of the presiding officers arose.

The APA clarified many of these points by insisting on a strict separation of functions (presiding officers may not exercise prosecutorial functions) and establishing heavy restrictions on ex parte contacts between the presiding officer, the rest of the agency and the parties to the adjudication. To shore up this independence, control over many of the personnel matters relating to presiding officers was taken out of the hands of the individual agencies and transferred to the Civil Service Commission (now the Office of Personnel Management). In 1972, the title of these presiding officers was changed dramatically. The Civil Service Commission, by rule, changed the term from hearing examiner to *administrative law judge*, a change that was codified in Title 5 of the United States Code in 1978.[88] While the ALJs remain assigned to specific agencies, negative personnel actions against ALJs are now handled by the Merit Systems Protection Board.[89]

Assignment of ALJ's to specific agencies is something that has been debated at length on the federal level. To a certain extent, an agency assignment still leaves the ALJs at the mercy of the agencies for things such as office assignments, secretarial services and staff support. By contrast, removing ALJs from individual

---

[87] *See* Ernest Gellhorn & Glen Robinson, *Summary Judgment in Administrative Adjudication*, 84 Harv. L. Rev. 612 (1971). (This report was used as the basis for an Administrative Conference recommendation that all agencies that conduct evidentiary hearings adopt a summary judgment rule.)

[88] 5 U.S.C. § 3105. For a discussion of the separation of functions doctrine, *see* Benjamin W. Mintz, *Administrative Separation of Functions: OSHA and the NLRB*, 47 Cath. U. L. Rev. 877 (1998).

[89] 5 U.S.C. § 7521.

agencies and assigning them to a central board which would then farm out individual judges to agencies on a case-by-case basis would diminish their expertise in specific areas of regulation.

This issue continues to be debated within the agencies, at the Administrative Conference, by the judges themselves and in Congress. However, every attempt so far to create an independent corps of ALJs for federal agencies has failed to get out of Congress, although some states take the opposite approach. Florida, for example, maintains a central pool of administrative law judges available for assignment to any agency that requires an adjudication.[90] New Jersey has a similar system. Both these systems seem to be working satisfactorily, although the opponents of a similar change on the federal level like to point out that the typical state adjudication is far less complicated than one at the federal level. Agency-specific expertise has its advantages. A central assignment facility has different advantages.[91]

Federal ALJs are subject to an elaborate appointment process. Successful applicants normally have substantial trial or hearing experience. Many appointees come out of the agencies' general counsel offices. The rules of the Office of Personnel Management and the Merit Systems Protection Board make it difficult to remove or discipline ALJs, so, to that extent, they are fairly well insulated from specific agency pressures, although ALJs assigned to the Social Security Administration (the largest single group of ALJs in the federal government) have frequently complained about undue agency pressure to dispose of cases quickly and without thorough consideration.[92]

[B] The Role of the ALJ

Section 556(c) details the role of the ALJ during the hearing process-a task which can extend from issuing subpoenas to administering oaths to witnesses to regulating the course of the hearing. Be aware that an ALJ is referred to as "judge" or "your honor," and most of them now wear judicial robes when presiding at hearings and related proceedings. For an assessment of the role of the ALJ from the perspective of an ALJ of long experience, consult Judge Merritt Ruhlen's small but nicely done monograph, *Manual for Administrative Law Judges*, now in a revised edition.[93]

---

[90] *See* Fla. Stat. § 120.57.

[91] *See* James F. Flanagan, *Redefining the Role of the State Administrative Law Judge: Central Panels and Their Impact on State ALJ Authority and Standards of Agency Review*, 54 Admin. L. Rev. 1355 (2002).

[92] For a specific case on point, *see Ass'n of Admin. Law Judges v. Heckler*, 594 F. Supp. 1132 (D.D.C. 1984). For more extensive narrative commentary, *see, e.g.*, Jerry L. Mashaw & Richard Merrill, The American Public Law System 239–50 (2d ed. 1985). Professor Mashaw has done extensive research and writing in the work of the social security system. *See, e.g.*, Jerry L. Mashaw, Social Security Hearings and Appeals (1978) (with others). For additional insight into the ALJs and their problems, *see* Daniel J. Gifford, *Federal Administrative Law Judges: The Relevance of Past Choices to Future Directions*, 49 Admin. L. Rev. 1 (1997). The system found in many state processes of assigning ALJs from a central pool of judges is extensively analyzed in Allen C. Hoberg, *Administrative Hearings: State Central Panels in the 1990s*, 46 Admin. L. Rev. 75 (1994).

[93] Ruhlen, *supra* note 53.

While the duties of the judge at a hearing are highly important, probably the most significant responsibility of the ALJ is to write the initial agency decision.[94] These decisions, while subject to review at higher levels in the agency and nearly always subject to judicial review, are frequently left intact by the reviewing authorities. To that extent, lawyers take their dealings with the judge seriously. For many clients, this is the only meaningful agency hearing that they will receive; and, as we will see in subsequent chapters, an agency decision is rarely overturned by a reviewing court.[95]

[C]   Separation of Functions

The problem of combining the duties of an investigator and prosecutor with those of a presiding officer at hearing have been carefully eliminated in the federal system through the enactment of some specific provisions in the APA. Section 554(d) separates functions very dramatically. Persons in an agency who have investigative or prosecutorial duties "may not, in that or a factually related case, participate or advise in the decision . . . except as witnesses or counsel in public proceedings." ALJs, on the other hand, are not permitted to be supervised by agency investigators or prosecutors. The other provisions in Title 5, discussed *above* in subsection [A], make ALJs effectively independent of their agencies. Some agencies, such as the Federal Energy Regulatory Commission, take these commands so seriously that they physically separate their ALJs from the rest of the agency.

It is clear that the Supreme Court views separation of function as extremely important, although the Court's perception of the problem differs depending on whether it is reviewing a federal or a state case. Shortly after the APA was enacted, the Court decided that the APA's separation of functions provisions applied to a deportation proceeding in *Wong Yang Sung v. McGrath*,[96] even though Congress overruled the decision by subsequent legislation directed specifically at the Immigration and Naturalization Service (INS).[97] At present, the separation of function problems occur mainly at the state level. For state administrative actions, the Court seems to be somewhat more casual about separation of functions, taking more of a pragmatic, rather than theoretical, approach to the problem. In *Withrow v. Larkin*,[98] a physician licensed to practice medicine in Wisconsin was subject to a disciplinary hearing because he allegedly performed abortions in violation of state law. The proceeding took place before the state's Medical Examining Board, an entity that conducted investigations of the doctor's conduct and then presided at the administrative hearing on the allegations. The doctor went into federal court, arguing that this combination of functions in a single entity was unconstitutional.

---

[94] Initial decisions are discussed *supra* § 8.01.

[95] *See* Jim Rossi, *Final, but Often Fallible: Recognizing Problems with ALJ Finality*, 56 ADMIN. L. REV. 53 (2004).

[96] 339 U.S. 33 (1950).

[97] *See Marcello v. Bonds*, 349 U.S. 302 (1955) (upholding the amendments to the Immigration and Naturalization Act's procedures as constitutional).

[98] 421 U.S. 35 (1975).

The Court decided otherwise, mainly because the doctor could not specify any actual bias on the part of the Board. The justices presumed regularity and integrity on the part of the Board, absent some showing to the contrary. On top of that, the Court was clearly reluctant to intrude into the internal mechanisms of all state administrative agencies, wherever and however situated. As the Court stated: "No single answer [on combination of functions] has been reached. Indeed, the growth, variety and complexity of the administrative processes have made any one solution highly unlikely."

This opinion does not suggest that the Court is completely callous about these issues, however. First, when actual bias has been shown, the Court has not hesitated to strike down agency action.[99] Second, even in *Withrow*, the Court hinted strongly that in a case in which a single person both prosecuted and judged, the result might be different. Nonetheless, it left the final solution to the wisdom of the various state legislatures.

§ 8.07   BIAS AND EX PARTE CONTACTS IN AGENCY PROCEEDINGS

[A]   Poisoning of Agency Hearing

There are plenty of ways to poison an agency hearing. Both Congress and the courts have been very sensitive to questions of bias on the part of decision makers and inappropriate ex parte contacts between the deciders and third parties.

[B]   Bias and Disqualification

[1]   Need for Impartiality

No one wants important disputes decided by people who cannot approach the issues with an open mind. Federal judges are held to scrupulous standards of impartiality. One of the reasons for the separation of functions discussed in § 8.06[C], *above*, is to avoid the appearance of bias in favor of the agency that might occur if someone performed several different functions that crossed the line between judging and prosecuting.

The APA itself recognizes this by permitting parties to get rid of deciders who may not be impartial: "On the filing in good faith of a timely and sufficient affidavit of personal bias or other disqualification of a presiding or participating employee, the agency shall determine the [allegations of bias] as a part of the record and decision in the case."[100] Note that this means that the agency will dispose of your motion to disqualify and will do it on the same record as your original case. Under normal circumstances, an issue of bias does not give rise to a wholly separate proceeding, but goes up on review along with the remainder of the dispute.

---

[99] *See Gibson v. Berryhill*, 411 U.S. 564 (1973).

[100] APA § 556(b).

Analyzing any question of bias is easier if you carefully distinguish between the two types of bias that may affect an agency hearing: pre-decisional bias and bias at hearing.[101] Pre-decisional bias arises mainly from remarks of agency personnel, either ALJs or persons higher up in the agency who have decisional responsibilities, outside of the hearing that suggest that they may have already made up their minds on the dispute at issue in the hearing. Bias at hearing is a little harder to describe, but can be just as damaging. It is a matter of personal bias on the part of the ALJ toward one or more parties or issues in the hearing.

Bias can be any type of mind-set or personal circumstance that suggests a decider cannot be impartial. Obviously, the type of bias that almost inevitably provokes a disqualification is pecuniary bias. People who have a financial stake in the outcome of a case will have a very difficult time surviving as decision makers. The Supreme Court has contended with this problem for years and has spoken with a single voice. *Gibson v. Berryhill*[102] involved a state board charged with licensing optometrists staffed entirely by already-licensed optometrists. A federal district court held that admitting new optometrists could dilute the earnings of the existing optometrists in the state, thereby giving the members of the board a personal financial stake in the issue of new licenses. The Supreme Court affirmed that decision, holding that financial stake does not even have to be a direct interest if it is sufficient to suggest possible bias.

Gibson is a good case and perfectly consistent with a long line of Supreme Court authority on pecuniary bias, but there is very little pecuniary bias present in most agency proceedings because most agency personnel who function in a decision making capacity are salaried government employees. Most bias that agency practitioners encounter is ideological bias-*i.e.*, bias that suggests that because of a decider's personal predilections, he or she has already made a decision prior to the hearing.

Before we examine the nuances of these issues, be aware of the bottom line: for anyone seeking to overturn an agency action because of bias of any kind, this is one of the most difficult fights in the book. It is rare that either pre-decisional bias or bias at hearing is sufficient to disqualify a decision maker. Understand that even if you do show bias, that does not mean you automatically win your case. The effect of successfully arguing that a decider is biased is merely to disqualify that person. The case itself will then simply be reassigned to an unbiased decider. In a few cases, even when you can demonstrate bias, the rule of necessity, discussed below, permits a decider to continue to sit. Recall the adage: "He who shoots at the king should aim carefully." Charging a judge with bias and not winning a disqualification on that point will guarantee you a very uncomfortable hearing.

---

[101] This distinction stems from the discussion on bias in Peter L. Strauss, Todd D. Rakoff, Roy A. Schotland & Cynthia R. Farina, Gellhorn & Byse's Administrative Law: Cases, Comments & Materials 993–1010 (9th ed. 1995).

[102] 411 U.S. 564 (1973).

[2] Pre-Decisional Bias

Issues of pre-decisional bias usually involve people at the top of the agency. These are the employees who make public statements on behalf of the agency, including their own views as to what the agency should be doing. Cabinet secretaries, independent regulatory commissioners and general counsels are normally the people who are asked to speak in public. Lower-ranking employees are usually too cautious or too low-profile to provoke the issues discussed here. Virtually all the cases of bias in this category involve commissioners and agency executives who display particular points of view before sitting on actual cases. On the federal level, for many reasons, the majority of the reported cases have involved Federal Trade Commissioners.

One of the principle cases of pre-decisional bias was decided by the Supreme Court in 1948. In *FTC v. Cement Institute*,[103] the FTC brought an enforcement action against various cement companies, alleging certain antitrust violations. Prior to launching the enforcement action, some of the Commissioners had given testimony before Congress on the practices of the cement industry and had filed reports with the President. A number of these statements suggested that the industry's practices violated the law. The industry argued that these statements constituted pre-decisional bias that made it impossible for the Commission to decide the enforcement case. The Court did not struggle with this issue. It simply commented that if agency members were precluded from launching enforcement actions just because they had earlier spoken on these issues to Congress and the President, the entire administrative process would come to a halt. Worse, if the entire Commission were somehow disqualified, no administrative agency could pass on the legal issues. (This last comment invokes the doctrine of necessity discussed below.)

Cement Institute remains a landmark case, in part because the Supreme Court rarely accepts bias cases. Consequently, most of the recent case law on bias has been disposed of by the federal courts of appeals. The Second Circuit has articulated the most frequently quoted test for bias — "whether a disinterested observer may conclude that [the agency] has in some measure adjudged the facts as well as the law of a particular case in advance of hearing it."[104]

A fair amount of pre-decisional bias case law has grown out of the actions of just one FTC member. In one case, former Chair Paul Rand Dixon gave a speech mentioning certain specific oil companies, including Texaco, as violators of certain FTC policies while the Commission had a case pending against Texaco on those same issues. Dixon was disqualified by the Court.[105] Two years later (1966) a drug company had Dixon disqualified because he had participated in a Congressional investigation of a drug company while committee counsel and subsequently, as FTC chair, he sat on an FTC enforcement proceeding involving that same drug company.[106]

---

[103] 333 U.S. 683 (1948).

[104] *Gilligan, Will & Co. v. SEC*, 267 F.2d 461 (2d Cir.), *cert. denied*, 361 U.S. 896 (1959).

[105] *Texaco, Inc. v. FTC*, 336 F.2d 754 (D.C. Cir. 1964), *vacated on other grounds*, 381 U.S. 739 (1965).

[106] *American Cyanamid Co. v. FTC*, 363 F.2d 757 (6th Cir. 1966).

Four years later (1970), in *Cinderella Career & Finishing Schools, Inc. v. FTC*,[107] the D.C. Circuit seemed to lose its temper. There, Dixon sat on a cease-and-desist proceeding against the company, a for-profit school, that allegedly did not live up to its promises to its students. Dixon sat on that case after having made a speech to the National Newspaper Association condemning proprietary charm schools, among others. The court concluded that Dixon must be disqualified. Its decision is characterized by exceptionally strong terms about Dixon's conduct. For example, in the court's words: "[Dixon] was sensitive to theory but insensitive to reality." Worse, his actions indicated that he was "indifferent" to the court's pronouncements on bias. The court determined that it had to speak in these terms because "of Mr. Dixon's flagrant disregard of prior decisions."

Do not conclude that these cases make it easy to disqualify agency personnel. The Court indicated in *Cement Institute* that statements made in the course of a commissioner's duties do not require disqualification, even if those statements suggest that a member has made up her mind. Most agency employees know about these cases and are more careful in their public statements than was Mr. Dixon. To the extent that agency personnel have particular problems with bias, they tend to recuse themselves voluntarily, either of their own volition or because a party suggests that they are biased and recommends recusal.

[3] Bias at Hearing

What happens when an ALJ makes faces when your witnesses testify? What do you do when a presiding officer talks about the untrustworthiness of pharmacists in a hearing in which your client is a pharmacist? This is bias at hearing. In theory, the answer is easy: you can obtain a disqualification of that presiding officer.[108] In practice, the much more difficult task is proving it. You must somehow place this bias on the record if you wish to make an issue of it. For example, non-verbal behavior on the part of the judge must be described sufficiently in words so that a reviewing body can understand precisely what was going on, merely by reading the transcript. A lawyer must state, for the record, "your honor made faces when my client's witnesses were on the stand" or "your honor read the newspaper while my expert was testifying." Remember, reviewing bodies see only the paper record; they are not present at the initial hearing.

[4] The Rule of Necessity

There can be occasions in which parties can show unquestionable bias on the part of the deciders and still not be able to obtain a disqualification. The Supreme Court hinted at this idea in *Cement Institute*, when it pointed out that disqualifying all the FTC commissioners would make it impossible ever to get the dispute heard. Thirty-two years later, the Court was forced to apply the rule to itself.

---

[107] 425 F.2d 583 (D.C. Cir. 1970).

[108] *See, e.g.,* a case in which a federal judge presiding in a case alleging espionage against a person of German descent described German-Americans as having hearts "reeking with disloyalty." *Berger v. United States,* 255 U.S. 22 (1921).

In *United States v. Will*,[109] a number of federal judges filed an action in federal court, arguing that the lack of pay raises for federal judges, including members of the Supreme Court, coupled with the ravages of inflation, was an unconstitutional diminution in their pay while in office. This case obviously affected the salaries of the justices themselves because their salary increases had not kept pace with the cost of living. The Court took a matter-of-fact approach to the dilemma. They simply pointed out that if they were all to be disqualified, no one in the country could decide the case. They kept it and decided the question on the merits. This is the rule of necessity. The rule of necessity rarely comes up in agency practice because it is rare to seek the disqualification of an entire decision making body. If you are trying to disqualify a single ALJ, the issue would simply not arise.

[C]   Ex Parte Contacts in Trial-Type Hearings

The drafters of the APA took this issue quite seriously. The Act contains a number of express provisions on ex parte contacts that should not be forgotten. First, § 554(d) prohibits an ALJ from consulting "a person or party on a fact in issue, unless on notice and opportunity for all parties to participate . . . ." Second, § 557(d)(1) sets out ex parte contact rules applicable to all agency employees who participate in the decision. At first glance, the language looks a little cumbersome, but it's really fairly easy to outline.

1. Remember that ex parte contacts go both ways; parties are prohibited from contacting the agency deciders, and the agency deciders are prohibited from contacting the parties.

2. Understand that this does not prohibit you from saying "good morning" to an ALJ. Ex parte contacts are those contacts that relate "to the merits of the proceeding." At the same time, it makes no difference whether the contacts are made orally or in written form. Either type of contact is forbidden.

3. Agency employees have an express obligation to docket and explain all such ex parte contacts or attempts at ex parte contacts in the hearing record.

4. It is not clear that an ex parte contact will destroy every case. The APA requires the agency or ALJ to convene a show cause hearing in which the person who initiated the contact must show why his claim or participation in the case should not be dismissed or sanctioned in some fashion.

Courts do not like ex parte contacts, so you can expect them to deal harshly with any abuses of these rules. In one instance, the D.C. Circuit vacated an agency action because the agency heard from an interested company in secret, after the record was ostensibly closed and other companies had concluded their participation.[110] Moreover, ex parte contacts, even among agency personnel, may threaten the validity of an agency action. The FCC, for example, draws some tight distinctions between decisional and non-decisional staff and prohibits contacts between the two categories of employees on matters subject to formal hearing

---

[109] 449 U.S. 200 (1980).

[110] *United States Lines, Inc. v. Fed. Maritime Comm'n*, 584 F.2d 519 (D.C. Cir. 1978).

requirements.[111] In *Seacoast Anti-Pollution League v. Costle*,[112] an Environmental Protection Agency presiding officer listened to some EPA scientists off the record. The agency action was vacated because of these contacts. In perhaps the worst recorded abuse of ex parte contacts, a participant in a television licensing proceeding contacted FCC commissioners at home, bought them dinners and gave them Christmas turkeys. As you can imagine, the reviewing court had no trouble vacating this proceeding.[113]

Hopefully, no reader of this book will go that far. Be extremely cautious. In the heat of lawyering, some of these concepts can get lost in the shuffle. You do, after all, have an ethical obligation to zealously represent your clients. But if you violate these commands, you can get bitten both by the agency and by bar disciplinary organizations. Remember that the ethical command tells you to represent your clients zealously *within* the bounds of the law.

§ 8.08 PREPARING THE INITIAL DECISION

[A] Preliminary Matters

This is the point at which the ALJ really earns her salary. Everything we have discussed in this chapter merely leads up to an agency decision. As usual, the APA contains some important provisions bearing on the entire process. To begin with, under normal circumstances, the ALJ who presided at the evidentiary hearing is the person who is to prepare the initial or recommended decision in the case "unless he becomes unavailable to the agency."[114] Understand that an ALJ does not have to preside. Section 556(b) permits the ALJ, "one or more members of the body which comprises the agency" (*e.g.*, one or two commissioners on an independent regulatory commission) or "the agency" to preside.

These last two options are rarely exercised. When a serious controversy arose over whether the supersonic transport aircraft, the Concorde, could land at Dulles Airport, the final decision was to be made by the Department of Transportation. In the interests of speed and efficiency (he knew he was going to get the dispute in any event), Secretary of Transportation William Coleman presided at the evidentiary hearing. Most cases, of course, will be presided over by an ALJ.

The initial decision becomes the final decision of the agency if it is not taken further within the agency on appeal. Before the ALJ drafts the initial decision, the parties are required to have an opportunity to proffer (1) proposed findings and conclusions, and (2) exceptions, with supporting reasons, to the initial decisions.[115] The final decision is normally reviewable by a federal court.

---

[111] 47 C.F.R. §§ 1.1208 *et seq.*

[112] 572 F.2d 872 (1st Cir.), *cert. denied*, 439 U.S. 824 (1978).

[113] *Sangamon Valley Television Corp. v. United States*, 269 F.2d 221 (D.C. Cir. 1959).

[114] APA § 554(d).

[115] APA § 557(c).

[B]   A Decision Based Exclusively on the Record

Section 556(e) makes clear that a decision in a §§ 556–557 proceeding is to be based exclusively on the record of the hearing. The record consists of the "transcript of testimony and exhibits, together with all papers and requests filed in the proceeding." This is an important facet of a mature system of administrative procedure. The Supreme Court believes so strongly in this element of the hearing process that it made the exclusivity requirement a matter of constitutional due process for AFDC termination hearings in *Goldberg v. Kelly.*[116]

The reasons for this requirement are obvious. Trial-type hearings are important to the participants. There is no place for secret ex parte contacts (this is one of the reasons why the APA requires ex parte contacts to be docketed), and all the participants should know before the initial decision is prepared exactly what the presiding officer is going to rely upon for the decision.

Moreover, it is a recognition that agency adjudication is an adversarial process before a neutral decider. The parties are the ones who create the record, so an agency record is just as bad or good as the lawyers make it. An ALJ cannot add to the record after it is formally closed. Lawyers should take comfort from this requirement. They have a great deal to do with the record's composition and thereby with the ultimate decision.

Good lawyers, however, also recognize that the exclusivity requirement contains pitfalls. Once the record closes, that's it. The record is reopened only on petition to the ALJ. These requests are often denied. You must get all of your material into the record before it closes, or risk a decision based upon less material than you think necessary. Don't let the ALJ close the record if you believe important things are still missing. Even if you don't get everything in at the hearing, documents and other material may still be submitted in writing with the judge's permission and with copies to opposing counsel.

[C]   Preparing the Initial Decision-The Requirement of Findings and Conclusions

[1]   The APA Requirements

The APA provides expressly that an initial decision reveal the ultimate decision, show the ALJ's rulings on objections and exceptions and be accompanied by "findings and conclusions, and the reasons or basis therefore, on all the material issues of fact, law, or discretion presented on the record."[117] This is a point at which many students with little or no trial experience become confused. What are findings and conclusions? How does an ALJ structure this part of the decision?

There is no specific format for a decision. Some judges utilize two outline headings, *Findings of Fact*, and *Conclusions of Law* and write individually numbered paragraphs within these headings. Other judges write what looks very

---

[116] 397 U.S. 254 (1970).

[117] APA § 557(c).

much like an appellate opinion, which they label *findings and conclusions.* The actual structure or appearance of the decision is not nearly as important as understanding something about the judge's mental processes in thinking through a decision. This is also a point at which a lengthy illustration may be more helpful than mere narrative explanation.

[2] An Illustration of ALJ Decision Making

At this point, you may be thinking that you will never be an ALJ, so why pay any attention to an ALJ's decisional process. First, you should try to understand as much as you can about the way a judge thinks through a case because that helps you, as a litigator, try cases. Appreciating a judge's problems will help you build a far better record. Second, look again at the APA. Counsel are generally permitted (indeed sometimes *required*) to draft proposed findings and conclusions. Knowing how to work through a record to arrive at a decision will help with that task as well. The following illustration is a bit fanciful and so short that it doesn't typify the voluminous agency records with which many lawyers and judges work. Even so, it will give you some insights into this fascinating and rarely taught process. The fact pattern is loosely based on the dismissal of a fourth-year medical student from a state-supported medical school in *Board of Curators of the University of Missouri v. Horowitz.*[118] Consider what might have happened if "Ms. H.," a medical student subject to dismissal, was given a trial-type proceeding governed by the Federal APA with the following record resulting from that hearing.

RECORD

A. *Complaint:*

A letter from the medical school dean informing Ms. H that she is being excluded for (1) non-payment of bills, and (2) poor dress and deportment while performing her clinical duties.

B. *Testimony:*

There were two pieces of testimony in the record on the non-payment-of-bills charge:

(1) The University Bursar testified that the last day for payment of bills was April 10, 1984, and Ms. H had not paid as of the close of business that day.

(2) Ms. H testified that she proffered payment in full by certified check at 9:30 a.m. on April 11, 1984, but the Bursar's office refused to accept payment.

On the dress and deportment charge:

(1) Clinical Supervisor No. 1 testified that Ms. H never had a problem with dress and deportment and that he found her clinical performance acceptable.

(2) Clinical Supervisor No. 2 testified that Ms. H was always sloppy and scruffy. She found Ms. H.'s clinical performance far below a minimum acceptable level.

---

[118] 435 U.S. 78 (1978).

Assume the record has been closed and that you are the ALJ assigned to write the initial opinion. What do you do?

Findings are generally findings of fact: the who, what, where and when aspects of a case. *Conclusions* are conclusions of law — *i.e.*, those parts of a decision in which you either apply fact to law or decide questions of pure law (*e.g.*, is the underlying statute constitutional on its face?). Applying the same analysis to the initial decision in the Ms. H. case will help you organize the initial decision. A finding of fact on issue No. 1 (non-payment of bills) would probably be a simple recitation of both pieces of testimony:

Finding of Fact:

1. The deadline for payment was April 10, 1984. Ms. H had not paid by the close of business that day, but Ms. H did proffer payment the next day. That payment was refused.

Notice that the record (which must be the exclusive basis for your decision) contains only two pieces of evidence on this point. Since your decision must be based on the entire record, you would probably not be free to disregard either piece of testimony without explaining why you are disregarding it. You probably don't have to disregard any of it, regardless of your ultimate conclusion on this point, because the testimony is not mutually exclusive.

The problem on this point is not your finding of fact, but your conclusion of law. It would not be improbable for an ALJ to write a conclusion such as the following:

Conclusion of Law:

Even though Ms. H. did not pay her bill as of the normal deadline, she did attempt to pay the next day. There is no further explanation from the bursar as to why payment could not be accepted the next day, particularly because the payment was in the form of a certified check and for the full amount. I conclude that, on the evidence, these facts do not provide a lawful basis on which to exclude Ms. H. from her fourth year of medical school.

Note that you used all the record but did not add to it, because it is impermissible to do so other than by taking official notice of some fact. Here, you resolved any defects in the record against the party who contributed to the defect. (If there was some legitimate reason for not accepting payment, should not the University have provided a reason?) If the University never does so as a matter of policy, should it not have articulated that policy? A hearing is an adversarial process. While an ALJ may not be quite as neutral as a federal judge, because she is also expected to be an expert in the agency's work, she can get into trouble on review if she attempts to help one of the parties try his case.

Non-payment is not the only ground for exclusion. The University has also asserted in the charging paper that she is being excluded for poor dress and deportment in clinical duties. In this case, you might first address the question of whether the University may exclude Ms. H on either ground (non-payment or dress and deportment) or whether it must prove both grounds. There may be prior cases to which you could refer, but if this is a case of first impression, you would have to decide on your own. There is no further explanation in the record; but you might permissibly take official notice (after informing the parties and permitting comment) of the fact that the University has excluded students on either of the two grounds. If you officially notice this fact, you must address the second ground for exclusion.

In this instance, there are two supervisors each giving contradictory testimony — a very common occurrence in administrative practice, especially when expert testimony is proffered. At the hearing, the lawyers might have helped you on this point by performing sufficient direct and cross-examination to tell you how often each supervisor saw Ms. H and to give you information on the experience and credentials of each supervisor.

If there was a substantial difference in credentials or the length of time each of them supervised Ms. H.'s work, you might base a finding of whom to believe on those differences. A supervisor who saw Ms. H thirty minutes in each week might be less plausible on the question of dress and deportment than someone who worked with her ten hours a day, four days each week. But again, the record does not help. Don't try to fill in missing details with personal speculation on your part. That will cause your decision to be reversed by someone higher up. You must, because of the exclusivity of the record, work with the record as it stands.

How do you handle contradictory and mutually exclusive testimony? One way is to make an express finding of credibility by simply stating as a finding of fact: "I believe Supervisor Number One. I do not believe Supervisor Number Two, and I do not find his testimony credible." Judges often have to do this when two witnesses give contradictory testimony on a crucial point. ALJs generally have to give reasons for this, and you can be assured that if your reasons are at all shaky, the case may be remanded to you for further action.

There is another way to deal with it, however. You can write a finding that simply restates the record, e.g., "Supervisor Number One testified [and recite that testimony]. Supervisor Number Two testified [and recite that testimony]." When you write your conclusion, you can also work with this testimony in conjunction with the burden of proof. The proponent of a rule or order has the burden under the APA. Indisputably, the University has the burden here. A preponderance of the evidence is proof which makes a proposition more likely than not. Can you say that it is more likely than not, on this record, that her clinical performance was unacceptable? If you cannot, your conclusion might be simply: "The University has not carried its burden of proof on the issue of clinical performance."

There is one last thing you must do. There has to be an ultimate conclusion in the decision on the controversy. Should Ms. H. be excluded? Again, based on this record and your preceding findings and conclusions, you would probably be hard pressed to exclude her. But whatever you conclude, your final conclusion on the exclusion issue must be placed in the decision itself.

Concededly, the foregoing illustration is too short to be completely realistic. Most agency records are far longer and most issues are far more complex. However, it is helpful as a brief compendium of techniques for working with a record and developing findings and conclusions. Lawyers and judges involved in the administrative process do this all the time.

§ 8.09   REVIEW OF AN INITIAL DECISION WITHIN THE AGENCY

[A]   The APA Provisions

Virtually all federal agencies provide for review of an initial decision within the agency. The APA acknowledges this by stating: "On appeal from or review of the initial decision, the agency has all the powers which it would have in making the initial decision except as it may limit the issues on notice or by rule."[119] The *Attorney General's Manual* makes clear that this gives the agency almost unfettered authority to do anything it wishes with the decision. It may review only those things objected to by the parties. It may set aside the entire decision and make its own findings with or without the taking of additional evidence.[120]

This is the theory of the APA, but in practice, matters are more closely confined on intra-agency review. Most agencies pay close attention to the initial decision for at least two reasons: first, as a practical matter, agencies don't have the time or the resources to completely reconsider every case that is appealed by the losing party. Second, the Supreme Court has written a series of decisions that place some constraints on what the agency can do with the case after the ALJ has conducted the initial hearing.

[B]   The Impact of *Universal Camera* and the *Morgan Quartet*

The Supreme Court has paid considerable attention to the weight to be given the ALJ's decision in the agency decisional process. In *Universal Camera Corp. v. NLRB*,[121] one of the most famous American administrative law cases, the Supreme Court reviewed a case in which a worker alleged that he had been unlawfully discharged by his employer because he filed a grievance against the company. The discharged worker invoked several of the federal labor statutes as protection against this kind of retaliatory termination. The employer said the worker was fired because he had a fist fight with the company's personnel manager. The ALJ believed the company's witnesses; the NLRB reversed and upheld the employee's side of the story.

The question that reached the Supreme Court was how much weight an ALJ's findings must be given on intra-agency review. In this case, the reviewing body was the Board itself. In an opinion authored by Justice Frankfurter, the Court conceded that the ALJ's decision did not have to be treated in the same way that a

---

[119] APA § 557(b).

[120] ATTORNEY GENERAL'S MANUAL ON THE ADMINISTRATIVE PROCEDURE ACT 84–85 (1947). For additional discussion on the issues involved with what is called intra-agency review, *see* Russell L. Weaver, *Appellate Review in Executive Departments and Agencies*, 48 ADMIN. L. REV. 251 (1996).

[121] 340 U.S. 474 (1951).

court might treat the findings of a special master. As Justice Frankfurter stated in a somewhat backhanded fashion: an ALJ's findings are "not as unassailable as a master's." Nor does the agency have to approach an ALJ's findings as an appellate court deals with the findings of a trial court (reversing a trial court's findings only if it determines that the findings are *clearly erroneous*).

At the same time, the ALJ's findings cannot be disregarded. Surely, the findings of someone who presided over the evidentiary hearing, heard the witnesses and presumably reviewed the entire record is deserving of some weight. The Court agreed that the Board should pay at least some attention to "the [ALJ's] opportunity to observe the witnesses he hears and sees and the Board does not." But precisely how much weight should be accorded? Here, the Court becomes unclear.

Cutting through Justice Frankfurter's verbiage, the message of this part of *Universal Camera* seems to be: a reviewing entity should be extremely careful when it reverses an ALJ who has heard the witnesses, when the ALJ's findings turn heavily on the credibility of the witnesses and when credibility is a significant factor in the case. This part of *Universal Camera* is not unique. It is, in part, an elaboration on another line of cases that are regarded as classics in administrative law and referred to collectively as the *Morgan Quartet.*

The *Morgan* cases began as a consolidated group of fifty individual actions that challenged an order of the Secretary of Agriculture setting maximum rates charged for buying and selling cattle in the Kansas City stockyards under the Packers and Stockyard Act. The cases reached the Supreme Court the first time in 1936; the fourth *Morgan* decision was handed down by the Court in 1941. The three cases of principal interest to administrative law scholars are *Morgan I*, *Morgan II* and *Morgan IV*.[122] The *Morgan Quartet* cases can take hours to read in the original, but can be quickly distilled for our purposes:

1. *Morgan I* says: "He who decides must hear." This pronouncement by Chief Justice Hughes was made because the Secretary of Agriculture based his final decision on meetings with agency personnel without ever examining the record, without himself presiding at the hearing, or without even being briefed on evidence adduced at the hearing. But even Hughes did not want his pronouncement taken literally. That would mean that the Secretary would have to preside at every hearing held by the Department in which he wanted to make the final decision.

2. *Morgan II* clarified this issue: The Secretary need not preside over the gathering of the evidence in order to make a final decision, so long as he reads the record or is briefed on the contents of the record by someone who has reviewed it.

3. *Morgan IV* was almost a matter of sour grapes. The packers didn't like the Secretary's decision in *Morgan II* and *III* and asked to take his deposition to discover the reasons for his decision, even though the *Morgan II* decision was accompanied by formal findings. The Court held that aggrieved parties could not

---

[122] The case citations are, respectively: 298 U.S. 468 (1936), 304 U.S. 1 (1938), and 313 U.S. 409 (1941). A good article on the *Quartet* is Daniel J. Gifford, *The* Morgan *Cases: A Retrospective View*, 30 ADMIN. L. REV. 237 (1978).

go behind the record to examine the mental processes of the decider, so long as there were reasons for that decision stated on the record.

Morgan IV was modified somewhat in 1971 by the Court's decision in *Citizens to Preserve Overton Park, Inc. v. Volpe*,[123] a case that did not involve a trial-type hearing. In *Overton Park*, the Court decided that the categorical refusal of *Morgan IV* to permit deposing the decider was to be limited solely to agency actions in which there had been formal findings. The *Overton Park* record had no formal findings, so the Court agreed that discovery of the administrator's mental process could be taken if there was no other way to understand how the agency's decision came to be made.

There is a good message in all of this for agency reviewers. First, do not totally disregard the findings of the ALJ. When you do so, make absolutely sure you have good reasons for doing so and that you place those reasons somewhere in your decision. Be especially cautious of reversing the ALJ's findings on credibility and demeanor. Second, if you want to decide but don't want to preside, at least make sure someone reviews the record for you and explains its contents. If you do at least this, you should not have to be deposed by losing parties, and your decision should stand if it is otherwise correct. Some careful thought and conduct on the part of the agency at this stage of the proceeding should alleviate a lot of problems discussed in the following chapters on judicial review of agency action.

---

[123] 401 U.S. 402 (1971).

Chapter 9

INFORMAL AGENCY ACTION

§ 9.01 INTRODUCTION

It may come as a surprise to some readers to find one of the shortest chapters in this book devoted to agency activities that comprise around 90 percent of all administrative action.[1] The problem is that it is very difficult to generalize about these agency actions, other than to call attention to supportive provisions in the Administrative Procedure Act and to survey court decisions affecting informal action. The following analysis may help to identify many of those instances of agency decision making that fit under the heading of *informal agency action*:

1. Is the agency required to take action, *i.e.*, to make some kind of decision?

2. Does the action affect a private person?

3. If both 1 and 2 are "yes", does the agency action constitute rulemaking? [If the action is rulemaking, it is beyond the scope of this chapter.]

4. If not, does the agency provide a trial-type hearing (APA §§ 556–557) before a decision is made?

5. If no trial-type hearing, the agency is engaged in what we will call informal agency action.

There is not even a great deal of agreement on the labels to be applied to informal agency action. A number of administrative law scholars have concluded that most informal agency action should be referred to as *informal adjudication* because an "order" under APA § 551 is a residual category (essentially any agency decision that is not a rule) and an order, again by definition, results from an adjudication.

The problem with the use of the term, *adjudication* is that it frequently suggests — to persons unfamiliar with the APA terminology — some type of elaborate, time-consuming adversarial proceeding. In reality, the bulk of informal agency determinations are relatively quick, almost Solomonic decisions. More importantly, the term does not really convey the wide spectrum of procedures used in informal action, which can run the gamut from almost no procedures whatsoever to a process that is nearly as elaborate as §§ 556–557 hearings.

Two examples provide a good illustration of the significant differences in informal agency procedures. Most actions taken by the Social Security Administration involve accepting, reviewing and processing various benefits applications. Occasion-

---

[1] Wendell Gardner, *The Procedures by Which Informal Action Is Taken*, 24 ADMIN. L. REV. 155 (1972).

ally, some of these actions result in an applicant's sitting down with an agency employee for a face-to-face conversation, but others are handled solely on the basis of a few pieces of paper. These applications result in some kind of decision, and the agency normally gives reasons for its decision. This action fits within the definition of *order* in the APA, and yet, the procedures afforded the applicants are skeletal at best. The applicant may, at a later point in time, get a trial-type proceeding but the initial determination for benefits is informal.

By contrast, the Department of Veterans Affairs Board of Veterans' Appeals (BVA) decides thousands of disability cases each year and a full §§ 556–557 evidentiary hearing is not required by statute. Nonetheless, the BVA procedures provide most of the elements of a trial-type proceeding without actually slipping over the line into formal adjudication. One of the distinctions between BVA procedures and formal adjudication is the absence of an administrative law judge. Most of the other BVA procedures are nearly the same as those required under §§ 556 and 557.[2]

Administrative law scholars have never resolved two issues involved in the study and analysis of informal agency action. One school of thought postulates it is better to study these actions from the standpoint of the substantive decisions made by the agency because these are the matters that are of primary concern to most affected parties. Most individuals who appear before the Social Security Administration are concerned with their eligibility for benefits and the amount of those benefits. They are not typically concerned with the agency's actual decisional process. The second school of thought recommends that we study informal action strictly on the basis of the procedures afforded affected persons because the main concern of the general public is that an agency deal fairly and equitably with persons who come before it, irrespective of whether a particular applicant receives his or her benefits.

Some of the most incisive and controversial commentary in this area is attributable to the administrative law scholar, the late Kenneth Culp Davis, who pioneered research efforts in this area. Evident from his nearly fifty years of writing and research, Professor Davis's ultimate concern was that a democratic society be able to develop *standards* governing substantive agency decisions and *procedures* governing the making of those decisions. The promulgation of satisfactory standards and procedures will insure two separate goals: (1) they curb unfettered agency discretion and (2) they promote agency accountability. In one of his landmark books in the area, DISCRETIONARY JUSTICE,[3] Professor Davis contended that the major focus of public concern ought to be on creating boundaries for the exercise of agency discretion. In his view, "[a] public officer has discretion whenever the effective limits on his power leave him free to make a choice among possible courses of action or inaction."[4]

To be sure, Professor Davis did not confine himself to a critique of discretion solely within administrative agencies, although the majority of unpoliced govern-

---

[2] *See, e.g.*, WILLIAM F. FOX, THE UNITED STATES BOARD OF VETERANS' APPEALS: THE UNFINISHED STRUGGLE TO RECONCILE SPEED AND JUSTICE DURING INTRA-AGENCY REVIEW (Paralyzed Veterans of America 2004).

[3] KENNETH CULP DAVIS, DISCRETIONARY JUSTICE: A PRELIMINARY INQUIRY (1971).

[4] *Id.* at 4.

ment discretion is probably in the hands of administrative agency officials. Most agency action, in Davis's view, may not be subject to meaningful control under our legal system.

But if any controls on informal action do exist, where might they be found? The answer lies in many of the issues already discussed in this book. Controls on agency behavior run the gamut from the express language of an agency's enabling act delegating specific duties to agencies, to procedural statutes such as the APA, to an agency's own substantive and procedural rules (recall that an agency's internal rules control the agency's activities unless and until the agency changes the rules), to court decisions.

Professor Davis feared, and observed many instances of, vast unfettered discretion in the hands of government administrators.[5] But many other commentators are more sanguine about agency activity. Most agency administrators who have to cope with a multitude of statutes, congressional oversight committees, the Government Accountability Office, the Office of Management and Budget, the Office of Personnel Management, internal watchdogs such as the agency inspectors general, and external watchdogs such as the press, the Chamber of Commerce and Common Cause, would probably tell you that their discretion is confined to the point of agency paralysis.

To a certain extent, these questions turn on whose ox is being gored. The citizen who cannot get a city commissioner to explain precisely why a dog license fee in his county is set higher than the fee in an adjacent county may agree with Davis and mutter about the lack of accountability and rationality on the part of government officials. The mid-level agency supervisor bombarded with what looks to her like patently frivolous demands for release of a commission hearing-transcript may conclude that there is too much citizen access to government. This is one of those issues in modern administrative law for which there are easy questions but no easy answers. The following discussion will help a new lawyer cope with some of the problems of agency discretion and informal agency action.

§ 9.02 APA PROVISIONS AFFECTING INFORMAL ACTION

In Chapter 8, § 8.05[I], we discussed the paper hearing process that some agencies use, even under the constraints of §§ 556–557. Recall that, under § 556(d), an agency is permitted to adopt procedures for the submission of all evidence in written form when it is determining claims for money or benefits or passing on applications for initial licenses. This is not, strictly speaking, informal agency action, but rather an exception within the formal adjudication process. Nonetheless, it does permit an agency to establish something other than a full-blown trial-type process for certain specified agency actions. Another example is § 555(e) in which the APA requires that:

> [P]rompt notice shall be given of the denial in whole or in part of a written application, petition, or other request of an interested person made in connection with any agency proceeding. Except in affirming a prior denial

---

[5] *Id.* at 8.

or when the denial is self-explanatory, the notice shall be accompanied by a brief statement of the grounds for denial.

On its face, it would seem that § 555(e) gives the agency enormous discretion. Unfortunately, the *Attorney General's Manual* states that § 555(e) "has no application to matters which do not relate to rulemaking, adjudication or licensing. Generally, it is not applicable to the mass of administrative routine unrelated to those proceedings."[6]

On the other hand, when courts have reviewed agency action under § 555(e) — and there have been relatively few such decisions — they have construed this subsection so broadly that almost any agency action satisfies its requirements. For example, one federal circuit has commented that § 555(e) is satisfied if a statement of grounds for denial of a petition is general, rather than specific, and is sufficient even if it does not address all of the arguments raised by the petitioner.[7]

Beyond § 555(e), there is virtually nothing else in the APA governing informal action. There are other statutory constraints, but, as noted above, those provisions are found in the individual agency enabling acts and thus, have no bearing on federal administrative procedure generally. Agencies are not totally insensitive to issues of fair dealing, so there are many internal agency rules that provide more informal process than may be mandated either by the APA or by the agency's enabling act. It is simply impossible to generalize about these matters. Such matters can be properly understood only in a specific agency context.

The *Model State Administrative Procedure Act* takes a slightly different approach to informal adjudication.[8] The MSAPA first requires an agency to conduct an adjudicative proceeding as its process for issuing an order.[9] However, the *Model Act* then establishes a number of choices depending on the matter in controversy. An agency proceeds by what the Act calls a formal adjudicative hearing unless a separate statute or agency rule permits an alternative proceeding.[10] The alternative proceedings recognized by the *Model Act* include a conference hearing, which may be utilized in situations in which there is no disputed issue of material fact.[11] Another alternative is what the Act calls an emergency or summary adjudicative proceeding. In this instance, the agency may issue an emergency order with virtually no due process afforded prior to the order, except in circumstances that pose an immediate danger to the public health, safety or welfare.[12]

This attempt to deal with informal agency action by express statutory provisions stands in dramatic contrast to the deliberate refusal of the Federal APA to deal

---

[6] Attorney General's Manual on the Administrative Procedure Act 70 (1947).

[7] *Estate of French v. FERC*, 603 F.2d 1158 (5th Cir. 1979). *But see Gillette v. FERC*, 737 F.2d 883 (10th Cir. 1984) (holding that a person who requests a commission waiver is entitled to a statement sufficiently detailed to permit a court to review the agency action).

[8] *The Model Act* is set out in full text in Appendix B.

[9] Model State Admin. P. Act § 102 (2010).

[10] Model State Admin. P. Act § 401 ("contested case") (2010).

[11] Model State Admin. P. Act § 102 (2010).

[12] Model State Admin. P. Act § 407 (2010).

expressly with informal action (apart, of course, from the minimalist provisions in § 555).[13] Most commentators on this issue have been hard-pressed to say which alternative is preferable. Most administrative law scholars tend to stay away from research on informal agency action.

§ 9.03   THE CONTROL OF INFORMAL AGENCY ACTION BY THE COURTS

[A]   Control of the Substance of Informal Agency Action

Reviewing courts ordinarily defer to the substance of agency action. Among many other decisions, the Supreme Court's opinion in *Vermont Yankee Nuclear Power Corp. v. Natural Resources Defense Council, Inc.*[14] admonished the federal judiciary that reviewing courts should avoid substituting their judgment for the scientific and technical determinations of administrative agencies.[15] But that does not mean that an agency's actions are no longer reviewable. At bottom, the APA imposes a duty on a court to reverse agency action that it finds arbitrary and capricious, even if it cannot substitute its judgment on certain matters for that of the agency.

The Supreme Court addressed judicial review of informal agency action in *Citizens to Preserve Overton Park, Inc. v. Volpe*,[16] a case in which the Secretary of Transportation decided to release federal funds to construct a highway through a municipal park in Memphis, Tennessee. *Overton Park* is a major Supreme Court administrative law opinion and will be cited repeatedly in several of the following chapters. For the purposes of this chapter, however, it suffices to know that a statute required the Secretary to take two steps before releasing funds for road construction: (1) to consider alternatives to the routing of the highway through the park, and (2) to insure that steps had been taken to minimize environmental damage.

Initially, the Supreme Court determined that the federal courts had jurisdiction to review the Department of Transportation's (DOT) actions, at least as to whether the agency action was arbitrary or capricious. The Court, however, went on to

---

[13] Dean Acheson, a well-known Washington lawyer (and later Secretary of State in the Truman Administration), chaired the 1941 Attorney General's Committee on Administrative Procedure (whose report ultimately led to the enactment of the Federal APA). Mr. Acheson commented that the Committee had deliberately avoided codifying informal procedures to avoid overly formalizing that process: "It was perfectly clear to us that that was not the thing to do; that that would not be of service to the citizen; that it would not be of service to the Government and it was an entirely futile thing to do so . . ." *Hearings Before Subcomm. of Comm. on the Judiciary on S.674, S.675 and S.918*, 77th Cong., 1st Sess. 804 (1941).

[14] 435 U.S. 519 (1978).

[15] Actually, the second Supreme Court decision in the *Vermont Yankee* dispute made this even clearer. *See Baltimore Gas & Elec. Co. v. Natural Res. Def. Council, Inc.*, 462 U.S. 87 (1983) ("[A] reviewing court must remember that the [Nuclear Regulatory Commission] is making predictions, within its area of special expertise, at the frontiers of science. When examining this kind of scientific determination, as opposed to simple findings of fact, a reviewing court must generally be at its most deferential." *Id.* at 103.).

[16] 401 U.S. 402 (1971).

conclude that the administrative record submitted by DOT was not sufficient for the Court to reach any conclusions as to the validity of the Secretary's actions. In essence, the Court determined that there was insufficient explanation by the DOT on the actions taken by the agency.

Because of deficiencies in the record, the Supreme Court remanded the case for further explanation of the Secretary's actions. The Court noted that a decision stemming from informal agency action need not be accompanied by formal findings and conclusions (as would be required in formal adjudication); but the agency must nonetheless give *reasons* for its action. At the same time, the Court realized that the remand gave the DOT a perfect opportunity simply to concoct plausible explanations for its actions long after the decision was made, so the Court took the additional step of cautioning the agency that any new explanation proffered on remand would be reviewed suspiciously by the Court as merely a "post hoc" explanation.

Overton Park made other contributions to review of informal action. The decision requires that a court reviewing agency action take what the Court terms a *hard look* at the agency record to determine whether there has been compliance with the underlying statutes and whether proper procedures have been followed. If this hard look shows that the agency has explained itself properly and has not abused its discretion or violated any mandatory procedures, the reviewing court's work is finished.[17]

The difficult question is whether this form of judicial review is sufficient to protect against that unfettered agency discretion that has caused Professor Davis so much apprehension. Most observers would probably agree that *Overton Park*-style review is sufficient. Often, the mere threat of taking a case into court makes agencies as careful as possible.

There is, of course, some agency action that is totally subject to agency discretion and that may not be reviewed by courts. Some examples are: an agency's decision to terminate an investigation, an agency's decision not to proceed with an enforcement matter and an agency's determination in areas that are so complicated and multifaceted that they simply cannot be reviewed by a non-expert court. Chapter 10, § 10.05 discusses this kind of non-reviewability. Although there are some minor exceptions not applicable here, non-reviewability, by definition, means that a party cannot seek recourse from the courts for an adverse agency decision.

Is there any way to cope with agency action that is categorically non-reviewable? The short answer is "yes." You can deal with it, but you must deal with it *inside* the agency or in the legislative branch, rather than through the courts. One way to approach actions that are not reviewable is to begin from the perspective that agencies are composed of human beings, most of whom try to perform their duties in good faith and who are subject to the limitations placed on them by Congress and by the courts. In this author's experience, there may be considerable tension

---

[17] A number of administrative law scholars believe that the Overton Park principles place a number of curbs on totally unfettered agency discretion. *See, e.g.*, Mariano-Florentino Cuellar, *Auditing Executive Discretion*, 82 Notre Dame L. Rev. 227 (2006); Barry Friedman, *The Politics of Judicial Review*, 84 Tex. L. Rev. 257 (2005).

between the regulators and the regulated, but there are few instances of downright ugly, malicious or irrational behavior on the part of government officials that cannot be challenged in some fashion or that will not be corrected at some other level within the agency.

Agency supervisors often reverse improper decisions by low-echelon agency employees. Agency inspectors general are authorized by statute to investigate allegations of unacceptable agency behavior.[18] On the federal level, Congress has authorized the Government Accountability Accounting Office (GAO) to investigate agency actions upon the request of individual members of Congress. Some state legislatures have offices, much like the GAO, that perform similar duties on the state level. So, even if you cannot challenge the substance of an agency decision in court, you are not completely powerless. To this extent, Professor Davis's fears of *totally* unconfined agency discretion have not been realized.

[B]   Control of the Process of Informal Action

There are three grounds on which a court may review the procedural aspects of informal action: (1) whether the action complies with procedures set out in the enabling act or in the APA; (2) whether the procedure complies with existing agency procedural regulations; and (3) whether the procedure is compatible with constitutional due process. The only way to examine grounds one and two is to look closely at the applicable statutes and the rules structure of individual agencies. Obviously, a violation of either the statutes or the rules may invalidate the action itself.

The issue of whether an agency's informal action procedures satisfy constitutional due process requires another look at all the cases and materials analyzed in Chapter 5. There is no need to repeat that material here, except to point out that after 1976 and the Court's articulation of the three-part *Mathews v. Eldridge*[19] *balancing test*, a court will review agency procedures in light of:

1.   the private interest affected;

2.   the risk of error inherent in the existing procedures; and

3.   the interest of the government.

Two administrative law scholars have examined the issue of informal action procedures and have arrived at nearly identical conclusions, albeit by slightly different routes. Professor Paul Verkuil studied forty-two instances of informal action in four federal agencies and compared those procedures with the ten *Goldberg v. Kelly* elements.[20] He found that while only two actions he studied had

---

[18]   *See* the Inspector General Act, 5 U.S.C. App. §§ 1–12 (2000).

[19]   424 U.S. 319 (1976).

[20]   Paul R. Verkuil, *A Study of Informal Adjudication Procedures*, 43 U. Chi. L. Rev. 739 (1976). The *Goldberg* procedures as he enumerates them are: (1) timely and adequate notice, (2) confrontation of adverse witnesses, (3) oral presentation of arguments, (4) oral presentation of evidence, (5) cross-examination of adverse witnesses, (6) disclosure of opposing evidence, (7) right to retain an attorney, (8) a determination on the record of the hearing, (9) a statement of reasons for the decision and evidence relied upon, and (10) an impartial decision maker. *Id.* at 760.

all of the *Goldberg* elements, more than half the actions studied provided between three and four of the elements. Only two actions, certain inspections conducted by the Department of Agriculture, had none of the elements.[21]

As discussed in Chapter 5, *Goldberg* is now viewed as an extreme case. There has been no other instance of the Court's prescribing, as a matter of constitutional law, more elements than those required in *Goldberg*. Most recent Supreme Court decisions, including *Mathews*, have approved far fewer procedural elements. Verkuil's study and recent Supreme Court decisions involving constitutional due process suggest that informal agency action affording minimal due process to persons affected by the agency action is going to pass constitutional muster.

The Supreme Court revisited these issues in a 1990 decision, *Pension Benefit Guaranty Corp. v. LTV Corp.*[22] The Pension Benefit Guaranty Corporation (PBGC) is a government corporation that becomes responsible for the payment of certain corporate pension benefits when the private businesses are not able to pay them. In this case, PBGC determined that certain pension plans initially in existence between LTV and some of its labor force were to be restored, even though LTV had been reorganized in bankruptcy. Among many other issues in the case, the court of appeals had struck down PBGC's restoration orders because PBGC's procedures did not afford LTV an adequate opportunity to participate in the decision. Specifically, the court of appeals determined that LTV was not apprised of the material on which PBGC based its decision, was not afforded an adequate opportunity to submit contradictory evidence, and did not provide LTV with a statement setting out PBGC's reasoning in issuing the restoration orders.

On review by the Supreme Court, the justices took a much milder view of the proceeding. The *PBGC* opinion, authored by Justice Blackmun, first determined that, contrary to LTV's assertions, there was really very little tension between the *Overton Park* and *Vermont Yankee* opinions. *Vermont Yankee* continues to stand for the proposition that courts may not impose specific procedural requirements on agencies "that have no basis in the APA." *Overton Park* simply requires an agency to provide a reviewing court with a record adequate for judicial review, not necessarily a record compiled through the use of specific procedures. Stated differently, the Court made clear that the thrust of *Vermont Yankee* (a decision involving rulemaking procedure) also applies to informal adjudication. In the Court's words,

> the determination in this case, however, was lawfully made by informal adjudication, the minimal requirements for which are set forth in § 555 of the APA, and do not include such elements. A failure to provide them where the Due Process Clause itself does not require them (which has not been asserted here) is therefore not unlawful.

But this, of course, analyzes only the constitutional minimums placed upon informal action. Neither agencies nor legislatures need confine themselves to minimum procedures if they believe that more process is necessary to insure fair

---

[21] *Id.* at 760–71. Even here, it is arguable that inspections are not subject to the requirements of constitutional due process because they are substitutes for a hearing.

[22] 496 U.S. 633 (1990).

and accurate decisions. Professor Davis has identified what he believes are four necessary ingredients for an acceptable system of informal action procedures: (1) parties be apprised of and have an opportunity to comment on evidence against them, (2) agencies should be as open as possible in reaching their decisions, (3) any action be accompanied by a statement of findings and reasons, and (4) agencies try, insofar as possible, to remain consistent through the application of precedent to their decisions. Professor Davis believes that ombudsmen and advisory opinions would also contribute to fairness in the decisional process.[23]

Each of these ingredients is dealt with elsewhere in this book, and each is generally considered to be a central facet of fair administrative procedure. Notice is probably the first among equals and is required under the APA, both when an agency initiates a rulemaking and when an agency commences an adjudication against a specific individual.[24] Virtually all agencies provide reasons (*see* § 555(e) discussed *above*), and courts normally require consistency in agency action.[25] So, none of the *Davis* ingredients for proper informal action really imposes any new requirements on administrative agencies. The problem is that, on occasion, lawyers will encounter agency process that lacks one or more of these ingredients. If a court challenge is impossible, remember the suggestions set out above in § 9.03[A]. You can still try to deal with agency personnel on an individual basis; you may be able to invoke internal corrective devices such as an intra-agency appeal or a plea to the inspector general; or you can take try to take your problem to the legislature for correction. These are not perfect solutions for agency abuses, but they at least provide some minimal leverage for persons aggrieved by informal agency action.

---

[23] Kenneth Culp Davis, Cases, Text & Problems on Administrative Law 514 (6th ed. 1977).

[24] *See* Chapter 7 for a discussion of rule making procedures and Chapter 8 for a discussion of agency adjudications.

[25] *See* Chapter 12, § 12.06 for a discussion of consistency. For a fresh look at some of these issues using a slightly different perspective, *see* Thomas O. Sargentich, *Informal Agency Decision Making: Problems of Delay and Public Information*, 3 Admin. L.J. 223 (1989). For yet another look at informal adjudication, see Ronald J. Krotoszynski, Jr., *Taming the Tail that Wags the Dog: Ex Post and Ex Ante Constraints on Informal Adjudication*, 56 Admin. L. Rev. 1057 (2004).

Chapter 10

JUDICIAL REVIEW OF AGENCY ACTION: GETTING INTO COURT

§ 10.01 AN ANALYTICAL FRAMEWORK FOR JUDICIAL REVIEW ISSUES

The topics covered here and in Chapters 11 and 12 are favorites of law professors and bar examiners. Although many of the concepts are based upon statutes, a substantial number of the important doctrines are judge-made, making it very easy to work through the material on a case-by-case basis. This may erroneously suggest, however, that reviewing courts look at vast numbers of agency decisions and frequently set aside agency action. This is simply not true.

New attorneys often get themselves into trouble by approaching an agency case with this attitude. If readers take away a fundamental message from this portion of the book, it should be: (1) courts review a relatively small percentage of agency decisions, and (2) courts set aside an even smaller percentage of agency decisions. The permissible grounds for overturning agency action are so narrow that most courts have very little room to maneuver. Remember cardinal rule number two of administrative practice: the place to win your case is at the agency. Don't expect a court to reward you for sloppy or casual lawyering at the agency level.

Of course, any time a lawyer says something this dramatic, he has to retrench a bit. Judicial review can have a disproportionate impact on agency action because a court's holding will often affect large numbers of individual agency actions. While the role of courts in reviewing agency action has been circumscribed in the last several years by a number of important Supreme Court decisions, courts remain an important component of federal agency practice. Their role, while somewhat diminished, cannot be disregarded.

Think for a moment about the Supreme Court's decision in *Goldberg v. Kelly*[1] requiring certain minimum procedures before a recipient's welfare benefits may be terminated. In one fell swoop, *Goldberg* redrafted agency procedures throughout the country and called into question literally hundreds of other procedural schemes involving similar types of agency action. We still have not seen the last of the administrative due process cases. At present, an agency may not be governed by the *Goldberg* holding, but it cannot afford to disregard the Supreme Court's pronouncements on procedural due process.

---

[1] 397 U.S. 254 (1970). *Goldberg* is discussed at length in Chapter 5, § 5.03. For good general discussion of most of the issues in this chapter, *see* Ronald M. Levin, *Understanding Unreviewability in Administrative Law*, 74 Minn. L. Rev. 689 (1990).

There are a number of ways to spot issues in a judicial review setting. The questions to ask yourself, in the following order, are:

1.   *Whether* the case may be taken to court?

2.   *When* judicial review is appropriate (discussed in Chapter 11)?

3.   *What kind* of review the court will perform on the merits (discussed in Chapter 12)?

This chapter is concerned with the *whether* issues. The components of the *whether* inquiry are: (1) jurisdiction, (2) form of action, (3) sovereign immunity, (4) preclusion, and (5) standing. Each of these issues will be discussed in order.

§ 10.02   JURISDICTION

[A]   Generally

On the federal level, any problem involving judicial review of agency action must begin with this inquiry. Recall some fundamental propositions of our system of government and particularly, what you learned about federal courts in other courses in law school. First, federal courts are courts of limited jurisdiction. Second, the limits on that jurisdiction are imposed by Article III of the Constitution, which, among other things, limits the federal courts to a consideration of cases or controversies arising under the laws, treaties or Constitution of the United States. Congress has also enacted certain jurisdictional limitations on the federal courts apart from the basic commands in Article III, including, for example, the amount in controversy requirement for diversity of citizenship actions. By contrast, state courts are usually courts of general jurisdiction, so the highly technical questions you must resolve on questions of federal jurisdiction may not be necessary in state court.[2]

For judicial review of agency action, these principles mean that no one may enter federal court unless Congress has enacted a statutory permission to use the federal courts.[3] Unfortunately, a number of administrative law scholars have developed a term, *non-statutory* review, that suggests that there may be instances in which a person injured by agency action can enter federal court without an underlying jurisdictional statute. When the law professors use the term *non-*

---

[2] It may be theoretically possible to enter federal court to challenge the action of a federal agency in the context of a lawsuit based on diversity of citizenship; but this almost never happens, because the *arising under* language in § 1331 normally includes the actions of all federal agencies. By contrast, diversity jurisdiction has been used frequently as a basis for testing the validity of state administrative action in federal court. *See, e.g., Burford v. Sun Oil Co.*, 319 U.S. 315 (1943). For a discussion of the manner in which an attorney might make various decisions relating to judicial review, *see* Toni M. Fine, *Appellate Practice on Review of Agency Action: A Guide for Practitioners*, 28 U. Tol. L. Rev. 1 (1996).

[3] It is conceivable that no statute is necessary to trigger the original jurisdiction of the Supreme Court because that jurisdiction is set out expressly in Article III and does not require congressional action. There are, however, very few instances in which federal agency action fits within that jurisdictional category.

statutory review, they are usually talking about federal court jurisdiction that is found outside the agency's enabling act.

Don't be confused by this terminology. Stick with the fundamental requirements for getting into federal court. Every case filed in a federal court requires a jurisdictional statute. That statement of jurisdiction must appear on the face of your complaint. You find those statutes in different places in the *United States Code*. The better approach is to think through a jurisdictional problem on the following lines. If you want to get into federal court, there are essentially two places to look for jurisdictional authority: (1) the enabling act and (2) the general jurisdictional statutes set out in Title 28 of the U.S.C., such as 28 U.S.C. § 1331 (basic federal question jurisdiction) or 28 U.S.C. § 1337 (jurisdiction arising out of any act of Congress regulating commerce).

[B]　Enabling Act Jurisdiction

Most federal enabling acts of any vintage, and virtually all modern enabling acts, contain language providing for judicial review. Under most circumstances, these are the provisions to be invoked in challenging agency action. That is, look first at the enabling act for a grant of subject matter jurisdiction and go to the general jurisdictional statutes in Title 28 only if the enabling act is silent.

Be aware, of course, that few practitioners take any chances here; defects in subject matter jurisdiction are fatal and may be brought up at any stage of the litigation by either party or by the court itself. Most lawyers challenging agency action write an allegation of jurisdiction that invokes as many jurisdictional statutes as may plausibly relate to the case.

There is no particular rhyme or reason for Congress' selection of various routes for judicial review. The selection of a judicial review scheme depends very heavily upon the views of judicial review held by the members of Congress who draft that particular enabling act. Some examples: (1) disputes out of the Securities and Exchange Commission generally go into federal district court; (2) most disputes coming out of the Federal Energy Regulatory Commission go into an appropriate federal court of appeals (the circuits), depending on the geographical location of the original dispute; (3) most disputes involving the Federal Communications Commission may be taken only into the United States Court of Appeals for the District of Columbia Circuit.

These agencies are all major federal regulatory agencies that perform similar regulatory tasks for different industries in the United States. They are all independent regulatory commissions and were created about the same time. The headquarters of each agency is in Washington, although some of the agencies have regional offices that transact a certain amount of agency business. The businesses that each agency regulates are scattered throughout the United States. There is no discernible reason, other than the whim of the legislators, that explains the vastly different routes of judicial review established for each agency.

Congress can make things even more complicated. Consider the jurisdictional provisions governing challenges to the actions of the Environmental Protection

Agency under the Clean Air Act:[4]

1.   Pre-enforcement challenges to EPA rulemaking may be taken to an appropriate circuit;

2.   Challenges to certain specific EPA actions, such as promulgation of national emission standards, may be taken only to the D.C. Circuit;

3.   EPA subpoena enforcement actions are docketed in a federal district court in which the subpoenaed person resides; and

4.   Certain EPA orders prohibiting retaliatory actions against employees may be enforced in appropriate federal district courts.

The message of this recitation is plain. Even within a single enabling act, such as the Clean Air Act, Congress may have inserted a multiplicity of jurisdictional provisions. Moreover, Congress may, in certain instances, make a certain jurisdictional provision mandatory — i.e., may forbid persons from using other statutory routes for judicial review. If you elect an impermissible jurisdictional statute, your case will be dismissed for lack of subject matter jurisdiction. That kind of dismissal may not hurt if you can refile in the proper court before the statute of limitations runs out, but you will look very silly in any event. Pay close attention to the jurisdictional provisions in agency enabling acts.

[C]   Review Under General Jurisdictional Statutes

The most frequently invoked general jurisdictional statute providing for review of agency action is 28 U.S.C. § 1331, which now provides: "The district courts shall have original jurisdiction of all civil actions arising under the Constitution, laws, or treaties of the United States."[5] Prior to October, 1976, § 1331 was not as useful as it is today because it limited district court jurisdiction to cases in which the amount in controversy was in excess of $10,000. Accordingly, it was possible to have federal agency action that arguably did not fit within any jurisdictional statute because the amount in controversy was not large enough.

Because of this pre-1976 loophole, a claimant who tried to have the Social Security Administration re-open a previously denied claim for benefits invoked the Administrative Procedure Act itself as an alternative jurisdictional basis for challenging the agency's action.[6] The Supreme Court took up this question in *Califano v. Sanders*.[7] The Court looked at the relevant APA language in § 702, which provides, in part: "A person suffering legal wrong because of agency action . . . is entitled to seek judicial review thereof." Because the APA is a Congressional enactment and because that portion of § 702 sounds very much like a guarantee of judicial review, it is arguable that Congress was writing, for federal agency action,

---

[4]   42 U.S.C. § 7607(b).

[5]   If an enabling act rests on the Commerce Clause, it is also possible to invoke 28 U.S.C. § 1337. Civil rights claims may come in under 28 U.S.C. § 1343.

[6]   The Social Security Act contains its own jurisdictional provision for cases of denied benefits. The claimant here had not challenged the original denial, so he could not use that provision.

[7]   430 U.S. 99 (1977).

a grant of jurisdiction for cases involving the APA.

However, the problem is this: that statement does not look exactly like conventional jurisdictional statutes, such as § 1331, because it does not contain language explicitly conferring jurisdiction on the federal courts. Section 1331 begins: "The district courts shall have original jurisdiction over . . . ." Most enabling act jurisdictional provisions contain the same sort of language.

This could have been a tricky question for the Court; but in this instance, in October, 1976 — just before *Sanders* was decided — Congress bailed the Court out by repealing the jurisdictional amount requirement in § 1331. The elimination of the amount in controversy made § 1331 essentially a catch-all or residual jurisdictional statute. In other words, to the extent that someone has a claim arising out of the laws, treaties or Constitution of the United States (virtually any challenge to agency action fits this language), a federal district court may hear the claim without worrying about the dollar amount of the claim. With the § 1331 amendment as a way out, the Court was then free to hold squarely: "We thus conclude that the APA does not afford an implied grant of subject-matter jurisdiction permitting federal judicial review of agency action." As a result of § 1331 and *Sanders*, this component of the *whether* question rarely presents a problem to someone seeking to challenge agency action.

§ 10.03   VENUE, SERVICE OF PROCESS AND A PROPER FORM OF ACTION

It is not enough to identify a proper federal jurisdictional statute. A litigator who wishes to challenge agency action must resolve the issues of *venue, service of process* and must invoke some type of remedial mechanism that the court can use to grant the relief sought. Venue and service of process are seldom major points of dispute when suing federal agencies. An enabling act may contain specific venue provisions-as does the Clean Air Act, discussed above. If the enabling act is silent on venue, 28 U.S.C. § 1391(e) provides that venue in these instances is proper in any federal judicial district where: (1) the defendant resides, (2) a substantial part of the events or omissions giving rise to the claim occurred, or a substantial part of property that is the subject of the action is situated, or (3) the plaintiff resides, if no real property is involved. This is one of the broadest venue provisions on the books and makes it possible in many cases to do a little forum shopping.

Service of process is equally uncomplicated, although you must work carefully through Rule 4 of the *Federal Rules of Civil Procedure* to make sure all persons are properly served. For most actions involving a federal agency, Rule 4 provides for service on the United States attorney in the district in which the action is being brought and service by certified or registered mail on the Attorney General in Washington. If the case involves a lawsuit against an agency or officer of the U.S., the plaintiff must serve the U.S. Attorney, the Attorney General and the agency itself. If the case involves an attack on an agency order when the agency is not named as a party to the lawsuit, the agency must also be notified by registered or certified mail.[8]

When the relief sought is simply an injunction asking the court to halt the challenged agency practice or a request that the court make a declaration as to the validity of the agency action, there is normally no problem. Section 703 of the APA now expressly permits a court to utilize "any applicable form of legal action including actions for declaratory judgments or writs of prohibitory or mandatory injunction or habeas corpus . . . ." In addition, the agency's action can normally be challenged in the context of a defense to an agency's civil or criminal enforcement action.

This last proposition has been discussed, but not conclusively resolved in a 1978 Supreme Court decision, *Adamo Wrecking Co. v. United States,*[9] an action brought by the federal government to enforce an Environmental Protection Agency penalty for violating the Clean Air Act. The company challenged the legitimacy of the EPA order by asserting, in part, that the emission standard itself was invalid (rather than merely arguing that it had not committed the offense in question). In *Adamo,* the EPA invoked an earlier Supreme Court decision, *Yakus v. United States,*[10] for the proposition that once the time has passed for challenging the agency's rulemaking-as it had passed in *Adamo* because the Clean Air Act set specific time limitations on challenging an EPA rule-a reviewing court should not consider attacks on the validity of the rule in a subsequent enforcement action. In other words, the only thing Adamo should be able to argue is whether it committed the act in question, not whether the EPA's emission standard was validly promulgated.

The Supreme Court looked carefully at this argument and held in favor of the company. The Court then went on to reach the merits, determined that the EPA rule was not a proper emission standard and ordered the district court to dismiss the indictment.

The *Adamo* decision seems to support the proposition that a regulated party can bring up the question of the validity of an agency's rules whenever a rule is used as the basis for an enforcement action, even if, under the statute, the time for challenging the rule's validity has long since run. For lawyers representing private parties involved in agency enforcement actions, this may be a dangerous view of the case. For example, the Court's reasoning in *Adamo* appears to be grounded heavily on the fact that the case was a criminal prosecution, rather than a mere civil enforcement action.[11]

The Court also seemed not to like the extremely short time period (thirty days after promulgation) in which a party could challenge the rule. And while Justice Powell suggested in a concurring opinion that a regulated party may have a *constitutional* right to attack the validity of a rule any time that rule is applied to the party, no other justice joined Powell in this part of his separate opinion. Lawyers who represent clients with regular business before particular agencies

---

[8] FED. R. CIV. P. 4(i)(2)(a).

[9] 434 U.S. 275 (1978).

[10] 321 U.S. 414 (1944).

[11] *See, e.g., FTC v. Morton Salt Co.,* 334 U.S. 37 (1948).

should challenge rules within the time frame established by Congress. Waiting until the agency attempts to enforce the rule may choke off some of the client's available arguments.

Federal courts no longer place a great deal of stock in the now-obsolete concepts of form of action, and § 703 makes clear that form of action is not to be an insuperable barrier to mounting a challenge to agency action. A party challenging agency action may invoke any remedy within the court's power to grant. Labels, such as *mandamus, injunction, declaratory judgment* and the like, are less important than the ground on which the action is challenged. Of course, you should also consider the matter of sovereign immunity, particularly if the remedy your client seeks is monetary relief.

§ 10.04 SOVEREIGN IMMUNITY

In years past, administrative law courses spent much time on sovereign immunity because there were a number of instances in which the Supreme Court blocked challenges to agency action on the ground that the government was sovereign and had not consented to being sued. Many times, challenging parties had to invoke various legal fictions as, for example, in *Ex parte Young*,[12] that an agency officer who is acting in excess of statutory authority (*ultra vires*) loses the cloak of immunity given to government officers. The standard case cited in administrative law casebooks on this point, *Larson v. Domestic and Foreign Commerce Corp.*,[13] was a Supreme Court opinion permitting a lawsuit against an agency official in his personal capacity based on "unconstitutional administration."

In 1976, Congress amended § 702 of the APA to eliminate the defense of sovereign immunity in cases in which the plaintiffs are seeking "other than money damages." So, those actions that seek only injunctions or declaratory relief no longer have to face a sovereign immunity defense.

But what if the client wants money damages? If you are suing for some kind of constitutional violation and if you seek a judgment against a federal officer or employee personally — *i.e.*, out of his or her personal pocketbook — you may be able to invoke the *Bivens* remedy.[14] However, a *Bivens*-type recovery is only against the employees and may not be satisfied out of the federal treasury. Most government employees are effectively judgment proof because their only income is their salary.

Those clients who seek to recover money damages satisfied out of the federal treasury must proceed under one or another of the statutes, such as the Federal Tort Claims Act or the Tucker Act — enactments by which Congress has relaxed the doctrine of sovereign immunity. These statutes are tricky, have a number of

---

[12] 209 U.S. 123 (1908).

[13] 337 U.S. 682 (1949).

[14] *Bivens v. Six Unknown Named Agents of Federal Bureau of Narcotics*, 403 U.S. 388 (1971) (when federal agents violate a citizen's constitutional rights and the citizen seeks money damages against the individual agents, a court may fashion a common-law remedy, even if Congress has not enacted a statute permitting such relief).

exceptions that must be confronted and are fully discussed in Chapter 13.[15]

§ 10.05 PRECLUSION

[A] Section 701 of the APA

Even when you find a proper jurisdictional statute and resolve all the issues previously discussed in this chapter, the action may not be reviewable because it has been precluded from review by § 701 of the APA. Section 701(a) distinguishes between two types of preclusion: (1) matters that are precluded *by statute*, and (2) matters that are precluded because they are *committed to agency discretion.*

Preclusion deals with the subject matter of a dispute, rather than the parties to the action. In a setting involving preclusion, it normally makes no difference who brings the case to court: if the issue is precluded from review, a court may not act. Much like all the other doctrines in this chapter, preclusion is a door-closing proposition. Courts are powerless to act on a matter that is properly precluded.

Preclusion sometimes poses both conceptual and analytical problems. There are some ways to sort out most of the problems, however. First, take some comfort from the fact that the vast bulk of agency actions are reviewable in some fashion. The cases that are precluded under § 701 are, by definition, the exceptions.

Second, be aware that courts do not take kindly to being told that they cannot examine action taken by the executive branch. Remember the message of *Marbury v. Madison*[16] and the exceptionally strong views of Chief Justice John Marshall on the proper role of the Supreme Court as a component of the federal government. Finally, consider two more recent cases, *Abbott Laboratories v. Gardner*[17] and *Citizens to Preserve Overton Park, Inc. v. Volpe,*[18] both cases in which the Supreme Court established a presumption in favor of judicial review.

[B] The Presumption in Favor of Judicial Review

Abbott Labs, discussed at length in § 11.04 *below*, was a case involving a challenge by various drug companies to certain labeling requirements imposed on them by the Food and Drug Administration. The Court, at the urging of the government, looked closely at whether there was any statute or part of a statute that might be interpreted as somehow precluding the Court from reviewing the companies' claims at that point in time. The Court could find no such pronouncement and held that there was no statute expressly prohibiting judicial review and that there was most certainly no "showing of clear and convincing

---

[15] There are instances in which the doctrine of sovereign immunity will prohibit lawsuits against state administrative agencies in federal court. Those issues are beyond the scope of this chapter and this book. Some excellent discussion of these matters may be found in Roger C. Hartley, *Enforcing Federal Civil Rights Against Public Entities After* Garrett, 28 J.C. & U.L. 41 (2001); Roger C. Hartley, *Alden Trilogy: Praise and Protest*, 23 HARV. J.L. & PUB. POL'Y 323 (2000).

[16] 5 U.S. (1 Cranch) 137 (1803).

[17] 387 U.S. 136 (1967).

[18] 401 U.S. 402 (1971).

evidence" of any intent on the part of Congress to restrict review.

Four years later, in *Overton Park*, the Court said virtually the same thing, this time in a case in which the government argued that the decision of the Secretary of Transportation to permit the use of federal funds to construct a highway through a municipal park was an action committed to agency discretion and thereby, precluded from review. Once again, the Court invoked the presumption in favor of review, and once again, the Court invoked the principle that this presumption is so strong that it can be overcome only by clear and convincing evidence to the contrary.

This is a strong statement from the 1970 Supreme Court, a Court that even then was developing an aversion to permitting courts to undermine agency action. The clear and convincing proof requirement makes it even plainer that the Court is rarely willing to accept an argument that federal courts cannot review an agency dispute.[19] Nonetheless, the Court has occasionally concluded that judicial review is prohibited. Preclusion is best understood by separately analyzing the two types of preclusion: statutory preclusion and preclusion because a decision is committed to agency discretion.

[C]   Statutory Preclusion

This component of preclusion analysis normally requires identification of a statute outside the APA that expressly prohibits a court from reviewing an agency decision, although on occasion, the Supreme Court has seen fit to examine a statute's legislative history to find the requisite evidence of intent to preclude. *Switchmen's Union v. National Mediation Board*[20] is one of very few instances in which the Court performed an intense search through a statute's legislative history (as contrasted with the statute's express language) to find the requisite evidence of preclusion. A 1984 Supreme Court decision, *Block v. Community Nutrition Institute*,[21] is another instance of the Court's discerning a statutory preclusion without express statutory language. But *Block* was, in truth, a case involving standing to challenge agency action, rather than the sort of preclusion issue under discussion here.

Most of the statutory preclusions appear on the face of the statute. There are a number of these statutes in the *United States Code.* For example, until 1988 there was a blanket preclusion for decisions on veterans benefits made by the Veterans Administration.[22] Some statutes, however, only partially preclude review, for

---

[19] *Compare* the clear and convincing requirement here with the Court's decision in *Steadman v. SEC*, 450 U.S. 91 (1981), holding that the standard of proof in agency actions is generally only the preponderance of the evidence test.

[20] 320 U.S. 297 (1943).

[21] 467 U.S. 340 (1984).

[22] 38 U.S.C. § 211(a) which provided in part:

"[T]he decisions of the [VA] on any question of law or fact . . . providing benefits for veterans . . . shall be final and conclusive and no other official or any court of the United States shall have power or jurisdiction to review any such decision by an action in the nature of mandamus or otherwise."

example, by placing strict limits on the timing of judicial review or by requiring review to be brought only in particular courts at particular times. When the Selective Service System was actively drafting young men for military service, many people in the United States became aware of a statutory preclusion that prohibits pre-induction review of selective service decisions. Under the preclusion, the only way a draftee could challenge the draft board's decision was: (1) to refuse to report for induction and bring up the challenge in the context of a defense to a criminal action (this, by the way, is what Muhammad Ali did), or (2) to enter the military service and then bring a habeas corpus action challenging the Board's actions. Selective service preclusions have generally been upheld by the Supreme Court.[23]

In a second example, a provision in the Clean Air Act purports to require that challenges to EPA emission standards be brought within thirty days of promulgation of the standard and only in the D.C. Circuit. While the government urged that this time limit statutorily precluded any subsequent challenge to EPA rules, the Supreme Court in *Adamo* (discussed in § 10.04 *above*) permitted a company to challenge the validity of an EPA rule in a criminal enforcement proceeding brought long after the thirty-day period had run.

Even when the Court encounters such statutes, it is reluctant to accept the preclusion as a total barrier to judicial review. For example, the Veterans Administration preclusion came up in *Johnson v. Robison*,[24] a case in which the plaintiff had done alternative service in lieu of serving in the military. He argued that the VA's refusal to give alternative service people the same veteran's benefits given to persons who served in the military was a violation of his right to equal protection. The Court looked closely at the statutory language and determined that when the person challenging agency action challenges the constitutionality of the enabling act on its face, the preclusion does not apply. It is applicable only to challenges of agency action in which the statute's validity is accepted.[25] The Supreme Court has hinted in *Adamo Wrecking Co. v. United States*[26] that a preclusion, such as the Clean Air Act preclusion, might not prohibit a court from examining the validity of an agency rule in the context of a criminal proceeding.

In certain instances, however, the Supreme Court appears to be more amenable to precluding review. In *Block v. Community Nutrition Institute*,[27] the Court prohibited certain consumers of milk from challenging milk market orders issued by the Secretary of Agriculture (milk market orders set minimum prices for milk as part of the federal government's price support program for milk). In a curiously

---

This section has been repealed by the Veterans Benefits and Program Improvement Act, 38 U.S.C. §§ 101 *et seq.* Limited judicial review of VA cases is now permitted.

[23] *See, e.g.,* the discussion of this topic in *Oestereich v. Selective Serv. System Bd. No. 11*, 393 U.S. 233 (1968).

[24] 415 U.S. 361 (1974).

[25] The *Oestereich* case, *supra* note 23, went the same way. When a person challenged certain interpretations of his draft board, the Court applied the preclusion. *See Clark v. Gabriel*, 393 U.S. 256 (1968).

[26] 434 U.S. 275 (1978).

[27] 467 U.S. 340 (1984).

written opinion, the Court used the term *preclusion* as the linguistic basis for prohibiting a federal court from entertaining the consumers' challenges, but spent most of the opinion discussing *standing* cases, such as *Data Processing v. Camp* and *Barlow v. Collins* (discussed in § 10.06). To the extent that it invoked the *Abbott Labs* presumption, it did so only to reiterate that the statutes authorizing the market orders appear to show a Congressional intent to prohibit challenges from a particular class of potential plaintiffs-namely, milk consumers.

There's no need to mince words here. The *Community Nutrition* opinion is weird. This is doubly so because the lower courts took up the case entirely on the basis of standing. Preclusion *is not* standing. Preclusion deals with the issues in a case and determines whether those issues are precluded either by statute or because they are committed to agency discretion. Standing, a concept discussed at length below, investigates the ability of a particular plaintiff or group of plaintiffs to bring a particular action. Both doctrines are door-closing doctrines in that they block any analysis of the merits of the case, but they are conceptually distinct. Do not be misled by the Court's mislabeling of the *Community Nutrition* dispute. The Court determined that *consumers* could not challenge Department of Agriculture marketing orders; it did not determine that those orders could never be reviewed. The result in this case may be the same-in either case the market orders stand as entered by the Secretary of Agriculture-but the doctrines are entirely different.

Few people know for sure what was going through the minds of the justices when they published this opinion. One explanation is that they might have believed that the *Community Nutrition* plaintiffs could not be kicked out on conventional standing principles, even though the Court did not want to let the consumers be heard in court on a challenge to those milk market orders. Another explanation is that the Court invoked the doctrine of preclusion in a wholly inappropriate case to send a signal that the *clear and convincing* component of preclusion analysis is less meaningful than it might have been when the Court decided *Abbott Labs* and *Overton Park*. The final, least drastic possibility, is that the Court is now using the term *preclusion* as a generic concept to describe many instances in which judicial review is prohibited. If this is now the case, the justices are doing a disservice to their audience because preclusion is a statutory term used in the APA in a much narrower sense.

The Supreme Court revisited statutory preclusion in a 2010 case involving the Attorney General of the United States. *Kucana v. Holder*[28] involved the Illegal Immigration Reform and Immigrant Responsibility Act of 1996.[29] The statute prohibits judicial review of any actions by the Attorney General "the authority for which is specified [under the Act which is] to be in the discretion of the Attorney General." Mr. Kucana, the petitioner, attempted to reopen his deportation proceeding on the basis of new evidence that would support his petition for asylum. The Seventh Circuit denied review under the preclusion articulated in the statute.

However, when the case came before the Supreme Court, the Court took a different view. The Attorney General had issued regulations that defined certain of

---

[28] 130 S. Ct. 827 (2010).

[29] 8 U.S.C. § 1252.

his actions as falling under the "discretionary" provisions of the statute. The Court concluded that the executive branch could not, by rule, define its own jurisdiction. It commented : "Separation of powers concerns . . . caution us against reading legislation, absent clear statement, to place in executive hands authority to remove cases from the Judiciary's domain."[30]

Whatever the explanation, the basic principle of statutory preclusion still exists. If Congress wants to preclude review by statute, it must say so in plain terms.

[D]   Preclusion of Action Committed to Agency Discretion

This component of preclusion is the site of a major battle between two giants of American administrative law scholarship. Begin your analysis by first noting the structure of this part of the APA. Section 701 constitutes a list of exceptions to judicial review. Section 701(a)(2), the committed-to-agency-discretion preclusion, is one of those exceptions. Professor K.C. Davis insists that Congress must be taken at its word and that when Congress says "thou shalt not review" that means *no review.*[31]

However, another portion of the judicial review provisions in the APA, § 706, provides in part that agency action may be reviewed for *abuse of discretion.* The late Professor Louis Jaffe argued for years that this provision, and the Constitution of the United States, guarantee judicial review at least to test whether the administrator's discretion has been abused.[32] There has been no conclusive resolution of the Jaffe/Davis dispute; but recent opinions by the Supreme Court suggest that Professor Davis's view may ultimately prevail.

There has been some additional scholarly analysis in this area. One law review article, published a number of years ago, suggested a number of factors that enter into determining whether action has been committed to agency discretion. These factors include:

- whether broad agency discretion already exists;

- the expertise and experience necessary to understand the subject matter;

- the managerial nature of the agency;

- the propriety of judicial intervention and the ability of a court to insure correct results;

- the need for informality and speed in agency decisions; and/or

- whether other controls on agency discretion exist.[33]

---

[30]   130 S. Ct. at 836.

[31]   *See, e.g.*, Kenneth Culp Davis, *Administrative Arbitrariness Is Not Always Reviewable*, 51 MINN. L. REV. 643 (1967).

[32]   LOUIS L. JAFFE, JUDICIAL CONTROL OF ADMINISTRATIVE ACTION 359 (1965).

[33]   Howard Saferstein, *Nonreviewability: A Functional Analysis of "Committed to Agency Discretion,"* 82 HARV. L. REV. 367 (1968).

Each of these factors has derived from a judicial decision on point, and the factors may be helpful in working through new fact patterns that raise a preclusion issue. However, most of the cases cited in this article are lower federal court cases that predate the truly important Supreme Court case law discussed below.

In *Overton Park*, the Supreme Court examined the committed-to-agency-discretion preclusion in light of the underlying statute. In that case, there were two applicable statutory provisions: (1) the Department of Transportation should consider alternatives to building the highway through the park and, (2) any decision to build through the park should include thorough planning to minimize environmental disruptions. After working through the *Abbott Labs* presumption in favor of review and looking closely at this statutory language, the Court concluded that there was "law to apply" and determined that the decision could be reviewed.[34]

The Court arrived at this conclusion in a commonsensical fashion. The notion of *committed to agency discretion* implies that the agency's decision making is completely unfettered — *i.e.*, that there is absolutely nothing limiting the agency except, perhaps, the good sense and judgment of the administrator. But here, while the statutory language was somewhat ambiguous, it did provide two factors that must be considered: (1) alternatives and (2) planning for minimal disruption. The statutory language suggested to the Court that there were some boundaries on agency discretion and that judicial review could be performed, at least to see whether the Secretary's decision satisfied these criteria. Presumably, if other statutes contain similar language, there will be law to apply and the action will not be precluded.

Complexity seems to be a principal reason for invoking the preclusion. One D.C. Circuit decision, *Curran v. Laird*,[35] reviewed a case involving the Cargo Preference Act-a statute requiring that American military cargo be shipped in American flagged vessels unless no such vessels are available. The court looked at everything the agency had to consider, simply to determine whether American flagged vessels were available, and just threw up its hands. The court concluded that the facts and problems faced by the agency in making the determination of availability were so multifaceted and complex that a court could not possibly perform meaningful review. Complexity also persuaded the First Circuit to invoke preclusion in *Hahn v. Gottlieb*,[36] a case involving certain agency decisions in the construction of low-income subsidized housing.

Of course, what appears to be impenetrable complexity to one court may be merely a challenging assignment to another court. The Department of Agriculture's Forest Service often grants permits to private individuals to use Forest Service lands for things such as access roads, pipeline rights-of-way and other non-governmental purposes. The Service's consideration of these land use permit applications involves analysis of a large number of different factors, ranging from the purpose of the use, the alternatives available to the private party, and the

---

[34] For a discussion of this concept, *see* Kenneth Culp Davis, *"No Law to Apply,"* 25 SAN DIEGO L. REV. 1 (1988).

[35] 420 F.2d 122 (D.C. Cir. 1969).

[36] 430 F.2d 1243 (1st Cir. 1970).

environmental consequences of permitting private usage. One federal circuit has held these decisions to be committed to agency discretion and thus not reviewable, while another circuit has held them subject to judicial review.[37] These two examples point up the occasional lack of consistency on the reviewability question, even when the courts are looking at precisely the same government program.

A pronouncement by the Supreme Court in *Webster v. Doe*[38] suggests that the Court may have a renewed interest in using the committed-to-agency-discretion exception to avoid unpopular causes of action. In *Webster*, an anonymous plaintiff who had been terminated from the Central Intelligence Agency (CIA) challenged the termination in court. There, the plaintiff argued that his dismissal exceeded the CIA's statutory authority and constituted an abuse of agency discretion. The plaintiff also raised a number of constitutional due process issues. In this instance, the Court quoted some very loose statutory language: an employee may be terminated whenever the CIA "shall deem such termination necessary or advisable in the interest of the United States." This language, in the Court's view, "fairly exudes deference to the [CIA] Director, and appears to us to foreclose the application of any meaningful judicial standard of review." At the same time, however, the Court held plaintiff's constitutional claims to be reviewable because there was no clear congressional intent to block review of constitutional issues. The effect of this holding is clear: a terminated employee may be able to challenge the *procedure* by which he was terminated (this is not yet clear in *Webster* because the case was remanded), but if the termination is procedurally correct, that final decision on the merits is precluded from judicial review.

Other sensitive factors may impinge on a court's decision not to review. For example, in *Department of Navy v. Egan*,[39] the Court considered the matter of revocation of a federal employee's security clearance. The considerations of national security, the multiplicity of complicated factors that enter into granting or denying (or revoking) a clearance and the plain fact that federal judges are simply not experts in intelligence or national security matters prompted the Court to hold that security clearance decisions are indisputably within the discretion of the agency charged with clearance responsibility. To be precise, the Court in *Egan* held that the Merit Systems Protection Board did not have the authority to substitute its opinion on a security clearance revocation for that of the appropriate agency, but the language pertaining to agency discretion is so clear and uncompromising that there is virtually no doubt that the same rule applies to reviewing courts.

At the same time, you should keep the *Webster* principle in mind. A court might be able to review a constitutional challenge to the procedures an agency followed in terminating a clearance, but it would not be able to review the merits of the decision to grant or deny the clearance.

---

[37] *Compare Ness Investment Corp. v. Dep't of Agriculture*, 512 F.2d 706 (9th Cir. 1975) (Forest Service land use permit decisions are committed to agency discretion), *with Sabin v. Butz*, 515 F.2d 1061 (10th Cir. 1975) (permits are reviewable).

[38] 486 U.S. 592 (1988). For a recent comment on *Webster* and a number of related issues, *see* Harel Arnon, *Legal Reasoning: Justifying Tolerance in the United States Supreme Court*, 2 N.Y.U. J.L. & LIBERTY 262 (2007).

[39] 484 U.S. 518 (1988).

All the cases discussed above have involved an affirmative decision on the part of a government agency. What happens when an agency simply refuses to act? Are those decisions committed to agency discretion and thereby not reviewable? The next subsection discusses this important topic.

[E] Discretion to Take No Agency Action

[1] Discretion Not To Make a Rule

Agencies sometimes refuse to promulgate rules even though they have been asked to do so by various private groups. Is such a refusal reviewable or is it committed to agency discretion under § 701 (a)(2)? Two panels of the D.C. Circuit writing only two years apart came to slightly different conclusions. In *Natural Resources Defense Council, Inc. v. SEC*,[40] the NRDC had petitioned the SEC to draft rules requiring publicly-held corporations to disclose to their shareholders and to the general public their environmental and equal employment opportunity policies. After considering the NRDC's request for *seven years*, the SEC finally denied the petition. The Natural Resources Defense Council filed suit, arguing that the agency's refusal to promulgate the rule was arbitrary and capricious.

The D.C. Circuit agreed. After working through the relevant case law and looking at the agency's record, the court noted that the SEC had spent seven years on the question, had held extensive proceedings and explained in detail why it was not going to adopt the rule. All of this activity made the actions reviewable in the very peculiar setting of the NRDC's petition for rulemaking. But the court took the trouble to state that its opinion should not be mistaken for a general principle that an agency's refusal to promulgate rules is a reviewable action. In another case, two years later, the D.C. Circuit held that the Federal Communications Commission's decision not to commence a rulemaking proceeding was reviewable on the *Jaffe* theory that agency discretion not to initiate rulemaking is at least reviewable for an abuse of that discretion.[41]

It is difficult to make much sense out of these two cases. More recent decisions of the D.C. Circuit suggest that the Circuit now believes that agency refusals to make a rule are not entitled to any presumption of non-reviewability.[42]

Recent signals sent by the Supreme Court (discussed below) in the context of an agency's refusal to take an enforcement action tell us that the current Supreme Court might not have spent too much time on either of these cases and might well have held that an agency has unreviewable discretion: (1) not to initiate rulemaking and (2) perhaps not to promulgate a rule after commencing the proceeding.

---

[40] 606 F.2d 1031 (D.C. Cir. 1979).

[41] *WWHT v. FCC*, 656 F.2d 807 (D.C. Cir. 1981).

[42] *See, e.g., Nat'l Customs Brokers v. United States*, 883 F.2d 93 (D.C. Cir. 1989); *Am. Horse Protection Ass'n v. Lyng*, 812 F.2d 1 (D.C. Cir. 1987).

[2]   Discretion Not to Take Enforcement Action

In 1975, the Supreme Court decided *Dunlop v. Bachowski*,[43] a case in which the Department of Labor had investigated alleged abuses in a union election and after the investigation, refused to pursue the matter further through the National Labor Relations Board. The Department defended its refusal on the basis of the agency's discretion not to take action. The Court held that the agency's refusal to act was reviewable, presumably, because a close look at the relevant statutes showed some factors that the agency was required to apply in deciding whether or not to take the case further. In other words, there was *law to apply* in the sense that the *Overton Park* decision used that term. Consequently, the decision not to take enforcement action was deemed judicially reviewable.

The *Dunlop* opinion lurked in the backwaters of Supreme Court case law for a number of years without causing much excitement. The situation changed dramatically in 1985 when the Court decided *Heckler v. Chaney.*[44] By any standard, *Chaney* has an unusual fact pattern. The case arose when death row prisoners in Texas and Oklahoma challenged the authority of prison officials to kill them with lethal injections. The prisoners' challenge was not brought on conventional cruel and unusual punishment or due process grounds, but rather on the ground that the chemical substances used in the lethal injections had not been approved for executions by the Food and Drug Administration. When the FDA refused to proceed with their complaint, the prisoners challenged the FDA in court. The FDA defended its actions, in part, on the ground that its refusal to take enforcement action was not reviewable, because it was committed to agency discretion under § 701(a)(2).

In a sweeping decision that clearly makes new law in this area, the Supreme Court agreed with the agency. With Justice Rehnquist writing a unanimous opinion, the Court held that agency refusals to pursue enforcement cases are not reviewable because they are committed to agency discretion. In reaching this conclusion, the Court distinguished *Dunlop* on the basis of the statutory provisions involved in that case that arguably placed some limits on totally unfettered agency discretion not to enforce.

But that is not the important part of *Chaney*. The Court went on to fashion a new analytical framework for this facet of committed-to-agency discretion.[45] Henceforth, the presumption to be applied in cases of agency refusals to pursue enforcement actions is just the opposite of the *Abbott Labs/Overton Park* presumption. An agency's refusal to take enforcement action is presumptively *not* reviewable. While concurring in the result in *Chaney*, Justice Marshall objected to the creation of this new presumption because he saw it as a device that might be used to swallow the entire *Overton Park* presumption and might permit the rapid

---

[43] 421 U.S. 560 (1975).

[44] 470 U.S. 821 (1985).

[45] *See, e.g.*, Daniel P. Selmi, *Jurisdiction to Review Agency Inaction Under Federal Environmental Law*, 72 IND. L.J. 65 (1996); Cass R. Sunstein, *Reviewing Agency Inaction After* Heckler v. Chaney, 52 U. CHI. L. REV. 653 (1985).

expansion of the § 701(a)(2) preclusion well beyond any limitations envisioned by the drafters of the APA.

All the ramifications of *Chaney* are difficult to parse. Probably to capture the votes of some of the other justices, Justice Rehnquist was careful to note that the preclusion itself "remains a narrow one." He also left the door open for Congress to change the result by legislation because *Dunlop* was not overruled and presumably remains good law. Thus, Congress may set aside *Chaney* anytime it wants to do so. That aspect of *Chaney* is not an unhealthy result. It is best for Congress to create statutory standards that permit judicial review if Congress believes judicial review to be a good thing.

Remember also, *Chaney* goes only to the initial decision whether to take action. A refusal to commence an enforcement action is not normally reviewable under *Chaney*. If, however, an agency proceeds with enforcement, the enforcement action itself will normally be subject to judicial review under the traditional standards discussed in this chapter and in Chapters 11 and 12.

A number of lower federal courts have addressed the *Chaney* presumption in the context of agency rulemaking and refused to apply it in that context.[46] However, the courts are enormously deferential to the agency even if they decide that the action is reviewable. Indeed, Judge Stephen Williams of the District of Columbia Circuit has noted that courts review an agency's determination not to initiate rulemaking "with a deference so broad as to make the process akin to [*Chaney*] non-reviewability."[47]

The Supreme Court has recently sent out some signals on review of agency inaction that are difficult to reconcile. In *Norton v. Southern Utah Wilderness Alliance*,[48] the plaintiffs, a public interest group, objected to the refusal of the Department of Interior's Bureau of Land Management to protect certain wilderness areas that the group asserted were being harmed by the use of off-road vehicles. Reviewing the claim under the APA[49] and the Wilderness Act,[50] the Court noted that such an action could proceed if and only if the plaintiffs could show that the agency failed to take a discrete agency action that it was required to take. In *Norton*, the Court concluded that there was no such requirement.

However, in *Massachusetts v. EPA*,[51] a significant case on a number of different levels, the Court examined the Environmental Protection Agency's failure to promulgate rules regulating greenhouse gas emissions from new motor vehicles under the Clean Air Act. In this instance, the Court ruled against EPA, noting that the EPA's refusal to promulgate rules was unacceptable: "EPA has offered no reasoned explanation for its refusal to decide whether greenhouse gases cause or

---

[46] *See, e.g., Am. Horse Prot. Ass'n v. Lyng*, 812 F.2d 1 (D.C. Cir. 1987).

[47] *Cellnet Communications, Inc. v. FCC*, 965 F.2d 1106, 1111 (D.C. Cir. 1992). For some recent *Chaney* scholarship, *see* Ashutosh Bhagwat, *Three-Branch Monte*, 72 NOTRE DAME L. REV. 157 (1996).

[48] 542 U.S. 55 (2004).

[49] 5 U.S.C. § 706(1).

[50] 43 U.S.C. § 1782(c).

[51] 549 U.S. 497 (2007).

contribute to climate change . . . We hold that EPA must ground its reasons for action or inaction in the statute."[52]

Parsing these two decisions is somewhat difficult. At bottom, it would seem that the Court viewed BLM's duties in Norton to be largely discretionary while viewing the EPA's duty to promulgate greenhouse gases as non-discretionary. Moreover, it would seem that the BLM was engaged in constant monitoring of the off-road usages in *Norton* while the EPA flatly refused to promulgate any kind of a rule in *Massachusetts v. EPA*.[53]

§ 10.06   STANDING

[A]   The Basic Concepts

Standing is a doctrine that springs from the case and controversy requirement set out in Article III, section 2 of the United States Constitution. The Supreme Court has always paid close attention to this limitation on the jurisdiction of federal courts because of the Court's long-standing belief that the Framers inserted the case and controversy requirement to insure that the courts spend their time only with disputes in which the litigants actually stand to lose or gain something from the case.

Keep in mind, as you read through this section, that the question of whether a plaintiff has standing to get into federal court is a proposition far different from the question of whether that same person might be permitted to participate in federal agency action. Participation in agency action is discussed separately in Chapter 8 so that no one confuses the two concepts. As we shall see, federal court standing poses a more difficult threshold burden.

When the Court is troubled by the subject matter of a dispute, it frequently looks at the case's justiciability in terms of whether it is moot, whether it involves a political question and whether the Court is being asked to give an advisory opinion. When the Court takes up a standing issue, it examines whether the persons bringing the lawsuit have what *Baker v. Carr*[54] called "a personal stake in the outcome." To a very large extent, the *Baker* test sets the bottom line for federal court standing. It is the minimum showing necessary for a plaintiff to survive a motion to dismiss for lack of standing.

---

[52] *Id.* at 534–35.

[53] For additional insights on these issues, *see, e.g.*, Jacob E. Gersen & Anne Joseph O'Connell, *Deadlines in Administrative Law*, 156 U. Pa. L. Rev. 923 (2008); Eric Biber, *Two Sides of the Same Coin: Judicial Review of Administrative Agency Action and Inaction*, 26 Va. Envt'l L.J. 461 (2008); Lisa S. Bressman, *Judicial Review of Agency Inaction: An Arbitrariness Approach*, 79 N.Y.U. L. Rev. 1657 (2004).

[54] 369 U.S. 186 (1962).

[B]   The Early Cases

Baker v. Carr is now one of the fundamental cases on federal court standing, but the basic principles articulated in *Baker* had been consistently invoked by the Supreme Court long before *Baker* was decided. The first level of analysis in any standing inquiry is simply to determine whether the plaintiff was really hurt. For example, a few years before *Baker*, the Court was able to conclude that the Department of Justice's inclusion of an organization's name on a list of subversive organizations could arguably injure that organization's reputation. Permitting a publicly-owned power project to sell electricity to customers of a privately-owned utility will arguably cause out-of-pocket financial losses (and thus *injury*) for the private utility. Frequently, the Court simply assumed injury and went on to discuss the merits of the case.

In a few early cases, the Court took the analysis to another level. In these cases, the vocabulary is slightly different from *Baker*, but the gist of the Court's reasoning is the same. In cases such as *Joint Anti-Fascist Refugee Committee v. McGrath*[55] (the listing of an organization as subversive) and *Perkins v. Lukens Steel Co.*[56] (financial losses for a private utility), the Court discussed whether the plaintiffs had a *legal interest* or a *legally protected right* in the dispute. The Court recognized that such interests could flow from a federal program established by statute (*Perkins*),[57] the Constitution (*Baker*) or the common law (*McGrath*).

Congress occasionally becomes involved by writing statutory standing provisions. For example, § 702 of the APA provides that "[a] person suffering legal wrong because of agency action, or adversely affected or aggrieved by agency action within the meaning of a relevant statute, is entitled to seek judicial review thereof." Congress has also written standing requirements in a number of enabling acts. A typical provision in a number of environmental protection statutes limits standing to bring pre-enforcement challenges to agency rules *solely* to persons who have participated in the *agency's* rulemaking for the rule that they are attempting to challenge in court.[58] Although the federal courts have never considered themselves absolutely bound by Congress' idea of who ought to have standing, they tend, by and large, to defer to Congressional pronouncements, even when those pronouncements concern who may come into federal court.[59]

These early cases seem to be both plausible and rational. While the Court looked closely at standing and while it took the doctrine very seriously, there is little evidence that the Court agonized over the doctrine. Nonetheless, it is clear that the Court was less than happy about the way the test for standing was formulated. Determining whether a person has a legal interest in a dispute is sometimes a very fuzzy matter. Moreover, because the doctrine of standing evolved on a case-by-case

---

[55] 341 U.S. 123 (1951).

[56] 310 U.S. 113 (1940).

[57] *See also Hardin v. Kentucky Utilities Co.*, 390 U.S. 1 (1968).

[58] *See, e.g.*, the Clean Air Act, 42 U.S.C. § 7607 (1990).

[59] *Associated Indus. of New York State, Inc. v. Ickes*, 134 F.2d 694 (2d Cir. 1943) (consumers of coal were "persons aggrieved" as defined in the statute and had standing to challenge certain actions of the Department of the Interior relating to the coal industry).

basis, it was frequently difficult to harmonize the case law. This dissatisfaction set the stage for the landmark 1970 decisions on standing to challenge agency action.

[C] The *Data Processing* Test

The Court's current test for standing to challenge agency action was first articulated in two cases decided the same day in 1970, *Association of Data Processing Service Organizations v. Camp*,[60] and *Barlow v. Collins*.[61] Neither of the two cases is factually complicated. *Data Processing* began when companies that sold data processing services challenged regulations issued by the Comptroller of the Currency that permitted banks to begin selling these services. The data processing companies asserted that they would lose money if banks got into this business and that the Comptroller's new rules violated the Bank Service Corporation Act of 1962.[62] The plaintiffs in *Barlow* were tenant farmers who alleged pocketbook injury stemming from regulations of the Department of Agriculture that affected the farmers' subsidy payments. The farmers argued that the new rules exceeded the department's jurisdiction.

Justice Douglas, writing both majority opinions, noted the Court's dissatisfaction with the legal injury test. In his view, it was difficult to apply and, more importantly, tended to go to the merits of the controversy when a standing analysis-being a threshold determination-should only examine the plaintiff's allegations of injury. Douglas then substituted a two-part test for the older analysis, but without overruling any previous cases.

The *Data Processing* test is relatively simple to state: In order to get into federal court to challenge federal agency action[63] the plaintiff must allege that:

1. the defendant's acts have caused plaintiff personal injury in fact-economic or otherwise; *and*

2. the plaintiff is arguably within the zone of interests to be protected by the statute or constitutional provision in question.

Note the three major elements of the test. First, it incorporates the *Baker* personal injury requirement while adding some curious language at the end: "economic or otherwise" — a phrase that is pure dicta in *Data Processing* and *Barlow* because both cases alleged only financial injury. Second, the test is stated in the conjunctive. Both parts one and two must be satisfied before a plaintiff may remain in court for a decision on the merits. Third, the *Data Processing* test adds the concept of "zone of interest" (discussed more fully below) to the basic injury in fact concept set out in *Baker v. Carr.*

---

[60] 397 U.S. 150 (1970).

[61] 397 U.S. 159 (1970).

[62] 12 U.S.C. § 1864 (1962). The Act provides: "No bank service corporation may engage in any activity other than the performance of bank services for banks."

[63] Note carefully that this is a test for challenges to federal agency action. The more elementary "personal stake in the outcome" test governs challenges to state administrative agencies brought in federal court.

Most of the other members of the Court agreed with this new formulation, although Justice Brennan, who had written the majority opinion in *Baker*, argued that grafting the second part of the test (zone of interest) onto the personal injury requirement stated in *Baker* came too close to forcing the plaintiff to try his or her entire case on the merits in the context of a preliminary motion to dismiss for lack of standing. In other words, Brennan believed that there was precious little difference between zone of interest and legal interest and that both were inappropriate and unworkable concepts. But the proof of the pudding is in the eating. The Court has refined the application of *Data Processing* for the last several years while never suggesting that there is anything fundamentally wrong with the two-part test itself.

[D] The Post-*Data Processing* Refinements-The Journey from *Sierra Club to Valley Forge*

When *Data Processing* was first published, a number of environmental organizations immediately picked up on that interesting and then-unnecessary language in Douglas' opinion, "economic or otherwise." The environmental movement was, at that point in time, building up considerable momentum, and there had been many articles wondering if normal standing requirements might be somehow relaxed when a dispute involved environmental injury that arguably affected large numbers of people. In other words, as one law review article put it, "should trees have standing?"[64]

Two years after *Data Processing*, the Supreme Court said "no." In that case, the Sierra Club brought an action challenging the decision of the Department of the Interior to allow construction of a commercial resort in the Mineral King Valley of the Sequoia National Forest. The club steadfastly refused to allege personal injury and instead argued that environmental lawsuits should have a standing test of their own. In a 5-4 decision, *Sierra Club v. Morton*,[65] the Court disagreed, holding that an allegation of personal injury to at least one member of the Sierra Club was indispensable to pursuing a federal court lawsuit.[66]

No one takes a chance on this any longer. Some law students at George Washington University, carrying out a project in their administrative law course, set up an organization called "Students Challenging Regulatory Agency Procedures" (SCRAP) to challenge certain rate making policies of the Interstate Commerce Commission. Their allegations, while somewhat "attenuated" (in the parlance of the Supreme Court), went something like this: (1) we are law students in the Washington metropolitan area who like to walk in the public parks in the D.C. metropolitan area; (2) when we walk in the parks we see discarded cans and bottles all over the place; (3) seeing this trash offends our sense of aesthetics (recall: personal injury in fact, economic *or otherwise*); (4) the reason this trash is

---

[64] Christopher D. Stone, *Should Trees Have Standing? Toward Legal Rights for Natural Objects*, 45 S. CAL. L. REV. 450 (1972).

[65] 405 U.S. 727 (1972).

[66] The right of an organization to stand up for the rights of its injured members-so long as at least one member is injured-has long since been settled. *See, e.g., NAACP v. Button*, 371 U.S. 415 (1963).

not picked up is because it is not economically feasible to do so; (5) the reason it is not economically feasible to do so is because the defendant, ICC, has approved freight rates for recycled goods that are excessively high (remember: the allegations of injury must be directly traceable to the defendant).

Of course, these allegations go only to Part One of *Data Processing.* How about Part Two? Here, everyone needs to know a little environmental law. The National Environmental Policy Act of 1969 (NEPA)[67] requires any federal agency engaged in major federal action significantly affecting the quality of the human environment to prepare an environmental impact statement (EIS) prior to taking the action. To explain this in the acronym — speak that substitutes for civilized conversation in Washington: SCRAP alleged that the ICC had not promulgated an EIS. Thus, the Commission's recycled goods rate structure was invalid. NEPA is the statute whose zone of interest arguably protected the SCRAP plaintiffs. In *United States v. SCRAP*,[68] without reaching the merits of the case, the Supreme Court agreed that the plaintiffs had made sufficient allegations in the complaint to accommodate both parts of *Data Processing.*

Still, no one should make too much of the *SCRAP* case. After reading the next several cases, it's entirely reasonable to conclude that there is very little left of *SCRAP*, even though the decision itself has never been overruled. Standing is normally disposed of as a pretrial motion in which the allegations stated in the complaint are taken as true for the purposes of the motion. This means that there must be sufficient facts alleged in the complaint to satisfy all the relevant requirements of the *Data Processing* test. *SCRAP* shows how these allegations can be framed to meet the standing issue.

An analysis of the "law" of standing can't stop with *SCRAP*, however. *SCRAP* is probably the most extreme decision in this area; and the Court seems to be tightening up considerably on the application of the standing test. This tightening-up effect is evidenced by a number of recent cases.

In *Simon v. Eastern Kentucky Welfare Rights Organization*,[69] indigent plaintiffs and a number of welfare organizations challenged the issuance of an Internal Revenue Service Revenue Ruling that, in their view, caused private hospitals to stop providing free medical care for indigents. The Supreme Court carefully scrutinized the standing allegations and determined that there was simply no possible way the allegations of injury ("we are not getting free medical care") were directly traceable to *any* actions of the defendant, the Department of the Treasury (of which the IRS is a component). The Court decided against the plaintiffs without even reaching Part Two of *Data Processing.*

Some people regard *Simon* as a case that simply showed the hostility of the Court to welfare cases; but smart lawyers should look at it in less ideological terms because it contains some important messages on the issue of standing. First, the Court looked at the allegations of the welfare rights organizations and reiterated

---

[67] 42 U.S.C. §§ 4331 *et seq.* (1969).

[68] 412 U.S. 669 (1973).

[69] 426 U.S. 26 (1976).

the holding of *Sierra Club* that mere abstract concerns do not substitute for the concrete personal injury required of federal court plaintiffs. The indigent plaintiffs' allegations did not survive because the Court was unwilling to conclude that any of the actions taken by the defendant IRS could plausibly have caused plaintiffs' injury. In other words, there may be a multiplicity of reasons why particular hospitals stop treating poor people for free. There was no showing here-and, hinted the Court, there probably could be no such showing-that anything the IRS did led directly to the denial of this medical care.

For practicing lawyers, *Simon* has an important message: your complaint must contain allegations that plausibly and directly connect your client's injuries to the actions of the defendant. Without such allegations, the complaint will be dismissed.[70]

A reading of the standing cases clearly indicates that plaintiffs must allege injury that is either actual or imminent. But what happens when a client wants to challenge the constitutionality of a federal statute setting an upper limit on damages flowing from a single nuclear power plant incident? There is such a statute; it's called the Price-Anderson Act,[71] and it caps monetary recovery at approximately $600 million. The case in which the constitutional attack was made is *Duke Power Co. v. Carolina Environmental Study Group*,[72] in which the Supreme Court quickly granted standing to the plaintiffs and then went on to hold the Price-Anderson Act constitutional.

Applying conventional standing reasoning to *Duke Power*, it is arguable that no one can have standing to challenge Price-Anderson until a nuclear incident actually occurs.[73] In other words, a limit upon tort damages following a nuclear accident cannot confer injury in fact until at least one person is actually hurt by that accident. But the Court may have looked beyond the record to take a kind of judicial notice of the fact that if the Price-Anderson Act were subject to any question, the nuclear power industry would encounter great difficulty raising money to maintain and operate nuclear power plants. To cope with this problem, the Court decided to focus on the activities surrounding the construction of the plant (these are massive facilities whose construction causes considerable environmental disruption, even if the disruptions are not necessarily permanent). The injury caused to persons in the neighborhood from plant construction, in the

---

[70] For a case in which the Court decided that none of the plaintiffs alleged sufficient personal injury, *see Warth v. Seldin*, 422 U.S. 490 (1975). The *Warth* plaintiffs were challenging a local zoning ordinance in Rochester, New York that they claimed had a disparate impact on racial minorities. But in a very curious turnabout just two years later, the Court granted standing on almost the same facts to a black man who said he had tried to buy housing in the exclusive area and would have done so but for the ordinance which eliminated low-cost housing. In that case, *Village of Arlington Heights v. Metro. Hous. Dev. Corp.*, 429 U.S. 252 (1977), the Court brushed past the issue of standing, jumped quickly into the merits of the case and held that persons charging racial discrimination in this setting must show an intent to discriminate.

[71] 42 U.S.C. § 2012(i).

[72] 438 U.S. 59 (1978).

[73] For example, if a Price-Anderson Act had been in place in the former Soviet Union, those persons injured at Chernobyl would clearly have standing to challenge the act.

Court's view, is sufficient injury to provide standing to challenge the Act itself, even if no nuclear incident has occurred.

In *Duke Power*, the Court treated standing gently, perhaps because it wanted to reach the merits quickly and to uphold the Act. However, the Court can, when it wants to do so, hold plaintiffs to enormously stringent standing requirements. One recent standing case, *Valley Forge Christian College v. Americans United for Separation of Church and State, Inc.*,[74] offers a useful compendium of recent standing decisions and provides a good example of how tough the Court can be on this issue. The plaintiffs alleged that the giving of surplus federal property to a church-related school violated the First Amendment's Establishment Clause.

Valley Forge stands for the proposition that when persons try to challenge agency action with allegations of injury only as taxpayers or as citizens of the United States, they face an almost insuperable task. The taxpayer standing aspects of *Valley Forge* will be discussed below. For our purposes here, note that the Court states expressly that the injury alleged must be personal and must be more than that suffered by every other citizen in the country. The mere fact that this organization has an interest in church-state affairs, or that some of the organization's members pay taxes, is not enough.

In *Block v. Community Nutrition Inst.*,[75] the Court refused to grant standing to consumers of milk products who wanted to challenge payments of milk subsidies to dairy farmers by the Department of Agriculture. The Court used the wholly inappropriate label, "preclusion," to describe the case; but there can be no mistaking *Community Nutrition*'s message: the Supreme Court may examine standing very closely when it chooses to address the issue directly. In *Allen v. Wright*,[76] the Court denied standing to parents of black public school children who challenged the IRS for its failure to develop appropriate standards for delaying tax-exempt status to private schools that discriminate on the basis of race. Using much the same approach as in *Simon*, the Court ruled that the parents could not come into court simply as persons generally interested in enforcing the laws and, more importantly, they had not alleged sufficient personal injury to bring them within *Data Processing*.

[E]   Tightening Standing: The Contributions of *Lujan*, *Clarke* and *Air Courier*

Supreme Court watchers now have a good sense of the considerable impact of Justice Scalia on the administrative law decisions of the Court. Justice Scalia wrote the opinion for the Court in an important recent standing case, *Lujan v. National Wildlife Federation*,[77] that may have sounded the death knell for *SCRAP*, even though the opinion did not expressly overrule *SCRAP*. In *Lujan*, an environmental group sued the Department of the Interior over agency action involving the

---

[74] 454 U.S. 464 (1982).

[75] 467 U.S. 340 (1984).

[76] 468 U.S. 737 (1984).

[77] 504 U.S. 555 (1992).

reclassification of certain federal lands. The functional effect of the reclassification was to open up a large amount of territory to commercial development, including mining operations. The National Wildlife Federation argued that, in doing so, Interior had violated both the National Environmental Policy Act (NEPA, the same statute at issue in *SCRAP*), some of the procedural requirements of the APA and a number of related federal land use statutes. The total number of reclassifications at issue in the lawsuit was 1250.

The Wildlife Federation tried to establish standing by filing two affidavits from Federation members who stated that they had visited locations in the vicinity of two of the reclassified areas for the purpose of recreation and aesthetic enjoyment, and that their aesthetic enjoyment had been adversely affected by the reclassification.

At this point, the procedural posture of the case becomes important. The government moved, in federal district court, for summary judgment. The district court granted summary judgment on the basis that the injured party's affidavit, alleging only visits in "the vicinity" of a single challenged land area, was insufficiently precise. As the district court put it: "The affidavit on its face contains only a bare allegation of injury, and fails to show specific facts supporting the affiant's allegation." The D.C. Circuit, however, overturned the grant of summary judgment. The effect of the D.C. Circuit's reversal was to suspend the entire reclassification program for over two years.

When *Lujan* finally reached the Supreme Court, the Court first looked at the sufficiency of the affidavit and found it sorely lacking. The Court distinguished *SCRAP* from *Lujan* by noting that *SCRAP* was a case involving a motion to dismiss on the pleadings while *Lujan* was a summary judgment matter. A motion to dismiss on the pleadings may consider nothing other than the face of the pleadings themselves. By contrast, in a summary judgment evaluation, the court may consider the facts and arguments presented by both parties and virtually all other information in the record and then it must grant summary judgment unless the party opposed to the summary judgment can point to specific-and controverted-facts that require a finding in its favor. In other words, in a summary judgment motion, the Court may look at everything, not just the face of the complaint and answer.

On the question of the sufficiency of the affidavit, the Court determined that the bare bones allegations were not sufficient. The requirements are

> assuredly not satisfied by averments which state only that one of respondent's members uses unspecified portions of an immense tract of territory, on some portions of which mining activity has occurred or probably will occur by virtue of the governmental action. It will not do to 'presume' the missing facts because without them the affidavits would not establish the injury that they generally allege.

But the Court did not stop there, even though the case could have been remanded solely on this basis. The Court next addressed the Federation's attack on the entirety of the reclassification program and concluded that there could be virtually no allegations of injury that would give the Federation standing to challenge the program as a whole. For one reason, the reclassification program is not a single, unified program, but rather constitutes a label that the Federation developed to describe large numbers of individual reclassification decisions under a myriad of Interior regulations. Beyond this, even to the extent that there is a reclassification "program," the Court determined that agency action is not complete and that the *final* agency action required to confer jurisdiction on the federal courts does not exist.

The sharp distinction Justice Scalia drew between the procedural posture of *SCRAP* and *Lujan* (*i.e.*, between a judgment on the pleadings and summary judgment) probably should not carry this much weight. A better explanation is that there are probably one or two justices left on the Court who want to keep what's left of *SCRAP.* The procedural distinctions may have been the price Justice Scalia had to pay for the votes of these justices in *Lujan.* There is no doubt that the Court is somewhat hostile to these broad attacks on large-scale federal programs by environmental groups. But on the other side of the coin, one senses an ill-advised hubris on the part of the environmentalists-an attitude that all they have to do is to make a minimalist presentation on actual injury in order to litigate the validity of an entire program. The current Supreme Court is having none of that.

Another Supreme Court decision permitted the plaintiffs to bring a law suit against the Federal Election Commission essentially to force the FEC to make public disclosure of information filed by a group that the plaintiffs alleged had violated the underlying statute. In *FEC v. Akins,*[78] the Court granted standing to the plaintiffs, reasoning that the "injury in fact" that the plaintiffs suffered "consists of their inability to obtain information." In the Court majority's view, this is not a mere generalized grievance widely shared with other members of the general public, but rather is an injury that directly relates "to voting, the most basic of political rights [and] is sufficiently concrete and specific" to permit judicial action.

In addition to scrutinizing much more closely the allegations of injury, the current Supreme Court has shown an interest in elaborating on the second part of *Data Processing,* namely the *zone of interest* test. In *Clarke v. Securities Industry Ass'n,*[79] the Court granted certiorari to review a case in which an association of securities dealers sued the Comptroller of the Currency. The association was, in essence, testing the jurisdictional limitations of the comptroller in a setting in which the comptroller permitted two national banks to sell discount brokerage services. The more technical legal argument was a matter of statutory construction. The relevant statute defined a bank's branch as a place where "deposits are received, . . . checks paid, or money lent." The statute says nothing about permission to sell stock, but the comptroller had nonetheless permitted the activity by claiming that the discount brokerage offices were not "branches" under the statute.

The Supreme Court dealt with the matter in terms of the standing issues. Personal injury was essentially conceded. There is no doubt that competitive harm would ensue to the securities dealers if banks were permitted to open discount sales offices. However, the zone of interest analysis proved somewhat more troublesome.

---

[78] 524 U.S. 11 (1998).

[79] 479 U.S. 388 (1987).

The Court began its analysis by citing and discussing *Block v. Community Nutrition Institute*, the case discussed above that uses the terminology of "preclusion of review" but reaches all of its conclusions on the basis of a somewhat surreptitious standing discussion. In *Community Nutrition*, the Court determined that while sellers of milk may be within the zone of interest of the milk market order program, consumers of milk are not.

In *Clarke*, the Court seemed to be searching for a refinement of that very elusive zone of interest concept by commenting:

> In cases where the plaintiff is not itself the subject of the contested regulatory action, the [zone of interest test] denies a right of review if the plaintiff's interests are so marginally related to or inconsistent with the purposes implicit in the statute that it cannot reasonably be assumed that Congress intended to permit the suit. The test is not meant to be especially demanding; in particular, there need be no indication of congressional purpose to benefit the would-be plaintiff.

Perhaps what the Court has given us is merely a lengthier formulation of the test: zone of interest does not extend to plaintiffs who are (1) only *marginally related* to the statute, or (2) whose interests are *inconsistent with* the statute's purposes. But at the same time, a plaintiff does not have to be an expressly intended beneficiary of the statutory scheme.

This analysis is helpful, but just paragraphs later in *Clarke*, the Court seems to adopt an *additional test* for those plaintiffs who survive the zone of interest analysis. The Court's own words are vitally important here:

> The inquiry into reviewability does not end with the "zone of interest" test. In *Community Nutrition Institute*, the interests of consumers were arguably within the zone of interests meant to be protected by the Act, but the Court found that point not dispositive, because at bottom the reviewability question turns on congressional intent, and all indicators helpful in discerning that intent must be weighed.

Overall, the Court's analysis is both troubling and unclear. Several things are apparent, however. First, the Court now seems to regard *Community Nutrition* as a major standing case, even though, either deliberately or unintentionally, it blurred the standing discussion in that opinion with an overuse of the term "preclusion." As noted in the preceding section, the Court may be using the term "preclusion" simply as a generic term for many different types of barriers to judicial review. Second, the combination of *Clarke* and *Community Nutrition* suggests that a federal court is now free to deny judicial review even if a plaintiff survives the two-part *Data Processing* test, so long as it perceives some vague, amorphous congressional intent beyond everything else already reviewed that suggests that the plaintiffs shouldn't be allowed in court. Third, beyond making the quoted statement, *Clarke* does not help much because the securities dealers were ultimately granted standing, although the decision of the comptroller was affirmed on the merits. To be completely fair to the Court, the remainder of the standing discussion in *Clarke* does involve examination of the intent of Congress in restricting and narrowly defining branch banking. The Court seems to conclude that these express limitations on the activities of banks suggest that securities dealers should be able to be heard when the activities of banks encroach on their own activities.

There is another possible analysis. In a separate plurality opinion in *Warth v. Seldin* (discussed above), Justice Blackmun suggested that in some cases standing may turn on what he termed *prudential considerations*. Justice Blackmun's opinion in *Warth* went on to suggest that, even if a plaintiff survives both parts of *Data Processing*, "prudential considerations" may still warrant a dismissal for lack of standing. Some members of the Court seem to have a renewed interest in this concept because in footnote 16 in *Clarke*, the Court hints that *Data Processing* may not be all that strict a standard for judging access to federal court. In footnote 16, the Court comments: "We have occasionally listed the 'zone of interest' inquiry among general prudential considerations bearing on standing . . . ." If this is the case, *zone of interest* is arguably only one of perhaps many inquiries that can be used to determine standing.

That does not mean, of course, that the Court will not place considerable weight on zone of interest when it chooses to do so. In a 1991 decision, *Air Courier Conference v. American Postal Workers Union*,[80] union members challenged an action by the U.S. Postal Service that permitted private couriers to deliver letters to government postal services in other countries. The effect of this action is to take what had been a monopoly out of the hands of the postal service-which would in turn lose business which would in turn result in the cutting back of postal service employees. Once again, the Court was willing to accept injury in fact, but denied standing on the basis of a zone of interest analysis. Briefly stated, the Court was simply unwilling to concede that the relevant statute-and the reformulation of that statute in a new Congressional enactment-gave any protection whatsoever to the postal workers. *Air Courier* uses much of the same language as *Clarke*.

Thus, we see a fascinating tension emerging on the Court. In his separate opinion attached to the *Data Processing/Barlow* opinions, Justice Brennan objected to the zone of interest test as going too far because it essentially forces a plaintiff to try the merits of his or her case during the standing inquiry. Now, some members of the Court seem to suggest that zone of interest is not going far enough-that the courts should be given additional grounds (*prudential considerations*) to deny standing, even when plaintiffs meet the traditional requirements. This muddle is deepened further by the suggestions, in an article by Justice O'Connor,[81] that standing is a component of separation of powers doctrine. If standing is a constitutional concept, her analysis then leads to the question of whether constitutional matters can ever be disposed of on the basis of a prudential considerations analysis. In other words,

---

[80] 498 U.S. 517 (1991).

[81] Sandra Day O'Connor, *Reflections on Preclusion of Judicial Review in England and the United States*, 27 WM. & MARY L. REV. 643, 658 (1986); Sidney A. Shapiro, United Church of Christ v. FCC: *Private Attorneys General and the Rule of Law*, 58 ADMIN. L. REV. 939 (2006). For a much different viewpoint, see Robert A. Anthony, *Zone-Free Standing for Private Attorneys General*, 7 GEO. MASON L. REV. 237 (1999). There is increasing worry among legal scholars that the standing doctrine, once seen as a purely legal issue is now turning on the political persuasions of various federal judges. *See generally* Richard J. Pierce, *Is Standing Law or Politics?*, 77 N.C.L. REV. 1741 (1999). For a recent Supreme Court case involving the zone of interest test, see *National Credit Union Administration v. First Nat'l Bank and Trust*, 522 U.S. 479 (1998).

if the Constitution grants a person the right to be in court if he can show personal injury, do federal courts have the additional "discretion" to keep him out? One would think not.

The Supreme Court continues to decide standing cases, many of which are difficult to harmonize. In *Summers v. Earth Island Institute*,[82] a private group devoted to environmental protection filed suit in federal court against the United States Forest Service to prevent the Forest Service from enforcing rules that created exemptions for small fire-rehabilitation and timber-salvage projects from the standard notice, comment and intra-agency appeal procedures that the Forest Service used for large-scale land management decisions.

While conceding that an association such as the Earth Island Institute had the right to assert the legal interests of its individual members (citing *Sierra Club v. Morton, supra*), the Court looked closely at the individual affidavits (alleging specific personal harm) and could not discern any concrete, specific injury that any of the affiants would suffer based on the Forest Service's exemptions, mainly because the affiants had essentially settled their grievances with the Forest Service. Writing for the majority, Justice Scalia noted: "We know of no precedent for the proposition that when a plaintiff has sued to challenge the lawfulness of certain action or threatened action but has settled that suit, he retains standing to challenge the basis for that action . . . in the abstract, apart from any concrete application that threatens imminent harm to his interests."[83]

Viewing standing a bit differently in a subsequent case, the Court granted standing to the plaintiffs in an opinion that was fraught with dissent on both standing and merits grounds. The plaintiffs in *Salazar v. Buono*,[84] invoked the Establishment Clause to challenge the erection of a Latin cross on Sunrise Rock in the Mojave National Preserve — a federal enclave in California. The cross had been erected by private citizens in 1934 as part of a memorial to American soldiers who were killed in World War One. While the initial lawsuit was moving through the federal courts, Congress entered the fray by enacting a land-transfer statute that authorized the transfer of this plot of land to a private group, The Veterans of Foreign Wars, in exchange for other lands in the Preserve on which no cross existed.

A deeply divided Court ultimately concluded that Mr. Buono had standing, but strangely did not invoke the three-part Lujan analysis. Instead, three justices (Justice Kennedy, Chief Justice Roberts and Justice Alito) articulated a test that seems to go back to *Baker v. Carr, supra*: "[T]o demonstrate standing, a plaintiff must have alleged such a personal stake in the outcome of the controversy as to warrant his invocation of federal court jurisdiction." However, there was a serious issue as to exactly what Mr. Buono was objecting to. At one point the three justices commented: "Buono does not find the cross itself objectionable but instead takes offense at the presence of a religious symbol on Federal land. Buono does not claim

---

[82] 555 U.S. 488 (2009).

[83] *Id.* at 494.

[84] 130 S. Ct. 1803 (2010)

that, as a personal matter, he has been made to feel excluded or coerced."[85] But if that was the case, the reader of this book might plausibly ask: "Where is the concrete injury"? Justice Kennedy (writing for himself, Roberts and Alito) seems to have ducked this central question by prohibiting the Government from asserting Buono's lack of standing because the Government had not, in earlier proceedings, sought review of Buono's standing. By contrast, Justices Scalia and Thomas would have dismissed the case because, in their view, Buono did not have standing to pursue his arguments relating to the injunction granted below. If the readers of this book are somewhat confused, you're in good company. It is entirely possible that the Buono case should be restricted to its facts and not regarded as any kind of shift in the Supreme Court's creation and application of its traditional standing principles.

This last assertion may have been confirmed by an even more recent case, *Bond v. United States*,[86] that granted standing to a plaintiff who challenged the criminal statute under which she was indicted on Tenth Amendment grounds. In *Bond*, the plaintiff entered a conditional plea of guilty to various violations of the Chemical Weapons Convention Implementation Act of 1998.[87] The lower court, the United States Court of Appeals for the Third Circuit, denied her standing to bring any challenge to this statute on Tenth Amendment grounds because she herself was not a state, and the Tenth Amendment relates only to powers reserved to states, not to individuals. In this instance, the Supreme Court was unanimous in granting her standing by simply applying Lujan and concluding: (1) injury-in-fact is present here because of her prospective incarceration; (2) she alleges that she will be incarcerated under an unconstitutional statute; and (3) a federal court can grant a full remedy by holding the statute unconstitutional.

On the troublesome issue of whether Ms. Bond could invoke the Tenth Amendment as the basis for her argument against the statute, the Court elaborated: "[The Tenth Amendment and related concepts of federalism] protects the liberty of all persons within a State by ensuring that laws enacted in excess of delegated governmental power cannot direct or control their actions . . . The limitations that federalism entails are not therefore a matter of rights belonging only to the States. States are not the sole intended beneficiaries of federalism. An individual has a direct interest in objecting to laws that upset the constitutional balance between the National Government and the States when the enforcement of those laws causes injury that is concrete, particular, and redressable."[88]

[F]   Taxpayer Standing

For years, the Supreme Court simply refused to grant standing to persons who sought to challenge government action merely on the basis that their tax dollars were being somehow misspent.[89] However, the Court altered its approach

---

[85] *Id.* at 1814.

[86] 131 S. Ct. 2355 (2011).

[87] 18 U.S.C. § 229.

[88] 131 S. Ct. at 2364.

[89] *See Frothingham v. Mellon*, 262 U.S. 447 (1923).

somewhat in *Flast v. Cohen*,[90] a 1968 case involving an attack on certain Department of Health, Education and Welfare (HEW) payments to religious schools. (HEW was later split into two different cabinet level departments: Health and Human Services and Education). The plaintiffs attacked the expenditures under the First Amendment's Establishment Clause, but the only injury they could allege involved their status as taxpayers and the expenditure of funds created from tax revenues.

In *Flast*, the Court articulated a two-part test that opens the window of taxpayer standing only slightly-taxpayer plaintiffs must allege: (1) a connection between status as taxpayers and the legislation attacked (*i.e.*, the legislation must spend tax dollars), and (2) a connection between their status as taxpayers and the constitutional infringement alleged (*i.e.*, that an absolute prohibition on the expenditure of tax dollars, such as the Establishment Clause, is being violated). The *Flast* plaintiffs satisfied both parts of this test.

Since *Flast*, however, the Court has been scrupulously careful to restrict the test to *Flast*-type facts. For example, taxpayer challenges to Vietnam War expenditures were rejected in 1974.[91]

As noted earlier, the *Valley Forge* decision prohibited taxpayer/citizens from challenging, on the basis of the Establishment Clause, the validity of the government's giving surplus federal government property to a religious school; first, because of some qualms the Court had about the true extent of personal injury suffered by the plaintiffs; and second, because the plaintiffs as taxpayers did not meet the first part of the *Flast* test. The Court determined that disposal of surplus property is not an exercise of congressional power, but rather the exercise of agency power (but Congress establishes the agencies, does it not?), and the actual disposal of the property is made under the Property Clause in Article I of the Constitution rather than the Spending and Taxation Clause in Article I (the clause at issue in *Flast*). Irrespective of anyone's views on the First Amendment, *Valley Forge* stands for the clear principle that if the only injury a person can allege is his status as taxpayer or citizen, he is not likely to get into federal court.

In 2011, the Supreme Court once again addressed taxpayer standing and concluded that the taxpayers lacked standing to go forward with their federal court lawsuit. In *Arizona Christian School Tuition Organization v. Winn*,[92] a number of Arizona taxpayers objected to the state's granting of tax credits for the support of "school tuition organizations." While a somewhat complex topic, these school tuition organizations funded scholarships for Arizona students to attend private schools, including schools that were created and operated by religious organizations. The plaintiff-taxpayers objected to this action as a violation of the Establishment Clause and invoked basic standing principles and the special rule of *Flast v. Cohen* as the basis for their standing to sue.

---

[90] 392 U.S. 83 (1968).

[91] *United States v. Richardson*, 418 U.S. 166 (1974); *Schlesinger v. Reservists*, 418 U.S. 208 (1974).

[92] 131 S. Ct. 1436 (2011).

In a 5-4 decision, the Court majority applied both the *Lujan* three-part standing test and *Flast*. Under *Lujan*, the Court noted that mere status as a taxpayer is normally not sufficient for standing. Moreover, the majority was unwilling to discern any palpable, specific injury to the State of Arizona due to the program. Further, merely because the State permitted the tax credits, there appeared to be no showing that the taxpayers themselves would have their individual state tax liabilities increased. In rejecting the argument that standing was conferred under the Establishment Clause exception in *Flast*, the Court discerned a significant difference between the tax credits at issue here and specific government *expenditures* that were at issue in *Flast*. The Court commented that: "When the government declines to impose a tax . . . there is no such connection between dissenting taxpayers and alleged [acts in violation of the Establishment Clause.]" As the Court pointed out, "any financial injury remains speculative."[93] Notably, two Justices in the majority, Justices Scalia and Thomas, would have overruled *Flast* in its entirety.

[G] Third-party Standing

May one person assert the rights of another person in federal court? Usually, the answer is no; but in a few limited circumstances the Court has permitted-or suggested-that it might permit the assertion of one person's rights by another. In *Craig v. Boren*,[94] the Court permitted a bar owner to assert the rights of young men in Oklahoma between the ages of 18 and 21 to drink beer containing 3.2% alcohol. Under an Oklahoma statute, women over 18 were permitted to buy the beer; men had to be 21. Reaching the merits, the Court decided that this was an impermissible gender discrimination under the Equal Protection Clause.

Craig is difficult to explain, however. In virtually all other cases in which the Court has permitted third-party standing, there has been a very close relationship between the plaintiff and the person whose rights are being advanced. In *Singleton v. Wulff*,[95] a plurality of four Justices thought that obstetricians should be permitted to assert the rights of their pregnant patients in attacking a federal prohibition on the use of Medicaid funds for abortions. In *Eisenstadt v. Baird*,[96] the relationship at issue was also physician-patient (prescribing contraceptives for minors). As a general rule, the Court will forbid most attempts to use third-party standing.

Would it make any difference if Congress enacted a third-party or so-called "citizen suit" provision? Approximately sixteen environmental and energy statutes contain such provisions. The Clean Air Act is prototypical: "Except [as otherwise provided] . . . any person may commence a civil action on his own behalf-against any person [violating the act] . . . [or]-against the [EPA] administrator . . . ."[97] Recall that the conventional statutory language is *any person aggrieved*. The Clean

---

[93] *Id.* at 1447.

[94] 429 U.S. 190 (1976).

[95] 428 U.S. 106 (1976).

[96] 405 U.S. 438 (1972).

[97] 42 U.S.C. § 7604 (1990).

Air Act language is not just sloppy drafting; Congress was deliberately trying to set up a statutory provision that would substitute for what the plaintiffs thought they were going to get out of the Supreme Court in *Sierra Club v. Morton.*

The difficult question is whether these statutes survive constitutional scrutiny. If *Baker* sets the minimum — *i.e.*, that Article III requires at least personal injury in fact — it is impermissible for Congress to try to broaden Article III by conventional legislation. The only proper way to expand the Article is by constitutional amendment.

Some courts view third-party or citizen suit provisions as unconstitutional. Others believe that Congress was making a scientific determination of injury - if there is polluted air or water anywhere in the country it (arguably) affects ("injures") all of us eventually. Other courts refer to a separate opinion by Justice Harlan in *Flast* which states that Congress does have the power to create a private-attorney general action, and when Congress does so the courts should respect that enactment.[98]

In the past several years, the Supreme Court has seen fit to review a number of citizen suit provisions. In perhaps the most striking case, *Bennett v. Spear,*[99] the Court reviewed a portion of the Endangered Species Act that permits "any person" the right to "commence a civil suit on his own behalf" in circumstances in which that person seeks to enjoin any person who is alleged to be in violation of the Act. In *Bennett*, the petitioners were two State of Oregon irrigation districts that sued the Fish and Wildlife Service. An interesting twist in this case is that the petitioners were suing not to enforce the Endangered Species Act, but rather, to force the Service to return to its traditional practices because there was (in the view of the petitioners) no harm ensuing to endangered species-here an endangered fish species known as "suckers." The Court saw absolutely no problem with this aspect of the case. There is nothing in the statute that suggests that only persons seeking to enhance the protection of endangered species were to have access to the federal courts.

At the court of appeals level, the petitioners were denied standing on the basis of *Lujan* and the zone of interest test. The Supreme Court disagreed with the circuit on several grounds with Justice Scalia writing for the Court. After working through many of the standing concepts already set out in this section, Justice Scalia noted:

> Our readiness to take the term 'any person' at face value is greatly augmented by two interrelated considerations: that the overall subject matter of this legislation is the environment (a matter in which it is common to think all persons have an interest) and that the obvious purpose of the [statute] is to encourage enforcement by so-called 'private attorneys general.'[100]

---

[98] For a good exposition of these issues, *see* Richard Schwartz & David Hackett, *Citizen Suits in Environmental Cases*, 14 Nat. Res. L. 225 (1984).

[99] 520 U.S. 154 (1997).

[100] *Id.* at 165. The Court noted further that granting standing to the Bennett petitioners flows

Given that the opinion was written by Justice Scalia — a justice who has been exceptionally strict on standing requirements — one might think that citizens' suits provisions are secure for the foreseeable future. That might not necessarily be the case. One needs to look closely at a decision also written by Justice Scalia just one year later in which the Court ruled that a statute with the cumbersome title, "The Emergency Planning and Community Right-to-Know Act," did not permit lawsuits by citizens who challenged the past failure of companies to file annual reports on hazardous chemical use. In *Steel Company v. Citizens for a Better Environment*,[101] Justice Scalia, writing for a six-Justice majority, denied standing to a group of citizens who filed suit to complain of past violations of the Act's requirement that companies file annual reports on their use of hazardous chemicals. The Court majority concluded, essentially, that the statute contained no mechanism that permitted an agency-respondent to redress the grievances (past violations) cited by the petitioners. Focusing on the "redressability" concept permitted the Court to avoid making sharp distinctions between the citizen suit provision in the Endangered Species Act and the much more ambiguous provision in the Emergency Planning Act that simply established jurisdiction in the district courts of "actions brought . . . against an owner or operator of a facility to enforce the requirement concerned and to impose any civil penalty."

While *Bennett* gives some comfort as to the validity of citizen suit statutory provisions, in the ordinary case, lawyers should not rest completely on such allegations. It would seem that the better, safer practice is not to force a confrontation on this issue. The simpler approach, following *SCRAP*, *Sierra Club* and *Lujan*, is to find at least one person with the requisite personal injury for the lawsuit to go forward.

[H]   Standing on the Part of State Governments

Do individual states have standing to sue federal administrative agencies in federal court? In 2007 the Supreme Court answered that question in the context of a dispute over global warming and its impact on individual states. In *Massachusetts v. Environmental Protection Agency*,[102] a consortium of states, local government, and private groups asserted that the Environmental Protection Agency (EPA) had abdicated its regulatory responsibilities under the Clean Air Act relating to global warming. Specifically, the petitioners argued that the EPA had failed to regulate four emissions of greenhouse gases including carbon dioxide emissions from automobiles. Note at the outset that this case was one of an agency's withholding agency action.

Justice Stevens wrote the majority opinion and began by reciting the normal doctrines of standing including the *Baker v. Carr* requirement of personal stake in the outcome and the *Lujan* need for "a concrete and particularized injury that is

---

inexorably from a previous Court decision, *Trafficante v. Metropolitan Life Ins. Co.*, 409 U.S. 205 (1972) (granting standing to a plaintiff under the Civil Rights Act of 1968 under a statutory provision that permits a federal action by "any person who claims to have been injured by a discriminatory housing practice").

[101] 523 U.S. 83 (1998).

[102] 549 U.S. 497 (2007).

either actual or imminent, that the injury is fairly traceable to the defendant, and that it is likely that a favorable decision will redress that injury." The difficulty here was the presence of Massachusetts as a sovereign state. The Court noted that "states are not normal litigants for the purposes of invoking federal jurisdiction." But even so, Justice Stevens recognized that in this particular action, Massachusetts "is entitled to special solicitude in our standing analysis."

The Court first examined the possibility of actual injury and concluded that the "harms associated with climate change are serious and well recognized." It examined some of the scientific studies on the climate, noting, among other things, that there is a strong consensus among respected scientists with regard to global warming and the harms that stem from warming, including a sharp rise in sea levels. These rising seas, according to the Court, "have already begun to swallow Massachusetts' coastal land. Since Massachusetts owns a large amount of this land, it is able to allege the requisite particularized injury in fact.

The Court went on to examine the element of causation to conclude that EPA's failure to regulate auto emissions is a substantial element in the chain of causation, and — with regard to an adequate remedy — "while it may be true that regulating motor-vehicle emissions will not by itself *reverse* global warming, it by no means follows that we lack jurisdiction to decide whether EPA has a duty to take steps *to slow or reduce* it." Given the current harm and the potential harm to Massachusetts by way of the EPA's inaction, the Court concluded that the state had standing to pursue the litigation.

Four dissenters, Chief Justice Roberts plus Justices Scalia, Thomas and Alito, disagreed sharply with the Stevens' analysis. Their basic point is that there is no room in the Court's standing doctrines for "special solicitude" for a state government. In their view, the state suffers no more harm than the harm that accrues to humanity at large. Here, in the dissenter's view, there is no immediate particularized injury in fact.[103]

§ 10.07 RESOLVING THRESHOLD JUDICIAL REVIEW ISSUES

Lawyers pay close attention to all the issues discussed in this chapter because even slight errors or poor client counseling at this stage of judicial review can result in a case's dismissal long before a court begins to sort out the merits. The easiest way to begin your analysis is to recall that the question being asked here is *whether* judicial review can be had at all. Only when you answer that question in the affirmative may you proceed with the *when* and *what kind* analysis.

---

[103] In a 2011 case subsequent to *Massachusetts v. EPA*, the Supreme Court split 4-4 on the issue of standing in a setting where a number of states, the City of New York and three private-sector land trusts sued four private electric utilities and the Tennessee Valley Authority on claims of common law nuisance. In *American Electric Power Co. v. Connecticut*, 131 S. Ct. 2527 (2011)), at least four of the justices concluded that at least some of the plaintiffs had standing under the principles articulated in *Massachusetts v. EPA*. Since the Second Circuit had held that some of the plaintiffs had standing, this part of the lower court opinion was upheld by an equally divided Court.

Use the sections and subsections in this chapter as a checklist. The first thing you must do is to identify and invoke a proper grant of federal subject matter jurisdiction. This will be found either in the enabling act or in one of the sections of Title 28, U.S.C. If the enabling act specifies the proper court or other requirements for getting into that court, you must abide by it. If all else fails, a lawyer may use 28 U.S.C. § 1331 to get into district court. Once in court under a jurisdictional statute, issues such as venue and service of process are normally disposed of under 28 U.S.C. § 1391 and the *Federal Rules of Civil Procedure.*

But you are still not home free. You must ask the court for some kind of remedy. This requires you to think through the twin issues of form of action and sovereign immunity. Federal courts normally have the power to award a winning plaintiff anything she asks for, but if you want an award of money damages from the federal treasury, you may proceed only under a statute, such as the Tucker Act or the Federal Tort Claims Act, which relaxes the doctrine of sovereign immunity and permits you to obtain monetary relief. If all you wish is a declaration and injunction, you should not encounter any difficulty, because the 1976 amendments to the APA solved the problem with sovereign immunity.

Once you resolve these issues, consider preclusion. Preclusion asks whether the issues you are bringing to the court are properly reviewable under the APA. Preclusion is applicable only to a few types of agency action, and the vast majority of agency decisions are reviewable. Both the APA and the case law make this clear. The courts, in particular, tend to shy away from holding that any case is precluded. But when Congress has written a precluding statute or when a court determines that the agency action is committed to the agency's discretion, the lawsuit must be dismissed.

Even if your *issues* are not precluded from judicial review, your *client* may give you further problems. Standing is an issue that goes to the identity of the plaintiff and addresses the question of whether the party bringing the lawsuit has personally suffered the requisite injury in fact. In drafting a complaint, you must be able to allege facts sufficient to meet both parts of the *Data Processing* test. Don't forget the hidden component in Part One of the *Data Processing* test. The injury suffered by the plaintiff must be directly traceable and attributable to the defendant. Finally, you must find some constitutional provision, statute or principle of common law which gives your client the protection sought — *i.e.*, creates a legal interest on your client's behalf.

Only after you have addressed and resolved all of these issues are you ready to proceed to the questions of timing of judicial review and review of the merits of the controversy.

Chapter 11

JUDICIAL REVIEW: STAYING IN COURT

§ 11.01 INTRODUCTION

This chapter covers some of the intermediate judicial review issues-those taken up after resolution of the issues discussed in Chapter 10 and before a court gets to the merits of the controversy. The standard question lawyers ask when reaching this point in a judicial review analysis is *when* judicial review can be had. These issues are often referred to as the *timing* issues because their resolution does not prohibit judicial review but simply establishes the point in time when a court can get its hands on the matter.

The three issues have universally-accepted labels: primary jurisdiction, exhaustion and ripeness. Briefly stated, *primary jurisdiction* is a question of whether a court can be the first avenue of resolution of a dispute or whether the dispute must be given to an agency first and taken into court only when the agency action is concluded. Stated a bit simplistically, this doctrine is like a fork in the road. The primary jurisdiction principles determine which fork a particular dispute must take. The following is a primary jurisdiction road map:

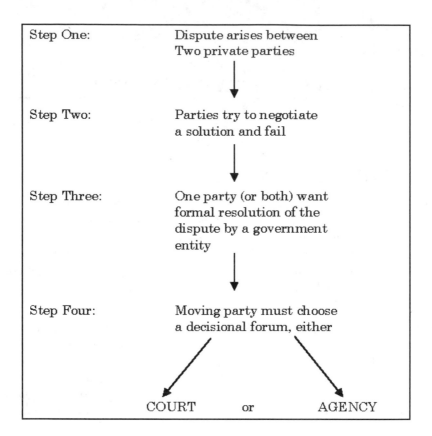

Step One: Dispute arises between
                   Two private parties

Step Two: Parties try to negotiate
                   a solution and fail

Step Three: One party (or both) want
                   formal resolution of the
                   dispute by a government
                   entity

Step Four: Moving party must choose
                   a decisional forum, either

              COURT   or   AGENCY

If the question of primary jurisdiction is resolved in favor of agency action — that is, if primary jurisdiction principles require an agency to take the first look at the dispute, judicial review will obviously be postponed for some time, normally until such time as final agency action is completed. The problem is that some cases are taken into court before the agency has completed action. Usually, a reviewing court faced with agency action that is not complete will order the case remanded to the agency. Occasionally, the dispute is framed in such a way as to eliminate the requirement of final agency action, thereby permitting a court to review the problem without having the parties go to the agency first.

The twin doctrines of *exhaustion* and *ripeness* also involve issues of the timing of judicial review. *Exhaustion* asks whether a person currently before the agency must stay within the agency until all possible agency procedures — or levels of decision making — are completed (or *exhausted*). *Ripeness*, essentially the other side of the same coin, asks whether the issues in dispute are sufficiently matured to permit a court to review the case — *i.e.*, whether there is a properly-framed *legal* issue in the case that the court may review. If the pending issues in the case are still matters of, say, scientific or technical judgment, rather than issues of law, the case will not be *ripe* for judicial review.

There are three possible variations on this theme. First, it is possible to have an issue that is ripe for review, even though there may be additional procedures available at the agency. This is a problem of exhaustion. Second, a case that has exhausted all possible procedures at the agency level is normally also ripe for judicial review. Third, there are many cases at the agency level that are not yet ripe for review nor have satisfied the exhaustion requirements. Some cases in category one (ripe but not exhausted) may be reviewed in the courts because the doctrine of exhaustion — essentially a judge-made concept-contains a great deal of discretion. Cases in category two (all agency proceedings completed) generally satisfy all "final agency action" requirements and can go immediately into court. Cases in category three (neither exhausted nor ripe) normally cannot get into court in their present posture. Category three cases must await further agency action to become final, judicially-reviewable disputes. The main thing to remember is that both doctrines, ripeness and exhaustion, can be used to block (or perhaps more accurately to postpone) judicial review, so both doctrines must be analyzed as you consider *when* a court may pass judgment on the matter.

§ 11.02 PRIMARY JURISDICTION

[A] Analysis of the Fundamentals

This topic frequently confuses law students because it is a somewhat obscure and difficult concept of administrative law that is often confused and misapplied by both courts and practitioners. Most confusion can be dispelled, however, by focusing on the fundamentals. First, look again at that primary jurisdiction road map in the preceding section. Primary jurisdiction issues arise as the disputing parties try to decide where to take their dispute. The party pushing for formal dispute resolution in this context has two choices: she may go first to court or she may go first to the agency. If she goes first to the agency, there is normally no issue of primary jurisdiction; all subsequent questions of the timing of judicial review will turn on application of the doctrines of exhaustion and ripeness, not on primary jurisdiction. Sometimes a party with a grievance will try to go to court first, completely avoiding the agency. When that happens, the issue of primary jurisdiction must be considered.

The next step in the analysis is to keep the doctrine itself firmly in mind. Stated concisely, the doctrine of primary jurisdiction requires that a dispute that fits within the jurisdiction of an administrative agency should be taken first to that agency, even if the case-or certain issues within the case-might in theory be taken into court initially.

The final step is to grasp the fact that the doctrine of primary jurisdiction is judge-made. There is no primary jurisdiction statute as such (at least not on the federal level), although in resolving a primary jurisdiction issue the courts will obviously look closely at the applicable enabling act and administrative procedure act.

In all of this analysis, you should be sensitive to the underlying tensions inherent in the doctrine. Congress established administrative agencies to deal with certain problems because courts were not always up to the task at hand. Unlike courts, agencies are expected to be experts in the technical matters within their jurisdiction. Frequently, the resolution of a dispute can be enhanced by a proper understanding of the technical aspects of the dispute-this is something at which an agency is usually more skilled than is a court.

However, you must consider a countervailing factor. Congress also confers many kinds of subject matter jurisdiction on the courts that give them the power to resolve certain categories of dispute. For example, the federal district courts are permitted to resolve disputes between parties who are citizens of different states when the amount in controversy exceeds the sum of $75,000 (so-called diversity jurisdiction).[1] Another statute permits a federal district court to decide cases that arise under a statute, treaty or the constitution of the United States (so-called federal question jurisdiction).[2] Yet another statute permits the federal district courts to hear cases involving interstate commerce or the federal antitrust statutes.[3] Thus, many disputes may arguably go first into court under one or another of these jurisdictional statutes, rather than to an appropriate agency. In each of the primary jurisdiction cases discussed below, the party trying to go into court without having gone to the agency invoked an appropriate jurisdictional statute, so they had at least the theoretical right to be in court in the first instance. In most of these cases, however, the Supreme Court ordered the party out of court and into the agency for initial resolution of the dispute.

[B]   The Landmark Case - *Abilene Cotton*

There may have been primary jurisdiction cases decided by the Supreme Court before *Texas & Pacific Railway v. Abilene Cotton Oil Co.*,[4] but they seem to be lost to human memory. *Abilene Cotton* itself has been relegated to a note case in most administrative law casebooks, even though it is the model for everything that follows and remains one of the clearer expositions of the primary jurisdiction doctrine.

Part of the reason for the decision's current unpopularity is that the Court's opinion is exceedingly lengthy, written in a turn-of-the-century judicial style that puts most law students and even a few law professors to sleep. It's possible, however, to state the case plainly and simply. The case evolved from a dispute between a shipper of goods and a railroad (the carrier of those goods) over whether the railroad was charging reasonable rates (prices) to haul the shipper's freight. Armed with this grievance, the shipper chose to go directly into a federal district court to challenge the reasonableness of the rates, even though a perfectly good federal agency, the Interstate Commerce Commission, existed with statutory authority to determine the reasonableness of interstate freight rates. Prior to the

---

[1]   28 U.S.C. § 1332. For a good discussion of many of the topics set out in this chapter, *see* R. George Wright, *The Timing of Judicial Review of Administrative Decisions: The Use and Abuse of Overlapping Doctrines*, 11 AM. J. TRIAL ADVOC. 83 (1987).

[2]   28 U.S.C. § 1331.

[3]   28 U.S.C. § 1337.

[4]   204 U.S. 426 (1907).

creation of the ICC, a federal district court was the only place where a shipper could challenge a railroad's rates. Invoking, among other things, the basic interstate commerce jurisdictional statute (28 U.S.C. § 1337), the shipper went directly to court.

The Supreme Court conceded that the shipper had the theoretical right to be in district court in the first instance, but concluded that the ICC had been set up expressly to handle rate disputes and was expected to be an expert on matters such as rail transportation and freight rates. Just as importantly, the Court reasoned that the ICC was a federal agency with national jurisdiction over the nation's transportation industry whose decisions and policies would have nationwide scope and effect. Letting a single federal district court take the first look at this kind of dispute could lead to literally hundreds and possibly thousands of conflicting and inconsistent court decisions on what constituted a reasonable rate, whereas the ICC could make a single pronouncement and thus settle the matter throughout the country.

Apparently for the first time, the Court invoked the doctrine of primary jurisdiction and ordered the district court to dismiss the case with an invitation to the parties to take their grievance to the ICC for resolution. If one or another of the parties disliked what the ICC did, they could always return to the courts for judicial review of the agency's action. If the Supreme Court had never said another word about primary jurisdiction beyond its decision in *Abilene Cotton*, there would probably be little quibbling about the doctrine today. Unfortunately, the Court later decided a number of primary jurisdiction cases whose total impact has produced far less satisfactory results.

[C]   The Case Law After *Abilene Cotton*

One of the cases often reproduced in casebooks as the main focus for analyzing primary jurisdiction is the case in which the Supreme Court made its second major statement on the primary jurisdiction doctrine, *United States v. Western Pacific Railroad Co.*[5] In terms of its subject matter, *Western Pacific* is not significantly different from *Abilene Cotton*. In this case, a shipper, the federal government, wanted to ship napalm bombs on the Western Pacific Railroad. Under the Interstate Commerce Act, railroads set their prices by filing tariffs (schedules of prices) with the ICC. There are two basic components to these prices, *i.e.*, the nature of the commodity to be shipped, and the distance traveled. Applying the first component requires a railroad to determine into which commodity classification the goods are to be placed. The classifications depend on such factors as density, perishability and dangerousness. In other words, a good that is highly perishable or extremely dangerous to transport will cost more to ship than a good that does not have those characteristics. Once the good is placed into an appropriate classification, the railroad then determines the number of miles the good is to be shipped and arrives at the final price to be charged for the shipment.

In the *Western Pacific* case, the government and the railroad disagreed over the proper classification of the goods. The railroad insisted that the napalm should be

---

[5] 352 U.S. 59 (1956).

classified as "incendiary bombs," a classification that triggered a higher price than the classification sought by the government — "gasoline in drums."[6] The railroad made more money if the napalm was classified as incendiary bombs. Given that the government shipped a significant amount of napalm, the amount in controversy was considerable.

The government insisted on paying the lower price for the shipments, so the railroad took the government to the Court of Claims (now the United States Court of Federal Claims), seeking reimbursement for the higher price. This lawsuit avoided the ICC entirely. On review, the Supreme Court determined that the doctrine of primary jurisdiction applied and that the railroad should have gone first to the ICC. The Supreme Court ordered the lawsuit dismissed with opportunity to the railroad to resolve the dispute first in the agency. That's the bottom line in *Western Pacific*. The Court's reasoning, however, requires further explanation.

In essence, the Court decided that federal courts were simply not experts on such arcane matters as railroad tariffs and the computation of freight rates. By contrast, the ICC possessed acknowledged expertise in these issues. The dispute itself went to the very heart of those complicated railroad tariffs and to the interpretation of specific tariff language in light of common industry practices. So why not have the expert agency, the ICC, look at the issue, make some pronouncement on the dispute within its expertise and, if necessary, hand the case back to the federal courts which could then decide other issues armed with the expert judgment of the Commission? If there is a fundamental rationale for the result in *Western Pacific*, it is probably "agency expertise."

It was about this same time, however, that the primary jurisdiction doctrine started getting a little blurred. It became a more cluttered doctrine than might appear merely from reading *Abilene Cotton* and *Western Pacific*. A case decided some four years before *Western Pacific*, *Far East Conference v. United States*,[7] was an antitrust action for violations of the Sherman Act brought by the Department of Justice against a group of ocean carriers. Justice objected to a system of dual rates established by the companies that appeared to penalize some shippers and to reward other shippers (mainly those who agreed to give all their transportation business to a single carrier). There is a federal agency, the Federal Maritime Commission (FMC), that has authority to regulate the rates charged by the ocean carriers in much the same fashion that the ICC regulates the rates of railroads. Moreover, ocean carriers operating under a license issued by the FMC (including all the carriers involved in this case) enjoy an immunity from the federal antitrust statutes. This immunity permits the carriers to form groups to promulgate tariffs that are often referred to as *conferences* (hence "Far East Conference") without running afoul of the federal price-fixing statutes. The rationale for the antitrust immunity is that FMC scrutiny of the conference's tariffs is an appropriate substitute for antitrust controls.

---

[6] Those readers who find this stuff impossibly turgid might just want to take something on faith from the author, who spent several years working as a freight rate clerk under Interstate Commerce rate regulation. It really used to work like this.

[7] 409 U.S. 289 (1973).

The FMC was never given a chance to review these dual rate systems because the Justice Department took the ocean carriers directly to court. On review, the Supreme Court invoked the doctrine of primary jurisdiction and directed the parties first to the FMC for its review of the rate structure. The Court cited the expertise and specialized knowledge of the agency as the main reason for seeking its guidance before permitting a court to rule on the antitrust questions. But the difficulty with the Court's rationale is this: while the FMC may know a lot about ocean carriers, it is not an expert on the Sherman Act-the statute underlying the Justice Department's antitrust claim against Far East Conference. Indeed, because FMC jurisdiction conferred certain antitrust immunity, the Commission had never had to deal with any of these concepts. Nonetheless, the Court invoked the doctrine of primary jurisdiction and ordered the parties to pursue the dispute first at the agency level.

At this point, you may be asking yourself whether the doctrine is wholly wise. The Justice Department had every right to be in federal court on the antitrust claim. Agencies can give advisory opinions, unlike the federal courts; and the agency could have participated, perhaps as an amicus curiae, in the federal court proceeding. Because FMC expertise was probably not central to the antitrust issues, it could have provided guidance and could have had input in federal court. Forcing the parties into the agency always delays final resolution of the dispute, sometimes by several years.

Antitrust allegations were also involved in a more recent primary jurisdiction case, *Ricci v. Chicago Mercantile Exchange.*[8] A private citizen, Ricci, brought an antitrust action in federal court, alleging that the Mercantile Exchange and various other persons conspired against him in violation of the Sherman Act's prohibition against conspiracies in restraint of trade. There was a federal agency, then the Commodities Exchange Commission (CEC) (now known as the Commodities Futures Trading Commission) with a certain amount of jurisdiction over exchanges. But one major difference between this case and *Far East Conference* is that the CEC had no power to confer antitrust immunity, and its regulatory authority was somewhat limited. Nevertheless, the Supreme Court invoked the doctrine of primary jurisdiction and insisted that the dispute begin in the agency.

At this point, consider the following chart:

---

[8] 409 U.S. 289 (1973).

Name of Case	Parties	Controversy	Agency	Primary Jurisdiction Invoked	Rational
Abilene	shpr/carrier	fgt rates	ICC	Yes	uniformity
Western Pacific		tariff. desc.	"	Yes	expertise
Far East Conference	U.S./carner	antitrust	FMC	Yes	knowledge of industry
Ricci	indiv/exch		CEC	Yes	

The progression of these cases shows exceptional deference on the part of the Supreme Court to the agencies.[9] However, this deference almost reaches the point, as suggested by a number of critics of *Far East Conference* and *Ricci*, of total abdication of the responsibilities of federal courts to resolve certain disputes within the subject matter expressly conferred on those courts by Congress. This is a point made most strongly by the dissenters in *Ricci*. Three years after *Ricci*, the Court appeared to rethink the entire doctrine and to retreat just a little bit from the extremes of *Ricci*.

---

[9] One federal circuit has courageously attempted to articulate a three-part test for primary jurisdiction: (1) whether the agency determination lay at the heart of the task assigned the agency by Congress; (2) whether agency expertise was required to unravel intricate, technical facts; and (3) whether, though perhaps not [dispositive], the agency determination would materially aid the court. *Mashpee Tribe v. New Seabury Corp.*, 592 F.2d 575, 580–81 (1st Cir. 1979). Justice Antonin Scalia distinguished between the doctrines of primary jurisdiction and exhaustion in *Reiter v. Cooper*, 507 U.S. 258 (1993). He stated that

> primary jurisdiction . . . is a doctrine specifically applicable to claims properly cognizable in court that contain some issue within the special competence of an administrative agency [while on the other hand] where relief is available from an administrative agency, the plaintiff is ordinarily required to pursue that avenue of redress before proceeding to the courts; and until that recourse is exhausted, suit is premature and must be dismissed.

Id. at 267–69. For a discussion of a number of cases that touch on many of the topics in this chapter, *see* Bernard Schwartz, *Timing of Judicial Review: A Survey of Recent Cases*, 8 ADMIN. L.J. AM. U. 261 (1994). *See* Michael Penney, *Application of the Primary Jurisdiction Doctrine to Clean Air Act Citizen Suits*, 29 B.C. ENVT'L L. REV. 399 (2002).

[D]   The Impact of *Nader*

In late April 1972, the regulatory activist, Ralph Nader, got bumped from a flight on Allegheny Airlines (now U.S. Airways) between Washington, D.C. and Hartford, Connecticut. Mr. Nader rarely takes things like this lightly, so he sued the airline in federal district court, invoking the court's diversity jurisdiction and claiming that Allegheny had committed fraud and misrepresentation by not telling him that he might be bumped. There was then an agency in existence, the Civil Aeronautics Board, with the power to regulate the economic aspects of the airline industry. The Board had, a short time before Nader got bumped, promulgated specific rules on airline bumping practices. This rulemaking followed a lengthy investigation of airlines' overbooking practices. The rules called for, among other things, the paying of certain compensation to passengers who were bumped. Armed with this regulatory structure, Allegheny asked the district court to dismiss Nader's suit on primary jurisdiction grounds and to turn the dispute over to the CAB for initial resolution.

The airline did not get its way. For the first time in a major primary jurisdiction case, the Supreme Court, in *Nader v. Allegheny Airlines, Inc.*,[10] refused to invoke the doctrine and permitted the district court to keep and decide the law suit. What is particularly interesting about this case is that the majority opinion in *Nader* is virtually a carbon copy of the dissent in *Ricci.* Many readers of the two cases believe that they simply cannot be harmonized-that the two decisions are not reconcilable. Other commentators have observed that the decision in *Nader* may have turned on the manner in which Mr. Nader framed his complaint. In his diversity action, Mr. Nader did not seek compensation for the bumping itself, but rather, he accused the airline of committing fraud in failing to warn him that he might possibly be bumped. Thus, one might view the case as a simple tort action that just happens to involve a carrier regulated by the CAB, rather than an action that somehow turns on what the CAB knows about the industry or what the CAB might have contributed to a proper resolution of the dispute.

This, then, is the doctrine of primary jurisdiction as construed by the Supreme Court. *Nader* clearly represents a bit of retrenching on the Court's part, and as such, most scholars view it as a healthy development. While most disputes should begin in an agency when an agency is directly involved, not every imaginable dispute should be sent to an agency merely because, in some peripheral fashion, the agency has something to do with one or another of the parties. While the Supreme Court has not revisited the doctrine since its decision in the *Nader* case, the federal circuits occasionally deal with primary jurisdiction issues. At least one federal circuit has suggested that the invocation of primary jurisdiction is no longer discretionary with the federal courts, but rather might be categorically required under the deferential doctrines of judicial review set out in the Supreme Court's decision in *Chevron U.S.A., Inc. v. Natural Resources Defense Council, Inc.*[11] *Chevron* held that a reviewing court must perform a two-part analysis (the famous *Chevron* "two-step") whenever it reviews an agency's interpretation of its own

---

[10]   426 U.S. 290 (1976).

[11]   467 U.S. 837 (1984).

statutes. In the first step, the court must consider whether the statute is ambiguous or silent on the point in question. If there is no ambiguity or silence, the court simply applies the statutory language irrespective of any different interpretation given that statute by the agency. However, if the court determines in step one that the statute is silent or ambiguous, the court must defer to the agency's interpretation so long as that interpretation is reasonable.[12]

The United States Court of Appeals for the District of Columbia Circuit suggested, in *Ayuda v. Thornburgh*:[13]

> Although the doctrine of primary jurisdiction was originally rooted in the notion that agencies have greater expertise, experience, and flexibility than courts in dealing with regulatory matters . . . abstention in favor of agencies charged with resolving conflicting statutory policies also promotes the proper relationships between courts and administrative agencies. This follows naturally from *Chevron*, which explained that deference to agencies was appropriate not only because of agency expertise but also because Congress is presumed to delegate the policy choices inherent in resolving statutory ambiguities to the agency charged with implementation of the statute.[14]

> If anything, these remarks suggest that courts, in the future, will be even less inclined to permit a party to go into court in the first instance so long as an agency has anything to contribute.

In practice, primary jurisdiction disputes arise infrequently because most parties automatically start with the agency and because so many disputes begin only when the agency itself initiates some kind of investigation or enforcement action. When this occurs, the doctrine of primary jurisdiction is simply irrelevant. Nonetheless, primary jurisdiction is an appropriate initial question for resolving the issue of *when* judicial review may take place.[15] In the vast number of cases, the issue of primary jurisdiction is going to be answered in the affirmative (*i.e.*, the case must originate in the agency) and then go to court. If your answer to the primary jurisdiction is in the affirmative, you must then confront the twin concepts of ripeness and exhaustion.

---

[12] The *Chevron* decision is discussed extensively in Chapter 12, § 12.05 *below*.

[13] 880 F.2d 1325 (D.C. Cir. 1989), *vacated on other grounds*, 498 U.S. 1117 (1991).

[14] *Id.* at 1344. In ruling on a petition for certiorari, the Supreme Court made a similar suggestion, commenting that an agency is "equipped, as courts are not, to survey the field nationwide, and to regulate based on a full view of the relevant facts and circumstances. If we had the benefit of the [agency's] reasoned decisions . . . we would accord [the agency's] decision substantial deference" *Northwest Airlines, Inc. v. County of Kent*, 510 U.S. 355 (1994) (citing *Chevron*).

[15] For a good analysis of primary jurisdiction, *see* Nicholas A. Lucchetti, *One Hundred Years of the Doctrine of Primary Jurisdiction: But What Standard of Review Is Appropriate for It*, 59 ADMIN. L. REV. 849 (2008).

§ 11.03   THE APA'S FINAL ORDER REQUIREMENT

The APA contains a final order provision in § 704: "Agency action made reviewable by statute and final agency action for which there is no other adequate remedy in a court are subject to judicial review. A preliminary, procedural, or intermediate agency action or ruling not directly reviewable is subject to review on the review of the final agency action."

This language is relatively clear on its face but still leads to problems when it becomes necessary to determine when *final agency action* has occurred. Sometimes a statute dictates when action is final or at least reviewable. For example, the Freedom of Information Act allows judicial review when an agency fails to comply with certain statutory deadlines.[16] A number of agencies have provisions in their rules structure stating that a particular action by a particular component of the agency constitutes final agency action for the purposes of judicial review. When your case falls under one of those provisions, there is usually no question of final agency action raised at any subsequent stage of the dispute by any of the parties. Both agencies and courts tend to accept these pronouncements at face value.

Some problems can arise when neither a statute (such as the FOIA) nor an agency rule makes a definitive pronouncement on when agency action is truly "final." In those cases, you must analyze the case in terms of the judge-made doctrines of ripeness and exhaustion to determine when it is permissible to take a dispute out of an agency and into court. Underlying the final order requirement and the judge-made doctrines of ripeness and exhaustion is the idea that a court generally should not interfere with ongoing agency operations. It is one thing for a court to review a case after the agency is finished with it. It is much more intrusive for a court to take a case out of the agency before agency action is completed.

§ 11.04   RIPENESS

[A]   Limitations on Court's Analysis of Issues

Any inquiry into ripeness asks whether the issue that is presented to the court is sufficiently mature and sufficiently crystallized to be a dispute with which a court can deal. When you analyze a fact pattern for ripeness issues, remember that this doctrine looks at the characteristics of the issue to be presented to the court. The exhaustion doctrine, by contrast, is more concerned with where the dispute lies within the agency's organizational structure. When you think through questions of ripeness, remember that judges are not pharmacologists or safety engineers or experts in television broadcasting. Agencies are experts in many of these things. They are the ones who are supposed to resolve the scientific and technical questions, such as whether a particular pollutant is truly harmful to human health, whether a mine roofing bolt is strong enough, or whether one radio station's broadcast signal will interfere with the signal broadcast by another station.

---

[16] 5 U.S.C. § 552(a)(6)(C). *See infra* Chapter 14, § 14.02.

Courts cannot decide complex technical questions. By and large, all they can do is look at the agency's determinations on such questions and consider whether they were made in a procedurally correct fashion, whether the agency's determination is explained sufficiently and whether that determination appears to be reasonable in light of all the things that the agency considered in the record of the proceeding. If you keep these limitations in mind, a ripeness issue rarely presents overwhelming analytical problems.

[B]   The Impact of *Abbott Laboratories*

Virtually every case involving ripeness begins and ends with a discussion of the landmark case in this area, *Abbott Laboratories v. Gardner*,[17] and its two companion cases, *Toilet Goods Ass'n v. Gardner* and *Gardner v. Toilet Goods Ass'n*.[18] The three cases are almost always referred to collectively as *Abbott Labs*, even though each of them involved entirely different forms of agency action. Moreover, the lead case, *Abbott Labs*, was the only opinion of the three that held agency action ripe for review.

In *Abbott Labs*, the Supreme Court took up a pre-enforcement challenge to rules promulgated by the Food and Drug and Cosmetic Act. In the late 1950s and early 1960s, Congress conducted an extensive investigation of the pharmaceutical industry, resulting in significant amendments to the FDC Act. One of the things that Congress sought to remedy was the practice followed by virtually all pharmaceutical manufacturers of discouraging the sale of what are known as *generic* pharmaceuticals. Generic drugs are produced and marketed in bulk to retail stores to be sold under the retail store's name. Because they are sold in bulk and because the manufacturer does not incur any advertising and promotion costs, the generic pharmaceuticals tend to sell for far less per pill than the pharmaceuticals sold under the manufacturer's brand name. You can test this proposition on your next visit to a large drug store. Compare the cost of 100 aspirin in bottles carrying the drug store's name as opposed to similar bottles carrying the brand of major drug manufacturers. There is usually a significant difference.

The drug companies, for many years, tried to encourage the sale of brand name drugs by promoting those brand names among doctors and other health care professionals. These promotional activities were accompanied by large-scale advertising programs designed to enhance the name-recognition of their branded products to the detriment of the generic products. At the same time, because pharmaceutical manufacturing is heavily regulated by the Food and Drug Administration, there was virtually no difference in the safety, effectiveness or chemical composition of the generic drugs as compared with the brand name drugs.[19]

---

[17]   387 U.S. 136 (1967).

[18]   387 U.S. 158 (1967) and 387 U.S. 167 (1967), respectively.

[19]   This part of the *Abbott Labs* fact pattern can seem almost unintelligible to lay people. Think of it this way: There are a number of ways that pharmaceuticals can be identified. The first is simply by reference to the chemical formula for that particular substance (recall your high school chemistry: the formula would be something like C2O6H8). Another way to identify the product is by its generic name.

In its investigation, Congress determined that one of the reasons generic drugs were not prescribed more often by doctors is that doctors simply did not know the generic name for many products and consequently wrote a prescription for the manufacturer's brand name, because those heavy advertising campaigns led to instant recognition and recall of the brand names. Congress decided that one way to encourage the sale of generic drugs was to educate physicians on generic names. To do this, they decided to enact legislation that required drug companies to include a pharmaceutical's generic name in parentheses alongside the brand name used by that particular manufacturer in all the literature and advertising for that particular product.

Beyond stating this, however, the statute was somewhat unclear in terms of how often the generic name had to be inserted. When the FDA promulgated regulations under the amendments, it decided to require the use of the generic name *every time* the drug's name was used. The drug companies objected to the every-time rule on the grounds that nothing in the Act's amendments required an every-time format. In other words, in the view of the companies, the FDA was acting *ultra vires*-in excess of statutory authority.

But recall this was a pre-enforcement action. The every-time rule was so new that the FDA had not yet begun to enforce it against any company through individual enforcement actions. As a result, when the rules were challenged in court, the government argued that the dispute was not yet ready for judicial review-not ripe-because the agency had not yet charged even a single company with a violation of the rule. The drug companies countered with the argument that they would prefer not to be charged with a violation, that they thought they had an on-going obligation to comply with the rule even if the rule were later to be deemed invalid and that they would incur substantial costs if they had to change all their containers and labels to accommodate the every-time requirement.[20]

In this posture, the case came before the Supreme Court.[21] The Court decided that the case was indeed ripe for review and wrote a decision that is probably one of the most cited opinions in modern American administrative law. On the issue of ripeness, the Court formulated a two-part test:

1. Whether the issue presented to the court is *fit* for review (the so-called "legal fitness" test);

The generic name for aspirin is *acetesalycilic acid, 5 grains*. A third way to identify aspirin is by a major manufacturer's brand name: Bayer Aspirin.

[20] Probably the real motivating factor behind this lawsuit was not the printing costs, but the considerably greater returns accruing to the companies the longer they could keep prescribing physicians ignorant of generic names. Given the usually significant differences in the per-pill price, the additional income accruing from *any* delay in the enforcement of the every-time rule would have run into millions of dollars nationwide.

[21] The companion case, *Toilet Goods*, was a challenge to different FDA rules promulgated under the Color Additive Amendments to the FDC Act. These rules governed the inspection of manufacturing facilities and the power to suspend certificates of permission to manufacture products by those companies that refused the inspector's entry. The Court held that while the rules were final, any legal dispute over the validity of the rules would not crystallize until the FDA brought at least one enforcement action because these rules, unlike the every-time rule at issue in *Abbott Labs*, did not affect a company's primary business conduct.

and

2. Whether withholding review would impose a *substantial hardship* on the party seeking review.

These are not difficult factors to parse. The hardship factor addresses the specific impact on the party challenging the rule if that party either (1) has to comply with a rule that it believes is invalid, or (2) has to risk an enforcement action and the inherent penalties for failure to comply. The Court determined that the drug companies' printing expenses incurred in complying with the rule and the monetary penalties they would face if they refused to comply were a sufficient hardship.

The fitness test is essentially what we have been discussing all along. The reviewing court looks at the issue presented and determines whether it is the sort of *legal* issue-as opposed to, say, a scientific issue-that a court is equipped to resolve. In *Abbott Labs*, the challenge to the rules was one that is extremely familiar to reviewing courts-was the agency's action *ultra vires*? In analyzing this question, a court will look at the statute, its legislative history, the agency's explanation for the rule, the language of the rule itself and other similar matters. This is something courts do every day and are perfectly capable of dealing with. Using this methodology in *Abbott Labs*, the Supreme Court decided that the issue of *ultra vires* conduct was indeed fit for review.

Occasionally, first-time readers of *Abbott* have a hard time with this issue. It is possible to ask whether there is any issue that comes out of an agency that a court could not review. The answer is one that leads into a discussion of review on the merits, a topic taken up in the next chapter. For the purposes of understanding *Abbott Labs* at this point in time, it is enough to know that the answer is "yes," courts may look at nearly anything that any agency does, but only if the question is presented in the proper form. As noted earlier, a court may not, of its own accord, declare a particular drug to be safe and effective. Judges are not scientists; they simply cannot make these decisions, and this is a purely scientific determination. However, a court may review the FDA's determination that a drug is safe and effective to see whether the agency's decision is reasonable, given everything in the record of the agency proceeding. This distinction may strike the uninitiated as mere hair-splitting, but it is a vitally important one for preserving a healthy relationship between agencies and courts.

Abbott Labs always sets the stage for any ripeness inquiry. Occasionally, other questions arise in a ripeness context. For example, in *Environmental Defense Fund v. Hardin*,[22] the D.C. Circuit held that agency action that is unreasonably delayed can be ripe for review if the agency is under a non-discretionary duty to act. In *Hardin*, the Secretary of Agriculture had not yet issued registration notices under the Federal Insecticide, Fungicide, and Rodenticide Act (FIFRA).

Even agency pronouncements that are not formal rules may, in certain circumstances, be ripe for review, irrespective of whether the agency has implemented the policy statements. *National Automatic Laundry and Cleaning Council v. Shultz*[23]

---

[22] 428 F.2d 1093 (D.C. Cir. 1970).

[23] 443 F.2d 689 (D.C. Cir. 1971).

approved judicial review of a Wage and Hour Administration's interpretative bulletin, even though the bulletin was labeled "informal" by the agency. The court reasoned that the bulletin was a final pronouncement by the head of the agency, no matter what the agency chose to call the document.

There may be instances when Congress passes an extraordinarily complex statute giving such a large amount of discretion to an agency that no pre-enforcement challenge to the agency's rules is possible. This was one of the issues addressed by the Supreme Court in *Reno v. Catholic Social Services, Inc.*[24] In this case, a private welfare office challenged a substantial number of regulations issued by the Immigration and Naturalization Service under the 1986 Immigration Reform and Control Act. Addressing the issue of whether anyone could challenge the rules before enforcement commenced, the Court commented that the ripeness doctrine has two separate underpinnings: the case and controversy requirement in the constitution and the notion that courts should exercise prudence in taking on agency disputes prematurely. The Court went on to state:

> As we said in *Abbott Laboratories*, . . . the presumption of available judicial review is subject to an implicit limitation: 'injunctive and declaratory judgment remedies,' what the respondents seek here, 'are discretionary, and courts traditionally have been reluctant to apply them to administrative determinations unless these arise in the context of a controversy "ripe" for judicial resolution.[25]

The Court compared the INS regulations being challenged by Catholic Social Services and the regulations that permissibly led to pre-enforcement judicial review in *Abbott* and concluded that the INS regulations were not sufficiently ripe because "[t]hey impose no penalties for violating any newly imposed restriction, but limit access to a benefit created by the [Immigration] Reform Act but not automatically bestowed on eligible aliens."[26] Therefore, the controversy was not ripe for review as the current record was composed. However, the Court went on to note that there might be members of the class of plaintiffs who were attacking the regulations who had ripe claims by virtue of being, in the parlance of the INS, "front-desked." These persons would have their applications rejected instantly by an INS employee who sat at the agency's "front desk" irrespective of the contents of the application. For these aliens, the Court was willing to concede injury "in a particularly concrete manner [accordingly, those persons' challenges] should not fail for lack of ripeness." Ultimately, the case was remanded for a determination of which of the members of the plaintiffs' class were to be given the front desk treatment by the agency.[27]

The *Catholic Social Services* decision shows how importantly the Supreme Court regards the ripeness doctrine, but it really does not appear to break any new

---

[24] 509 U.S. 43 (1993).

[25] *Id.* at 57.

[26] *Id.* at 57.

[27] *Id.* at 62. The Supreme Court denied judicial review on ripeness grounds in a case involving a dispute between the U.S. Forest Service and the Sierra Club. In *Ohio Forestry Ass'n v. Sierra Club*, 523 U.S. 726 (1998), the Court applied the *Abbott* test to conclude that judicial review of a forest management plan was premature.

ground. Note that the Court simply applied the *Abbott* test to a new fact pattern. At the same time, Justice O'Connor was not quite so sanguine. She pointed out that nothing in *Abbott* suggested that rules that confer benefits could never be attacked until the plaintiff applied for those benefits. She believes, to the contrary, that when adverse agency action is both "patent" and "inevitable," there may be a dispute "that the Court may find prudent to resolve."[28] If Justice O'Connor's view of the *Catholic Social Services* case is correct, it is possible that the Court has created a ripeness test for persons who are seeking agency benefits that is different and clearly more restrictive than the ripeness test applied to the *Abbott* plaintiffs who were asking, in essence, not to be regulated. However, there is virtually nothing to be found in the majority opinion that would support the notion that a new ripeness test has been created. The majority seems to go out of its way to show a total congruence between its decision in *Abbott* and its decision in *Catholic Social Services*.

In 1998, the Supreme Court decided not to review a case filed by the Sierra Club against the United States Forest Service because the issues were not ripe for judicial review. In *Ohio Forestry Association, Inc. v. Sierra Club*,[29] the Sierra Club challenged a resource management plan developed by the Forest Service because it permitted too much logging and too much clearcutting of timber. The Court applied the two-part Abbott Laboratories test and concluded that, at the point in time at which the lawsuit was filed, there was no appreciable, tangible harm to the Sierra Club. The Court seems to suggest that the Club would have to wait until this generic plan was given effect by way of specific prohibitions or permissions for logging on specific tracts of land before it could challenge the agency action.

The Supreme Court has often confirmed the validity of the *Abbott* ripeness principles. In 2003, the Court decided *National Park Hospitality Association v. Department of Interior*,[30] a case involving a rule promulgated by the agency that required concession operators in public parks to resolve their contractual claims under a federal statute called the Contracts Disputes Act of 1978.[31] The narrow issue in that case was whether the rule itself constituted final agency action even though it did not directly affect specific concessionaires with specific contracts. The Court invoked the ripeness doctrine, applied the *Abbott* doctrine, denied the plaintiffs judicial review, and commented: "Ripeness is a justiciabilty doctrine designed to prevent the courts, through avoidance of premature adjudication, from entangling themselves in abstract disagreements over administrative policies and also to protect the agencies from judicial interference until an administrative decision has been formalized and its effects felt in a concrete way by the challenging parties. . . . The ripeness doctrine is drawn both from Article III limitations on judicial power and from prudential reasons for refusing to exercise jurisdiction."[32]

---

[28] *Id.* at 68.

[29] 523 U.S. 726 (1998).

[30] 538 U.S. 803 (2003).

[31] 41 U.S.C. §§ 601 *et seq.*

[32] 538 U.S. at 807–08.

§ 11.05 EXHAUSTION

[A] An Analytical Framework for Exhaustion Issues

This doctrine is not all that different from ripeness. As mentioned earlier, it is just the other side of the same coin. Both ripeness and exhaustion are principles designed to prevent premature judicial review and to permit an agency to resolve cases in their own time and under their own procedures without unwarranted interference from the courts.

Because both ripeness and exhaustion are questions of finality, they are sometimes difficult to distinguish in application. Obviously, you should look closely at the issue presented for judicial review, first in terms of the two-part *Abbott Labs* test. Most of the time, it is best to analyze a dispute for ripeness problems before moving to the exhaustion issue. If you can discern no problems with ripeness, you should then look at the agency's organizational chart. You will likely find something such as the following diagram:

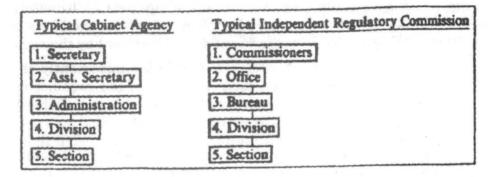

Granting that not every agency has this precise organization, you can still regard it as a typical agency structure. It may be that the agency, by rule, has resolved your exhaustion problem. The rule may state, expressly, that a certain matter constitutes final agency action when a final decision has been made by, say, the relevant bureau or assistant secretary. If you cannot find the answer in the agency's rules, you should then examine the organizational chart and identify the component of the agency that is currently dealing with your case.

As a general rule, if your case is anywhere below level 1, you will have to cope with an exhaustion issue because there are higher echelons of authority within the agency that have not yet acted upon your case. Presumably, they have the authority to review the matter and, if necessary to reverse a decision made by someone at a lower level. If your case is at levels 4 or 5, in all likelihood you will have to continue to pursue your remedies within the agency because it is unlikely, in most agencies, that components sitting that low on the organizational chart have any kind of final decision making authority.

This is the essence of the exhaustion question. The basic premise is that an aggrieved party should be required to pursue his or her remedies within the agency as high as the agency will permit before trying to jump into court. If your organizational analysis suggests that you have an exhaustion problem, you should apply the factors discussed below to determine how the exhaustion issue might be resolved by a court.

[B] Some Exhaustion Case Law

The case law on exhaustion is somewhat scant. The Supreme Court has issued very few decisions on point, and there is nothing in the area of exhaustion that is as helpful as the two-part test for ripeness that stems from *Abbott Labs*. Instead, what we have is a kind of general presumption that a dispute should remain within an agency until *all* levels of decision making have been pursued.[33]

If, however, a litigant wishes to move into court from some place lower on the chart than the highest level — *i.e.*, before he or she has exhausted agency remedies — a court will analyze the propriety of judicial review in light of various factors gleaned from the case law. In *McKart v. United States*,[34] a troublesome selective service case, the Court waxed eloquent on the desirability of having a litigant stay inside the agency as long as possible. The factors set out in *McKart* and enumerated below are decidedly pro-exhaustion. They include:

1. Letting the agency apply its expertise to the matter;

2. Respecting the autonomy of the agency (a kind of separation of powers argument);

3. Preventing review on an incomplete record; and

4. Cutting down on the workload of the courts on the assumption that the agency may take care of the problem at a higher level within the agency.

McKart and other cases also identify a number of factors that mitigate in favor of exhaustion. These include:

1. If the agency has no power, or insufficient power to grant the remedy sought;

2. If the agency has already made up its mind on the issue (frequently referred to as the *futility* factor);

3. If the federal court plaintiff (the person seeking judicial review) would be irreparably injured by the withholding of judicial review;

4. If the attack mounted in court goes to the constitutionality of the entire agency's structure.[35]

---

[33] For a lengthy judicial discussion of both exhaustion and ripeness by three excellent judges, *see Ticor Title Ins. Co. v. FTC*, 814 F.2d 731 (D.C. Cir. 1987).

[34] 395 U.S. 185 (1969).

[35] For example, in *Weinberger v. Salfi*, 422 U.S. 749 (1975), the Supreme Court stated that when all nonconstitutional arguments have been resolved and when the only issue remaining is the constitutionality of a statute, exhaustion is not necessary.

Recall that *Abbott* determined that an agency acting in excess of jurisdiction might create a situation where a dispute was ripe for review. By contrast, in one of the principal cases discussing that same issue in the context of exhaustion, *Myers v. Bethlehem Shipbuilding Corp.*,[36] the Court went the other way, reasoning that the *ultra vires* issue could always be taken up in court after exhausting administrative remedies.

During the 1990s the Supreme Court decided two cases involving the exhaustion doctrine. In the first, *McCarthy v. Madigan*,[37] the Court addressed the issue of whether a prisoner who brings an action for money damages against the warden for depriving the prisoner of medical care must first exhaust internal prison administrative remedies. In not requiring exhaustion in this case, the Court concluded that the central component of the prisoner's lawsuit (*i.e.*, the prayer for monetary relief and the invocation of the Eighth Amendment's prohibitions against cruel and unusual punishment) could not possibly be adjudicated within the prison system. Nor, according to the Court, would a decision on his complaint involve important agency (prison) interests or require the contribution of the agency's special expertise.

In another case, *Darby v. Cisneros*,[38] the Supreme Court looked at its earlier exhaustion cases and § 704 of the APA to conclude that courts should not impose additional exhaustion requirements beyond the normal final order requirement set out in § 704. In this case, a real estate developer challenged the Department of Housing and Urban Development's conclusion that he should be prohibited from participating in federal housing programs. The agency determination was made by an administrative law judge. Under HUD rules, the ALJ's decision becomes final unless the developer seeks intra-agency review within 15 days of the ALJ's decision. Darby did no such thing, permitted the ALJ's decision to become the final agency action and then went to court. At that point, HUD argued that Darby should be denied judicial review because he did not pursue his intra-agency appeal prerogatives. The Supreme Court disagreed, holding that seeking further review within the agency can be made a prerequisite to judicial review only when such intra-agency review is required by statute or when an agency rule requires an appeal before judicial review and when the agency's action is effectively stayed pending that intra-agency review.

Federal courts deal with an enormous number of filings on the part of federal prisoners. In an attempt to keep a lid on these cases, Congress, in 1995, enacted the Prison Litigation Reform Act.[39] Among other things, the statute prohibits any actions in federal court challenging prison conditions "until such administrative remedies as are available are exhausted." In *Jones v. Bock*,[40] the Supreme Court dealt with the issue of whether this statutory requirement required a federal court

---

[36] 303 U.S. 41 (1938).

[37] 503 U.S. 140 (1992). *See* Sonya Gidumal, Note, McCarthy v. Madigan: *Exhaustion of Administrative Agency Remedies and Bivens*, 7 ADMIN. L.J. AM. U. 373 (1993).

[38] 509 U.S. 137 (1993). *See* William Funk, *Exhaustion of Administrative Remedies — New Dimensions Since* Darby, 18 PACE ENVT'L L. REV. 1 (2000).

[39] 42 U.S.C. §§ 1997e *et seq.*

[40] 549 U.S. 199 (2007).

to dismiss a lawsuit if it contained both exhausted and unexhausted claims (so-called "total exhaustion") or whether a court could entertain in the initial lawsuit those claims that had been administratively exhausted while dismissing only those claims that had not been fully dealt with at the agency level. Looking closely at the statutory language and delving into some of the policy reasons for each approach, the Court rejected the total exhaustion doctrine, albeit with a heavy dose of sympathy for the lower federal courts: "We are not insensitive to the challenges faced by the lower federal courts in managing their dockets and attempting to separate, when it comes to prisoner suits, not so much wheat from chaff as needles from haystacks."[41]

Even though § 704 of the APA seemingly codifies the exhaustion principle through the final order requirement, exhaustion remains largely a judge-made concept. The entire doctrine of exhaustion is typified by somewhat inconsistent case-by-case development. When a legal doctrine is bottomed on factor analysis, the only thing a lawyer can do is identify the factors, emphasize those that cut in the client's favor, and hope for the best. Once all of these timing issues are resolved, the case is ready for judicial review on the merits of the agency action.

---

[41] *Id.* at 217. *Jones* was preceded by a similar case, *Woodford v. Ngo*, 548 U.S. 81 (2006).

Chapter 12

JUDICIAL REVIEW: ON THE MERITS

§ 12.01 INTRODUCTION

This is the final stage of judicial review. Applying the analytical structure and the vocabulary begun in Chapters 10 and 11, you reach this point in your analysis of any judicial review problem only if the answer to the *whether* question is "yes" and only if the answer to the *when* question is "now." If a court agrees to review the merits of the dispute, it makes a determination as to the substantive validity of the agency's action.

Inept lawyers think that this is the point at which any and all defects in an agency case will be remedied. In practice, it almost never works out that way. Many agency decisions never reach the court because the losing party cannot afford judicial review. A number of cases that try to go to court will be waylaid by the door-closing or delaying doctrines discussed in Chapters 10 and 11. Thus, only a few cases ever reach this stage.

If an agency record is appallingly incomplete, if some bad evidence or impermissible ex parte contract has totally poisoned a case, or if there are points of view not fully considered or drastic changes in agency policy not fully explained, a court might possibly reverse and remand; but as we shall see, the grounds on which agency action may be reversed are so narrow that the party who loses before the agency has precious little hope of prevailing in court. Most importantly, keep in mind that the normal disposition of a case in which the courts find a reversible defect is simply to remand to the agency for corrective proceedings. It is extremely rare for a court to declare a winner in an agency action on its own initiative.

Is there any good way to approach judicial review on the merits? As usual, the best place to begin is with the agency's enabling act. Congress quite often specifies the terms of judicial review on the merits. It is not unusual to find a provision in an enabling act instructing a court to review agency action on the basis of the *substantial evidence* test or a statutory command to reverse agency action only if the court finds the agency action *arbitrary and capricious*. If the enabling act is silent on grounds for review, § 706 of the Administrative Procedure Act fills the gap by providing a laundry list of grounds (discussed *below* in § 12.02) on which a court may evaluate the agency's decision.

In addition to the statutory limitations, the courts have fashioned a number of principles of review that must be taken into account in many cases. Over the past twenty or thirty years, the Supreme Court has taken a very strong position against courts substituting their judgment for that of the agency, whether it be on substantive or procedural grounds. The Court's opinions in this area have been increasingly less subtle. The message that has emerged from the Supreme Court in the last two decades of the twentieth century is that reviewing courts ought to leave agency decisions alone, absent significant and palpably harmful defects in the proceedings below.

At this point in the typical administrative law course, students are often asked to compare a statement made over thirty years ago by Judge David Bazelon, who sat on the D.C. Circuit with an equally strong pronouncement made in 1984 by the Supreme Court. Judge Bazelon commented:

> We stand on the threshold of a new era in the history of the long and fruitful collaboration of administrative agencies and federal courts. [Historically, courts have been highly deferential to agency decisions.] [Now] courts are increasingly asked to review administrative action that touches on fundamental personal interests in life, health, and liberty. These interests have always had a special claim to judicial protection . . . . To protect these interests from administrative arbitrariness, it is necessary . . . to insist on strict judicial scrutiny of administrative action.[1]

Note the sharp contrast in both tone and content between Judge Bazelon's sentiments and a Supreme Court comment in 1984, reversing a D.C. Circuit decision that had overturned an Environmental Protection Agency rulemaking. In the 1984 case, *Chevron U.S.A., Inc. v. Natural Resources Defense Council, Inc.*,[2] the Supreme Court stated:

> Judges are not experts in the field [being regulated], and are not part of either political branch of government. Courts must, in some cases, reconcile competing political interests, but not on the basis of the judges' personal policy preferences . . . . While agencies are not directly accountable to the people, the Chief Executive [and Congress] is, and it is entirely appropriate for [the political branches of government] to make such policy choices.

A year earlier, reversing the D.C. Circuit for holding a Nuclear Regulatory Commission environmental rule arbitrary and capricious, the Court pointed out that when an agency is making policy "at the frontiers of science, a reviewing court must generally be at its most deferential."[3]

It is not hard to decide which of the two statements deserves the most attention. If the Bazelon partnership ever existed — and many observers of federal administrative law believe that this "partnership" lived only in the mind of a single, albeit brilliant jurist and was never truly accepted by other federal judges — it no longer has much currency. The Supreme Court does not permit lower federal courts to blithely and casually reverse agency decisions. Keep this concept firmly in mind as you work through the rest of this chapter.

---

[1] *Environmental Def. Fund v. Ruckelshaus*, 439 F.2d 584 (D.C. Cir. 1971).

[2] *Chevron U.S.A., Inc. v. Natural Res. Def. Council, Inc.*, 467 U.S. 837 (1984).

[3] *Baltimore Gas & Elec. Co. v. Natural Res. Def. Council, Inc.*, 462 U.S. 87 (1983).

§ 12.02 JUDICIAL REVIEW UNDER THE APA

Section 706, the APA's scope of review provision, contains a long list of grounds on which a court may review agency action. In general, a court has the power to "decide all relevant questions of law, interpret constitutional and statutory provisions and determine the meaning or applicability of the terms of an agency action." Having performed this review, the court is permitted to:

compel agency action unlawfully withheld or unreasonably delayed; [or]

hold unlawful and set aside agency action [which is]:

- – arbitrary [and] capricious;

- – an abuse of discretion;

- – or otherwise not in accordance with law; [or is]

- – contrary to constitutional right, power, privilege, or immunity;

- – in excess of statutory jurisdiction, authority or limitations; or

- – short of statutory right;

- – without observation of procedure required by law;

- – unsupported by substantial evidence [in a §§ 556, 557 case]; or

- – unwarranted by the facts [in a *de novo* court proceeding].

Most first-time readers of § 706 look at this list of possibilities and wonder if there is anything else a court *cannot* do. Section 706 gives a reviewing court a sweeping laundry list of reasons to reverse the agency. But in truth, the better way to read these provisions is simply as a list of *possibilities*, not a list of *probabilities*. The *Attorney General's Manual* on the APA makes clear that, while the APA's drafters were trying to write a comprehensive list of grounds for review on the merits, the list was nothing more than a compendium of principles derived from existing statutes and court decisions.[4] The *Manual* itself is quite cautious as to when a court may substitute its judgment for that of an agency. Except in *de novo* review proceedings, § 706 "does not purport to empower a court to substitute its discretion for that of an administrative agency and thus exercise administrative duties. In fact, with respect to constitutional [Article III] courts, it could not do so."[5]

Beyond setting out the list of grounds, the APA says very little about the use of each of the grounds, how they relate to each other and how some of the terms ought to be defined. After 1946, the courts simply groped their way through the § 706 laundry list on a ground-by-ground, case-by-case basis, deciding, for example, what was meant by *substantial evidence* or *de novo*. It was not until 1971 that the Supreme Court provided a useful road map for § 706.

---

[4] Attorney General's Manual on the Administrative Procedure Act 93 (1947).

[5] *Id.* at 108. For some provocative thoughts on selecting an appropriate standard for review, *see* Paul R. Verkuil, *An Outcomes Analysis of Scope of Review Standards*, 44 Wm. & Mary L. Rev. 679 (2002).

§ 12.03   THE *OVERTON PARK* ROADMAP FOR § 706

[A]   Introduction

We have already seen *Citizens to Preserve Overton Park, Inc. v. Volpe*[6] in a number of other settings. *Overton Park* gives us an understanding of how the Court will deal with agency action that is neither rulemaking nor formal adjudication (Chapter 9); it contributed a great deal to our understanding of APA § 701(a)(2) (action committed to agency discretion and thus precluded from judicial review) (Chapter 10), and it also says a great deal about § 706. Indeed, it is so prominent and so frequently cited that many administrative lawyers and law professors find that they have memorized the *Overton Park* citation.

Recall that *Overton Park* involved a decision by the Secretary of Transportation to allow the expenditure of federal funds to construct a highway through a public park in Memphis, Tennessee. A number of citizens objected to the environmental and social disruption the highway would cause and filed suit to block construction. When the case reached the Supreme Court, Justice Thurgood Marshall, writing for a unanimous Court, looked first at the underlying statutory requirements. In this instance, the statute required the Secretary to consider alternatives to the project and to take steps (all possible planning) to minimize environmental damage. Given that there were some statutory standards, the Court was then able to conclude that there was "law to apply." This meant that the Secretary's decision was not completely committed to agency discretion and was thereby reviewable under the APA. But this determination only addresses the issue of preclusion. If a reviewing court actually reaches the merits of a dispute arising in an agency, where does it begin?

[B]   Reviewing the Agency Record

The *Overton Park* Court first determined that a reviewing court is required to make a thorough examination of the entire record. This conclusion is regarded as establishing as a basic principle of judicial review the so-called *hard look* doctrine. As the Court explained it, the reviewing court's "inquiry into the facts is to be searching and careful." In other words, it is to take a close and rigorous look at everything the agency has done. The hard look requirement flows directly from additional language in § 706, which obliges a court to "review the whole record." A court may not simply look at those contents of the record that support the agency's decision; it must examine both sides of the record before arriving at any conclusions.

This formulation sounds nice. At first glance, it may even appear to the Bazelon theory of a partnership between agencies and courts. But no one should take it too literally. Records developed by the major federal regulatory agencies can run into the thousands of pages, and virtually no court ever looks at every page. The hard look doctrine works properly only when capable lawyers for both sides prepare court documents that pinpoint the issues and that call the court's attention to any

---

[6]   401 U.S. 402 (1971).

information, problems, or deficiencies in the record that support their respective positions. The tedious page-by-page searching of the record is normally counsels' job, not the court's.

Recently, there has been some question as to whether the hard look doctrine retains its original vitality and speculation as to the purposes served by the doctrine.[7] Over time, the Supreme Court has unquestionably rejected David Bazelon's notion of a grand partnership between agencies and courts. Nonetheless, in *Motor Vehicle Manufacturers Ass'n v. State Farm Mutual Automobile Insurance Co.*,[8] the Court subjected an attempt by the Reagan Administration to rescind certain Department of Transportation seat-belt rules to exceptionally close scrutiny — a classic *hard look*. Without relying heavily on *Overton Park*, the Court very carefully and very precisely examined the agency record to find that there was no reasonable basis for the rescission of the rules.

The hard look doctrine may be somewhat like other principles of judicial review. When the Court wishes to invoke it, it will; when it wishes to be much more lenient with regard to an agency's action, the doctrine will be disregarded. This is not to accuse the Court of unprincipled decision making; the Court just suffers, as do all of us, from an occasional lack of consistency.

[C]   Picking the Appropriate Standard for Review

[1]   Parties' Choices

Because there was no standard in the enabling act for review on the merits, the *Overton Park* Court had to pick one out of § 706. It is obvious that the Court dispensed with any elaborate inquiry on grounds such as constitutional right, excess of statutory authority, procedural defects and untimeliness. The only three standards that were arguably applicable in this case were: (1) the *arbitrary/capricious* standard, (2) the *substantial evidence* standard, or (3) *de novo* review. It should come as no surprise that the *Overton Park* citizens' group argued that either the substantial evidence test should be applied or that a reviewing court should provide a de novo hearing. The government, by contrast, preferred use of the arbitrary/capricious standard.

[2]   *De Novo* Review

Justice Marshall dealt with the problem of selecting an appropriate ground for judicial review by walking through these provisions as they are set out in the APA. First, in the *Overton Park* setting, does a court have the authority to provide a *de*

---

[7] *See, e.g.,* Harold Bruff, *Legislative Formality, Administrative Rationality,* 63 Tex. L. Rev. 207 (1984).

[8] 463 U.S. 29 (1983). Even in the face of Supreme Court rejection of the partnership, Senior Judge Patricia Wald of the District of Columbia Circuit believes that certain aspects of the partnership survive. Patricia M. Wald, *Judicial Review in Midpassage: The Uneasy Partnership Between Courts and Agencies Plays On,* 32 Tulsa L.J. 221 (1996). For some additional creative thinking on the current state of judicial review, *see* Richard J. Pierce, Jr., *Judicial Review of Agency Actions in a Period of Diminishing Agency Resources,* 49 Admin. L. Rev. 61 (1997).

novo hearing? The answer is "no." In the Court's view, a *de novo* proceeding is normally permissible only when a statute specifically authorizes it.[9] However, even in the absence of a separate statute, *de novo* review might be warranted under the APA in two other instances: (1) "when the action is adjudicatory in nature and the agency's fact-finding procedures are inadequate"; or (2) "when issues that were not before the agency are raised in a proceeding to enforce nonadjudicatory agency action." The Court concluded that neither of the two conditions existed in this case.

These two exceptions to the no *de novo* review doctrine come directly from the APA's legislative history. The exceptions have been rarely invoked because if an agency properly applies the APA's adjudication procedures, it is virtually impossible to attack the procedural posture of the case. If the agency has made some kind of procedural mistake in its adjudication, a reviewing court is much more likely to invoke the different ground of *without observance of procedure required by law* and remand the case for a rehearing at the agency level. *De novo* review when an agency's fact finding procedures are inadequate is almost never granted because virtually all federal agencies' fact-finding procedures are within what might be called the "zone of reasonableness." Chapter 9 contains additional discussion on informal fact-finding procedures in various agencies.

The second exception is equally uncommon. It might be raised in the context of reviewing an agency sanction imposed not through a hearing but on the basis of a test or inspection by the agency. While there are instances of this type of agency action, under normal agency procedures, some kind of hearing is usually made available at the agency level in enforcement proceedings irrespective of whether the case arises out of a test or inspection. And even if a case fits within this exception, the *de novo* review is authorized only for those issues that were *not before the agency* during the enforcement proceeding. This phrase addresses new facts that were uncovered after the agency proceeding is concluded or facts that the agency deliberately disregarded.

[3]   Substantial Evidence Review

If the *de novo* standard does not apply, what about applying the *substantial evidence* standard? Here again, Justice Marshall simply went back to the express language of § 706 for the answer. Recall that under the terms of § 706, substantial evidence review is performed "in a case subject to sections 556 and 557 [formal adjudication or formal rulemaking] of this title or otherwise reviewed on the record of an agency hearing provided by statute . . . ." The Secretary's decision in *Overton Park* was not the result of formal adjudication, and there was no separate statutory requirement that forced him to conduct a trial-type proceeding to make his decision. Under the express language of § 706, it is only formal rulemaking or an individual trial-type proceeding that is subject to the substantial evidence standard. The agency's decision in *Overton Park* is classified as *informal adjudication (see*

---

[9] Remember, the statute triggering de novo review must normally be found outside the APA itself. There are very few statutes in the United States Code that contain de novo review provisions. Perhaps the most frequently invoked example is judicial review of agency decisions under the Freedom of Information Act, 5 U.S.C. § 552. See Chapter 14 for a discussion of de novo review in the context of the FOIA.

Chapter 9). Thus, substantial evidence review is not permissible.

[4] Arbitrary/Capricious Review

If *de novo* review is not permitted, and the substantial evidence test does not apply on its terms, what is left? Justice Marshall took a matter-of-fact approach to this question. Because the Court had already decided that the Secretary's decision was reviewable and because the first two standards (*de novo* and substantial evidence) were not applicable, there was only one test left: whether the decision was "arbitrary, capricious or an abuse of agency discretion." In other words, the arbitrary/capricious standard is simply the *residual* ground in § 706. If the case is reviewable and if no other standard fits, a court may always review under the arbitrary/capricious test.

That's the *Overton Park* road map. Most lawyers have found it a very helpful framework for working through the issue of review on the merits. Strangely enough, all of this language was mere dicta in *Overton Park* itself.[10] After deciding that the case was reviewable and after determining that the arbitrary/capricious standard applied, the Court took a hard look at the record. What the Court found was a record so deficient in explaining the Secretary of Transportation's decision the Court could not perform any meaningful review whatsoever, irrespective of the standard of review to be applied.[11] The case was remanded to DOT with the admonition that a subsequent explanation would be viewed suspiciously by a reviewing court as, perhaps, a mere "*post hoc*" rationalization for the original decision.

In another part of the opinion that was pure dicta but nonetheless fascinating, the Court held out an even more drastic possibility for agency action on remand. If after further analysis, the paper record still lacked a sufficient explanation, a reviewing court might determine that it is necessary to take the agency official's deposition to determine the reasons for funding the highway. This last possibility, of course, is a variation on the general rule stated in *Morgan IV* (*see* Chapter 8) that normally prohibits anyone attacking an agency action to attempt to probe the mind of the administrator.

---

[10] The *Overton Park* dicta (namely, that arbitrary/capricious works if nothing else fits) became the holding in the next term when the Court, in a simple per curiam opinion, applied the arbitrary/capricious standard to a decision of the Comptroller of the Currency. *Camp v. Pitts*, 411 U.S. 138 (1973).

[11] While the Court took a very matter-of-fact approach to the subsequent compilation of the record, the actual compilation of the record by the DOT after remand took four months. Professor Nathanson was one of the first to point this out. *See* Nathaniel L. Nathanson, *Probing the Mind of the Administrator: Hearing Variations and Standards of Judicial Review Under the Administrative Procedure Act and Other Federal Statutes*, 75 COLUM. L. REV. 722 (1975).

§ 12.04   JUDICIAL REVIEW OF AN AGENCY'S FACTUAL DETERMINATIONS

[A]   Introduction

The three standards of review described above apply to an agency's factual determinations. There are somewhat different tests applied to a review of questions of law. Distinguishing between questions of fact and law is sometimes difficult, but always important in trying to gauge a court's reaction to an agency record. To make these distinctions, it is sometimes helpful to move completely out of the realm of administrative law and simply think about these distinctions in the context of a garden-variety automobile accident that results in a lawsuit. Consider that there are essentially three categories of issues that might emerge from that accident: (1) questions of basic fact, (2) mixed questions of law and fact, and (3) questions of what might be called *pure* law.

There are no bright lines between these categories, but a brief analysis of the automobile accident will likely demonstrate that the questions of basic fact are the *who*, *what*, *where* and *when* questions that a newspaper reporter might ask in writing an article on the accident. Answers to those questions will probably reveal the details of the accident. For example, it may be that the accident occurred at 10 a.m., July 21, 1992, at the intersection of Maple Avenue and First Street in the village of Middletown and involved two cars. In one of the cars, a Chevrolet sedan, there were a driver named Smith and a passenger named Jones. The other car, a Ford, was driven by Brown, who was its sole occupant. It was a sunny day with a dry pavement. One car was heading north, the other car was heading west.

Now put this concept into an agency context. At this point, don't worry about the type of agency action. Just pay attention to what the agency determines. For example, the Environmental Protection Agency once determined that a level of 1 gram per gallon of lead in gasoline is the highest level that can be tolerated without endangering human health. The National Labor Relations Board may find that foreman X punched worker Y in the nose in the State Street plant on November 4, 1983 in the course of Y's picketing the plant during a labor disruption. The Federal Communications Commission might decide that a broadcast signal from proposed TV station WRXQ will not interfere with the reception of signals that are broadcast by existing station WXXY.

Identifying mixed questions of fact and law (sometimes referred as *application of fact to law* or questions of *ultimate fact*) requires you to determine — at least preliminarily — some of the legal issues in the case and the impact the specific facts of the case are going to have on those issues. In our automobile accident, we found that as a matter of basic fact there were two persons in the Chevrolet. Assume that the injured passenger wants to sue her own driver, rather than the driver of the other car. If the passenger was riding in the car as part of a car pool for which the passenger pays the driver, does the state's guest statute apply? Recall that the typical guest statute prohibits a passenger from suing the driver of the car in which the passenger is riding except for acts of gross negligence and willful and wanton conduct. Guest statutes were enacted to forestall lawsuits between passengers and drivers when the ride in question was for social purposes

— going to church on Sunday, for example, or being driven to a party to which both driver and passenger were invited. But if the ride in question is for commercial purposes (i.e., when the driver is remunerated by the passenger for the trip), the guest statute does not normally apply.

Applying the mixed fact and law concept to agency determinations, the questions might be stated as: (1) does the 1 gram per gallon lead content standard protect the public health with an *adequate margin of safety* (the standard set out in the Clean Air Act); (2) does the company's refusal to discipline the foreman constitute an *unfair labor practice* (the jurisdictional basis for NLRB enforcement action); (3) is the FCC's determination that there will be no signal interference between the two broadcast stations consistent with the *public interest* language of the Federal Communications Act?

A question of *pure* law in the auto accident case might be: Is the state's guest statute constitutional on its face? In an agency context, a question that would likely be regarded as *pure* law is: Does the Clean Air Act violate the non-delegation doctrine? Recall that a nondelegation issue does not require reference to underlying facts; it is solely an analysis of the express language of the statute. This is often a test for a question of pure law: whether a reviewing court can decide the issue without reference to the facts of the case. Concededly, in the federal system even facial challenges to the constitutionality of a statute must be brought in the context of an actual case or controversy (implicating an underlying fact pattern) but the court's decision does not have to reference any of the facts to arrive at a conclusion as to the statute's constitutionality. Moreover, a number of state courts have the power to issue so-called advisory opinions — a device that permits a court to examine such questions even before an individual lawsuit is filed.

Keeping each of these hypotheticals in mind may make it easier to understand the following discussion on the individual standards of review and the mechanics of the reviewing process.

[B] *De Novo* Review

This standard leaves no room for doubt. A reviewing court need not pay any attention whatsoever to any of the agency's findings or conclusions. The case comes into the court as if there were no decision at the agency level. There is typically a brand new fact finding proceeding. The court is perfectly free to substitute its judgment for any of the agency's findings and conclusions. Remember, however, that there are very few instances in which agency action is subject to *de novo* review.

[C] Substantial Evidence Review

This standard has been around for a long time. It is the standard of review in a number of enabling acts as well as one of the standards in the APA. The express language of § 706 and the *Overton Park* decision make clear that it applies only to formal (§§ 556, 557) agency action.

What appears to be the first attempt by the Supreme Court to define *substantial evidence* was a pre-World War Two case, *Consolidated Edison Co. v.*

NLRB,[12] a case in which the Court construed the term *evidence* as that word was used in the part of the Labor Management Relations Act dealing with judicial review. The Court concluded that the use of "evidence" was understood to mean *substantial evidence* and defined *substantial evidence* as: "something more than a mere scintilla. It means such relevant evidence as a reasonable mind might accept as adequate to support a conclusion . . . ."[13] Thus, substantial evidence is something in the record supporting the agency's decision, although only God knows what a "scintilla" is. You probably should not waste too much time worrying about it. Presumably, *Consolidated Edison* means that an agency decision supported by *no evidence whatsoever* would not meet the substantial evidence test. It may be that an agency decision supported only by a tiny bit of evidence is no good. In most instances, an agency's determination is supported by a lot of evidence, even if there is strong evidence on the other side of the case. For the most part, you will probably recognize substantial evidence when you see it.

The important factor to stress here is the idea of reasonableness. Never forget that reasonableness is largely an objective factor. It makes no difference what the reviewing judge thinks personally about the case. If a *reasonable* person could have arrived at the same conclusion as the agency based on the record before the agency, the agency's decision will stand.

If *Consolidated Edison* resolved the definition of substantial evidence, what did *Universal Camera Corp. v. NLRB*[14] contribute to our understanding of that concept? It is by far the more famous case, in part because it was written by Justice Frankfurter, a distinguished professor of administrative law prior to being named to the Court. In addition, *Universal Camera* had an impact because (1) it was written just after the APA was enacted, and (2) it determined that Congress' use of the term *substantial evidence* in the then-new APA was consistent with Congress' use of the same term in other statutes enacted around the same time. In other words, because the term *substantial evidence* predated the APA, Congress, in all likelihood, was using it in the same sense that the Court construed it in *Consolidated Edison.* Prior to the Court's *Universal Camera* decision, there had been much speculation that Congress had something different in mind when it wrote *substantial evidence* into the APA. After a lengthy exposition of the APA's legislative history, Frankfurter, writing for the Court, concluded that Congress intended the substantial evidence as used in the APA to be synonymous with earlier usages of the term.

At the same time, the *Universal Camera* opinion added more language to the *Consolidated Edison* test without making much more sense. Justice Frankfurter

---

[12] 305 U.S. 197 (1938).

[13] As you work through this definition of substantial evidence — a concept applicable to *judicial review* of agency action — make sure you distinguish it from the standard of proof such as *preponderance* of the evidence (discussed in Chapter 8). Preponderance of the evidence is the standard of proof applicable at the agency hearing. It helps the administrative law judge decide whether a party has proven a specific fact (*e.g.*, whether the existence of the fact is more probable than not). Substantial evidence is an analysis performed by a reviewing court to see what, if anything, in the record supports the agency's decision.

[14] 340 U.S. 474 (1951).

was happy to invoke the "more-than-a-scintilla" idea but he went further. To constitute substantial evidence, the evidence "must do more than create a suspicion of the existence of the fact to be established . . . . [I]t must be enough to justify, if the trial were to a jury, a refusal to direct a verdict when the conclusion sought to be drawn from it is one of fact for the jury."

Be careful with the statement relating to directed verdicts. Frankfurter obviously knew what he had in mind, but one of the more dangerous practices in working with administrative law concepts is drawing too many analogies to court litigation. Recall that administrative agencies were often created because courts were not doing an adequate job. Besides, does the directed verdict analogy make things any clearer? It may help a trial judge with experience in granting or denying motions for directed verdict. It probably doesn't help persons who are not judges. Perhaps the best way to think about substantial evidence as a quantitative concept is simply to keep in mind that there must be an adequate amount of evidence in the record that supports the agency's decision.

Beyond this, *Universal Camera* made a major contribution to the *process* of substantial evidence review. The Court found earlier attempts at substantial evidence review by the federal courts to be too casual and lacking in appropriate rigor. The Court separated substantial evidence review into two stages: stage one is the fact gathering stage — the proceeding before the administrative law judge (back then ALJs were referred to as hearing examiners). Stage two is the final decision made by the agency. With regard to stage one, the Court determined that while the findings of fact submitted to higher-ups in an agency by the administrative law judge were important and could not be totally disregarded, they could be set aside in certain circumstances by reviewing personnel in the agency. The Court's reasoning here is that agency action involves all the expertise within an agency, not merely that vested in its ALJs. Agencies, however, were cautioned to be sensitive to an ALJ's findings on issues such as the credibility of witnesses because it is the ALJ who presides over the evidentiary hearing and who hears and sees the witnesses.[15]

In *Universal Camera*, the Court used a somewhat backhanded formula of words to describe the weight that must be given to an ALJ's findings by a reviewing court. The Court said that an ALJ's findings were "not as unassailable as a master's." This refers to a *special master* appointed by a court to make a fact-finding inquiry on the record that is later submitted to the court for its review. Special masters are used at every level of the judiciary. The Supreme Court frequently resorts to masters in cases arising under its original jurisdiction because the Court itself will not sit to gather evidence. When receiving a report from its own special masters, the Court rarely questions the master's factual findings.

In substantial evidence review, both the agency and a reviewing court must pay attention to the work of the ALJ, but the ALJ's findings are not totally beyond questioning. With regard to further agency review, the persons in the agency above the ALJ (*i.e.*, those who perform a reviewing function) are permitted to consider

---

[15] This point is also discussed in Chapter 8, § 8.09.

the dispute in light of their own expertise as well as being required to pay attention to the pronouncements of the ALJ.

The second major contribution of *Universal Camera* concerns the manner in which the court educates itself on the agency record. Recall that many agency records run to hundreds if not thousands of pages. On this point, the Court took a pragmatic approach to the assignment of responsibilities for examining the record. The Supreme Court did not want to find itself groping through thousands of pages of agency record looking for the presence or absence of a "scintilla" of proof. As a result, in a companion case, *NLRB v. Pittsburgh Steamship Co.*,[16] the Court made clear that the burden of closely examining the agency record would fall mainly on the lower federal courts. Even more realistically, the Court concluded that the important contents of the record, either favoring or cutting against the agency's action, would of necessity have to be brought to the court's attention by skilled counsel. Even the lower federal courts could not be expected to dig through each and every page of material that had been before the agency.

Third, the Court acknowledged that the technique that the federal courts had been using for substantial evidence review in the past was not consistent with § 706 of the APA. Recall that the language at the end of § 706 requires the court to review *the whole record*. Prior to *Universal Camera*, a typical reviewing court would obtain the agency record and would start reading the record from page one onward. However, as soon as the court came to some evidence (more than a scintilla, of course) that supported the agency's decision, it would halt its review and would then declare the agency decision to be supported by substantial evidence.

Universal Camera teaches us that this technique is not sufficient under the APA. In this respect, it is a harbinger of the hard look doctrine enunciated in *Overton Park*. As commanded by *Universal Camera*, a court performing substantial evidence review must review the record as a whole, examining both the evidence supporting and opposing the agency's decision, to determine whether the decision is supported *on the entire record* by substantial evidence.

There is still some uncertainty as to which court is obliged to perform the substantial evidence review. Recall the *Pittsburgh Steamship* case, companion to *Universal Camera*, in which the Court suggested that it would not perform such a task, and that substantial evidence review was to be conducted by the lower federal courts, including the courts of appeals. However, in 1998, the Supreme Court engaged in a thorough-going (some might say nit-picking) review of a decision by the National Labor Relations Board to conclude, among many other things, that the NLRB's decision is not supported by substantial evidence. In *Allentown Mack Sales & Svc., Inc. v. NLRB*,[17] the Court dug into the record to discuss specific testimony by individual witnesses at the hearing before the administrative law judge and to compare the manner in which the ALJ and the Board dealt with that testimony. The Court itself weighed some of the witness testimony in terms that are more often found in decisions by ALJs themselves:

---

[16] 340 U.S. 498 (1951).

[17] 522 U.S. 359 (1998).

Allentown [the company and a party to the action] would reasonably have given great credence to Mohr's [an employee/witness] assertion of lack of union support, since he was not hostile to the union, and was in a good position to assess antiunion sentiment . . . . It seems to us [the Supreme Court] that Mohr's statement has undeniable and substantial probative value on the issue of 'reasonable doubt.'[18]

The Court majority went on to conclude that the test established by the Board (the so-called "reasonable doubt" test) was rational and consistent with the statute, but the Board's decision was fatally flawed because its finding that Allentown lacked such doubt was not supported by substantial evidence on the record as a whole. Justice Breyer, himself a former professor of administrative law, writing for four dissenters, had a much different perspective: "[The majority] has rewritten a Board decision without adequate justification. It has ignored certain evidentiary presumptions . . . And it has failed to give the kind of leeway to the Board's fact-finding authority that the Court's precedents mandate."[19]

The Supreme Court has had very little more to say about substantial evidence review since *Universal Camera*. The fundamental propositions advanced in that case have rarely been questioned. There is, however, some question these days as to whether there is any meaningful difference between substantial evidence and the arbitrary/capricious test. That issue is discussed in the following subsection.

[D]　The Arbitrary/Capricious Test

As the residual test for review of an agency's factual determinations, you would think that this test has been clearly articulated and evenly applied. That is not the case. *Overton Park* suggested that the test meant whether "the decision was based on a consideration of the relevant factors and whether there has been a clear error of judgment." A footnote in *Overton Park*, appended to the discussion of the arbitrary and capricious test analogized to Rule 52(a) of the *Federal Rules of Civil Procedure* which creates the *clearly erroneous* test for overturning a trial court's findings of fact. The analogy itself is clearly erroneous and illustrates once again the dangers of drawing too heavily on civil litigation principles to answer administrative law questions. Most administrative law professors encourage their students to delete that footnote from their casebook's extract of *Overton Park*. The Rule 52(a) analogy is simply not accepted by any academic who has commented on *Overton Park*, and the concept has not been revisited or further approved by the Supreme Court. Whatever arbitrary/capricious might mean, it is not to be judged by the court-based concept of clearly erroneous.

---

[18] *Id.* at 372.

[19] *Id.* at 381. Recently, the Supreme Court ordered the United States Court of Appeals for the Federal Circuit to use APA review standards (including, presumably, the substantial evidence test) to decisions involving the Patent and Trademark Office. The Federal Circuit had sought to apply what it believed to be the more rigorous "clearly erroneous" test under the Federal Rules of Civil Procedure on the basis that the clearly erroneous test was found in the common law, that it predated the APA, and that the APA was not an exclusive set of grounds for judicial review. The Supreme Court, in *Dickinson v. Zurko*, 527 U.S. 150 (1999).

Nonetheless, it is difficult to tell where things stand in the second decade of the twenty-first century. The D.C. Circuit, writing five years after *Overton Park*, expressed some qualms about the Court's definition of arbitrary/capricious because prior to *Overton Park*, most observers believed that the substantial evidence test was somehow more rigorous than the arbitrary/capricious test. The circuit called *Overton Park*'s attempt at a definition "difficult to plumb and its standard even more uncertain of application."[20] Until the Supreme Court clarifies its use of "clear error of judgment," the Circuit has decided to equate arbitrary/capricious with rational basis. In other words, the test is a standard that is highly deferential to the agency. Agency action will be reversed only if that action lacks a rational basis. Rational basis is used here in the same sense that it is used in review of non-suspect classifications under the Equal Protection Clause of the United States Constitution. It is very unusual for an agency action to lack a rational basis.

In 1984, one of the newer members of the D.C. Circuit (now a Supreme Court Justice), Antonin Scalia, took the bull by the horns and decided that there simply was no difference between the substantial evidence test and the arbitrary/capricious test. Writing for the court in *Association of Data Processing Service Organizations v. Federal Reserve Board*,[21] then-Circuit Judge Scalia reviewed a case in which part of the record was an outgrowth of an individualized Federal Reserve Board action which, by statute, was to be reviewed on the basis of the substantial evidence test. The remainder of the record was the product of the agency's informal rulemaking and thereby subject to the arbitrary/capricious test. As Judge Scalia put it:

> [Substantial evidence] is only a specific application of [arbitrary/capricious] separately recited in the APA not to establish a more rigorous standard of factual support but to emphasize that in the case of formal proceedings, the factual support must be found in the closed [hearing] record as opposed to elsewhere.

In Scalia's opinion, the distinction is mainly one of semantics. The touchstone for both tests is *reasonableness*. The differences between the two are differences of analytical technique rather than analytical substance. While not all courts of appeals have adopted Justice Scalia's language, most courts appear to accept his message. At present, there seems not to be much agonizing among the federal courts over the distinction between arbitrary/capricious and substantial evidence. If the agency's action is reasonable, it must be upheld.

Reading these cases might give the reader the idea that arbitrary/capricious review is nearly totally deferential to the agency. Most of the time that's probably a sound conclusion. But in 2007, the Supreme Court took up the highly contentious issue of global warming and decided that an agency's failure to promulgate rules comprised arbitrary and capricious agency action. In *Massachusetts v. EPA*,[22] a

---

[20] *Ethyl Corp. v. Environmental Protection Agency*, 541 F.2d 1 (D.C. Cir.), *cert. denied*, 426 U.S. 941 (1976).

[21] 745 F.2d 677 (D.C. Cir. 1984).

[22] 549 U.S. 497 (2007). This case is also important for some pronouncements on when states have "standing" in federal court. Those issues are discussed in Chapter 10 at § 10.06(H).

large number of plaintiffs, including individual states (e.g., Massachusetts), local governments and private environmental protection groups sued the Environmental Protection Agency for its refusal to make rules regulating the emission of four greenhouse gases, including carbon dioxide, by new motor vehicles. The plaintiffs had earlier petitioned EPA to make such rules and the EPA denied the petition for rulemaking, arguing that it did not have sufficient statutory authority to do so and, even if there was statutory authority, that the scientific issues were so uncertain that it could not fashion a proper rule.

On review by the Supreme Court with Justice Stevens writing the majority opinion, the Court conceded that the *Chevron* doctrine required federal courts to defer to agency interpretations of its own statute (see *Chevron, infra*). It further conceded that the *Heckler v. Chaney* doctrine (see *Heckler, supra*) made it difficult for a reviewing court to second-guess an agency's decision not to pursue an enforcement action. However, in *Massachusetts*, the Court first determined that an agency's refusal to initiate a rulemaking was judicially reviewable, albeit in circumstances where a reviewing court's review was required to be "highly deferential" and "extremely limited."[23]

Having resolved the issues of standing and reviewability in favor of the plaintiffs, the Court then turned to the question of whether the EPA had statutory authority to promulgate an emissions rule. The Court looked at the express language of the Clean Air Act which provides, in part: "The [EPA] Administrator shall by regulation prescribe . . . standards applicable to the emission of any air pollutant from . . . new motor vehicles . . . which in his judgment cause, or contribute to, air pollution which may reasonably be anticipated to endanger public health or welfare."[24] The Act then defines "air pollutant" to include "any air pollution agent or combination of such agents, including any physical, chemical, biological, radioactive . . . substance or matter which is emitted into or otherwise enters the ambient air."[25] In defining "welfare," the Clean Air Act provides a broad definition including: "effects on . . . weather . . . and climate."[26]

To avoid the rulemaking, the EPA tried to argue, among other things, that these issues primarily affected automobile mileage, which regulatory mission was vested in the Department of Transportation. The Court quickly dispensed with these arguments to state, unequivocally: "Because greenhouse gases fit well within the Clean Air Act's capacious definition of 'air pollutant,' we hold that EPA has the statutory authority to regulate the emission of such gases from new motor vehicles."[27]

Having resolved the statutory authority issue, the Court then moved to an analysis of whether the EPA's refusal constituted arbitrary/capricious agency action. Recall that the EPA had argued that the science was too uncertain to permit

---

[23] *Id.* at 523. *See* Jack M. Beermann, *The Turn Toward Congress in Administrative Law*, 89 B.U. L. Rev. 727 (2009).

[24] Clean Air Act, § 202(a)(1).

[25] *Id.* § 7602(g).

[26] *Id.* § 7602(h).

[27] 549 U.S. at 523.

it to proceed in this area. On this point, Justice Stevens hammered the agency on both the science and the administrative law issues. He cited all of the scientific commentary on global warming to demonstrate the existence of the problem. He noted "the enormity of the potential consequences associated with man-made climate change." He commented that "The risk of catastrophic harm, though remote, is nevertheless real." He then chastised EPA for arguing that whatever action EPA could take on automobile emissions was merely "incremental." In Justice Steven's words: "Agencies, like legislatures, do not generally resolve massive problems in one fell regulatory swoop. . . . That[28] a first step might be tentative does not by itself support the notion [that a rule should not be made.]"

And, finally, on the issue of whether the EPA's refusal to promulgate the rule constituted arbitrary and capricious action, he concluded: "EPA has offered no reasoned explanation for its refusal to decide whether greenhouse gases cause or contribute to climate change. Its action was therefore 'arbitrary, capricious . . . or not in accordance with law,' [However,] we need not and do not reach the question whether on remand EPA must make an endangerment finding . . . We hold only that EPA must ground its reasons for action or inaction in the statute . . . ."[29]

§ 12.05 JUDICIAL REVIEW OF QUESTIONS OF LAW AND MIXED QUESTIONS OF LAW AND FACT

[A] Formulating the Issues

This is a good time to review those hypotheticals set out just before the substantial evidence discussion because at this point things can start getting a little complicated and, unfortunately, more than a little fuzzy. But don't despair; these issues have puzzled more than one reviewing court, and there are not a lot of really good answers.

It also makes sense at this point to distinguish between what a court is *obliged* to do and what a court *may* do in reviewing some of these issues. On the first issue — those things that a court is obliged to do — consider that a court must give an agency's substantive rules the force and effect of law.[30] On the second issue — what a court may do in performing judicial review in this area — consider the following question. Is a reviewing court required to defer to an agency's determination that the agency's own enabling act does not violate the non-delegation doctrine or that the agency's procedures are compatible with constitutional due process? Most commentators would probably say "no."

But as a practical matter there is nothing to prevent a court from at least hearing what the agency has to say on these points. Irrespective of the language in

---

[28] *Id.* at 526.

[29] *Id.* As any reader will concede, this case was fraught with politics and involved the transition from the administration of President George W. Bush into the administration of Barack Obama. The EPA under President Obama made an endangerment finding and is proceeding with final rules for automobile emissions.

[30] *See* the discussion on this concept in Chapter 7, § 7.09.

a court's opinion, if a reviewing court agrees with an agency on the delegation or due process issues, some people reading the opinion might conclude that the court paid at least some deference to the agency. If a court disagrees with the agency, readers of the opinion might conclude that the court felt free to substitute its own judgment on the issue. This is one of the reasons why mere labels do not suffice. This is also one of the areas of administrative law that clearly illustrate that homily of Mark Twain's, quoted by Justice Jackson in his separate opinion in *Chenery II*: "I give up. Now I know what Mark Twain meant when he said, 'the more you explain it, the less I understand it.' "[31]

There are a number of alternate approaches to formulating the issue. Professor Bernard Schwartz suggests setting up the same type of spectrum described in § 12.04, *above*, albeit using a slightly different vocabulary. Begin by listing the three possibilities:

1. Questions of basic fact

2. Mixed questions of fact and law (application of law to fact) (ultimate facts)

3. Questions of *pure* law.[32]

Having set up this spectrum, place the issue under review in its appropriate category: either 1, 2, or 3. Then, simply consider that as your analysis moves from category 1 to category 3, it becomes easier for a court to substitute its judgment for that of the agency irrespective of the label placed on the review.

Under this analysis, it is easy to understand why courts almost never secondguess the resolution of basic facts by an agency. Would a court really want to revisit an ALJ's finding that Foreman X punched Worker Y in the nose on June 13, 1991?

Universal Camera also provides an answer. A court may not reverse unless, after a thorough search of the entire record, it concludes that the finding was not supported by substantial evidence and that a reasonable person looking at the same record would not have found the same thing. Reversing the agency's findings of basic fact exposes the lower court to being reversed by a higher court for tampering with an agency's fact-finding process. Moreover, except in *de novo* review proceedings, why would a court want to deal with factual questions that have already been addressed, and presumably resolved, by the agency? This simply is not the court's proper role in most instances.

There may be a little more leeway on mixed questions of law and fact. Is a buyer an *employee* as that term is used in the Labor Management Relations Act? The agency might say "yes," and a reviewing court looking at the same record might be inclined to say "no." May the court reverse the agency on this point?

There is no easy answer here. There are many cases in which courts have reversed the agency and, conversely, many in which they have felt obliged to give deference to the agency's determination. There is not even much agreement on the

---

[31] *See* the discussion of *Chenery II* in Chapter 6, § 6.03.

[32] BERNARD SCHWARTZ, ADMINISTRATIVE LAW, Ch. 10 (3d ed. 1991).

standard of review to be applied to these issues. Some courts insist that they use either the substantial evidence or arbitrary/capricious test; nevertheless, they seem to defer far less to the agency's position than they do on the basic factual questions.

The APA is of absolutely no help here. It simply does not distinguish between the three types of issues outlined above, although the fact that the structure of § 706 sets grounds such as *in excess of statutory authority* and *short of statutory right* apart from the substantial evidence and arbitrary/capricious grounds may be a hint that a court is not required to use these last two tests to review questions of law, mixed or otherwise. Similarly, there is precious little help in most agency enabling acts, probably because neither Congress, nor the courts, nor the judges, nor the administrative law scholars have yet resolved these problems.

One of the preeminent circuit judges, the late Henry Friendly, broke the problem down into even more subtle categories than are outlined above. In *NLRB v. Marcus Trucking Co.*,[33] he suggested three categories based on his review of a large number of Supreme Court cases:

1.   Cases involving an agency finding on the who, what, where, when "raw" facts in the statutory framework are not in dispute;

2.   Cases in which there are disputes as to "raw" facts and as to the application of a statutory term, such as *course of employment* (*e.g.*, was the truck driver drunk, and being drunk after regular working hours, was he functioning in the course of his employment?);

3.   Cases in which the primary dispute is not over the "raw" facts, but rather over how to interpret and apply the statutory term (*e.g.*, are newsboys *employees* under the Labor Management Relations Act).

Judge Friendly has no problem with categories 1 and 3. He concludes that Category 1 issues are subject to either the substantial evidence test or arbitrary/capricious test, as appropriate. Category 3 issues, he believes, comprise questions of law that may require some deference to the agency's position but need not be reviewed under the extremely deferential substantial evidence test. However, with regard to Category 2-type issues, and even after this brilliant preliminary analysis, he too becomes unclear. All that Judge Friendly can say is that if there is little dispute over the statutory terms but a lot of argument over whether the party fits within the statute, the substantial evidence test applies. If the dispute is mainly over what the statute says, a court may properly be less deferential to the agency.

[B]   The Constitutional Fact/Jurisdictional Fact Muddle

Some older administrative law casebooks and treatises spend a great deal of time discussing issues of constitutional/jurisdictional fact, mainly because of some early Supreme Court decisions that appear to suggest that there are special rules governing judicial review of such questions. The tension here is caused primarily

---

[33] 286 F.2d 583 (2d Cir. 1961).

by two cases that remain on the books, but appear to have been overruled *sub silentio* by the Court. Note that both these cases predate the New Deal. Note further that neither of these decisions appear to be favored by the current Supreme Court. In *Ohio Valley Water Co. v. Ben Avon Borough*,[34] the Court reviewed a claim stemming from an alleged unconstitutional taking of private property by a state agency and concluded that when constitutional facts are at issue, a court is empowered to review those facts *de novo* — *i.e.*, without any deference to anything said or done by the agency.

In *Crowell v. Benson*,[35] the Court looked at a federal workers compensation statute and noted that the two main issues were (1) whether the claimant was injured in the course of his employment, and (2) whether the injury suffered was "upon the navigable waters of the United States." The Court determined that the statute had no force and effect — *i.e.*, the agency was simply without jurisdiction to proceed-if these facts were not properly proved. Because it concluded that a reviewing court could always look at whether an agency is functioning within its jurisdiction and because these were so-called *jurisdictional* facts, a reviewing court could take up the issue *de novo*. *Crowell* may have been done in by a 1965 per curiam decision, *O'Keeffe v. Smith, Hinchman & Grylls Associates, Inc.*,[36] in which the Court reviewed an agency decision dealing with whether a person was within the scope of his employment under exactly the same statute involved in *Crowell* and concluded: "While this Court may not have reached the same conclusion as the [agency] it cannot be said that [the agency's decision] is irrational or without substantial evidence on the record as a whole." However, the much more recent *Chevron* opinion (discussed at length in the next subsection) has muddied the waters once again.

[C]   An Agency's Interpretation of Its Own Statutes: *NLRB v. Hearst* and *Gray v. Powell*

The Supreme Court has contributed to the confusion. Examine the remainder of this chapter before you come to any personal conclusions as to what the law is. In *NLRB v. Hearst Publications, Inc.*,[37] the Court addressed the issue of whether newsboys were employees under the Labor Management Relations Act (LMRA) — a question that Judge Friendly puts into his "law" category. In *Hearst*, there seemed to be virtually no dispute about what the "newsboys" did. They were, in truth, adult males who had permanent newsstands in various locations in the City of Los Angeles and sold Hearst newspapers. However, the newsboys were generally compensated only for papers sold — *i.e.*, they were not on salary, and they had no guarantee of employment. If the newsboys didn't sell Hearst papers, they didn't get paid. Moreover, there was no dispute at the other end of the interpretative spectrum. Hearst was not asserting that the underlying statute was

---

[34] 253 U.S. 287 (1920).

[35] 285 U.S. 22 (1932).

[36] 380 U.S. 359 (1965).

[37] 322 U.S. 111 (1944).

unconstitutional — the LMRA's constitutionality had been conclusively resolved a few years earlier.

The Hearst management regarded newsboys as independent contractors rather than employees of the Hearst newspapers.[38] When the newsboys in Los Angeles tried to organize themselves into a union under the Labor Management Relations Act, Hearst fought the unionization attempt by claiming (1) that the newsboys were not employees but independent contractors, (2) the LMRA applied only to the employer/employee relationship, (3) therefore, there could be no union, and (4) if there could be no union, Hearst had no obligation to bargain with this group that called itself a "union." The NLRB concluded otherwise and cited Hearst for an unfair labor practice.

When the case reached the Ninth Circuit, the court looked at the dispute and took a wholly new approach to the definitional problem — i.e., are newsboys *employees* — by going outside LMRA case law and examining common law principles governing the employer-employee relationship, mainly in the area of *respondeat superior* doctrine — a doctrine that grows out of the convergence of common law agency and tort principles. The circuit believed that it was authorized to apply these common law definitions because it concluded, as a threshold matter, that the LMRA incorporated common law *respondeat superior* concepts in its definitional structure. Based on a review of the common law cases, the circuit reversed the NLRB decision, concluding that the newsboys were not employees and therefore not eligible to bargain collectively with Hearst.

In this posture, the *Hearst* case reached the Supreme Court. The Court concluded that the Ninth Circuit had erred in applying common law decisional criteria since the entire legislative history of the LMRA indicates that it was enacted because the common law *was not* dealing capably with the problems of labor-management relations. Any reliance on common law concepts to interpret this brand new statute was, therefore, totally misplaced.

The Court, moreover, decided that this was an instance in which the reviewing court should defer to the agency, stating:

> [W]here the question is one of specific application of a broad statutory term in a proceeding in which the agency administering the statute must determine it initially, the reviewing court's function is limited . . . . The Board's determination that specified persons are 'employees' under this Act is to be accepted if it has 'warrant in the record' and a reasonable basis in law.

This sounds very much like substantial evidence review even though as distinguished a jurist as Friendly placed the *Hearst* issue in a category of *law* where, he suggests, a court need grant the agency only a little deference in its interpretation of the statute.

---

[38] To get a better feel for the entire situation, take another look at the movie, *Citizen Kane.*

The reasonableness test was articulated in slightly less dramatic form just three years prior to *Hearst* in *Gray v. Powell*,[39] a case in which a New Deal agency determined that a railroad was a *producer* as that term was defined in the Bituminous Coal Act. In *Gray*, the Court pointed out that a reviewing court's work is done when it determines that the agency applied the enabling act to the regulated party in "a just and reasonable manner." A reversal is justified only when a court can conclude that the agency went haywire — *i.e.*, when its application of the statute to the private party is "so unrelated to the tasks entrusted by Congress . . . to deny a sensible exercise of judgment." But under either *Hearst* or *Gray*, the test appears to be stated in two parts: (1) what criteria did the agency use in interpreting the statute? and (2) if the interpretative criteria are consistent with the legislative history of the statute, was the agency's ultimate decision reasonable?

[D] An Agency's Interpretation of Its Own Statutes: From *Chevron* Through *Brown & Williamson* and *Mead* and Beyond

Most people would think that by the first decade of the twenty-first century, the Court or Congress or both would have gotten their act together on a point as crucial as judicial review of questions of law. There was an ill-fated attempt to write some new standards of review in the 97th Congress. Senator Bumpers introduced a regulatory reform bill, S. 1080, that included a provision requiring courts to make an independent review of an agency's interpretation of its own statutes and prohibiting the courts from indulging any presumption in favor or against agency action. The bill did not survive, however, and this type of regulatory reform by way of amendments to the APA has ceased to be a hot topic in Congress.

A line of Supreme Court decisions show that the Court has not yet completely made up its mind on the issue. The most prominent case, the one most often cited and the one most often written about is *Chevron U.S.A., Inc. v. Natural Resources Defense Council, Inc.*,[40] a case involving the Environmental Protection Agency's interpretation of the term *stationary source* in the Clean Air Act.[41] The EPA permitted the states to define a *stationary source* as an entire plant (rather than, say, a single smokestack in a plant with multiple smokestacks) for the purposes of working out a state implementation plan to cut down on air pollution. The effect of this interpretation left the plant owners free to determine on their own how to cope with certain pollution control requirements under the Clean Air Act, so long as the entire plant met the standards. As so frequently happens with the EPA, various environmental groups challenged the policy in court, and the case eventually made its way to the Supreme Court.

In *Chevron*, a 6-0 decision with three justices not participating, the Court reviewed the entire rulemaking record and concluded that the EPA's interpretation "represents a reasonable accommodation of manifestly competing interests and is entitled to deference [in a situation in which] the regulatory scheme is technical

[39] 314 U.S. 402 (1941).

[40] 467 U.S. 837 (1984).

[41] 42 U.S.C. §§ 7410, 7411.

and complex." The Court then proceeded to comment on the fact that judges are not expert and are not politically accountable, as are both Congress and the agencies (through the President).

But the most important contribution of Chevron is the two-step formula for dealing with these issues.[42] First, the Court determines "whether Congress has spoken to the precise question at issue." If this is the case, neither the agency nor the courts can alter this pronouncement. In other words, both agency and courts must defer to the Congressional position irrespective of their own views on the subject. But as the Court acknowledged in *Chevron*, Congress has a history of writing relatively ambiguous statutes that permit the agencies to fill in many of the gaps through agency policy making and interpretation. This is step two: if Congress has not directly addressed the matter — i.e., if the statutory language is either silent or ambiguous — the reviewing court then examines the agency's construction of its statutory mandate. The court must defer to the agency's position if the court concludes that the agency's action is reasonable. In *Chevron*, the Supreme Court concluded that the EPA's so-called bubble policy was a reasonable interpretation of the Clean Air Act.

This seems on its face to be a rational way to deal with a constantly perplexing problem of review of agency policy making. It is also consistent with the whole line of Supreme Court opinions discussed earlier in this chapter, holding that courts should not lightly overturn agency action on any grounds. It certainly seems consistent with *NLRB v. Hearst*, probably its closest relation. The problem is that *Chevron* may not be followed, even by the Supreme Court itself, as religiously as the *Chevron* Court and some commentators might prefer; and the opinion has become a favorite of law professors, generating more writing than virtually any administrative law decision of recent vintage.[43]

Interestingly, just before deciding *Chevron* in a case that most commentators seem to have forgotten about the Court had no qualms whatsoever reversing an

---

[42] This phrase was quoted in an insightful article on *Chevron* by Professor Richard Pierce. It is probably inevitable that some of the following discussion in this section derives from Professor Pierce's comments on *Chevron* in Richard J. Pierce, Jr., *Chevron and Its Aftermath: Judicial Review of Agency Interpretations of Statutory Provisions*, 41 VAND. L. REV. 301 (1988).

[43] For an example of a case in which the Supreme Court overturned an agency's interpretation of its own statute in a unanimous opinion that never once even cited *Chevron*, see *Brotherhood of Locomotive Engineers v. A.T. & S.F. RR. Co.*, 516 U.S. 152 (1996). For some of the best of the now-burgeoning Chevron scholarship, see, e.g., Robert A. Anthony, *Which Agency Interpretations Should Bind the Courts?*, 7 YALE J. ON REG. 1 (1990); Antonin Scalia, *Judicial Deference to Administrative Interpretations of Law*, 1989 DUKE L.J. 511; Clark Byse, *Judicial Review of Administrative Interpretation of Statutes*, 2 ADMIN. L.J. 255 (1988); Stephen J. Breyer, *Judicial Review of Questions of Law and Policy*, 38 ADMIN L. REV. 363 (1986); Kenneth Starr, *Judicial Review in the Post-*Chevron *Era*, 3 YALE J. ON REG. 283 (1986); Maureen B. Callahan, *Must Federal Courts Defer to Agency Interpretations of Statutes?: A New Doctrinal Basis for* Chevron U.S.A. v. Natural Resources Defense Council, 1991 WIS. L. REV. 1275 (concluding that the *Chevron* doctrine is based neither in the Constitution nor in governing statutes and that the doctrine is merely a "flexible" guide, selectively applied to agency interpretations). *Chevron* continues to generate an enormous amount of scholarship. *See, e.g.*, Orin S. Kerr, *Shedding Light on* Chevron: *An Empirical Study of the* Chevron *Doctrine in the U.S. Courts of Appeals*, 15 YALE J. ON REG. 1 (1998); John F. Manning, *Constitutional Structure and Judicial Deference to Agency Interpretations of Agency Rules*, 96 COLUM. L. REV. 612 (1996).

agency's interpretation of its own statute. In *Public Service Commission of New York v. Mid-Louisiana Gas Co.*,[44] the Court reviewed a decision by the Federal Energy Regulatory Commission (FERC) involving an arcane issue of natural gas pricing under the Natural Gas Policy Act.[45] Specifically, a number of large natural gas pipelines that also owned natural gas wells asked FERC to give their companies the same pricing benefits that were enjoyed by independent gas well owners (*i.e.*, those owners who were not affiliated with pipelines). The controversy, frequently referred to as the "first sale" dispute, represented literally hundreds of millions of dollars in additional revenues for the pipeline companies if they could persuade FERC to give them these benefits.

FERC refused to treat the pipelines and the independent owners similarly. The Supreme Court, in a 5-4 decision, paid lip service to the proposition that "the interpretation of an agency charged with administering a statute is entitled to substantial deference," but ultimately concluded that the Commission's position on first sale was "contrary to the history, structure and basic philosophy of the [Natural Gas Policy Act]."

There may be ways to distinguish these two cases. For example, it is arguable that the Natural Gas Policy Act (NGPA) is less ambiguous on the *first sale* issue than the Clean Air Act was on the concept of stationary source, although reasonable minds may differ on this proposition. Thus, Mid-Louisiana may simply be a Chevron *first step* case and nothing more. By contrast, there is no question that the NGPA is at least as complex and technical a statute as the Clean Air Act, and that FERC is supposed to be the expert on regulation of the natural gas industry.[46] In other words, why did the Court defer to the EPA's expertise while running roughshod over FERC's expertise? Moreover, the tone and style of the two decisions is difficult to fathom. Why would the Court brush so quickly past the substantial deference principle in *Mid-Louisiana* while carrying on at length about the necessity for deference in *Chevron*? There are inconsistencies in these two decisions (and a substantial number of others, quite frankly) that are almost impossible to explain. Worse, if the Supreme Court is inconsistent in its review of questions of law, everyone else is going to equally confused.[47]

Just a few years after *Chevron*, the Court decided *Immigration and Naturalization Service v. Cardoza-Fonseca*,[48] holding that the INS had interpreted an immigration statute wrongly and quoted its own language in *Chevron*: "The judiciary is the final authority on issues of statutory construction and must reject administrative constructions which are contrary to clear congressional intent." Some readers of *Cardoza-Fonseca* believe that this opinion may be a slight stepping back from the strong message of deference set out in *Chevron*. On its face, the opinion does not seem to represent a retrenching. Rather,

---

[44] 463 U.S. 319 (1983).

[45] 15 U.S.C. §§ 3301 *et seq.*

[46] *See, e.g.*, WILLIAM FOX, FEDERAL REGULATION OF ENERGY 423–72 (1983).

[47] For a well-thought-out approach to these questions, *see* Colin S. Diver, *Statutory Interpretation in the Administrative State*, 133 U. PA. L. REV. 549 (1985).

[48] 480 U.S. 421 (1987).

the Court seems to be saying that there was no doubt about congressional intent in the statute, and that the INS' interpretation was contrary to that intent. That is the first of *Chevron*'s two steps so, at least analytically if not substantively, the *Cardoza-Fonseca* Court appears consistent with *Chevron*.

In another case, the Court struck down a policy of the Federal Energy Regulatory Commission when it decided that the agency's policy was inconsistent with the clear language of the statute.[49] In that case, the Court held that there was no ambiguity whatsoever in the underlying statute. By contrast, in *American Hospital Ass'n v. NLRB*,[50] in reviewing virtually the first substantive rule ever promulgated by the National Labor Relations Board, the Court deferred to the Board's policy, holding that its rule was consistent with the underlying statutory scheme.

A few peripheral issues seem to crop up from time to time under *Chevron*. Under the Occupational Safety and Health Act, the Occupational Safety and Health Administration (OSHA), a component of the Department of Labor, develops safety and health policy and investigates businesses for compliance with OSHA rules. If a business cited with an OSHA violation disagrees with the citation, it may have an adjudication of its penalty in the Occupational Safety and Health Review Commission. In *Martin v. Occupational Safety and Health Review Commission*,[51] the Court was faced with interpretations of the statute by OSHA and the Commission that were in direct conflict. In this case, the Court had to decide to whom to defer, OSHA or the Commission. The Court chose to accept OSHA's interpretation as the entity charged under the statute with the obligation to make policy. The Commission, in the Court's view, performed only an adjudicatory function, not a policy making one.

These cases make clear that all the nuances of *Chevron* have not yet been explored. It is equally important to understand that *Chevron* does not mean total capitulation or unprincipled deference to an agency. While deference is required for an agency's substantive rules and most if not all interpretations of those rules, deference is not required for "agency litigating positions that are wholly unsupported by regulations, rulings, or administrative practice. To the contrary, we have declined to give deference to an agency counsel's interpretation of a statute where the agency itself has articulated no position on the question."[52]

At the same time, it is clear that courts are affirming more agency determinations than they seemed to have done prior to *Chevron*.[53] Patricia Wald, a scholarly, now-retired judge on the District of Columbia Circuit has performed her own analysis of *Chevron* to conclude, among many other things:

---

[49] *Mobil Oil Exploration v. United Distribution Cos.*, 498 U.S. 211 (1991).

[50] 499 U.S. 606 (1991).

[51] 499 U.S. 144 (1991).

[52] *Bowen v. Georgetown Univ. Hosp.*, 488 U.S. 204 (1988). *See* Anthony, *supra* note 43.

[53] Two law professors performing empirical research for the Administrative Conference have determined that affirmances of agency interpretations have grown by over 10 percent after *Chevron*. Peter Schuck & Donald Elliott, *To the* Chevron *Station: An Empirical Study of Federal Administrative Law*, 1990 DUKE L.J. 984.

A study I conducted of the D.C. Circuit's administrative law decisions over a seven-month period confirmed the conventional wisdom that the bulk of reversals of agency action under Chevron occur at the Chevron [*first step*] stage. Thus, it would appear that Congress, and not the judiciary, is the true source of many of the administrative law decisions . . . in which the courts refused to defer to the agency.[54]

In an earlier study performed by Judge Wald, she found that the D.C. Circuit disposed of eleven out of twenty-nine cases (over a one-year period) on Chevron first step grounds. Of these eleven decisions, the circuit reversed the agency 73 percent of the time. When that same circuit disposed of a case on Chevron second step grounds, the agency was reversed only 11 percent of the time.[55] Another study of all the circuits concluded that of 223 published circuit cases that applied *Chevron* between 1995 and 1996, 38 percent of the decisions were resolved at step one and 62 percent at step two. Of the step one cases, 58 percent reversed the agency, but when the circuits went to step two to conclude the case, only 11 percent of the agencies' positions were reversed by the reviewing court.[56]

A decision by the Supreme Court holding that the Food and Drug Administration does not have jurisdiction to regulate tobacco products is a good example of the Court's stopping at *Chevron's* first step to resolve the case against the interpretation proffered by the agency's. In *Food & Drug Administration v. Brown & Williamson Tobacco Corp.*,[57] the Court examined the FDA's assertion that terms, such as "drugs" and "devices," used in the Food, Drug, and Cosmetic Act gave the FDA the power to regulate tobacco products under the theory that nicotine is a "drug" and that cigarettes and smokeless tobacco are "devices" that deliver the drug, nicotine. The court examined both the express language of the Act and an enormous amount of materials and information external to the Act. Looking only at the Act itself, the Court concluded:

> In view of the FDA's conclusions regarding the health effects of tobacco use, the agency would have no basis for finding any such reasonable assurances of safety [the Act permits the FDA to authorize the sale of drugs and devices when it can be shown that such drugs or devices are 'safe' and 'effective']. The [Act's] misbranding and device classification provisions therefore make evident that were the FDA to regulate cigarettes and smokeless tobacco, the Act would require the agency to ban them.

If this were the only thing the Court examined, it might well have simply confirmed the agency's interpretation of its own power and authority. However, the Court did not stop at this point. It went on to examine various statutes and other Congressional actions external to the Food, Drug, and Cosmetic Act, such as the Federal Cigarette Labeling and Advertising Act and the Comprehensive Smoking Education Act, to conclude that "Congress . . . has foreclosed the removal of

---

[54] Patricia M. Wald, *A Response to Tiller and Cross*, 99 COLUM. L. REV. 235, 243 (1999).

[55] Patricia M. Wald, *Judicial Review in Mid-Passage: The Uneasy Partnership Between Courts and Agencies Plays On*, 32 TULSA L.J. 221, 242 (1996).

[56] Kerr, *supra*, note 43, at 30–31.

[57] 529 U.S. 120 (2000).

tobacco products from the market."[58] The Court summed up by pointing out: "Taken together, these actions by Congress over the past 35 years preclude an interpretation of the [Act] that grants the FDA jurisdiction to regulate tobacco products."[59]

The Court might have stopped at this point, but because of an exceptionally strong dissenting opinion, the majority went on to comment:

> [O]ur inquiry into whether Congress has directly spoken to the precise question at issue is shaped, at least in some measure, by the nature of the question presented. Deference under *Chevron* to an agency's construction of a statute that it administers is premised on the theory that a statute's ambiguity constitutes an implicit delegation from Congress to the agency to fill in the statutory gaps.[60]

> This is hardly an ordinary case . . . . Given this history [that since 1914 until the present controversy arose, the FDA asserted that it did *not* have jurisdiction over tobacco products] and the breadth of the authority that the FDA has asserted, we are obliged to defer not to the agency's expansive construction of the statute, but to Congress' consistent judgment to deny the FDA this power.[61]

There was, as noted, a sharp dissent by four Justices joining an opinion authored by Justice Breyer (whose scholarship as a law professor was cited by the majority). The dissenters would have relied almost exclusively on the plain language of the Act to conclude that tobacco products fit easily within the Act's statutory definitions. They discount almost entirely the use of the other statutes invoked by the majority and the tobacco companies as "based on erroneous assumptions." As Justice Breyer put it:

> The inferences that the majority draws [from these other statutes and] from later legislative history are not persuasive, since . . . one can just as easily infer from the later laws that Congress did not intend to affect the FDA's tobacco-related authority at all. And the fact that the FDA changed its mind about the scope of its own jurisdiction is legally insignificant because . . . the agency's reasons for changing course are fully justified. Finally, . . . the degree of accountability that likely will attach to the FDA's action in this case should alleviate any concern that Congress, rather than an administrative agency, ought to make this important regulatory decision.[62]

The *Brown and Williamson* decision is an important one for the nation and the nation's health. Obviously, the FDA and its supporters must now go to Congress for

---

[58] *Id.* at 137. The Court noted in passing that since 1965 Congress dealt with problems of tobacco and health six separate times and throughout this 35-year period, the health consequences of smoking were well understood.

[59] *Id.* at 155.

[60] *Id.* at 159.

[61] *Id.* at 160.

[62] *Id.* at 163–64.

a legislative solution-a solution that is not likely to be granted in the present mood and make-up of Congress. But, at the same time, nothing in *Brown and Williamson* undercuts the basic legitimacy of *Chevron* itself.

In 2011, the Supreme Court issued yet another decision involving *Chevron* Step One in *Mayo Foundation for Medical Education and Research v. United States*.[63] In *Mayo*, a number of physicians who were serving as medical residents argued that they should be given a student exemption under the Federal Insurance Contribution Act (FICA) because they were not yet fully board-certified physicians. The Treasury Department denied the exemption by promulgating rules that provided that employees who were scheduled to work 40 or more hours each week were not to be considered for the student exemption. Ultimately, the case was decided in favor of Treasury under the second step of *Chevron* because the underlying statute did not expressly define "student." However, before reaching that conclusion, the Court offered a number of striking comments on Step One of *Chevron*: "We have repeatedly held that agency inconsistency is not a basis for declining to analyze the agency's interpretation under the *Chevron* framework. [Further] we have instructed that neither antiquity nor contemporaneity with a statute is a condition of the regulation's validity. And we have found it immaterial . . . that [the promulgation of] a regulation was prompted by litigation."[64] Among other things, most readers of this case see it as confirming the full applicability of *Chevron* to tax regulations.

A example of the Supreme Court's overturning agency action on the basis of the second step in the *Chevron* test is *AT&T Corp. v. Iowa Utilities Board*.[65] In AT&T, a number of parties brought challenges to Federal Communications Commission rules implementing the Telecommunications Act of 1996. Specifically challenged were rules that set out the obligations of certain companies to provide access to their telecommunications networks to their own competitors. In a lengthy opinion, the Court agreed that the statute was ambiguous (thus moving past *Chevron* step one), but went on to overturn the Commission's rules because those rules were not consistent with a reasonable interpretation of the 1996 Act.

Moreover, it would appear that the Supreme Court draws no distinction between executive branch agencies under the control of the President (e.g., EPA and FDA) and the independent regulatory commissions when it comes to an application of *Chevron*. In *National Cable & Telecommunications Association v. Brand X Internet Services*,[66] the Court affirmed a decision by the Federal Communications Commission that classified broad band services provided by a cable television service as an "information service."

The Court's analytical path is standard fare. They found the underlying statute ambiguous (step one) and the FCC's interpretation reasonable (step two). At first glance, the Court's reasoning would not surprise anyone. But you should be aware that there is a sliver of academic and practitioner commentary to the effect that

---

[63] 131 S. Ct. 704 (2011).

[64] *Id.* at 711–12 (internal quotation marks and citations omitted).

[65] 525 U.S. 366 (1999).

[66] 545 U.S. 967 (2005).

independent regulatory commissions should receive less deference than presidential agencies.[67] The Court may see fit in the near future to speak more extensively on this issue.

At bottom, the Supreme Court itself seems totally comfortable with both the analytical process of *Chevron* and its ultimate impact on judicial review of agency action. Some commentators suggest that *Chevron* has eroded the hard look requirement of *Overton Park*. The following discussion would seem to indicate that such is not the case.

[B] An Agency's Interpretation of Its Own Rules: *Skidmore, Christensen* and *Mead*

The preceding subsection discussed the concepts and analysis that applies to an agency's interpretation of its own enabling statutes. Somewhat different considerations operate when an agency interprets its own rules. There are times when this issue becomes almost a labyrinth because an agency may issue an *interpretative* rule that explains a substantive rule. It may issue a *statement of policy* that is not related to any of its pre-existing substantive rules. Agencies have been known to issue *rulings* that explain *interpretative* rules that construe *substantive* rules. Some of these matters are discussed in Chapter 7 (rulemaking), § 7.09. This subsection continues that discussion in terms of the many ways in which reviewing courts have reacted to an agency's interpretation of its own rules.

The starting point is the frequently cited case of *Skidmore v. Swift.*[68] In *Skidmore*, the Supreme Court dealt with an interpretative bulletin issued by the Department of Labor's Wage and Hour Administration. The Court noted:

> We consider that the rulings, interpretations and opinions of the Administrator under this Act, while not controlling upon the courts by reason of their authority, do constitute a body of experience and informed judgment to which courts and litigants may properly resort for guidance. The weight of such a judgment [the interpretation] . . . will depend upon the thoroughness evident in its consideration, the validity of its reasoning, its consistency with earlier and later pronouncements [in other words, the agency's consistency (see the discussion of consistency immediately below)], and all those factors which give it power to persuade, if lacking power to control.[69]

This pronouncement became known in the administrative law literature as the *great deference* rule. In other words, an agency's interpretation will be both helpful and perhaps persuasive, but it is not necessarily controlling. Contrast this approach

---

[67] *See, e.g.*, Randolph J. May, *Defining Deference Down: Independent Agencies and* Chevron *Deference*, 58 ADMIN. L. REV. 429 (2006); David M. Gossett, Chevron, *Take Two: Deference to Revised Agency Interpretations of Statutes*, 64 U. CHI. L. REV. 681 (1997). *See also* Richard J. Pierce, Jr., & Joshua Weiss, *An Empirical Study of Judicial Review of Agency Interpretations of Agency Rules*, 63 ADMIN. L. REV. 515 (2011).

[68] 323 U.S. 134 (1944). A very good article on this topic is Robert A. Anthony, *The Supreme Court and the APA: Sometimes They Just Don't Get It*, 10 ADMIN. L.J. AM. U. 1 (1996).

[69] 323 U.S. at 140.

with the *Chevron* doctrine. Under *Chevron*, an agency's interpretation of a *statute* may indeed be controlling; and a court may not substitute its judgment for that of the agency.

This creates a bit of a puzzlement. Why should an agency's interpretation of a statute be controlling, at least in some circumstances, when its interpretation of its own rules is not? The Supreme Court has persistently muddied these waters. For example, in *Udall v. Tallman*,[70] concededly a pre-*Chevron* case, the Court suggested: "When the construction of an administrative regulation rather than a statute is in issue, deference is even more clearly in order."[71]

But there is another problem. Under § 553 of the APA, interpretative rules do not necessarily have to be put through the conventional notice and comment process, which means that the agency can issue them on almost an off-the-cuff fashion. Put a little differently, the public is not necessarily given advanced notice of an interpretative rule, and, simultaneously, does not enjoy the benefit of public input before the interpretation is announced. This would suggest that less deference ought to be due to these types of agency pronouncements in contrast to the considerable deference given to an agency's substantive rules which have, at the very least, survived the fire of notice and comment.[72]

In a frequently cited 1997 case, *Auer v. Robbins*,[73] the Supreme Court reviewed the interpretation of rules issued under the Fair Labor Standards Act by the Department of Labor. The Court held that deference is required for agency interpretations of regulations unless the interpretation is "plainly erroneous or inconsistent with the regulation."[74]

In *Christensen v. Harris*,[75] the Court resolved an important question under *Chevron*. The issue was whether *Chevron* deference is required for agency pronouncements in the form of interpretative rules or statements of policy. The Court's answer was clearly "no." The Department of Labor's Wage and Hour Division had issued an opinion letter in a narrow question relating to the use of compensatory time by an employee. The statute itself and the implementing regulations were ambiguous on the point. The Court pointed out that *Chevron* deference is required only for agency rules that have the force of law. Review of such pronouncements as "opinion letters" is conducted under the much weaker deference established by *Skidmore v. Swift*.

There is yet another problem. What exactly do we mean by the term *deference*? One judge sitting on the Seventh Circuit has distinguished between three different concepts that may fit within the definition of deference. Judge Frank Easterbrook

---

[70] 380 U.S. 1 (1965).

[71] *Id.* at 16.

[72] This is an issue that Professor Anthony has addressed in several different settings. *See, e.g.,* Anthony, *supra* note 43, at 4–16.

[73] 519 U.S. 452 (1997).

[74] *Id.* at 465. For a lengthy analysis of *Auer*, see Kristin E. Hickman & Matthew D. Krueger, *In Search of the Modern* Skidmore *Standard*, 107 COLUM. L. REV. 1235 (2007).

[75] 529 U.S. 576 (2000).

suggests that when judges use the term deference, they may have in mind any one of the following three notions: a. *delegation*: "the court must accept action within the scope of the delegated power"; b. *respect*: "The President rather than a judge decides how to execute the laws, and a court therefore must respect the discretionary choices a coordinate branch of government has made . . . ."; c. *persuasion*: "On a pure question of law, an agency's views may persuade [even] when they cannot compel . . . . To the extent other factors . . . matter, the agency may have better access to indicators [of such things as legislative intent, etc.,] than do judges."[76] Judge Easterbrook finds the use of a single term, deference, to encompass all three of these concepts is not terribly helpful. Most other commentators would concur.

Recall, once again, that *Skidmore* held that an agency's interpretation of its own rules is persuasive but not necessarily controlling. Reviewing courts may defer to the agency's interpretation, but are not necessarily bound by it. In 1994, the Supreme Court issued a decision, *Thomas Jefferson University v. Shalala*,[77] a case involving the interpretation of agency regulations by the Department of Health and Human Services. In *Thomas Jefferson* the Court used language that Professor Anthony views as "an indulgent if not downright abject standard of deference."[78] There, the Court stated:

> [T]he agency's interpretation must be given "controlling weight unless it is plainly erroneous or inconsistent with the regulation." . . . [W]e must defer to the [agency's] interpretation unless an 'alternative reading is compelled by the regulation's plain language or by other indications of the [agency's] intent at the time of the regulation's promulgation.[79]

Does this quotation make things any clearer? This author thinks not.

In 2001, in *United States v. Mead Corporation*,[79a] the Supreme Court took a look at the issue of whether a tariff classification issued by the United States Customs Service triggered judicial deference. The first paragraph of *Mead* says almost all that needs saying: "We agree that a tariff classification has no claim to judicial deference under *Chevron*, there being no indication that Congress intended such a ruling to carry the force of law, but we hold that under *Skidmore v. Swift* . . . the ruling is eligible to claim respect according to its persuasiveness."[79b] But this language did not necessarily save the tariff ruling. The Court remanded to the Federal Circuit for an inquiry under *Skidmore*.

There was a sharp dissent by Justice Scalia who called *Mead* "an avulsive change in judicial review of federal administrative action. In Scalia's opinion "What was previously a general presumption of authority in agencies to resolve ambiguity in the [their] statutes . . . has been changed to a presumption of no such authority . . . henceforth the court must supposedly give the agency some indeterminate

---

[76] *Atchison, Topeka & Santa Fe Ry. Co. v. Pena*, 44 F.3d 437, 445 (7th Cir. 1994) (en banc).

[77] 512 U.S. 504 (1994).

[78] Anthony, *supra* note 43, at 4.

[79] 512 U.S. at 521.

[79a] 533 U.S. 218 (2001).

[79b] *Id.* at 221.

amount of so-called Skidmore deference."[79c] In his dissent, Justice Scalia predicted that the Court would need years to sort all of this out. His prediction seems to be coming true.[80]

Of course, exceptional deference does not mean total deference. In *Gonzales v. Oregon*,[81] the Supreme Court looked at an interpretative rule issued by the Department of Justice under the Controlled Substances Act. The interpretation prohibited physicians working in the context of the State of Oregon's physician-assisted suicide act from prescribing drugs that those doctors use in assisting suicide. The Court majority refused to give the interpretation either *Auer* deference or *Chevron* deference, holding that an interpretation that is defective is not cured by the agency's merely invoking statutory language. In the Court's words, "Simply put, the existence of a parroting regulation does not change the fact that the question here is not the meaning of the regulation but the meaning of the statute. An agency does not acquire special authority to interpret its own words when, instead of using its expertise and experience to formulate a regulation, it has elected merely to paraphrase the statutory language."[82]

One respected professor of administrative law, Richard Pierce, has concluded that "it is now at least arguable that (1) courts accord greater deference to policy statements and interpretative rules than to [an agency's] legislative rules; and, (2) in important contexts, interpretative rules and policy statements bind judges and the public to the same extent as do legislative rules."[83] The final statement on this issue has yet to be written.

In a 2011 case, the Supreme Court held that an agency's interpretation may be found in a legal brief. It does not necessarily have to be in some more formal pronouncement. In *Talk America, Inc. v. Michigan Bell Telephone Co.*,[84] the Court reviewed a challenge to rules issued by the Federal Communications Commission involving providers of local telephone services. The FCC itself did not participate as a party in the action but filed an amicus curiae brief with the Court giving the Court its interpretation of its own rules. While this case is technically an Auer deference case rather than a Chevron deference case, the Court made clear that "we defer to an agency's interpretation of its regulations, even in a legal brief, unless the doctrine is 'plainly erroneous or inconsistent with the regulations or there is any other reason to suspect that the interpretation does not reflect the agency's fair and

---

[79c] *Id.* at 239.

[80] *See, e.g., Barnhart v. Walton*, 535 U.S. 212 (2002) (the Court upheld the Social Security Administration's interpretation of a rule defining "disability" over a *Mead*-type dissent by Justice Scalia). *See* Lisa Schultz Bressman, *How* Mead *Has Muddled Judicial Review of Agency Action*, 58 VAND. L. REV. 1443 (2005).

[81] 546 U.S. 243 (2006).

[82] *Id.* at 257. For some excellent commentary on Gonzales, see Jacob E. Gersen, *Overlapping and Underlapping Jurisdiction in Administrative Law*, 2006 SUP. CT. REV. 201. Professor Gersen discusses a concept that many observers are now referring to as Chevron "Step Zero." Step Zero involves an inquiry into the fundamental authority of an agency to act — essentially an ultra vires notion — that must be resolved before we even get to either Chevron or Auer.

[83] Richard J. Pierce, Jr., *Seven Ways to Deossify Agency Rulemaking*, 47 ADMIN. L. REV. 59, 83 (1995).

[84] 131 S. Ct. 2254 (2011).

considered judgment on the matter in question."[85]

[C] Agency Consistency

The place to begin this analysis is with a case that was first discussed in Chapter 6, *SEC v. Chenery Corp.*,[86] the so-called *Chenery I* decision. There, the Court overturned an SEC order because the SEC did not sufficiently explain its new policy. The SEC asserted that it was simply affirming what had always been its policy on certain aspects of holding company reorganization. The Court noted that the record was barren of the sort of "findings [that] might have been made and considerations disclosed which would justify its [new] order."

Eleven years after *Chenery I*, in *Secretary of Agriculture v. United States*,[87] the Court reviewed an Interstate Commerce Commission order which, for the first time, permitted railroads to charge shippers for certain unloading expenses that previously had been considered part of the normal freight rate. In this instance, the Court held the rates invalid because "the Commission has not adequately explained its departure from prior norms and has not sufficiently spelled out the legal basis of its decision."

These two decisions, among many others, establish a fairly clear general rule. Agencies are supposed to be experts, and they are permitted to adapt to changing conditions. Indeed, one of the central reasons for creating administrative agencies was the failure of the judicial system-with its rigid focus on *stare decisis* and *res judicata*--to deal flexibly with pressing social problems. However, the element of fairness demands consistent, evenly-applied action. Change, improperly implemented, can do a great deal of violence to members of the regulated industry and will go a long way towards undermining public confidence in government institutions.

The Supreme Court showed an awareness of all these considerations in deciding *Motor Vehicle Manufacturers Ass'n v. State Farm Mutual Automobile Insurance Co.*,[88] in 1983. In *State Farm*, the Court reviewed the rescission of a Department of Transportation standard imposing a passive restraint requirement on automobile manufacturers. In promulgating the original standard (worked out during the Ford and Carter administrations) the DOT had determined, among many other things, that car seat belts that required people to buckle up weren't very effective. What really was needed was some kind of passenger safety device that did not require any specific action on the part of a car's occupants. The Department waxed and waned on air bags versus belt restraints and finally promulgated, by rule, Modified Standard 208, that permitted manufacturers to choose between belt restraints and air bags, so long as they installed one or the other.

---

[85] *Id.* at 2268. In *Talk America*, Justice Scalia wrote separately to comment: "It is comforting to know that I would reach the Court's result even without Auer. For while I have in the past uncritically accepted [the Auer] rule, I have become increasingly doubtful of its validity."

[86] 318 U.S. 80 (1943).

[87] 347 U.S. 645 (1954).

[88] 463 U.S. 29 (1983).

When President Reagan's newly appointed Secretary of Transportation took office, he commissioned a rulemaking to repeal Modified Standard 208 and after considering written comments and holding some oral hearings, the Department rescinded Standard 208. A number of insurance companies challenged the rescission in court. After granting certiorari, the Supreme Court looked at the entire history of the proceeding — *i.e.*, both the promulgation of the Standard and its rescission — and concluded that, while an agency always has the authority to reconsider its policies, here it failed to articulate plausible reasons for rescission.

As the Court put it: "An agency's view of what is in the public interest may change, either with or without a change in circumstances. But an agency changing its course must supply a reasoned analysis." One interesting phenomenon in *State Farm* is that even the three justices who filed a partial dissent concluded that the DOT had provided no reasoned analysis whatsoever of the decision to rescind.[89]

No one can say with any certainty what sort of reasoned explanation for changes in rules will satisfy the Court in the future. In *State Farm*, the Court seemed to be troubled by the fact that there appeared to be absolutely no change in external circumstances. In other words, people still were being killed and maimed in car accidents in the early 1980s with about the same frequency as in the mid-1970s. If this is the case, why is the earlier rule now unnecessary? The Department of Transportation really didn't address this issue in its rescission.

In addition, the comments filed during the rescission proceeding did not differ substantially from the comments filed when the Modified Standard was promulgated. It was just that the insurance companies prevailed in the earlier rulemaking, and the automobile manufacturers prevailed in the rescission. Finally, there had been no changes in the agency's enabling act. The legislature had taken no action compelling the rescission.

The Supreme Court recently reiterated many of these principles in *INS v. Yang*.[90] In *Yang*, the Immigration Service refused to grant a waiver in the deportation of Mr. Yang. The Service asserted that he had committed fraud in entering the United States in the first instance. While Mr. Yang argued, and later, the Ninth Circuit, concluded, that the statute did not permit the INS to consider this type of fraud, the Supreme Court disagreed. If the Court had simply stopped with an outright reversal, the case would have been totally unremarkable; but in this instance, the Court used the opportunity to make additional comments about agency consistency:

> Though the agency's discretion is unfettered at the outset, if it announces and follows-by rule or settled course of adjudication-a general policy by which its exercise of discretion will be governed, an irrational departure from that policy . . . could constitute action that [is arbitrary, capricious or an abuse of discretion].[91]

---

[89] Justice Rehnquist was probably the most candid. He preferred to explain the case solely in terms of the change in Presidential administrations.

[90] 519 U.S. 26 (1996).

[91] *Id.* at 33. For some very persuasive writing on this point, *see* Harold Krent, *Reviewing Agency*

The message of *State Farm* is clear. It is unquestionable that the Court will permit agencies to modify and rescind rules. But it is equally clear that changes have to be elaborately and plausibly explained.

[D]   Agency Policy and Political Considerations

No one can plausibly argue that administrative agencies are, or should be, insulated from politics. As we saw in the introductory chapters, agencies were created with the understanding that they would, much more than would courts, reflect current political realities. But how much should politics influence an agency's policy making. And, should politics ever influence an agency's policymaking in an adjudication context?

In one of the more important Supreme Court decisions in the past decade, the Court proffered some answers in the case of *Federal Communications Commission v. Fox Television Stations, Inc.*[92] In *Fox*, the Court examined the language in 18 U.S.C. § 1464 that prohibits the broadcasting of "any obscene, indecent, or profane language by means of radio communication." Under the various federal communication statutes, the holder of a license to operate a television station assumes what the Court has referred to as "enforceable public obligations" including the proscription on indecency. In its various indecency rules, the FCC discussed the use of the "S-word" and the "F-word" and determined that enforcement actions could be taken against a broadcaster even when those words were used as expletives and not repeated.

The *Fox* case arose out of two separate programs. The first was the entertainer Cher who commented: "I've also had critics for the last 40 years saying that I was on my way out every year. Right. So f*** 'em." The second was the entertainer Nicole Richie who stated: "Why do they even call it 'The Simple Life'? Have you ever tried to get cow s*** out of a Prada purse. It's not so f***ing simple." The FCC issued indecency enforcement notices against Fox Broadcasting for these two incidents. In resisting the enforcement action, Fox Broadcasting invoked its rights under the free speech provisions of the First Amendment of the U. S. Constitution.

On review at the United States Court of Appeals for the Second Circuit, the court concluded that the FCC could not provide an adequate explanation and rationale for its prohibition of so-called "fleeting expletive" (the one-time utterance) phenomenon. The one-time "fleeting expletive" policy was seen as new and a departure from previous FCC policy that seemed to accept, as not violating the underlying statute, one-time utterances. The Second Circuit held that the enforcement action could not proceed because the FCC's explanation was inadequate and therefor arbitrary and capricious under the Administrative Procedure Act's standards of judicial review.

At the Supreme Court, the majority opinion was written by Justice Scalia who made three points. First, the concept of arbitrary and capricious review remains the same even when First Amendment issues are involved. Second, just because a

---

Action for Inconsistency with Prior Rules and Regulations, 72 CHI-KENT L. REV. 1187 (1997).

[92] 556 U.S. 502 (2009).

policy differs sharply from an older policy, as here, the new policy should be upheld so long as the agency proffers an adequate explanation for its new policy. Third, just because the FCC is an independent regulatory commission and just because this case was an adjudication rather than a rulemaking, the concept of *Chevron* deference remains the same.

The four dissenters (Justices Breyer, Stevens, Ginsberg and Souter) sharply disagreed viewing the case as one involving a policy shift made for "purely political reasons."

Fox has created something of a furor in administrative law. At least one commentator sees the opinion as a "watershed precedent that charts a new course for administrative law."[93] Another, because of Justice Scalia's pronouncements on the place of independent regulatory agencies in our scheme of government, sees Fox as profoundly affecting concepts of separation of powers.[94]

§ 12.07   RESOLVING PROBLEMS INVOLVING REVIEW ON THE MERITS

By now, everyone should be keenly aware of how difficult it is to persuade a court to overturn agency action. The statutory standards are narrow on their face and they have probably been made even a little narrower by judicial construction. Although it is difficult to pin down the Supreme Court on these issues, the prevalent mood, with one or two aberrations, appears to be very much a "let-the-agencies-alone" philosophy.

In other words, any attempt to predict the outcome of judicial review on the merits should begin with an assumption that the court is likely *not* to overturn an agency decision. After that, the analysis can proceed in any number of ways, although most lawyers try first to identify the applicable test for review (*e.g.*, substantial evidence, arbitrary/capricious, etc.), and second, to decide where the issue lies on the scale from basic facts to questions of law. Professor Schwartz' analytical framework is particularly healthy and helpful.

Just don't expect a lot of bright lines to emerge. This type of analysis is never easy. Consider that your case is on a kind of continuum: the more your dispute turns on basic facts, the less likely you are to get a reversal; the closer your issue is to a pure question of law, the more a reviewing court may be willing to substitute its judgment for that of the agency. When you dispute the facial constitutionality of the enabling act itself, you are likely to find virtually no deference to the agency. This whole area, like so much of lawyering, is a matter of predictions and probabilities. There are no final answers.

---

[93] Scott A. Keller, *Depoliticizing Judicial Review of Agency Rulemaking*, 84 Wash. L. Rev. 419, 424–25 (2009).

[94] Randolph J. May, *Defining Deference Down, Again: Independent Agencies*, Chevron *Deference, and* Fox, 62 Admin. L. Rev. 433, 448–49 (2010). For yet another view, *see* Kathryn A. Watts, *Proposing a Place for Politics in Arbitrary and Capricious Review*, 119 Yale L.J. 2 (2009).

Chapter 13

PRIVATE ACTIONS AGAINST THE GOVERNMENT AND GOVERNMENT OFFICIALS

§ 13.01 INTRODUCTION

The matter of bringing tort actions and breach of contract lawsuits against the government is not, strictly speaking, a topic of administrative law. Actions against the government are a sub-set within the general topic of federal litigation and are usually studied in those courses. However, most administrative law casebooks at least touch upon the subject, and a lawyer who proposes to represent clients in federal agency practice does not have a complete understanding of the entire field until she has some grasp of these topics. Private actions constitute a kind of control on action of administrative agencies, even if they do not fit squarely within the concepts discussed previously in this book.

There are a number of things to consider. First, under our Constitution, the government may not be sued for anything unless it consents to be sued. This is known as the doctrine of *sovereign immunity*. Many students first encounter sovereign immunity in constitutional law because it is derived from, although not specifically expressed in, the federal and many state constitutions. However, modern sovereign immunity must also take into consideration the various statutes discussed below. Second, the only way consent may be given-*i.e.*, the only way sovereign immunity may be abrogated-is through an Act of Congress. No agency employee, no member of the executive branch, and no judge may provide the required consent. If there is any question about the government's consent, you must be able to identify a specific statute giving that consent. Moreover, the consent may not be inferred from a creative reading of statutes. Under normal circumstances, Congress' consent to be sued must be plain on the face of the applicable statute.

Early in the history of the United States, sovereign immunity was nearly absolute. But in the two hundred years since the formation of our constitutional system, Congress has written a number of statutes that unambiguously relax the doctrine of sovereign immunity. We have already covered one in § 10.04, namely the 1976 amendment to § 702, prohibiting the government from invoking sovereign immunity in agency actions in which the plaintiff does not seek money damages. In instances in which a plaintiff seeks money damages, Congress has provided two separate sources of relief, the Federal Tort Claims Act,[1] providing for certain rights

---

[1] 28 U.S.C. §§ 1346(b), 2671–2680. For a solid exposition of FTCA issues and concepts, *see* L. S. JAYSON, HANDLING FEDERAL TORT CLAIMS: ADMINISTRATIVE AND JUDICIAL REMEDIES (1992). For a solid discussion of sovereignty immunity issues, see Vicki C. Jackson, *Suing the Federal Government: Sovereignty, Immunity, and Judicial Independence*, 35 GEO. WASH. INT'L L. REV. 521 (2003).

of action akin to private tort actions, and the Tucker Act,[2] a statute that permits certain kinds of recovery against the government in actions for breach of contract. Each of these statutes will be discussed below.

§ 13.02   SOVEREIGN IMMUNITY AND SUITS AGAINST FEDERAL OFFICERS

[A]   *Ex Parte Young*

The idea that the government cannot be sued without its consent is often understood even by high school civics students, but it comes as a surprise to most people when they discover that there is no express language in the Constitution that establishes the doctrine. While the Supreme Court hinted as early as 1846 that the doctrine existed, it did not articulate sovereign immunity as a constitutional principle until a number of years later.[3] The doctrine stems from English jurisprudence and is frequently is expressed in its most distasteful fashion as "The King can do no wrong." In the United States, most courts approach it as a rule of reason rather than as a command of written law, *i.e.*, it makes sense not to expose the government to the same sort of liability faced by private citizens. Shortly after the turn of the century, Justice Holmes first articulated this approach on behalf of the Supreme Court. He described the doctrine as a matter of common sense: there can be no recovery against the government because of the "logical and practical ground that there can be no legal right as against the authority that makes the law on which the right stands."[4]

Most early courts applied the doctrine absolutely: the government simply could not be sued. But as the country moved into the twentieth century, it became clear that the government was assuming a role far different from that exercised by the English kings. The government began entering into more and more contracts with private persons. Those contracts were sometimes breached by the government. Government employees drove automobiles on official business; those automobiles were occasionally involved in accidents. These activities were much like parallel activities in the private sector; they indisputably caused economic and physical harm, and yet the government simply could not be held accountable. This lack of accountability when the government engaged in essentially private sector activity caused a great deal of political pressure to be exerted on all three branches of government.[5]

---

[2] 24 Stat. 505 (codified in scattered sections of Title 28). For an excellent handbook covering, in depth, virtually all the major issues involving both the Federal Tort Claims Act and the Tucker Act and many other matters, *see* URBAN A. LESTER & MICHAEL F. NOONE, LITIGATION WITH THE FEDERAL GOVERNMENT (3d ed. 1994).

[3] *See, e. g.*, the discussion in *Kawananakoa v. Polyblank*, 205 U.S. 349 (1907).

[4] *Id.* at 353.

[5] For an excellent exposition of the doctrine of sovereign immunity and the history of the United States Court of Federal Claims, *see* Richard J. Fallon, Jr., *Claims Court at the Crossroads*, 40 CATH. U. L. REV. 517 (1991).

Unfortunately, Congress was reluctant to act, so the Supreme Court in *Ex parte Young*,[6] a case deserving of criticism on many grounds, decided that a state attorney general who acted under an allegedly unconstitutional statute lost his cloak of immunity as a government officer because his actions were outside the scope of his authority (*ultra vires*). In reality, the opinion signaled a great deal of hostility on the part of the Court toward states that were then attempting to curb the worst excesses of the railroads. The State of Minnesota at the time was trying to regulate certain railroad freight rates. The attorney general of the state brought an enforcement action only to have his actions branded by the Supreme Court as *ultra vires*, thereby making him subject to being sued for his actions in the same manner that private citizens could be sued.

[B] Immunity on the Part of Federal Officers-*Larson* and *Barr*

The *Young* decision quickly became unpopular around the country, particularly in the state legislatures. Even the Supreme Court eventually lost its affection for *Young*, although the case itself has never been expressly overruled. Nearly forty years later, the Court took up a case involving a federal officer who manipulated a government contract to purchase coal to the detriment of the seller of the coal. The seller invoked the *Young* decision to argue that a government official interfering with a contract for the sale of goods loses his cloak of sovereign immunity. In *Larson v. Domestic and Foreign Commerce Corp.*,[7] the Court examined the facts of the case, essentially conceded that the officer had erred and nevertheless conferred immunity, holding: "[I]f the actions of an officer do not conflict with the terms of his valid statutory authority, then they are the actions of the sovereign, whether or not they are tortious under general law . . . ."

The *Larson* holding struck most people as almost incredible. A government official can commit an act that would be plainly a tort or an act of breach of contract - and cause serious injury to a private citizen — and yet not be held accountable for his actions in any judicial forum. *Larson* caused a stir but, unfortunately, did not trigger Congressional action.

In 1959, the Court took up another case, *Barr v. Matteo*,[8] in which an agency official, Barr, issued a press release to the effect that he had suspended two other agency employees, Matteo and Madigan, because they had allegedly violated various agency personnel regulations by permitting certain temporary employees to take accrued annual leave in the form of cash. The two employees asserted that Barr lied about their activities and damaged their professional reputations. They sued Barr for defamation. The case eventually made its way to the Supreme Court where, in a plurality opinion, the Court appeared to hold that the press release was at least tangentially related to Barr's official duties and for that reason he enjoyed immunity from this type of lawsuit.

---

[6] 209 U.S. 123 (1908).

[7] 337 U.S. 682 (1949).

[8] 360 U.S. 564 (1959).

Using the parlance of defamation law rather than the language of sovereign immunity, the *Barr* Court reviewed an earlier decision that held that the Postmaster General of the United States (then a member of the executive branch with cabinet rank) was absolutely immune from a defamation action. In this instance, the Court acknowledged that Barr was not even at the top of his own agency, much less a cabinet level official, so it might seem that some of the rationale for sovereign immunity-that the highest government officials ought not to be bothered by private law suits when they are attempting to carry out important governmental functions-did not apply. Even so, the Court stated:

> We do not think that the principle announced in [the case involving the Postmaster General] can properly be restricted to executive officers of cabinet rank. The privilege is not a badge or emolument of exalted office, but an expression of a policy designed to aid in the effective functioning of government.

Mr. Barr was thus held to be immune from the tort action.[9]

[C] Immunity for Constitutional Violations-the Progeny of *Bivens* and *Butz*

Even though *Barr* was only a plurality opinion, the case brought all such lawsuits to a halt for a number of years. In 1971, a sliver of daylight appeared when the Supreme Court in *Bivens v. Six Unknown Named Agents of Federal Bureau of Narcotics*,[10] held that federal courts have jurisdiction over suits against federal employees such as narcotics agents for constitutional violations. In this instance, the narcotics agents broke into Bivens' house, beat him up and handcuffed him in front of members of his own family-all without a warrant or probable cause. The Court held that federal jurisdiction existed for this type of constitutional violation by federal officers; and, moreover, that a federal court had inherent (essentially common law) powers to order that Bivens be awarded money damages, even though there was no federal statute providing for such relief. *Bivens* was recently one of the focal points of Congressional action. In amending the Federal Tort

---

[9] For an intriguing analysis of agency tort liability for false statements made on a website, see James T. O'Reilly, *Libel by Website: Federal Agency Liability for False Website Statements*, 29 ADMIN. & REG. L. NEWS 2 (2004).

[10] 403 U.S. 388 (1971). One of the questions law students frequently ask about *Bivens* is how the caption of the case came to be written as it did. The answer lies in Federal Rule of Civil Procedure 15. Bivens' counsel knew that federal narcotics agents had broken into Bivens' apartment and bound him and hauled him away, but he did not know the names of any of the officers. He needed pre-trial discovery to get the names, but before he could commence his discovery, the government filed a 12(b)(1) motion to dismiss for lack of subject matter jurisdiction and a 12(b)(6) motion to dismiss for failure to state a claim upon which relief can be granted. It was the lower courts' rulings on these dispositive motions that the Supreme Court reviewed. The complaint that was initially filed ("Six unknown named agents") is what is known as a John Doe complaint. In many cases, a court will permit the actual names to be added at a later date. See FED. R. CIV. P. 15(c). For a provocative discussion of Bivens in modern dress, *see* Michael B. Hedrick, *New Life for a Good Idea: Revitalizing Efforts to Replace the Bivens Action with a Statutory Waiver of the Sovereign Immunity of the United States for Constitutional Tort Suits*, 71 GEO. WASH. L. REV. 1055 (2003), and Susan Bandes, *Reinventing Bivens: The Self-Executing Constitution*, 68 S. CAL. L. REV. 289 (1995).

Claims Act to reverse a recent Supreme Court decision (*see* the discussion of *Westfall v. Erwin* below), Congress expressly provided that *Bivens* was still good law. The injuries litigated in *Bivens*-type cases, the so-called; constitutional (as contrasted with *common law*) torts, may continue to be litigated against individual federal employees and officers.[11]

However, many readers of *Bivens* do not understand that any forthcoming relief would have to be satisfied against the agents personally. Recall *Ex parte Young* — officers who act unconstitutionally lose their immunity but may be sued only as individuals. Probably because of its holding in *Young*, the Court spent very little time on the question of immunity.[12]

But remember, *Bivens* only addressed the questions of whether the federal court had jurisdiction and whether it could fashion a remedy. While the opinion called attention to the doctrinal weaknesses of *Barr*, it did not, for example, deal with the question of whether the immunity of federal officers is absolute or qualified. The Supreme Court finally came to grips with *Barr*'s shortcomings and the general lack of fairness that grows out of a grant of absolute immunity in a 1978 case, *Butz v. Economou*.[13] In *Butz*, a private citizen sued a number of officials in the Department of Agriculture, including the Secretary of Agriculture, on a number of grounds, some alleging various kinds of defamation and others alleging constitutional violations, such as failure of the agency to afford the plaintiff Due Process and infringement of his right to freedom of speech. The government argued that the agency personnel, including the Secretary, enjoyed an absolute immunity, even when constitutional infringements were alleged.

In a 5-4 decision, the Supreme Court approached the case with a strong dose of common sense and determined the following: (1) for these officials, the immunity is merely qualified, not absolute (to overcome the qualified immunity the plaintiff would have to prove malice, but at least the officials were subject to being sued); and (2) for certain officials such as judges, prosecutors or agency attorneys litigating enforcement cases, the immunity remains absolute. Agency activities that are analogous to the office of judge or prosecutor require, in the Court's view, complete and categorical immunity from lawsuits.

---

[11] 28 U.S.C. § 2679(b)(2).

[12] The Court has extended the *Bivens* principle to other civilian officers of the federal government for Eighth Amendment violations, *Carlson v. Green*, 446 U.S. 14 (1980), and for gender discrimination that violates the Fifth Amendment, *Davis v. Passman*, 442 U.S. 228 (1979). However, it refused to do the same for military officers, citing the special nature and needs of the military services. *Chappell v. Wallace*, 462 U.S. 296 (1983). In *United States v. Stanley*, 483 U.S. 669 (1987), the Court refused to grant a *Bivens*-type remedy to a former army sergeant who, without his knowledge or consent, had been given LSD as part of the army's chemical warfare experiments. Writing for the Court, Justice Scalia emphasized the special considerations that, in the Court's view, attend military service and commented that entertaining *Bivens*-type lawsuits growing out of the military would be an impermissible intrusion on military matters. In a civilian federal employee's disability case, the Court determined that there already existed administrative mechanisms for dealing with disability claims and refused to permit the plaintiffs to bring a *Bivens* claim against the Department of Health and Human Services. *Schweiker v. Chilicky*, 487 U.S. 412 (1988).

[13] 438 U.S. 478 (1978).

Butz, of course, was only a preliminary decision. Like many similar opinions, it left open nearly as many questions as it answered. For example, are there any other executive branch officers who still enjoy absolute immunity other than those functioning as judges or prosecutors? The answer is "yes." The Court has held that the President of the United States is absolutely immune for any actions taken within the "outer perimeter of his official responsibility."[14] However, that absolute immunity does not extend to presidential assistants.[15] In the legislative branch, members of Congress performing their legislative duties enjoy absolute immunity.[16]

Is there anything more to be said about the dimensions of qualified immunity? In *Harlow v. Fitzgerald*,[17] the Court noted that the basic test-whether the government official was acting in good faith-has both subjective and objective components. The combination of the objective and subjective tests, in the Court's words, works like this:

> [Q]ualified immunity would be defeated if an official knew or should have known that the action he took within his sphere of official responsibility would violate the constitutional rights of the [plaintiff], or if he took the action with malicious intention to cause a deprivation of constitutional rights or other injury . . . .[18]

Applying these standards, the official's knowledge would be measured by the standard of the reasonable administrator, rather than that of the specific administrator. By contrast, the question of malicious behavior would turn on the state of mind of the specific official sued. In a later case, *Anderson v. Creighton*,[19] the Court stated that qualified immunity would extend to an FBI agent accused of violating the plaintiff's Fourth Amendment rights if a "reasonable officer" could have believed the search to be lawful. The Court further stated that the officer's subjective beliefs as to the lawfulness of the search are irrelevant to an inquiry into the issue of qualified immunity.[20]

Is there anything left of *Barr*? At this point in time the *answer* is most assuredly "yes." The more recent cases, including *Bivens* and *Butz*, have drawn a sharp distinction between constitutional injuries and common law tort injuries. *Barr*, however, remains the basic statement on non-constitutional torts; and the Court shows no present intention of doing away with that decision. Although the ultimate

---

[14] *Nixon v. Fitzgerald*, 457 U.S. 731 (1982).

[15] *Harlow v. Fitzgerald*, 457 U.S. 800 (1982).

[16] *Gravel v. United States*, 408 U.S. 606 (1972).

[17] 457 U.S. 800 (1982).

[18] *Id.* at 821.

[19] 483 U.S. 635 (1987).

[20] In *Richardson v. McKnight*, 521 U.S. 399 (1997), the Supreme Court refused to grant qualified immunity to prison guards who are employees of a private prison management firm. Along the same lines, the Court has refused to grant prisoners of a private correctional facility a *Bivens*-type remedy against the private prison's correctional officers. *Correctional Servs. Corp. v. Malesko*, 534 U.S. 61 (2001). *See* Mariana C. Pastore, *Running from the Law: Federal Contractors Escape* Bivens *Liability*, 4 U. PA. J. CONST. L. 850 (2002).

result may seem exceptionally harsh, this judge-made immunity may be less important today because Congress has seen fit to broaden the range of claims against federal officers that may be litigated under the Federal Tort Claims Act.

§ 13.03 THE FEDERAL TORT CLAIMS ACT

Enacted in 1946, about the same time as the Administrative Procedure Act, the Federal Tort Claims Act (FTCA) provides a right of action in federal court for certain torts caused by federal employees and permits any damage award to be satisfied out of the federal treasury, rather than out of the personal funds of the employees sued. Recall that this is the Achilles' Heel of *Bivens* — a cause of action and a possible remedy may be created by the court, but the plaintiff satisfies the judgment out of the back pockets of the employees concerned, not out of the U.S. Treasury. Most low-ranking federal employees are probably judgment-proof.

The FTCA contains some crucial statutory provisions and has accrued a sizable body of case law.[21] The best way to understand the Act is to walk through the relevant statutory provisions. Title 28 U.S.C. § 1346 gives the federal district courts jurisdiction over civil actions for tort claims against the United States where the plaintiff is seeking money damages. This provision is not a blanket relaxation of sovereign immunity, however, because § 1346 goes on to limit the provision to actions against federal employees:

> [F]or [personal injury or death or loss of property] caused by the negligent or wrongful act . . . of any employee of the Government while acting within the scope of his office or employment, under circumstances where the United States, if a private person, would be liable to the claimant in accordance with the law of the place where the act or omission occurred.

Note the important elements of this section. The statute applies to personal injury or property damage caused by a federal employee only when the employee is acting within the scope of his duties. This means, for example, that an off-duty federal employee who has an automobile accident while on vacation is not liable under the FTCA. She is not functioning within the scope of her duties at that time. However, a government chauffeur who is involved in an automobile accident while driving a cabinet secretary to a Senate hearing is definitely covered.

Note further that the statute essentially incorporates local tort law as the choice of law for FTCA actions (the government is liable if a private person would be liable under the law of the place of the tort). If you can bring an FTCA action, you handle it essentially as you would handle a negligence action between two private persons. Under the FTCA, however, the government is always the defendant (the Act cannot be used by the government to bring a tort action against a private citizen) and is always represented by the Justice Department.

---

[21] For a good introduction to the FTCA, *see* Paul F. Figley, *Understanding the Federal Tort Claims Act: A Different Metaphor*, 44 Tort & Ins. L.J. 1105 (2009).

Congress amended the FTCA expressly to overrule the Supreme Court decision in *Westfall v. Erwin.*[22] In *Westfall*, the plaintiff, a federal employee, brought a common law tort action against his supervisors, alleging that they were negligent in permitting him to be exposed to certain toxic wastes. The district court held that federal employees enjoyed an absolute immunity from common law tort actions for ordinary torts committed within the scope of their employment. The Eleventh Circuit reversed, and on further review, the Supreme Court agreed with the Circuit, holding that absolute immunity attaches only if the challenged act is discretionary and is within the outer perimeter of the employee's line of duty. The Court's decision in *Westfall* triggered quick congressional action. In the Federal Employees Liability Reform and Tort Compensation Act,[23] Congress amended § 2679 (part of the FTCA) to provide that *employees* enjoy an absolute immunity. For injuries such as those suffered by the plaintiff in *Westfall*, the FTCA-which as you will recall provides for a claim against the United States and not against individual employees-constituted the exclusive remedy. However, to avoid overruling *Bivens*, Congress also provided that this absolute immunity does not extend to a civil action brought against a government employee for a violation of someone's constitutional rights.[24]

There is one other general restriction. While the government is liable in the same manner as a private citizen, § 2674 provides expressly that no court may award either punitive damages or pre-judgment interest to the prevailing party. In early 1992, the Supreme Court seems to have expanded the permissible range of recovery, however. In *Molzof v. United States*,[25] the first opinion authored by Justice Clarence Thomas, Molzof suffered permanent brain damage when his oxygen was cut off during lung surgery performed in a veterans hospital. The government admitted negligence; but Molzof's wife asked for over $1 million for future care, even though his care was being provided by the Veterans Administration, plus an additional $60,000 for his "loss of enjoyment of life." Mr. Molzof himself died during the litigation.

The lower federal courts held that the recovery for future care and enjoyment of life would constitute punitive damages prohibited by the FTCA. The Supreme Court reversed, holding that the damages sought by Molzof's wife were not truly punitive damages, but rather were in a kind of "gray zone" — *i.e.*, they were neither purely compensatory nor punitive, thus not expressly prohibited by the FTCA. The Court remanded the case for a determination of whether under Wisconsin law, Molzof would have been permitted to obtain such relief in a private state tort action.

Appended to the general elements of the FTCA, Congress has written a long list of exceptions. You may not recover under the FTCA in any case in which the employee is performing a discretionary function (such as setting agency policy) or on claims arising out of (1) activities in a foreign country, (2) the collection of any tax or duty, (3) libel, slander, misrepresentation, deceit or interference with contract, (4) assault, battery, false imprisonment, false arrest, malicious prosecution or abuse

---

[22] 484 U.S. 292 (1988).

[23] Pub. L. No. 100-694, 102 Stat. 4562.

[24] 28 U.S.C. § 2679(b)(2).

[25] 502 U.S. 301 (1992).

of process, "except where based upon acts or omissions of federal investigative officers occurring after 1974" [recall *Bivens*] or (5) where other statutes bar a claim.[26] Other provisions in the FTCA establish a procedure for the processing of claims by the individual agencies against whom the claims are lodged.

One of the exceptions in the FTCA that has given the courts the most trouble is the *discretionary* versus *ministerial* distinction. Some of the boundaries are readily apparent. A government driver who injures someone is performing a ministerial task and is fully within the FTCA. A cabinet secretary signing a final agency rulemaking is performing a discretionary function because she is engaged in making policy. The Supreme Court has dealt with this distinction over the more than forty years that the FTCA has been in existence and has generally labeled functions as discretionary or ministerial on a case-by-case basis.[27]

In an important Supreme Court FTCA decision, *United States v. S.A. Empresa de Viacao Aerea (Varig Airlines)*,[28] the Court reviewed a claim stemming from the crash of a Varig Airlines 707 built by the Boeing Company that had been issued a safety certificate by the predecessor of the Federal Aviation Administration. The plaintiffs argued that the FAA had been negligent in issuing that safety certificate because the aircraft's construction did not conform to established fire safety standards. The government argued, among other things, that the FTCA action was barred under the discretionary function exception in the Act.

After a long discussion of both the manner in which the FAA issues certificates and of earlier case law on the discretionary exception, the Court concluded that the inspection of the aircraft for safety compliance and the ultimate issuance of the certificate were policy determinations and regulatory functions that the FAA and its employees are required to perform. As the Court stated:

> Judicial intervention in such decision making through private tort suits would require the courts to "second-guess" the political, social, and economic judgments of an agency exercising its regulatory function. It was precisely this sort of [act] that the discretionary function exception was designed to prevent.

In a more recent decision, *United States v. Gaubert*,[29] the Supreme Court reviewed the activities of the now-abolished Federal Home Loan Bank Board (the agency that formerly regulated the activities of federally-chartered savings and loan institutions (S & L's)). The Board had been sued under the FTCA for negligent supervision of a financially-distressed Texas S & L. The plaintiffs argued that, while the FTCA's discretionary function might apply to the Board's setting of policy, it did

---

[26] 28 U.S.C. § 2680. In *United States v. Smith*, 499 U.S. 160 (1991), a military doctor was held to be not subject to a malpractice suit brought against him, even though the injuries were sustained in a foreign country.

[27] For some good reading on the discretionary exception, see Stephen L. Nelson, *The King's Wrongs and the Federal District Courts: Understanding the Discretionary Function Exception to the Federal Tort Claims Act*, 51 S. Tex. L. Rev. 259 (2009); Andrew Hyer, Comment, *The Discretionary Function Exception to the Federal Tort Claims Act: A Proposal for a Workable Analysis*, 2007 B.Y.U. L. Rev. 1091.

[28] 467 U.S. 797 (1984).

[29] 499 U.S. 315 (1991).

not extend to the nuts-and-bolts, day-to-day supervision that the Board was supposed to exercise over the S & L's. The Court disagreed, holding that the discretionary function is not limited to the uppermost reaches of agency policymaking. Supervising the daily activities of the S & L's also involved the exercise of agency judgment and discretion sufficient to bring those activities within the FTCA's discretionary act exception.

There is a substantial amount of case law on this exception and on the other important elements of the FTCA. As a rule of thumb, the FTCA is a useful statute for recovery against the government for car accidents, but not for injuries occurring when the government official is taking steps to carry out a statutory obligation. There is a very narrow range of justiciable tort claims that can be brought under the FTCA. While the Act has some effect on certain agency activities, it has very little effect on agency policymaking.

§ 13.04   THE TUCKER ACT

The Tucker Act predates the FTCA by about fifty years. It permits suits against the government when the claim is founded "either on the Constitution, or any Act of Congress, or any regulation of an executive department, upon any express or implied contract with the United States, or for liquidated or unliquidated damages in cases not sounding in tort."[30] Initial jurisdiction rests with the United States Claims Court with appeals taken to the United States Court of Appeals for the Federal Circuit. For cases in which there is less than $10,000 in controversy, there is concurrent jurisdiction in the federal district courts. These cases are sometimes referred to as *Little Tucker Act* lawsuits.

The Act or parallel statutes have been used in the context of tax refund claims, suits on government contracts and Indian land claims. However, the Act itself has been held to be merely jurisdictional. Other statutes must be consulted to determine whether an action will lie for a particular contract or agreement. In *United States v. Testan*,[31] the Supreme Court held that the Tucker Act did not confer any right of action in a claim for increased federal salaries by two lawyers employed by the government. The Court noted the jurisdictional nature of the Tucker Act and pointed out that in order to approve a right of action, "[w]e therefore must determine whether [other statutes] . . . confer a substantive right to recover money damages from the United States . . . ."

In *United States v. Mitchell*,[32] the Court reviewed money damage claims made by individual members of a Northwest Indian tribe who asserted that the Department of the Interior had mismanaged timber reserves that it was managing on behalf of the tribe. The difficult legal issue was whether the special relationship of trust that existed between the Department and the tribal members under both

---

[30] 28 U.S.C. § 1491. For an excellent article distinguishing between contracts implied-in-fact and implied-in-law as those terms relate to Claims Court jurisdiction, *see* Willard L. Boyd III & Robert K. Huffman, *The Treatment of Implied-in-Law and Implied-in-Fact Contracts and Promissory Estoppel in the United States Claims Court*, 40 Cath. U. L. Rev. 605 (1991).

[31] 424 U.S. 392 (1976).

[32] 463 U.S. 206 (1983).

treaties and statutes gave rise to a claim by the tribal members on an express or implied contract theory under the Tucker Act. The Court concluded that it did, determining that the regulation of Indian lands had created what were essentially fiduciary relationships between the government and the tribes. If the government breached that trust by mismanaging the timber reserves on these lands, the claimants had a right to claim money damages.

It is not presently clear which is the better approach. There is a very special relationship that exists between the federal government and Indian tribes. Part of this relationship springs from a somewhat patronizing attitude historically shown by the government toward the tribes; another part derives from the fact that the earliest juridical relationships between the tribes and the government grew out of treaties (essentially a diplomatic relationship), rather than out of purely domestic legislation. That special relationship is evidenced by these treaties (most of which were abrogated at one time or another), the special statutes written by Congress for the tribes and in a large number of Supreme Court decisions. In Chapter 5, readers were warned not to generalize from cases involving immigration and naturalization. The same warning holds true for Supreme Court decisions involving Indian tribes. For all claims other than those made by tribal members, the *Testan* decision probably provides the predictable rule.

The Supreme Court has written another opinion that troubles many observers of the Tucker Act and the United States Court of Federal Claims. In *Bowen v. Massachusetts*,[33] the State of Massachusetts sued the Secretary of Health and Human Services, Otis Bowen, in *federal district court* seeking an injunction that would force HHS to release millions of dollars in federal Medicaid funds to the state because, allegedly, the funds had been improperly withheld from the state. The federal government defended, in part, on subject matter jurisdiction grounds, asserting that suits such as this could not be brought in federal district court because the amount in controversy exceeded $10,000 and the nature of the lawsuit was essentially one of breach of contract. Under this theory, the Claims Court (now the United States Court of Federal Claims) was the only appropriate forum for the action.

The Supreme Court disagreed, holding that it was appropriate for the case to be entertained by the district court. The Court reasoned that this action was not truly a Tucker Act case, but rather was an action seeking injunctive and declaratory relief under § 702 of the Administrative Procedure Act. Moreover, the Court determined that any appeal from this type of action would lie in the regional courts of appeals rather than the Court of Appeals for the Federal Circuit. In dissent, Justice Scalia suggested that the ultimate result of *Bowen* would be the evisceration of Claims Court jurisdiction, because the Supreme Court majority did not really provide any principled means to distinguish between *Bowen*-type suits and other actions seeking money damages against the government. A number of highly-regarded commentators have similar reservations about the *Bowen* holding,[34] but over 15

---

[33] 487 U.S. 879 (1988).

[34] *See, e.g.,* Michael F. Noone & Urban A. Lester, *Defining Tucker Act Jurisdiction After* Bowen v. Massachusetts, 40 CATH. U. L. Rev. 571 (1991). The two authors believe *Bowen* creates far more jurisdictional problems than the Court may have envisioned. In the absence of any clarification from

years after *Bowen*, Congress has yet to provide any legislative clarification. The final impact of *Bowen* on the Tucker Act and the jurisdiction of what is now called the United States Court of Federal Claims have yet to be determined.

Both the FTCA and the Tucker Act are not only useful for recovering money from the government for acts and omissions of federal officers, but they also provide a backdrop against which the legitimacy of certain types of agency action may be tested. Obviously, if a federal agency is deemed to have violated the FTCA or to have breached a contract subject to the Tucker Act, it is likely to clean up its act in the future. There are few judicial sanctions more attention-getting and more compelling than forcing an agency to pay money for its misdeeds. While the vast bulk of cases challenging agency action will continue to be brought under the judicial review provisions of the APA, these two remedial statutes have a salutary effect on the manner in which the federal government conducts its business.

Congress, they suggest a number of tests that may minimize any violence done to the Claims Court by the *Bowen* decision.

Chapter 14

OBTAINING GOVERNMENT INFORMATION

§ 14.01 INTRODUCTION

Chapter 4 discussed the process by which government agencies obtain information from the public and from the entities that they regulate. This chapter discusses the reverse of that proposition: the process by which private citizens obtain information from the federal government. Prior to 1966, there was very little a citizen could do to obtain information from the government. The government could give out information voluntarily, and many agencies did so. But there was little consistency among the agencies in terms of what they might or might not willingly disclose. People who were able to sue the government could sometimes obtain information by using litigation discovery techniques against an agency. Some of this discovery might be available through the agency's own rules of discovery in the context of adjudication within the agency. Some of it might be obtained in civil litigation against the government in federal court.

There were a few devices for obtaining information built into the federal administrative system even before the Administrative Procedure Act (APA) was enacted. The Federal Register Act,[1] enacted in the mid-1930s, with additional language codified in 1946 as a component of the APA,[2] required agencies to publish in the *Federal Register* a certain amount of material, usually having something to do with proposed and final agency rules. The impetus for the Federal Register Act arose out of *Panama Refining Co. v. Ryan*,[3] one of the major New Deal decisions in which the Supreme Court struck down a portion of the National Industrial Recovery Act. When the solicitor general and some other government attorneys began to write their Supreme Court brief,[4] they discovered that the underlying agency rules had been amended out of existence by a lapse in regulatory drafting. One of the reasons that the lawyers discovered the error so late in the game was the lack of any statutory requirement that agency rules be published in any generally available format. When the lawyers for the government tried to unravel the agency rules, they found the text of those rules in the desk drawers of agency officials. Only after examining the desk drawer copies of the rules did the lawyers learn that the rules did not actually exist because they had been inadvertently repealed.

---

[1] 44 U.S.C. §§ 1501 *et seq.*

[2] Formerly § 3 of the APA.

[3] 293 U.S. 388 (1935).

[4] The case is discussed in Chapter 2.

One unfortunate result of this inadvertent repeal of the NRA's rules was that the Supreme Court held that because the rules did not exist, the Court could not review them for any substantive or procedural deficiencies. This might have had a major impact on the ultimate decision had the Supreme Court taken a different approach to the case because the government argued, among other things, that the rules promulgated by the NRA were reasonable. However, because the Supreme Court held the underlying statute unconstitutional as a violation of the non-delegation doctrine, the lack of any implementing rules had no effect on the outcome of the case. The intense embarrassment suffered by the executive branch, along with a subsequent uproar in Congress, led to the enactment of the Federal Register Act and the later incorporation of the Act's publication requirements in both §§ 552 and 553 (rulemaking) of the APA.[5]

The current version of § 552(a) sets out an elaborate list of materials that must be published. Section 552(a) also provides expressly that if certain rules are not published and are not served upon the affected individuals, those rules are not enforceable. The list of items required to be published includes far more than the proposed and final rules of an agency and includes documents such as:

– descriptions of an agency's central and field organization;

– statements of the general course and method by which an agency's functions are carried out; and

– rules of procedure and sample forms.

Since the enactment of the Regulatory Flexibility Act[6] in 1980, agencies are also required to publish semi-annual regulatory agendas. An agency's regulatory agenda includes a review of rules published by the agency, the status of on-going rulemaking proceedings and target dates for the completion of the rulemaking activity. Presently, the *Federal Register* and other agency information required to be published under § 552(a) comprises a sizeable compendium of agency data especially useful for lawyers with agency business. This published information is easily accessible by mail or in agency reading rooms and is automatically released. Persons seeking this information are not required to invoke the more elaborate procedures necessary to process a request under the Freedom of Information Act, the Government in the Sunshine Act or the Federal Privacy Act, discussed below. Lawyers new to the federal administrative process should remember that there is an enormous amount of agency information available on a regular basis. Many administrative law neophytes make unnecessary formal requests for information when the data they need is readily at hand in agency publications. This is terribly inefficient lawyering that often proves costly for the client.

---

[5] This story is entertainingly told in Louis L. Jaffe, *An Essay on Delegation of Legislative Power*, 47 Colum. L. Rev. 561 (1947).

[6] 5 U.S.C. §§ 601–612. *See also* Michelle Goldberg-Cahn, Note, Associated Fisheries of Maine, Inc. v. Daley: *A Balanced Approach to Judicial Review Under the Regulatory Flexibility Act*, 51 Admin. L. Rev. 663 (1999).

§ 14.02 THE FREEDOM OF INFORMATION ACT

[A] Background

Prior to 1966, § 3 of the APA merely provided: "Except as otherwise required by statute, matters of official record shall be made available, in accordance with published rule, to persons properly and directly concerned, except information held confidential for good cause found."[7] Note the elements of the statute: certain matters must be released *by statute* (essentially those matters required to be published under § 552(a); there were a handful of other statutes requiring disclosure, but they did not govern access to the vast bulk of agency information).

The requester of the information had to show that he or she was "properly and directly concerned." An agency could refuse access to information if it concluded that the requester had not shown this requisite concern. Even if a requester were directly concerned, the request could be refused if the agency concluded that there was *good cause* for the refusal. The statute also recognized a *public interest* exception (*i.e.*, information could be withheld if non-disclosure was deemed to be in the public interest) to disclosure that was probably the most frequently invoked reason for withholding information. The cumulative effect of the original version of APA § 3 gave the agencies a virtual *carte blanche* to withhold information from whomever they pleased and to set up what amounted to a *de facto* presumption against disclosure. Agencies read § 3 as permitting them to do almost anything they wanted with their data. In other words, the agencies could release information if they felt like it; otherwise they could refuse access.

After nearly a decade of debate, Congress enacted the Freedom of Information Act (FOIA)[8] to reverse these presumptions against disclosure and to give private persons unprecedented access to government information. For many reasons, the FOIA has become one of the most heavily litigated components of the APA. The FOIA was significantly amended in 1974 to make even more information available, and it is, even in the first decade of the twenty-first century, a wonderment to persons in other countries who have far less access to government information.

[B] A FOIA Roadmap

The FOIA is not as well organized in its codified form as one might hope. Someone reading the Act for the first time can easily become hopelessly bogged down in statutory language that should have been more artfully drafted and better organized. Sometimes, it can be difficult to separate even the principal elements of the FOIA from the material in § 552 that existed before the FOIA was enacted. The extract from § 552 set out below shows where to start reading the FOIA.

---

[7] 5 U.S.C. § 552(d) (repealed 1996).

[8] 5 U.S.C. § 552(a)(3). The reader should review the following discussion in the text to spot the division in § 552(a) between the pre-existing portion of the statute granting automatic access to certain agency information and the FOIA.

§ 552. Public information; agency rules, opinions, orders, records, and proceedings

(a) Each agency shall make available to the public information as follows:

. . . .

(2) Each agency, in accordance with published rules, shall make available for public inspection and copying-

(A) final opinions, including concurring and dissenting opinions, as well as orders, made in the adjudication of cases;

(B) those statements of policy and interpretations which have been adopted by the agency and are not published in the Federal Register; and

(C) administrative staff manuals and instructions to staff that affect a member of the public;

unless the materials are promptly published and copies offered for sale. To the extent required to prevent a clearly unwarranted invasion of personal privacy, an agency may delete identifying details when it makes available or publishes an opinion, statement of policy, interpretation, or staff manual or instruction. However, in each case the justification for the deletion shall be explained fully in writing. Each agency shall also maintain and make available for public inspection and copying current indexes providing identifying information for the public as to any matter issued, adopted or promulgated after July 4, 1967, and required by this paragraph to be made available or published. Each agency shall promptly publish, quarterly or more frequently, and distribute (by sale or otherwise) copies of each index or supplements thereto unless it determines by order published in the *Federal Register* that the publication would be unnecessary and impracticable, in which case the agency shall nonetheless provide copies of such index on request at a cost not to exceed the direct cost of duplication. A final order, opinion, statement of policy, interpretation, or staff manual or instruction that affects a member of the public may be relied on, used, or cited as precedent by an agency against a party other than an agency only if-

(i) it has been indexed and either made available or published as provided by this paragraph; or

(ii) the party has actual and timely notice of the terms thereof.

[NOTE TO THE READER: **THE TEXT OF THE FOIA BEGINS HERE.**]

(3) Except with respect to the records made available under paragraphs (1) and (2) of this subsection, each agency, upon any request for records which (A) reasonably describes such records and (B) is made in accordance with published rules stating the time, place, fees (if any), and procedures to be followed, shall make the records promptly available to any person.

(4)(A) In order to carry out the provisions of this section, each agency shall promulgate regulations, pursuant to notice and receipt of public comment, specifying a uniform schedule of fees applicable to all constituent units of such agency. Such fees shall be limited to reasonable standard charges for document search and duplication and provide for recovery of only the direct costs of such search and duplication. Documents shall be furnished without charge or at a reduced charge where the agency determines that waiver or reduction of the fee is in the public interest because furnishing the information can be considered as primarily benefiting the general public.

. . . .

[NOTE TO THE READER: THIS IS ONLY THE FIRST PORTION OF THE FOIA. PLEASE EXAMINE THE REMAINDER OF THE FOIA IN THE APPENDIX AS YOU READ THE FOLLOWING SECTIONS OF TEXT.]

Once you have reviewed the express language of the FOIA, the following discussion provides a walk-through of the Act. The questions posed in each of the subsections below will provide a framework for spotting and resolving FOIA issues.[9]

§ 14.03   WHO MAY REQUEST GOVERNMENT INFORMATION?

[A]   Generally

The Act is clear on this point: *any person* may request information. Note the striking contrast between the unmodified *any person* in the FOIA and the much more confined definition (any person *properly and directly concerned*) in the original § 3 of the APA. Even so, there are occasions when *person* must be defined for FOIA purposes. To define *person*, you must leave the FOIA itself and go to § 551 of the APA to discover that *person* is "an individual, partnership, corporation, association, or public or private organization *other than an agency* [emphasis supplied]."

Note that this is essentially a residual definition. A *person* appears to be any entity that is capable of making a request and that is not a federal agency. The difficulty with interpreting this term is that it appears in § 551, the basic definitional section of the entire APA, rather than as a separate definition in the

---

[9] The authoritative commercial publication on the FOIA is JAMES T. O'REILLY, FEDERAL INFORMATION DISCLOSURE. The Department of Justice published two *Attorney General's Memoranda* on the FOIA, one in 1967 and the second in 1974, that are standard references and frequently regarded by the courts as part of the legislative history of the FOIA. However, many FOIA scholars view the Attorney General's memoranda as excessively deferential toward protection of information and thus not fully consistent with the FOIA's basic principle of full disclosure. There is a mass of law review literature on various parts of the Act. For a provocative article, *see* Fred H. Cate, D. Annette Fields & James K. McBain, *The Right to Privacy and the Public's Right to Know: The "Central Purpose" of the Freedom of Information Act*, 46 ADMIN. L. REV. 41 (1994). For some empirical data on the FOIA, see Minjeong Kim, *Numbers Tell Part of the Story: A Comparison of FOIA Implementation Under the Clinton and Bush Administrations*, 12 COMM. L. & POL'Y 313 (2007).

FOIA itself. Nonetheless, there are ways to cope with this problem. Begin with the fundamental purposes of the FOIA: to promote as much disclosure of information as possible. Then, recall that the FOIA contains a presumption in favor of disclosure. Taken together, the definition of *person* ought to be struck as broadly as possible. Virtually all courts agree, although there is sometimes a question as to whether a foreign government is a person under the FOIA. This last issue has been rarely litigated because individuals and law firms are persons within the terms of the Act. A foreign government may simply have its request filed in the name of an entity that is squarely recognized under the FOIA.

This broad definition of *person* has other advantages. For law firms, one of the profound benefits of the FOIA is that a request may be made in the name of the firm or in the name of an individual employee of a firm. This means that the firm does not have to disclose the identity of the client for whom the request is being made. By contrast, if information were being sought from an agency in the context of litigation, the client's name would likely have to be revealed. This is one reason why the FOIA has become an important confidential discovery tool for private parties.

[B]   Which Agencies Are Subject to the FOIA?

Here, as in so many other parts of the FOIA, Congress cast as broad a net as possible in favor of disclosure. In contrast to the definition of *person*, the FOIA contains its own definition of *agency* that differs substantially from the definition of agency in § 551 of the APA. For FOIA purposes, § 552(e) defines *agency* as including independent regulatory commissions, the executive office of the president, all other executive departments, all government corporations and the military. It is now conceded that this definition includes the Central Intelligence Agency and the Federal Bureau of Investigation-two agencies that now process proportionately more FOIA requests than any other federal agency. Both of these agencies have frequently asked Congress to create specific exceptions to narrow the range of information that they have to disclose because they deal constantly with highly sensitive criminal and national security material. While the courts have been sympathetic to the special needs of both the FBI and the CIA, Congress has created few special exceptions solely for the benefit of those two agencies. However, merely accepting federal funds does not necessarily convert a private entity into an agency for FOIA purposes.[10] Note finally, that the definition of *agency* includes only entities within the executive branch of government and does not include either Congress or the judiciary.

[C]   How and With Whom Do You File an FOIA Request?

FOIA requests are generally made in the form of a letter directed to an agency's FOIA officer. The name of the FOIA officer and the precise address for FOIA requests are published in the *Federal Register* and the *Code of Federal Regulations.*

---

[10] *Forsham v. Harris*, 445 U.S. 169, 178–79 (1980).

One of the singular advantages of the FOIA is that a requester need give no reasons for making the request. Recall that § 3 of the original APA required an agency to entertain information requests only from a person properly and directly concerned. Prior to the FOIA, a requester frequently had to provide a substantial justification for wanting the information. There is no longer such a requirement, and an explanation is no longer necessary. Because no explanation is necessary, many agencies have established Public Information Reading Rooms containing copies of many regularly requested documents that may be read and copied in the reading room. No formal written request has to be made for these documents. If you file a written request, you are required, under the Act, to *reasonably describe* the records sought, and if gathering or photocopying the records takes agency time, you are expected to pay for both copying and search fees.[11]

When the Act was first passed, it was estimated that the total cost to the Government would be slightly over $150,000 per year because the FOIA is supposed to pay for itself by placing the fee and cost burden on the requesters of information rather than on the agency. It has not worked out that way. Because many agencies waive fees and because fee schedules rarely reflect the actual search and retrieval costs, the costs to many agencies have been substantial-far in excess of the original projections. Recent congressional inquiries indicate that the FOIA is costing agencies millions of dollars each year in processing expenses.

[D]   What Documents May Be Requested?

The FOIA permits any person to request disclosure of an *agency record.* The term *agency record* is not expressly defined in the FOIA or elsewhere in the APA. It has fallen to the federal courts to elaborate on what constitutes an agency record. The Supreme Court suggested that the term ought to be broadly construed to effectuate the basic purposes of the FOIA. In *Department of Justice v. Tax Analysts,*[12] the Court addressed the question of whether copies of federal district court opinions in the files of the Department of Justice constituted agency records that must be disclosed under the FOIA. The decisions were sought by the publisher of a tax newsletter; and the Justice Department refused the request on essentially two grounds: (1) because the documents were generated by the courts, a court is not an *agency* for FOIA purposes; and (2) because the opinions were not initially created by the executive branch, they were not *records* as that term is used in the FOIA. Recall that the FOIA does not apply to the federal judiciary.

The Supreme Court reviewed its earlier case law and concluded that even court decisions, if they were regularly collected and held by the Justice Department, constituted agency records for FOIA purposes. Among other things, the Court emphasized that an agency resisting disclosure of the records carries the burden of proving that information in its hands is not an agency record. Here, the Justice Department did not carry its burden.

---

[11] Congress has issued a handbook on the FOIA that contains some sample letters for requesting documents under the FOIA: *A Citizens Guide on How to Use the Freedom of Information Act and the Privacy Act in Requesting Government Documents,* H.R. 95-793 (1977).

[12] 492 U.S. 136 (1989).

Another issue can arise with regard to the nature of the agency record. Since 1974, the FOIA has expressly stated that an agency must provide a requester with those portions of a record that are not protected from disclosure, even when some other part of the document is protected. In the parlance of the Act: "Any *reasonably segregable* portion of a record shall be provided . . . after deletion of the portions which are [protected]." Eliminating protected data from the entire document (also discussed in subsection [6] below) is referred to as *redaction* and can be an extremely time-consuming and expensive task for the agency. Nonetheless, since 1974, all agencies must redact or must argue that a particular document is not reasonably segregable. Reviewing courts frequently examine documents *in camera* to ascertain whether redaction has been properly carried out.

There is a third problem that frequently arises when an agency argues that no part of any of the requested documents may properly be disclosed. Since a 1973 decision by the D.C. Circuit, *Vaughn v. Rosen*,[13] agencies are required to provide a list or an index of the documents (such list is now referred to as a *Vaughn* index) unless the list or index itself may not be disclosed. A *Vaughn* index can be a powerful tool in terms of ascertaining what is in the agency's hands, even if the documents themselves are not disclosable. It has become a principal feature of FOIA activity, particularly in those agencies such as the FBI, CIA and State Department that deal with large amounts of otherwise classified or protected data.

[E]   How Long Does an Agency Have to Act on Your Request?

Here we begin to see the teeth Congress put into the Act. Under normal circumstances, until October, 1997, an agency had ten days from receipt of an FOIA request to tell the requester (on a "yes" or "no" basis) whether they will honor the request for information. If the answer is *no*, or only a partial *yes*, the requester may appeal the denial of access to another level of the agency (the agency's FOIA rules state where and how to take an intra-agency appeal). The agency has twenty days to process the appeal. In late 1996, Congress finally came to terms with the totally unworkable ten day deadline and increased the agency's initial response time to twenty days.[14]

The statutory language is extremely tight, giving the agency very little leeway to avoid compliance with these strict deadlines. If the agency needs extra time to work with field offices or another agency, or if the request is particularly voluminous, it can notify the requester in writing that it will pass on her request within an additional ten days beyond the normal ten days for the initial request. The agency, with explanation to the requester, may also obtain a ten-day extension for processing the intra-agency appeal. Given that so many agencies work at a glacial speed in many of their other activities, ten or twenty days for doing

---

[13] 484 F.2d 820 (D.C. Cir. 1973), *cert. denied*, 415 U.S. 977 (1974).

[14] The Electronic Freedom of Information Act Amendments of 1996, 104-231, 110 Stat. 3048. In addition, the agencies are now admonished to gather frequently requested documents for which FOIA requests have already been honored into a collection that the general public will have easier access to.

anything is not much time. These exceptionally strict time limits show the seriousness of Congress in enacting the FOIA.

If the agency violates any of these deadlines, the Act expressly provides that the requester is deemed to have exhausted[15] his administrative remedies. The requester may go immediately into federal court to challenge the lack of timely agency action and to pursue the FOIA request directly with the court. A court, however, is empowered to give the agency more time if the agency can show due diligence and unusual circumstances.

Read the FOIA carefully. The provisions establishing time requirements for responding and processing intra-agency appeals apply only to the agency's decision to disclose or to refuse disclosure. These deadlines have nothing to do with how quickly the agency must provide the documents. For most of the lifespan of the FOIA, the only provision governing the time in which the agency must give over the records stated: "[The agency] shall make the records *promptly available* [emphasis supplied]." This is a much looser term than the ten and twenty-day periods specified for passing on requests and, in many cases, has given back to the agency almost everything that was taken away by the ten and twenty-day deadlines.

In late 1996, Congress finally addressed the problem of delay in the Electronic Freedom of Information Act Amendments.[16] The Electronic Amendments Act permits an agency to handle different FOIA requests on different timetables, rather than merely using a first in/first out schedule. Routine requests may be handled differently from large volume requests. In certain instances, an agency will be required to give expedited processing (defined as processing on an "as soon as practicable" basis) to requests in which the requester makes a showing of compelling need. Of course, if the agency delays excessively, a requester may always seek judicial review for agency action unreasonably delayed, but federal courts are now quite sympathetic to agencies that are heavily burdened with FOIA requests.

[F] How Must a Court Deal with Judicial Review of a Denial?

This is another place where the FOIA's pro-disclosure bias is evident. Subject matter jurisdiction is vested in the federal district courts with an exceptionally broad venue provision: any denial or partial denial of an FOIA request may be taken into a federal district court in the district (1) where the requester resides or has her place of business, or (2) where the records are physically located, or (3) in the District of Columbia. An action is commenced by filing a complaint (often subtitled "Freedom of Information Act Action"). The complaint must be answered within thirty days by the government. Recall that the government normally has sixty days to answer a complaint under the *Federal Rules of Civil Procedure*.[17]

---

[15] *See* Chapter 11, § 11.05 for a discussion of exhaustion.

[16] Pub. L. No. 104-231, 110 Stat. 3048 (codified in scattered subsections of 5 U.S.C. § 552).

[17] *See* FED. R. CIV. P. 12(b).

To insure that courts do not delay FOIA cases, the Act originally provided that FOIA actions are to be given expedited treatment on the court's docket. Of course, this last provision did not work all that well in practice. Many other federal statutes — e.g., some of the civil rights cases, the Speedy Trial Act (criminal prosecutions) — also require expedited treatment. In 1984, Congress repealed this provision. FOIA lawsuits no longer get expedited treatment.

When an agency denies access to the records or provides only partial release, that denial is to be reviewed by the court on a *de novo* standard.[18] If the agency contends that the records are protected from disclosure-for example, because the documents contain data involving national security or trade secrets-the court is permitted to examine the documents *in camera* as part of its *de novo* review. Of course, once again the language of the Act sounds better than the *in camera* review process works in practice. Parties are normally not permitted to participate in the in camera review; the actual review involves a federal judge sitting in her chambers, without the presence of counsel, and examining the documents. Most federal judges thoroughly detest this burden on their time and avoid *in camera* review whenever possible.

The reviewing court has the power to enjoin the agency from withholding records or to order the production of records properly disclosable under the Act. The court may award attorneys' fees to a private litigant who *substantially prevails* in FOIA litigation, but a request for attorneys' fees must be sought in a separate piece of litigation after the basic FOIA case has been resolved.

[G]   What Information Is Protected from Disclosure?

The FOIA case law is voluminous. However, most of the reported FOIA cases involve issues of what information is disclosable and what is protected. The FOIA itself deals with this aspect of disclosure under nine separate exemptions. In the FOIA case law and among FOIA practitioners, these exemptions are usually referred to by their subsection numbers in the Act. They are:

   b(1)- national security information;

   b(2)- internal personnel rules and files;

   b(3)- exempted by separate statute;

   b(4)- commercial/financial information and trade secrets;

   b(5)- inter/intra-agency memoranda;

   b(6)- personnel/medical and other files disclosure of which would violate personal privacy;

   b(7)- law enforcement and investigation files;[19]

---

[18] *See* the scope of review discussion in Chapter 12. In FOIA cases, *de novo* means that the reviewing court is not bound by any of the assertions or explanations proffered by the agency for refusing disclosure. It may substitute its own judgment as to the propriety of disclosure.

[19] In 2003, the D.C. Circuit reviewed a request submitted to the Department of Justice by various interest groups for the names, attorneys, dates of arrest and release, etc., of persons detained by the

b(8)- data on financial institutions; and

b(9)- certain geological and geophysical information on oil and natural gas wells.

In working through these exemptions, the actual language of the exemption must be carefully analyzed. There are very few types of federal information that are categorically protected from disclosure. Many of the exemptions were amended in 1974 specifically to overrule court decisions that, in the view of Congress and many commentators, were making it excessively difficult to obtain information.

Since 1974, for example, the b(1) exemption protects documents that are: "(A) specifically authorized under criteria established by an Executive Order to be kept secret in the interest of national defense or foreign policy and (B) are in fact properly classified pursuant to such Executive Order." This exemption was rewritten to circumvent some of the more cumbersome aspects of *Environmental Protection Agency v. Mink*,[20] a Supreme Court decision that attempted as a matter of statutory interpretation to create a blanket exemption for all classified documents (*i.e.*, national security materials that bear a classified document stamp) generated by the executive branch. This is not to say the Court's interpretation was disingenuous. The original language of b(1) prohibited the disclosure of documents "specifically required by Executive Order to be kept secret in the interest of the national defense or foreign policy." Patsy Mink, a member of Congress, and others asked for agency information on nuclear weapons testing then in the hands of the EPA. The Supreme Court determined that all such documents carried a classified stamp and held that such a stamp ended the court's inquiry. In other words, when a document bears a stamp, it has been specifically required to be kept secret.

Congress reversed the *Mink* decision in 1974 by substantially amending the b(1) language. Note the current language of b(1). First, there must be in existence — at the time the document is classified — an executive order that provides for classifying national security documents and that specifies the criteria for classifying these documents in some category such as *confidential, secret* or *top secret.* Second, the documents in question must have been classified properly within the executive order's substantive criteria and must also have been classified in a procedurally correct fashion — *i.e.*, a document that is classified only after an FOIA request is received, where the executive order requires classification when the document is created, arguably is not exempt under b(1).

A similar analysis must be performed for each of the FOIA's exemptions. The exemptions are supposed to protect as little information as possible, consistent with

---

federal government after the September 11, 2001 attack on the Pentagon and the World Trade Center. After a lengthy review, the Circuit concluded that the Department properly withheld all of the information under 7(A)(law enforcement records the release of which would interfere with enforcement proceedings). *Center for National Security Studies v. United States Department of Justice*, 331 F.3d 918 (D.C. Cir. 2003). For analysis of the impact of the war against terrorism, the formation of the Department of Homeland Security and other issues, *see* Christina E. Wells, *"National Security" Information and the Freedom of Information Act*, 56 ADMIN. L. REV. 1195 (2004), and Stephen Gidiere & Jason Forrester, *Balancing Homeland Security and Freedom of Information*, 16 NAT. RESOURCES & ENV'T 139 (2002).

[20] 410 U.S. 73 (1973).

the exemption's language, and are to be read in light of the fundamental purpose and presumption of the FOIA favoring disclosure of information. Recall that the burden of convincing the court that the document should not be disclosed is always on the government.[21] The Supreme Court states this requirement in terms of requiring the agency to show that the records have not been "improperly withheld."[22] The government frequently invokes more than one exemption, when appropriate, because of the stringent burdens on justifying non-disclosure. The agency only has to prevail on one of several exemptions.

[H] Some Representative FOIA Case Law

[1] Introduction

The federal courts have had a major impact on the FOIA, although one of the main reasons for the 1974 amendments to the FOIA was to reverse a number of judicial decisions that Congress regarded as protecting too much information. As a consequence, most FOIA practitioners view pre-1974 cases with caution. There are any number of major post-1974 FOIA decisions extracted and discussed in the major administrative law casebooks. Three of the frequently included cases are discussed below: *NLRB v. Sears, Roebuck & Co.*, *Department of Air Force v. Rose* and *Chrysler Corp. v. Brown.*

[2] *NLRB v. Sears, Roebuck & Co.*[23]

In *Sears*, a case involving the b(5) inter/intra-agency memorandum exemption, the company filed an FOIA request with the National Labor Relations Board requesting memoranda on how the Board's general counsel made decisions to pursue unfair labor practice complaints. The Board resisted, invoking the b(5) exemption and arguing, under the language of b(5), that these were documents that would not normally be available to a party in litigation against the agency.

The Court worked through the express language of the exemption to determine that merely labeling a document "inter/intra-agency memorandum" will not suffice to protect a document. Instead, the proper focus for a b(5) analysis is on the "available to a party in litigation" phrase. This, the Court concluded, was Congress's way of incorporating civil discovery rules into the FOIA. Under Federal Rule of Civil Procedure 26, a party may normally discover any material that is relevant and not privileged. The concept of relevance has no bearing on an FOIA analysis because a requester need give no reasons for an FOIA request. However, the term *privilege* does have an impact.

Clearly, the Court stated, the b(5) exemption was to encompass the doctrine of executive privilege.[24] The exemption is also related to the attorney-client privilege

---

[21] *Dep't of Justice v. Tax Analysts*, 492 U.S. 136 (1989).

[22] *GTE Sylvania, Inc. v. Consumers Union of the United States*, 445 U.S. 375 (1980).

[23] 421 U.S. 132 (1975).

[24] *See* Chapter 8, § 8.04.

and the attorney work-product doctrine.[25] However, one of the problems in FOIA work is that there is no precedential litigation to provide a focal point for evaluating a claim of privilege. To resolve this dilemma, the Court took a commonsense approach and provided simply that documents that are not privileged would be those that are "routinely disclosed" in private litigation.

Examining more closely Sears' request and the two different types of memoranda in question, the Court held that b(5) did not protect from disclosure memoranda "which conclude that no complaint should be filed and which have the effect of finally denying relief to the charging party" because those documents no longer need any of the protections afforded by the various privileges. By contrast, b(5) did protect those memoranda that are used as the basis for actually filing an unfair labor practice charge. The latter memoranda, in the Court's view, were in the nature of attorney work-product documents prepared by agency lawyers to assist the Board in deciding whether to pursue administrative litigation before the Board. Consequently, those documents would not be discoverable even in litigation.[26]

[3] *Department of Air Force v. Rose*[27]

This case is a favorite of both law professors and law students because it is one of the few Supreme Court decisions involving the writing (as opposed to the citing) of a law review article. *Rose* has become one of the principal decisions construing the b(2) (internal agency rules) and b(6) (personal privacy) exemptions. It is an important statement on the manner in which the Court prefers to work with the Act's legislative history. It also has a lot to say about the matter of *redaction* — *i.e.*, the process by which protected information is excised from documents.

The *Rose* case grew out of an FOIA request filed by an Air Force officer who was then enrolled in law school. The officer intended to write a law review article on discipline in the military academies.[28] The law student wanted to examine Air Force Academy documents that constituted summaries of Academy honor board disciplinary actions involving individual cadets. Copies of the summaries were posted at the Academy but were not published. Each summary was also stamped "for official use only."

---

[25] *See, e.g., Hickman v. Taylor*, 329 U.S. 495 (1947).

[26] The D.C. Circuit has noted that a fundamental purpose of the b(5) exemption is to protect the confidentiality of the pre-decisional agency deliberative process. Unwarranted disclosure of certain pre-decisional matters would have the effect of inhibiting broad-brush discussion of all kinds of alternatives. However, in order to be protected, such documents have to be *both* pre-decisional *and* part of the agency's deliberative process. *See Mead Data Central, Inc. v. Dep't of the Air Force*, 566 F.2d 242 (D.C. Cir. 1977). A recent decision of the United States Court of Appeals for the District of Columbia Circuit, *In re Sealed Case*, 121 F.3d 729 (D.C. Cir. 1997), contains an excellent discussion of the pre-decisional/post-decisional distinction, albeit in the context of a grand jury subpoena.

[27] 425 U.S 352 (1976).

[28] Readers will note, in Chief Justice Burger's separate opinion in *Rose*, a statement by the Chief Justice showing that he was outraged and scandalized by the fact that vast amounts of government and Court time could be taken up helping a law student write a law review article. The Chief Justice and other commentators have suggested that Congress force FOIA requesters to state their reasons for making a request and that those reasons be taken into account when passing on the request itself. So far, Congress has not taken the hint.

The Air Force resisted disclosure by relying upon both the b(2) and b(6) exemptions. By invoking the b(2) exemption, the Air Force asserted that the summaries were for internal use only and held no interest for the general public. The Air Force cited the House Report on the FOIA, a piece of legislative history that arguably protected the summaries, while the requester cited the Senate Report — a report stating that b(2) was to protect only minor or trivial agency matters, such as sick leave policy and the assignment of agency parking spaces. The Court examined the disciplinary summaries in light of b(2) and concluded that there was a legitimate public interest in knowing something about cadet discipline in the Nation's military academies. The academies, after all, are created by Congress and the executive branch, enroll students from all over the country for the important task of military service and are funded by U.S. taxpayers.

The Court then proceeded to examine b(2)'s legislative history. There were, concededly, significant differences between the House and Senate Reports on the FOIA. When legislative history conflicts in this fashion, it is usually up to the courts to determine which piece of legislative history should be given the most credence on judicial review. In this case, the b(2) language originated in the Senate-which wrote a committee report-and was then passed on to the House, which wrote its own report. Here, the Court determined that it would give more weight to the Senate Report because it was the only one of the two to have been considered by, and available to, both houses of Congress. Using the Senate Report, the Court held that b(2) protects only the trivia of government activity, not something as important as the administration of the nation's service academies.

The b(6) (personal privacy) exemption was more troublesome for the *Rose* court. The b(6) language protects agency files on individuals, the "disclosure of which would constitute a clearly unwarranted invasion of personal privacy." The Court first concluded that b(6) is not a categorical exemption for all personnel and medical files. Its discussion of this point was akin to its refusal to accept merely labeling a document as an inter-agency memorandum as grounds for refusing to disclose the memorandum. Next, the Court determined that the *clearly unwarranted* language in the exemption should be read in light of the requirement that agencies *reasonably segregate* protected information from non-protected information. These two FOIA provisions create a need to balance an individual's interests in privacy against the public's right to know what the government is doing. Balancing these interests is not easy in any event, but can be made easier by simply removing the sensitive material from the document by the process of redaction and then releasing the remainder of the document to the requester.

Addressing the redaction issue, the Court acknowledged that even the most heavily-redacted document might still contain enough personal information to permit someone somewhere to identify an individual cadet. Other cadets might be able to identify the disciplined cadet with the slimmest information because they were at the Air Force Academy at the same time and knew a great deal about their classmates. But, according to the Court, that is not the test for redaction under the FOIA. Release of information will not constitute a *clearly unwarranted* privacy invasion so long as members of the *general public* cannot identify the person(s) to whom the information pertains. As the Court pointed out, "redaction cannot eliminate all risks of identifiability," but given the balancing necessary under the b(6) exemption and the fact that redaction is a fairly well known process, the analysis ought to foster "practical workable concepts." The FOIA, however, does not require absolute protection of identity.

[4] *Chrysler Corp. v. Brown*[29]

Not all FOIA requests are intended merely to help law students write law review articles. Businesses quickly realized that the FOIA could provide a gold mine of data on competitors because so many businesses in the United States are subject to comprehensive agency reporting requirements. Although some commentators believe that business has used the FOIA as part of an industrial espionage strategy with good success, an objective view of the FOIA suggests this is not as much of an abuse as some might believe. Nonetheless, because most businesses have no choice in providing information to the government,[30] they become understandably worried when it appears that their competitors may obtain access to proprietary information and trade secrets.

On its face, the b(4) exemption protects from disclosure "trade secrets and commercial or financial information obtained from a person and which is privileged or confidential." Agencies are generally quite sensitive to the release of competitive information. But the problem has an additional dimension: an agency is not obligated to refuse to disclose information even if it is protected by one of the FOIA exemptions. In many instances, the agency has the discretion not to invoke the FOIA. Also, a number of courts have held that if information is disclosed erroneously, it loses its protection under the FOIA, even if the disclosure was unintentional.

These problems led a number of companies in the first ten years of the FOIA to bring what became known as *reverse-FOIA* lawsuits by which they would invoke the jurisdictional provisions of the FOIA and ask a federal court to enjoin disclosure. The Supreme Court finally took up the issue in *Brown* and decided that, while the issue of industrial espionage was quite sensitive, the FOIA did not provide a *jurisdictional* basis for a reverse-FOIA action.

In reaching its conclusion, the Court took a plain language approach to the statute. Justice Rehnquist, writing for a unanimous Court, determined first that the FOIA "is exclusively a disclosure statute." While the Act permits a court to enjoin the withholding of records and to order an agency to make disclosure, nowhere on its face does the FOIA give a court express permission to *prohibit* disclosure.

Chrysler argued in the alternative that even if the FOIA did not contain express authority for a court to prohibit disclosure, a separate federal statute, the Trade Secrets Act,[31] did provide a court with the statutory authority to forbid the release of sensitive business information. The Supreme Court disagreed, reasoning that because the Trade Secrets Act did not create a private right of action, it could not

---

[29] 441 U.S 281 (1979).

[30] *See* Chapter 4, § 4.05.

[31] 18 U.S.C. § 1905.

be invoked as a basis for a reverse-FOIA action.[32]

At this point, the Court seems to have wanted to make a minor concession to American business. Even if the FOIA or the Trade Secrets Act could not be used as a basis for a reverse-FOIA action, an agency's act of disclosure was reviewable under § 706 of the APA. This conclusion provides the seeds for an alternative route toward halting unauthorized disclosure. If a company is fortunate enough to hear that the agency is about to reveal some of its sensitive data, it is permitted to file a lawsuit challenging the agency decision under some other statute (for example, basic federal question jurisdiction[33]) and to request, under § 702 of the APA, a stay of agency action pending judicial review.[34] If the stay is issued and if the company ultimately prevails on its arguments that the disclosure is forbidden under, for example, the Trade Secrets Act, the documents will not be released. Using the §§ 702/706 procedure under the APA creates what amounts to a reverse-FOIA action, even if one cannot be brought under the FOIA itself. Such an action necessarily requires continuous policing of agency activity. This is one reason why large companies so closely monitor the FOIA requests filed by their competitors. Executive branch agencies must now tell affected companies that information concerning their business practices has become the subject of an FOIA request and permit the affected company to respond before releasing the information.[35]

[4] *National Archives and Records Administration v. Favish*[36]

Favish involves that part of FOIA exemption 7(C) — "records or information compiled for law enforcement purpose" — that excuses from disclosure material whose disclosure "could reasonably be expected to constitute an unwarranted invasion of personal privacy."[37] In this case, a requester sought records involving the suicide of Vincent Foster, a member of President Clinton's White House staff. Mr. Favish, a journalist, sought the release of several color photographs taken at the site of the suicide and including views of Mr. Foster's body.

On review by the Supreme Court, the Court noted that the photographs had been taken pursuant to an investigation by the FBI, thus constituting "law enforcement records." On the additional issue of whether the release of the photos would compromise personal privacy issues, the Court noted that a family, such as that of Mr. Foster, had a clear interest in protecting itself from "public intrusions long deemed impermissible under the common law and in our cultural traditions." While a family might not necessarily have the same privacy interests as the person whose

---

[32] On the issue of private right of action, the Court worked through the criteria set out in *Cort v. Ash*, 422 U.S. 66 (1975). The Trade Secrets Act, in the Court's judgment, simply did not satisfy the *Cort* criteria.

[33] 28 U.S.C. § 1331.

[34] *See* the discussion of § 702 in Chapter 10, § 10.03.

[35] *See* Exec. Order No. 12,600, 52 Fed. Reg. 23,781 (1987).

[36] 541 U.S. 157 (2004).

[37] 5 U.S.C. § 552(b)(7)(C).

information is at stake, the family here had a clear interest in protecting the death scene photographs.

As in all other FOIA personal privacy cases, the Court acknowledged the need to balance the privacy issues against the basic presumption in favor of disclosure to conclude that the photos need not be disclosed. In these cases, the requester has a burden of showing that the public disclosure interests exceed the personal privacy interests. In this case, the requester had not met his burden and the photos did not have to be disclosed.

[5] Conclusion

These are not the only important Supreme Court FOIA decisions. They are included here as representative examples of the way in which the Court approaches FOIA disputes. Both the Court and Congress seem to be generally happy with the way the Act is working. At present, there seem to be no major problems with the FOIA of great concern to either the Court or Congress. Recently, Congress inserted additional language in § 552(a)(3)(c)(1) pertaining to access to information involving on-going criminal proceedings and informant information. But the language of that amendment makes abundantly clear that it is to be narrowly construed to conceal as little information as possible.

We could continue to analyze individual FOIA cases without much productive result. As the United States moves into the twenty first century, the concern has begun to shift from printed data, what we now have begun to call "hard copy" records, to electronic data collection and retrieval. Indeed, at least one commentator believes that electronic data is beginning to re-shape all of administrative law.[38] In late 1996, Congress enacted the Electronic Freedom of Information Act Amendments.[39] But as discussed earlier, this statute relates more to delays in processing FOIA requests than to the special problems of electronic data. Whether the FOIA can be made truly responsive to the Internet age remains to be seen.

§ 14.04 THE GOVERNMENT IN THE SUNSHINE ACT

In 1976, in the aftermath of the Watergate scandal, Congress became concerned that too much government decision-making was taking place in secret. The FOIA requires disclosure of written information in the hands of the federal agencies, but there was no parallel disclosure statute requiring that agency meetings (where much of the business is transacted orally) be open to the public. The statute that resulted from this concern, the Government in the Sunshine Act (sometimes also referred to as the Open Meeting Act),[40] has met with a very mixed reception.

---

[38] Henry H. Perritt, Jr., *The Electronic Agency and the Traditional Paradigms of Administrative Law*, 44 ADMIN. L. REV. 79 (1992).

[39] Pub. L. No. 104-231, 110 Stat. 3048. While the Act mainly extends the FOIA to any agency record kept in "an electronic format," its implications for the future are far more intriguing. For a discussion of the impact of the Internet on agency functioning, *see* Stephen M. Johnson, *The Internet Changes Everything: Revolutionizing Public Participation and Access to Government Information Through the Internet*, 50 ADMIN. L. REV. 277 (1998).

[40] 5 U.S.C. § 552b.

Stated briefly, the Act requires agencies headed by a collegial body (this includes all the major independent regulatory commissions) to conduct their meetings in a format that is open to the public. Meeting times and topics are to be published in advance, generally in the *Federal Register*. If the agency wishes to close a meeting, it may do so only by invoking certain specified procedures, and only if that meeting involves a topic that is covered by one of the Act's ten exemptions.

Unfortunately, the number and extent of the exemptions in the Sunshine Act essentially overpower the statute's basic presumption in favor of open meetings. Eight of the ten exemptions are virtually identical to the exemptions in the FOIA, although there is no exemption in the Sunshine Act for inter/intra-agency memoranda. However, the ninth Sunshine Act exemption permits any agency to close a meeting if holding an open meeting would "be likely to significantly frustrate implementation of a proposed agency action." The tenth Sunshine Act exemption concerns commission discussion of matters that are currently in litigation.

There has been very little significant litigation involving the Sunshine Act, even though the Act expressly provides for judicial review. However, the Supreme Court clarified the definition of *meeting* under the Act in *FCC v. ITT World Communications*.[41] In *ITT*, the Supreme Court reviewed a claim that the FCC had violated the Sunshine Act by setting up a series of conferences known as the "Consultative Process." This process was a device by which FCC members and representatives of foreign governments met to work out joint statements and proposals on the development of certain international telecommunications policies.

ITT claimed that meetings should have been open to the public under the terms of the Sunshine Act. The Supreme Court held in favor of the agency, determining that the meetings were not subject to the unilateral control of the FCC and thus were not meetings *of an agency* as that term is used in the Sunshine Act.

Federal circuit court case law involving the Sunshine Act has been relatively inconsequential. In one case, *Common Cause v. Nuclear Regulatory Commission*,[42] the D.C. Circuit concluded that the Commission's budget deliberations were not, in and of themselves, exempted from the open meeting requirement. In *Pan American Airways, Inc. v. Civil Aeronautics Board*,[43] the court suggested that the proper remedy for a Sunshine Act violation is to order the release of the deliberation transcript, rather than to invalidate the agency action taken during the closed meeting.

The idea of open meetings is healthy in concept but appears to be completely unworkable in practice. To the extent that agencies must hold open meetings, their true deliberations generally take place elsewhere-in hallway conversations or exchanges of memoranda. In practice, the Sunshine Act appears to make open meetings merely proceedings which confirm agency decisions made elsewhere.

---

[41] 466 U.S. 463 (1984).

[42] 674 F.2d 921 (D.C. Cir. 1982).

[43] 684 F.2d 31 (D.C. Cir. 1982).

§ 14.05   THE FEDERAL PRIVACY ACT

Another reaction to the problems of the Watergate era was the enactment in 1974 of the Federal Privacy Act.[44] Much like the Sunshine Act, the motives of Congress were salutary. The executive branch was playing far too fast and loose with personal information. Yet, the result of this concern, the Federal Privacy Act, leaves much to be desired, irrespective of whether one favors more or less disclosure of government information.

The Privacy Act may have some impact, even though certain aspects of its definitional structure limit its effectiveness. The Act does three things for private persons. First, it restricts the manner in which the Government may collect and disseminate personal information. Second, it provides penalties for wrongful disclosure of that information. Third, it gives a person a statutory right to obtain and review information collected on that person and the right for that person to correct, or at least to supplement, information in the file to which the person objects.

Ironically, other parts of the Privacy Act may compromise an individual's complete right to privacy. The entire act turns on the definition of *system of records* — a set of agency records by which information on individuals is collected and may be retrieved by using a person's name or some type of individual identifying number, such as a social security number or tax identification number. While this definition covers a substantial number of government records, it does not reach all personal information in the hands of the federal government. Thus, a defamatory letter on an individual in the files of an agency administrator that is not in a system of records is arguably not protected by the Privacy Act.

The Act essentially establishes a presumption against disclosure-exactly the opposite of the FOIA-and provides exceptions by which certain requesters can obtain data. These exceptions are somewhat like the FOIA's. For example, a system of records can be entered and information retrieved for certain national security and law enforcement purposes. Personal data properly redacted may be used for certain statistical and research purposes.

Yet, for all of its detail, and given the sensitivity of the material which the Privacy Act touches upon, it has not been heavily litigated. The Supreme Court has yet to review a Privacy Act case. This may be due to the fact that the Privacy Act, containing both criminal sanctions and civil monetary penalties, may have frightened agencies into compliance right from the beginning. Thus, there may not be very many actual instances of violations of the Act and even fewer litigated instances of violations. For persons directly affected, however, it remains a useful statute.

---

[44] 5 U.S.C. § 552(a).

Chapter 15

NEW DIRECTIONS IN ADMINISTRATIVE LAW

§ 15.01 INTRODUCTION

With the media filled with talk of deregulation, devolution, budget cuts and privatization, anyone who wonders where administrative law is headed in the next decades of the twenty first century is asking a very astute and probably unanswerable question. Law students in particular ought to be concerned because one of the worst possible things to do is to become deeply and exclusively involved early in one's professional career with a body of law that proves to be a professional dead end. This is especially true for anyone who chooses a career in a particular segment of administrative practice. In the past there have been Washington lawyers who made a lucrative specialty out of obtaining export licenses. Changes in that regulatory program by the Department of Commerce have virtually eliminated export licensing as a viable full-time specialty for anyone. No one knows for sure what has happened to all the lawyers who practiced exclusively before the now-defunct Interstate Commerce Commission. Hopefully, those attorneys found something else to do.

It is possible, of course, to worry *too* much about future prospects. We all realize that there are no guarantees that any particular body of law is going to survive thirty or forty years of professional life. One of the central premises of our legal system is that it is subject to change in many areas. For example, students looking forward to litigation should also consider other forms of dispute resolution, such as arbitration and mediation-as courts become more and more congested-disputes will inevitably be channeled into other systems of dispute resolution. Those of you who anticipate a lucrative personal injury practice should monitor any state or federal legislation that closes off various causes of action and various types of damages awards.

In administrative law, there are a few discernible trends, but there have been no drastic alterations in the basic model of American administrative law over the past fifty years. Budget cuts and revenue shortfalls may sharply curtail certain areas of administrative activity, but legislative bodies and the general public do not seem to be constantly troubled by the way in which agencies function. In early 1994, some very aggressive freshman members of Congress announced sweeping plans to do away with several cabinet-level departments and other federal agencies. However, contrary to certain prognostications, the only federal administrative agency to be closed down was the Interstate Commerce Commission, an agency that had precious few supporters in the last years of its existence. There is always change on the state level, and there is strong support both within and without the government for devolution (the transfer of regulatory powers from the federal government to the state or local governments). But one of the consequences of devolution is that many states have actually seen their regulatory burdens increase over the past several years.

The United States is a very complex society. Legislators do not have the staff or the time to master the details of every aspect of government. The detail of government on both the federal and state levels, most, of necessity, be vested in the executive branch. The executive branch is invariably going to delegate most of the day-to-day functions of government to administrative agencies. The notion of the *fourth branch* of government has become so deeply ingrained in the American consciousness that few sweeping changes are likely in the foreseeable future. At the same time, there seems to be little interest in creating new agencies or new regulatory programs at any level of government. The one exception in the George W. Bush Administration was the creation of the cabinet Department of Homeland Security, a reaction to the traumatic events of September 11, 2001 but, in truth, mainly a repositioning (and in certain cases a renaming) of existing agencies. The single exception in President Obama's first term is the new Consumer Financial Protection Bureau in the Department of the Treasury. What the lack of change may reflect is the fact that the current system of administrative law, while concededly not perfect, is functioning rather well.

To the extent that substantive changes occur, the most vulnerable regulatory programs appear to be those devoted to economic regulation. As we develop a more sophisticated political system and become more adept at precise economic analysis, traditional economic regulation, as exemplified by the work of the late Interstate Commerce Commission or the somewhat shaky Federal Maritime Commission, is more and more difficult to justify. Regulation in the form of price controls is doomed to almost certain failure. There have been virtually no examples of truly successful price regulation in U.S. history. As we watched the disintegration of the former Soviet Union and so many other socialist systems, we see even more striking examples of the failures of price controls. Heavy-handed economic regulation may well be a thing of the past; but many types of government supervision of business are likely to continue. The savings and loan debacle suggests that government will pay close attention to the activities of financial institutions for many years to come. Crowded frequencies and new technological developments in broadcast and tele-communications dictate government oversight in those areas.

Increasing public awareness will likely trigger continuing health and safety regulation at various levels of government. Indeed, more and more academicians are referring to this type of regulation as *public interest* or *quality of life* regulation. Because environmental and safety issues cross jurisdictional lines, there will be an even greater need for creative thinking in these areas. As we appreciate the fact that these problems cross international boundaries — *e.g.*, the nuclear accidents at Chernobyl and Fukushima and the problem of transboundary air and water pollution — we must devise international solutions. It is likely that many of the solutions will have an administrative component.

If matters such as employee and consumer product safety are to be regulated by government, rather than the marketplace, the regulations must apply equally to all firms in order to minimize the economic problems that result from only a single firm's attempt to do the right thing in the face of industry-wide non-compliance. The economic concept of *externalities* demands across-the-board, even-handed regulation. Coping with externalities frequently calls for some regulation by the national government.

It is possible that American administrative law principles may begin to have impact on political systems outside the United States. The European Union is facing many of the same problems of federalism, government regulation of business and public accountability that engages the various governments within the U.S. The increasing "internationalization" of business may foster administrative schemes that are truly transnational in scope. While there is a fair amount of what might be labeled comparative administrative law scholarship, there are only a few persons who are beginning to think in truly global terms.[1]

This may be an overly sanguine view of administrative law in the twenty first century. Writing on the same topic, Professor Richard Stewart perceives "regulatory administrative fatigue" that, in his opinion, stems from "public demands [for] higher and higher regulatory protection, yet regulatory administrative government seems less and less capable of providing such protection in an efficient and effective manner. . . . Regulatory results often fall short of expectations at the same time that regulatory requirements grow ever more burdensome."[2] Professor Stewart urges more reliance on at least two new concepts: government-stakeholder network structures and economic incentive systems. He cites a number of initiatives involving habitat conservation plans (implicating the Endangered Species Act) on the part of federal natural resource agencies, state and local governments, and private sector actors.[3] Examples of economic incentive systems include the newly-established markets for trading pollution permits.[4] But, once again, at bottom he sees few gigantic changes: "Administrative law will continue to be evolutionary and strongly conserving in character. The several existing forms and remedies will be maintained, although their applications may change . . . ."[5]

---

[1] One person doing work in this area is Professor Alfred C. Aman, Jr. of the School of Law Bloomington, Indiana University. *See, e.g.*, Alfred C. Aman, Jr., *Globalization, Democracy, and the Need for a New Administrative Law*, 10 IND. J. GLOBAL LEGAL STUD. 125 (2003); *Proposals for Reforming the Administrative Procedure Act: Globalization, Democracy and the Furtherance of a Global Public Interest*, 6 IND. J. GLOBAL LEGAL STUD. 397 (1999); ALFRED C. AMAN, JR., ADMINISTRATIVE LAW IN A GLOBAL ERA (1992).

[2] Richard B. Stewart, *Administrative Law in the Twenty-First Century*, 78 N.Y.U. L. REV. 437, 446 (2003).

[3] *Id.* at 448.

[4] *Id.*

[5] *Id.* at 453. *See also* Jody Freeman, *Collaborative Governance in the Administrative State*, 45 UCLA L. REV. 1 (1997).

§ 15.02   DEREGULATION

[A]   Introduction

Deregulation was a hot topic during the eight years of the Reagan Administration. And deregulation has continued to be discussed in many areas of governmental activity.[6]

[B]   Legislative Action

Because agencies are creatures of the legislature, efforts to deregulate seem to work best when the initial impetus comes from the legislature. Congress has deregulated a number of activities over the past several years. Two entire independent regulatory commissions that engaged in economic regulation of the transportation industry, the Civil Aeronautics Board and the Interstate Commerce Commission, have been completely eliminated by act of Congress. Some of the safety and consumer protection functions were transferred to other components within the Department of Transportation.[7] Some of the legislative deregulation has not been completely consistent. In the area of energy and natural resources, Congress, in 1989, repealed Title I of the Natural Gas Policy Act of 1978, effectively removing all price controls from natural gas at the wellhead,[8] even though natural gas pipelines remain subject to limited economic regulation and state public utility commissions continue to regulate the sale of natural gas to commercial and residential consumers.

These deregulation statutes have had their proponents and their detractors. Some commentators attribute many of the current woes of the U.S. airline industry to the abolition of the CAB, although the voices attacking trucking and railroad deregulation have been far weaker. There have been some attempts in Congress to re-regulate in all three industries, although none of those moves has a large probability of success. Viewed another way, the statutes preserve the integrity of the American administrative model in that they represent changes in our regulatory structure mandated by Congress. Agencies are constitutionally required to follow Congressional directives. Apart from the economic disruptions that have occurred because of deregulation in a number of industries, notably among the airlines, the process has run fairly smoothly.

---

[6] For some excellent articles on many of these issues, *see* Richard W. Parker, *The Empirical Roots of the "Regulatory Reform" Movement: A Critical Appraisal*, 58 ADMIN. L. REV. 359 (2006); Thomas O. Sargentich, Symposium, *The Future of the American Administrative Process: The Question of the Future of the Administrative Process*, 49 ADMIN. L. REV. 149 (1997); Richard H. Pildes & Cass R. Sunstein, *Reinventing the Regulatory State*, 62 U. CHI. L. REV. 1 (1995); Robert L. Rabin, *Federal Regulation in Historical Perspective*, 38 STAN. L. REV. 1189 (1986). For an article that argues that not all regulation is bad, *see* Peter L. Kahn, *The Politics of Unregulation: Public Choice and Limits on Government*, 75 CORNELL L. REV. 280 (1990).

[7] Airline Deregulation Act of 1978, Pub. L. No. 95-504, 92 Stat. 1705 (codified in various portions of Title 49, U.S.C.).

[8] Pub. L. No. 101-60, 103 Stat. 157 (1989).

On the state level, after more than two decades, the Model State Administrative Procedure Act has been revised and a new formulation promulgated in 2010 by the National Conference of Commissioners on Uniform State Laws (full text of the 2010 Model Act is found in Appendix B, *infra*). While too voluminous to quote here, the 2010 revision:

1. continues and enhances some of the innovative rulemaking procedures found in the earlier iterations of the Model Act including a detailed description of what comprises a rulemaking record, relatively unconfined permission for oral contacts between the agency and the public, the requirement of a "regulatory analysis," and time limits for the promulgation of the final rule;

2. acknowledges the role of so-called "guidance documents" which may be issued outside the rulemaking process;

3. simplifies a number of adjuciation procedures, and

4. clarifies some of the issues involving judicial review of agency action.

Most observers are highly complimentary of the new iteration of the MSAPA.

[C]   The Executive Branch

On the federal level, a number of attempts to deregulate, or at least to put a halt to new regulation, have been fostered by the Office of Management and Budget (OMB) in the context of its supervisory role over executive branch agencies. Many agencies, acting on their own, have initiated deregulation efforts. There are a number of ways for agencies to deregulate. They can amend or repeal rules. The Federal Energy Regulatory Commission has taken giant steps to develop a market mechanism form of regulation for natural gas pipelines without any change in the underlying statutes.[9] Agencies may, when permitted by statute, preempt the field and then refuse to regulate. The Federal Communications Commission has done this, on occasion, in certain areas of broadcasting activity, such as regulation of satellite dishes.

Agencies can attempt a form of deregulation by doing nothing or by deliberately delaying agency action. Slowing the pace of agency activity sends subtle yet powerful signals to the regulated industry. When word gets out that the regulators are no longer paying much attention, industry tends to disregard those agency controls that exist on paper-witness the actions of the nation's savings and loan institutions during the 1980's.

An agency can also regulate in a way that is more consistent with existing conditions and more palatable to the regulated industry. The Federal Communications Commission awards certain types of licenses by lottery and auction to eliminate the need for a comparative evidentiary hearing in every case. Those attempts were frequently criticized. When an agency tries to innovate without an accompanying change in its underlying statute, it may get into trouble.

---

[9] *See, e.g.*, William Fox, *Transforming an Industry by Agency Rulemaking: Regulation of Natural Gas by the Federal Energy Regulatory Commission*, 23 LAND & WATER L. REV. 113 (1988).

Two case histories deserve review. In the first example, the Environmental Protection Agency set out to regulate the lead content of gasoline under a mandate in the Clean Air Act.[10] Congress recognized that the only effective way to deal with lead in gasoline is to force petroleum refiners to reduce or eliminate lead from the gasoline they manufacture. There are no cost-effective devices for controlling lead emissions at any other point in the gasoline fuel cycle.

EPA engaged in a massive rulemaking effort and was taken to court a number of times by the various contending parties. EPA won a definitive victory in court. The D.C. Circuit wrote a strong opinion upholding the agency's attempts to gradually reduce lead in gasoline and took the unusual step of telling the agency that the record it had accumulated on the detrimental effects of lead on the public's health would have permitted the agency to ban lead entirely.[11] Armed with this mandate, EPA might have been able to shove virtually anything down the refiners' throats. Instead, EPA devised an innovative scheme to phase out lead while creating the least possible disruption to the industry. Refiners were permitted to buy and sell rights to put additional lead in gasoline over a period of years.[12] At the end of that transitional period, lead would be banned from gasoline.

This rulemaking was one of the first instances of a federal agency's permitting a regulated industry to trade in what are now called *pollution rights*. EPA itself avoided much heavy-handed command and control regulation over that period, and the phase-out of lead over a several-year period permitted the refiners to spread their investment in lead-removal equipment over a longer time than they might have had under a different regulatory program. Although the refiners did not like any of this, the impact of the D.C. Circuit decision (the refiners had virtually no ammunition left to fight the phaseout program) and the low-key market oriented approach of the EPA made everything much more palatable for all concerned. There was very little industry resistance to the EPA's market-oriented program-at least as compared with the massive battles waged earlier by the industry. The phaseout, to both EPA's and the refiner's credit, has run smoothly. If there is a message here, it is probably this: when regulation is made more compatible with industry practices and with basic market mechanisms, it works. The United States is now one of the few countries in the world where lead is totally banned from gasoline. The nation's health will benefit considerably.

The second case history reveals what an agency may be able to accomplish simply by a change in agency philosophy caused by new appointments at the highest agency level. During the 1980's, President Reagan was able to change the entire membership of the Federal Energy Regulatory Commission though his appointment powers. Virtually all of these appointees took office committed to eliminating or modifying a great deal of the Commission's traditional forms of regulation. In particular, Reagan's appointees determined that they would develop

---

[10] 42 U.S.C. 7545.

[11] *See Small Refiner Lead Phase-Down Task Force v. Environmental Protection Agency*, 705 F.2d 506 (D.C. Cir. 1983).

[12] *See, e.g.*, William Fox, *Getting the Lead out of American Gasoline*, 4 J. ENERGY & NAT. RESOURCES L. I (1986).

market-oriented rules for natural gas pipelines.[13] The Commission controlled natural gas pipeline rates through traditional public utility ratemaking models. Thus, rates were tightly controlled and rate changes required a cumbersome, adjudicatory proceeding that often took years to conclude. The ultimate result, in the view of the Reagan-era commissioners, was that natural gas consumers paid artificially high prices for natural gas. Moreover, the traditional ratemaking mechanisms artificially sheltered the pipeline companies from appropriate market incentives and business decisions. These are salutary goals, but in this case, FERC launched its rulemaking with no change in its underlying statutory authority. As a result, the history of FERC's attempt to deregulate by rule is much more troubled than the EPA's experience in the lead phase-down program-a program triggered by legislative changes.

To implement their market-oriented goals, the commissioners set out to convert natural gas pipelines from *contract carriers* to *common carriers*. What may appear to be a mere change in label would actually have profound changes in the industry because the change to common carrier status meant that pipelines would be required to transport natural gas for anyone who requested their services, rather than only for those natural gas producers who had signed long-term contracts with the pipeline. This, in turn, meant that natural gas producers could contract directly with natural gas consumers almost anywhere in the country. The pipelines would provide only a transportation function instead of a price-setting function, permitting the ultimate price of the natural gas to reflect market prices more accurately. FERC knew that it would have to proceed gently because Congress had not modified the Federal Power Act to give them express authority to make these changes. The Commission worked up an innovative carrot-and-stick approach, offering certain benefits (such as nearly unfettered permission to abandon certain pipeline routes or to construct new pipelines) to those pipelines that voluntarily switched to common carrier status. The Commission's reasoning was that a voluntary change in status would undercut any argument that the Commission was not complying with its enabling act.

The implementation of these changes has not been nearly as trouble-free as EPA's lead phase-down program, largely because FERC has been functioning without a clear mandate issued by Congress. A few industry and consumer dissidents continue to fight a kind of guerilla war against FERC's innovations; but, in part because of the voluntary nature of the program and in part because the industry itself recognized that changes were required, the bulk of FERC's program has been put into effect and has survived judicial review.[14]

These experiments suggest that other agencies may innovate, even without new legislative authority. There is only one drawback. As the following discussion shows, agencies will have to move carefully in order to avoid being overturned by the courts.

In the first week of his administration, President Obama issued a memorandum to presidential agencies that seeks to implement and enhance transparency and

---

[13] *See, e.g.*, Fox, *supra* note 12.

[14] *See, e.g.*, *American Gas Ass'n v. FERC*, 912 F.2d 1496 (D.C. Cir. 1990).

openness in government.[15] Based solidly in electronic media and communication through the Internet, the memorandum promotes transparency and openness in all agencies under the guidance and supervision of the Office of Management and Budget. It focuses mainly on these goals in the context of release of federal information and the agency rulemaking process. While subject to some criticism and even now, in 2011, not fully implemented, the mere issuance of the memorandum signals a striking departure from earlier presidential administrations. If and when fully implemented, it has the potential of being truly transformative.[16]

[D]   The Courts

Some deregulation battles have been fought in the courts. These fights have been particularly troublesome because courts have only the traditional models of judicial review to apply to such cases and, since the mid 1970's, the Supreme Court has admonished the lower federal courts to keep their hands off the agencies. As a result, no one is quite sure how courts should approach these agency experiments in deregulation.

Probably the best recent example of this dilemma-one that had to be resolved by the Supreme Court itself-is the twenty-year fight over requiring passive restraints in automobiles. In resolving a part of the controversy, the Supreme Court decided that judicial review of an agency's attempt to revoke or rescind an existing rule is to be governed by the hard look-arbitrary/capricious doctrine discussed at length in Chapter 12. In *Motor Vehicle Manufacturers Ass'n v. State Farm Mutual Automobile Insurance Co.*,[17] the Court reviewed one of the longest running industry/agency battles in American history. In the late 1960s, the Department of Transportation (DOT) initiated a rulemaking to force automobiles sold in the United States to install passive restraints (automatic seat belts or air bags). DOT had concluded that seat belts that had to be fastened by passengers were not being used and were ineffective in preventing injury. The passive-restraint rulemaking extended through the Nixon, Ford and Carter administrations, culminating in a DOT rule that made passive restraints mandatory. However, DOT personnel appointed by President Reagan attempted to rescind the rule after it had been properly promulgated by the Carter administration. After taking the requisite *hard look* at both the record of the Reagan administration's rescission proceeding and the prior rulemaking history, the Supreme Court concluded that the DOT had not provided an adequate explanation for the rescission. Thus, the attempted rescission of the passive-restraint rule was invalid.

Some commentators have suggested that *State Farm* represents nothing more than the Court's hostile reaction to deregulation in the absence of express statutory authority. The better view is that the decision represents a clear signal to

---

[15] Transparency and Open Government: Memorandum for the Heads of Executive Departments and Agencies, 74 Fed. Reg. 4685 (Jan. 21, 2009).

[16] *See, e.g.,* Cary Coglianese et al., *Transparency and Public Participation in the Federal Rulemaking Process: Recommendations for the New Administration,* 77 Geo. Wash. L. Rev. 924 (2009).

[17] 463 U.S. 29 (1983).

the agencies that they may change their substantive policies, but must do so in a reasoned, procedurally correct fashion.[18] As former judge Mikva has put it, "[a]s long as administrative decisions to regulate or deregulate result from reasoned decision-making and are compatible with congressional instructions, they should be upheld."[19]

§ 15.03 DEVOLUTION

There is much talk these days about promoting the sovereignty of state governments and, derivatively, giving back a substantial part of the federal government's regulatory burden to the states.[20] Now styled as *devolution* and known in Europe as *subsidiarity*, the concept is perhaps best illustrated by the legislation enacted by Congress abolishing the often-criticized Aid to Families with Dependent Children (AFDC) program and moving the welfare burden to the states in the form of relatively unstructured block grants.[21] There is no question that AFDC had many defects and shortcomings. Basically, the program provided money to the states for needy recipients, but accompanied that money with rigid and, some would argue, exceptionally cumbersome substantive and procedural requirements. In essence, states under the AFDC program were not much more than conduits for the transmission of money from the federal government to the ultimate recipients.

The Personal Responsibility Act stands in sharp contrast to AFDC. Under this act, there are a few rather rudimentary guidelines imposed on the states; but the states are permitted for the most part to design and implement their own welfare programs, paid for in large part by federal *block grants*. Presumably, many of the procedures under which the state programs are administered may be flexibly tailored to accommodate the wishes of individual states. There may, however, be some procedural minimums either dictated by the statute itself or imposed under constitutional due process.

Devolution appears to be a popular topic with both academics and members of Congress. Professor Breger, for example, believes that devolution and its corollary, privatization, "have created not only a more efficient government but one far more accountable to the public."[22] If the concept of devolution includes a requirement that the federal government be more sensitive to the burdens of the states imposed by federal actions, then another example of devolution is the recent Unfunded

---

[18] The D.C. Circuit sent similar signals to the Federal Energy Regulatory Commission when it struck down a FERC natural gas rulemaking in *Maryland People's Counsel v. FERC*, 761 F.2d 768 (D.C. Cir. 1985), and 761 F.2d 780 (D.C. Cir. 1985) (companion case). For a comment on both *State Farm* and *Maryland People's Counsel, see* Abner J. Mikva, *The Changing Role of Judicial Review*, 38 ADMIN. L. REV. 115 (1986).

[19] Mikva, *Id.* at 134.

[20] A great deal of the discussion in this section is taken from Marshall J. Breger, *Government Accountability in the Twenty-First Century*, 57 U. PITT. L. REV. 423 (1996). *See also* Patrick J. Gibbons, *Too Much of a Good Thing? Federal Supremacy and the Devolution of Regulatory Power: The Case of the Coastal Zone Management Act*, 48 NAVAL L. REV. 84 (2001).

[21] The statute is the Personal Responsibility and Work Opportunity Reconciliation Act of 1996, Pub. L. No. 104-193, 110 Stat. 2105 (codified in scattered portions of U.S.C.).

[22] Breger, *supra* note 20, at 432.

Mandates Reform Act,[23] admonishing federal agencies "to begin consideration of the effect of previously imposed Federal mandates" on state and local government and Indian tribes; and to require agencies to prepare and consider the budgetary impact of their regulations on state and local governments.

§ 15.04 PRIVATIZATION

Another currently popular notion is that many of the functions performed by government, at any level, could be done far better and far more efficiently by the private sector. State and local governments have experimented with privatizing schools and jails, among many other things. There is mixed evidence as to whether privatization actually results in cost savings and at least some commentary to the effect that privatization severely erodes the power of the least among us.[24]

§ 15.05 REGULATORY FLEXIBILITY

It's possible that government regulation is too stiff and too structured and that this excessive detail stifles creative private sector approaches to dealing with various problems. Part of the thinking emphasizes government cooperating with the private sector, rather than forcing the private sector to comply with rigid, command-and-control style regulations. A number of commentators are currently exploring the concept of regulatory flexibility as an antidote to government "heavy-handedness." Regulatory flexibility would have an agency explore voluntary compliance measures, the negotiation of what are called "individuated" regulations (regulations tailored specifically to a particular company) and the setting of performance standards as a substitute for traditional regulations.[25] Once again, these are provocative ideas; although in this author's personal experience, many members of the business community get very nervous when the government does not spell out its requirements with great specificity. If flexibility translates in practice into ambiguity or special treatment for particular individuals, it may not survive either political accountability or judicial review.

---

[23] 2 U.S.C. §§ 1501–1503. For some good commentary on this statute, see Daniel E. Troy, *The Unfunded Mandates Reform Act of 1995*, 49 Admin. L. Rev. 139 (1997).

[24] Professor Nancy Ehrenreich has cataloged some of these qualms in Nancy Ehrenreich, *A Trend? The Progressive Potential in Privatization*, 73 Denv. U. L. Rev. 1235 (1996). For an article focusing on privatization in a single federal program, see Elizabeth C. Price, *Teaching the Elephant to Dance: Privatizing the FDA Review Process*, 51 Food & Drug L.J. 651 (1996). An indication that there may be some backlash building against privatization of prison facilities is Warren L. Ratliff, *The Due Process Failure of America's Prison Privatization Statutes*, 21 Seton Hall Legis. J. 371 (1997). *See also* Gillian E. Metzger, *Privatization as Delegation*, 103 Colum. L. Rev. 1367 (2003).

[25] Good discussion of many of the nuances of regulatory flexibility may be found in Michael C. Dorf & Charles F. Sabel, *A Constitution of Democratic Experimentalism*, 98 Colum. L. Rev. 267 (1998), and Marshall J. Breger, *Regulatory Flexibility and the Administrative State*, 32 Tulsa L.J. 325 (1996).

§ 15.06 PROCEDURAL INNOVATIONS

In 1991, Congress enacted two statutes, discussed extensively in earlier chapters, that may have a positive, perhaps even a striking, impact on the manner in which agencies make their decisions. The Negotiated Rulemaking Act[26] and the Administrative Dispute Resolution Act[27] represent codifications of procedural experiments that have been taking place within individual agencies for years. To a certain extent, each statute is a curious development, given that administrative agencies were originally established because the then-existing forums for dispute resolution were not doing the job. When the Interstate Commerce Commission was first set up, courts were viewed as too slow, too expensive and too inexpert in the details of a then-expanding government. Unfortunately, as agencies have proliferated, they have made themselves more and more like the courts they were designed to supplant. Slightly more than 100 years later, these two new statutes constitute a similar finding that agencies do not now measure up to their assigned tasks. Both negotiated rulemaking and the use of such procedures as arbitration and mediation to resolve agency disputes are healthy developments. At the very least, they suggest that agencies can also change with the times in a procedural sense. At the same time, there have been few proposals for massive revision of the basic Federal Administrative Procedure Act, even though the APA is almost 60 years old. For example, Professor Bernard Schwartz, commenting on the APA system of adjudication, first points out that "the APA has effected a quantum improvement in the administrative adjudicatory process" and then states: "As a general proposition, [APA adjudication] should be maintained."[28]

There is a strong possibility that the Internet may provoke sweeping changes in the manner in which agencies deliver information to the public, engage in rulemaking and frame and disseminate agency policy. But at bottom, the Internet is mainly a new communications media. As discussed in Chapter 7, the Internet has had a significant effect on agency rulemaking to the extent that it seems to have very nearly replaced the old hard copy system of notice and comment, but apart from rulemaking — so far at least — relatively little has changed in basic administrative law concepts simply because of the Internet.[29]

---

[26] 5 U.S.C. §§ 561–570. *See* § 7.05[A], *above*, for a more elaborate discussion of the act.

[27] 5 U.S.C. §§ 571–581 (with substantial amendments in 1996); *see* § 8.02, *above*, for a more elaborate discussion of the act. *See, e.g.*, D. Aaron Lacy, *Alternative Dispute Resolution or Appropriate Dispute Resolution: Will ADR Help or Hurt the EEO Complaint Process?*, 80 U. Det. Mercy L. Rev. 31 (2002).

[28] Bernard Schwartz, *Adjudication and the Administrative Procedure Act*, 32 Tulsa L.J. 203 (1996). Some agencies, notably the Board of Veterans' Appeals (the intra-agency review body within the Department of Veterans Affairs) is conducting a substantial number of hearings by videoconference.

[29] For a good article discussing these matters, *see* Stephen M. Johnson, *The Internet Changes Everything: Revolutionizing Public Participation and Access to Government Information Through the Internet*, 50 Admin. L. Rev. 277 (1998).

§ 15.07   OTHER PROPOSALS FOR LEGISLATIVE CHANGE

Over the past three decades, there has been a great deal of interest and a fair amount of activity in both Congress and the state legislatures on various proposals for regulatory reform. These proposals ranged from requiring agencies to perform cost-benefit analysis for virtually all rulemakings,[30] to proposals to use a paper hearing (non-oral) process for a greater number of agency matters, to comprehensive revisions of the entire Administrative Procedure Act. But then also consider that most observers of the federal scene appear to be relatively comfortable with the existing Administrative Procedure Act.[31] The Model State Administrative Procedure Act has not been modified since 1981.

Today, Congress finds itself consumed mainly by budget and tax matters and in a kind of legislative versus executive gridlock on many other matters. It is now clear that matters of budget-which are, of course, matters of legislation-are going to have a far more profound effect on the functioning of agencies than any of the minor tinkering in which Congress may indulge with regard to the APA. So, the answer to the question "where are we going with administrative law" might be "it's too early to tell."

---

[30] Consider, for example, the proposal of Professor Sunstein to enact legislation requiring cost benefit analysis for virtually all federal regulations: Cass R. Sunstein, *Congress, Constitutional Moments, and the Cost-Benefit State*, 48 STAN. L. REV. 247 (1996), and the somewhat different views expressed by two other commentators: Richard Whisnant & Diane DeWitt Cherry, *Economic Analysis of Rules: Devolution, Evolution, and Realism*, 31 WAKE FOREST L. REV. 693 (1996).

[31] For example, Richard J. Pierce, Jr., Symposium, *The Fiftieth Anniversary of the Administrative Procedure Act: Past and Prologue: Rulemaking and the Administrative Procedure Act*, 32 TULSA L.J. 185 (1996).

Appendix A

Administrative Procedure Act

§ 551. Definitions

For the purpose of this subchapter —

(1) "agency" means each authority of the Government of the United States, whether or not it is within or subject to review by another agency, but does not include —

(A) the Congress;

(B) the courts of the United States;

(C) the governments of the territories or possessions of the United States;

(D) the government of the District of Columbia; or except as to the requirements of section 552 of this title —

(E) agencies composed of representatives of the parties or of representatives of organizations of the parties to the disputes determined by them;

(F) courts martial and military commissions;

(G) military authority exercised in the field in time of war or in occupied territory; or

(H) functions conferred by sections 1738, 1739, 1743, and 1744 of title 12; chapter 2 of title 41; subchapter II of chapter 471 of title 49; or sections 1884, 1891–1902, and former section 1641(b)(2), of title 50, appendix;

(2) "person" includes an individual, partnership, corporation, association, or public or private organization other than an agency;

(3) "party" includes a person or agency named or admitted as a party, or properly seeking and entitled as of right to be admitted as a party, in an agency proceeding, and a person or agency admitted by an agency as a party for limited purposes;

(4) "rule" means the whole or a part of an agency statement of general or particular applicability and future effect designed to implement, interpret, or prescribe law or policy or describing the organization, procedure, or practice requirements of an agency and includes the approval or prescription for the future of rates, wages, corporate or financial structures or reorganizations thereof, prices, facilities, appliances, services or allowances therefor or of valuations, costs, or accounting, or practices bearing on any of the foregoing;

(5) "rule making" means agency process for formulating, amending, or repealing a rule;

(6) "order" means the whole or a part of a final disposition, whether

affirmative, negative, injunctive, or declaratory in form, of an agency in a matter other than rule making but including licensing;

(7) "adjudication" means agency process for the formulation of an order;

(8) "license" includes the whole or a part of an agency permit, certificate, approval, registration, charter, membership, statutory exemption or other form of permission;

(9) "licensing" includes agency process respecting the grant, renewal, denial, revocation, suspension, annulment, withdrawal, limitation, amendment, modification, or conditioning of a license;

(10) "sanction" includes the whole or a part of an agency —

(A) prohibition, requirement, limitation, or other condition affecting the freedom of a person;

(B) withholding of relief;

(C) imposition of penalty or fine;

(D) destruction, taking, seizure, or withholding of property;

(E) assessment of damages, reimbursement, restitution, compensation, costs, charges, or fees;

(F) requirement, revocation, or suspension of a license; or

(G) taking other compulsory or restrictive action;

(11) "relief" includes the whole or a part of an agency —

(A) grant of money, assistance, license, authority, exemption, exception, privilege, or remedy;

(B) recognition of a claim, right, immunity, privilege, exemption, or exception; or

(C) taking of other action on the application or petition of, and beneficial to, a person;

(12) "agency proceeding" means an agency process as defined by paragraphs (5), (7), and (9) of this section;

(13) "agency action" includes the whole or a part of an agency rule, order, license, sanction, relief, or the equivalent or denial thereof, or failure to act; and

(14) "ex parte communication" means an oral or written communication not on the public record with respect to which reasonable prior notice to all parties is not given, but it shall not include requests for status reports on any matter or proceeding covered by this subchapter.

§ 552. Public information; agency rules, opinions, orders, records, and proceedings

(a) Each agency shall make available to the public information as follows:

(1) Each agency shall separately state and currently publish in the Federal Register for the guidance of the public —

(A) descriptions of its central and field organization and the established places at which, the employees (and in the case of a uniformed service, the members) from whom, and the methods whereby, the public may obtain information, make submittals or requests, or obtain decisions;

(B) statements of the general course and method by which its functions are channeled and determined, including the nature and requirements of all formal and informal procedures available;

(C) rules of procedure, descriptions of forms available or the places at which forms may be obtained, and instructions as to the scope and contents of all papers, reports, or examinations;

(D) substantive rules of general applicability adopted as authorized by law, and statements of general policy or interpretations of general applicability formulated and adopted by the agency; and

(E) each amendment, revision, or repeal of the foregoing.

Except to the extent that a person has actual and timely notice of the terms thereof, a person may not in any manner be required to resort to, or be adversely affected by, a matter required to be published in the Federal Register and not so published. For the purpose of this paragraph, matter reasonably available to the class of persons affected thereby is deemed published in the Federal Register when incorporated by reference therein with the approval of the Director of the Federal Register.

(2) Each agency, in accordance with published rules, shall make available for public inspection and copying —

(A) final opinions, including concurring and dissenting opinions, as well as orders, made in the adjudication of cases;

(B) those statements of policy and interpretations which have been adopted by the agency and are not published in the Federal Register;

(C) administrative staff manuals and instructions to staff that affect a member of the public;

(D) copies of all records, regardless of form or format, which have been released to any person under paragraph (3) and which, because of the nature of their subject matter, the agency determines have become or are likely to become the subject of subsequent requests for substantially the same records; and

(E) a general index of the records referred to under subparagraph (D);

unless the materials are promptly published and copies offered for sale. For records created on or after November 1, 1996, within one year after such date, each agency shall make such records available, including by computer telecommunications or, if computer telecommunications means have not been established by the agency, by other electronic means. To the extent required to prevent a clearly unwarranted invasion of personal privacy, an agency may delete identifying details when it makes available or publishes an opinion, statement of policy, interpretation, staff manual, instruction, or copies of records referred to in subparagraph (D). However, in each case the justification for the deletion shall be explained fully in writing, and the extent of such deletion shall be indicated on the portion of the record which is made available or published, unless including that indication would harm an interest protected by the exemption in subsection (b) under which the deletion is made. If technically feasible, the extent of the deletion shall be indicated at the place in the record where the deletion was made. Each agency shall also maintain and make available for public inspection and copying current indexes providing identifying information for the public as to any matter issued, adopted, or promulgated after July 4, 1967, and required by this paragraph to be made available or published. Each agency shall promptly publish, quarterly or more frequently, and distribute (by sale or otherwise) copies of each index or supplements thereto unless it determines by order published in the Federal Register that the publication would be unnecessary and impracticable, in which case the agency shall nonetheless provide copies of such index on request at a cost not to exceed the direct cost of duplication. Each agency shall make the index referred to in subparagraph (E) available by computer telecommunications by December 31, 1999. A final order, opinion, statement of policy, interpretation, or staff manual or instruction that affects a member of the public may be relied on, used, or cited as precedent by an agency against a party other than an agency only if —

> (i) it has been indexed and either made available or published as provided by this paragraph; or

> (ii) the party has actual and timely notice of the terms thereof.

(3) (A) Except with respect to the records made available under paragraphs (1) and (2) of this subsection, and except as provided in subparagraph (E), each agency, upon any request for records which (i) reasonably describes such records and (ii) is made in accordance with published rules stating the time, place, fees (if any), and procedures to be followed, shall make the records promptly available to any person.

(B) In making any record available to a person under this paragraph, an agency shall provide the record in any form or format requested by the person if the record is readily reproducible by the agency in that form or format. Each agency shall make reasonable efforts to maintain its records in forms or formats that are reproducible for purposes of this section.

(C) In responding under this paragraph to a request for records, an agency shall make reasonable efforts to search for the records in electronic form or format, except when such efforts would significantly interfere with the operation of the agency's automated information system.

(D) For purposes of this paragraph, the term "search" means to review, manually or by automated means, agency records for the purpose of locating those records which are responsive to a request.

(E) An agency, or part of an agency, that is an element of the intelligence community (as that term is defined in section 3(4) of the National Security

Act of 1947 (50 U.S.C. 401a(4))) shall not make any record available under this paragraph to —

(i) any government entity, other than a State, territory, commonwealth, or district of the United States, or any subdivision thereof; or

(ii) a representative of a government entity described in clause (i).

(4) (A) (i) In order to carry out the provisions of this section, each agency shall promulgate regulations, pursuant to notice and receipt of public comment, specifying the schedule of fees applicable to the processing of requests under this section and establishing procedures and guidelines for determining when such fees should be waived or reduced. Such schedule shall conform to the guidelines which shall be promulgated, pursuant to notice and receipt of public comment, by the Director of the Office of Management and Budget and which shall provide for a uniform schedule of fees for all agencies.

(ii) Such agency regulations shall provide that —

(I) fees shall be limited to reasonable standard charges for document search, duplication, and review, when records are requested for commercial use;

(II) fees shall be limited to reasonable standard charges for document duplication when records are not sought for commercial use and the request is made by an educational or noncommercial scientific institution, whose purpose is scholarly or scientific research; or a representative of the news media; and

(III) for any request not described in (I) or (II), fees shall be limited to reasonable standard charges for document search and duplication.

(iii) Documents shall be furnished without any charge or at a charge reduced below the fees established under clause (ii) if disclosure of the information is in the public interest because it is likely to contribute significantly to public understanding of the operations or activities of the government and is not primarily in the commercial interest of the requester.

(iv) Fee schedules shall provide for the recovery of only the direct costs of search, duplication, or review. Review costs shall include only the direct costs incurred during the initial examination of a document for the purposes of determining whether the documents must be disclosed under this section and for the purposes of withholding any portions exempt from disclosure under this section. Review costs may not include any costs incurred in resolving issues of law or policy that may be raised in the course of processing a request under this section. No fee may be charged by any agency under this section —

(I) if the costs of routine collection and processing of the fee are likely to equal or exceed the amount of the fee; or

(II) for any request described in clause (ii) (II) or (III) of this subparagraph for the first two hours of search time or for the first one hundred pages of duplication.

(v) No agency may require advance payment of any fee unless the requester has previously failed to pay fees in a timely fashion, or the agency has determined that the fee will exceed $250.

(vi) Nothing in this subparagraph shall supersede fees chargeable under a statute specifically providing for setting the level of fees for particular types of records.

(vii) In any action by a requester regarding the waiver of fees under this section, the court shall determine the matter de novo:

Provided, That the court's review of the matter shall be limited to the record before the agency.

(B) On complaint, the district court of the United States in the district in which the complainant resides, or has his principal place of business, or in which the agency records are situated, or in the District of Columbia, has jurisdiction to enjoin the agency from withholding agency records and to order the production of any agency records improperly withheld from the complainant. In such a case the court shall determine the matter de novo, and may examine the contents of such agency records in camera to determine whether such records or any part thereof shall be withheld under any of the exemptions set forth in subsection (b) of this section, and the burden is on the agency to sustain its action. In addition to any other matters to which a court accords substantial weight, a court shall accord substantial weight to an affidavit of an agency concerning the agency's determination as to technical feasibility under paragraph (2)(C) and subsection (b) and reproducibility under paragraph (3)(B).

(C) Notwithstanding any other provision of law, the defendant shall serve an answer or otherwise plead to any complaint made under this subsection within thirty days after service upon the defendant of the pleading in which such complaint is made, unless the court otherwise directs for good cause shown.

[(D) Repealed. Pub. L. 98-620, title IV, Sec. 402(2), Nov. 8, 1984, 98 Stat. 3357.]

(E) The court may assess against the United States reasonable attorney fees and other litigation costs reasonably incurred in any case under this section in which the complainant has substantially prevailed.

(F) Whenever the court orders the production of any agency records improperly withheld from the complainant and assesses against the United States reasonable attorney fees and other litigation costs, and the court additionally issues a written finding that the circumstances surrounding the withholding raise questions whether agency personnel acted arbitrarily or capriciously with respect to the withholding, the Special Counsel shall promptly initiate a proceeding to determine whether disciplinary action is warranted against the officer or employee who was primarily responsible for the withholding. The Special Counsel, after investigation and consideration of the evidence submitted, shall submit his findings and recommendations to the administrative authority of the agency concerned and shall send copies of the findings and recommendations to the officer or employee or his representative. The administrative authority shall take the corrective action that the Special Counsel recommends.

(G) In the event of noncompliance with the order of the court, the district court may punish for contempt the responsible employee, and in the case of a uniformed service, the responsible member.

(5) Each agency having more than one member shall maintain and make available for public inspection a record of the final votes of each member in every agency proceeding.

(6) (A) Each agency, upon any request for records made under paragraph (1), (2), or (3) of this subsection, shall —

(i) determine within 20 days (excepting Saturdays, Sundays, and legal public holidays) after the receipt of any such request whether to comply with such request and shall immediately notify the person making such request of such determination and the reasons therefor, and of the right of such person to appeal to the head of the agency any adverse determination; and

(ii) make a determination with respect to any appeal within twenty days (excepting Saturdays, Sundays, and legal public holidays) after the receipt of such appeal. If on appeal the denial of the request for records is in whole or in part upheld, the agency shall notify the person making such request of the provisions for judicial review of that determination under paragraph (4) of this subsection.

(B) (i) In unusual circumstances as specified in this subparagraph, the time limits prescribed in either clause (i) or clause (ii) of subparagraph (A) may be extended by written notice to the person making such request setting forth the unusual circumstances for such extension and the date on which a determination is expected to be dispatched. No such notice shall specify a date that would result in an extension for more than ten working days, except as provided in clause (ii) of this subparagraph.

(ii) With respect to a request for which a written notice under clause (i) extends the time limits prescribed under clause (i) of subparagraph (A), the agency shall notify the person making the request if the request cannot be processed within the time limit specified in that clause and shall provide the person an opportunity to limit the scope of the request so that it may be processed within that time limit or an opportunity to arrange with the agency an alternative time frame for processing the request or a modified request. Refusal by the person to reasonably modify the request or arrange such an alternative time frame shall be considered as a factor in determining whether exceptional circumstances exist for purposes of subparagraph (C).

(iii) As used in this subparagraph, "unusual circumstances" means, but only to the extent reasonably necessary to the proper processing of the particular requests —

(I) the need to search for and collect the requested records from field facilities or other establishments that are separate from the office processing the request;

(II) the need to search for, collect, and appropriately examine a voluminous amount of separate and distinct records which are demanded in a single request; or

(III) the need for consultation, which shall be conducted with all practicable speed, with another agency having a substantial interest in the determination of the request or among two or more components of the agency having substantial subject-matter interest therein.

(iv) Each agency may promulgate regulations, pursuant to notice and receipt of public comment, providing for the aggregation of certain requests by the same requestor, or by a group of requestors acting in concert, if the agency reasonably believes that such requests actually constitute a single request, which would otherwise satisfy the unusual circumstances specified in this subparagraph, and the requests involve clearly related matters. Multiple requests involving unrelated matters shall not be aggregated.

(C) (i) Any person making a request to any agency for records under paragraph (1), (2), or (3) of this subsection shall be deemed to have exhausted his administrative remedies with respect to such request if the agency fails to comply with the applicable time limit provisions of this paragraph. If the Government can show exceptional circumstances exist and that the agency is exercising due diligence in responding to the request, the court may retain jurisdiction and allow the agency additional time to complete its review of the records. Upon any determination by an agency to comply with a request for records, the records shall be made promptly available to such person making such request. Any notification of denial of any request for records under this subsection shall set forth the names and titles or positions of each person responsible for the denial of such request.

(ii) For purposes of this subparagraph, the term "exceptional Circumstances" does not include a delay that results from a predictable agency workload of requests under this section, unless the agency demonstrates reasonable progress in reducing its backlog of pending requests.

(iii) Refusal by a person to reasonably modify the scope of a request or arrange an alternative time frame for processing a request (or a modified request) under clause (ii) after being given an opportunity to do so by the agency to whom the person made the request shall be considered as a factor in determining whether exceptional circumstances exist for purposes of this subparagraph.

(D) (i) Each agency may promulgate regulations, pursuant to notice and receipt of public comment, providing for multitrack processing of requests for records based on the amount of work or time (or both) involved in processing requests.

(ii) Regulations under this subparagraph may provide a person making a request that does not qualify for the fastest multitrack processing an opportunity to limit the scope of the request in order to qualify for faster processing.

(iii) This subparagraph shall not be considered to affect the requirement under subparagraph (C) to exercise due diligence.

(E) (i) Each agency shall promulgate regulations, pursuant to notice and receipt of public comment, providing for expedited processing of requests for records —

   (I) in cases in which the person requesting the records demonstrates a compelling need; and

   (II) in other cases determined by the agency.

(ii) Notwithstanding clause (i), regulations under this subparagraph must ensure —

   (I) that a determination of whether to provide expedited processing shall be made, and notice of the determination shall be provided to the person making the request, within 10 days after the date of the request; and

   (II) expeditious consideration of administrative appeals of such determinations of whether to provide expedited processing.

(iii) An agency shall process as soon as practicable any request for records to which the agency has granted expedited processing under this subparagraph. Agency action to deny or affirm denial of a request for expedited processing pursuant to this subparagraph, and failure by an agency to respond in a timely manner to such a request shall be subject to judicial review under paragraph (4), except that the judicial review shall be based on the record before the agency at the time of the determination.

(iv) A district court of the United States shall not have jurisdiction to review an agency denial of expedited processing of a request for records after the agency has provided a complete response to the request.

(v) For purposes of this subparagraph, the term "compelling need" means —

   (I) that a failure to obtain requested records on an expedited basis under this paragraph could reasonably be expected to pose an imminent threat to the life or physical safety of an individual; or

   (II) with respect to a request made by a person primarily engaged in disseminating information, urgency to inform the public concerning actual or alleged Federal Government activity.

(vi) A demonstration of a compelling need by a person making a request for expedited processing shall be made by a statement certified by such person to be true and correct to the best of such person's knowledge and belief.

(F) In denying a request for records, in whole or in part, an agency shall make a reasonable effort to estimate the volume of any requested matter the provision of which is denied, and shall provide any such estimate to the person making the request, unless providing such estimate would harm an interest protected by the exemption in subsection (b) pursuant to which the denial is made.

(b) This section does not apply to matters that are —

(1) (A) specifically authorized under criteria established by an Executive order to be kept secret in the interest of national defense or foreign policy and (B) are in fact properly classified pursuant to such Executive order;

(2) related solely to the internal personnel rules and practices of an agency;

(3) specifically exempted from disclosure by statute (other than section 552b of this title), provided that such statute (A) requires that the matters be withheld from the public in such a manner as to leave no discretion on the issue, or (B) establishes particular criteria for withholding or refers to particular types of matters to be withheld;

(4) trade secrets and commercial or financial information obtained from a person and privileged or confidential;

(5) inter-agency or intra-agency memorandums or letters which would not be available by law to a party other than an agency in litigation with the agency;

(6) personnel and medical files and similar files the disclosure of which would constitute a clearly unwarranted invasion of personal privacy;

(7) records or information compiled for law enforcement purposes, but only to the extent that the production of such law enforcement records or information (A) could reasonably be expected to interfere with enforcement proceedings, (B) would deprive a person of a right to a fair trial or an impartial adjudication, (C) could reasonably be expected to constitute an unwarranted invasion of personal privacy, (D) could reasonably be expected to disclose the identity of a confidential source, including a State, local, or foreign agency or authority or any private institution which furnished information on a confidential basis, and, in the case of a record or information compiled by criminal law enforcement authority in the course of a criminal investigation or by an agency conducting a lawful national security intelligence investigation, information furnished by a confidential source, (E) would disclose techniques and procedures for law enforcement investigations or prosecutions, or would disclose guidelines for law enforcement investigations or prosecutions if such disclosure could reasonably be expected to risk circumvention of the law, or (F) could

reasonably be expected to endanger the life or physical safety of any individual;

(8) contained in or related to examination, operating, or condition reports prepared by, on behalf of, or for the use of an agency responsible for the regulation or supervision of financial institutions; or

(9) geological and geophysical information and data, including maps, concerning wells.

Any reasonably segregable portion of a record shall be provided to any person requesting such record after deletion of the portions which are exempt under this subsection. The amount of information deleted shall be indicated on the released portion of the record, unless including that indication would harm an interest protected by the exemption in this subsection under which the deletion is made. If technically feasible, the amount of the information deleted shall be indicated at the place in the record where such deletion is made.

(c) (1) Whenever a request is made which involves access to records described in subsection (b)(7)(A) and —

(A) the investigation or proceeding involves a possible violation of criminal law; and

(B) there is reason to believe that (i) the subject of the investigation or proceeding is not aware of its pendency, and (ii) disclosure of the existence of the records could reasonably be expected to interfere with enforcement proceedings,

the agency may, during only such time as that circumstance continues, treat the records as not subject to the requirements of this section.

(2) Whenever informant records maintained by a criminal law enforcement agency under an informant's name or personal identifier are requested by a third party according to the informant's name or personal identifier, the agency may treat the records as not subject to the requirements of this section unless the informant's status as an informant has been officially confirmed.

(3) Whenever a request is made which involves access to records maintained by the Federal Bureau of Investigation pertaining to foreign intelligence or counterintelligence, or international terrorism, and the existence of the records is classified information as provided in subsection (b)(1), the Bureau may, as long as the existence of the records remains classified information, treat the records as not subject to the requirements of this section.

(d) This section does not authorize withholding of information or limit the availability of records to the public, except as specifically stated in this section. This section is not authority to withhold information from Congress.

(e) (1) On or before February 1 of each year, each agency shall submit to the Attorney General of the United States a report which shall cover the preceding fiscal year and which shall include —

(A) the number of determinations made by the agency not to comply with requests for records made to such agency under subsection (a) and the reasons for each such determination;

(B) (i) the number of appeals made by persons under subsection (a)(6), the result of such appeals, and the reason for the action upon each appeal that results in a denial of information; and

(ii) a complete list of all statutes that the agency relies upon to authorize the agency to withhold information under subsection (b)(3), a description of whether a court has upheld the decision of the agency to withhold information under each such statute, and a concise description of the scope of any information withheld;

(C) the number of requests for records pending before the agency as of September 30 of the preceding year, and the median number of days that such requests had been pending before the agency as of that date;

(D) the number of requests for records received by the agency and the number of requests which the agency processed;

(E) the median number of days taken by the agency to process different types of requests;

(F) the total amount of fees collected by the agency for processing requests; and

(G) the number of full-time staff of the agency devoted to processing requests for records under this section, and the total amount expended by the agency for processing such requests.

(2) Each agency shall make each such report available to the public including by computer telecommunications, or if computer telecommunications means have not been established by the agency, by other electronic means.

(3) The Attorney General of the United States shall make each report which has been made available by electronic means available at a single electronic access point. The Attorney General of the United States shall notify the Chairman and ranking minority member of the Committee on Government Reform and Oversight of the House of Representatives and the Chairman and ranking minority member of the Committees on Governmental Affairs and the Judiciary of the Senate, no later than April 1 of the year in which each such report is issued, that such reports are available by electronic means.

(4) The Attorney General of the United States, in consultation with the Director of the Office of Management and Budget, shall develop reporting and performance guidelines in connection with reports required by this subsection by October 1, 1997, and may establish additional requirements for such reports as the Attorney General determines may be useful.

(5) The Attorney General of the United States shall submit an annual report on or before April 1 of each calendar year which shall include for the prior calendar year a listing of the number of cases arising under this section, the exemption involved in each case, the disposition of such case, and the cost, fees, and penalties assessed under subparagraphs (E), (F), and (G) of subsection

(a)(4). Such report shall also include a description of the efforts undertaken by the Department of Justice to encourage agency compliance with this section.

(f) For purposes of this section, the term —

(1) "agency" as defined in section 551(1) of this title includes any executive department, military department, Government corporation, Government controlled corporation, or other establishment in the executive branch of the Government (including the Executive Office of the President), or any independent regulatory agency; and

(2) "record" and any other term used in this section in reference to information includes any information that would be an agency record subject to the requirements of this section when maintained by an agency in any format, including an electronic format.

(g) The head of each agency shall prepare and make publicly available upon request, reference material or a guide for requesting records or information from the agency, subject to the exemptions in subsection (b), including —

(1) an index of all major information systems of the agency;

(2) a description of major information and record locator systems maintained by the agency; and

(3) a handbook for obtaining various types and categories of public information from the agency pursuant to chapter 35 of title 44, and under this section.

§ 552a.   Records maintained on individuals

(a)   Definitions.— For purposes of this section —

(1) the term "agency" means agency as defined in section 552(e)of this title;

(2) the term "individual" means a citizen of the United States or an alien lawfully admitted for permanent residence;

(3) the term "maintain" includes maintain, collect, use, or disseminate;

(4) the term "record" means any item, collection, or grouping of information about an individual that is maintained by an agency, including, but not limited to, his education, financial transactions, medical history, and criminal or employment history and that contains his name, or the identifying number, symbol, or other identifying particular assigned to the individual, such as a finger or voice print or a photograph;

(5) the term "system of records" means a group of any records under the control of any agency from which information is retrieved by the name of the individual or by some identifying number, symbol, or other identifying particular assigned to the individual;

(6) the term "statistical record" means a record in a system of records maintained for statistical research or reporting purposes only and not used in whole or in part in making any determination about an identifiable individual, except as provided by section 8 of title 13;

(7) the term "routine use" means, with respect to the disclosure of a record, the use of such record for a purpose which is compatible with the purpose for which it was collected;

(8) the term "matching program"—

(A) means any computerized comparison of —

(i) two or more automated systems of records or a system of records with non-Federal records for the purpose of —

(I) establishing or verifying the eligibility of, or continuing compliance with statutory and regulatory requirements by, applicants for, recipients or beneficiaries of, participants in, or providers of services with respect to, cash or in-kind assistance or payments under Federal benefit programs, or

(II) recouping payments or delinquent debts under such Federal benefit programs, or

(ii) two or more automated Federal personnel or payroll systems of records or a system of Federal personnel or payroll records with non-Federal records,

(B) but does not include —

(i) matches performed to produce aggregate statistical data without any personal identifiers;

(ii) matches performed to support any research or statistical project, the specific data of which may not be used to make decisions concerning the rights, benefits, or privileges of specific individuals;

(iii) matches performed, by an agency (or component thereof) which performs as its principal function any activity pertaining to the enforcement of criminal laws, subsequent to the initiation of a specific criminal or civil law enforcement investigation of a named person or persons for the purpose of gathering evidence against such person or persons;

(iv) matches of tax information (I) pursuant to section 6103(d) of the Internal Revenue Code of 1986, (II) for purposes of tax administration as defined in section 6103(b)(4) of such Code, (III) for the purpose of intercepting a tax refund due an individual under authority granted by section 404(e), 464, or 1137 of the Social Security Act; or (IV) for the purpose of intercepting a tax refund due an individual under any other tax refund intercept program authorized by statute which has been determined by the Director of the Office of Management and Budget to contain verification, notice, and hearing requirements that are substantially similar to the procedures in section 1137 of the Social Security Act;

(v) matches —

(I) using records predominantly relating to Federal personnel, that are performed for routine administrative purposes (subject to guidance provided by the Director of the Office of Management and Budget pursuant to subsection (v)); or

    (II) conducted by an agency using only records from systems of records maintained by that agency;

if the purpose of the match is not to take any adverse financial, personnel, disciplinary, or other adverse action against Federal personnel;

    (vi) matches performed for foreign counterintelligence purposes or to produce background checks for security clearances of Federal personnel or Federal contractor personnel;

    (vii) matches performed incident to a levy described in section 6103(k)(8) of the Internal Revenue Code of 1986; or

    (viii) matches performed pursuant to section 202(x)(3) or 1611(e)(1) of the Social Security Act (42 U.S.C. 402(x)(3), 1382(e)(1));

(9) the term "recipient agency" means any agency, or contractor thereof, receiving records contained in a system of records from a source agency for use in a matching program;

(10) the term "non-Federal agency" means any State or local government, or agency thereof, which receives records contained in a system of records from a source agency for use in a matching program;

(11) the term "source agency" means any agency which discloses records contained in a system of records to be used in a matching program, or any State or local government, or agency thereof, which discloses records to be used in a matching program;

(12) the term "Federal benefit program" means any program administered or funded by the Federal Government, or by any agent or State on behalf of the Federal Government, providing cash or in-kind assistance in the form of payments, grants, loans, or loan guarantees to individuals; and

(13) the term "Federal personnel" means officers and employees of the Government of the United States, members of the uniformed services (including members of the Reserve Components), individuals entitled to receive immediate or deferred retirement benefits under any retirement program of the Government of the United States (including survivor benefits).

(b)   Conditions of Disclosure.— No agency shall disclose any record which is contained in a system of records by any means of communication to any person, or to another agency, except pursuant to a written request by, or with the prior written consent of, the individual to whom the record pertains, unless disclosure of the record would be —

(1) to those officers and employees of the agency which maintains the record who have a need for the record in the performance of their duties;

(2) required under section 552 of this title;

(3) for a routine use as defined in subsection (a)(7) of this section and described under subsection (e)(4)(D) of this section;

(4) to the Bureau of the Census for purposes of planning or carrying out a census or survey or related activity pursuant to the provisions of title 13;

(5) to a recipient who has provided the agency with advance adequate written assurance that the record will be used solely as a statistical research or reporting record, and the record is to be transferred in a form that is not individually identifiable;

(6) to the National Archives and Records Administration as a record which has sufficient historical or other value to warrant its continued preservation by the United States Government, or for evaluation by the Archivist of the United States or the designee of the Archivist to determine whether the record has such value;

(7) to another agency or to an instrumentality of any governmental jurisdiction within or under the control of the United States for a civil or criminal law enforcement activity if the activity is authorized by law, and if the head of the agency or instrumentality has made a written request to the agency which maintains the record specifying the particular portion desired and the law enforcement activity for which the record is sought;

(8) to a person pursuant to a showing of compelling circumstances affecting the health or safety of an individual if upon such disclosure notification is transmitted to the last known address of such individual;

(9) to either House of Congress, or, to the extent of matter within its jurisdiction, any committee or subcommittee thereof, any joint committee of Congress or subcommittee of any such joint committee;

(10) to the Comptroller General, or any of his authorized representatives, in the course of the performance of the duties of the Government Accountability Office;

(11) pursuant to the order of a court of competent jurisdiction; or

(12) to a consumer reporting agency in accordance with section 3711(e) of title 31.

(c) Accounting of Certain Disclosures.— Each agency, with respect to each system of records under its control, shall —

(1) except for disclosures made under subsections (b)(1) or (b)(2) of this section, keep an accurate accounting of —

(A) the date, nature, and purpose of each disclosure of a record to any person or to another agency made under subsection (b) of this section; and

(B) the name and address of the person or agency to whom the disclosure is made;

(2) retain the accounting made under paragraph (1) of this subsection for at least five years or the life of the record, whichever is longer, after the disclosure for which the accounting is made;

(3) except for disclosures made under subsection (b)(7) of this section, make

the accounting made under paragraph (1) of this subsection available to the individual named in the record at his request; and

(4) inform any person or other agency about any correction or notation of dispute made by the agency in accordance with subsection (d) of this section of any record that has been disclosed to the person or agency if an accounting of the disclosure was made.

(d) Access to Records.— Each agency that maintains a system of records shall —

(1) upon request by any individual to gain access to his record or to any information pertaining to him which is contained in the system, permit him and upon his request, a person of his own choosing to accompany him, to review the record and have a copy made of all or any portion thereof in a form comprehensible to him, except that the agency may require the individual to furnish a written statement authorizing discussion of that individual's record in the accompanying person's presence;

(2) permit the individual to request amendment of a record pertaining to him and —

(A) not later than 10 days (excluding Saturdays, Sundays, and legal public holidays) after the date of receipt of such request, acknowledge in writing such receipt; and

(B) promptly, either —

(i) make any correction of any portion thereof which the individual believes is not accurate, relevant, timely, or complete; or

(ii) inform the individual of its refusal to amend the record in accordance with his request, the reason for the refusal, the procedures established by the agency for the individual to request a review of that refusal by the head of the agency or an officer designated by the head of the agency, and the name and business address of that official;

(3) permit the individual who disagrees with the refusal of the agency to amend his record to request a review of such refusal, and not later than 30 days (excluding Saturdays, Sundays, and legal public holidays) from the date on which the individual requests such review, complete such review and make a final determination unless, for good cause shown, the head of the agency extends such 30-day period; and if, after his review, the reviewing official also refuses to amend the record in accordance with the request, permit the individual to file with the agency a concise statement setting forth the reasons for his disagreement with the refusal of the agency, and notify the individual of the provisions for judicial review of the reviewing official's determination under subsection (g)(1)(A) of this section;

(4) in any disclosure, containing information about which the individual has filed a statement of disagreement, occurring after the filing of the statement under paragraph (3) of this subsection, clearly note any portion of the record which is disputed and provide copies of the statement and, if the agency deems

it appropriate, copies of a concise statement of the reasons of the agency for not making the amendments requested, to persons or other agencies to whom the disputed record has been disclosed; and

(5) nothing in this section shall allow an individual access to any information compiled in reasonable anticipation of a civil action or proceeding.

(e) Agency Requirements.— Each agency that maintains a system of records shall —

(1) maintain in its records only such information about an individual as is relevant and necessary to accomplish a purpose of the agency required to be accomplished by statute or by executive order of the President;

(2) collect information to the greatest extent practicable directly from the subject individual when the information may result in adverse determinations about an individual's rights, benefits, and privileges under Federal programs;

(3) inform each individual whom it asks to supply information, on the form which it uses to collect the information or on a separate form that can be retained by the individual —

(A) the authority (whether granted by statute, or by executive order of the President) which authorizes the solicitation of the information and whether disclosure of such information is mandatory or voluntary;

(B) the principal purpose or purposes for which the information is intended to be used;

(C) the routine uses which may be made of the information, as published pursuant to paragraph (4)(D) of this subsection; and

(D) the effects on him, if any, of not providing all or any part of the requested information;

(4) subject to the provisions of paragraph (11) of this subsection, publish in the Federal Register upon establishment or revision a notice of the existence and character of the system of records, which notice shall include —

(A) the name and location of the system;

(B) the categories of individuals on whom records are maintained in the system;

(C) the categories of records maintained in the system;

(D) each routine use of the records contained in the system, including the categories of users and the purpose of such use;

(E) the policies and practices of the agency regarding storage, retrievability, access controls, retention, and disposal of the records;

(F) the title and business address of the agency official who is responsible for the system of records;

(G) the agency procedures whereby an individual can be notified at his request if the system of records contains a record pertaining to him;

(H) the agency procedures whereby an individual can be notified at his request how he can gain access to any record pertaining to him contained in the system of records, and how he can contest its content; and

(I) the categories of sources of records in the system;

(5) maintain all records which are used by the agency in making any determination about any individual with such accuracy, relevance, timeliness, and completeness as is reasonably necessary to assure fairness to the individual in the determination;

(6) prior to disseminating any record about an individual to any person other than an agency, unless the dissemination is made pursuant to subsection (b)(2) of this section, make reasonable efforts to assure that such records are accurate, complete, timely, and relevant for agency purposes;

(7) maintain no record describing how any individual exercises rights guaranteed by the First Amendment unless expressly authorized by statute or by the individual about whom the record is maintained or unless pertinent to and within the scope of an authorized law enforcement activity;

(8) make reasonable efforts to serve notice on an individual when any record on such individual is made available to any person under compulsory legal process when such process becomes a matter of public record;

(9) establish rules of conduct for persons involved in the design, development, operation, or maintenance of any system of records, or in maintaining any record, and instruct each such person with respect to such rules and the requirements of this section, including any other rules and procedures adopted pursuant to this section and the penalties for noncompliance;

(10) establish appropriate administrative, technical, and physical safeguards to insure the security and confidentiality of records and to protect against any anticipated threats or hazards to their security or integrity which could result in substantial harm, embarrassment, inconvenience, or unfairness to any individual on whom information is maintained;

(11) at least 30 days prior to publication of information under paragraph (4)(D) of this subsection, publish in the Federal Register notice of any new use or intended use of the information in the system, and provide an opportunity for interested persons to submit written data, views, or arguments to the agency; and

(12) if such agency is a recipient agency or a source agency in a matching program with a non-Federal agency, with respect to any establishment or revision of a matching program, at least 30 days prior to conducting such program, publish in the Federal Register notice of such establishment or revision.

(f)   Agency Rules.— In order to carry out the provisions of this section, each agency that maintains a system of records shall promulgate rules, in accordance with the requirements (including general notice) of section 553 of this title, which shall —

(1) establish procedures whereby an individual can be notified in response to his request if any system of records named by the individual contains a record pertaining to him;

(2) define reasonable times, places, and requirements for identifying an individual who requests his record or information pertaining to him before the agency shall make the record or information available to the individual;

(3) establish procedures for the disclosure to an individual upon his request of his record or information pertaining to him, including special procedure, if deemed necessary, for the disclosure to an individual of medical records, including psychological records, pertaining to him;

(4) establish procedures for reviewing a request from an individual concerning the amendment of any record or information pertaining to the individual, for making a determination on the request, for an appeal within the agency of an initial adverse agency determination, and for whatever additional means may be necessary for each individual to be able to exercise fully his rights under this section; and

(5) establish fees to be charged, if any, to any individual for making copies of his record, excluding the cost of any search for and review of the record.

The Office of the Federal Register shall biennially compile and publish the rules promulgated under this subsection and agency notices published under subsection (e)(4) of this section in a form available to the public at low cost.

(g) (1)   Civil Remedies.— Whenever any agency

(A) makes a determination under subsection (d)(3) of this section not to amend an individual's record in accordance with his request, or fails to make such review in conformity with that subsection;

(B) refuses to comply with an individual request under subsection (d)(1) of this section;

(C) fails to maintain any record concerning any individual with such accuracy, relevance, timeliness, and completeness as is necessary to assure fairness in any determination relating to the qualifications, character, rights, or opportunities of, or benefits to the individual that may be made on the basis of such record, and consequently a determination is made which is adverse to the individual; or

(D) fails to comply with any other provision of this section, or any rule promulgated thereunder, in such a way as to have an adverse effect on an individual,

the individual may bring a civil action against the agency, and the district courts of the United States shall have jurisdiction in the matters under the provisions of this subsection.

(2) (A) In any suit brought under the provisions of subsection (g)(1)(A) of this section, the court may order the agency to amend the individual's record in accordance with his request or in such other way as the court may direct.

In such a case the court shall determine the matter de novo.

(B) The court may assess against the United States reasonable attorney fees and other litigation costs reasonably incurred in any case under this paragraph in which the complainant has substantially prevailed.

(3) (A) In any suit brought under the provisions of subsection (g)(1)(B) of this section, the court may enjoin the agency from withholding the records and order the production to the complainant of any agency records improperly withheld from him. In such a case the court shall determine the matter de novo, and may examine the contents of any agency records in camera to determine whether the records or any portion thereof may be withheld under any of the exemptions set forth in subsection (k) of this section, and the burden is on the agency to sustain its action.

(B) The court may assess against the United States reasonable attorney fees and other litigation costs reasonably incurred in any case under this paragraph in which the complainant has substantially prevailed.

(4) In any suit brought under the provisions of subsection (g)(1)(C) or (D) of this section in which the court determines that the agency acted in a manner which was intentional or willful, the United States shall be liable to the individual in an amount equal to the sum of —

(A) actual damages sustained by the individual as a result of the refusal or failure, but in no case shall a person entitled to recovery receive less than the sum of $1,000; and

(B) the costs of the action together with reasonable attorney fees as determined by the court.

(5) An action to enforce any liability created under this section may be brought in the district court of the United States in the district in which the complainant resides, or has his principal place of business, or in which the agency records are situated, or in the District of Columbia, without regard to the amount in controversy, within two years from the date on which the cause of action arises, except that where an agency has materially and willfully misrepresented any information required under this section to be disclosed to an individual and the information so misrepresented is material to establishment of the liability of the agency to the individual under this section, the action may be brought at any time within two years after discovery by the individual of the misrepresentation. Nothing in this section shall be construed to authorize any civil action by reason of any injury sustained as the result of a disclosure of a record prior to September 27, 1975.

(h)   Rights of Legal Guardians.— For the purposes of this section, the parent of any minor, or the legal guardian of any individual who has been declared to be incompetent due to physical or mental incapacity or age by a court of competent jurisdiction, may act on behalf of the individual.

(i) (1)   Criminal Penalties.— Any officer or employee of an agency, who by virtue of his employment or official position, has possession of, or access to, agency records which contain individually identifiable information the disclosure of which is prohibited by this section or by rules or regulations established thereunder, and who knowing that disclosure of the specific material is so prohibited, willfully discloses the material in any manner to any person or agency not entitled to receive it, shall be guilty of a misdemeanor and fined not more than $5,000.

(2) Any officer or employee of any agency who willfully maintains a system of records without meeting the notice requirements of subsection (e)(4) of this section shall be guilty of a misdemeanor and fined not more than $5,000.

(3) Any person who knowingly and willfully requests or obtains any record concerning an individual from an agency under false pretenses shall be guilty of a misdemeanor and fined not more than $5,000.

(j)   General Exemptions.— The head of any agency may promulgate rules, in accordance with the requirements (including general notice) of sections 553(b)(1), (2), and (3), (c), and (e) of this title, to exempt any system of records within the agency from any part of this section except subsections (b), (c)(1) and (2), (e)(4)(A) through (F), (e)(6), (7), (9), (10), and (11), and (i) if the system of records is —

(1) maintained by the Central Intelligence Agency; or

(2) maintained by an agency or component thereof which performs as its principal function any activity pertaining to the enforcement of criminal laws, including police efforts to prevent, control, or reduce crime or to apprehend criminals, and the activities of prosecutors, courts, correctional, probation, pardon, or parole authorities, and which consists of (A) information compiled for the purpose of identifying individual criminal offenders and alleged offenders and consisting only of identifying data and notations of arrests, the nature and disposition of criminal charges, sentencing, confinement, release, and parole and probation status; (B) information compiled for the purpose of a criminal investigation, including reports of informants and investigators, and associated with an identifiable individual; or (C) reports identifiable to an individual compiled at any stage of the process of enforcement of the criminal laws from arrest or indictment through release from supervision.

At the time rules are adopted under this subsection, the agency shall include in the statement required under section 553(c) of this title, the reasons why the system of records is to be exempted from a provision of this section.

(k)   Specific Exemptions.— The head of any agency may promulgate rules, in accordance with the requirements (including general notice) of sections 553(b)(1), (2), and (3), (c), and (e) of this title, to exempt any system of records within the agency from subsections (c)(3), (d), (e)(1), (e)(4)(G), (H), and (I) and (f) of this section if the system of records is —

(1) subject to the provisions of section 552(b)(1) of this title;

(2) investigatory material compiled for law enforcement purposes, other than material within the scope of subsection (j)(2) of this section: Provided, however, That if any individual is denied any right, privilege, or benefit that he would otherwise be entitled by Federal law, or for which he would otherwise

be eligible, as a result of the maintenance of such material, such material shall be provided to such individual, except to the extent that the disclosure of such material would reveal the identity of a source who furnished information to the Government under an express promise that the identity of the source would be held in confidence, or, prior to the effective date of this section, under an implied promise that the identity of the source would be held in confidence;

(3) maintained in connection with providing protective services to the President of the United States or other individuals pursuant to section 3056 of title 18;

(4) required by statute to be maintained and used solely as statistical records;

(5) investigatory material compiled solely for the purpose of determining suitability, eligibility, or qualifications for Federal civilian employment, military service, Federal contracts, or access to classified information, but only to the extent that the disclosure of such material would reveal the identity of a source who furnished information to the Government under an express promise that the identity of the source would be held in confidence, or, prior to the effective date of this section, under an implied promise that the identity of the source would be held in confidence;

(6) testing or examination material used solely to determine individual qualifications for appointment or promotion in the Federal service the disclosure of which would compromise the objectivity or fairness of the testing or examination process; or

(7) evaluation material used to determine potential for promotion in the armed services, but only to the extent that the disclosure of such material would reveal the identity of a source who furnished information to the Government under an express promise that the identity of the source would be held in confidence, or, prior to the effective date of this section, under an implied promise that the identity of the source would be held in confidence.

At the time rules are adopted under this subsection, the agency shall include in the statement required under section 553(c) of this title, the reasons why the system of records is to be exempted from a provision of this section.

(l) (1) Archival Records.— Each agency record which is accepted by the Archivist of the United States for storage, processing, and servicing in accordance with section 3103 of title 44 shall, for the purposes of this section, be considered to be maintained by the agency which deposited the record and shall be subject to the provisions of this section. The Archivist of the United States shall not disclose the record except to the agency which maintains the record, or under rules established by that agency which are not inconsistent with the provisions of this section.

(2) Each agency record pertaining to an identifiable individual which was transferred to the National Archives of the United States as a record which has sufficient historical or other value to warrant its continued preservation by the United States Government, prior to the effective date of this section, shall,

for the purposes of this section, be considered to be maintained by the National Archives and shall not be subject to the provisions of this section, except that a statement generally describing such records (modeled after the requirements relating to records subject to subsections (e)(4)(A) through (G) of this section) shall be published in the Federal Register.

(3) Each agency record pertaining to an identifiable individual which is transferred to the National Archives of the United States as a record which has sufficient historical or other value to warrant its continued preservation by the United States Government, on or after the effective date of this section, shall, for the purposes of this section, be considered to be maintained by the National Archives and shall be exempt from the requirements of this section except subsections (e)(4)(A) through (G) and (e)(9) of this section.

(m) (1) Government Contractors.— When an agency provides by a contract for the operation by or on behalf of the agency of a system of records to accomplish an agency function, the agency shall, consistent with its authority, cause the requirements of this section to be applied to such system. For purposes of subsection (i) of this section any such contractor and any employee of such contractor, if such contract is agreed to on or after the effective date of this section, shall be considered to be an employee of an agency.

(2) A consumer reporting agency to which a record is disclosed under section 3711(e) of title 31 shall not be considered a contractor for the purposes of this section.

(n) Mailing Lists.— An individual's name and address may not be sold or rented by an agency unless such action is specifically authorized by law. This provision shall not be construed to require the withholding of names and addresses otherwise permitted to be made public.

(o) Matching Agreements.— (1) No record which is contained in a system of records may be disclosed to a recipient agency or non-Federal agency for use in a computer matching program except pursuant to a written agreement between the source agency and the recipient agency or non-Federal agency specifying —

(A) the purpose and legal authority for conducting the program;

(B) the justification for the program and the anticipated results, including a specific estimate of any savings;

(C) a description of the records that will be matched, including each data element that will be used, the approximate number of records that will be matched, and the projected starting and completion dates of the matching program;

(D) procedures for providing individualized notice at the time of application, and notice periodically thereafter as directed by the Data Integrity Board of such agency (subject to guidance provided by the Director of the Office of Management and Budget pursuant to subsection (v)), to —

(i) applicants for and recipients of financial assistance or payments under Federal benefit programs, and

(ii) applicants for and holders of positions as Federal personnel,

that any information provided by such applicants, recipients, holders, and individuals may be subject to verification through matching programs;

(E) procedures for verifying information produced in such matching program as required by subsection (p);

(F) procedures for the retention and timely destruction of identifiable records created by a recipient agency or non-Federal agency in such matching program;

(G) procedures for ensuring the administrative, technical, and physical security of the records matched and the results of such programs;

(H) prohibitions on duplication and redisclosure of records provided by the source agency within or outside the recipient agency or the non-Federal agency, except where required by law or essential to the conduct of the matching program;

(I) procedures governing the use by a recipient agency or non-Federal agency of records provided in a matching program by a source agency, including procedures governing return of the records to the source agency or destruction of records used in such program;

(J) information on assessments that have been made on the accuracy of the records that will be used in such matching program; and

(K) that the Comptroller General may have access to all records of a recipient agency or a non-Federal agency that the Comptroller General deems necessary in order to monitor or verify compliance with the agreement.

(2) (A) A copy of each agreement entered into pursuant to paragraph (1) shall —

(i) be transmitted to the Committee on Governmental Affairs of the Senate and the Committee on Government Operations of the House of Representatives; and

(ii) be available upon request to the public.

(B) No such agreement shall be effective until 30 days after the date on which such a copy is transmitted pursuant to subparagraph (A)(i).

(C) Such an agreement shall remain in effect only for such period, not to exceed 18 months, as the Data Integrity Board of the agency determines is appropriate in light of the purposes, and length of time necessary for the conduct, of the matching program.

(D) Within 3 months prior to the expiration of such an agreement pursuant to subparagraph (C), the Data Integrity Board of the agency may, without additional review, renew the matching agreement for a current, ongoing matching program for not more than one additional year if —

(i) such program will be conducted without any change; and

(ii) each party to the agreement certifies to the Board in writing that the program has been conducted in compliance with the agreement.

(p) Verification and Opportunity to Contest Findings.— (1) In order to protect any individual whose records are used in a matching program, no recipient agency, non-Federal agency, or source agency may suspend, terminate, reduce, or make a final denial of any financial assistance or payment under a Federal benefit program to such individual, or take other adverse action against such individual, as a result of information produced by such matching program, until —

(A) (i) the agency has independently verified the information; or

(ii) the Data Integrity Board of the agency, or in the case of a non-Federal agency the Data Integrity Board of the source agency, determines in accordance with guidance issued by the Director of the Office of Management and Budget that —

(I) the information is limited to identification and amount of benefits paid by the source agency under a Federal benefit program; and

(II) there is a high degree of confidence that the information provided to the recipient agency is accurate;

(B) the individual receives a notice from the agency containing a statement of its findings and informing the individual of the opportunity to contest such findings; and

(C) (i) the expiration of any time period established for the program by statute or regulation for the individual to respond to that notice; or

(ii) in the case of a program for which no such period is established, the end of the 30-day period beginning on the date on which notice under subparagraph (B) is mailed or otherwise provided to the individual.

(2) Independent verification referred to in paragraph (1) requires investigation and confirmation of specific information relating to an individual that is used as a basis for an adverse action against the individual, including where applicable investigation and confirmation of —

(A) the amount of any asset or income involved;

(B) whether such individual actually has or had access to such asset or income for such individual's own use; and

(C) the period or periods when the individual actually had such asset or income.

(3) Notwithstanding paragraph (1), an agency may take any appropriate action otherwise prohibited by such paragraph if the agency determines that the public health or public safety may be adversely affected or significantly threatened during any notice period required by such paragraph.

(q) Sanctions.— (1) Notwithstanding any other provision of law, no source agency may disclose any record which is contained in a system of records to a recipient agency or non-Federal agency for a matching program if such source agency has reason to believe that the requirements of subsection (p), or any matching agreement entered into pursuant to subsection (o), or both, are not being met by such recipient agency.

(2) No source agency may renew a matching agreement unless —

(A) the recipient agency or non-Federal agency has certified that it has complied with the provisions of that agreement; and

(B) the source agency has no reason to believe that the certification is inaccurate.

(r)   Report on New Systems and Matching Programs.— Each agency that proposes to establish or make a significant change in a system of records or a matching program shall provide adequate advance notice of any such proposal (in duplicate) to the Committee on Government Operations of the House of Representatives, the Committee on Governmental Affairs of the Senate, and the Office of Management and Budget in order to permit an evaluation of the probable or potential effect of such proposal on the privacy or other rights of individuals.

(s)   Biennial Report.— The President shall biennially submit to the Speaker of the House of Representatives and the President pro tempore of the Senate a report —

(1) describing the actions of the Director of the Office of Management and Budget pursuant to section 6 of the Privacy Act of 1974 during the preceding 2 years;

(2) describing the exercise of individual rights of access and amendment under this section during such years;

(3) identifying changes in or additions to systems of records;

(4) containing such other information concerning administration of this section as may be necessary or useful to the Congress in reviewing the effectiveness of this section in carrying out the purposes of the Privacy Act of 1974.

(t) (1)   Effect of Other Laws.— No agency shall rely on any exemption contained in section 552 of this title to withhold from an individual any record which is otherwise accessible to such individual under the provisions of this section.

(2) No agency shall rely on any exemption in this section to withhold from an individual any record which is otherwise accessible to such individual under the provisions of section 552 of this title.

(u)   Data Integrity Boards.— (1) Every agency conducting or participating in a matching program shall establish a Data Integrity Board to oversee and coordinate among the various components of such agency the agency's implementation of this section.

(2) Each Data Integrity Board shall consist of senior officials designated by the head of the agency, and shall include any senior official designated by the head of the agency as responsible for implementation of this section, and the inspector general of the agency, if any. The inspector general shall not serve as chairman of the Data Integrity Board.

(3) Each Data Integrity Board —

(A) shall review, approve, and maintain all written agreements for receipt or disclosure of agency records for matching programs to ensure compliance with subsection (o), and all relevant statutes, regulations, and guidelines;

(B) shall review all matching programs in which the agency has participated during the year, either as a source agency or recipient agency, determine compliance with applicable laws, regulations, guidelines, and agency agreements, and assess the costs and benefits of such programs;

(C) shall review all recurring matching programs in which the agency has participated during the year, either as a source agency or recipient agency, for continued justification for such disclosures;

(D) shall compile an annual report, which shall be submitted to the head of the agency and the Office of Management and Budget and made available to the public on request, describing the matching activities of the agency, including —

(i) matching programs in which the agency has participated as a source agency or recipient agency;

(ii) matching agreements proposed under subsection (o) that were disapproved by the Board;

(iii) any changes in membership or structure of the Board in the preceding year;

(iv) the reasons for any waiver of the requirement in paragraph (4) of this section for completion and submission of a cost-benefit analysis prior to the approval of a matching program;

(v) any violations of matching agreements that have been alleged or identified and any corrective action taken; and

(vi) any other information required by the Director of the Office of Management and Budget to be included in such report;

(E) shall serve as a clearinghouse for receiving and providing information on the accuracy, completeness, and reliability of records used in matching programs;

(F) shall provide interpretation and guidance to agency components and personnel on the requirements of this section for matching programs;

(G) shall review agency recordkeeping and disposal policies and practices for matching programs to assure compliance with this section; and

(H) may review and report on any agency matching activities that are not matching programs.

(4) (A) Except as provided in subparagraphs (B) and (C), a Data Integrity Board shall not approve any written agreement for a matching program unless the agency has completed and submitted to such Board a cost-benefit analysis of the proposed program and such analysis demonstrates that the program is likely to be cost effective.

(B) The Board may waive the requirements of subparagraph (A) of this paragraph if it determines in writing, in accordance with guidelines prescribed by the Director of the Office of Management and Budget, that a cost-benefit analysis is not required.

(C) A cost-benefit analysis shall not be required under subparagraph (A) prior to the initial approval of a written agreement for a matching program that is specifically required by statute. Any subsequent written agreement for such a program shall not be approved by the Data Integrity Board unless the agency has submitted a cost-benefit analysis of the program as conducted under the preceding approval of such agreement.

(5) (A) If a matching agreement is disapproved by a Data Integrity Board, any party to such agreement may appeal the disapproval to the Director of the Office of Management and Budget. Timely notice of the filing of such an appeal shall be provided by the Director of the Office of Management and Budget to the Committee on Governmental Affairs of the Senate and the Committee on Government Operations of the House of Representatives.

(B) The Director of the Office of Management and Budget may approve a matching agreement notwithstanding the disapproval of a Data Integrity Board if the Director determines that —

(i) the matching program will be consistent with all applicable legal, regulatory, and policy requirements;

(ii) there is adequate evidence that the matching agreement will be cost-effective; and

(iii) the matching program is in the public interest.

(C) The decision of the Director to approve a matching agreement shall not take effect until 30 days after it is reported to committees described in subparagraph (A).

(D) If the Data Integrity Board and the Director of the Office of Management and Budget disapprove a matching program proposed by the inspector general of an agency, the inspector general may report the disapproval to the head of the agency and to the Congress.

(6) In the reports required by paragraph (3)(D), agency matching activities that are not matching programs may be reported on an aggregate basis, if and to the extent necessary to protect ongoing law enforcement or counterintelligence investigations.

(v)   Office of Management and Budget Responsibilities.— The Director of the Office of Management and Budget shall —

(1) develop and, after notice and opportunity for public comment, prescribe guidelines and regulations for the use of agencies in implementing the provisions of this section; and

(2) provide continuing assistance to and oversight of the implementation of this section by agencies.

§ 552b.   Open meetings

(a) For purposes of this section —

(1) the term "agency" means any agency, as defined in section 552(e) of this title, headed by a collegial body composed of two or more individual members, a majority of whom are appointed to such position by the President with the advice and consent of the Senate, and any subdivision thereof authorized to act on behalf of the agency;

(2) the term "meeting" means the deliberations of at least the number of individual agency members required to take action on behalf of the agency where such deliberations determine or result in the joint conduct or disposition of official agency business, but does not include deliberations required or permitted by subsection (d) or (e); and

(3) the term "member" means an individual who belongs to a collegial body heading an agency.

(b) Members shall not jointly conduct or dispose of agency business other than in accordance with this section. Except as provided in subsection (c), every portion of every meeting of an agency shall be open to public observation.

(c) Except in a case where the agency finds that the public interest requires otherwise, the second sentence of subsection (b) shall not apply to any portion of an agency meeting, and the requirements of subsections (d) and (e) shall not apply to any information pertaining to such meeting otherwise required by this section to be disclosed to the public, where the agency properly determines that such portion or portions of its meeting or the disclosure of such information is likely to —

(1) disclose matters that are (A) specifically authorized under criteria established by an Executive order to be kept secret in the interests of national defense or foreign policy and (B) in fact properly classified pursuant to such Executive order;

(2) relate solely to the internal personnel rules and practices of an agency;

(3) disclose matters specifically exempted from disclosure by statute (other than section 552 of this title), provided that such statute (A) requires that the matters be withheld from the public in such a manner as to leave no discretion on the issue, or (B) establishes particular criteria for withholding or refers to particular types of matters to be withheld;

(4) disclose trade secrets and commercial or financial information obtained

from a person and privileged or confidential;

(5) involve accusing any person of a crime, or formally censuring any person;

(6) disclose information of a personal nature where disclosure would constitute a clearly unwarranted invasion of personal privacy;

(7) disclose investigatory records compiled for law enforcement purposes, or information which if written would be contained in such records, but only to the extent that the production of such records or information would (A) interfere with enforcement proceedings, (B) deprive a person of a right to a fair trial or an impartial adjudication, (C) constitute an unwarranted invasion of personal privacy, (D) disclose the identity of a confidential source and, in the case of a record compiled by a criminal law enforcement authority in the course of a criminal investigation, or by an agency conducting a lawful national security intelligence investigation, confidential information furnished only by the confidential source, (E) disclose investigative techniques and procedures, or (F) endanger the life or physical safety of law enforcement personnel;

(8) disclose information contained in or related to examination, operating, or condition reports prepared by, on behalf of, or for the use of an agency responsible for the regulation or supervision of financial institutions;

(9) disclose information the premature disclosure of which would —

(A) in the case of an agency which regulates currencies, securities, commodities, or financial institutions, be likely to (i) lead to significant financial speculation in currencies, securities, or commodities, or (ii) significantly endanger the stability of any financial institution; or

(B) in the case of any agency, be likely to significantly frustrate implementation of a proposed agency action,

except that subparagraph (B) shall not apply in any instance where the agency has already disclosed to the public the content or nature of its proposed action, or where the agency is required by law to make such disclosure on its own initiative prior to taking final agency action on such proposal; or

(10) specifically concern the agency's issuance of a subpena, or the agency's participation in a civil action or proceeding, an action in a foreign court or international tribunal, or an arbitration, or the initiation, conduct, or disposition by the agency of a particular case of formal agency adjudication pursuant to the procedures in section 554 of this title or otherwise involving a determination on the record after opportunity for a hearing.

(d) (1) Action under subsection (c) shall be taken only when a majority of the entire membership of the agency (as defined in subsection (a)(1)) votes to take such action. A separate vote of the agency members shall be taken with respect to each agency meeting a portion or portions of which are proposed to be closed to the public pursuant to subsection (c), or with respect to any information which is proposed to be withheld under subsection (c). A single vote may be taken with respect to a series of meetings, a portion or portions of which are proposed to be closed to the public, or with respect to any information concerning such series of meetings, so long as each meeting in such series involves the same particular matters and is scheduled to be held no more than thirty days after the initial meeting in such series. The vote of each agency member participating in such vote shall be recorded and no proxies shall be allowed.

(2) Whenever any person whose interests may be directly affected by a portion of a meeting requests that the agency close such portion to the public for any of the reasons referred to in paragraph (5), (6), or (7) of subsection (c), the agency, upon request of any one of its members, shall vote by recorded vote whether to close such meeting.

(3) Within one day of any vote taken pursuant to paragraph (1) or (2), the agency shall make publicly available a written copy of such vote reflecting the vote of each member on the question. If a portion of a meeting is to be closed to the public, the agency shall, within one day of the vote taken pursuant to paragraph (1) or (2) of this subsection, make publicly available a full written explanation of its action closing the portion together with a list of all persons expected to attend the meeting and their affiliation.

(4) Any agency, a majority of whose meetings may properly be closed to the public pursuant to paragraph (4), (8), (9)(A), or (10) of subsection (c), or any combination thereof, may provide by regulation for the closing of such meetings or portions thereof in the event that a majority of the members of the agency votes by recorded vote at the beginning of such meeting, or portion thereof, to close the exempt portion or portions of the meeting, and a copy of such vote, reflecting the vote of each member on the question, is made available to the public. The provisions of paragraphs (1), (2), and (3) of this subsection and subsection (e) shall not apply to any portion of a meeting to which such regulations apply: Provided, That the agency shall, except to the extent that such information is exempt from disclosure under the provisions of subsection (c), provide the public with public announcement of the time, place, and subject matter of the meeting and of each portion thereof at the earliest practicable time.

(e) (1) In the case of each meeting, the agency shall make public announcement, at least one week before the meeting, of the time, place, and subject matter of the meeting, whether it is to be open or closed to the public, and the name and phone number of the official designated by the agency to respond to requests for information about the meeting. Such announcement shall be made unless a majority of the members of the agency determines by a recorded vote that agency business requires that such meeting be called at an earlier date, in which case the agency shall make public announcement of the time, place, and subject matter of such meeting, and whether open or closed to the public, at the earliest practicable time.

(2) The time or place of a meeting may be changed following the public announcement required by paragraph (1) only if the agency publicly announces such change at the earliest practicable time. The subject matter of a meeting, or the determination of the agency to open or close a meeting, or portion of a meeting, to the public, may be changed following the public

announcement required by this subsection only if (A) a majority of the entire membership of the agency determines by a recorded vote that agency business so requires and that no earlier announcement of the change was possible, and (B) the agency publicly announces such change and the vote of each member upon such change at the earliest practicable time.

(3) Immediately following each public announcement required by this subsection, notice of the time, place, and subject matter of a meeting, whether the meeting is open or closed, any change in one of the preceding, and the name and phone number of the official designated by the agency to respond to requests for information about the meeting, shall also be submitted for publication in the Federal Register.

(f) (1) For every meeting closed pursuant to paragraphs (1) through (10) of subsection (c), the General Counsel or chief legal officer of the agency shall publicly certify that, in his or her opinion, the meeting may be closed to the public and shall state each relevant exemptive provision. A copy of such certification, together with a statement from the presiding officer of the meeting setting forth the time and place of the meeting, and the persons present, shall be retained by the agency. The agency shall maintain a complete transcript or electronic recording adequate to record fully the proceedings of each meeting, or portion of a meeting, closed to the public, except that in the case of a meeting, or portion of a meeting, closed to the public pursuant to paragraph (8), (9)(A), or (10) of subsection (c), the agency shall maintain either such a transcript or recording, or a set of minutes. Such minutes shall fully and clearly describe all matters discussed and shall provide a full and accurate summary of any actions taken, and the reasons therefor, including a description of each of the views expressed on any item and the record of any rollcall vote (reflecting the vote of each member on the question). All documents considered in connection with any action shall be identified in such minutes.

(2) The agency shall make promptly available to the public, in a place easily accessible to the public, the transcript, electronic recording, or minutes (as required by paragraph (1)) of the discussion of any item on the agenda, or of any item of the testimony of any witness received at the meeting, except for such item or items of such discussion or testimony as the agency determines to contain information which may be withheld under subsection (c). Copies of such transcript, or minutes, or a transcription of such recording disclosing the identity of each speaker, shall be furnished to any person at the actual cost of duplication or transcription. The agency shall maintain a complete verbatim copy of the transcript, a complete copy of the minutes, or a complete electronic recording of each meeting, or portion of a meeting, closed to the public, for a period of at least two years after such meeting, or until one year after the conclusion of any agency proceeding with respect to which the meeting or portion was held, whichever occurs later.

(g) Each agency subject to the requirements of this section shall, within 180 days after the date of enactment of this section, following consultation with the Office of the Chairman of the Administrative Conference of the United States and published notice in the Federal Register of at least thirty days and opportunity for written comment by any person, promulgate regulations to implement the requirements of subsections (b) through (f) of this section. Any person may bring a proceeding in the United States District Court for the District of Columbia to require an agency to promulgate such regulations if such agency has not promulgated such regulations within the time period specified herein. Subject to any limitations of time provided by law, any person may bring a proceeding in the United States Court of Appeals for the District of Columbia to set aside agency regulations issued pursuant to this subsection that are not in accord with the requirements of subsections (b) through (f) of this section and to require the promulgation of regulations that are in accord with such subsections.

(h) (1) The district courts of the United States shall have jurisdiction to enforce the requirements of subsections (b) through (f) of this section by declaratory judgment, injunctive relief, or other relief as may be appropriate. Such actions may be brought by any person against an agency prior to, or within sixty days after, the meeting out of which the violation of this section arises, except that if public announcement of such meeting is not initially provided by the agency in accordance with the requirements of this section, such action may be instituted pursuant to this section at any time prior to sixty days after any public announcement of such meeting. Such actions may be brought in the district court of the United States for the district in which the agency meeting is held or in which the agency in question has its headquarters, or in the District Court for the District of Columbia. In such actions a defendant shall serve his answer within thirty days after the service of the complaint. The burden is on the defendant to sustain his action. In deciding such cases the court may examine in camera any portion of the transcript, electronic recording, or minutes of a meeting closed to the public, and may take such additional evidence as it deems necessary. The court, having due regard for orderly administration and the public interest, as well as the interests of the parties, may grant such equitable relief as it deems appropriate, including granting an injunction against future violations of this section or ordering the agency to make available to the public such portion of the transcript, recording, or minutes of a meeting as is not authorized to be withheld under subsection (c) of this section.

(2) Any Federal court otherwise authorized by law to review agency action may, at the application of any person properly participating in the proceeding pursuant to other applicable law, inquire into violations by the agency of the requirements of this section and afford such relief as it deems appropriate. Nothing in this section authorizes any Federal court having jurisdiction solely on the basis of paragraph (1) to set aside, enjoin, or invalidate any agency action (other than an action to close a meeting or to withhold information under this section) taken or discussed at any agency meeting out of which the violation of this section arose.

(i) The court may assess against any party reasonable attorney fees and other litigation costs reasonably incurred by any other party who substantially prevails in any action brought in accordance with the provisions of subsection (g) or (h) of this section, except that costs may be assessed against the plaintiff only where the court finds that the suit was initiated by the plaintiff primarily for frivolous or dilatory purposes. In the case of assessment of costs against an agency, the costs may be assessed by the court against the United States.

(j) Each agency subject to the requirements of this section shall annually report to the Congress regarding the following:

(1) The changes in the policies and procedures of the agency under this section that have occurred during the preceding 1-year period.

(2) A tabulation of the number of meetings held, the exemptions applied to close meetings, and the days of public notice provided to close meetings.

(3) A brief description of litigation or formal complaints concerning the implementation of this section by the agency.

(4) A brief explanation of any changes in law that have affected the responsibilities of the agency under this section.

(k) Nothing herein expands or limits the present rights of any person under section 552 of this title, except that the exemptions set forth in subsection (c) of this section shall govern in the case of any request made pursuant to section 552 to copy or inspect the transcripts, recordings, or minutes described in subsection (f) of this section. The requirements of chapter 33 of title 44, United States Code, shall not apply to the transcripts, recordings, and minutes described in subsection (f) of this section.

(l) This section does not constitute authority to withhold any information from Congress, and does not authorize the closing of any agency meeting or portion thereof required by any other provision of law to be open.

(m) Nothing in this section authorizes any agency to withhold from any individual any record, including transcripts, recordings, or minutes required by this section, which is otherwise accessible to such individual under section 552a of this title.

§ 553. Rule making

(a) This section applies, according to the provisions thereof, except to the extent that there is involved —

(1) a military or foreign affairs function of the United States; or

(2) a matter relating to agency management or personnel or to public property, loans, grants, benefits, or contracts.

(b) General notice of proposed rule making shall be published in the Federal Register, unless persons subject thereto are named and either personally served or otherwise have actual notice thereof in accordance with law. The notice shall include —

(1) a statement of the time, place, and nature of public rule making proceedings;

(2) reference to the legal authority under which the rule is proposed; and

(3) either the terms or substance of the proposed rule or a description of the

subjects and issues involved.

Except when notice or hearing is required by statute, this subsection does not apply —

(A) to interpretative rules, general statements of policy, or rules of agency organization, procedure, or practice; or

(B) when the agency for good cause finds (and incorporates the finding and a brief statement of reasons therefor in the rules issued) that notice and public procedure thereon are impracticable, unnecessary, or contrary to the public interest.

(c) After notice required by this section, the agency shall give interested persons an opportunity to participate in the rule making through submission of written data, views, or arguments with or without opportunity for oral presentation. After consideration of the relevant matter presented, the agency shall incorporate in the rules adopted a concise general statement of their basis and purpose. When rules are required by statute to be made on the record after opportunity for an agency hearing, sections 556 and 557 of this title apply instead of this subsection.

(d) The required publication or service of a substantive rule shall be made not less than 30 days before its effective date, except —

(1) a substantive rule which grants or recognizes an exemption or relieves a restriction;

(2) interpretative rules and statements of policy; or

(3) as otherwise provided by the agency for good cause found and published with the rule.

(e) Each agency shall give an interested person the right to petition for the issuance, amendment, or repeal of a rule.

§ 554. Adjudications

(a) This section applies, according to the provisions thereof, in every case of adjudication required by statute to be determined on the record after opportunity for an agency hearing, except to the extent that there is involved —

(1) a matter subject to a subsequent trial of the law and the facts de novo in a court;

(2) the selection or tenure of an employee, except a administrative law judge appointed under section 3105 of this title;

(3) proceedings in which decisions rest solely on inspections, tests, or elections;

(4) the conduct of military or foreign affairs functions;

(5) cases in which an agency is acting as an agent for a court; or

(6) the certification of worker representatives.

(b) Persons entitled to notice of an agency hearing shall be timely informed of —

(1) the time, place, and nature of the hearing;

(2) the legal authority and jurisdiction under which the hearing is to be held; and

(3) the matters of fact and law asserted.

When private persons are the moving parties, other parties to the proceeding shall give prompt notice of issues controverted in fact or law; and in other instances agencies may by rule require responsive pleading. In fixing the time and place for hearings, due regard shall be had for the convenience and necessity of the parties or their representatives.

(c) The agency shall give all interested parties opportunity for —

(1) the submission and consideration of facts, arguments, offers of settlement, or proposals of adjustment when time, the nature of the proceeding, and the public interest permit; and

(2) to the extent that the parties are unable so to determine a controversy by consent, hearing and decision on notice and in accordance with sections 556 and 557 of this title.

(d) The employee who presides at the reception of evidence pursuant to section 556 of this title shall make the recommended decision or initial decision required by section 557 of this title, unless he becomes unavailable to the agency. Except to the extent required for the disposition of ex parte matters as authorized by law, such an employee may not —

(1) consult a person or party on a fact in issue, unless on notice and opportunity for all parties to participate; or

(2) be responsible to or subject to the supervision or direction of an employee or agent engaged in the performance of investigative or prosecuting functions for an agency.

An employee or agent engaged in the performance of investigative or prosecuting functions for an agency in a case may not, in that or a factually related case, participate or advise in the decision, recommended decision, or agency review pursuant to section 557 of this title, except as witness or counsel in public proceedings. This subsection does not apply —

(A) in determining applications for initial licenses;

(B) to proceedings involving the validity or application of rates, facilities, or practices of public utilities or carriers; or

(C) to the agency or a member or members of the body comprising the agency.

(e) The agency, with like effect as in the case of other orders, and in its sound discretion, may issue a declaratory order to terminate a controversy or remove uncertainty.

§ 555. Ancillary matters

(a) This section applies, according to the provisions thereof, except as otherwise provided by this subchapter.

(b) A person compelled to appear in person before an agency or representative thereof is entitled to be accompanied, represented, and advised by counsel or, if permitted by the agency, by other qualified representative. A party is entitled to appear in person or by or with counsel or other duly qualified representative in an agency proceeding. So far as the orderly conduct of public business permits, an interested person may appear before an agency or its responsible employees for the presentation, adjustment, or determination of an issue, request, or controversy in a proceeding, whether interlocutory, summary, or otherwise, or in connection with an agency function. With due regard for the convenience and necessity of the parties or their representatives and within a reasonable time, each agency shall proceed to conclude a matter presented to it. This subsection does not grant or deny a person who is not a lawyer the right to appear for or represent others before an agency or in an agency proceeding.

(c) Process, requirement of a report, inspection, or other investigative act or demand may not be issued, made, or enforced except as authorized by law. A person compelled to submit data or evidence is entitled to retain or, on payment of lawfully prescribed costs, procure a copy or transcript thereof, except that in a nonpublic investigatory proceeding the witness may for good cause be limited to inspection of the official transcript of his testimony.

(d) Agency subpenas authorized by law shall be issued to a party on request and, when required by rules of procedure, on a statement or showing of general relevance and reasonable scope of the evidence sought. On contest, the court shall sustain the subpena or similar process or demand to the extent that it is found to be in accordance with law. In a proceeding for enforcement, the court shall issue an order requiring the appearance of the witness or the production of the evidence or data within a reasonable time under penalty of punishment for contempt in case of contumacious failure to comply.

(e) Prompt notice shall be given of the denial in whole or in part of a written application, petition, or other request of an interested person made in connection with any agency proceeding. Except in affirming a prior denial or when the denial is self-explanatory, the notice shall be accompanied by a brief statement of the grounds for denial.

§ 556. Hearings; presiding employees; powers and duties; burden of proof; evidence; record as basis of decision

(a) This section applies, according to the provisions thereof, to hearings required by section 553 or 554 of this title to be conducted in accordance with this section.

(b) There shall preside at the taking of evidence —

(1) the agency;

(2) one or more members of the body which comprises the agency; or

(3) one or more administrative law judges appointed under section 3105 of this title.

This subchapter does not supersede the conduct of specified classes of proceedings, in whole or in part, by or before boards or other employees specially provided for by or designated under statute. The functions of presiding employees and of employees participating in decisions in accordance with section 557 of this title shall be conducted in an impartial manner. A presiding or participating employee may at any time disqualify himself. On the filing in good faith of a timely and sufficient affidavit of personal bias or other disqualification of a presiding or participating employee, the agency shall determine the matter as a part of the record and decision in the case.

(c) Subject to published rules of the agency and within its powers, employees presiding at hearings may —

(1) administer oaths and affirmations;

(2) issue subpenas authorized by law;

(3) rule on offers of proof and receive relevant evidence;

(4) take depositions or have depositions taken when the ends of justice would be served;

(5) regulate the course of the hearing;

(6) hold conferences for the settlement or simplification of the issues by consent of the parties or by the use of alternative means of dispute resolution as provided in subchapter IV of this chapter;

(7) inform the parties as to the availability of one or more alternative means of dispute resolution, and encourage use of such methods;

(8) require the attendance at any conference held pursuant to paragraph (6) of at least one representative of each party who has authority to negotiate concerning resolution of issues in controversy;

(9) dispose of procedural requests or similar matters;

(10) make or recommend decisions in accordance with section 557 of this title; and

(11) take other action authorized by agency rule consistent with this subchapter.

(d) Except as otherwise provided by statute, the proponent of a rule or order has the burden of proof. Any oral or documentary evidence may be received, but the agency as a matter of policy shall provide for the exclusion of irrelevant, immaterial, or unduly repetitious evidence. A sanction may not be imposed or rule or order issued except on consideration of the whole record or those parts thereof cited by a party and supported by and in accordance with the reliable, probative, and substantial evidence. The agency may, to the extent consistent with the interests of justice and the policy of the underlying statutes administered by the agency, consider a violation of section 557(d) of this title sufficient grounds for a decision adverse to a party who has knowingly committed such violation or knowingly caused such violation to occur. A party is entitled to present his case or defense by oral or documentary evidence, to submit rebuttal evidence, and to conduct such cross-examination as may be required for a full and true disclosure of the facts. In rule making or determining claims for money or benefits or applications for initial licenses an agency may, when a party will not be prejudiced thereby, adopt procedures for the submission of all or part of the evidence in written form.

(e) The transcript of testimony and exhibits, together with all papers and requests filed in the proceeding, constitutes the exclusive record for decision in accordance with section 557 of this title and, on payment of lawfully prescribed costs, shall be made available to the parties. When an agency decision rests on official notice of a material fact not appearing in the evidence in the record, a party is entitled, on timely request, to an opportunity to show the contrary.

§ 557. Initial decisions; conclusiveness; review by agency; submissions by parties; contents of decisions; record

(a) This section applies, according to the provisions thereof, when a hearing is required to be conducted in accordance with section 556 of this title.

(b) When the agency did not preside at the reception of the evidence, the presiding employee or, in cases not subject to section 554(d) of this title, an employee qualified to preside at hearings pursuant to section 556 of this title, shall initially decide the case unless the agency requires, either in specific cases or by general rule, the entire record to be certified to it for decision. When the presiding employee makes an initial decision, that decision then becomes the decision of the agency without further proceedings unless there is an appeal to, or review on motion of, the agency within time provided by rule. On appeal from or review of the initial decision, the agency has all the powers which it would have in making the initial decision except as it may limit the issues on notice or by rule. When the agency makes the decision without having presided at the reception of the evidence, the presiding employee or an employee qualified to preside at hearings pursuant to section 556 of this title shall first recommend a decision, except that in rule making or determining applications for initial licenses —

(1) instead thereof the agency may issue a tentative decision or one of its responsible employees may recommend a decision; or

(2) this procedure may be omitted in a case in which the agency finds on the record that due and timely execution of its functions imperatively and unavoidably so requires.

(c) Before a recommended, initial, or tentative decision, or a decision on agency review of the decision of subordinate employees, the parties are entitled to a reasonable opportunity to submit for the consideration of the employees participating in the decisions —

(1) proposed findings and conclusions; or

(2) exceptions to the decisions or recommended decisions of subordinate employees or to tentative agency decisions; and

(3) supporting reasons for the exceptions or proposed findings or conclusions.

The record shall show the ruling on each finding, conclusion, or exception presented. All decisions, including initial, recommended, and tentative decisions, are a part of the record and shall include a statement of —

(A) findings and conclusions, and the reasons or basis therefor, on all the material issues of fact, law, or discretion presented on the record; and

(B) the appropriate rule, order, sanction, relief, or denial thereof.

(d) (1) In any agency proceeding which is subject to subsection (a) of this section, except to the extent required for the disposition of ex parte matters as authorized by law —

(A) no interested person outside the agency shall make or knowingly cause to be made to any member of the body comprising the agency, administrative law judge, or other employee who is or may reasonably be expected to be involved in the decisional process of the proceeding, an ex parte communication relevant to the merits of the proceeding;

(B) no member of the body comprising the agency, administrative law judge, or other employee who is or may reasonably be expected to be involved in the decisional process of the proceeding, shall make or knowingly cause to be made to any interested person outside the agency an ex parte communication relevant to the merits of the proceeding;

(C) a member of the body comprising the agency, administrative law judge, or other employee who is or may reasonably be expected to be involved in the decisional process of such proceeding who receives, or who makes or knowingly causes to be made, a communication prohibited by this subsection shall place on the public record of the proceeding:

(i) all such written communications;

(ii) memoranda stating the substance of all such oral communications; and

(iii) all written responses, and memoranda stating the substance of all oral responses, to the materials described in clauses (i) and (ii) of this subparagraph;

(D) upon receipt of a communication knowingly made or knowingly caused to be made by a party in violation of this subsection, the agency, administrative law judge, or other employee presiding at the hearing may, to the extent consistent with the interests of justice and the policy of the underlying statutes, require the party to show cause why his claim or interest in the proceeding should not be dismissed, denied, disregarded, or otherwise adversely affected on account of such violation; and

(E) the prohibitions of this subsection shall apply beginning at such time as the agency may designate, but in no case shall they begin to apply later than the time at which a proceeding is noticed for hearing unless the person responsible for the communication has knowledge that it will be noticed, in which case the prohibitions shall apply beginning at the time of his acquisition of such knowledge.

(2) This subsection does not constitute authority to withhold information from Congress.

§ 558. Imposition of sanctions; determination of applications for licenses; suspension, revocation, and expiration of licenses

(a) This section applies, according to the provisions thereof, to the exercise of a power or authority.

(b) A sanction may not be imposed or a substantive rule or order issued except within jurisdiction delegated to the agency and as authorized by law.

(c) When application is made for a license required by law, the agency, with due regard for the rights and privileges of all the interested parties or adversely affected persons and within a reasonable time, shall set and complete proceedings required to be conducted in accordance with sections 556 and 557 of this title or other proceedings required by law and shall make its decision. Except in cases of willfulness or those in which public health, interest, or safety requires otherwise, the withdrawal, suspension, revocation, or annulment of a license is lawful only if, before the institution of agency proceedings therefor, the licensee has been given —

(1) notice by the agency in writing of the facts or conduct which may warrant the action; and

(2) opportunity to demonstrate or achieve compliance with all lawful requirements.

When the licensee has made timely and sufficient application for a renewal or a new license in accordance with agency rules, a license with reference to an activity of a continuing nature does not expire until the application has been finally determined by the agency.

§ 559. Effect on other laws; effect of subsequent statute

This subchapter, chapter 7, and sections 1305, 3105, 3344, 4301(2)(E), 5372, and 7521 of this title, and the provisions of section 5335(a)(B) of this title that relate to administrative law judges, do not limit or repeal additional requirements imposed by statute or otherwise recognized by law. Except as otherwise required by law, requirements or privileges relating to evidence or procedure apply equally to agencies and persons. Each agency is granted the authority necessary to comply with the requirements of this subchapter through the issuance of rules or otherwise. Subsequent statute may not be held to supersede or modify this subchapter, chapter 7, sections 1305, 3105, 3344, 4301(2)(E), 5372, or 7521 of this title, or the provisions of section 5335(a)(B) of this title that relate to administrative law judges, except to the extent that it does so expressly.

SUBCHAPTER III NEGOTIATED RULEMAKING PROCEDURE

§ 561. Purpose

The purpose of this subchapter is to establish a framework for the conduct of negotiated rulemaking, consistent with section 553 of this title, to encourage agencies to use the process when it enhances the informal rulemaking process. Nothing in this subchapter should be construed as an attempt to limit innovation and experimentation with the negotiated rulemaking process or with other innovative rulemaking procedures otherwise authorized by law.

§ 562. Definitions

For the purposes of this subchapter, the term —

(1) "agency" has the same meaning as in section 551(1) of this title;

(2) "consensus" means unanimous concurrence among the interests represented on a negotiated rulemaking committee established under this subchapter, unless such committee —

(A) agrees to define such term to mean a general but not unanimous concurrence; or

(B) agrees upon another specified definition;

(3) "convener" means a person who impartially assists an agency in determining whether establishment of a negotiated rulemaking committee is feasible and appropriate in a particular rulemaking;

(4) "facilitator" means a person who impartially aids in the discussions and negotiations among the members of a negotiated rulemaking committee to develop a proposed rule;

(5) "interest" means, with respect to an issue or matter, multiple parties which have a similar point of view or which are likely to be affected in a similar manner;

(6) "negotiated rulemaking" means rulemaking through the use of a negotiated rulemaking committee;

(7) "negotiated rulemaking committee" or "committee" means an advisory committee established by an agency in accordance with this subchapter and the Federal Advisory Committee Act to consider and discuss issues for the purpose of reaching a consensus in the development of a proposed rule;

(8) "party" has the same meaning as in section 551(3) of this title;

(9) "person" has the same meaning as in section 551(2) of this title;

(10) "rule" has the same meaning as in section 551(4) of this title; and

(11) "rulemaking" means "rule making" as that term is defined in section 551(5) of this title.

§ 563. Determination of need for negotiated rulemaking committee

(a) Determination of Need by the Agency. — An agency may establish a negotiated rulemaking committee to negotiate and develop a proposed rule, if the head of the agency determines that the use of the negotiated rulemaking procedure is in the public interest. In making such a determination, the head of the agency shall consider whether —

(1) there is a need for a rule;

(2) there are a limited number of identifiable interests that will be significantly affected by the rule;

(3) there is a reasonable likelihood that a committee can be convened with a balanced representation of persons who —

(A) can adequately represent the interests identified under paragraph (2); and

(B) are willing to negotiate in good faith to reach a consensus on the proposed rule;

(4) there is a reasonable likelihood that a committee will reach a consensus on the proposed rule within a fixed period of time;

(5) the negotiated rulemaking procedure will not unreasonably delay the notice of proposed rulemaking and the issuance of the final rule;

(6) the agency has adequate resources and is willing to commit such resources, including technical assistance, to the committee; and

(7) the agency, to the maximum extent possible consistent with the legal obligations of the agency, will use the consensus of the committee with respect to the proposed rule as the basis for the rule proposed by the agency for notice and comment.

(b) Use of Conveners.—

(1) Purposes of conveners.— An agency may use the services of a convener to assist the agency in —

(A) identifying persons who will be significantly affected by a proposed rule, including residents of rural areas; and

(B) conducting discussions with such persons to identify the issues of concern to such persons, and to ascertain whether the establishment of a negotiated rulemaking committee is feasible and appropriate in the particular rulemaking.

(2) Duties of conveners.— The convener shall report findings and may make recommendations to the agency. Upon request of the agency, the convener shall ascertain the names of persons who are willing and qualified to represent interests that will be significantly affected by the proposed rule, including residents of rural areas. The report and any recommendations of the convener shall be made available to the public upon request.

§ 564. Publication of notice; applications for membership on committees

(a) Publication of Notice.— If, after considering the report of a convener or conducting its own assessment, an agency decides to establish a negotiated rulemaking committee, the agency shall publish in the Federal Register and, as appropriate, in trade or other specialized publications, a notice which shall include —

(1) an announcement that the agency intends to establish a negotiated rulemaking committee to negotiate and develop a proposed rule;

(2) a description of the subject and scope of the rule to be developed, and the issues to be considered;

(3) a list of the interests which are likely to be significantly affected by the rule;

(4) a list of the persons proposed to represent such interests and the person or persons proposed to represent the agency;

(5) a proposed agenda and schedule for completing the work of the committee, including a target date for publication by the agency of a proposed rule for notice and comment;

(6) a description of administrative support for the committee to be provided by the agency, including technical assistance;

(7) a solicitation for comments on the proposal to establish the committee, and the proposed membership of the negotiated rulemaking committee; and

(8) an explanation of how a person may apply or nominate another person for membership on the committee, as provided under subsection (b).

(b) Applications for Membership or Committee.— Persons who will be significantly affected by a proposed rule and who believe that their interests will not be adequately represented by any person specified in a notice under subsection (a)(4) may apply for, or nominate another person for, membership on the negotiated rulemaking committee to represent such interests with respect to the proposed rule. Each application or nomination shall include —

(1) the name of the applicant or nominee and a description of the interests such person shall represent;

(2) evidence that the applicant or nominee is authorized to represent parties related to the interests the person proposes to represent;

(3) a written commitment that the applicant or nominee shall actively participate in good faith in the development of the rule under consideration; and

(4) the reasons that the persons specified in the notice under subsection (a)(4) do not adequately represent the interests of the person submitting the application or nomination.

(c) Period for Submission of Comments and Applications.— The agency shall provide for a period of at least 30 calendar days for the submission of comments and applications under this section.

§ 565. Establishment of committee

(a) Establishment.—

(1) Determination to establish committee. — If after considering comments and applications submitted under section 564, the agency determines that a negotiated rulemaking committee can adequately represent the interests that will be significantly affected by a proposed rule and that it is feasible and appropriate in the particular rulemaking, the agency may establish a negotiated rulemaking committee. In establishing and administering such a committee, the agency shall comply with the Federal Advisory Committee Act with respect to such committee, except as otherwise provided in this subchapter.

(2) Determination not to establish committee. — If after considering such comments and applications, the agency decides not to establish a negotiated rulemaking committee, the agency shall promptly publish notice of such decision and the reasons therefor in the Federal Register and, as appropriate, in trade or other specialized publications, a copy of which shall be sent to any person who applied for, or nominated another person for membership on the negotiating rulemaking committee to represent such interests with respect to the proposed rule.

(b) Membership.— The agency shall limit membership on a negotiated rulemaking committee to 25 members, unless the agency head determines that a greater number of members is necessary for the functioning of the committee or to achieve balanced membership. Each committee shall include at least one person representing the agency.

(c) Administrative Support.— The agency shall provide appropriate administrative support to the negotiated rulemaking committee, including technical assistance.

§ 566. Conduct of committee activity

(a) Duties of Committee.— Each negotiated rulemaking committee established under this subchapter shall consider the matter proposed by the agency for consideration and shall attempt to reach a consensus concerning a proposed rule with respect to such matter and any other matter the committee determines is relevant to the proposed rule.

(b) Representatives of Agency on Committee.— The person or persons representing the agency on a negotiated rulemaking committee shall participate in the deliberations and activities of the committee with the same rights and responsibilities as other members of the committee, and shall be authorized to fully represent the agency in the discussions and negotiations of the committee.

(c) Selecting Facilitator.— Notwithstanding section 10(e) of the Federal Advisory Committee Act, an agency may nominate either a person from the Federal Government or a person from outside the Federal Government to serve as a facilitator for the negotiations of the committee, subject to the approval of the committee by consensus. If the committee does not approve the nominee of the agency for facilitator, the agency shall submit a substitute nomination. If a committee does not approve any nominee of the agency for facilitator, the committee shall select by consensus a person to serve as facilitator. A person designated to represent the agency in substantive issues may not serve as facilitator or otherwise chair the committee.

(d)   Duties of Facilitator.— A facilitator approved or selected by a negotiated rulemaking committee shall —

(1) chair the meetings of the committee in an impartial manner;

(2) impartially assist the members of the committee in conducting discussions and negotiations; and

(3) manage the keeping of minutes and records as required under section 10(b) and (c) of the Federal Advisory Committee Act, except that any personal notes and materials of the facilitator or of the members of a committee shall not be subject to section 552 of this title.

(e)   Committee Procedures.— A negotiated rulemaking committee established under this subchapter may adopt procedures for the operation of the committee. No provision of section 553 of this title shall apply to the procedures of a negotiated rulemaking committee.

(f)   Report of Committee.— If a committee reaches a consensus on a proposed rule, at the conclusion of negotiations the committee shall transmit to the agency that established the committee a report containing the proposed rule. If the committee does not reach a consensus on a proposed rule, the committee may transmit to the agency a report specifying any areas in which the committee reached a consensus. The committee may include in a report any other information, recommendations, or materials that the committee considers appropriate. Any committee member may include as an addendum to the report additional information, recommendations, or materials.

(g)   Records of Committee.— In addition to the report required by subsection (f), a committee shall submit to the agency the records required under section 10(b) and (c) of the Federal Advisory Committee Act.

§ 567.   Termination of committee

A negotiated rulemaking committee shall terminate upon promulgation of the final rule under consideration, unless the committee's charter contains an earlier termination date or the agency, after consulting the committee, or the committee itself specifies an earlier termination date.

§ 568.   Services, facilities, and payment of committee member expenses

(a)   Services of Conveners and Facilitators.—

(1)   In general.— An agency may employ or enter into contracts for the services of an individual or organization to serve as a convener or facilitator for a negotiated rulemaking committee under this subchapter, or may use the services of a Government employee to act as a convener or a facilitator for such a committee.

(2)   Determination of conflicting interests.— An agency shall determine

whether a person under consideration to serve as convener or facilitator of a committee under paragraph (1) has any financial or other interest that would preclude such person from serving in an impartial and independent manner.

(b) Services and Facilities of Other Entities.— For purposes of this subchapter, an agency may use the services and facilities of other Federal agencies and public and private agencies and instrumentalities with the consent of such agencies and instrumentalities, and with or without reimbursement to such agencies and instrumentalities, and may accept voluntary and uncompensated services without regard to the provisions of section 1342 of title 31. The Federal Mediation and Conciliation Service may provide services and facilities, with or without reimbursement, to assist agencies under this subchapter, including furnishing conveners, facilitators, and training in negotiated rulemaking.

(c) Expenses of Committee Members.— Members of a negotiated rulemaking committee shall be responsible for their own expenses of participation in such committee, except that an agency may, in accordance with section 7(d) of the Federal Advisory Committee Act, pay for a member's reasonable travel and per diem expenses, expenses to obtain technical assistance, and a reasonable rate of compensation, if —

(1) such member certifies a lack of adequate financial resources to participate in the committee; and

(2) the agency determines that such member's participation in the committee is necessary to assure an adequate representation of the member's interest.

(d) Status of Member as Federal Employee.— A member's receipt of funds under this section or section 569 shall not conclusively determine for purposes of sections 202 through 209 of title 18 whether that member is an employee of the United States Government.

§ 569. Encouraging negotiated rulemaking

(a) The President shall designate an agency or designate or establish an interagency committee to facilitate and encourage agency use of negotiated rulemaking. An agency that is considering, planning, or conducting a negotiated rulemaking may consult with such agency or committee for information and assistance.

(b) To carry out the purposes of this subchapter, an agency planning or conducting a negotiated rulemaking may accept, hold, administer, and utilize gifts, devises, and bequests of property, both real and personal if that agency's acceptance and use of such gifts, devises, or bequests do not create a conflict of interest. Gifts and bequests of money and proceeds from sales of other property received as gifts, devises, or bequests shall be deposited in the Treasury and shall be disbursed upon the order of the head of such agency. Property accepted pursuant to this section, and the proceeds thereof, shall be used as nearly as possible in accordance with the terms of the gifts, devises, or bequests.

§ 570. Judicial review

Any agency action relating to establishing, assisting, or terminating a negotiated rulemaking committee under this subchapter shall not be subject to judicial review. Nothing in this section shall bar judicial review of a rule if such judicial review is otherwise provided by law. A rule which is the product of negotiated rulemaking and is subject to judicial review shall not be accorded any greater deference by a court than a rule which is the product of other rulemaking procedures.

SUBCHAPTER IV   ALTERNATIVE MEANS OF DISPUTE RESOLUTION IN THE ADMINISTRATIVE PROCESS

§ 571.   Definitions

For the purposes of this subchapter, the term —

(1) "agency" has the same meaning as in section 551(1) of this title;

(2) "administrative program" includes a Federal function which involves protection of the public interest and the determination of rights, privileges, and obligations of private persons through rule making, adjudication, licensing, or investigation, as those terms are used in subchapter II of this chapter;

(3) "alternative means of dispute resolution" means any procedure that is used to resolve issues in controversy, including, but not limited to, conciliation, facilitation, mediation, factfinding, minitrials, arbitration, and use of ombuds, or any combination thereof;

(4) "award" means any decision by an arbitrator resolving the issues in controversy;

(5) "dispute resolution communication" means any oral or written communication prepared for the purposes of a dispute resolution proceeding, including any memoranda, notes or work product of the neutral, parties or nonparty participant; except that a written agreement to enter into a dispute resolution proceeding, or final written agreement or arbitral award reached as a result of a dispute resolution proceeding, is not a dispute resolution communication;

(6) "dispute resolution proceeding" means any process in which an alternative means of dispute resolution is used to resolve an issue in controversy in which a neutral is appointed and specified parties participate;

(7) "in confidence" means, with respect to information, that the information is provided —

(A) with the expressed intent of the source that it not be disclosed; or

(B) under circumstances that would create the reasonable expectation on behalf of the source that the information will not be disclosed;

(8) "issue in controversy" means an issue which is material to a decision concerning an administrative program of an agency, and with which there is disagreement —

(A) between an agency and persons who would be substantially affected by the decision; or

(B) between persons who would be substantially affected by the decision;

(9) "neutral" means an individual who, with respect to an issue in controversy, functions specifically to aid the parties in resolving the controversy;

(10) "party" means —

(A) for a proceeding with named parties, the same as in section 551(3) of this title; and

(B) for a proceeding without named parties, a person who will be significantly affected by the decision in the proceeding and who participates in the proceeding;

(11) "person" has the same meaning as in section 551(2) of this title; and

(12) "roster" means a list of persons qualified to provide services as neutrals.

§ 572. General authority

(a) An agency may use a dispute resolution proceeding for the resolution of an issue in controversy that relates to an administrative program, if the parties agree to such proceeding.

(b) An agency shall consider not using a dispute resolution proceeding if —

(1) a definitive or authoritative resolution of the matter is required for precedential value, and such a proceeding is not likely to be accepted generally as an authoritative precedent;

(2) the matter involves or may bear upon significant questions of Government policy that require additional procedures before a final resolution may be made, and such a proceeding would not likely serve to develop a recommended policy for the agency;

(3) maintaining established policies is of special importance, so that variations among individual decisions are not increased and such a proceeding would not likely reach consistent results among individual decisions;

(4) the matter significantly affects persons or organizations who are not parties to the proceeding;

(5) a full public record of the proceeding is important, and a dispute resolution proceeding cannot provide such a record; and

(6) the agency must maintain continuing jurisdiction over the matter with authority to alter the disposition of the matter in the light of changed circumstances, and a dispute resolution proceeding would interfere with the agency's fulfilling that requirement.

(c) Alternative means of dispute resolution authorized under this subchapter are voluntary procedures which supplement rather than limit other available agency dispute resolution techniques.

§ 573. Neutrals

(a) A neutral may be a permanent or temporary officer or employee of the Federal Government or any other individual who is acceptable to the parties to a dispute resolution proceeding. A neutral shall have no official, financial, or personal conflict of interest with respect to the issues in controversy, unless such interest is fully disclosed in writing to all parties and all parties agree that the neutral may serve.

(b) A neutral who serves as a conciliator, facilitator, or mediator serves at the will of the parties.

(c) The President shall designate an agency or designate or establish an interagency committee to facilitate and encourage agency use of dispute resolution under this subchapter. Such agency or interagency committee, in consultation with other appropriate Federal agencies and professional organizations experienced in matters concerning dispute resolution, shall —

(1) encourage and facilitate agency use of alternative means of dispute resolution; and

(2) develop procedures that permit agencies to obtain the services of neutrals on an expedited basis.

(d) An agency may use the services of one or more employees of other agencies to serve as neutrals in dispute resolution proceedings. The agencies may enter into an interagency agreement that provides for the reimbursement by the user agency or the parties of the full or partial cost of the services of such an employee.

(e) Any agency may enter into a contract with any person for services as a neutral, or for training in connection with alternative means of dispute resolution. The parties in a dispute resolution proceeding shall agree on compensation for the neutral that is fair and reasonable to the Government.

§ 574. Confidentiality

(a) Except as provided in subsections (d) and (e), a neutral in a dispute resolution proceeding shall not voluntarily disclose or through discovery or compulsory process be required to disclose any dispute resolution communication or any communication provided in confidence to the neutral, unless —

(1) all parties to the dispute resolution proceeding and the neutral consent in writing, and, if the dispute resolution communication was provided by a nonparty participant, that participant also consents in writing;

(2) the dispute resolution communication has already been made public;

(3) the dispute resolution communication is required by statute to be made public, but a neutral should make such communication public only if no other person is reasonably available to disclose the communication; or

(4) a court determines that such testimony or disclosure is necessary to —

(A) prevent a manifest injustice;

(B) help establish a violation of law; or

(C) prevent harm to the public health or safety,

of sufficient magnitude in the particular case to outweigh the integrity of dispute resolution proceedings in general by reducing the confidence of parties in future cases that their communications will remain confidential.

(b) A party to a dispute resolution proceeding shall not voluntarily disclose or through discovery or compulsory process be required to disclose any dispute resolution communication, unless —

(1) the communication was prepared by the party seeking disclosure;

(2) all parties to the dispute resolution proceeding consent in writing;

(3) the dispute resolution communication has already been made public;

(4) the dispute resolution communication is required by statute to be made public;

(5) a court determines that such testimony or disclosure is necessary to —

(A) prevent a manifest injustice;

(B) help establish a violation of law; or

(C) prevent harm to the public health and safety,

of sufficient magnitude in the particular case to outweigh the integrity of dispute resolution proceedings in general by reducing the confidence of parties in future cases that their communications will remain confidential;

(6) the dispute resolution communication is relevant to determining the existence or meaning of an agreement or award that resulted from the dispute resolution proceeding or to the enforcement of such an agreement or award; or

(7) except for dispute resolution communications generated by the neutral, the dispute resolution communication was provided to or was available to all parties to the dispute resolution proceeding.

(c) Any dispute resolution communication that is disclosed in violation of subsection (a) or (b), shall not be admissible in any proceeding relating to the issues in controversy with respect to which the communication was made.

(d) (1) The parties may agree to alternative confidential procedures for disclosures by a neutral. Upon such agreement the parties shall inform the neutral before the commencement of the dispute resolution proceeding of any modifications to the provisions of subsection (a) that will govern the confidentiality of the dispute resolution proceeding. If the parties do not so inform the neutral, subsection (a) shall apply.

(2) To qualify for the exemption established under subsection (j), an alternative confidential procedure under this subsection may not provide for less disclosure than the confidential procedures otherwise provided under this section.

(e) If a demand for disclosure, by way of discovery request or other legal process, is made upon a neutral regarding a dispute resolution communication, the neutral shall make reasonable efforts to notify the parties and any affected nonparty participants of the demand. Any party or affected nonparty participant who receives such notice and within 15 calendar days does not offer to defend a refusal of the neutral to disclose the requested information shall have waived any objection to such disclosure.

(f) Nothing in this section shall prevent the discovery or admissibility of any evidence that is otherwise discoverable, merely because the evidence was presented in the course of a dispute resolution proceeding.

(g) Subsections (a) and (b) shall have no effect on the information and data that are necessary to document an agreement reached or order issued pursuant to a dispute resolution proceeding.

(h) Subsections (a) and (b) shall not prevent the gathering of information for research or educational purposes, in cooperation with other agencies, governmental entities, or dispute resolution programs, so long as the parties and the specific issues in controversy are not identifiable.

(i) Subsections (a) and (b) shall not prevent use of a dispute resolution communication to resolve a dispute between the neutral in a dispute resolution proceeding and a party to or participant in such proceeding, so long as such dispute resolution communication is disclosed only to the extent necessary to resolve such dispute.

(j) A dispute resolution communication which is between a neutral and a party and which may not be disclosed under this section shall also be exempt from disclosure under section 552(b)(3).

§ 575.　Authorization of arbitration

(a) (1) Arbitration may be used as an alternative means of dispute resolution whenever all parties consent. Consent may be obtained either before or after an issue in controversy has arisen. A party may agree to —

(A) submit only certain issues in controversy to arbitration; or

(B) arbitration on the condition that the award must be within a range of possible outcomes.

(2) The arbitration agreement that sets forth the subject matter submitted to the arbitrator shall be in writing. Each such arbitration agreement shall specify a maximum award that may be issued by the arbitrator and may specify other conditions limiting the range of possible outcomes.

(3) An agency may not require any person to consent to arbitration as a condition of entering into a contract or obtaining a benefit.

(b) An officer or employee of an agency shall not offer to use arbitration for the resolution of issues in controversy unless such officer or employee —

(1) would otherwise have authority to enter into a settlement concerning the matter; or

(2) is otherwise specifically authorized by the agency to consent to the use of

arbitration.

(c) Prior to using binding arbitration under this subchapter, the head of an agency, in consultation with the Attorney General and after taking into account the factors in section 572(b), shall issue guidance on the appropriate use of binding arbitration and when an officer or employee of the agency has authority to settle an issue in controversy through binding arbitration.

§ 576. Enforcement of arbitration agreements

An agreement to arbitrate a matter to which this subchapter applies is enforceable pursuant to section 4 of title 9, and no action brought to enforce such an agreement shall be dismissed nor shall relief therein be denied on the grounds that it is against the United States or that the United States is an indispensable party.

§ 577. Arbitrators

(a) The parties to an arbitration proceeding shall be entitled to participate in the selection of the arbitrator.

(b) The arbitrator shall be a neutral who meets the criteria of section 573 of this title.

§ 578. Authority of the arbitrator

An arbitrator to whom a dispute is referred under this subchapter may —

(1) regulate the course of and conduct arbitral hearings;

(2) administer oaths and affirmations;

(3) compel the attendance of witnesses and production of evidence at the hearing under the provisions of section 7 of title 9 only to the extent the agency involved is otherwise authorized by law to do so; and

(4) make awards.

§ 579. Arbitration proceedings

(a) The arbitrator shall set a time and place for the hearing on the dispute and shall notify the parties not less than 5 days before the hearing.

(b) Any party wishing a record of the hearing shall —

(1) be responsible for the preparation of such record;

(2) notify the other parties and the arbitrator of the preparation of such record;

(3) furnish copies to all identified parties and the arbitrator; and

(4) pay all costs for such record, unless the parties agree otherwise or the arbitrator determines that the costs should be apportioned.

(c) (1) The parties to the arbitration are entitled to be heard, to present evidence material to the controversy, and to cross-examine witnesses appearing at the hearing.

(2) The arbitrator may, with the consent of the parties, conduct all or part of the hearing by telephone, television, computer, or other electronic means, if each party has an opportunity to participate.

(3) The hearing shall be conducted expeditiously and in an informal manner.

(4) The arbitrator may receive any oral or documentary evidence, except that irrelevant, immaterial, unduly repetitious, or privileged evidence may be excluded by the arbitrator.

(5) The arbitrator shall interpret and apply relevant statutory and regulatory requirements, legal precedents, and policy directives.

(d) No interested person shall make or knowingly cause to be made to the arbitrator an unauthorized ex parte communication relevant to the merits of the proceeding, unless the parties agree otherwise. If a communication is made in violation of this subsection, the arbitrator shall ensure that a memorandum of the communication is prepared and made a part of the record, and that an opportunity for rebuttal is allowed. Upon receipt of a communication made in violation of this subsection, the arbitrator may, to the extent consistent with the interests of justice and the policies underlying this subchapter, require the offending party to show cause why the claim of such party should not be resolved against such party as a result of the improper conduct.

(e) The arbitrator shall make the award within 30 days after the close of the hearing, or the date of the filing of any briefs authorized by the arbitrator, whichever date is later, unless —

(1) the parties agree to some other time limit; or

(2) the agency provides by rule for some other time limit.

§ 580.　Arbitration awards

(a) (1) Unless the agency provides otherwise by rule, the award in an arbitration proceeding under this subchapter shall include a brief, informal discussion of the factual and legal basis for the award, but formal findings of fact or conclusions of law shall not be required.

(2) The prevailing parties shall file the award with all relevant agencies, along with proof of service on all parties.

(b) The award in an arbitration proceeding shall become final 30 days after it is served on all parties. Any agency that is a party to the proceeding may extend this 30-day period for an additional 30-day period by serving a notice of such extension on all other parties before the end of the first 30-day period.

(c) A final award is binding on the parties to the arbitration proceeding, and may be enforced pursuant to sections 9 through 13 of title 9. No action brought to enforce such an award shall be dismissed nor shall relief therein be denied on the grounds that it is against the United States or that the United States is an indispensable party.

(d) An award entered under this subchapter in an arbitration proceeding may not serve as an estoppel in any other proceeding for any issue that was resolved in the proceeding. Such an award also may not be used as precedent or otherwise be considered in any factually unrelated proceeding, whether conducted under this subchapter, by an agency, or in a court, or in any other arbitration proceeding.

§ 581. Judicial Review

(a) Notwithstanding any other provision of law, any person adversely affected or aggrieved by an award made in an arbitration proceeding conducted under this subchapter may bring an action for review of such award only pursuant to the provisions of sections 9 through 13 of title 9.

(b) A decision by an agency to use or not to use a dispute resolution proceeding under this subchapter shall be committed to the discretion of the agency and shall not be subject to judicial review, except that arbitration shall be subject to judicial review under section 10(b).

Section 582 was repealed. Sections 583 (support services) and 584 (authorization of appropriations) are not reproduced.

CHAPTER 6   THE ANALYSIS OF REGULATORY FUNCTIONS

§ 601.   Definitions

For purposes of this chapter —

(1) the term "agency" means an agency as defined in section 551(1) of this title;

(2) the term "rule" means any rule for which the agency publishes a general notice of proposed rulemaking pursuant to section 553(b) of this title, or any other law, including any rule of general applicability governing Federal grants to State and local governments for which the agency provides an opportunity for notice and public comment, except that the term "rule" does not include a rule of particular applicability relating to rates, wages, corporate or financial structures or reorganizations thereof, prices, facilities, appliances, services, or allowances therefor or to valuations, costs or accounting, or practices relating to such rates, wages, structures, prices, appliances, services, or allowances;

(3) the term "small business" has the same meaning as the term "small business concern" under section 3 of the Small Business Act, unless an agency, after consultation with the Office of Advocacy of the Small Business Administration and after opportunity for public comment, establishes one or more definitions of such term which are appropriate to the activities of the agency and publishes such definition(s) in the Federal Register;

(4) the term "small organization" means any not-for-profit enterprise which is independently owned and operated and is not dominant in its field, unless an agency establishes, after opportunity for public comment, one or more definitions of such term which are appropriate to the activities of the agency and publishes such definition(s) in the Federal Register;

(5) the term "small governmental jurisdiction" means governments of cities, counties, towns, townships, villages, school districts, or special districts, with a population of less than fifty thousand, unless an agency establishes, after opportunity for public comment, one or more definitions of such term which are appropriate to the activities of the agency and which are based on such factors as location in rural or sparsely populated areas or limited revenues due to the population of such jurisdiction, and publishes such definition(s) in the Federal Register;

(6) the term "small entity" shall have the same meaning as the terms "small business", "small organization" and "small governmental jurisdiction" defined in paragraphs (3), (4) and (5) of this section; and

(7) the term "collection of information"—

(A) means the obtaining, causing to be obtained, soliciting, or requiring the disclosure to third parties or the public, of facts or opinions by or for an agency, regardless of form or format, calling for either —

(i) answers to identical questions posed to, or identical reporting or recordkeeping requirements imposed on, 10 or more persons, other than agencies, instrumentalities, or employees of the United States; or

(ii) answers to questions posed to agencies, instrumentalities, or employees of the United States which are to be used for general statistical purposes; and

(B) shall not include a collection of information described under section 3518(c)(1) of title 44, United States Code.

(8) Recordkeeping requirement. — The term "recordkeeping requirement" means a requirement imposed by an agency on persons to maintain specified records.

§ 602. Regulatory agenda

(a) During the months of October and April of each year, each agency shall publish in the Federal Register a regulatory flexibility agenda which shall contain —

(1) a brief description of the subject area of any rule which the agency expects to propose or promulgate which is likely to have a significant economic impact on a substantial number of small entities;

(2) a summary of the nature of any such rule under consideration for each subject area listed in the agenda pursuant to paragraph (1), the objectives and legal basis for the issuance of the rule, and an approximate schedule for completing action on any rule for which the agency has issued a general notice of proposed rulemaking, and

(3) the name and telephone number of an agency official knowledgeable concerning the items listed in paragraph (1).

(b) Each regulatory flexibility agenda shall be transmitted to the Chief Counsel for Advocacy of the Small Business Administration for comment, if any.

(c) Each agency shall endeavor to provide notice of each regulatory flexibility agenda to small entities or their representatives through direct notification or publication of the agenda in publications likely to be obtained by such small entities and shall invite comments upon each subject area on the agenda.

(d) Nothing in this section precludes an agency from considering or acting on any matter not included in a regulatory flexibility agenda, or requires an agency to consider or act on any matter listed in such agenda.

§ 603. Initial regulatory flexibility analysis

(a) Whenever an agency is required by section 553 of this title, or any other law, to publish general notice of proposed rulemaking for any proposed rule, or publishes a notice of proposed rulemaking for an interpretative rule involving the internal revenue laws of the United States, the agency shall prepare and make available for public comment an initial regulatory flexibility analysis. Such analysis shall describe the impact of the proposed rule on small entities. The initial regulatory flexibility analysis or a summary shall be published in the Federal Register at the time of the publication of general notice of proposed rulemaking for the rule. The agency shall transmit a copy of the initial regulatory flexibility analysis to the Chief Counsel for Advocacy of the Small Business Administration. In the case of an interpretative rule involving the internal revenue laws of the United States, this chapter applies to interpretative rules published in the Federal Register for codification in the Code of Federal Regulations, but only to the extent that such interpretative rules impose on small entities a collection of information requirement.

(b) Each initial regulatory flexibility analysis required under this section shall contain —

(1) a description of the reasons why action by the agency is being considered;

(2) a succinct statement of the objectives of, and legal basis for, the proposed rule;

(3) a description of and, where feasible, an estimate of the number of small entities to which the proposed rule will apply;

(4) a description of the projected reporting, recordkeeping and other compliance requirements of the proposed rule, including an estimate of the classes of small entities which will be subject to the requirement and the type of professional skills necessary for preparation of the report or record;

(5) an identification, to the extent practicable, of all relevant Federal rules which may duplicate, overlap or conflict with the proposed rule.

(c) Each initial regulatory flexibility analysis shall also contain a description of any significant alternatives to the proposed rule which accomplish the stated objectives of applicable statutes and which minimize any significant economic impact of the proposed rule on small entities. Consistent with the stated objectives of applicable statutes, the analysis shall discuss significant alternatives such as —

(1) the establishment of differing compliance or reporting requirements or timetables that take into account the resources available to small entities;

(2) the clarification, consolidation, or simplification of compliance and reporting requirements under the rule for such small entities;

(3) the use of performance rather than design standards; and

(4) an exemption from coverage of the rule, or any part thereof, for such small entities.

§ 604. Final regulatory flexibility analysis

(a) When an agency promulgates a final rule under section 553 of this title, after being required by that section or any other law to publish a general notice of proposed rulemaking, or promulgates a final interpretative rule involving the internal revenue laws of the United States as described in section 603(a), the agency shall prepare a final regulatory flexibility analysis. Each final regulatory flexibility analysis shall contain —

(1) a succinct statement of the need for, and objectives of, the rule;

(2) a summary of the significant issues raised by the public comments in response to the initial regulatory flexibility analysis, a summary of the assessment of the agency of such issues, and a statement of any changes made in the proposed rule as a result of such comments;

(3) a description of and an estimate of the number of small entities to which the rule will apply or an explanation of why no such estimate is available;

(4) a description of the projected reporting, recordkeeping and other compliance requirements of the rule, including an estimate of the classes of small entities which will be subject to the requirement and the type of professional skills necessary for preparation of the report or record; and

(5) a description of the steps the agency has taken to minimize the significant economic impact on small entities consistent with the stated objectives of applicable statutes, including a statement of the factual, policy, and legal reasons for selecting the alternative adopted in the final rule and why each one of the other significant alternatives to the rule considered by the agency which affect the impact on small entities was rejected.

(b) The agency shall make copies of the final regulatory flexibility analysis available to members of the public and shall publish in the Federal Register such analysis or a summary thereof.

§ 605. Avoidance of duplicative or unnecessary analyses

(a) Any Federal agency may perform the analyses required by sections 602, 603, and 604 of this title in conjunction with or as a part of any other agenda or analysis required by any other law if such other analysis satisfies the provisions of such sections.

(b) Sections 603 and 604 of this title shall not apply to any proposed or final rule if the head of the agency certifies that the rule will not, if promulgated, have a significant economic impact on a substantial number of small entities. If the head of the agency makes a certification under the preceding sentence, the agency shall publish such certification in the Federal Register at the time of publication of general notice of proposed rulemaking for the rule or at the time of publication of the final rule, along with a statement providing the factual basis for such certification. The agency shall provide such certification and statement to the Chief Counsel for Advocacy of the Small Business Administration.

(c) In order to avoid duplicative action, an agency may consider a series of closely related rules as one rule for the purposes of sections 602, 603, 604 and 610 of this title.

§ 606. Effect on other law

The requirements of sections 603 and 604 of this title do not alter in any manner standards otherwise applicable by law to agency action.

§ 607. Preparation of analyses

In complying with the provisions of sections 603 and 604 of this title, an agency may provide either a quantifiable or numerical description of the effects of a proposed rule or alternatives to the proposed rule, or more general descriptive statements if quantification is not practicable or reliable.

§ 608. Procedure for waiver or delay of completion

(a) An agency head may waive or delay the completion of some or all of the requirements of section 603 of this title by publishing in the Federal Register, not later than the date of publication of the final rule, a written finding, with reasons therefor, that the final rule is being promulgated in response to an emergency that makes compliance or timely compliance with the provisions of section 603 of this title impracticable.

(b) Except as provided in section 605(b), an agency head may not waive the requirements of section 604 of this title. An agency head may delay the completion of the requirements of section 604 of this title for a period of not more than one hundred and eighty days after the date of publication in the Federal Register of a final rule by publishing in the Federal Register, not later than such date of publication, a written finding, with reasons therefor, that the final rule is being promulgated in response to an emergency that makes timely compliance with the provisions of section 604 of this title impracticable. If the agency has not prepared a final regulatory analysis pursuant to section 604 of this title within one hundred and eighty days from the date of publication of the final rule, such rule shall lapse and have no effect. Such rule shall not be repromulgated until a final regulatory flexibility analysis has been completed by the agency.

§ 609. Procedures for gathering comments

(a) When any rule is promulgated which will have a significant economic impact on a substantial number of small entities, the head of the agency promulgating the rule or the official of the agency with statutory responsibility for the promulgation of the rule shall assure that small entities have been given an opportunity to participate in the rulemaking for the rule through the reasonable use of techniques such as —

(1) the inclusion in an advanced notice of proposed rulemaking, if issued, of a statement that the proposed rule may have a significant economic effect on a substantial number of small entities;

(2) the publication of general notice of proposed rulemaking in publications likely to be obtained by small entities;

(3) the direct notification of interested small entities;

(4) the conduct of open conferences or public hearings concerning the rule for small entities including soliciting and receiving comments over computer networks; and

(5) the adoption or modification of agency procedural rules to reduce the cost or complexity of participation in the rulemaking by small entities.

(b) Prior to publication of an initial regulatory flexibility analysis which a covered agency is required to conduct by this chapter —

(1) a covered agency shall notify the Chief Counsel for Advocacy of the Small Business Administration and provide the Chief Counsel with information on the potential impacts of the proposed rule on small entities and the type of small entities that might be affected;

(2) not later than 15 days after the date of receipt of the materials described in paragraph (1), the Chief Counsel shall identify individuals representative of affected small entities for the purpose of obtaining advice and recommendations from those individuals about the potential impacts of the proposed rule;

(3) the agency shall convene a review panel for such rule consisting wholly of full time Federal employees of the office within the agency responsible for carrying out the proposed rule, the Office of Information and Regulatory Affairs within the Office of Management and Budget, and the Chief Counsel;

(4) the panel shall review any material the agency has prepared in connection with this chapter, including any draft proposed rule, collect advice and recommendations of each individual small entity representative identified by the agency after consultation with the Chief Counsel, on issues related to subsections 603(b), paragraphs (3), (4) and (5) and 603(c);

(5) not later than 60 days after the date a covered agency convenes a review panel pursuant to paragraph (3), the review panel shall report on the comments of the small entity representatives and its findings as to issues related to subsections 603(b), paragraphs (3), (4) and (5) and 603(c), provided that such report shall be made public as part of the rulemaking record; and

(6) where appropriate, the agency shall modify the proposed rule, the initial regulatory flexibility analysis or the decision on whether an initial regulatory flexibility analysis is required.

(c) An agency may in its discretion apply subsection (b) to rules that the agency intends to certify under subsection 605(b), but the agency believes may have a greater than de minimis impact on a substantial number of small entities.

(d) For purposes of this section, the term "covered agency" means the Environmental Protection Agency and the Occupational Safety and Health Administration of the Department of Labor.

(e) The Chief Counsel for Advocacy, in consultation with the individuals identified in subsection (b)(2), and with the Administrator of the Office of Information and Regulatory Affairs within the Office of Management and Budget, may waive the requirements of subsections (b)(3), (b)(4), and (b)(5) by including in the rulemaking record a written finding, with reasons therefor, that those requirements would not advance the effective participation of small entities in the rulemaking process. For purposes of this subsection, the factors to be considered in making such a finding are as follows:

(1) In developing a proposed rule, the extent to which the covered agency consulted with individuals representative of affected small entities with respect to the potential impacts of the rule and took such concerns into consideration.

(2) Special circumstances requiring prompt issuance of the rule.

(3) Whether the requirements of subsection (b) would provide the individuals identified in subsection (b)(2) with a competitive advantage relative to other small entities.

§ 610.   Periodic review of rules

(a) Within one hundred and eighty days after the effective date of this chapter, each agency shall publish in the Federal Register a plan for the periodic review of the rules issued by the agency which have or will have a significant economic impact upon a substantial number of small entities. Such plan may be amended by the agency at any time by publishing the revision in the Federal Register. The purpose of the review shall be to determine whether such rules should be continued without change, or should be amended or rescinded, consistent with the stated objectives of applicable statutes, to minimize any significant economic impact of the rules upon a substantial number of such small entities. The plan shall provide for the review of all such agency rules existing on the effective date of this chapter within ten years of that date and for the review of such rules adopted after the effective date of this chapter within ten years of the publication of such rules as the final rule. If the head of the agency determines that completion of the review of existing rules is not feasible by the established date, he shall so certify in a statement published in the Federal Register and may extend the completion date by one year at a time for a total of not more than five years.

(b) In reviewing rules to minimize any significant economic impact of the rule on a substantial number of small entities in a manner consistent with the stated objectives of applicable statutes, the agency shall consider the following factors —

(1) the continued need for the rule;

(2) the nature of complaints or comments received concerning the rule from the public;

(3) the complexity of the rule;

(4) the extent to which the rule overlaps, duplicates or conflicts with other Federal rules, and, to the extent feasible, with State and local governmental rules; and

(5) the length of time since the rule has been evaluated or the degree to which technology, economic conditions, or other factors have changed in the area affected by the rule.

(c) Each year, each agency shall publish in the Federal Register a list of the rules which have a significant economic impact on a substantial number of small entities, which are to be reviewed pursuant to this section during the succeeding twelve months. The list shall include a brief description of each rule and the need for and legal basis of such rule and shall invite public comment upon the rule.

§ 611. Judicial review

(a) (1) For any rule subject to this chapter, a small entity that is adversely affected or aggrieved by final agency action is entitled to judicial review of agency compliance with the requirements of sections 601, 604, 605(b), 608(b), and 610 in accordance with chapter 7. Agency compliance with sections 607 and 609(a) shall be judicially reviewable in connection with judicial review of section 604.

(2) Each court having jurisdiction to review such rule for compliance with section 553, or under any other provision of law, shall have jurisdiction to review any claims of noncompliance with sections 601, 604, 605(b), 608(b), and 610 in accordance with chapter 7. Agency compliance with sections 607 and 609(a) shall be judicially reviewable in connection with judicial review of section 604.

(3) (A) A small entity may seek such review during the period beginning on the date of final agency action and ending one year later, except that where a provision of law requires that an action challenging a final agency action be commenced before the expiration of one year, such lesser period shall apply to an action for judicial review under this section.

(B) In the case where an agency delays the issuance of a final regulatory flexibility analysis pursuant to section 608(b) of this chapter, an action for judicial review under this section shall be filed not later than —

(i) one year after the date the analysis is made available to the public, or

(ii) where a provision of law requires that an action challenging a final agency regulation be commenced before the expiration of the 1-year period, the number of days specified in such provision of law that is after the date the analysis is made available to the public.

(4) In granting any relief in an action under this section, the court shall order the agency to take corrective action consistent with this chapter and chapter 7, including, but not limited to —

(A) remanding the rule to the agency, and

(B) deferring the enforcement of the rule against small entities unless the court finds that continued enforcement of the rule is in the public interest.

(5) Nothing in this subsection shall be construed to limit the authority of any court to stay the effective date of any rule or provision thereof under any other provision of law or to grant any other relief in addition to the requirements of this section.

(b) In an action for the judicial review of a rule, the regulatory flexibility analysis for such rule, including an analysis prepared or corrected pursuant to paragraph (a)(4), shall constitute part of the entire record of agency action in connection with such review.

(c) Compliance or noncompliance by an agency with the provisions of this chapter shall be subject to judicial review only in accordance with this section.

(d) Nothing in this section bars judicial review of any other impact statement or similar analysis required by any other law if judicial review of such statement or analysis is otherwise permitted by law.

§ 612. Reports and intervention rights

(a) The Chief Counsel for Advocacy of the Small Business Administration shall monitor agency compliance with this chapter and shall report at least annually thereon to the President and to the Committees on the Judiciary and Small Business of the Senate and House of Representatives.

(b) The Chief Counsel for Advocacy of the Small Business Administration is authorized to appear as amicus curiae in any action brought in a court of the United States to review a rule. In any such action, the Chief Counsel is authorized to present his or her views with respect to compliance with this chapter, the adequacy of the rulemaking record with respect to small entities and the effect of the rule on small entities.

(c) A court of the United States shall grant the application of the Chief Counsel for Advocacy of the Small Business Administration to appear in any such action for the purposes described in subsection (b).

§ 701. Application; definitions

(a) This chapter applies, according to the provisions thereof, except to the extent that —

(1) statutes preclude judicial review; or

(2) agency action is committed to agency discretion by law.

(b) For the purpose of this chapter —

(1) "agency" means each authority of the Government of the United States, whether or not it is within or subject to review by another agency, but does not include —

(A) the Congress;

(B) the courts of the United States;

(C) the governments of the territories or possessions of the United States;

(D) the government of the District of Columbia;

(E) agencies composed of representatives of the parties or of representatives of organizations of the parties to the disputes determined by them;

(F) courts martial and military commissions;

(G) military authority exercised in the field in time of war or in occupied territory; or

(H) functions conferred by sections 1738, 1739, 1743, and 1744 of title 12; chapter 2 of title 41; subchapter II of chapter 471 of title 49; or sections 1884, 1891–1902, and former section 1641(b)(2), of title 50, appendix; and

(2) "person", "rule", "order", "license", "sanction", "relief", and "agency action" have the meanings given them by section 551 of this title.

§ 702. Right of review

A person suffering legal wrong because of agency action, or adversely affected or aggrieved by agency action within the meaning of a relevant statute, is entitled to judicial review thereof. An action in a court of the United States seeking relief other than money damages and stating a claim that an agency or an officer or employee thereof acted or failed to act in an official capacity or under color of legal authority shall not be dismissed nor relief therein be denied on the ground that it is against the United States or that the United States is an indispensable party. The United States may be named as a defendant in any such action, and a judgment or decree may be entered against the United States: Provided, That any mandatory or injunctive decree shall specify the Federal officer or officers (by name or by title), and their successors in office, personally responsible for compliance. Nothing herein (1) affects other limitations on judicial review or the power or duty of the court to dismiss any action or deny relief on any other appropriate legal or equitable ground; or (2) confers authority to grant relief if any other statute that grants consent to suit expressly or impliedly forbids the relief which is sought.

§ 703. Form and venue of proceeding

The form of proceeding for judicial review is the special statutory review proceeding relevant to the subject matter in a court specified by statute or, in the absence or inadequacy thereof, any applicable form of legal action, including actions for declaratory judgments or writs of prohibitory or mandatory injunction or habeas corpus, in a court of competent jurisdiction. If no special statutory review proceeding is applicable, the action for judicial review may be brought against the United States, the agency by its official title, or the appropriate officer. Except to the extent that prior, adequate, and exclusive opportunity for judicial review is provided by law, agency action is subject to judicial review in civil or criminal proceedings for judicial enforcement.

§ 704. Actions reviewable

Agency action made reviewable by statute and final agency action for which there is no other adequate remedy in a court are subject to judicial review. A preliminary, procedural, or intermediate agency action or ruling not directly reviewable is subject to review on the review of the final agency action. Except as otherwise expressly required by statute, agency action otherwise final is final for the purposes of this section whether or not there has been presented or determined an application for a declaratory order, for any form of reconsideration, or, unless the agency otherwise requires by rule and provides that the action meanwhile is inoperative, for an appeal to superior agency authority.

§ 705. Relief pending review

When an agency finds that justice so requires, it may postpone the effective date of action taken by it, pending judicial review. On such conditions as may be required and to the extent necessary to prevent irreparable injury, the reviewing court, including the court to which a case may be taken on appeal from or on application for certiorari or other writ to a reviewing court, may issue all necessary and appropriate process to postpone the effective date of an agency action or to preserve status or rights pending conclusion of the review proceedings.

§ 706. Scope of review

To the extent necessary to decision and when presented, the reviewing court shall decide all relevant questions of law, interpret constitutional and statutory provisions, and determine the meaning or applicability of the terms of an agency action. The reviewing court shall —

(1) compel agency action unlawfully withheld or unreasonably delayed; and

(2) hold unlawful and set aside agency action, findings, and conclusions found to be —

(A) arbitrary, capricious, an abuse of discretion, or otherwise not in accordance with law;

(B) contrary to constitutional right, power, privilege, or immunity;

(C) in excess of statutory jurisdiction, authority, or limitations, or short of statutory right;

(D) without observance of procedure required by law;

(E) unsupported by substantial evidence in a case subject to sections 556 and 557 of this title or otherwise reviewed on the record of an agency hearing provided by statute; or

(F) unwarranted by the facts to the extent that the facts are subject to trial de novo by the reviewing court.

In making the foregoing determinations, the court shall review the whole record or those parts of it cited by a party, and due account shall be taken of the rule of prejudicial error.

CHAPTER 8 CONGRESSIONAL REVIEW OF AGENCY RULEMAKING

§ 801. Congressional review

(a) (1) (A) Before a rule can take effect, the Federal agency promulgating such rule shall submit to each House of the Congress and to the Comptroller General a report containing —

(i) a copy of the rule;

(ii) a concise general statement relating to the rule, including whether it is a major rule; and

(iii) the proposed effective date of the rule.

(B) On the date of the submission of the report under subparagraph (A), the Federal agency promulgating the rule shall submit to the Comptroller General and make available to each House of Congress —

(i) a complete copy of the cost-benefit analysis of the rule, if any;

(ii) the agency's actions relevant to sections 603, 604, 605, 607, and 609;

(iii) the agency's actions relevant to sections 202, 203, 204, and 205 of the Unfunded Mandates Reform Act of 1995; and

(iv) any other relevant information or requirements under any other Act and any relevant Executive orders.

(C) Upon receipt of a report submitted under subparagraph (A), each House shall provide copies of the report to the chairman and ranking member of each standing committee with jurisdiction under the rules of the House of Representatives or the Senate to report a bill to amend the provision of law under which the rule is issued.

(2) (A) The Comptroller General shall provide a report on each major rule to the committees of jurisdiction in each House of the Congress by the end of 15 calendar days after the submission or publication date as provided in section 802(b)(2). The report of the Comptroller General shall include an assessment of the agency's compliance with procedural steps required by paragraph (1)(B).

(B) Federal agencies shall cooperate with the Comptroller General by providing information relevant to the Comptroller General's report under subparagraph (A).

(3) A major rule relating to a report submitted under paragraph (1) shall take effect on the latest of —

(A) the later of the date occurring 60 days after the date on which —

(i) the Congress receives the report submitted under paragraph (1); or

(ii) the rule is published in the Federal Register, if so published;

(B) if the Congress passes a joint resolution of disapproval described in section 802 relating to the rule, and the President signs a veto of such resolution, the earlier date —

(i) on which either House of Congress votes and fails to override the veto of the President; or

(ii) occurring 30 session days after the date on which the Congress received the veto and objections of the President; or

(C) the date the rule would have otherwise taken effect, if not for this section (unless a joint resolution of disapproval under section 802 is enacted).

(4) Except for a major rule, a rule shall take effect as otherwise provided by law after submission to Congress under paragraph (1).

(5) Notwithstanding paragraph (3), the effective date of a rule shall not be delayed by operation of this chapter beyond the date on which either House of Congress votes to reject a joint resolution of disapproval under section 802.

(b) (1) A rule shall not take effect (or continue), if the Congress enacts a joint resolution of disapproval, described under section 802, of the rule.

(2) A rule that does not take effect (or does not continue) under paragraph (1) may not be reissued in substantially the same form, and a new rule that is substantially the same as such a rule may not be issued, unless the reissued or new rule is specifically authorized by a law enacted after the date of the joint resolution disapproving the original rule.

(c) (1) Notwithstanding any other provision of this section (except subject to paragraph (3)), a rule that would not take effect by reason of subsection (a)(3) may take effect, if the President makes a determination under paragraph (2) and submits written notice of such determination to the Congress.

(2) Paragraph (1) applies to a determination made by the President by Executive order that the rule should take effect because such rule is —

(A) necessary because of an imminent threat to health or safety or other emergency;

(B) necessary for the enforcement of criminal laws;

(C) necessary for national security; or

(D) issued pursuant to any statute implementing an international trade agreement.

(3) An exercise by the President of the authority under this subsection shall have no effect on the procedures under section 802 or the effect of a joint resolution of disapproval under this section.

(d) (1) In addition to the opportunity for review otherwise provided under this chapter, in the case of any rule for which a report was submitted in accordance with subsection (a)(1)(A) during the period beginning on the date occurring —

(A) in the case of the Senate, 60 session days, or

(B) in the case of the House of Representatives, 60 legislative days, before the date the Congress adjourns a session of Congress through the date on which the same or succeeding Congress first convenes its next session, section 802 shall apply to such rule in the succeeding session of Congress.

(2) (A) In applying section 802 for purposes of such additional review, a rule described under paragraph (1) shall be treated as though —

(i) such rule were published in the Federal Register (as a rule that shall take effect) on —

(I) in the case of the Senate, the 15th session day, or

(II) in the case of the House of Representatives, the 15th legislative day,

after the succeeding session of Congress first convenes; and

(ii) a report on such rule were submitted to Congress under subsection (a)(1) on such date.

(B) Nothing in this paragraph shall be construed to affect the requirement under subsection (a)(1) that a report shall be submitted to Congress before a rule can take effect.

(3) A rule described under paragraph (1) shall take effect as otherwise provided by law (including other subsections of this section).

(e) (1) For purposes of this subsection, section 802 shall also apply to any major rule promulgated between March 1, 1996, and the date of the enactment of this chapter.

(2) In applying section 802 for purposes of Congressional review, a rule described under paragraph (1) shall be treated as though —

(A) such rule were published in the Federal Register on the date of enactment of this chapter; and

(B) a report on such rule were submitted to Congress under subsection (a)(1) on such date.

(3) The effectiveness of a rule described under paragraph (1) shall be as otherwise provided by law, unless the rule is made of no force or effect under section 802.

(f) Any rule that takes effect and later is made of no force or effect by enactment of a joint resolution under section 802 shall be treated as though such rule had never taken effect.

(g) If the Congress does not enact a joint resolution of disapproval under section 802 respecting a rule, no court or agency may infer any intent of the Congress from any action or inaction of the Congress with regard to such rule, related statute, or joint resolution of disapproval.

§ 802.   Congressional disapproval procedure

(a) For purposes of this section, the term "joint resolution" means only a joint resolution introduced in the period beginning on the date on which the report referred to in section 801(a)(1)(A) is received by Congress and ending 60 days thereafter (excluding days either House of Congress is adjourned for more than 3 days during a session of Congress), the matter after the resolving clause of which is as follows: "That Congress disapproves the rule submitted by the _____ relating to _____, and such rule shall have no force or effect." (The blank spaces being appropriately filled in).

(b) (1) A joint resolution described in subsection (a) shall be referred to the committees in each House of Congress with jurisdiction.

(2) For purposes of this section, the term "submission or publication date" means the later of the date on which —

(A) the Congress receives the report submitted under section 801(a)(1); or

(B) the rule is published in the Federal Register, if so published.

(c) In the Senate, if the committee to which is referred a joint resolution described in subsection (a) has not reported such joint resolution (or an identical joint resolution) at the end of 20 calendar days after the submission or publication date defined under subsection (b)(2), such committee may be discharged from further consideration of such joint resolution upon a petition supported in writing by 30 Members of the Senate, and such joint resolution shall be placed on the calendar.

(d) (1) In the Senate, when the committee to which a joint resolution is referred has reported, or when a committee is discharged (under subsection (c)) from further consideration of a joint resolution described in subsection (a), it is at any time thereafter in order (even though a previous motion to the same effect has been disagreed to) for a motion to proceed to the consideration of the joint resolution, and all points of order against the joint resolution (and against consideration of the joint resolution) are waived. The motion is not subject to amendment, or to a motion to postpone, or to a motion to proceed to the consideration of other business. A motion to reconsider the vote by which the motion is agreed to or disagreed to shall not be in order. If a motion to proceed to the consideration of the joint resolution is agreed to, the joint resolution shall remain the unfinished business of the Senate until disposed of.

(2) In the Senate, debate on the joint resolution, and on all debatable motions and appeals in connection therewith, shall be limited to not more than 10 hours, which shall be divided equally between those favoring and those opposing the joint resolution. A motion further to limit debate is in order and not debatable. An amendment to, or a motion to postpone, or a motion to proceed to the consideration of other business, or a motion to recommit the joint resolution is not in order.

(3) In the Senate, immediately following the conclusion of the debate on a joint resolution described in subsection (a), and a single quorum call at the conclusion of the debate if requested in accordance with the rules of the Senate, the vote on final passage of the joint resolution shall occur.

(4) Appeals from the decisions of the Chair relating to the application of the rules of the Senate to the procedure relating to a joint resolution described in

subsection (a) shall be decided without debate.

(e) In the Senate the procedure specified in subsection (c) or (d) shall not apply to the consideration of a joint resolution respecting a rule —

(1) after the expiration of the 60 session days beginning with the applicable submission or publication date, or

(2) if the report under section 801(a)(1)(A) was submitted during the period referred to in section 801(d)(1), after the expiration of the 60 session days beginning on the 15th session day after the succeeding session of Congress first convenes.

(f) If, before the passage by one House of a joint resolution of that House described in subsection (a), that House receives from the other House a joint resolution described in subsection (a), then the following procedures shall apply:

(1) The joint resolution of the other House shall not be referred to a committee.

(2) With respect to a joint resolution described in subsection (a) of the House receiving the joint resolution —

(A) the procedure in that House shall be the same as if no joint resolution had been received from the other House; but

(B) the vote on final passage shall be on the joint resolution of the other House.

(g) This section is enacted by Congress —

(1) as an exercise of the rulemaking power of the Senate and House of Representatives, respectively, and as such it is deemed a part of the rules of each House, respectively, but applicable only with respect to the procedure to be followed in that House in the case of a joint resolution described in subsection (a), and it supersedes other rules only to the extent that it is inconsistent with such rules; and

(2) with full recognition of the constitutional right of either House to change the rules (so far as relating to the procedure of that House) at any time, in the same manner, and to the same extent as in the case of any other rule of that House.

§ 803.   Special rule on statutory, regulatory, and judicial deadlines

(a) In the case of any deadline for, relating to, or involving any rule which does not take effect (or the effectiveness of which is terminated) because of enactment of a joint resolution under section 802, that deadline is extended until the date 1 year after the date of enactment of the joint resolution. Nothing in this subsection shall be construed to affect a deadline merely by reason of the postponement of a rule's effective date under section 801(a).

(b) The term "deadline" means any date certain for fulfilling any obligation or exercising any authority established by or under any Federal statute or regulation, or by or under any court order implementing any Federal statute or regulation.

§ 804. Definitions

For purposes of this chapter —

(1) The term "Federal agency" means any agency as that term is defined in section 551(1).

(2) The term "major rule" means any rule that the Administrator of the Office of Information and Regulatory Affairs of the Office of Management and Budget finds has resulted in or is likely to result in —

(A) an annual effect on the economy of $100,000,000 or more;

(B) a major increase in costs or prices for consumers, individual industries, Federal, State, or local government agencies, or geographic regions; or

(C) significant adverse effects on competition, employment, investment, productivity, innovation, or on the ability of United States-based enterprises to compete with foreign-based enterprises in domestic and export markets.

The term does not include any rule promulgated under the Telecommunications Act of 1996 and the amendments made by that Act.

(3) The term "rule" has the meaning given such term in section 551, except that such term does not include —

(A) any rule of particular applicability, including a rule that approves or prescribes for the future rates, wages, prices, services, or allowances therefor, corporate or financial structures, reorganizations, mergers, or acquisitions thereof, or accounting practices or disclosures bearing on any of the foregoing;

(B) any rule relating to agency management or personnel; or

(C) any rule of agency organization, procedure, or practice that does not substantially affect the rights or obligations of non-agency parties.

§ 805. Judicial review

No determination, finding, action, or omission under this chapter shall be subject to judicial review.

§ 806. Applicability; severability

(a) This chapter shall apply notwithstanding any other provision of law.

(b) If any provision of this chapter or the application of any provision of this chapter to any person or circumstance, is held invalid, the application of such provision to other persons or circumstances, and the remainder of this chapter, shall not be affected thereby.

§ 807. Exemption for monetary policy

Nothing in this chapter shall apply to rules that concern monetary policy proposed or implemented by the Board of Governors of the Federal Reserve System or the Federal Open Market Committee.

§ 808.　Effective date of certain rules

Notwithstanding section 801—

(1) any rule that establishes, modifies, opens, closes, or conducts a regulatory program for a commercial, recreational, or subsistence activity related to hunting, fishing, or camping, or

(2) any rule which an agency for good cause finds (and incorporates the finding and a brief statement of reasons therefor in the rule issued) that notice and public procedure thereon are impracticable, unnecessary, or contrary to the public interest,

shall take effect at such time as the Federal agency promulgating the rule determines.

CHAPTER 13　SPECIAL AUTHORITY

§ 1305.　Administrative law judges

For the purpose of sections 3105, 3344, 4301(2)(D), and 5372 of this title and the provisions of section 5335(a)(B) of this title that relate to administrative law judges, the Office of Personnel Management may, and for the purpose of section 7521 of this title, the Merit Systems Protection Board may investigate, prescribe regulations, appoint advisory committees as necessary, recommend legislation, subpena witnesses and records, and pay witness fees as established for the courts of the United States.

CHAPTER 31　AUTHORITY FOR EMPLOYMENT

SUBCHAPTER I　EMPLOYMENT AUTHORITIES

§ 3105.　Appointment of administrative law judges

Each agency shall appoint as many administrative law judges as are necessary for proceedings required to be conducted in accordance with sections 556 and 557 of this title. Administrative law judges shall be assigned to cases in rotation so far as practicable, and may not perform duties inconsistent with their duties and responsibilities as administrative law judges.

CHAPTER 33　EXAMINATION, SELECTION, AND PLACEMENT

SUBCHAPTER III　DETAILS, VACANCIES, AND APPOINTMENTS

§ 3344.　Details; administrative law judges

An agency as defined by section 551 of this title which occasionally or temporarily is insufficiently staffed with administrative law judges appointed under section 3105 of this title may use administrative law judges selected by the Office of Personnel Management from and with the consent of other agencies.

CHAPTER 53   PAY RATES AND SYSTEMS

§ 5372.   Administrative law judges

(a) For the purposes of this section, the term "administrative law Judge" means an administrative law judge appointed under section 3105.

(b) (1) (A) There shall be 3 levels of basic pay for administrative law judges (designated as AL-1, 2, and 3, respectively), and each such judge shall be paid at 1 of those levels, in accordance with the provisions of this section.

(B) Within level AL-3, there shall be 6 rates of basic pay, designated as AL-3, rates A through F, respectively. Level AL-2 and level AL-1 shall each have 1 rate of basic pay.

(C) The rate of basic pay for AL-3, rate A, may not be less than 65 percent of the rate of basic pay for level IV of the Executive Schedule, and the rate of basic pay for AL-1 may not exceed the rate for level IV of the Executive Schedule.

(2) The Office of Personnel Management shall determine, in accordance with procedures which the Office shall by regulation prescribe, the level in which each administrative-law-judge position shall be placed and the qualifications to be required for appointment to each level.

(3) (A) Upon appointment to a position in AL-3, an administrative law judge shall be paid at rate A of AL-3, and shall be advanced successively to rates B, C, and D of that level at the beginning of the next pay period following completion of 52 weeks of service in the next lower rate, and to rates E and F of that level at the beginning of the next pay period following completion of 104 weeks of service in the next lower rate.

(B) The Office of Personnel Management may provide for appointment of an administrative law judge in AL-3 at an advanced rate under such circumstances as the Office may determine appropriate.

(4) Subject to paragraph (1), effective at the beginning of the first applicable pay period commencing on or after the first day of the month in which an adjustment takes effect under section 5303 in the rates of basic pay under the General Schedule, each rate of basic pay for administrative law judges shall be adjusted by an amount determined by the President to be appropriate.

(c) The Office of Personnel Management shall prescribe regulations necessary to administer this section.

CHAPTER 75   ADVERSE ACTIONS

SUBCHAPTER III   ADMINISTRATIVE LAW JUDGES

§ 7521.   Actions against administrative law judges

(a) An action may be taken against an administrative law judge appointed under section 3105 of this title by the agency in which the administrative law judge is employed only for good cause established and determined by the Merit

Systems Protection Board on the record after opportunity for hearing before the Board.

(b) The actions covered by this section are —

    (1) a removal;

    (2) a suspension;

    (3) a reduction in grade;

    (4) a reduction in pay; and

    (5) a furlough of 30 days or less;

but do not include —

        (A) a suspension or removal under section 7532 of this title;

        (B) a reduction-in-force action under section 3502 of this title; or

        (C) any action initiated under section 1215 of this title.

Appendix B

Uniform Law Commissioners'
Model State Administrative Procedure Act (2010)

[ARTICLE] 1 GENERAL PROVISIONS

SECTION 101. SHORT TITLE. This [act] may be cited as the [State] Administrative Procedure Act.

SECTION 102. DEFINITIONS. In this [act]:

(1) "Adjudication" means the process for determining facts or applying law pursuant to which an agency formulates and issues an order. "Adjudicate" has a corresponding meaning.

(2) "Adopt", with respect to a rule, includes to adopt a new rule and to amend or repeal an existing rule. "Adoption" has a corresponding meaning.

(3) "Agency" means a state board, authority, commission, institution, department, division, office, officer, or other state entity that is authorized by law of this state to make rules or to adjudicate. The term does not include the Governor, the [Legislature], or the Judiciary.

(4) "Agency action" means:

(A) the whole or part of an order or rule;

(B) the failure to issue an order or rule; or

(C) an agency's performing or failing to perform a duty, function, or activity or to make a determination required by law.

(5) "Agency head" means the individual in whom, or one or more members of the body of individuals in which, the ultimate legal authority of an agency is vested.

(6) "Agency record" means the agency rulemaking record required by Section 302, the hearing record in adjudication required by Section 406, the hearing record in an emergency adjudication under Section 407, or the record for review compiled under Section 507(b).

(7) "Contested case" means an adjudication in which an opportunity for an evidentiary hearing is required by the federal constitution, a federal statute, or the constitution or a statute of this state.

(8) "Electronic" means relating to technology having electrical, digital, magnetic, wireless, optical, electromagnetic, or similar capabilities.

(9) "Electronic record" means a record created, generated, sent, communicated, received, or stored by electronic means.

(10) "Emergency adjudication" means an adjudication in a contested case when the public health, safety, or welfare requires immediate action.

(11) "Evidentiary hearing" means a hearing for the receipt of evidence on issues on which a decision of the presiding officer may be made in a contested case.

(12) "Final order" means the order issued by the agency head sitting as the presiding officer in a contested case, the order issued following the agency head review of a recommended order, the order issued following the agency head review of an initial order, or the order issued by the presiding officer when the presiding officer has been delegated final decisional authority with no subsequent agency head review.

(13) "Final rule" means a rule adopted, amended, or repealed under Sections 304 through 308, an emergency rule adopted under Section 309, or a direct final rule adopted under Section 310.

(14) "Guidance document" means a record of general applicability developed by an agency which lacks the force of law but states the agency's current approach to, or interpretation of, law, or describes how and when the agency will exercise discretionary functions. The term does not include records described in paragraph (30)(A), (B), (C), or (D).

(15) "Index" means a searchable list in a record of subjects and titles with page numbers, hyperlinks, or other connectors that link each index entry to the text to which it refers.

(16) "Initial order" means an order that is issued by a presiding officer with final decisional authority if the order is subject to discretionary review by the agency.

(17) "Internet website" means a website on the Internet or other appropriate technology or successor technology that permits the public to search a database that archives materials required to be published by the [publisher] under this [act].

(18) "Law" means the federal or state constitution, a federal or state statute, a federal or state judicial decision, a federal or state rule of court, or an executive order that rests on statutory or constitutional authority.

(19) "License" means a permit, certificate, approval, registration, charter, or similar form of permission required by law and issued by an agency.

(20) "Licensing" means the grant, denial, renewal, revocation, suspension, annulment, withdrawal, or amendment of a license.

(21) "Notice" means a record containing information required to be sent to a person by this [act].

(22) "Notify" means to take steps reasonably required to inform a person, regardless of whether the person actually comes to know of the information.

(23) "Order" means an agency decision that determines or declares the rights, duties, privileges, immunities, or other interests of a specific person.

(24) "Party" means the agency taking action, the person against which the action is directed, any other person named as a party, or any person permitted to intervene and that does intervene.

(25) "Person" means an individual, corporation, business trust, statutory trust, estate, trust, partnership, limited liability company, association, joint venture, public corporation, government or governmental subdivision, agency, or instrumentality, or any other legal or commercial entity.

(26) "Presiding officer" means an individual who presides over the evidentiary hearing in a contested case.

(27) "Proceeding" means any type of formal or informal agency process or procedure commenced or conducted by an agency. The term includes adjudication, rulemaking, and investigation.

(28) "Recommended order" means an order issued by a presiding officer if the officer does not have final decisional authority and the order is subject to review by the agency head.

(29) "Record" means information that is inscribed on a tangible medium or that is stored in an electronic or other medium and is retrievable in perceivable form.

(30) "Rule" means the whole or a part of an agency statement of general applicability that implements, interprets, or prescribes law or policy or the organization, procedure, or practice requirements of an agency and has the force of law. The term includes the amendment or repeal of an existing rule. The term does not include:

(A) a statement that concerns only the internal management of an agency and which does not affect private rights or procedures available to the public;

(B) an intergovernmental or interagency memorandum, directive, or communication that does not affect private rights or procedures available to the public;

(C) an opinion of the Attorney General;

(D) a statement that establishes criteria or guidelines to be used by the staff of an agency in performing audits, investigations, or inspections, settling commercial disputes, negotiating commercial arrangements, or defending, prosecuting, or settling cases, if disclosure of the criteria or guidelines would enable persons violating the law to avoid detection, facilitate disregard of requirements imposed by law, or give an improper advantage to persons that are in an adverse position to the state;

(E) a form developed by an agency to implement or interpret agency law or policy; or

(F) a guidance document.

(31) "Rulemaking" means the process for the adoption of a new rule or the amendment or repeal of an existing rule.

(32) "Sign" means, with present intent to authenticate or adopt a record:

(A) to execute or adopt a tangible symbol; or

(B) to attach to or logically associate with the record an electronic symbol, sound, or process.

(33) "Writing" means a record inscribed on a tangible medium. "Written" has a corresponding meaning.

SECTION 103.   APPLICABILITY.

(a) This [act] applies to an agency unless the agency is expressly exempted by a statute of this state.

(b) This [act] applies to all agency proceedings and all proceedings for judicial review or civil enforcement of agency action commenced after [the effective date of this [act]]. This [act] does not apply to an adjudication for which notice was given before that date and rulemaking for which notice was given or a petition was filed before that date.

[ARTICLE] 2 PUBLIC ACCESS TO AGENCY LAW AND POLICY

SECTION 201. PUBLICATION, COMPILATION, INDEXING, AND PUBLIC INSPECTION OF RULEMAKING DOCUMENTS.

(a) The [publisher] shall administer this section and other sections of this [act] that require publication. The [publisher] shall publish the [administrative bulletin] and the [administrative code].

(b) The [publisher] shall publish in [electronic and written] [electronic or written] [electronic] [written] format all rulemaking-related documents listed in Section 202(c). The [publisher] shall prescribe a uniform numbering system, form, and style for proposed rules.

(c) The [publisher] shall maintain the official record of a rulemaking, including the text of the rule and any supporting documents, filed with the [publisher] by an agency. An agency engaged in rulemaking shall maintain the rulemaking record required by Section 302(b) for that rule.

(d) The [publisher] shall create and maintain an Internet website. The [publisher] shall make available on the Internet website the [administrative bulletin], the [administrative code], and any guidance document filed with the [publisher] by an agency.

(e) The [publisher] shall publish the [administrative bulletin] at least once [each month].

(f) The [administrative bulletin] must be provided in written form on request, for which the [publisher] may charge a reasonable fee.

(g) The [administrative bulletin] must contain:

(1) notices of proposed rulemaking prepared so that the text of the proposed rule shows the text of any existing rule proposed to be changed and the change proposed;

(2) newly filed final rules prepared so that the text of a newly filed amended rule shows the text of the existing rule and the change that is made;

(3) any other notice and material required to be published in the [administrative bulletin]; and

(4) an index.

(h) The [administrative code] must be compiled, indexed by subject, and published in a format and medium prescribed by the [publisher]. The rules of an agency must be published and indexed in the [administrative code].

(i) The [publisher] shall make the [administrative bulletin] and the [administrative code] available for public inspection and, for a reasonable charge, copying.

(j) The [publisher], with notification to the agency, may make minor nonsubstantive corrections in spelling, grammar, and format in a proposed or final rule. The [publisher] shall make a record of the corrections.

(k) The [publisher] shall make available on the [publisher's] Internet website, at no charge, all the documents provided by an agency under Section 202(c).

Legislative Note: Throughout this act the drafting committee has used the term [publisher] to describe the official or agency to which substantive publishing functions are assigned. All states have such an official, but their titles vary. Each state using this act should determine what that agency is, then insert its title in place of [publisher] throughout this act. Each state also has an [administrative bulletin] and an [administrative code]. The bulletin is similar to the Federal Register, and the code is similar to the Code of Federal Regulations. The names of the administrative bulletin and the administrative code vary from state to state. Each state should insert the proper title in place of [administrative bulletin], and [administrative code]. The [publisher] has statutory authority under subsections (f) and (i) to provide written materials for a reasonable charge. In many states, [publishers] have statutory authority under a public records act to adopt regulations setting fees for providing written copies of documents under this section.

SECTION 202.   PUBLICATION; AGENCY DUTIES.

(a) Unless the record is exempt from disclosure under law of this state other than this [act], an agency shall publish on its Internet website and, on request and for a reasonable charge, make available through the regular mail:

(1) each notice of a proposed rule under Section 304;

(2) each rule filed under Section 316;

(3) each summary of regulatory analysis required by Section 305;

(4) each declaratory order issued under Section 204;

(5) the index of declaratory orders prepared under Section 204(g);

(6) each guidance document issued under Section 311;

(7) the index of currently effective guidance documents prepared under Section 311(e);

(8) each final order in a contested case issued under Section 413, 414, or 415; and

(9) the index of final orders in contested cases prepared under Section 418(a).

(b) An agency may provide for electronic distribution to a person that requests electronic distribution of notices related to rulemaking or guidance documents. If a notice is distributed electronically, the agency need not transmit the actual notice but must send all the information contained in the notice.

(c) An agency shall file with the [publisher] in an electronic format acceptable to the [publisher]:

(1) notice of the adoption of a final rule;

(2) a summary of the regulatory analysis required by Section 305 for each proposed rule;

(3) each final rule;

(4) an index of currently effective guidance documents under Section 311(f); and

(5) any other notice or matter that an agency is required to publish under this [act].

Legislative Note: Agencies have statutory authority under subsection (a) to provide written materials for a reasonable charge. In many states, agencies have statutory authority under a public records act to adopt regulations setting reasonable charges for providing written copies of documents under this section.

SECTION 203.   REQUIRED AGENCY PUBLICATION AND RECORD-KEEPING. An agency shall:

(1) publish a description of its organization, stating the general course and method of its operations and the methods by which the public may obtain information or make submissions or requests;

(2) publish a description of all formal and informal procedures available, including a description of all forms and instructions used by the agency;

(3) publish a description of the process for application for a license, available benefits, or other matters for which an application is appropriate, unless the process is prescribed by law other than this [act];

(4) adopt rules for the conduct of public hearings [if the standard procedural rules adopted under Section 205 do not include provisions for the conduct of public hearings];

(5) maintain the agency's current rulemaking docket required by Section 301(b); and

(6) maintain a separate, official, current, and dated index and compilation of all final rules filed with the [publisher], make the index and compilation available for public inspection and, for a reasonable charge, copying at the principal office of the agency [and online on the [publisher]'s Internet website], update the index and compilation at least [monthly], and file the index and the compilation and all changes to both with the [publisher].

SECTION 204.   DECLARATORY ORDER.

(a) A person may petition an agency for a declaratory order that interprets or applies a statute administered by the agency or states whether or in what manner a rule, guidance document, or order issued by the agency applies to the petitioner.

(b) An agency shall adopt rules prescribing the form of a petition under subsection (a) and the procedure for its submission, consideration, and prompt disposition. The provisions of this [act] concerning formal, informal, or other applicable hearing procedure do not apply to an agency proceeding for a declaratory order, except to the extent provided in this [article] or to the extent the agency provides by rule or order.

(c) Not later than 60 days [or at the next regularly scheduled meeting of the agency, whichever is later,] after receipt of a petition under subsection (a), an agency shall issue a declaratory order in response to the petition, decline to issue the order, or schedule the matter for further consideration.

(d) If an agency declines to issue a declaratory order requested under subsection (a), it shall notify promptly the petitioner of its decision. The decision must be in a record and must include a brief statement of the reasons for declining. An agency decision to decline to issue a declaratory order is subject to judicial review for abuse of discretion. An agency failure to act within the applicable time under subsection (c) is subject to judicial action under Section 501(d).

(e) If an agency issues a declaratory order, the order must contain the names of all parties to the proceeding, the facts on which it is based, and the reasons for the agency's conclusion. If an agency is authorized not to disclose certain information in its records to protect confidentiality, the agency may redact confidential information in the order. The order has the same status and binding effect as an order issued in an adjudication and is subject to judicial review under Section 501.

(f) An agency shall publish each currently effective declaratory order.

(g) An agency shall maintain an index of all of its currently effective declaratory orders, file the index [annually] with the [publisher], make the index readily available for public inspection, and make available for public inspection and, for a reasonable charge, copying the full text of all declaratory orders to the extent inspection is permitted by law of this state other than this [act].

SECTION 205. STANDARD PROCEDURAL RULES.

(a) The [Governor] [Attorney General] [designated state agency] shall adopt standard procedural rules for use by agencies. The standard rules must provide for the procedural functions and duties of as many agencies as is practicable.

(b) Except as otherwise provided in subsection (c), an agency shall use the standard procedural rules adopted under subsection (a).

(c) An agency may adopt a rule of procedure that differs from the standard procedural rules adopted under subsection (a) if it explains with particularity the reasons for the variation.

[ARTICLE] 3   RULEMAKING; PROCEDURAL REQUIREMENTS AND EFFECTIVENESS OF RULES

SECTION 301.   RULEMAKING DOCKET.

(a) In this section, "rule" does not include an emergency rule adopted under Section 309 or a direct final rule adopted under Section 310.

(b) An agency shall maintain a rulemaking docket for all pending rulemaking proceedings that is indexed.

(c) The agency shall maintain a rulemaking docket under subsection (b) that must for each pending rulemaking proceeding state or contain:

(1) the subject matter of the proposed rule;

(2) notices related to the proposed rule;

(3) how comments on the proposed rule may be submitted;

(4) the time within which comments may be submitted;

(5) where comments may be inspected;

(6) requests for a public hearing;

(7) appropriate information concerning a public hearing, if any; and

(8) the timetable for action on the proposed rule.

(d) On request, the agency shall provide, for a reasonable charge, a written rulemaking docket maintained under subsection (c).

SECTION 302.   RULEMAKING RECORD.

(a) An agency shall maintain a rulemaking record for each proposed rule. Unless the record and any materials incorporated by reference are privileged or exempt from disclosure under law of this state other than this [act], the record and materials must be readily available for public inspection in the principal office of the agency and available for public display on the Internet website maintained by the [publisher]. If an agency determines that any part of the rulemaking record cannot be displayed practicably or is inappropriate for public display on the Internet website, the agency shall describe the part and note that the part is not displayed.

(b) A rulemaking record must contain:

(1) a copy of all publications in the [administrative bulletin] relating to the rule and the proceeding on which the rule is based;

(2) a copy of any part of the rulemaking docket containing entries relating to the rule and the proceeding on which the rule is based;

(3) a copy and, if prepared, an index, of all factual material, studies, and reports agency personnel relied on or consulted in formulating the proposed or final rule;

(4) any official transcript of oral presentations made in the proceeding on

which the rule is based or, if not transcribed, any audio recording or verbatim transcript of the presentations, and any memorandum summarizing the contents of the presentations prepared by the agency official who presided over the hearing;

(5) a copy of all comments received by the agency under Section 306(a) in response to the notice of proposed rulemaking;

(6) a copy of the rule and explanatory statement filed with the [publisher]; and

(7) any petition for agency action on the rule, except a petition governed by Section 204.

SECTION 303.   ADVANCE NOTICE OF PROPOSED RULEMAKING; NEGOTIATED RULEMAKING.

(a) An agency may gather information relevant to the subject matter of a potential rulemaking proceeding and may solicit comments and recommendations from the public by publishing an advance notice of proposed rulemaking in the [administrative bulletin] and indicating where, when, and how persons may comment.

(b) An agency may engage in negotiated rulemaking by appointing a committee to comment or make recommendations on the subject matter of a proposed rulemaking under active consideration within the agency. In making appointments to the committee, the agency shall make reasonable efforts to establish a balance in representation among members of the public known to have an interest in the subject matter of the proposed rulemaking. At least annually, the agency shall publish in the [administrative bulletin] a list of all committees with their membership. Notice of a meeting of the committee must be published in the [administrative bulletin] at least [15 days] before the meeting. A meeting of the committee is open to the public.

(c) A committee appointed under subsection (b), in consultation with one or more agency representatives, shall attempt to reach a consensus on the terms or substance of a proposed rule. The committee shall present the consensus recommendation, if any, to the agency.

The agency shall consider whether to use it as the basis for a proposed rule under Section 304, but the agency is not required to propose or adopt the recommendation.

(d) This section does not prohibit an agency from obtaining information and opinions from members of the public on the subject of a proposed rule by any other method or procedure.

SECTION 304.   NOTICE OF PROPOSED RULE.

(a) At least [30] days before the adoption of a rule, an agency shall file notice of the proposed rulemaking with the [publisher] for publication in the [administrative bulletin]. The notice must include:

(1) a short explanation of the purpose of the proposed rule;

(2) a citation or reference to the specific legal authority authorizing the proposed rule;

(3) the text of the proposed rule;

(4) how a copy of the full text of any regulatory analysis of the proposed rule may be obtained;

(5) where, when, and how a person may comment on the proposed rule and request a hearing;

(6) a citation to and summary of each scientific or statistical study, report, or analysis that served as a basis for the proposed rule, together with an indication of how the full text of the study, report, or analysis may be obtained; and

(7) any summary of a regulatory analysis prepared under Section 305(d).

(b) Not later than three days after publication of the notice of the proposed rulemaking in the [administrative bulletin], the agency shall mail the notice or send it electronically to each person that has made a timely request to the agency for a mailed or electronic copy of the notice. An agency may charge a reasonable fee for a mailed copy requested by a person.

SECTION 305.   REGULATORY ANALYSIS.

(a) An agency shall prepare a regulatory analysis for a proposed rule that has an estimated economic impact of more than $[ ]. The analysis must be completed before notice of the proposed rulemaking is published. The summary of the analysis prepared under subsection (d) must be published with the notice of proposed rulemaking.

(b) If a proposed rule has an economic impact of less than $[ ], the agency shall prepare a statement of minimal estimated economic impact.

(c) A regulatory analysis must contain:

(1) an analysis of the benefits and costs of a reasonable range of regulatory alternatives reflecting the scope of discretion provided by the statute authorizing the proposed rule; and

(2) a determination whether:

(A) the benefits of the proposed rule justify the costs of the proposed rule; and

(B) the proposed rule will achieve the objectives of the authorizing statute in a more cost-effective manner, or with greater net benefits, than other regulatory alternatives.

(d) An agency preparing a regulatory analysis under this section shall prepare a concise summary of the analysis.

(e) An agency preparing a regulatory analysis under this section shall submit the analysis to the [appropriate state agency].

(f) If an agency has made a good faith effort to comply with this section, a rule is not invalid solely because the regulatory analysis for the proposed rule is insufficient or inaccurate.

Legislative Note: State laws vary as to which state agency or body an agency preparing the regulatory analysis should submit the analysis. In some states, it is the department of finance or revenue; in others it is a regulatory review agency or regulatory review committee. The appropriate state agency in each state should be inserted into the brackets.

SECTION 306. PUBLIC PARTICIPATION.

(a) An agency proposing a rule shall specify a public comment period of at least [30] days after publication of notice of the proposed rulemaking during which a person may submit information and comment on the proposed rule. The information or comment may be submitted in an electronic or written format. The agency shall consider all information and comment on a proposed rule which is submitted pursuant to this subsection within the comment period.

(b) An agency may consider any other information it receives concerning a proposed rule during the rulemaking. Any information considered by the agency must be incorporated into the record under Section 302(b)(3). The information need not be submitted in an electronic or written format. Nothing in this section prohibits an agency from discussing with any person at any time the subject of a proposed rule.

(c) Unless a hearing is required by law of this state other than this [act], an agency is not required to hold a hearing on a proposed rule but may do so. A hearing must be open to the public, recorded, and held at least [10] days before the end of the public comment period.

(d) A hearing on a proposed rule may not be held earlier than [20] days after notice of its location, date, and time is published in the [administrative bulletin].

(e) An agency representative shall preside over a hearing on a proposed rule. If the representative is not the agency head, the representative shall prepare a memorandum summarizing the contents of the presentations made at the hearing for consideration by the agency head.

Legislative Note: State laws vary on the length of public comment periods and on whether a rulemaking hearing is required. The bracketed number of days in subsections (a) and (d) should be interpreted to require that if a rulemaking hearing is held, it will be held before the end of the public comment period. In that case, the minimum time period would be 50 days rather than 30 days.

SECTION 307. TIME LIMIT ON ADOPTION OF RULE.

(a) An agency may not adopt a rule until the public comment period has ended.

(b) Not later than [two years] after a notice of proposed rulemaking is published, the agency shall adopt the rule or terminate the rulemaking by publication of a notice of termination in the [administrative bulletin]. [The agency may extend the time for adopting the rule once for an additional [two years] by publishing a statement of good cause for the extension but must provide for additional public participation as provided in Section 306 before adopting the rule.]

(c) An agency shall file an adopted rule with the [publisher] not later than [ ] days after the adoption of the rule.

(d) A rule is void unless it is adopted and filed within the time limits in this section.

SECTION 308.   VARIANCE BETWEEN PROPOSED AND FINAL RULE. An agency may not adopt a rule that differs from the rule proposed in the notice of proposed rulemaking unless the final rule is a logical outgrowth of the rule proposed in the notice.

SECTION 309.   EMERGENCY RULE. If an agency finds that an imminent peril to the public health, safety, or welfare or the loss of federal funding for an agency program requires the immediate adoption of an emergency rule and publishes in a record its reasons for that finding, the agency, without prior notice or hearing or on any abbreviated notice and hearing that it finds practicable, may adopt an emergency rule without complying with Sections 304 through 307. The emergency rule may be effective for not longer than [180] days [renewable once for no more than [180] days]. The adoption of an emergency rule does not preclude the adoption of a rule under Sections 304 through 307. The agency shall file with the [publisher] a rule adopted under this section as soon as practicable given the nature of the emergency, publish the rule on its Internet website, and notify persons that have requested notice of rules related to that subject matter. This section does not prohibit the adoption of a new emergency rule if, at the end of the effective period of the original emergency rule, the agency finds that the imminent peril to the public health, safety, or welfare or the loss of federal funding for an agency program still exists.

SECTION 310.   DIRECT FINAL RULE. If an agency proposes to adopt a rule which is expected to be noncontroversial, it may use direct final rulemaking authorized by this section and must comply with Section 304(a)(1), (2), (3), and (5), Section 304(b), and Section 313(1). The proposed rule must be published in the [administrative bulletin] with a statement by the agency that it does not expect the adoption of the rule to be controversial and that the proposed rule takes effect 30 days after publication if no objection is received. If no objection is received, the rule becomes final under Section 317(e). If an objection to the rule is received from any person not later than [ ] days after publication of the notice of the proposed rule, the proposed rule does not become final. The agency shall file notice of the objection with the [publisher] for publication in the [administrative bulletin], and may proceed with rulemaking under Sections 304 through 307.

SECTION 311.   GUIDANCE DOCUMENT.

(a) An agency may issue a guidance document without following the procedures set forth in Sections 304 through 307.

(b) An agency that proposes to rely on a guidance document to the detriment of a person in any administrative proceeding shall afford the person an adequate opportunity to contest the legality or wisdom of a position taken in the document.

The agency may not use a guidance document to foreclose consideration of issues raised in the document.

(c) A guidance document may contain binding instructions to agency staff members if, at an appropriate stage in the administrative process, the agency's procedures provide an affected person an adequate opportunity to contest the legality or wisdom of a position taken in the document.

(d) If an agency proposes to act in an adjudication at variance with a position expressed in a guidance document, it shall provide a reasonable explanation for the variance. If an affected person in an adjudication may have relied reasonably on the agency's position, the explanation must include a reasonable justification for the agency's conclusion that the need for the variance outweighs the affected person's reliance interest.

(e) An agency shall maintain an index of all of its effective guidance documents, publish the index on its Internet website, make all guidance documents available to the public, and file the index [annually] with the [publisher]. The agency may not rely on a guidance document, or cite it as precedent against any party to a proceeding, unless the guidance document is published on its Internet website.

(f) A guidance document may be considered by a presiding officer or final decision maker in an agency adjudication, but it does not bind the presiding officer or the final decision maker in the exercise of discretion.

(g) A person may petition an agency under Section 318 to adopt a rule in place of a guidance document.

(h) A person may petition an agency to revise or repeal a guidance document. Not later than [60] days after submission of the petition, the agency shall:

(1) revise or repeal the guidance document;

(2) initiate a proceeding to consider a revision or repeal; or

(3) deny the petition in a record and state its reasons for the denial.

SECTION 312.   REQUIRED INFORMATION FOR RULE. A final rule filed by an agency with the [publisher] under Section 316 must contain the text of the rule and be accompanied by a record that contains:

(1) the date the final rule was adopted by the agency;

(2) a reference to the specific statutory or other authority authorizing the rule;

(3) any finding required by law as a prerequisite to adoption or effectiveness of the rule;

(4) the effective date of the rule; and

(5) the concise explanatory statement required by Section 313.

SECTION 313.   CONCISE EXPLANATORY STATEMENT. When an agency adopts a final rule, the agency shall issue a concise explanatory statement that contains:

(1) the agency's reasons for adopting the rule, including the agency's reasons for not accepting substantial arguments made in testimony and comments;

(2) subject to Section 308, the reasons for any change between the text of the proposed rule contained in the notice of proposed rulemaking and the text of the final rule; and

(3) the summary of any regulatory analysis prepared under Section 305(d).

SECTION 314.   INCORPORATION BY REFERENCE. A rule may incorporate by reference all or any part of a code, standard, or rule that has been adopted by an agency of the United States, this state, or another state, or by a nationally recognized organization or association, if:

(1) repeating verbatim the text of the code, standard, or rule in the rule would be unduly cumbersome, expensive, or otherwise inexpedient;

(2) the reference in the rule fully identifies the incorporated code, standard, or rule by citation, place of inspection, and date[, and states whether the rule includes any later amendments or editions of the incorporated code, standard, or rule];

(3) the code, standard, or rule is readily available to the public in written or electronic form at no charge or for a reasonable charge;

(4) the rule states where copies of the code, standard, or rule are available from the agency adopting the rule for a reasonable charge, if any, or where copies are available from the agency of the United States, this state, another state, or the organization or association originally issuing the code, standard, or rule; and

(5) the agency maintains a copy of the code, standard, or rule readily available for public inspection at the principal office of the agency.

SECTION 315.   COMPLIANCE. An action taken under this [article] is not valid unless taken in substantial compliance with this [article].

SECTION 316.   FILING OF RULE. An agency shall file in written and electronic form with the [publisher] each final rule. In filing a final rule, an agency shall use a standard form prescribed by the [publisher]. The agency shall file the rule not later than [ ] days after adoption. The [publisher] shall maintain a permanent register of all filed rules and concise explanatory statements for the rules. The [publisher] shall affix to each final rule a certification of the time and date of filing. The [publisher] shall publish the notice of each final rule in the [administrative bulletin].

SECTION 317.   EFFECTIVE DATE OF RULE.

(a) Except as otherwise provided in this section, [unless disapproved by the [rules review committee][,] [or] [withdrawn by the agency under Section 703,] a rule becomes effective [30] days after publication of the rule [in the administrative bulletin] [on the [publisher's] Internet website].

(b) A rule may become effective on a date later than that established by subsection (a) if that date is specified in the rule or required by law other than this [act].

(c) A rule becomes effective immediately on its filing with the [publisher] or on any subsequent date earlier than that established by subsection (a) if it is required to be implemented by a certain date by law other than this [act].

(d) An emergency rule under Section 309 becomes effective on adoption by the agency.

(e) A direct final rule under Section 310 to which no objection is made becomes effective [30] days after publication, unless the agency specifies a later effective date.

SECTION 318. PETITION FOR ADOPTION OF RULE. Any person may petition an agency to adopt a rule. An agency shall prescribe by rule the form of the petition and the procedure for its submission, consideration, and disposition. Not later than [60] days after submission of a petition, the agency shall:

(1) deny the petition in a record and state its reasons for the denial; or

(2) initiate rulemaking.

[ARTICLE] 4   ADJUDICATION IN CONTESTED CASE

SECTION 401.   CONTESTED CASE. This [article] applies to an adjudication made by an agency in a contested case.

SECTION 402.   PRESIDING OFFICER.

(a) A presiding officer must be an administrative law judge assigned in accordance with Section 604(2), the individual who is the agency head, a member of a multi-member body of individuals that is the agency head, or, unless prohibited by law of this state other than this [act], an individual designated by the agency head.

(b) An individual who has served as investigator, prosecutor, or advocate at any stage in a contested case or who is subject to the authority, direction, or discretion of an individual who has served as investigator, prosecutor, or advocate at any stage in a contested case may not serve as the presiding officer in the same case. An agency head that has participated in a determination of probable cause or other preliminary determination in an adjudication may serve as the presiding officer or final decision maker in the adjudication unless a party demonstrates grounds for disqualification under subsection (c).

(c) A presiding officer or agency head acting as a final decision maker is subject to disqualification for bias, prejudice, financial interest, ex parte communications as provided in Section 408, or any other factor that would cause a reasonable person to question the impartiality of the presiding officer or agency head. A presiding officer or agency head, after making a reasonable inquiry, shall disclose to the parties any known facts related to grounds for disqualification which are material to the impartiality of the presiding officer or agency head in the proceeding.

(d) A party may petition for the disqualification of a presiding officer or agency head promptly after notice that the person will preside or, if later, promptly on discovering facts establishing a ground for disqualification. The petition must state with particularity the ground on which it is claimed that a fair and impartial hearing cannot be accorded or the applicable rule or canon of practice or ethics that requires disqualification. The petition may be denied if the party fails to exercise due diligence in requesting disqualification after discovering a ground for disqualification.

(e) A presiding officer or agency head whose disqualification is requested shall decide whether to grant the petition and state in a record facts and reasons for the decision. The decision to deny disqualification is not subject to interlocutory judicial review.

(f) If a substitute presiding officer is required, the substitute must be appointed [as required by law, or if no law governs,] by:

(1) the Governor, if the original presiding officer is an elected official; or

(2) the appointing authority, if the original presiding officer is an appointed official.

(g) If participation of the agency head is necessary to enable the agency to take action, the agency head may continue to participate notwithstanding a ground for disqualification or exclusion.

Legislative Note: The first alternative under subsection (a) would be applicable in states that have adopted central panel hearing offices but would not apply to states that do not have central panel hearing offices. Article 6 governs central panel hearing offices under this act. If a state does not have a central panel hearing agency, presiding officers would include administrative law judges who are employees of the agency with final decision authority. States vary in the terms used to describe agency employees who are presiding officers. The term includes administrative judges, hearing officers, and hearing examiners. Administrative law judges can be employees of the central panel hearing office or of the agency with final decision authority.

SECTION 403. CONTESTED CASE PROCEDURE.

(a) This section does not apply to an emergency adjudication under Section 407.

(b) An agency shall give notice of the agency decision to a person when the agency takes an action as to which the person has a right to a contested case hearing. The notice must be in writing, set forth the agency action, inform the person of the right, procedure, and time limit to file a contested-case petition, and provide a copy of the agency procedures governing the contested case.

(c) In a contested case, the presiding officer shall give all parties a timely opportunity to file pleadings, motions, and objections. The presiding officer may give all parties the opportunity to file briefs, proposed findings of fact and conclusions of law, and proposed recommended, initial, or final orders. The presiding officer, with the consent of all parties, may refer the parties in a contested case to mediation or other dispute resolution procedure.

(d) In a contested case, to the extent necessary for full disclosure of all relevant facts and issues, the presiding officer shall give all parties the opportunity to respond, present evidence and argument, conduct cross-examination, and submit rebuttal evidence.

(e) Except as otherwise provided by law other than this [act], the presiding officer may conduct all or part of an evidentiary hearing or a prehearing conference by telephone, television, video conference, or other electronic means. The hearing may be conducted by telephone or other method by which the witnesses may not be seen only if all parties consent [or the presiding officer finds that this method will not impair reliable determination of the credibility of testimony]. Each party must be given an opportunity to attend, hear, and be heard at the proceeding as it occurs. This subsection does not prevent an agency from providing by rule for electronic hearings.

(f) Except as otherwise provided in subsection (g), a hearing in a contested case must be open to the public. A hearing conducted by telephone, television, video conference, or other electronic means is open to the public if members of the public have an opportunity to attend the hearing at the place where the presiding officer is located or to hear or see the proceeding as it occurs.

(g) A presiding officer may close a hearing to the public on a ground on which a court of this state may close a judicial proceeding to the public or pursuant to law of this state other than this [act].

(h) Unless prohibited by law of this state other than this [act], a party, at the party's expense, may be represented by counsel or may be advised, accompanied, or represented by another individual.

(i) A presiding officer shall ensure that a hearing record is created that complies with Section 406.

(j) The decision in a contested case must be based on the hearing record and contain a statement of the factual and legal bases of the decision. If a finding of fact is set forth in language of a statute of this state other than this [act], it must be accompanied by a concise and explicit statement of the underlying facts supporting the finding of fact. The decision must be prepared electronically and, on request, made available in writing.

(k) Subject to Section 205, the rules by which an agency conducts a contested case may include provisions more protective than the requirements of this section of the rights of parties other than the agency.

(l) Unless prohibited by law of this state other than this [act], an agency may dispose of a contested case without a hearing by stipulation, agreed settlement, consent order, or default.

SECTION 404.   EVIDENCE IN CONTESTED CASE. The following rules apply in a contested case:

(1) Except as otherwise provided in paragraph (2), all relevant evidence is admissible, including hearsay evidence, if it is of a type commonly relied on by a reasonably prudent individual in the conduct of the affairs of the individual.

(2) The presiding officer may exclude evidence in the absence of an objection if the evidence is irrelevant, immaterial, unduly repetitious, or excludable on constitutional or statutory grounds or on the basis of an evidentiary privilege recognized in the courts of this state. The presiding officer shall exclude the evidence if objection is made at the time the evidence is offered.

(3) If the presiding officer excludes evidence with or without objection, the offering party may make an offer of proof before further evidence is presented or at a later time determined by the presiding officer.

(4) Evidence may be received in a record if doing so will expedite the hearing without substantial prejudice to a party. Documentary evidence may be received in the form of a copy if the original is not readily available or by incorporation by reference. On request, parties must be given an opportunity to compare the copy with the original.

(5) Testimony must be made under oath or affirmation.

(6) Evidence must be made part of the hearing record of the case. Information or evidence may not be considered in determining the case unless

it is part of the hearing record. If the hearing record contains information that is confidential, the presiding officer may conduct a closed hearing to discuss the information, issue necessary protective orders, and seal all or part of the hearing record.

(7) The presiding officer may take official notice of all facts of which judicial notice may be taken and of scientific, technical, or other facts within the specialized knowledge of the agency. A party must be notified at the earliest practicable time of the facts proposed to be noticed and their source, including any staff memoranda or data. The party must be afforded an opportunity to contest any officially noticed fact before the decision becomes final.

(8) The experience, technical competence, and specialized knowledge of the presiding officer or members of an agency head that is a multi-member body that is hearing the case may be used in evaluating the evidence in the hearing record.

SECTION 405. NOTICE IN CONTESTED CASE.

(a) Except as otherwise provided in an emergency adjudication under Section 407, an agency shall give notice in a contested case that complies with this section.

(b) In a contested case initiated by a person other than an agency, not later than [five] days after filing, the agency shall give notice to all parties that the case has been commenced. The notice must contain:

(1) the official file or other reference number, the name of the proceeding, and a general description of the subject matter;

(2) contact information for communicating with the agency, including the agency mailing address [, electronic mail address,] [,] [facsimile number,] and telephone number;

(3) a statement of the date, time, place, and nature of the prehearing conference or hearing, if any;

(4) the name, official title, mailing address, [electronic mail address,] [facsimile number,] and telephone number of any attorney or employee who has been designated to represent the agency; and

(5) the names and last known addresses of all parties and other persons to which notice is being given by the agency.

(c) In a contested case initiated by an agency, the agency shall give notice to the party against which the action is brought. The notice must contain:

(1) a statement that a case that may result in an order has been commenced against the party;

(2) a short and plain statement of the matters asserted, including the issues involved;

(3) a statement of the legal authority under which the hearing will be held citing the statutes and any rules involved;

(4) the official file or other reference number and the name of the

proceeding;

(5) the name, official title, mailing address, [and] [electronic mail address,] [and] [facsimile number,] [and] [telephone number] of the presiding officer and the name, official title, mailing address, [electronic mail address,] [facsimile number,] and telephone number of the agency's representative;

(6) a statement that a party that fails to attend or participate in any subsequent proceeding in the case may be held in default;

(7) a statement that the party served may request a hearing and includes instructions in plain English about how to request a hearing; and

(8) the names and last known addresses of all parties and other persons to which notice is being given by the agency.

(d) When a hearing or a prehearing conference is scheduled, the agency shall give parties notice that contains the information required by subsection (c) at least [30] days before the hearing or prehearing conference.

(e) A notice under this section may include other matters that the presiding officer considers desirable to expedite the proceedings.

SECTION 406. HEARING RECORD IN CONTESTED CASE.

(a) An agency shall maintain the hearing record created under Section 403(i) in each contested case.

(b) The hearing record must contain:

(1) a recording of each proceeding;

(2) notice of each proceeding;

(3) any prehearing order;

(4) any motion, pleading, brief, petition, request, and intermediate ruling;

(5) evidence admitted;

(6) a statement of any matter officially noticed;

(7) any proffer of proof and objection and ruling thereon;

(8) any proposed finding, requested order, and exception;

(9) any transcript of the proceeding prepared at the direction of the agency;

(10) any recommended order, final order, or order on reconsideration; and

(11) any matter placed on the record after an ex parte communication under Section 408(f).

(c) The hearing record constitutes the exclusive basis for agency action in a contested case.

SECTION 407. EMERGENCY ADJUDICATION PROCEDURE.

(a) Unless prohibited by law of this state other than this [act], an agency may conduct an emergency adjudication in a contested case under this section.

(b) An agency may take action and issue an order under this section only to deal with an imminent peril to the public health, safety, or welfare.

(c) Before issuing an order under this section, an agency, if practicable, shall give notice and an opportunity to be heard to the person to which the agency action is directed. The notice of the hearing and the hearing may be oral or written and may be by telephone, facsimile, or other electronic means.

(d) An order issued under this section must briefly explain the factual and legal reasons for using emergency adjudication procedures.

(e) To the extent practicable, an agency shall give notice to the person to which the agency action is directed that an order has been issued. The order is effective when signed by the agency head or the designee of the agency head.

(f) After issuing an order pursuant to this section, an agency shall proceed as soon as practicable to provide notice and an opportunity for a hearing following the procedure under Section 403 to determine the issues underlying the order.

(g) An order issued under this section may be effective for not longer than [180] days or until the effective date of any order issued under subsection (f), whichever is shorter.

SECTION 408.   EX PARTE COMMUNICATIONS.

(a) In this section, "final decision maker" means the person with the power to issue a final order in a contested case.

(b) Except as otherwise provided in subsection (c), (d), (e), or (h), while a contested case is pending, the presiding officer and the final decision maker may not make to or receive from any person any communication concerning the case without notice and opportunity for all parties to participate in the communication. For the purpose of this section, a contested case is pending from the issuance of the agency's pleading or from an application for an agency decision, whichever is earlier.

(c) A presiding officer or final decision maker may communicate about a pending contested case with any person if the communication is required for the disposition of ex parte matters authorized by statute or concerns an uncontested procedural issue.

(d) A presiding officer or final decision maker may communicate about a pending contested case with an individual authorized by law to provide legal advice to the presiding officer or final decision maker and may communicate on ministerial matters with an individual who serves on the [administrative] [personal] staff of the presiding officer or final decision maker if the individual providing legal advice or ministerial information has not served as investigator, prosecutor, or advocate at any stage of the case, and if the communication does not augment, diminish, or modify the evidence in the record.

(e) An agency head that is the presiding officer or final decision maker in a pending contested case may communicate about that case with an employee or representative of the agency if:

(1) the employee or representative:

(A) has not served as investigator, prosecutor, or advocate at any stage of the case;

(B) has not otherwise had a communication with any person about the case other than a communication a presiding officer or final decision maker is permitted to make or receive under subsection (c) or (d) or a communication permitted by paragraph (2); and

(2) the communication does not augment, diminish, or modify the evidence in the agency hearing record and is:

(A) an explanation of the technical or scientific basis of, or technical or scientific terms in, the evidence in the agency hearing record;

(B) an explanation of the precedent, policies, or procedures of the agency; or (C) any other communication that does not address the quality or sufficiency of, or the weight that should be given to, evidence in the agency hearing record or the credibility of witnesses.

(f) If a presiding officer or final decision maker makes or receives a communication in violation of this section, the presiding officer or final decision maker:

(1) if the communication is in a record, shall make the record of the communication a part of the hearing record and prepare and make part of the hearing record a memorandum that contains the response of the presiding officer or final decision maker to the communication and the identity of the person that communicated; or

(2) if the communication is oral, shall prepare a memorandum that contains the substance of the verbal communication, the response of the presiding officer or final decision maker to the communication, and the identity of the person that communicated.

(g) If a communication prohibited by this section is made, the presiding officer or final decision maker shall notify all parties of the prohibited communication and permit parties to respond in a record not later than 15 days after the notice is given. For good cause, the presiding officer or final decision maker may permit additional testimony in response to the prohibited communication.

(h) If a presiding officer is a member of a multi-member body of individuals that is the agency head, the presiding officer may communicate with the other members of the body when sitting as the presiding officer and final decision maker. Otherwise, while a contested case is pending, no communication, direct or indirect, regarding any issue in the case may be made between the presiding officer and the final decision maker. Notwithstanding any provision of [state open meetings law], a communication permitted by this subsection is not a meeting.

(i) If necessary to eliminate the effect of a communication received in violation of this section, a presiding officer or final decision maker may be disqualified under Section 402(d) and (e), the parts of the record pertaining to the communication may be sealed by protective order, or other appropriate relief may be granted, including an adverse ruling on the merits of the case or dismissal of the application.

SECTION 409. INTERVENTION.

(a) A presiding officer shall grant a timely petition for intervention in a contested case, with notice to all parties, if:

(1) the petitioner has a statutory right under law of this state other than this [act] to initiate or to intervene in the case; or

(2) the petitioner has an interest that may be adversely affected by the outcome of the case and that interest is not adequately represented by existing parties.

(b) A presiding officer may grant a timely petition for intervention in a contested case, with notice to all parties, if the petitioner has a permissive statutory right to intervene under law of this state other than this [act] or if the petitioner's claim or defense is based on the same transaction or occurrence as the case.

(c) A presiding officer may impose conditions at any time on an intervener's participation in the contested case.

(d) A presiding officer may permit intervention provisionally and, at any time later in the contested case or at the end of the case, may revoke the provisional intervention.

(e) On request by the petitioners or a party or by action of the presiding officer, the presiding officer may hold a hearing on the intervention petition.

(f) A presiding officer shall promptly give notice of an order granting, denying, or revoking intervention to the petitioner for intervention and to the parties. The notice must allow parties a reasonable time to prepare for the hearing on the merits.

SECTION 410. SUBPOENAS.

(a) On a request in a record by a party in a contested case, the presiding officer or any other officer to whom the power to issue a subpoena is delegated pursuant to law, on a showing of general relevance and reasonable scope of the evidence sought for use at the hearing, shall issue a subpoena for the attendance of a witness and the production of books, records, and other evidence.

(b) Unless otherwise provided by law or agency rule, a subpoena issued under subsection (a) shall be served and, on application to the court by a party or the agency, enforced in the manner provided by law for the service and enforcement of a subpoena in a civil action.

(c) Witness fees shall be paid by the party requesting a subpoena in the manner provided by law for witness fees in a civil action.

SECTION 411. DISCOVERY.

(a) In this section, "statement" includes a record of a person's written statement signed by the person and a record that summarizes an oral statement made by the person.

(b) Except in an emergency hearing under Section 407, a party, on written notice to another party at least [30] days before an evidentiary hearing, unless otherwise provided by agency rule under subsection (g), may:

(1) obtain the names and addresses of witnesses the other party will present at the hearing to the extent known to the other party; and

(2) inspect and copy any of the following material in the possession, custody, or control of the other party:

(A) statements of parties and witnesses proposed to be called by the other party;

(B) all records, including reports of mental, physical, and blood examinations, and other evidence the other party proposes to offer;

(C) investigative reports made by or on behalf of the agency or other party pertaining to the subject matter of the adjudication;

(D) statements of expert witnesses proposed to be called by the other party;

(E) any exculpatory material in the possession of the agency; and

(F) other materials for good cause.

(c) Parties to a contested case have a duty to supplement responses provided under subsection (b) to include information thereafter acquired, to the extent that the information will be relied on in the hearing.

(d) On petition, the presiding officer may issue a protective order for any material for which discovery is sought under this section which is exempt, privileged, or otherwise made confidential or protected from disclosure by law of this state other than this [act] and material the disclosure of which would result in annoyance, embarrassment, oppression, or undue burden or expense to any person.

(e) On petition, the presiding officer shall issue an order compelling discovery for refusal to comply with a discovery request unless good cause exists for refusal. Failure to comply with the order may be enforced according to the rules of civil procedure.

(f) On petition and for good cause, the presiding officer shall issue an order authorizing discovery in accordance with the rules of civil procedure.

(g) An agency may provide by rule that some or all discovery procedures under this section do not apply to a specified program or category of cases if it finds that:

(1) the availability of discovery would unduly complicate or interfere with the hearing process in the program or cases, because of the volume of the applicable caseload and the need for expedition and informality in that process;

and

(2) alternative procedures for the sharing of relevant information are sufficient to ensure the fundamental fairness of the proceedings.

SECTION 412. DEFAULT.

(a) Unless otherwise provided by law of this state other than this [act], if a party without good cause fails to attend or participate in a prehearing conference or hearing in a contested case, the presiding officer may issue a default order.

(b) If a default order is issued, the presiding officer may conduct any further proceedings necessary to complete the adjudication without the defaulting party and shall determine all issues in the adjudication, including those affecting the defaulting party.

(c) A recommended, initial, or final order issued against a defaulting party may be based on the defaulting party's admissions or other evidence that may be used without notice to the defaulting party. If the burden of proof is on the defaulting party to establish that the party is entitled to the agency action sought, the presiding officer may issue a recommended, initial, or final order without taking evidence.

(d) Not later than [15] days after notice to a party subject to a default order that a recommended, initial, or final order has been rendered against the party, the party may petition the presiding officer to vacate the recommended, initial, or final order. If good cause is shown for the party's failure to appear, the presiding officer shall vacate the decision and, after proper service of notice, conduct another evidentiary hearing. If good cause is not shown for the party's failure to appear, the presiding officer shall deny the motion to vacate.

SECTION 413. ORDERS: RECOMMENDED, INITIAL, OR FINAL.

(a) If the presiding officer is the agency head, the presiding officer shall issue a final order.

(b) Except as otherwise provided by law of this state other than this [act], if the presiding officer is not the agency head and has not been delegated final decisional authority, the presiding officer shall issue a recommended order. If the presiding officer is not the agency head and has been delegated final decisional authority, the presiding officer shall issue an initial order that becomes a final order [30] days after issuance, unless reviewed by the agency head on its own initiative or on petition of a party.

(c) A recommended, initial, or final order must be served in a record on each party and the agency head not later than [90] days after the hearing ends, the record closes, or memoranda, briefs, or proposed findings are submitted, whichever is latest. The presiding officer may extend the time by stipulation, waiver, or for good cause.

(d) A recommended, initial, or final order must separately state findings of fact and conclusions of law on all material issues of fact, law, or discretion, the remedy prescribed, and, if applicable, the action taken on a petition for a stay. The presiding officer may permit a party to submit proposed findings of fact and conclusions of law. The order must state the available procedures and time limits for seeking reconsideration or other administrative relief and must state the time limits for seeking judicial review of the agency order. A recommended or initial order must state any circumstances under which the order, without further notice, may become a final order.

(e) Findings of fact must be based exclusively on the evidence and matters officially noticed in the hearing record in the contested case.

Alternative A

(f) Hearsay evidence may be used to supplement or explain other evidence, but on timely objection, is not sufficient by itself to support a finding of fact unless it would be admissible over objection in a civil action.

Alternative B

(f) Hearsay evidence is sufficient to support a finding of fact if it constitutes reliable, probative, and substantial evidence.

End of Alternatives

(g) An order is issued under this section when it is signed by the agency head, presiding officer, or an individual authorized by law of this state other than this [act] to sign the order.

(h) A final order is effective [30] days after all parties are notified of the order unless reconsideration is granted under Section 416 or a stay is granted under Section 417.

SECTION 414.   AGENCY REVIEW OF INITIAL ORDER.

(a) An agency head may review an initial order on its own initiative.

(b) A party may petition an agency head to review an initial order. On petition by a party, the agency head may review an initial order.

(c) A petition for review of an initial order must be filed with the agency head or with any person designated for this purpose by agency rule not later than [15] days after notice to the parties of the order. If the agency head decides to review an initial order on its own initiative, the agency head shall give notice in a record to the parties that it intends to review the order. The notice must be given not later than [15] days after the parties are notified of the order. If a petition for review is not filed or the agency head does not elect to review the initial order within the prescribed time limit, the initial order becomes a final order.

(d) The period in subsection (c) for a party to file a petition or for the agency head to notify the parties of its intention to review an initial order is tolled by the submission of a timely petition under Section 416 for reconsideration of the order. A new [15]-day period begins on disposition of the petition for reconsideration. If an order is subject both to a timely petition for reconsideration and a petition for review by the agency head, the petition for reconsideration must be disposed of first, unless the agency head determines that action on the petition for reconsideration has been unreasonably delayed.

(e) When reviewing an initial order, the agency head shall exercise the decision-making power that the agency head would have had if the agency head had conducted the hearing that produced the order, except to the extent that the issues subject to review are limited by law of this state other than this [act] or by order of the agency head on notice to the parties. In reviewing findings of fact in an initial order, the agency head shall consider the presiding officer's opportunity to observe the witnesses and to determine the credibility of witnesses. The agency head shall consider the hearing record or parts of the record designated by the parties.

(f) If an agency head reviews an initial order, the agency head shall issue a final order disposing of the proceeding not later than 120 days after the decision to review the initial order or remand the matter for further proceedings with instructions to the presiding officer who issued the initial order. On remanding a matter, the agency head may order such temporary relief as is authorized and appropriate.

(g) A final order or an order remanding the matter for further proceedings must identify any difference between the order and the initial order and must state the facts of record that support any difference in findings of fact, the law that supports any difference in legal conclusions, and the policy reasons that support any difference in the exercise of discretion. Findings of fact must be based exclusively on the evidence and matters officially noticed in the hearing record in the contested case. A final order under this section must include, or incorporate by express reference to the initial order, the matters required by Section 413(d). The agency head shall deliver the order to the presiding officer and notify the parties of the order.

SECTION 415.   AGENCY REVIEW OF RECOMMENDED ORDER.

(a) An agency head shall review a recommended order pursuant to this section.

(b) When reviewing a recommended order, the agency head shall exercise the decision-making power that the agency head would have had if the agency head had conducted the hearing that produced the order, except to the extent that the issues subject to review are limited by law of this state other than this [act] or by order of the agency head on notice to the parties. In reviewing findings of fact in a recommended order, the agency head shall consider the presiding officer's opportunity to observe the witnesses and to determine the credibility of witnesses. The agency head shall consider the hearing record or parts that are designated by the parties.

(c) An agency head may render a final order disposing of the proceeding or remand the matter for further proceedings with instructions to the presiding officer who rendered the recommended order. On remanding a matter, the agency head may order such temporary relief as is authorized and appropriate.

(d) A final order or an order remanding the matter for further proceedings must identify any difference between the order and the recommended order and must state the facts of record that support any difference in findings of fact, the law that supports any difference in legal conclusions, and the policy reasons that support any difference in the exercise of discretion. Findings of fact must be based exclusively on the evidence and matters officially noticed in the hearing record in the contested case. A final order under this section must include, or incorporate by express reference to the recommended order, the matters required by Section 413(d). The agency head shall deliver the order to the presiding officer and notify the parties of the order.

SECTION 416.   RECONSIDERATION.

(a) A party, not later than [15] days after notice to the parties that a final order has been issued, may file a petition for reconsideration that states the specific grounds on which relief is requested. The place of filing and other procedures, if any, must be specified by agency rule and must be stated in the final order.

(b) If a petition for reconsideration is timely filed, and if the petitioner has complied with the agency's procedural rules for reconsideration, if any, the time for filing a petition for judicial review does not begin until the agency disposes of the petition for reconsideration as provided in Section 503(d).

(c) Not later than [20] days after a petition is filed under subsection (a), the decision maker shall issue a written order denying the petition, granting the petition and dissolving or modifying the final order, or granting the petition and setting the matter for further proceedings. If the decision maker fails to respond to the petition not later than [30] days after filing, or a longer period agreed to by the parties, the petition is deemed denied. The petition may be granted only if the decision maker states findings of facts, conclusions of law, and the reasons for granting the petition.

SECTION 417.   STAY.
Except as otherwise provided by law of this state other than this [act], a party, not later than [seven] days after the parties are notified of the order, may request the agency to stay a final order pending judicial review. The agency may grant the request for a stay pending judicial review if the agency finds that justice requires. The agency may grant or deny the request for stay of the order before, on, or after the effective date of the order.

SECTION 418.   AVAILABILITY OF ORDERS; INDEX.

(a) Except as otherwise provided in subsections (b) and (c), an agency shall create an index of all final orders in contested cases and make the index and all final orders available for public inspection and copying, at cost, in its principal offices.

(b) Except as otherwise provided in subsection (c), final orders that are exempt, privileged, or otherwise made confidential or protected from disclosure by [the public records law of this state] are not public records and may not be indexed. The final order may be excluded from an index and disclosed only by order of the presiding officer with a written statement of reasons attached to the order.

(c) If the presiding officer determines it is possible to redact a final order that is exempt, privileged, or otherwise made confidential or protected from disclosure by law of this state other than this [act] so that it complies with the requirements of that law, the redacted order may be placed in the index and published.

(d) An agency may not rely on a final order adverse to a party other than the agency as precedent in future adjudications unless the agency designates the order as a precedent, and the order has been published, placed in an index, and made available for public inspection.

SECTION 419. LICENSES.

(a) If a licensee has made timely and sufficient application for the renewal of a license or a new license for any activity of a continuing nature, the existing license does not expire until the agency takes final action on the application and, if the application is denied or the terms of the new license are limited, until the last day for seeking review of the agency order or a later date fixed by the reviewing court.

(b) A revocation, suspension, annulment, or withdrawal of a license is not lawful unless, before the institution of agency proceedings, the agency notifies the licensee of facts or conduct that warrants the intended action, and the licensee is given an opportunity to show compliance with all lawful requirements for the retention of the license. If the agency finds that imminent peril to public health, safety, or welfare requires emergency action and incorporates a finding to that effect in its order, summary suspension of a license may be ordered pending proceedings for revocation or other action. These proceedings must be promptly instituted and concluded.

[ARTICLE] 5   JUDICIAL REVIEW

SECTION 501.   RIGHT TO JUDICIAL REVIEW; FINAL AGENCY ACTION REVIEWABLE.

(a) In this [article], "final agency action" means an act of an agency which imposes an obligation, grants or denies a right, confers a benefit, or determines a legal relationship as a result of an administrative proceeding. The term does not include agency action that is a failure to act.

(b) Except to the extent that a statute of this state other than this [act] limits or precludes judicial review, a person that meets the requirements of this [article] is entitled to judicial review of a final agency action.

(c) A person entitled to judicial review under subsection (b) of a final agency action is entitled to judicial review of an agency action that is not final if postponement of judicial review would result in an inadequate remedy or irreparable harm that outweighs the public benefit derived from postponing judicial review.

(d) A court may compel an agency to take action that is unlawfully withheld or unreasonably delayed.

SECTION 502.   RELATION TO OTHER JUDICIAL REVIEW LAW AND RULES.

(a) Except as otherwise provided by law of this state other than this [act], judicial review of final agency action may be taken only as provided by rules of [appellate] [civil] procedure [of this state]. The court may grant any type of legal and equitable remedies that are appropriate.

(b) This [article] does not limit use of or the scope of judicial review available under other means of review, redress, relief, or trial de novo provided by law of this state other than this [act]. Except to the extent that prior, adequate, and exclusive opportunity for judicial review is available under this [article] or under law of this state other than this [act], final agency action is subject to judicial review in civil or criminal proceedings for judicial enforcement.

SECTION 503.   TIME TO SEEK JUDICIAL REVIEW OF AGENCY ACTION; LIMITATIONS.

(a) Judicial review of a rule on the ground of noncompliance with the procedural requirements of this [act] must be commenced not later than [two] years after the effective date of the rule. Judicial review of a rule or guidance document on other grounds may be sought at any time.

(b) Judicial review of an order or other final agency action other than a rule or guidance document must be commenced not later than [30] days after the date the parties are notified of the order or other agency action.

(c) The time for seeking judicial review under this section is tolled during any time a party pursues an administrative remedy before the agency which must be exhausted as a condition of judicial review.

(d) A party may not petition for judicial review while seeking reconsideration under Section 416. During the time a petition for reconsideration is pending before an agency, the time for seeking judicial review in subsection (b) is tolled.

SECTION 504. STAYS PENDING APPEAL. A petition for judicial review does not automatically stay an agency decision. A challenging party may request the reviewing court for a stay on the same basis as stays are granted under the rules of [appellate] [civil] procedure [of this state], and the reviewing court may grant a stay regardless of whether the challenging party first sought a stay from the agency.

SECTION 505. STANDING. The following persons have standing to obtain judicial review of a final agency action:

(1) a person aggrieved or adversely affected by the agency action; and

(2) a person that has standing under law of this state other than this [act].

SECTION 506. EXHAUSTION OF ADMINISTRATIVE REMEDIES.

(a) Subject to subsection (d) or law of this state other than this [act] which provides that a person need not exhaust administrative remedies, a person may file a petition for judicial review under this [act] only after exhausting all administrative remedies available within the agency the action of which is being challenged and within any other agency authorized to exercise administrative review.

(b) Filing a petition for reconsideration or a stay of proceedings is not a prerequisite for seeking judicial review.

(c) A petitioner for judicial review of a rule need not have participated in the rulemaking proceeding on which the rule is based or have filed a petition to adopt a rule under Section 318.

(d) The court may relieve a petitioner of the requirement to exhaust any or all administrative remedies to the extent the administrative remedies are inadequate or the requirement would result in irreparable harm.

**SECTION 507. AGENCY RECORD ON JUDICIAL REVIEW;
                 EXCEPTIONS.**

(a) If an agency was required by [Article] 3 or 4, or by law of this state other than this [act], to maintain an agency record during the proceeding that gave rise to the action under review, the court review is confined to that record and to matters arising from that record.

(b) In any case to which subsection (a) does not apply, the record for review consists of the unprivileged materials that agency decision makers directly or indirectly considered, or which were submitted for consideration by any person, in connection with the action under review, including information that is adverse to the agency's position. If the agency action was ministerial or was taken on the basis of a minimal or no administrative record, the court may receive evidence relating to the agency's basis for taking the action.

(c) The court may supervise an agency's compilation of the agency record. If a challenging party makes a substantial showing of need, the court may allow discovery or other evidentiary proceedings and consider evidence outside the agency record to:

(1) ensure that the agency record is complete as required by this [act] and other applicable law;

(2) adjudicate allegations of procedural error not disclosed by the record; or

(3) prevent manifest injustice.

SECTION 508. SCOPE OF REVIEW.

(a) Except as provided by law of this state other than this [act], in judicial review of an agency action, the following rules apply:

(1) The burden of demonstrating the invalidity of agency action is on the party asserting invalidity.

(2) The court shall make a ruling on each material issue on which the court's decision is based.

(3) The court may grant relief only if it determines that a person seeking judicial review has been prejudiced by one or more of the following:

(A) the agency erroneously interpreted the law;

(B) the agency committed an error of procedure;

(C) the agency action is arbitrary, capricious, an abuse of discretion, or otherwise not in accordance with law;

(D) an agency determination of fact in a contested case is not supported by substantial evidence in the record as a whole; or

(E) to the extent that the facts are subject to a trial de novo by the reviewing court, the action was unwarranted by the facts.

(b) In making a determination under this section, the court shall review the agency record or the parts designated by the parties and shall apply the rule of harmless error.

[ARTICLE] 6   OFFICE OF ADMININISTRATIVE HEARINGS

SECTION 601.   CREATION OF OFFICE OF ADMINISTRATIVE HEARINGS.

(a) In this [article], "office" means the [Office of Administrative Hearings].

(b) The [Office of Administrative Hearings] is created in the executive branch of state government [within the [ ] agency].

SECTION 602.   CHIEF ADMINISTRATIVE LAW JUDGE; APPOINTMENT; QUALIFICATIONS; TERM; REMOVAL.

(a) The office is headed by a chief administrative law judge appointed by [the Governor] [with the advice and consent of the Senate].

(b) A chief administrative law judge serves a term of [five] years and until a successor is appointed and qualifies for office, is entitled to the salary provided by law, and may be reappointed.

(c) At the time of appointment, the chief administrative law judge must have been admitted to the practice of law in this state for at least five years and have substantial experience in administrative law.

(d) A chief administrative law judge:

(1) must take the oath of office required by law before beginning the duties of the office;

(2) shall devote full time to the duties of the office and may not engage in the private practice of law; and

(3) is subject to the code of conduct for administrative law judges adopted pursuant to Section 604(7).

(e) A chief administrative law judge may be removed from office only for cause and only after notice and an opportunity for a contested case hearing.

SECTION 603.   ADMININSTRATIVE LAW JUDGES; APPOINTMENT; QUALIFICATIONS; DISCIPLINE.

(a) The chief administrative law judge shall appoint administrative law judges pursuant to the [state merit system].

(b) In addition to meeting other requirements of the [state merit system], to be eligible for appointment as an administrative law judge, an individual must have been admitted to the practice of law in this state for at least [three] years.

(c) An administrative law judge:

(1) shall take the oath of office required by law before beginning duties as an administrative law judge;

(2) is subject to the code of conduct for administrative law judges adopted pursuant to Section 604(7);

(3) is entitled to the compensation provided by law; and

(4) may not perform any act inconsistent with the duties and responsibilities of an administrative law judge.

(d) An administrative law judge:

(1) is subject to the administrative supervision of the chief administrative law judge;

(2) may be disciplined pursuant to the [state merit system law];

(3) except as otherwise provided in paragraph (4), may be removed from office only for cause and only after notice and an opportunity for a contested case hearing; and

(4) is subject to a reduction in force in accordance with the [state merit system law].

(e) On [the effective date of this [act]], administrative law judges employed by agencies to which this [article] applies are transferred to the office and, regardless of the minimum qualifications imposed by this [article], are administrative law judges in the office.

SECTION 604.   CHIEF ADMINISTRATIVE LAW JUDGE; POWERS; DUTIES. The chief administrative law judge has the powers and duties specified in this section. The chief administrative law judge:

(1) shall supervise and manage the office;

(2) shall assign administrative law judges in a case referred to the office;

(3) shall assure the decisional independence of each administrative law judge;

(4) shall establish and implement standards for equipment, supplies, and technology for administrative law judges;

(5) shall provide and coordinate continuing education programs and services for administrative law judges and advise them of changes in the law concerning their duties;

(6) shall adopt rules pursuant to this [act] to implement [Article] 4 and this [article];

(7) shall adopt a code of conduct for administrative law judges;

(8) shall monitor the quality of adjudications conducted by administrative law judges;

(9) shall discipline [pursuant to the state merit system law] administrative law judges who do not meet appropriate standards of conduct and competence;

(10) may accept grants and gifts for the benefit of the office; and

(11) may contract with other public agencies for services provided by the office.

SECTION 605.   COOPERATION OF AGENCIES.

(a) Every agency shall cooperate with the chief administrative law judge in the discharge of the duties of the office.

(b) Subject to Section 402, an agency may not reject a particular administrative law judge for a particular hearing.

SECTION 606. ADMINISTRATIVE LAW JUDGES; POWERS; DUTIES; DECISION MAKING AUTHORITY.

(a) In a contested case, unless the hearing is conducted by a presiding officer assigned under Section 402(a) other than an administrative law judge, an administrative law judge must be assigned to be the presiding officer. If the administrative law judge is delegated final decisional authority, the administrative law judge shall issue a final order. If the administrative law judge is not delegated final decisional authority, the administrative law judge shall issue to the agency head a recommended order in the contested case.

(b) Except as otherwise provided by law of this state other than this [act], if a contested case is referred to the office by an agency, the agency may not take further action with respect to the proceeding, except as a party, until a recommended, initial, or final order is issued. [This subsection does not prevent an appropriate interlocutory review by the agency or an appropriate termination or modification of the proceeding by the agency when authorized by law of this state other than this [act].]

(c) In addition to acting as the presiding officer in contested cases under this [act], subject to the direction of the chief administrative law judge, an administrative law judge may perform duties authorized by law of this state other than this [act].

SECTION 607. AGENCIES EXCLUDED. [This [article] does not apply to the following agencies: [list agencies exempted]].

[ARTICLE] 7   RULES REVIEW

SECTION 701.   [LEGISLATIVE RULES REVIEW COMMITTEE]. There is created a standing committee of the [Legislature] designated the [rules review committee].

Legislative Note: States that have existing rules review committees can incorporate the provisions of Sections 701 and 702, using the existing number of members of their current rules review committee. Because state practice varies as to how these committees are structured, and how many members of the legislative body serve on this committee, as well as how they are selected, the act does not specify the details of the legislative review committee selection process. Details of the committee staff and adoption of rules to govern the rules review committee staff and organization are governed by law other than this act including the existing law in each state.

SECTION 702.   REVIEW BY [RULES REVIEW COMMITTEE].

(a) An agency shall file a copy of an adopted rule with the [rules review committee] at the same time it is filed with the [publisher]. An agency is not required to file an emergency rule adopted under Section 309 with the [rules review committee].

(b) The [rules review committee] may examine each rule in effect and each newly adopted rule to determine whether the:

(1) rule is a valid exercise of delegated legislative authority;

(2) statutory authority for the rule has expired or been repealed;

(3) rule is necessary to accomplish the apparent or expressed intent of the specific statute that the rule implements;

(4) rule is a reasonable implementation of the law as it applies to any affected class of persons; and

(5) agency complied with the regulatory analysis requirements of Section 305 and the analysis properly reflects the effect of the rule.

(c) The [rules review committee] may request from an agency information necessary to exercise its powers under subsection (b). The [rules review committee] shall consult with standing committees of the [Legislature] with subject matter jurisdiction over the subjects of the rule under examination.

(d) The [rules review committee] shall:

(1) maintain oversight over agency rulemaking; and

(2) exercise other duties assigned to it under this [article].

SECTION 703.   [RULES REVIEW COMMITTEE] PROCEDURE AND POWERS.

(a) Not later than [30] days after receiving a copy of an adopted rule from an agency under Section 702, the [rules review committee] may:

(1) approve the adopted rule;

(2) disapprove the rule and propose an amendment to the adopted rule; or

(3) disapprove the adopted rule.

(b) If the [rules review committee] approves an adopted rule or does not disapprove and propose an amendment under subsection (a)(2) or disapprove under subsection (a)(3), the adopted rule becomes effective on the date specified in Section 317.

(c) If the [rules review committee] proposes an amendment to an adopted rule under subsection (a)(2), the agency may make the amendment and resubmit the rule, as amended, to the [rules review committee]. The amended rule must be one that the agency could have adopted on the basis of the record in the rulemaking proceeding and the legal authority granted to the agency. The agency shall provide an explanation for the amended rule as provided in Section 313. An agency is not required to hold a hearing on an amendment made under this subsection. If the agency makes the amendment, it shall give notice to the [publisher] for publication of the rule, as amended, in the [administrative bulletin]. The notice must include the text of the rule as amended. If the [rules review committee] does not disapprove the rule, as amended, or propose a further amendment, the rule becomes effective on the date specified under Section 317.

(d) If the [rules review committee] disapproves the adoption of a rule under subsection (a)(3), the adopted rule becomes effective on adjournment of the next regular session of the [Legislature] unless before adjournment the [Legislature] [adopts a [joint] [concurrent] resolution] [enacts a bill] sustaining the action of the committee.

(e) Before the effective date specified in Section 317, the agency may withdraw the adoption of a rule by giving notice of the withdrawal to the [rules review committee] and to the [publisher] for publication in the [administrative bulletin]. A withdrawal under this subsection terminates the rulemaking with respect to the adoption but does not prevent the agency from initiating new rulemaking for the same or substantially similar adoption.]

Legislative Note: The 30-day time period in subsection (a) is the same as the 30-day period in Section 317. State constitutions vary as to whether or not a joint resolution is a valid way of disapproving an agency rule. In some states, the Legislature must use the bill process with approval by the Governor. In other states, the joint resolution process is proper. States should use the alternative that complies with their state constitution. State constitutions vary on the federal constitutional issue decided by the U.S. Supreme Court in I.N.S. v. Chadha (1983) 462 U.S. 919, 103 S. Ct. 2764. The U.S. Supreme Court held that the one house legislative veto provided for in Section 244(c)(2) violated the Article I requirement that legislative action requires passage of a law by both Houses of Congress (bicameralism) and presentation to the President for signing or veto (presentation requirement). Those state constitutions that require presentation to the Governor need an additional step, presentation of the joint resolution to the Governor for approval or disapproval. With state constitutions that do not require presentation of a resolution to the Governor, the rules review process can be completed with legislative adoption of a joint resolution.

[ARTICLE] 8　MISCELLANEOUS PROVISIONS

SECTION 801.　RELATION TO ELECTRONIC SIGNATURES IN GLOBAL AND NATIONAL COMMERCE ACT. This [act] modifies, limits, and supersedes the Electronic Signatures in Global and National Commerce Act, 15 U.S.C. Section 7001 et seq., but does not modify, limit, or supersede Section 101(c) of that act, 15 U.S.C. Section 7001(c), or authorize electronic delivery of any of the notices described in Section 103(b) of that act, 15 U.S.C. Section 7003(b).

SECTION 802.　REPEALS. [The State Administrative Procedure Act] is repealed.

SECTION 803.　EFFECTIVE DATE. This [act] takes effect [ ] . . . .

TABLE OF CASES

[References are to pages]

[References are to pages]

[References are to pages]

[References are to pages]

[References are to pages]

INDEX

[References are to sections.]

A

ADJUDICATION
Generally . . . 1.04[C]

ADMINISTRATIVE LAW(GENERALLY)
Generally . . . 1.01[A]; 15.01
Adjudication . . . 1.04[C]
Agencies (See AGENCIES(GENERALLY))
Alternative dispute resolution . . . 1.04[E]
Attorney General, opinions of . . . 1.06[B][7]
Code of Federal Regulations . . . 1.06[B][3]
Deregulation
    Generally . . . 15.02[A]
    Courts . . . 15.02[D]
    Executive branch . . . 15.02[C]
    Legislative action . . . 15.02[B]
Devolution . . . 15.03
Federal Register . . . 1.06[B][2]
Informal agency action . . . 1.04[D]
Official materials
    Agency
        Decisions . . . 1.06[B][4]
        Publications, other . . . 1.06[B][5]
    Attorney General, opinions of . . . 1.06[B][7]
    Code of Federal Regulations . . . 1.06[B][3]
    Federal Register . . . 1.06[B][2]
    Presidential documents . . . 1.06[B][6]
    United States Code . . . 1.06[B][1]
Practice of . . . 1.01[B]
Presidential documents . . . 1.06[B][6]
Privatization . . . 15.04
Procedural innovations . . . 15.06
Process, administrative
    Generally . . . 1.04[A]
    Adjudication . . . 1.04[C]
    Alternative dispute resolution . . . 1.04[E]
    Informal agency action . . . 1.04[D]
    Rulemaking . . . 1.04[B]
Proposals for legislative change, other . . . 15.07
Regulatory flexibility . . . 15.05
Researching
    Awareness of administrative materials, student
       . . . 1.06[A]
    Official materials
        Agency publications, other
          . . . 1.06[B][5]
        Attorney General, opinions of
          . . . 1.06[B][7]
        Code of Federal Regulations
          . . . 1.06[B][3]
        Decisions, agency . . . 1.06[B][4]
        Federal Register . . . 1.06[B][2]
        Presidential documents . . . 1.06[B][6]
        United States Code . . . 1.06[B][1]
    Student awareness of administrative materials
       . . . 1.06[A]
    Unofficial commercial services . . . 1.06[C]

ADMINISTRATIVE LAW(GENERALLY)—Cont.
Rulemaking . . . 1.04[B]
Student awareness of administrative materials
    . . . 1.06[A]
Study of . . . 1.01[B]
Substantive due process in
    Generally . . . 5.06[A]
    Takings doctrine, impact of . . . 5.06[B]
United States Code . . . 1.06[B][1]
Unofficial commercial services . . . 1.06[C]

ADMINISTRATIVE LAW JUDGES (ALJ)
Appointment of . . . 8.06[A]
Decision making, illustration of . . . 8.08[C][2]
Establishment of . . . 8.06[A]
Functions, separation of . . . 8.06[C]
Role of . . . 8.06[B]

ADMINISTRATIVE PROCEDURE ACT (APA)
Generally . . . App. A
Final order requirement . . . 11.03
Informal agency action, provisions affecting
    . . . 9.02
Initial decision preparation . . . 8.08[C][1]
Judicial review under . . . 12.02
Review of initial decision within agency
    . . . 8.09[A]
Rulemaking procedure under (See RULES AND
    RULEMAKING, subhead: Procedure under Ad-
    ministrative Procedure Act, basic rulemaking)
Section 701 of . . . 10.05[A]
Trial-type proceedings (See TRIAL-TYPE PRO-
    CEEDINGS, subhead: Administrative Procedure
    Act)

AGENCIES(GENERALLY)
Generally . . . 4.01
Acquisition of information
    Congress' and courts' recognition of
        . . . 4.05[A]
    Forms of information gathering, other
        . . . 4.05[F]
    Physical inspections . . . 4.05[E]
    Recordkeeping requirements . . . 4.05[B]
    Reporting requirements . . . 4.05[C]
    Subpoenas . . . 4.05[D]
Command-and-control regulation . . . 1.02[C]
Decision-making
    Constitutional limitations (See CONSTITU-
        TIONAL LIMITATIONS)
    Rule and order (See RULES AND RULE-
        MAKING, subhead: Order, rule and)
Exercise of legislative power . . . 4.03
External controls on
    Executive branch (See EXECUTIVE
        BRANCH)
    Legislative branch (See LEGISLATIVE
        BRANCH)
Informal action (See INFORMAL AGENCY AC-
    TION)

[References are to sections.]

[References are to sections.]

[References are to sections.]

[References are to sections.]

O

OFFICE OF INDEPENDENT COUNSEL
Ethical issues . . . 3.05[C]

OFFICE OF MANAGEMENT AND BUDGET (OMB)
Rulemaking of executive branch agencies, role in . . . 7.06

OFFICIAL NOTICE
Generally . . . 8.05[E]

ORDERS
Executive orders . . . 3.04[B]

P

PAPERWORK REDUCTION ACT
Generally . . . 4.06[C]

PHYSICAL INSPECTIONS
Generally . . . 4.08[A]
Agency acquisition of information, in . . . 4.05[E]
Preliminary analysis . . . 4.08[A]
Warrant requirement
    Analyzing . . . 4.08[C]
    Border searches . . . 4.08[B][4]
    Categories of exceptions . . . 4.08[B][1]
    Consent . . . 4.08[B][2]
    Exceptions to
        Border searches . . . 4.08[B][4]
        Categories of . . . 4.08[B][1]
        Consent . . . 4.08[B][2]
        Emergency . . . 4.08[B][3]
        Pervasively regulated industries . . . 4.08[B][7]
        Plain view inspections . . . 4.08[B][6]
        Welfare inspections . . . 4.08[B][5]
    Pervasively regulated industries, exception for searches to . . . 4.08[B][7]
    Plain view inspections . . . 4.08[B][6]
    Welfare inspections . . . 4.08[B][5]

POLICING ADMINISTRATIVE AGENCIES
Congressional devices for . . . 2.03[A]

PRECLUSION OF REVIEW (See JUDICIAL REVIEW, subhead: Preclusion)

PRE-HEARING ACTIVITIES
Administrative Procedure Act . . . 8.02[C]
Analysis of . . . 8.04[A]
Conference . . . 8.04[D]
Discovery . . . 8.04[C]
Participation . . . 8.04[B][1]
Right to counsel . . . 8.04[B][2]

PRESIDENTIAL DOCUMENTS
Generally . . . 1.06[B][6]

PRESIDENTIAL SIGNING STATEMENTS
Generally . . . 3.05[D]

PRIMARY JURISDICTION
Abilene Cotton
    Case law after . . . 11.02[C]
    Landmark case . . . 11.02[B]
Analysis of fundamentals . . . 11.02[A]
Fundamentals, analysis of . . . 11.02[A]
Nader, impact of . . . 11.02[D]

PRIVATIZATION
Generally . . . 15.04

PRIVILEGE
Doctrine of executive privilege . . . 2.03[B]

PROOF
Burden of proof . . . 8.05[G]
Standard of proof . . . 8.05[H]

R

RECORDKEEPING AND REPORTING REQUIREMENTS
Agency acquisition of information, in . . . 4.05[B]
Fifth Amendment Right against self-incrimination, limitations of . . . 4.06[B]
Information requests . . . 4.06[A]
Limitations
    Fifth Amendment Right against self-incrimination, of . . . 4.06[B]
    Paperwork Reduction Act, imposed by . . . 4.06[C]
Self-incrimination, limitations of Fifth Amendment Right against . . . 4.06[B]

RESEARCH ON ADMINISTRATIVE LAW (See ADMINISTRATIVE LAW(GENERALLY), subhead: Researching)

REVIEW OF ADMINISTRATIVE ACTION (See JUDICIAL REVIEW)

RIGHT TO COUNSEL
Generally . . . 8.04[B][2]

RIPENESS DOCTRINE
Abbott Laboratories, impact of . . . 11.04[B]
Limitations on court's analysis of issues . . . 11.04[A]

RULES AND RULEMAKING
Generally . . . 1.04[B]; 7.01
Administrative Procedure Act, basic rulemaking procedure under (See subhead: Procedure under Administrative Procedure Act, basic rulemaking)
Bias in agency rulemaking . . . 7.08[B]
Comments, consideration of . . . 7.02[D]
Cost-benefit analysis (See COST-BENEFIT ANALYSIS)
Drafting of rules . . . 7.12
Electronic rulemaking . . . 7.02[F]
Estoppel against government
    Generally . . . 7.10[A]
    Case law . . . 7.10[B]
    Practitioner, dealing with estoppel as . . . 7.10[C]

[References are to sections.]

[References are to sections.]